The Institute of Chartered Accountants in England and Wales

FINANCIAL REPORTING

Professional Stage Application Level

For exams in 2012

Study Manual

www.icaew.com

Financial Reporting
The Institute of Chartered Accountants in England and Wales Professional Stage

ISBN: 978-0-85760-239-8

First edition 2007
Second edition 2008
Third edition 2009
Fourth edition 2010
Fifth edition 2011

British Library Cataloguing-in-Publication Data
A catalogue record for this book has been applied for from the British Library

Printed in Great Britain

Your learning materials are printed on paper sourced from sustainable,
managed forests.

Welcome to ICAEW

Welcome to ICAEW

ICAEW is much more than just the accountancy body that awards you the ACA qualification.

As a world-leading professional accountancy body, we provide leadership and practical support to over 150,000 members and students in more than 160 countries. We work with governments, regulators and industry to ensure the highest professional standards are maintained, and the skills of our members are constantly developed, recognised and valued. In addition to the ACA and Certificate in Finance, Accounting and Business qualifications, ICAEW offers a suite of qualifications and development programmes designed to support you throughout your career.

Throughout your ACA training you will develop your professional skills through the initial professional development (IPD) programme. Once you are qualified, you will enhance these skills through continuing professional development (CPD), which ensures that you keep up-to-date in your relevant field.

ICAEW is recognised as a thought leader, and the Institute's technical operations and support services provide technical expertise and the latest knowledge of best practice. See page viii for more details, or visit icaew.com and go to 'Technical & Business Topics'.

ICAEW faculties, which include the **Financial Reporting** faculty, provide additional specialised support to their members in key areas and invaluable networking opportunities. The ICAEW special interest groups (SIGs) further extend the building of sector-specific knowledge within the profession. The groups provide support, conferences, information and representation for members working in – or working for clients in – specific sectors. As a student of ICAEW you can take advantage of free membership of a faculty and a special interest group for one year during your training – choose the faculty and group that best suit your career needs and see how they can help you.

After you qualify and become a member of ICAEW, our Young Professionals network is a vital resource to link you directly with peers and colleagues with similar interests and aspirations. Young Professional members meet regularly to share ideas, and to network. Furthermore, our Library & Information Service, available to all members and students, is there to guide you to the best sources of information on all subjects, utilising a wide range of online databases, books, journals, and the internet.

To help you with the latest information, topics of interest and guidance you can always turn to our free and confidential Ethics Advisory Service, our Institute magazine *Accountancy*, the dedicated student publication *VITAL* and the student support helpline on +44 (0)1908 248 040. The student area of the website – icaew.com/acastudents - gives you access to key resources for your exams and work experience requirements. You can also access additional resources and share your experiences of training and studies with fellow students on your online community; visit icaew.com/studentcommunity

You can, of course, find more information about all of the above at icaew.com

We wish you the very best of luck with your studies and look forward to welcoming you as a member of ICAEW and supporting you throughout your career.

Michael Izza
Chief Executive
ICAEW

Contents

- Introduction   vii
- Financial Reporting   viii
- Getting help   viii
- Skills assessment guide   ix
- Faculties and special interest groups   xxi
- ICAEW publications for further reading   xxii

1. Reporting framework   1
2. Reporting financial performance   43
3. Non-current assets   95
4. Investment properties, government grants and borrowing costs   163
5. Leases   205
6. Revenue and construction contracts   239
7. Financial instruments   265
8. Group financial statements   311
9. Earnings per share and distributable profits   387
10. Other standards   417
11. Financial statement analysis: introduction and ratios   453
12. Financial statement analysis: interpretation   493
13. Financial statement analysis examination techniques   529
14. Scenario-based, open-ended questions   565
15. Scenario-based, consequential questions   589

- Index   621

The Sample Paper questions for Financial Reporting appear as questions in this study manual as follows:

Sample paper question	Chapter
Q1 Calne plc	15 (self-test Q1)
Q2 Windgather plc	14 (section 3)
Q3 Lydford plc	13 (section 5)
Q4 Stragglethorpe Ltd	15 (section 3)

1 Introduction

1.1 What is Financial Reporting and how does it fit within the ACA Professional Stage?

Structure

The ACA syllabus has been designed to develop core technical, commercial, and ethical skills and knowledge in a structured and rigorous manner.

The diagram below shows the twelve modules at the ACA Professional Stage, where the focus is on the acquisition and application of technical skills and knowledge, and the ACA Advanced Stage which comprises two technical integration modules and the Case Study.

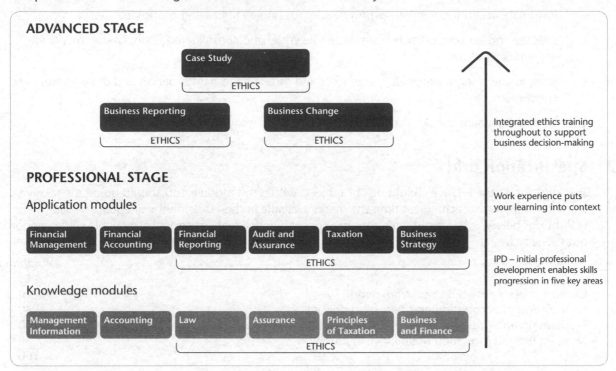

The knowledge level

In the Accounting paper you will have been introduced to the double entry system of recording transactions and the preparation of non-complex financial statements.

Progression to ACA application level

The knowledge base that is put into place here will be taken further in two application stage modules.

The Financial Accounting module develops these basic principles covered in Accounting, looking at the preparation of single entity financial statements in more complex situations and also introduces the issue of group financial statements.

The Financial Reporting paper then takes these issues a step further enabling students to prepare extracts from financial statements for entities undertaking a wide range of accounting transactions. The emphasis is also on understanding financial information as well as preparation with analysis and interpretation a key feature.

Progression to ACA Advanced Stage

The Advanced Stage papers – Business Reporting (BR) and Business Change (BC) – then take things further again. The aims of BR are to ensure that students can apply analysis techniques, technical knowledge and professional skills to resolve real-life compliance issues faced by businesses. In the BC paper the aim is to ensure that students can provide technical advice in respect of issues arising in business transformations eg mergers and acquisitions.

The above illustrates how the knowledge base of accounting gives a platform from which a progression of skills and technical expertise is developed.

2 Financial Reporting

2.1 Module aim

To enable students to prepare and present extracts from financial statements, including accounting policies, for entities undertaking a wide range of accounting transactions, and to conduct financial analysis.

On completion of this module, students will be able to:

- explain the current issues in the regulatory framework for reporting and identify key ethical issues for an accountant undertaking work in accounting and reporting

- formulate accounting and reporting policies for single entities and groups

- prepare and present extracts from the single entity and consolidated financial statements for accounting policies

- analyse and interpret financial statements and other financial information and draw appropriate conclusions.

This module builds on the skills acquired in the Financial Accounting module.

2.2 Specification grid

This grid shows the relative weightings of subjects within this module and should guide the relative study time spent on each. Over time the marks available in the assessment will equate to the weightings below, while slight variations may occur in individual assessments to enable suitably rigorous questions to be set.

	Weighting (%)
Current issues in the reporting framework	10
Formulation of accounting and reporting policies	30
Preparation and presentation of extracts from financial statements	30
Analysis and interpretation of financial information	30
	100

Your exam will last two and a half hours and will contain four questions, one question being rather longer than the other three. In past papers, one question has attracted around 32 marks, and the other three questions had marks in the range of 20 to 25.

3 Getting help

Firstly, if you are receiving structured tuition, make sure you know how and when you can contact your tutors for extra help.

Identify a work colleague who is qualified, or has at least passed the paper you are studying for, who is willing to help if you have questions.

Form a group with a small number of other students. You can help each other and study together, providing informal support. You can meet and share ideas and study tips with other ACA and CFAB students online – visit www.icaew.com/studentcommunity

Go to www.icaew.com/students and look under student societies, to find your local society and find out what additional support they offer.

If you need further information on studying, please refer to the Study Guide for each subject. This includes information on planning your studies. These can be found at www.icaew.com/students

Call +44 (0) 1908 248040 or email studentsupport@icaew.com with non-technical queries.

Watch the ICAEW website for future support initiatives.

4 Skills assessment guide

4.1 Introduction

As a Chartered Accountant in the business world, you will require the knowledge and skills to interpret financial and other numerical and business data, and communicate the underlying issues to your clients. In a similar way to the required knowledge, the ACA syllabus has been designed to develop your professional skills in a progressive manner. These skills are broadly categorised as:

- Assimilating and using information
- Structuring problems and solutions
- Applying judgement
- Drawing conclusions and making recommendations

4.2 Assessing your professional skills

Set out below is a pictorial representation of the different mix of knowledge and skills that will be assessed in the examinations that comprise the ACA qualification.

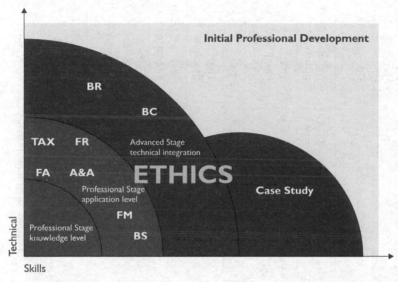

In the six Knowledge Modules of the Professional Stage, you will have experienced a limited amount of skills assessment, generally 'Assimilating and using information'. Most of the questions were set in a context that required you to identify the piece of knowledge that was being assessed. In the Application Modules of the Professional Stage, the context of the examination will be simple business situations, from which you will be required to determine the relevant information to answer the questions.

To be successful in the Financial Reporting examination, you will need a strong core of subject knowledge and a good understanding of how this knowledge should be applied in simple situations. You will be expected to apply your judgement to determine the relevance and importance of the different information provided and to recommend suitable courses of action.

4.3 Assessment grids

The following pages set out the learning outcomes for Financial Reporting that are addressed under each of the four skills areas. In addition, for each skills area, there is a description of:

- The specific skills that are assessed
- How these skills are assessed

Using these grids will enable you to determine how the examination paper will be structured and to consider whether your knowledge of Financial Reporting is sufficiently strong to enable you to apply it in the required manner.

SKILLS PROGRESSION THROUGH THE ACA QUALIFICATION

Assessed skills	Professional Stage		Advanced Stage	
	Knowledge modules	Application modules	Technical Integration	Case Study
Assimilating and using information				
Understanding the subject matter and identifying issues	Specific issues	Simple scenarios	Complex scenarios	Unstructured complex business scenarios
Accessing, evaluating and managing information	Information/data as provided	Single information source provided	Multiple information sources provided	Multiple information sources including own research
Using technical knowledge and professional experience	Highly structured application of non-integrated knowledge	Structured application of non-integrated knowledge	Structured application of integrated and non-integrated knowledge and experience	Unstructured application of integrated knowledge and experience
Structuring problems and solutions				
Using analytical tools	Specified tools	Specified tools	Tools inferred by nature of problem	Unspecified tools
Analysing and evaluating problems	Highly specified tasks	Specified non-integrated problems	Specified integrated and non-integrated problems	Defined output but unspecified problems
Applying judgement				
Assessing quality of information	Objective testing	Specified in simple scenario	Specified in complex scenario	Underlying requirement within complex scenario
Assessing options and priorities including ethical issues	Options given	Options included in simple scenario	Options included in complex scenario	Balanced judgement of priorities and risks in unstructured scenario
Considering other perspectives	Not assessed	Possible alternative provided	Alternative(s) provided	Alternatives identified using professional experience
Conclusions and recommendations and communication				
Drawing conclusions and making recommendations	Not assessed	Specified conclusions and recommendations in simple scenarios	Specified conclusions and recommendations in complex scenarios	Conclusions and recommendations supported by own evidence
Presenting data and written work	Prescribed exam format	Exam requirements, including some professional presentation	Short written professional presentations	Professional report with appendices and executive summary

4.4 Technical knowledge

The table contained in this section shows the technical knowledge covered in the ACA Syllabus by module.

For each individual standard the level of knowledge required in the relevant Professional Stage module and at the Advanced Stage is shown.

The knowledge levels are defined as follows:

Level D

An awareness of the scope of the standard.

Level C

A general knowledge with a basic understanding of the subject matter and training in its application sufficient to identify significant issues and evaluate their potential implications or impact.

Level B

A working knowledge with a broad understanding of the subject matter and a level of experience in the application thereof sufficient to apply the subject matter in straightforward circumstances.

Level A

A thorough knowledge with a solid understanding of the subject matter and experience in the application thereof sufficient to exercise reasonable professional judgement in the application of the subject matter in those circumstances generally encountered by Chartered Accountants.

Key to other symbols:

→   the knowledge level reached is assumed to be continued

Financial Reporting

Title	Professional Stage			Advanced Stage
	Accounting	Financial Accounting	Financial Reporting	
Preface to International Financial Reporting Standards		A	➡	➡
Conceptual Framework for Financial Reporting	C	A	➡	➡
IAS 1 Presentation of Financial Statements	B	A	➡	➡
IAS 2 Inventories		A	➡	➡
IAS 7 Statement of Cash Flows	C	B	A	➡
IAS 8 Accounting Policies, Changes in Accounting Estimates and Errors		A	➡	➡
IAS 10 Events after the Reporting Period		A	➡	➡
IAS 11 Construction Contracts			A	➡
IAS 12 Income Taxes			C	A
IAS 16 Property, Plant and Equipment		A	➡	➡
IAS 17 Leases		A	➡	➡
IAS 18 Revenue		A	➡	➡
IAS 19 Employee Benefits				A

Title	Accounting	Financial Accounting	Financial Reporting	Advanced Stage
IAS 20 Accounting for Government Grants and Disclosure of Government Assistance			A	➡
IAS 21 The Effects of Changes in Foreign Exchange Rates				A
IAS 23 Borrowing Costs			A	➡
IAS 24 Related Party Disclosures			A	➡
IAS 26 Accounting and Reporting by Retirement Benefit Plans				D
IAS 27 Consolidated and Separate Financial Statements		B	A	➡
IAS 28 Investments in Associates		B	A	➡
IAS 29 Financial Reporting in Hyperinflationary Economies				D
IAS 31 Interests in Joint Ventures			A	➡
IAS 32 Financial Instruments: Presentation		C	A	➡
IAS 33 Earnings per Share			B	A
IAS 34 Interim Financial Reporting				A
IAS 36 Impairment of Assets		B	A	➡
IAS 37 Provisions, Contingent Liabilities and Contingent Assets		A	➡	➡
IAS 38 Intangible Assets		B	A	➡
IAS 39 Financial Instruments: Recognition and Measurement		C	B	A
IAS 40 Investment Property			A	➡
IAS 41 Agriculture				D
IFRS 1 First-Time Adoption of IFRS				A
IFRS 2 Share-based Payment				A
IFRS 3 Business Combinations		B	B	A
IFRS 4 Insurance Contracts				D
IFRS 5 Non-current Assets Held for Sale and Discontinued Operations		B	A	➡
IFRS 6 Exploration for and Evaluation of Mineral Resources				D
IFRS 7 Financial Instruments: Disclosures			B	A
IFRS 8 Operating Segments			A	➡
IFRS 9 Financial Instruments				C
IFRS for SMEs				C

4.5 Differences between IFRS and UK GAAP

The following table identifies the scope of the differences examinable in the ACA qualification and where they will be introduced. In general, the differences will become examinable where the relevant IFRS is set at knowledge level 'A'. The differences may also be examined in subsequent modules but only in a different context, for example at the Advanced Stage where knowledge of the differences forms part of an integrated question. Where a general awareness only of an accounting standard is expected (knowledge level 'D') any differences will also be dealt with at this level.

Key: First Module

FR = Financial Reporting

AS = Advanced Stage

Title	First Module	Key *examinable differences* between IFRS and UK GAAP
Preface to International Financial Reporting Standards	FR	No examinable differences
Conceptual Framework for Financial Reporting	FR	**ASB Statement of Principles for Financial Reporting** • Qualitative characteristics are based on the IASB Framework rather than the revised chapters that form part of the new Conceptual Framework • Includes chapters on the reporting entity, presentation and accounting for interests in other entities where there is no direct equivalent in the Conceptual Framework • Measurement chapter is more detailed with an emphasis on the 'deprival value model'.
IAS 1 Presentation of Financial Statements	FR	**Companies Act** • Format 1 and 2 profit & loss account classifications of expenses are similar to IAS 1. However, IAS 1 requires further detail, but not necessarily as individual line items in the statement of comprehensive income. • CA balance sheet formats are less flexible than IAS 1 formats that allow a wider choice of classification formats. • Differences in terminology used, including a balance sheet which is described as a statement of financial position under IAS 1. **FRS 3 Reporting Financial Performance** • Specifies certain 'mezzanine' exceptional items that must be presented on the face of the profit & loss account after operating profit. IAS 1 doesn't specify items and doesn't contain the strict 'concept' of exceptional items. • Requires separate presentation of profit & loss account and STRGL. IAS 1 allows a single statement of comprehensive income which combines both. • Requires a sub-total for operating profit which is not explicitly required by IAS 1. **FRS 18 Accounting Policies** • The disclosure requirements for estimation techniques are not as extensive. FRS 18 only requires a discussion of significant estimation techniques. **FRS 28 Corresponding Amounts** • Does not specifically require comparative information for narrative and descriptive information to be disclosed.

Title	First Module	Key *examinable differences* between IFRS and UK GAAP
IAS 2 Inventories	FR	**SSAP 9 Stocks and Long-Term Contracts** • No examinable differences.
IAS 7 Statement of Cash Flows	FR	**FRS 1 Cash Flow Statements** • Allows certain exemptions from preparing a cash flow statement for certain subsidiaries and small companies. No exemptions in IAS 7. • The definition of cash is more restrictive and only includes cash and deposits repayable on demand (within 24 hours). IAS 7 uses the wider terminology of 'cash and cash equivalents'. • Cash flows are classified under eight standard headings rather than three. There is less flexibility as to where certain cash flows, such as interest paid, are presented.
IAS 8 Accounting Policies, Changes in Accounting Estimates and Errors	FR	**FRS 3 Reporting Financial Performance** • Comparative financial information is restated where a fundamental prior period error has occurred which is more restrictive than IAS 8 which requires restatement for material prior period errors. **FRS 18 Accounting Policies** • Impending changes to accounting policies are not required to be disclosed **FRS 28 Corresponding Amounts** • No examinable differences
IAS 10 Events after the Reporting Period	FR	**FRS 21 Events After the Balance Sheet Date** • No examinable differences
IAS 11 Construction Contracts	FR	**SSAP 9 Stocks and Long-Term Contracts** • Unlike IAS 11, service contracts may fall within its scope. • Requires the asset representing the gross amount due from customers for contract work to be split between amounts recoverable on contracts (debtors) and long-term contract balances (stocks). • Inequalities in profit generation from different stages of a contract should be considered in determining the attributable profit. IAS 11 is silent on this.
IAS 12 Income Taxes	AS	**FRS 19 Deferred tax** • Requires deferred taxation to be recognised on the basis of timing differences rather than IAS 12's temporary differences. • May require deferred taxation to be recognised at a different rate than IAS 12 for intra-group transactions eliminated on consolidation. • FRS 19 permits, but does not require, the discounting of deferred tax balances, whereas IAS 12 prohibits this. • FRS 19 does not normally recognise deferred taxation on the revaluation of assets

Title	First Module	Key *examinable differences* between IFRS and UK GAAP
IAS 16 Property, Plant and Equipment	FR	**FRS 15 Tangible Fixed Assets** • Where assets have been revalued FRS 15 requires the use of existing use value (EUV) rather than fair value. • FRS 15 specifies a maximum period of five years between full valuations and an interim valuation every three years. IAS 16 does not specify a maximum period and the timing of revaluations depends on changes in market values. • FRS 15 requires impairment losses to be debited first against any revaluation surplus in respect of the asset unless it reflects a consumption of economic benefits. IAS 16 does not include such a limitation. • The residual values of assets are assessed at the date of acquisition and not adjusted for expected future price changes. However, residual values should be reviewed at each balance sheet date and revised if appropriate. IAS 16 requires them to be reassessed at the end of each reporting period taking into account current price changes. This may affect the depreciation expense. • Annual impairment reviews are required for all assets, which are either depreciated over a period of more than 50 years or not depreciated. IAS 16 does not include such a requirement.
IAS 17 Leases	FR	**SSAP 21 Accounting For Leases and Hire Purchase Contracts** • SSAP 21 contains the '90% test' rebuttable presumption for determining the classification of finance and operating leases. • IAS 17 specifically requires leases of land and buildings to be split at inception as a separate lease of the land and a separate lease of the buildings. Under SSAP 21 they are considered together. • The net cash investment method is used for lessor accounting. IAS 17 requires the net investment method. • UK GAAP requires operating lease rental incentives to be spread over the shorter of the lease term and the period until the next rent review. IAS 17 requires any incentives to be spread over the whole lease term.
IAS 18 Revenue	FR	There is no comprehensive UK accounting standard covering revenue. The main principles in FRS 5 Reporting the Substance of Transactions and IAS 18 are consistent.
IAS 19 Employee Benefits	AS	**FRS 17 Retirement Benefits** • The scope of IAS 19 is wider and covers different types of employee compensation. • IAS 19 allows a similar immediate recognition approach to actuarial gains and losses as FRS 17. However, it alternatively permits the deferral from recognition of actuarial gains and losses that remain within a '10% corridor'. • Deferred tax balances are netted off the net pension scheme asset/liability under FRS 17. Under IAS 19 they must be shown separately.

Title	First Module	Key *examinable differences* between IFRS and UK GAAP
IAS 20 Accounting for Government Grants and Disclosure of Government Assistance	FR	**Companies Act** • No examinable differences.
IAS 21 The Effects of Changes in Foreign Exchange Rates	AS	**FRS 23 The Effects of Changes in Foreign Exchange Rates** • No examinable differences.
IAS 23 Borrowing Costs	FR	**FRS 15 Tangible Fixed Assets** • FRS 15 allows the option for borrowing costs to be capitalised and this is a choice of accounting policy. IAS 23 requires directly attributable costs, including borrowing costs, to form part of the cost of the asset. • FRS 15 limits the capitalisation of borrowing costs to the finance costs incurred on the expenditure incurred. IAS 23 limits the amount to the borrowing costs on the total related funds raised less the investment income from any temporary investment of those funds.
IAS 24 Related Party Disclosures	FR	**FRS 8 Related Party Disclosures** • Unlike under IAS 24, parent company's individual financial statements are exempt from providing disclosures when consolidated financial statements are presented. • Unlike under IAS 24, wholly owned UK subsidiaries are exempt from disclosing transactions with the parent entity. • Disclosure requirements differ. In general FRS 8 requires the disclosure of the name of the related party where a transaction has occurred whereas IAS 24 does not. • Management compensation disclosures are included in the Companies Act rather than FRS 8 as well as disclosures on loans and other transactions involving directors. • IAS 24 does not consider the materiality of related party transactions. FRS 8 considers materiality from the perspective of both the company and the related party.
IAS 26 Accounting and Reporting by Retirement Benefit Plans	AS	No examinable differences.

Title	First Module	Key *examinable differences* between IFRS and UK GAAP
IAS 27 Consolidated and Separate Financial Statements	FR & AS	FRS 2 Accounting for Subsidiary Undertakings • Includes an exclusion of a subsidiary from consolidation on the grounds of severe long-term restrictions. No exemption exists under IAS 27. (FR) • Under IAS 27 the existence of potential voting rights should be considered in assessing control. No consideration is required under UK GAAP. (FR) • Requires the non-controlling interest to be presented separately from shareholders' funds. IAS 27 requires it to be shown as a separate component of equity. (FR) • IAS 27 requires changes in a parent's ownership interest in a subsidiary that do not result in the loss of control to be accounted for within equity. (AS) • IAS 27 requires any investment retained in the former subsidiary following a loss of control to be measured at its fair value at the date when control is lost. FRS 2 does not require this. (AS)
IAS 28 Investments in Associates	FR	FRS 9 Associates and Joint Ventures • Prescribes detailed format for equity accounting. IAS 28 does not prescribe guidance for the statement of comprehensive income. However, IAS 1 provides limited guidance which uses a pre-tax presentation of the associate's income. FRS 9 shows the components separately. • Requires investors to recognise their share of any interest in net liabilities. IAS 28 only requires this where there is a legal or constructive obligation to make good those losses.
IAS 29 Financial Reporting in Hyperinflationary Economies	AS	FRS 24 Financial Reporting in Hyperinflationary Economies • No examinable differences
IAS 31 Interests in Joint Ventures	FR	FRS 9 Associates and Joint Ventures • Requires the use of the gross equity method rather than proportionate consolidation or equity methods allowed by IAS 31.
IAS 32 Financial Instruments: Presentation	FR	FRS 25 Financial Instruments: Presentation • No examinable differences.
IAS 33 Earnings per Share	FR	FRS 22 Earnings Per Share • No examinable differences.
IAS 34 Interim Financial Reporting	AS	No UK accounting standard on interim financial reporting. IAS 34 is broadly comparable with the ASB statement on interim reports.

Title	First Module	Key *examinable differences* between IFRS and UK GAAP
IAS 36 Impairment of Assets	FR	FRS 11 Impairment of fixed assets and goodwill • Impairment losses on previously revalued assets are taken to the profit & loss account where they relate to a consumption of economic benefits (see IAS 16/FRS 15 above) • Impairment losses are allocated to goodwill, intangible assets and tangible assets in that order. IAS 36 allocates the losses to goodwill first and then on a pro-rata basis to intangible and tangible assets. • FRS 11 is more restrictive on the recognition of the reversal of intangible assets other than goodwill. • Unlike IAS 36, where cash flows have been used to demonstrate the recoverable amount, FRS 11 requires future cash flows to be monitored against those forecasts for the 5 subsequent years (look back test).
IAS 37 Provisions, Contingent Liabilities and Contingent Assets	FR	FRS 12 Provisions, Contingent Liabilities and Contingent Assets • No examinable differences
IAS 38 Intangible Assets	FR	SSAP 13 Accounting for Research and Development • The capitalisation of development expenditure is optional. IAS 38 requires it to be capitalised where it meets the recognition criteria. • Development expenditure recognition criteria include a requirement to have a reasonable expectation of future benefits. IAS 38 is more stringent as the requirement is to demonstrate future benefits. FRS 10 Goodwill and Intangible Assets • Only intangible assets that can be sold separately from the business are recognised under UK GAAP. IAS 38 requires non-separable assets to be recognised where they arise from contractual or other legal rights. • Allows amortisation of intangibles over economic life or no amortisation where an indefinite life is assessed. Under IAS 38 goodwill and indefinite life assets should not be amortised but instead tested annually for impairment.
IAS 39 Financial Instruments: Recognition and Measurement	AS	FRS 26 Financial Instruments: Measurement • No examinable differences
IAS 40 Investment Property	FR	SSAP 19 Accounting for Investment Properties • Requires measurement at open market value. IAS 40 allows a choice between cost and fair value. • Investment gains and losses are taken to STRGL unless they represent a permanent deficit in fair value. Under IAS 40 all gains and losses are recognised in profit or loss.
IAS 41 Agriculture	AS	No equivalent UK accounting standard.

Title	First Module	Key *examinable differences* between IFRS and UK GAAP
IFRS 1 First-Time Adoption of IFRS	AS	Not applicable – not relevant to UK GAAP
IFRS 2 Share-based Payment	AS	FRS 20 Share-based Payment • No examinable differences
IFRS 3 Business Combinations	FR & AS	FRS 6 Acquisitions and Mergers • Merger accounting is required when criteria are met. Not permitted under IFRS. (FR) • Group reconstructions are merger accounted for (AS). • Common control transactions are not within scope of IFRS 3 (AS). • IFRS 3 contains explicit option (not in UK GAAP) to measure minority interest (or non-controlling interest (NCI)) at fair value. FRS 7 Fair Values in Acquisition Accounting • Provides specific guidance on fair value measurement. IFRS 3 only offers brief guidance on fair value measurement. (FR) • Only requires separable intangible assets to be fair valued. Hence, more intangibles could be recognised under IFRS 3. (FR) • Requires acquisition-related costs to be included in the cost of the investment. IFRS 3 requires them to be treated as period costs. • Post-acquisition changes to the estimates of contingent consideration affect the amounts of goodwill recognised. IFRS 3 permits few subsequent changes to be reflected in goodwill. (FR) FRS 10 Goodwill and Intangible Assets • Goodwill is often amortised over its estimated useful economic life. There is a rebuttable presumption that it is not more than 20 years. IFRS 3 prohibits amortisation and requires annual impairment reviews. (FR) • Negative goodwill is capitalised as a separate item within goodwill and amortised over the period over which any related losses are expected and as acquired non-monetary assets are realised. IFRS 3 requires immediate recognition as a gain in profit or loss. (FR)
IFRS 4 Insurance Contracts	AS	Companies Act • Contains specific requirements for insurance companies Specific requirements in SORP and FRS 27, Life Assurance

Title	First Module	Key *examinable differences* between IFRS and UK GAAP
IFRS 5 Non-current Assets Held for Sale and Discontinued Operations	FR	**FRS 3 Reporting Financial Performance** • Continuing and discontinued activities must be analysed. Unlike IFRS 5 detailed analysis is shown on face of P&L account. • Discontinued classification will often be at a later date than under IFRS 5 as disposal must be completed during the reporting period or before the earlier of the approval of the financial statements and three months after year-end. **FRS 15 Tangible Fixed Assets** • Classification and measurement of assets generally continues as normal without regard for the disposal. This includes depreciation until the date of disposal. IFRS 5 on the other hand requires depreciation to cease while a non-current asset is held for sale. **FRS 1 Cash Flow Statements** • Encourages the separate disclosure of cash flows from discontinued operations. This is required rather than encouraged by IFRS 5.
IFRS 6 Exploration for and Evaluation of Mineral Resources	AS	SORP discusses the issues surrounding oil and gas exploration and production.
IFRS 7 Financial Instruments: Disclosures	AS	**FRS 29 Financial Instruments: Disclosures** • No examinable differences
IFRS 8 Operating Segments	FR	**SSAP 25 Segmental Reporting** • Omission of segment information is allowed where disclosure may be seriously prejudicial to the entity's interests. No exemption exists under IFRS 8. • Requires disclosures for both geographic and business segments. IFRS 8 requires disclosure about the components of the entity that management uses to make decisions about resource allocation and to assess performance. • Requires segment information to be prepared in accordance with accounting policies. IFRS 8 requires the amounts reported to be on the same basis as for internal decision making. • SSAP 25 does not require unlisted subsidiaries of listed parents to disclose segment information where the parent has prepared such information.

IFRS in individual company accounts

Candidates may be required to discuss the key issues that need to be considered when considering whether UK companies should retain UK GAAP for their individual company accounts or to move to IFRS. This is examinable in the Financial Reporting module.

Ethics Codes and Standards

Ethics Codes and Standards	Level	Professional Stage modules
IFAC Code of Ethics for Professional Accountants (parts A, B and C and Definitions)	A	Assurance Business and Finance
ICAEW Code of Ethics	A	Law Principles of Taxation Audit and Assurance Business Strategy Financial Reporting Taxation
APB Ethical Standards 1-5 (revised) Provisions Available to Small Entities (revised)	A	Assurance Audit and Assurance

5 Faculties and special interest groups (SIGs)

The faculties and SIGs are specialist bodies within the ICAEW which offer members networking opportunities, influence and recognition within clearly defined areas of technical expertise. As well as providing accurate and timely technical analysis, they lead the way in many professional and wider business issues through stimulating debate, shaping policy and encouraging good practice. Their value is endorsed by over 40,000 members of the Institute who currently belong to one or more of the seven faculties:

- Audit and Assurance
- Corporate Finance
- Finance and Management
- Financial Reporting
- Financial Services
- Information Technology
- Tax

For example, the Financial Reporting Faculty is the focus for chartered accountants working in financial reporting. It represents the Institute on financial reporting matters, making representations to the government and other authorities, and public pronouncements on major issues affecting the profession. It is a free standing body with its own constitution.

The SIGs provide practical support, information and representation for chartered accountants working within a range of industry sectors, including:

- Charity and Voluntary sector
- Entertainment and Media
- Farming and Rural Business
- Forensic
- Healthcare
- Interim Management
- Non-Executive Directors
- Public Sector
- Solicitors
- Tourism and Hospitality
- Valuation

ACA and CFAB students can register for provisional faculty membership of one of the seven faculties free of charge. ACA students can also register for free membership of a SIG. To register and find out more, visit the student website at www.icaew.com/students and click on student support and services.

6 ICAEW publications for further reading

ICAEW produces publications and guidance for its students and members on a variety of technical and business topics. This list of publications has been prepared for students who wish to undertake further reading in a particular subject area and is by no means exhaustive. You are not required to study these publications for your exams. For a full list of publications, or to access any of the publications listed below, visit the Technical & Business Topics section of the ICAEW website at www.icaew.com.

ICAEW no longer prints a Members Handbook. ICAEW regulations, standards and guidance are available at www.icaew.com/regulations. This area includes regulations and guidance relevant to the regulated areas of audit, investment business and insolvency as well as materials that was previously in the handbook.

The TECH series of technical releases are another source of guidance available to members and students. Visit www.icaew.com/technicalreleases for the most up-to-date releases.

Audit and Assurance Faculty – www.icaew.com/aaf

- **Right First Time with the Clarified ISAs**, ICAEW 2010, ISBN 978-0-85760-063-9

  Clarified ISAs provide many opportunities for practitioners in terms of potential efficiencies, better documentation, better reporting to clients, and enhanced audit quality overall.

  This modular guide has been developed by ICAEW's ISA implementation sub-group to help medium-sized and smaller firms implement the clarified ISAs and take advantage of these opportunities. This modular guide is designed to give users the choice of either downloading the publication in its entirety, or downloading specific modules on which they want to focus

- **Quality Control in the Audit Environment**, ICAEW 2010, ISBN 0-497-80857-605-5

  The publication identifies seven key areas for firms to consider. Illustrative policies and procedures are provided for selected aspects of each key area, including some examples for sole practitioners. The guide also includes an appendix with answers to a number of frequently asked questions on the standard.

- **The Audit of Related Parties in Practice**, ICAEW 2010, ISBN 978-1-84125-565-6

  This practical guide to the audit of related party relationships and transactions is set in the context of the significant change in approach that is required under the revised ISA and highlights the importance of planning, the need to involve the entire audit team in this, to assign staff with the appropriate level of experience to audit this area and upfront discussions with the client to identify related parties.

- **Alternatives to Audit**, ICAEW 2009, ISBN 978-1-84152-819-9

  In August 2006, the ICAEW Audit and Assurance Faculty began a two-year consultation on a new assurance services (the ICAEW Assurance Service), an alternative to audit based on the idea of limited assurance introduced by the International Auditing and Assurance Standards Board (IAASB). This report presents findings from the practical experience of providing the ICAEW Assurance Service over the subsequent two years and views of users of financial information that help in assessing the relevance of the service to their needs.

- **Companies Act 2006 supplement** ICAEW, 2009, ISBN 978-1-84152-639-3

  This updated supplement originally published in December 2006, provides a brief summary of the key sections in the Companies Act 2006 which relate directly to the rights and duties of auditors. It covers the various types of reports issued by auditors and provides a comparison to the requirements and regulations in the Companies Act 1985 and Companies Act 1989. It is designed to be a signposting tool for practitioners and identifies the other pieces of guidance issued by ICAEW, APB, FRC, POB and others to support implementation of the Act, along with transitional provisions arising from the Act.

- **Auditing in a group context: practical considerations for auditors** ICAEW, 2008, ISBN 978-1-84152-628-7

  The guide describes special considerations for auditors at each stage of the group audit's cycle. The publication also covers matters in the IAASB's revised and redrafted 'ISA 600 Special Considerations - Audits of Group Financial Statements (Including the Work of Component Auditors)'. The revised publication contains suggestions for both group auditors and component auditors.

Corporate Finance Faculty – www.icaew.com/corpfinfac

- **Private equity demystified –an explanatory guide** Second Edition, Financing Change Initiative, ICAEW, March 2010, John Gilligan and Mike Wright

  This guide summarises the findings of academic work on private equity transactions from around the world. Hard copies of the abstract and full report are free and are also available by download from www.icaew.com/thoughtleadership

- **Best Practice Guidelines**

  The Corporate Finance Faculty publishes a series of guidelines on best-practice, regulatory trends and technical issues. Authored by leading practitioners in corporate finance, they are succinct and clear overviews of emerging issues in UK corporate finance. www.icaew.com/corpfinfac

- **Corporate Financier magazine**, ISSN 1367-4544

  The award-winning *Corporate Financier* magazine is published ten times a year for members, stakeholders and key associates of ICAEW's Corporate Finance Faculty. Aimed at professionals, investors and company directors involved in corporate finance, it covers a wide range of emerging regulatory, commercial and professional development issues. The magazine includes features, news, analysis and research, written by experts, experienced editors and professional journalists. In 2011, three major themes were introduced: Innovation & Corporate Finance; Financing Entrepreneurship; and Deal Leadership.

Corporate governance – www.icaew.com/corporategovernance

- **The UK Corporate Governance Code 2010**

  The UK Corporate Governance Code (formerly the Combined Code) sets out standards of good practice in relation to board leadership and effectiveness, remuneration, accountability and relations with shareholders. All companies with a Premium Listing of equity shares in the UK are required under the Listing Rules to report on how they have applied the UK Corporate Governance Code in their annual report and accounts.

  The first version of the UK Corporate Governance Code was produced in 1992 by the Cadbury Committee. In May 2010 the Financial Reporting Council issued a new edition of the Code which applies to financial years beginning on or after 29 June 2010.

  The UK Corporate Governance Code contains broad principles and more specific provisions. Listed companies are required to report on how they have applied the main principles of the Code, and either to confirm that they have complied with the Code's provisions or - where they have not - to provide an explanation.

- **Internal Control: Revised Guidance on Internal Control for Directors on the Combined Code (now the UK Corporate Governance Code)**

  Originally published in 1999, the Turnbull guidance was revised and updated in October 2005, following a review by the Financial Reporting Council. The updated guidance applies to listed companies for financial years beginning on or after 1 January 2006.

- **The FRC Guidance on Audit Committees** (formerly known as The Smith Guidance)

  First published by the Financial Reporting Council in January 2003, and most recently updated in 2010. It is intended to assist company boards when implementing the sections of the UK Corporate Governance Code dealing with audit committees and to assist directors serving on audit committees in carrying out their role. Companies are encouraged to use the 2010 edition of the guidance with effect from 30 April 2011.

- **The UK Stewardship Code**

    The UK Stewardship Code was published in July 2010. It aims to enhance the quality of engagement between institutional investors and companies to help improve long-term returns to shareholders and the efficient exercise of governance responsibilities by setting out good practice on engagement with investee companies to which the Financial Reporting Council believes institutional investors should aspire.

    A report summarising the actions being taken by the Financial Reporting Council and explaining how the UK Stewardship Code is intended to operate was also published in July 2010.

Corporate responsibility – www.icaew.com/corporateresponsibility

- **Sustainable Business** January 2009

    The new thought leadership prospectus acts as a framework for the work that ICAEW do in sustainability/corporate responsibility. It argues that any system that is sustainable needs accurate and reliable information to help it learn and adapt, which is where the accounting profession plays an important role. A downloadable pdf is available at www.icaew.com/sustainablebusiness

- **Environmental issues in annual financial statements** ICAEW, May 2009, ISBN 978-1-84152-610-2

    This report is a joint initiative with the Environment Agency. It is aimed at business accountants who prepare, use or audit the financial statements in statutory annual reports and accounts, or who advise or sit on the boards of the UK companies and public sector organisations. It offers practical advice on measuring and disclosing environmental performance. A downloadable pdf is available at www.icaew.com/sustainablebusiness

- **ESRC seminar series – When worlds collide: contested paradigms of corporate responsibility**

    ICAEW, in conjunction with the British Academy of Management, won an Economic and Social Research Council grant to run a seminar series which aims to bring academics and the business community together to tackle some of the big challenges in corporate responsibility. www.icaew.com/corporateresponsibility

- **The Business Sustainability Programme (BSP)**

    The Business Sustainability Programme is an e-learning package for accountants and business professionals who want to learn about the business case for sustainability. The course is spread across five modules taking users from definitions of sustainability and corporate responsibility, through case studies and finally towards developing an individually tailored sustainability strategy for their business. The first two modules are free to everyone. For more information and to download a brochure visit www.icaew.com/bsp

Ethics – www.icaew.com/ethics

- **Code of Ethics**

    The Code of Ethics helps ICAEW members meet these obligations by providing them with ethical guidance. The Code applies to all members, students, affiliates, employees of member firms and, where applicable, member firms, in all of their professional and business activities, whether remunerated or voluntary.

- **Instilling integrity in organisations**, ICAEW June 2009

    Practical guidance aimed at directors and management to assist them in instilling integrity in their organisations. This document may also be helpful to audit firms discussing this topic with clients and individuals seeking to address issues in this area with their employers.

- **Reporting with Integrity,** ICAEW May 2007, ISBN 978-1-84152-455-9

  This publication brings ideas from a variety of disciplines, in order to obtain a more comprehensive understanding of what is meant by integrity, both as a concept and in practice. Moreover, because this report sees reporting with integrity as a joint endeavour of individuals, organisations and professions, including the accounting profession, the concept of integrity is considered in all these contexts.

Finance and Management Faculty – www.icaew.com/fmfac

- **Finance's role in the organisation** November 2009, ISBN 978-1-84152-855-7

  This considers the challenges of designing successful organisations, written by Rick Payne, who leads the faculty's finance direction programme.

- **Investment Appraisal** SR27: December 2009, ISBN 978-1-84152-854-4

  This special report looks at the key issues and advises managers on how they can contribute effectively to decision making and control during the process of investment appraisal.

- **Starting a Business** SR28: March 2010, ISBN 978-1-84152-984-2

  This report provides accountants with a realistic and motivational overview of what to consider when starting a business.

- **Developing a vision for your business** SR30: September 2010, ISBN 978-0-85760-054-7

  This special report looks at what makes a good vision, the benefits of having one, the role of the FD in the process, leadership, storytelling and the use of visions in medium-sized businesses.

- **Finance transformation – the outsourcing perspective** SR31: December 2010, ISBN 978-0-85760-079-0

  The authors of this outsourcing special report share their expertise on topics including service level agreements, people management, and innovation and technology.

Financial Services Faculty – www.icaew.com/fsf

- **Audit of banks: lessons from the crisis,** (Inspiring Confidence in Financial Services initiative) ICAEW, June 2010 ISBN 978-0-85760-051-6

  This research has looked into the role played by bank auditors and examined improvements that can be made in light of lessons learned from the financial crisis. The project has included the publication of stakeholder feedback and development of a final report.

- **Measurement in financial services,** (Inspiring Confidence in Financial Services initiative) ICAEW, March 2008, ISBN 978-1-84152-546-4

  This report suggests that more work is required on matching measurement practices in the financial services industry to the needs of different users of financial information, despite the fact that the financial services industry has the greatest concentration of measurement and modelling skills of any industry. A downloadable pdf is available at www.icaew.com/thoughtleadership

- **Skilled Persons' Guidance – Reporting Under s166 Financial Services and Markets Act 2000 (Interim Technical Release FSF 01/08)**

  This interim guidance was issued by ICAEW in April 2008 as a revision to TECH 20/30 to assist chartered accountants and other professionals who are requested to report under s166 Financial Services and Markets Act 2000. A downloadable pdf is available at www.icaew.com/technicalreleases

Financial Reporting Faculty – www.icaew.com/frfac

- **EU Implementation of IFRS and the Fair Value Directive** ICAEW, October 2007, ISBN 978-1-84152-519-8

  The most comprehensive assessment to date of compliance with the requirements of IFRS and the overall quality if IFRS financial reporting.

  The Financial Reporting Faculty makes available to students copies of its highly-regarded factsheets on UK GAAP and IFRS issues, as well as its journal, *By All Accounts*, at www.icaew.com/frfac

Information Technology Faculty – www.icaew.com/itfac

The IT Faculty provides ongoing advice and guidance that will help students in their studies and their work. The online community (http://www.ion.icaew.com/itcountshome) provides regular free updates as well as a link to the faculty's Twitter feed which provides helpful updates and links to relevant articles. The following publications should also be of interest to students:

- **Business Continuity and Management – an introductory guide**, ICAEW 2010, ISBN 978-0-85760-080-6

  Business Continuity and Management provides a proven corporate discipline which helps small businesses to plan for, respond to, cope with and recover from sudden, unexpected and often traumatic events. By following the steps in this guide and focusing on the consequences of disruption, asking yourselves 'what if' more often than 'how much' you can reap significant benefits.

- **Cloud Computing – A guide for business managers** ICAEW, April 2010, ISBN 987-0-85760-000-4

  This publication outlines what is meant by cloud computing and how business people can take advantage of what it has to offer.

- **Information security – an essential today** ICAEW, December 2009, ISBN 978-1-84152-853-3

  This publication outlines what businesses should be doing to ensure the information assets of their businesses are properly identified, protected and secured. It introduces the information security management framework, ISO 27001, which can be used to implement verifiable system of information security.

Tax Faculty – www.icaew.com/taxfac

The Tax Faculty runs a Younger Members Tax Club which provides informal presentations, discussions and socialising. All young professionals interested in tax are welcome to attend. See the website for more details www.icaew.com/taxfac

- **Tax news service**

  You can keep up with the tax news as it develops on the Tax Faculty's news site www.icaew.com/taxnews. And you can subscribe to the free newswire which gives you a weekly round up. For more details visit www.icaew.com/taxfac

- **Demystifying XBRL**

  This booklet, produced jointly by KPMG, the Tax Faculty and the Information Technology Faculty, explains exactly what iXBRL is all about and what must be done in order to e-file corporation tax returns using the new standard.

CHAPTER 1

Reporting framework

Introduction
Examination context
Topic List

1 *Conceptual Framework*
2 Regulatory framework
3 Convergence process
4 Small and medium sized entities
5 Fair presentation
6 Ethical and professional issues

Summary and Self-test
Technical reference
Answers to Interactive questions
Answers to Self-test

Learning objectives

Tick off

- Explain the standard-setting process used by national and international bodies (IASB) and the authority of the national and international standards, using appropriate examples as an illustration ☐

- Explain the main ways in which national and international requirements (including FRSSE) affect financial reporting, performing simple calculations to illustrate the effects ☐

- Explain, in non-technical language and with appropriate examples, the current work to achieve convergence between UK GAAP and international reporting standards ☐

- Explain the sources of reporting requirements in different jurisdictions and the principles behind different reporting treatments, illustrating the principles with suitable calculations ☐

- Recognise the ethical and professional issues for a professional accountant undertaking work in and giving advice on accounting and financial reporting: explain the relevance and importance of these issues and evaluate the relative merits of different standpoints taken in debate ☐

- Discuss the concepts of 'fair presentation' and 'true and fair view' and the circumstances in which these concepts may override the detailed provisions of legislation or of accounting standards ☐

Specific syllabus references for this chapter are: 1a, 1b, 1c, 1d, 1e, and 2c.

Syllabus links

The basics of the IASB *Conceptual Framework for Financial Reporting* (previously the IASB *Framework for the Preparation and Presentation of Financial Statements*) were covered in Financial Accounting but this knowledge is still fundamental for Financial Reporting.

This chapter takes your knowledge of current issues and particularly the progress of the convergence process which aims to produce a set of global accounting standards much further. These are areas which are also likely to be highly relevant at the Advanced Stage. The ethical considerations at the end of the chapter are dealt with specifically here but will be pervasive across all areas of the Financial Reporting syllabus.

Examination context

In the examination, candidates may be required to:

- Discuss the standard setting process and the authority of national and international standards

- Discuss and comment on the convergence process and recent developments in this process

- Discuss and comment on the ASB's and the IASB's approach to dealing with the problem of small and medium sized companies

- Discuss the ethical and professional issues facing accountants within the context of any of the technical areas of the syllabus

- Compare and contrast the concepts of 'fair presentation' and 'true and fair view' and discuss the use of the true and fair override

- Discuss the key issues that need to be considered when considering whether UK companies should retain UK GAAP for their individual company financial statements or adopt IFRS

1 *Conceptual Framework*

Section overview

This section provides a brief revision of the *Conceptual Framework* which was covered in Financial Accounting; it also includes discussion of how well the major needs of users of financial statements are met.

1.1 Background

The IASB is in the process of completing the development of the *Conceptual Framework for Financial Reporting* (*Conceptual Framework*) in collaboration with the US Financial Accounting Standards Board (see below). This is to replace the *Framework for the Preparation and Presentation of Financial Statements* which was developed by the IASB's predecessor in 1989.

The *Conceptual Framework* is currently as follows:

Chapter 1: The objective of general purpose financial reporting
Chapter 2: The reporting entity (to be issued)
Chapter 3: Qualitative characteristics of useful financial information
Chapter 4: Remaining text of 1989 *Framework*:
- Underlying assumption
- The elements of financial statements
- Recognition of the elements of financial statements
- Measurement of the elements of financial statements
- Concepts of capital and capital maintenance

1.2 Status

The *Conceptual Framework* is not a standard; it does not override the specific requirements of any standard.

It sets out the concepts which underlie the preparation and presentation of financial information for external users, so that neither the IASB nor preparers, auditors and users have to re-debate basic principles every time a new standard is in the course of development.

1.3 Objective of general purpose financial reporting

The objective of general purpose financial reporting is to provide financial information about the reporting entity that is useful to existing and potential investors, lenders and other creditors in making decisions about providing resources to the entity. Those decisions involve buying, selling or holding equity and debt instruments, and providing or settling loans and other forms of credit.

Existing and potential investors, lenders and other creditors are defined as the primary users to whom this financial reporting is directed. Other parties (such as regulators and other members of the public) may find this reporting useful, but the reports are not primarily directed to them.

The primary users need information to help them assess the prospects for future net cash inflows to an entity, ie information about:

- the **resources of the entity**;
- the **claims against the entity**; and
- how **efficiently and effectively the entity's management** have used these resources.

1.4 Information about economic resources, claims and changes in resources and claims

Information about the entity's **financial position**, ie its **economic resources and the claims against it** helps users to assess the entity's financial strengths and weaknesses, including its liquidity and solvency and its likely needs for additional financing.

Information about a reporting entity's financial performance (the **changes in its economic resources and claims**) helps users to understand the return that the entity has produced on its economic resources. This is an indicator of how efficiently and effectively management has used the resources of the entity and is helpful in predicting future returns.

Information about a reporting entity's cash flows during a period also helps users assess the entity's ability to generate future net cash inflows and gives users a better understanding of its operations.

Point to note:

Economic resources include items such as property, plant and equipment, inventory and receivables as well as cash and cash equivalents, while claims include amounts payable. Information about resources and claims can therefore only be provided by accrual accounting.

1.5 Qualitative characteristics of useful financial information

If financial information is to be useful, it must be relevant and faithfully represent what it purports to represent. So the **two fundamental qualitative** characteristics are;

- Relevance

  Relevant financial information is capable of making a difference in the decisions of users, by its predictive value, its confirmatory value or by both. Materiality is an aspect of relevance. Information is material if its omission or misstatement could influence such decisions; materiality is entity-specific, being based upon the nature and/or the magnitude of the items involved in the context of the particular entity.

- Faithful representation

  Financial reports represent economic phenomena in words and numbers. To be useful, financial information must not only represent relevant phenomena, but must also faithfully represent the phenomena it purports to represent.

  Faithful representation requires information to be complete, neutral and free from error.

  Point to note:

  There is no need for separate identification of substance over form and prudence as components of faithful representation. A transaction or event can only be faithfully represented if its substance, rather than merely its legal form, is represented while prudence results in information which is not neutral.

The usefulness of relevant and faithfully represented information is increased by the **enhancing qualitative characteristics** of comparability, verifiability (meaning that different knowledgeable and independent observers could reach consensus, but not necessarily complete agreement, that something is faithfully represented), timeliness and understandability.

1.6 Cost constraint on useful financial reporting

Providers of financial information incur costs in collecting, processing, verifying and disseminating information; users then incur their own costs in analysing and interpreting it.

In applying the cost constraint the IASB assesses whether the benefits of reporting particular information are likely to justify the costs incurred in providing it. In developing a new IFRS the IASB seeks quantitative and qualitative information about expected costs and benefits from providers of financial information, users, auditors, academics and others.

1.7 Underlying assumption

The financial statements are normally prepared on the assumption that an entity is a going concern and will continue in operation for the foreseeable future.

- This results in non-current assets being measured, not at net realisable value, but at cost less depreciation calculated on the basis of reducing the carrying amount to the residual value (usually £nil) by the end of the assets' useful lives.

1.8 Elements of financial statements

The elements of financial statements are:

- Assets: resources controlled by the entity as a result of past events and from which future economic benefits are expected to flow to the entity.

- Liabilities: present obligations of the entity arising from past events, the settlement of which is expected to lead to outflows from the entity of resources embodying economic benefits.

- Equity: the residual interest in the assets of the entity after deducting all its liabilities.

- Income: increases in economic benefits in the form of assets increases and/or liabilities decreases, other than contributions from owners.

- Expenses: decreases in economic benefits in the form of assets decreases and/or liabilities increases, other than distributions to owners.

1.9 Recognition of elements in financial statements

An item that meets the definition of an element should be recognised in the financial statements if:

- It is probable that any future economic benefit associated with the item will flow to or from the entity, and

- The item has a cost or value which can be measured with reliability – information is reliable when it is complete, neutral and free from error.

1.10 Measurement in financial statements

Several different measurement bases are recognised:

- Historical cost: assets at what they cost on acquisition, liabilities at amount received.

- Current cost: assets at what they would cost if acquired now, liabilities at (undiscounted) amount to settle now.

- Realisable value: assets at what they would fetch if sold, liabilities at (undiscounted) amount to settle in normal course of business.

- Present value: assets and liabilities at discounted present value of future net cash inflows and outflows respectively.

In addition to those included in the *Conceptual Framework* a range of other measurement bases are utilised in financial reporting standards, such as:

- Depreciated replacement cost, which, for an asset, is its current replacement cost, reduced by reference to the proportion of its useful life already used up.

- Fair value, which is the amount at which an asset could be sold/a liability settled in a transaction between knowledgeable, willing parties in an arm's length transaction.

The different measurement bases of transactions form an important area of the Financial Reporting syllabus.

These measurement bases can also be combined to determine what is known as current value.

Current value (or deprival value or value to the business) is the lower of replacement cost and recoverable amount. Recoverable amount in turn is the higher of net realisable value and value in use.

- Replacement cost is the cost of replacing the capability of the asset.

- Net realisable value is what the entity could obtain by disposing of the asset now, less disposal costs.

- Value in use is the present value of the future cash flows from using the asset and from its ultimate disposal.

Worked example: Current value

(a) An asset has a replacement cost of £1m, a value in use of £1.5m and a net realisable value of £500,000. If the entity were to be deprived of the asset the sensible thing for it to do would be to replace the asset which would cost £1m. It would do this because it is able to generate a return with a present value of £1.5m.

The asset therefore has a current value of £1m.

(b) An asset has a replacement cost of £3m, a value in use of £2m and a net realisable value of £1m. If the entity were deprived of the asset it would not replace it, but would no longer be able to use it. It would therefore have lost its ability to generate returns of £2m.

The asset therefore has a current value of £2m.

(c) An asset has a replacement cost of £5m, a value in use of £3m and a net realisable value of £4m. If the entity were deprived of the asset, it would not replace it. If the entity still held the asset, it would be able to sell the asset for a net amount of £4m which would have been a more sensible course of action than continuing to use it to generate a return with a present value of only £3m.

The asset therefore has a current value of £4m.

1.11 Capital maintenance

The two concepts of capital maintenance dealt with are:

- Financial capital maintenance (FCM), either monetary FCM whereby capital is measured at the amounts put up by investors; or constant purchasing power FCM, whereby capital is carried at the amount originally put up uprated by a broadly based price index.

- Physical capital maintenance, whereby capital is measured by reference to the entity's physical productive capacity; if asset prices rise, capital rises, if they fall, it falls.

Capital is an important concept because, assuming no distributions are made to, or contributions from, the owners, a profit is only earned in any period if the capital (however measured) at the end of a period is greater than it was at the start.

1.12 UK equivalent of *Conceptual Framework*

The UK equivalent of the *Conceptual Framework* is the *Statement of Principles for Financial Reporting* published by the Accounting Standards Board (see below) in 1999. The ASB *Statement* contains more detail on measurement in financial statements, with an emphasis on the "deprival value model"; it also includes chapters (which do not yet have a direct equivalent in the *Conceptual Framework*) on the reporting entity, presentation of financial information and accounting for interests in other entities.

1.13 Major needs of users of financial statements

As noted, financial information is used by those making economic decisions, such as whether to buy, sell or hold equity and debt instruments, and provide or settle loans and other forms of credit. A purchase of equity results in a stake in the entity's future, not its past, so users really need information about how the entity will develop in the future. In deciding between entities, users measure one entity's performance against another's in terms of:

- Profitability: how profitable is each entity?

  The main measure of profitability is return on capital employed (ROCE) which at this stage (there is more detailed discussion of ROCE in a later chapter) is defined as profit before interest and tax as a percentage of the total capital employed (equity + interest-bearing liabilities).

- Gearing: how solvent is each entity?

  At this stage gearing is defined as interest-bearing liabilities as a percentage of equity.

- Cash flow: how good at creating cash inflows is each entity?

At this stage cash generation is defined as cash generated from operations, a heading in the statement of cash flows familiar from your Financial Accounting studies.

Interactive question 1: Two companies

[Difficulty level: Intermediate]

Extracts from the financial statements of two companies are as follows:

	Buckland £m	Ferrers £m
Profit from operations/profit before interest and tax	100	200
– after charging depreciation of	20	50
Equity	300	500
Interest bearing liabilities	200	700
Increase in working capital	5	60

Measure the performance of the two companies and explain which you think has performed better.

See **Answer** at the end of the chapter.

1.14 Meeting the needs of users

For decision making users need information which faithfully represents the transactions and events it purports to represent. The *Conceptual Framework* meets these needs in terms of:

- Its focus on the accrual basis of accounting, which is less easily manipulated than cash accounting.

- Its inclusion of faithful representation (which requires the application of substance over form) as one of the two qualitative characteristics which make information useful.

- Its definitions of assets and liabilities. Only items which meet these definitions should appear in financial statements, and assets must already be **controlled** by the entity, and liabilities arise from **past** events. The process of identifying what has occurred in the past leads to information which is more verifiable than estimating what might happen in the future.

- Its requirement that assets and liabilities should only be recognised when they can be measured **with reliability**.

- Its focus on historical cost as the measurement basis.

But users also need information which is **relevant** to their task of making economic decisions about the future and many argue that the *Conceptual Framework* has shortcomings in terms of:

- Not identifying a mechanism by which internally generated assets can be recognised. In an era when well-trained staff and product branding are key drivers of a successful business, an entity which develops its own staff/brands internally must treat the cost as an expense, on the basis that it is impossible to differentiate with reliability the cost of developing, say, a new brand from the cost of maintaining existing brands. So items which company executives often describe as their most important assets are not recognised as assets in financial statements.

- Not including budgeted information as part of the content of financial statements. Budgets reflect management's plans for the future. Users of financial statements are making economic decisions about the future and budgeted information would be an invaluable input to the process. But the *Conceptual Framework* rules out such information as not being sufficiently verifiable.

- Not adopting a policy of favouring the 'fair value' measurement basis. As noted above, fair value reflects the market price between willing buyer and willing seller and in a capitalist economy the market price is the true 'value' of any item. (This omission from the *Conceptual Framework* is all the more noticeable when the IASB seems to be favouring fair value in a number of the new IFRS it develops.)

2 Regulatory framework

Section overview

- Financial reporting is the provision of financial information to those outside the entity.

- The organisation responsible for setting IFRSs comprises the International Financial Reporting Standards Foundation (IFRS Foundation), the Monitoring Board, the International Accounting Standards Board (IASB), the IFRS Advisory Council (Advisory Council) and the IFRS Interpretations Committee (Interpretations Committee).

- The process of setting IFRSs is an open dialogue involving co-operation between national and international standard setters.

2.1 What is financial reporting?

Financial reporting is the provision of financial information about an entity to those outside the entity that is useful in making decisions about providing resources to the entity.

Typically this information is provided in the annual financial statements:

- Statement of financial position
- Statement of comprehensive income
- Statement of changes in equity
- Statement of cash flows
- Notes to the financial statements

in formats laid down by governments and national regulators in each national jurisdiction.

2.2 Structure and processes of the organisation setting IFRS

The international standard setting organisation is now made up of several inter-related bodies with different functions, as follows:

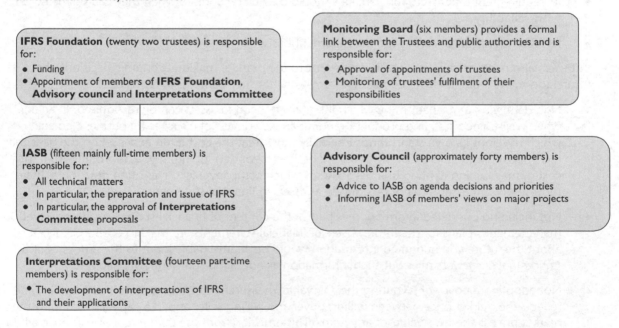

Point to note:

Names have recently been changed as follows: the IFRS Foundation was previously the IASCF, the IFRS Advisory Council was previously the Standards Advisory Council and the IFRS Interpretations Committee was previously the International Financial Reporting Interpretations Committee.

The **objectives** of the IFRS Foundation are set out in its *Constitution:*

- To develop, in the public interest, a single set of high quality, understandable, enforceable and globally accepted financial reporting standards based on clearly articulated principles. These standards should require high quality, transparent and comparable information in financial statements and other financial reporting to help investors, other participants in the world's capital markets and other users of financial information make economic decisions

- To promote the use and rigorous application of those standards

- In fulfilling the two preceding objectives to take account of, as appropriate, the needs of a range of sizes and types of entities in diverse economic settings

- To promote and facilitate the adoption of IFRSs, being the standards and interpretations issued by the IASB, through the convergence of national accounting standards and IFRSs.

2.3 The standard setting process

The IASB process for developing standards is set out in the *Preface to International Financial Reporting Standards* and involves some or all of the following stages (those marked with an * are required by the IFRS Foundation's Constitution).

- Identification by staff of all the issues associated with the topic and consideration of the application of the *Conceptual Framework* to the issues

- Study by staff of national requirements and practices and exchange of views with national standard setters

- Consultation with the Trustees and the Advisory Council as to whether the issue should be added to the IASB's agenda*

- Formation of an advisory group to give advice to the IASB on the project

- Publication for public comment of a discussion paper

- Publication for public comment of an exposure draft together with any dissenting opinions of IASB members (must be approved by at least nine of the IASB members). Normally a basis for conclusions should also be published*

- Consideration of all comments received on exposure draft within the comment period (usually 120 days)*

- Public hearings about, and field tests of, the exposure draft

- Approval of the standard, together with any dissenting opinions of IASB members (must be approved by at least nine of the IASB members)*

- Publication of the standard, a basis for conclusions and the dissenting opinion of any IASB member*

There is a great deal of openness about the entire standard setting process.

- Written contributions are welcomed from anyone throughout the process

- IASB meetings are held in public and anyone can attend as an observer

- There is much emphasis on exchanging views with national standard setters. The IASB seeks to work jointly with national standard setters

2.4 International Federation of Accountants

IFAC is the global organisation for the accountancy profession and comprises over 160 members and associates. It works to protect the public interest by encouraging high quality practices by the world's accountants. Its members and associates, which are primarily national professional accountancy bodies, represent 2.5 million accountants employed in public practice, industry and commerce, government, and academia. ICAEW is a member of IFAC.

IFAC develops international standards on ethics, auditing and assurance, education, and public sector accounting. It also issues guidance to support professional accountants in business, small and medium practices, and developing nations.

IFAC has a direct impact on your work life as the ICAEW ethical code has been developed from the IFAC guidance.

2.5 UK regulatory framework

UK companies produce their financial statements in line with the requirements of:

- The Companies Act 2006, and

- Accounting standards, whether IFRS or the UK's Financial Reporting Standards (issued by the UK's Accounting Standards Board (ASB)).

Companies whose shares or debt are traded on a regulated securities exchange have had to prepare their consolidated financial statements in accordance with IFRS from 2005. This requirement does not apply to the separate financial statements of the parent company or the separate financial statements of any subsidiaries, although it is permissible to use IFRS for these as well. From 2007 onwards this regulation also applies to companies whose shares/debt is traded on the London Alternative Investment Market (AIM).

All other companies have a choice of whether to prepare both consolidated and separate financial statements in accordance with UK GAAP or IFRS. However, when a company chooses to change the basis of preparation to IFRS, it cannot subsequently change back to using UK GAAP.

To date few companies have made a voluntary transition to IFRS. They have preferred to remain with UK GAAP.

3 Convergence process

Section overview

- There has been a drive in recent years towards increased harmonisation of accounting standards.

- Groups whose shares or debt are traded on a supervised securities exchange in EU countries must now prepare their consolidated financial statements under IFRS.

- The IASB Convergence programme includes collaboration with the US Financial Accounting Standards Board (FASB) in order to create a set of global reporting standards.

- In the UK the ASB is also working closely with the IASB in order to converge UK accounting standards with IFRS.

3.1 National and international financial reporting

In the past, companies have been required to prepare their financial statements according to the accounting requirements of the country in which the company is registered. In the UK this would mean compliance with:

- Companies Act 2006
- Statements of Standard Accounting Practice (SSAPs)
- Financial Reporting Standards (FRSs)

Many entities are large multi-national groups with their shares traded on stock exchanges around the world, and have often been required to prepare financial statements in line with a number of different, local reporting bases, before making adjustments prior to consolidating them in their home country.

US-based entities are required to prepare their financial statements in accordance with the financial reporting standards issued by the US FASB. Non-US entities which prepared their financial statements under different standards, such as IFRS, and whose shares are traded on a US stock exchange used to be required to prepare reconciliations of the profit and equity amounts measured under these different standards and the equivalent amounts under US GAAP. These restatements often required a substantial amount of work.

In recent years there has been increased pressure for the adoption of a single set of global accounting standards. This drive towards worldwide harmonisation of financial reporting has two main causes:

- Increased globalisation of trade and of capital markets, with the result that:

    - Management wants all group entities to produce financial statements on the same basis

    - Investors and lenders are now adopting an international approach to their activities and want to be spared the trouble of having to understand a number of different bases for the preparation of financial statements

- It is also the case that the increasing pace of information technology development now provides companies with the communications to take advantage of such harmonisation.

The benefits from the convergence of global financial reporting include:

- Reducing the cost of capital as investors/lenders understand all financial statements better
- Encouraging investment growth
- Improving the quality of financial reporting
- Reducing the time and cost of preparing financial statements.

There are some who would also argue that there are costs of global convergence, in particular:

- The cost of changing accounting practices and systems to suit IFRS
- A perceived dilution of national sovereignty
- A concern that the desire to converge with US requirements (see below) will lead to standards which are appropriate for the very largest, international companies, which regularly raise finance on the capital markets. Such standards are just too complex, and compliance with them too expensive, for companies operating only in their domestic markets and raising the finance they need from their clearing banks.

3.2 The European Union

For many years the European Union (EU) has had an overall objective of creating a properly functioning internal market. It has therefore set a specific objective in the financial arena of developing an integrated and efficiently operating capital market. The adoption of internationally accepted accounting standards with few measurement options, leading to a single set of global accounting standards, is a major contribution to the achievement of this objective.

In 2000, as part of this process, the International Organisation of Securities Commissions (IOSCO) adopted a core set of IFRS for use by multi-national entities. IOSCO represents the regulators of securities markets and keeps a watching brief over the major regulatory issues associated with international securities in general and with multi-national disclosure and accounting in particular.

In June 2002 the European Commission issued a Regulation requiring the **adoption of IFRS** for the preparation of consolidated financial statements for financial periods starting on or after 1 January 2005 for entities incorporated in a member state and whose securities, debt or equity, are traded on a regulated market in the EU.

To maintain some political control over standards and prevent them being solely under the control of unelected accountants, the European Commission set up an endorsement mechanism whereby the European Parliament and the Council of the EU must adopt new international accounting standards before companies are required to comply with them. In deciding whether to adopt a standard they take advice from two committees:

- The Accounting Regulatory Committee (ARC) which is made up of representatives of member states and works at a political level

- The European Financial Reporting Advisory Group (EFRAG) which is made up of technical experts such as national standard setters, national regulators and preparers and users of financial statements. This group is expected to contribute to the IASB's development work and identify early in the development of an IFRS whether the IASB proposals are going to cause significant problems for the EU.

Although the IASB issues IFRS, it has no legal authority to require compliance with them, so the use of IFRS requires specific legislation in each country or on the part of the EU. In the EU enforcement is also delegated to the regulatory authorities in member states, but must be carried out in line with the enforcement principles issued by the Committee for European Securities Regulators (CESR) which has now been renamed the European Securities and Markets Authority. These principles can be summarised as follows:

- The purpose of enforcement is to protect investors and promote securities market confidence

- Enforcement shall take the form of a review to see whether IFRS have been properly complied with

- Enforcement shall be 'ex-post', in that there shall be reviews of financial statements only after they have been published

- The selection of financial statements to be reviewed should combine a risk-based approach together with a sampling and/or rotation approach

- Total reliance on a risk-based approach may be acceptable, but total reliance on a rotation approach is not

- A purely reactive approach (conducting a review only when someone complains) is not acceptable

- Restatements of financial statements should be demanded where appropriate.

In the UK there are two main bodies which regulate financial statements:

- The Financial Services Authority (FSA) which is the UK regulator of financial services. The FSA supervises the provision of information to the investing public when an entity wishes to make a public offering of its securities.

- The Financial Reporting Review Panel (FRRP).

The FRRP is independent of the ASB but is, like it, answerable to the Financial Reporting Council. It was set up to enquire into financial statements and directors' reports which appear not to comply with the requirements laid down in the UK. In line with the CESR principles it adopts a proactive approach to the review of all financial information within its remit. The aim of the FRRP, if it considers that inappropriate accounting has been adopted, is to reach agreement with the directors so that they voluntarily agree to restate their financial statements. Failing voluntary correction, the FRRP does have the power to restate the financial statements through a court order.

3.3 IASB and US regulators

IFRS are leading the way as the generally accepted accounting standards for capital market reporting outside of the US. However, an overwhelming volume of financial capital is traded through US markets, and any attempts at global convergence must incorporate the US at its core.

After a joint meeting in September 2002, the US FASB and the IASB issued their Norwalk Agreement. In this agreement they each:

- Acknowledged their commitment to the development of high quality, compatible accounting standards that could be used for both domestic and cross-border financial reporting.

- Pledged to use their best efforts to make their existing financial reporting standards fully compatible as soon as is practicable, and

- Pledged to co-ordinate their future work programmes to ensure that once achieved, compatibility is maintained.

This is known as the **IASB Convergence Project** and IFRS 5 *Non-Current Assets Held for Sale and Discontinued Operations* was the first standard to be issued as a result of this agreement.

3.4 Progress in general convergence

In October 2004 and subsequent to the Norwalk Agreement there was an agreement between IASB and FASB to develop a common conceptual framework. The intention was to divide the project into two phases:

- The initial focus being on particular aspects of the framework such as objectives, qualitative characteristics, elements, recognition and measurement

- In the later stage to apply these aspects to other aspects (see below).

In February 2006 'A Roadmap for convergence between IFRSs and US GAAP 2006 – 2008 Memorandum of Understanding between the FASB and IASB' (known as the **Memorandum of Understanding** (MoU)) was issued. Progress on convergence was such that in November 2007 the Securities and Exchange Commission (SEC), the regulator of US securities markets removed the requirement referred to above for non-US companies to prepare the reconciliations of profit and equity.

In November 2008 the SEC produced for comment its proposals for a 'Roadmap for the Potential Use of Financial Statements Prepared in Accordance with International Financial Reporting Standards by US Issuers'. The proposals were revised in 2010 and now set out six headings on which progress needs to be made. These headings include:

- Further improvements to IFRS

- Changes to the accountability and funding arrangements for the IFRS Foundation, to demonstrate beyond doubt its independence

- Investor understanding and education regarding IFRS.

If these proposals are adopted and assuming that the SEC judges that sufficient progress has been made under the six headings, then the use of IFRS, as opposed to US financial reporting standards, would become **compulsory** for all US entities, starting in approximately 2015 or 2016. This would be a major step along the road to a single set of global reporting standards.

3.5 Conceptual framework

An essential part of harmonising US GAAP and IFRS is to create a common conceptual framework. An agreement on the underpinning concepts is seen as vital to international convergence.

The IASB and the US FASB are developing a **common conceptual framework** (that is a single converged framework) which is:

- Complete and internally consistent

- An improvement on the existing frameworks of both boards

- Capable of providing a sound foundation for developing future accounting standards

- Essential to fulfilling the boards' goal of **developing standards** that:

  – Are principles-based

  – Are internally consistent

  – Are internationally converged, and

  – Lead to financial reporting that provides the information needed for investment, credit, and similar decisions.

The boards are conducting the project in eight phases.

Phase	Topic
A	Objectives and qualitative characteristics
B	Definitions of elements, recognition and derecognition
C	Measurement
D	Reporting entity concept
E	Boundaries of financial reporting and presentation and disclosure
F	Purpose and status of the framework
G	Application to not-for-profit entities
H	Remaining issues, if any

Phase A has been completed and implemented (see above) and an exposure draft in respect of Phase D was published in March 2010. Work is in hand in relation to Phases B and C, but has not started in relation to Phases E to H. It is unlikely that this project will be completed for a number of years.

3.6 Other convergence projects

Over recent years convergence has been achieved in the areas of:

- Borrowing costs: IAS 23 *Borrowing Costs* has been converged with US requirements in that capitalisation of qualifying borrowing costs is now compulsory, rather than an option.
- Operating segments: IFRS 8 *Operating Segments* has converged segmental reporting with US requirements.
- Business combinations: the US equivalent of IFRS 3 *Business Combinations* has been revised very substantially to converge with the slightly modified IFRS.

In May 2011 the IASB issued converged or substantially converged standards as follows:

- IFRS 10 *Consolidated Financial Statements* (IAS 27 will in future only apply to separate financial statements)

- IFRS 11 *Joint Arrangements* (this will replace IAS 31 *Interests in Joint Ventures*)

- IFRS 12 *Disclosure of Interest in Other Entities*

- IFRS 13 *Fair Value Measurement*

These IFRS are to be applied for annual reporting periods commencing on or after 1 January 2013, with early adoption permitted.

By May 2011 work was well advanced on converged standards in respect of the presentation of other comprehensive income, financial instruments, revenue recognition and leasing.

As well as the work on convergence between IFRS and US standards, the IASB has also been working closely on projects with the national accounting standard setters of Canada, Japan and China, all of which countries are committed to adopting or converging their national financial reporting standards with, IFRS. Japan is expected to make a decision in or around 2012 on the mandatory use of IFRS by domestic entities.

3.7 IASB and the credit crisis

The IASB took a number of steps in response to the "credit crisis" which started emerging in mid-2007. Some of the steps were taken on its own initiative while others were in response to proposals from the G20 group of rich nations and the Financial Stability Board (which brings together senior representatives of national financial authorities (eg central banks, supervisory authorities and treasury departments), international financial institutions, international regulatory and supervisory groupings, committees of central bank experts and the European Central Bank). The IASB has:

- Amended IAS 39 *Financial Instruments: Recognition and Measurement* to permit the reclassification of certain financial assets at fair value through profit or loss to held-to-maturity investments or loans and receivables

- Issued several exposure drafts/standards which together will comprise a replacement for IAS 39.

- In conjunction with the FASB established the Financial Crisis Advisory Group (FCAG), to consider financial reporting issues arising from the global financial crisis. The Group reported a number of conclusions and recommendations, including:

  - Financial reporting should continue to provide information relevant to investors. Different information required by regulators concerned with financial stability should be provided to them separately, not by changing IFRS to focus on their needs.

  - Accounting standards were not the root cause of the financial crisis. The fair value measurement basis did not lead to an overstatement of the losses incurred by entities on their financial instruments. (Some have argued that requiring financial institutions to measure financial assets at fair value leads them in falling markets to sell off these assets to maintain capital, thereby further depressing fair values. To this extent the fair value measurement basis exacerbates downturns and is "pro-cyclical".) But the publication of simplified and improved standards on financial instruments, together with more application guidance on measuring fair value, should be the highest priority.

  - Dynamic provisioning (the setting aside of reserves in the good times to meet losses in the bad times) should be considered, but reserves re possible future losses should be separated from those in respect of losses already incurred.

  - Substantial progress should be made on converged and improved standards on consolidation (particularly the definition of "control") and derecognition (ie off-balance sheet issues).

  - All users should recognise the limitations of financial reporting: it provides only a snapshot in time of economic performance and cannot provide perfect insight into the effects of macro-economic developments.

  - National governments, financial market participants, and the global business community should support actively the development of a single set of high quality accounting standards.

  - Accounting standard setters should enjoy a high degree of independence from undue commercial and political pressures, but they must also have a high degree of accountability through appropriate due process.

  These proposals from FCAG are being considered by the IASB and FASB under their normal due process arrangements.

3.8 Convergence of UK standards and IFRS

For many years the ASB has been committed to narrowing the differences between UK GAAP and IFRS and has done so in many areas such as:

- FRS 12 *Provisions, Contingent Liabilities and Contingent Assets,* which is very similar to IAS 37 of the same name

- FRS 15 *Tangible Fixed Assets* which draws heavily on IAS 16 *Property, Plant and Equipment*

- FRS 29 *Financial Instruments*: *Disclosures* which embodies the requirements of IFRS 7.

However, there are still **differences** between some UK standard accounting treatments and those required by international standards, for example:

- IFRS 3 prohibits the annual amortisation of goodwill through profit or loss and requires annual impairment testing whereas FRS 10 requires annual amortisation of goodwill, which has a limited useful life and annual impairment testing for other goodwill.

- IAS 38 requires the capitalisation of certain items of development expenditure, whereas SSAP 13 permits either capitalisation or immediate recognition as an expense.

These and other differences between UK GAAP and IFRS are detailed at the end of each subsequent chapter under the heading of **UK GAAP comparison**.

3.9 The future role of the Accounting Standards Board

Now that certain UK groups are required to use IFRS rather than UK standards, it is widely recognised that maintaining the development of UK accounting standards may not be beneficial in relation to the costs as public companies now use a different reporting regime. This obviously impacts upon the role of the ASB and it now sees its future role as being:

- To contribute to the development and implementation of international standards

- To influence EU policy on accounting standards, including the endorsement of international standards

- To achieve **convergence** of UK accounting standards with international standards.

It will exert intellectual influence through thought leadership and as a hub for regional debate, drawing on its practical experience as an interpreter and implementer of standards. It will also carry out research and test theories on the market as useful contributions to international standard setting. For example, it issued a Discussion Paper on the financial reporting of pensions.

More specifically:

- It should support the work of the IASB and the Interpretations Committee. It will not therefore issue its own interpretations of international standards as this would usurp the role of the Interpretations Committee.

- It should continue to issue its own accounting rules in areas which would not be the concern of the IASB, for example for specific sectors, such as charities, through Statements of Recommended Practice.

The ASB accepts that there is no case for maintaining differences between two sets of GAAP, ie between UK accounting standards and IFRS. Consistency between UK standards and IFRS is not only important for the credibility and understandability of financial reporting; it is also important for those companies which, whilst choosing to continue to prepare their financial statements under UK standards, also wish to ensure that their financial statements are consistent with IFRS.

The ASB approach is to:

- Adopt UK standards with a minimum of differences from IFRS, other than when those differences are essential or justifiable such as to ensure compliance with company law.

- Issue 'new' IFRS as a UK standard, (for example, FRS 22, *Earnings per Share*). However, immediate adoption may be difficult where an IFRS-based UK standard would require consequential changes to several other UK standards.

- Delay the implementation of an existing IFRS where the IASB is in the process of research and development of a new standard. The new standard will be implemented. Otherwise, UK companies may need to change their accounting policies on two occasions (once to the existing IFRS and then to the revised version) rather than one (the revised version).

- Issue more prescriptive UK standards in rare cases. An example is in the area of life assurance where the UK government referred the issue to the ASB.

3.10 Future application of reporting requirements to UK companies

For some time the ASB has been concerned about the increasing complexity of UK accounting standards and the need to update them. UK standards have been developed over decades to reflect changing economic circumstances and corporate activity. They have also been adapted to include changes in international accounting standards. This has created an unwieldy book of 2,000 pages, which lacks a coherent framework. The ASB believes that the logical approach for a country whose standards have much in common with IFRS, and which continues to influence them, is to extend the IFRS-based framework. While full IFRS would place a disproportionate burden on the vast majority of companies, the advent of the IFRS for SMEs (see below) has presented an opportunity to adopt a simplified version.

In October 2010 the ASB issued an exposure draft (with a comment period ending in 30 April 2011) for the future of financial reporting in the UK and the Republic of Ireland. The exposure draft proposes a three tier system of reporting, as follows:

- Tier 1: All UK publicly traded and other publicly accountable entities would be required to apply full IFRS, irrespective of turnover and whether they present group accounts or not.

- Tier 2: An adapted version of the IFRS for Small and Medium-sized Entities (see below) would be applied by entities in this middle tier.

- Tier 3: The ASB's own Financial Reporting Standard for Smaller Entities (see below) would be applied by entities in the smallest tier. The FRSSE enables small entities to take advantage of simplified requirements.

This exposure draft included a draft Financial Reporting Standard for Medium-sized Entities (FRSME) which would be applied by Tier 2 entities; this took the form of the IFRS for Small and Medium-sized Entities modified to fit UK legislation.

3.11 Considerations for private companies considering moving from UK GAAP to IFRS

All UK companies have the choice to change to IFRS as their primary basis of reporting. In considering whether to change to IFRS companies should consider the advantages of each reporting basis.

The principal advantages of continuing to apply UK GAAP reporting requirements are listed below.

- Understood by user groups and familiar to those stakeholders who interact with private companies

- Established accounting systems do not require change and UK GAAP does not require changes to systems and retraining staff

- Sufficient reporting basis for the providers of capital to private companies

- Understandable by management

- Basis on which taxation and capital distributions are calculated is well established

The principal advantages of changing to IFRS reporting requirements are listed below.

- For private companies that are looking for venture capital, private equity or to make the transition to a public market, moving to IFRS reporting will be an advantage to potential investors in terms of making it easier to compare financial performance

- Improved transparency against international companies

- Assists overseas trade development with international partners

Once the transition is made it is permanent. There are many cost and operational advantages to remaining with UK GAAP at present. Few companies have made the transition on a voluntary basis.

4 Small and medium sized entities

Section overview

- In the UK the FRSSE recognises that the information needs of users of smaller entity financial statements are different from those of users of the financial statements of other entities.

- The FRSSE includes all of the accounting, disclosure and measurement requirements for smaller entities plus the related legal requirements.

- The IASB has published a separate IFRS for small and medium sized entities.

4.1 Financial Reporting Standard for Smaller Entities

The Financial Reporting Standard for Smaller Entities (FRSSE) was first issued in November 1997 and has been regularly updated since then as new FRS have been issued. Its purpose was to recognise that the accounting and disclosure requirements for larger entities were not necessarily appropriate for smaller entities.

The FRSSE applies to:

- Companies that qualify as small under the Companies Act 2006, and
- Other entities that would have qualified as small if they were incorporated.

The key point is that in the UK small companies are defined by size, in terms of having revenue, assets and number of employees below specified limits.

Such entities have a choice. They can adopt the FRSSE or they can choose not to adopt the FRSSE and to comply with the other accounting standards and UITF Abstracts instead.

4.2 Objective and contents of the FRSSE

The stated objective of the FRSSE is to ensure that reporting entities falling within its scope provide information about the financial position, performance and financial adaptability of the entity. This needs to be useful to users in assessing the stewardship of management and for making economic decisions, recognising that the balance between users' needs in respect of stewardship and economic decision-making for smaller entities is different from that for other reporting entities.

The FRSSE contains:

- The relevant **accounting requirements and disclosures** from the other accounting standards and UITF Abstracts simplified and modified as appropriate

- The same basic **measurement requirements** as in other accounting standards, although with some simplifications and without many of the disclosure and presentation requirements of other standards

- The accounting requirements of **companies legislation** but clearly distinguished from the requirements of accounting standards.

Worked example: Simplified accounting treatment

An example of a simplified accounting treatment in the FRSSE is the treatment of finance lease rental payments.

How does the FRSSE treatment differ from SSAP 21 for finance lease rental payments?

Solution

Under SSAP 21 these must be allocated to accounting periods so as to produce a constant periodic rate of charge on the remaining balance of the obligations for each accounting period.

However the FRSSE allows the straight line method of allocating these finance charges.

4.3 IASB and small and medium sized entities

It is a widely held belief that IFRS are most suitable for large multinational organisations that operate in capital markets (such as UK public companies). IFRS is often referred to as CapGAAP to reflect this belief. There has been strong international demand from both developed and emerging economies for a rigorous and common set of accounting standards for smaller and medium-sized businesses that is much simpler than IFRS. The IASB, which estimates that SMEs make up 95% of all companies, issued in July 2009 the *International Financial Reporting Standard for Small and Medium-sized Entities (SMEs)*, the result of a five-year development period.

The *IFRS for SMEs* runs to some 230 pages only, and is completely separate from all the other IFRS (which are termed "full IFRS"). It is structured by topic (eg statement of financial position, revenue and inventories) and draws from full IFRS to set out in respect of each topic:

- Simplified recognition and measurement rules. As an example, all development expenditure should be recognised as an expense in profit or loss, because an SME is unlikely to have the resources to assess whether a project is commercially viable on an ongoing basis.

- Omission of full IFRS rules in respect of situations unlikely to be encountered by SMEs. As an example, the IFRS for SMEs does not mention non-current assets held for sale.

It is for each local jurisdiction (probably the EU in the case of the UK) to decide which entities should be permitted or required to adopt the *IFRS for SMEs* and which should not be permitted to do so. The *IFRS for SMEs* defines SMEs as entities which:

- Do not have public accountability, and
- Publish general purpose financial statements for external users.

An entity has **public accountability** if:

- It has filed, or is in the process of filing, its financial statements with a securities commission or other regulatory organisation for the purpose of issuing any class of financial instruments in a public market, or

- It holds assets in a fiduciary capacity for a broad group of outsiders, such as a bank, insurance company, securities broker/dealer, pension fund, mutual fund or investment banking entity.

This definition is made as the basis for deciding which accounting and disclosure requirements are appropriate; it is also needed to prevent public accountability entities claiming that compliance with the IFRS for SMEs is approved of by the IASB.

The IASB believes that the *IFRS for SMEs* will:

- Provide improved comparability for users of accounts
- Enhance the overall confidence in the accounts of SMEs, and
- Reduce the significant costs involved of maintaining standards on a national basis.

The *IFRS for SMEs* will also provide a platform for growing businesses that are preparing to enter public capital markets, where application of full IFRSs is required.

It is important to note that the IFRS for SMEs applies to **medium-sized** (as well as small) entities, whereas the UK FRSSE only applies to small entities. This key difference is reflected in the way the IASB defines those who can take advantage of the IFRS in terms of whether or not they are publicly accountable, not in terms of their size. So UK companies which are too big for the FRSSE may well find they will be permitted or required to adopt the IFRS for SMEs, once the EU/UK has made decisions about its use.

4.4 Not-for-profit entities

A further question arises about the suitability of IFRS for not-for-profit entities. Currently not-for-profit entities are regulated by local legislation, SORPs (issued by the ASB) and IPSAS (International Public Sector Accounting Standards published by IFAC).

SORPs use existing UK GAAP and apply it to the specific circumstances of the industry. Given the recent convergence of IFRS and UK GAAP (for example in relation to financial instruments), it is unlikely that major differences between the two will continue to exist.

Increasingly not-for-profit entities, such as the ICAEW, are adopting IFRS as a basis for external financial reporting. This reflects the increasing global nature of not-for-profit entities.

The *Conceptual Framework* explicitly states that it applies to the financial statements of all commercial, industrial and business reporting entities, whether in the public or the private sectors. IAS 1 explains that it uses terminology which is suitable for profit-orientated entities and this includes public sector business entities. However, it does accept that not-for-profit entities in the private sector, public sector and government may need to amend the descriptions they use for particular line items in the financial statements and even the financial statements themselves.

5 Fair presentation

Section overview

- IAS 1 requires financial statements to present fairly the information provided.
- In the UK the Companies Act requires financial statements to show a true and fair view.

5.1 Introduction

IAS 1 *Presentation of Financial Statements* requires financial statements to 'present fairly' the financial position and performance of an entity.

5.2 Present fairly

'Present fairly' is explained as representing faithfully the effects of transactions. In general terms this will be the case if IFRS are adhered to. IAS 1 states that **departures** from international standards are only allowed:

- In extremely rare cases

- Where compliance with IFRS would be so misleading as to conflict with the objectives of financial statements as set out in the *Conceptual Framework*, that is to provide information about financial position, performance and changes in financial position that is useful to a wide range of users.

5.3 True and fair view

In the UK the Companies Act 2006 requires that financial statements give a true and fair view of a company's state of affairs (that is its financial position) and of its profit or loss for the period.

The concept of a true and fair view reflects:

- The fact that significant **judgements** are involved in the preparation of financial statements, for example determining the lives of non-current assets for depreciation calculations

- The fact that there could be **more than one true and fair view**, for example financial statements based upon historical cost can be true and fair but so can those incorporating revaluations.

5.4 The meaning of true and fair

'True' and 'fair' each have separate meanings:

- Truth is usually seen as an objective concept reflecting **factual accuracy** within the bounds of materiality.

- Fairness is usually seen as meaning that the view given is **objective** and unbiased.

Together, true and fair is usually defined in terms of generally accepted accounting practice (GAAP) which means:

- Compliance with accounting standards

- Adherence to the requirements of the Companies Act 2006

- In the absence of more specific requirements, application of general accounting principles and fundamental concepts and, where appropriate, adherence to accepted industry practices

- Where a choice of treatments or methods is permitted, the one selected should be the most appropriate to the company's circumstances

- The financial statements should reflect the economic position of the company reflecting the substance of transactions, not merely their legal form.

5.5 The statutory 'True and Fair Override'

The Companies Act 2006 requires that where compliance with its accounting rules would not lead to a true and fair view, then those rules should be departed from to the extent necessary to give a true and fair view.

Where the true and fair override is invoked, for example in order to comply with an accounting standard, the Act requires **disclosure** of:

- The particulars of the departure
- The reason for it, and
- The financial effect.

5.6 Comparison of UK GAAP and IFRS

As 'fair presentation' is explained as representing faithfully the effects of transactions, there is unlikely to be any substantial difference in practical terms between it and the true and fair concept.

Because international standards are designed to operate in all legal environments, they cannot provide for departures from the legal requirements in any particular country. IAS 1 indicates that there are few, if any, circumstances where compliance with IFRS will be fundamentally misleading. In effect, UK companies applying IFRS cannot take advantage of the true and fair override.

This is in marked contrast with UK GAAP where the true and fair override is embedded in certain accounting standards which conflict with the Companies Act. An example is SSAP 19 *Investment Properties* which does not allow depreciation of investment properties but requires them to be measured at open market value with the revaluation amounts taken to a separate investment property revaluation reserve. However the Companies Act states that all fixed assets with a limited useful life should be depreciated.

5.7 Judgements and financial statements

Although IFRS narrow down the range of acceptable alternative accounting treatments, there are still many areas which are left to the discretion of the directors of the company. On the whole, the concept of faithful representation should result in transactions being 'presented fairly'. However, commercial and financial considerations may result in pressure being brought to bear to account for and report transactions in accordance with their strict legal form. This can raise ethical questions for a professional accountant (see next section).

6 Ethical and professional issues

Section overview

- The ICAEW has issued a Code of Ethics which is principles-based and centres around five fundamental principles.

- A professional accountant is responsible for recognising and assessing the potential threats to these fundamental principles.

- A professional accountant must then implement safeguards to eliminate these threats or reduce them to an acceptable level.

6.1 ICAEW Code of Ethics

Chartered Accountants are expected to demonstrate the highest standards of professional conduct and to take into consideration the public interest. Ethical behaviour by Chartered Accountants plays a vital role in ensuring public trust in financial reporting and business practices and upholding the reputation of the accountancy profession.

The ICAEW's Code of Ethics (The Code) applies to all its members and is based upon the International Federation of Accountants (IFAC) Code of Ethics.

The Code is **principles-based** and members are responsible for:

- Identifying threats to compliance with the fundamental principles
- Evaluating the significance of these threats
- Implementing safeguards to eliminate them or reduce them to an acceptable level.

The guidance in The Code is given in the form of:

- Fundamental principles and
- Illustrations as to how they are to be applied in specific situations.

The Code applies to all members, students, affiliates, employees of member firms and, where applicable, member firms, in all of their professional and business activities, whether remunerated or voluntary. The ICAEW is committed to enforcing the Code through disciplining members who do not meet reasonable ethical and professional expectations of the public and other members.

A copy of the code is included in the Member's Handbook and is available at www.icaew.com.

Members (or students) who are in doubt as to their ethical position may seek advice from the following ICAEW sources:

- Ethics advisory service helpline
- Money laundering helpline
- Support Members Scheme

6.2 Fundamental principles

Professional accountants are expected to follow the guidance contained in the fundamental principles in all of their professional and business activities. The professional accountant should also follow the requirements in the illustrations. However, he/she should be guided not just by the terms but also by **the spirit of The Code.**

The Code sets out five fundamental principles, the spirit of which must always be complied with:

1 Integrity

A professional accountant should be straightforward and honest in all professional and business relationships.

A professional accountant should not be associated with reports, returns, communications or other information where they believe that the information:

- Contains a materially false or misleading statement

- Contains statements or information furnished recklessly

- Omits or obscures information required to be included where such omission or obscurity would be misleading.

2 Objectivity

A professional accountant should not allow bias, conflict of interest or undue influence of others to override professional or business judgements.

3 Professional competence and due care

A professional accountant has an obligation to:

- Maintain professional knowledge and skill at the level required to ensure that a client/employer receives competent professional services based upon current developments in practice, legislation and techniques

- Act diligently and in accordance with applicable technical and professional standards.

Professional competence may be divided into two separate phases:

- Attainment of professional competence – initial professional development
- Maintenance of professional competence – continuing professional development (CPD)

Diligence encompasses the responsibility to act in accordance with the requirements of an assignment, carefully, thoroughly and on a timely basis.

4 Confidentiality

A professional accountant should:

- Respect the confidentiality of information acquired as a result of professional and business relationships

- Not disclose any such information to third parties without proper and specific authority (unless there is a legal or professional duty to disclose)

- Not use such information for the personal advantage of himself or third parties.

The professional accountant must maintain confidentiality even in a social environment and even after employment with the client/employer has ended.

A professional accountant may be required to disclose confidential information:

- Where disclosure is permitted by law and is authorised by the client or employer
- Where disclosure is required by law, for example

  - Production of documents or other provision of evidence in the course of legal proceedings
  - Disclosure to the appropriate public authorities of infringements of the law that come to light.

5 Professional behaviour

A professional accountant should comply with relevant laws and regulations and should avoid any action that discredits the profession.

Two sets of legislation which may have a particular impact on the work of a professional accountant are:

- Money laundering regulations

  Money laundering is the process by which money from illegal sources is made to appear legally derived and it is a criminal offence for a person knowingly to help another person launder the proceeds of criminal activity.

  In addition, there is a **duty to report**. Where a person discovers in the course of his/her work information which makes him/her believe or suspect, or where a person has reasonable grounds for being suspicious, that money laundering is occurring, this must be reported to the police. It is a criminal offence not to make such a report. Making such a report does not breach any duty of confidentiality owed by a professional accountant.

- Bribery Act 2010

  For individuals it is a criminal offence to:

  - Offer, promise or give a financial or other advantage to another person where the advantage is intended to induce improper performance of an activity or a function or as a reward for the improper performance of an activity or a function.

  - Request, agree to receive or accept a financial or other advantage intending that, in consequence (or as reward for), a relevant function or activity be performed improperly (even if performance is by another person).

  - Offer, promise or give a financial or other advantage to a foreign public official in order to obtain or retain business or retain or gain an advantage in the conduct of business.

  The definition of function or activity is wide and includes any activity connected with a business.

  A commercial organisation is guilty of a criminal offence if an employee, agent or subsidiary of the organisation bribes another person to obtain/retain business.

  It should be noted that the Act includes offences committed outside of the UK by UK citizens.

In marketing and promoting themselves professional accountants should not bring the profession into disrepute that is they should not make:

- Exaggerated claims for the services they are able to offer, the qualifications they possess or experience they have gained

- Disparaging references or unsubstantiated comparisons to the work of others.

6.3 Threats

Compliance with these fundamental principles may potentially be threatened by a broad range of circumstances. Many of these threats fall into five categories:

A **Self-interest threats** may occur as a result of the financial or other interests of a professional accountant or of an immediate or close family member.

Examples of circumstances that may create such threats include:

- Financial interests, loans or guarantees
- Incentive compensation arrangements
- Inappropriate personal use of corporate assets
- Concern over employment security
- Commercial pressure from outside the employing organisation

B **Self-review threats** may occur when a previous judgement needs to be re-evaluated by the professional accountant responsible for that judgement.

C **Advocacy threats** may occur when a professional accountant promotes a position or opinion to the point that subsequent objectivity may be compromised.

D **Familiarity threats** may occur when, because of a close relationship, a professional accountant becomes too sympathetic to the interests of others.

Examples of circumstances that may create such threats include:

- A professional accountant in business, who is in a position to influence financial or non-financial reporting or business decisions, where an immediate or close family member would benefit from that influence

- Long association with business contacts influencing business decisions

- Acceptance of a gift or preferential treatment, unless the value is clearly insignificant.

E **Intimidation threats** may occur when a professional accountant may be deterred from acting objectively by threats, either actual or perceived.

Examples of circumstances that may create such threats include:

- Threat of dismissal or replacement in business, of yourself, or of a close or immediate family member, over a disagreement about the application of an accounting principle or the way in which financial information is to be reported
- A dominant personality attempting to influence the decision making process, for example, with regard to the awarding of contracts or the application of an accounting principle.

6.4 Safeguards

There are two broad categories of safeguards which may eliminate or reduce such threats to an acceptable level:

Safeguards created by the profession, legislation or regulation

Examples are:

- Educational, training and experience requirements for entry into the profession

- Continuing professional development requirements

- Corporate governance regulations

- Professional standards.

- Professional or regulatory monitoring and disciplinary procedures

- External review by a legally empowered third party of reports, returns, communication or information produced by a professional accountant

- Effective, well-publicised complaints systems operated by the employing organisation, the profession or a regulator, which enable colleagues, employers and members of the public to draw attention to unprofessional or unethical behaviour

- An explicitly stated duty to report breaches of ethical requirements.

Safeguards in the work environment

Examples are:

- The employing organisation's systems of corporate oversight or other oversight structures

- The employing organisation's ethics and conduct programmes

- Recruitment procedures in the employing organisation emphasising the importance of employing high calibre, competent staff

- Strong internal controls

- Appropriate disciplinary processes

- Leadership that stresses the importance of ethical behaviour and the expectation that employees will act in an ethical manner.

- Policies and procedures to implement and monitor the quality of employee performance

- Timely communication to all employees of the employing organisation's policies and procedures, including any changes made to them, and appropriate training and education given on such policies and procedures

- Policies and procedures to empower and encourage employees to communicate to senior levels within the employing organisation any ethical issues that concern them without fear of retribution

- Consultation with another appropriate professional accountant.

6.5 Ethical conflict resolution

When evaluating compliance with the fundamental principles, a professional accountant may be required to resolve a conflict in the application of the fundamental principles.

A professional accountant may face pressure to:

- Act contrary to law or regulation

- Act contrary to technical or professional standards

- Facilitate unethical or illegal earnings management strategies

- Lie to, or otherwise mislead, others in particular:

  - The auditor of the employing organisation
  - Regulators

- Issue, or otherwise be associated with, a financial or non-financial report that materially misrepresents the facts, for example:

  - Financial statements
  - Tax compliance
  - Legal compliance or
  - Reports required by securities regulators

When dealing with such a conflict resolution the following should be considered:

- Relevant facts
- Relevant parties
- Ethical issues involved
- Fundamental principles related to the matter in question
- Established internal procedures
- Alternative courses of action

In this case he/she should:

- Determine the appropriate course of action that is consistent with the fundamental principles
- Weigh up the possible consequences of each course of action
- Consult with other appropriate persons if the matter remains unresolved
- Obtain professional advice from the Institute or legal advisers, if it cannot be resolved
- Finally if it remains unresolved refuse to remain associated with the matter creating the conflict.

6.6 Preparation and reporting of information

Accountants will often be involved in the preparation and reporting of information that may be:

- Made public or
- Used by others inside or outside the employing organisation.

The accountant should:

- Prepare or present such information fairly, honestly and in accordance with relevant professional standards

- Present financial statements in accordance with applicable financial reporting standards

- Maintain information for which (s)he is responsible in a manner which:

  - Describes clearly the true nature of the business transactions, assets or liabilities
  - Classifies and records information in a timely and proper manner
  - Represents the facts accurately and completely in all material respects.

6.7 Acting with sufficient expertise

An accountant should only undertake significant tasks for which (s)he has, or can obtain, sufficient specific training or expertise.

Circumstances that threaten the ability of the accountant to perform duties with the appropriate degree of professional competence and due care include:

- Insufficient time for properly performing or completing the relevant duties
- Incomplete, restricted or otherwise inadequate information for performing the duties properly
- Insufficient experience, training and/or education
- Inadequate resources for the proper performance of the duties.

Safeguards that may be considered include:

- Obtaining additional advice or training
- Ensuring that there is adequate time available for performing the relevant duties
- Obtaining assistance from someone with the necessary expertise
- Consulting where appropriate with:
    - Superiors within the employing organisation
    - Independent experts, or
    - ICAEW

6.8 Financial interests

An accountant may have financial interests, or may know of financial interests of immediate or close family members, that could in certain circumstances, threaten compliance with the fundamental principles.

Examples of circumstances that may create self-interest threats, are if the accountant or family member:

- Holds a direct or indirect financial interest in the employing organisation and the value of that interest could be directly affected by decisions made by the accountant

- Is eligible for a profit related bonus and the value of that bonus could be directly affected by a decision made by the accountant

- Holds, directly or indirectly, share options in the employing organisation, the value of which could be directly affected by decisions made by the accountant

- Holds, directly or indirectly, share options in the employing organisation which are, or will soon be, eligible for conversion

- May qualify for share options in the employing organisation or performance-related bonuses if certain targets are achieved.

Safeguards against such threats may include:

- Policies and procedures for a committee independent of management to determine the level or form of remuneration of senior management

- Disclosure of all relevant interests and of any plans to trade in relevant shares to those charged with the governance of the employing organisation, in accordance with any internal policies

- Consultation, where appropriate, with superiors within the employing organisation

- Consultation, where appropriate, with those charged with the governance of the employing organisation or relevant professional bodies

- Internal and external audit procedures

- Up-to-date education on ethical issues and the legal restrictions and other regulations around potential insider trading.

6.9 Inducements

An accountant, or immediate or close family, may be offered an inducement such as:

- Gifts
- Hospitality
- Preferential treatment
- Inappropriate appeals to friendship or loyalty

An accountant should assess the risk associated with all such offers and consider whether the following actions should be taken:

- Immediately inform higher levels of management or those charged with governance of the employing organisation

- Inform third parties of the offer for example a professional body or the employer of the individual who made the offer, or seek legal advice

- Advise immediate or close family members of relevant threats and safeguards where they are potentially in positions that might result in offers of inducements (for example as a result of their employment situation)

- Inform higher levels of management or those charged with governance of the employing organisation where immediate or close family members are employed by competitors or potential suppliers of that organisation.

6.10 Conflicts of interest

An accountant should take reasonable steps to identify circumstances that could pose a conflict of interest.

Examples might be:

- An accountant in public practice, competing directly with a client, or having a joint venture or similar arrangement with a major competitor of a client

- An accountant performing services for clients whose interests are in conflict

- Clients are in dispute with each other in relation to the matter or transaction in question.

Safeguards should include:

- Notifying the client of the firm's business interest or activities that may represent a conflict of interest, and obtaining their consent to act in such circumstances

- Notifying all known relevant parties that the professional accountant is acting for two or more parties in respect of a matter where their respective interests are in conflict and obtaining their consent to so act

- Notifying the client that the accountant does not act exclusively for any one client in the provision of proposed services and obtaining their consent to so act.

Worked example: Ethical considerations

You are a reporting accountant in a company. Your immediate manager is a very forceful, domineering individual and you have accepted his views over the last two years on the level of work in progress. He has given you specific assurance that work in progress has increased by 200% during the current reporting period and instructed you to report this level in the monthly management accounts. The year end draft financial accounts show that the organisation has only just met its business plan financial targets.

Evidence then becomes available (which you were not aware of when the draft accounts were produced) to indicate that the work in progress had not increased by anywhere near the rate advised by your manager.

How should you approach this?

Solution

Key fundamental principles

Integrity – Will you be able to demonstrate that the accounts are true and fair without re-drafting?

Objectivity – How would you maintain your objectivity given that your immediate manager is such a forceful character?

Professional competence and due care – Are the draft accounts prepared in accordance with technical and professional standards?

Professional behaviour – How should you proceed so as not to discredit yourself?

Discussion

Identify relevant facts: Consider the business' policies, procedures and guidelines, accounting standards, best practice, Code of Ethics, applicable laws and regulations. Is the evidence that work in progress is incorrectly stated supported by other documentation, for example, any hard copy relating to the valuation, or analytical review of cost of sales, margins and cash flows?

Identify affected parties: Key affected parties are you and your immediate manager. Other possible affected parties are the next levels of management, recipients of management accounts and the draft financial accounts, finance, purchasing, accounts payable, human resources, internal audit, audit committee, the Board, external auditors, shareholders and financial backers.

Who would be involved in resolution? Consider not just who should be involved but also for what reason and the timing of their involvement. Have you thought of contacting the ICAEW for advice and guidance? Have you discussed this matter with your immediate line manager in light of all the available evidence and possible consequences? Can you discuss this matter with recipients of the management and financial accounts? At what point will you consider involving other affected parties?

Possible course of action

Check the relevant facts by corroborating with other available documentation, for example, cost of sales calculations, margins, previous inventory counts and other financial information.

Discuss the matter with your immediate line manager to determine an appropriate course of action, for example, undertaking another inventory count.

If you feel that your manager's response is not appropriate, discuss the matter with recipients of the management accounts and draft financial accounts and the next level of management.

Next stages could include discussion with senior management, internal audit, audit committee, the board of directors, external auditors or other actions indicated in internal whistle-blowing procedures.

During the resolution process it may be helpful to document your involvement, the substance of the discussions held, who else was involved, what decisions were made and why.

Interactive question 2: Ethical considerations [Difficulty level: Intermediate]

Your employer has put you in charge of a project which when you considered it carefully requires expertise that you do not have. You are uneasy about doing the job given that you do not have the necessary expertise and are uncertain about what to say to your employer.

Fill in the proforma below.

Key fundamental principles

Discussion

Possible course of action

See **Answer** at the end of this chapter.

6.11 Practical significance

Accountants working within a financial reporting environment can come under pressure to improve the financial performance or financial position of their employer. Finance managers who are part of the team putting together the results for publication must be careful to withstand pressures from their non-finance colleagues to indulge in reporting practices which dress up short-term performance and position. Financial managers must be conscious of their professional obligations and seek appropriate assistance from colleagues, peers or independent sources.

Summary and Self-test

Summary

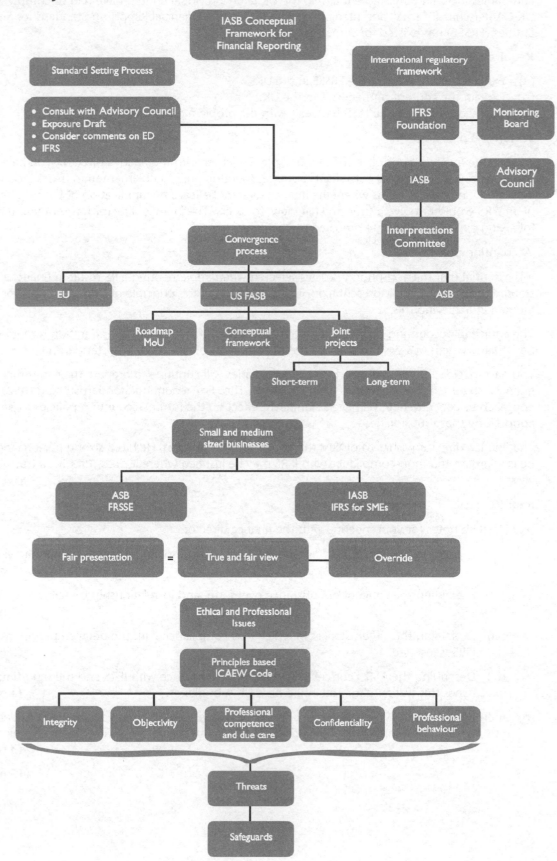

Self-test

Answer the following questions.

1 Discuss whether the move towards global accounting standards has been successful.

2 In the UK the majority of companies currently using IFRSs are listed groups. However in other countries IFRSs are used as national Generally Accepted Accounting Practices (GAAP) for all companies including unlisted entities. In the UK large individual entities have had to comply with UK GAAP, while for small and medium entities (SMEs) the Financial Reporting Standard for Smaller Entities (FRSSE) has existed for some years.

Requirements

(a) Explain the objective of the FRSSE in the UK.
(b) Explain the content of the FRSSE in the UK.
(c) Briefly explain how the IASB has dealt with the problem of accounting for SMEs.

3 **Tattanhoe plc**

You are the financial controller of Tattanhoe plc. Together with the finance director, you have held conversations with external consultants about accounting policy implementation issues. You have discussed a number of areas where the finance director believes the application of the requirements of an IFRS would not give a 'true and fair view' for users. The finance director has sent you the following extract from a note prepared by the consultants.

'Accounting policies

It is essential that the accounting policies selected when implementing IFRS result in financial statements that give a fair presentation. The application of the principle of substance over form is integral in achieving this.

The choice of accounting policies is a matter of judgement and careful consideration is required particularly where you wish to override the requirements of an accounting standard.

You have decided that Tattanhoe plc's UK subsidiaries will continue to prepare their statutory financial statements in accordance with UK GAAP. The UK Accounting Standards Board (ASB) approach to convergence will have a significant effect on the future accounting policies to be adopted by these subsidiaries.'

The finance director wishes to discuss the above extract with you. He has a strong personality and he is adamant that non-compliance with IFRS may be justified where it does not give a true and fair view.

Requirements

(a) Prepare notes for your meeting with the finance director:

   (i) Explaining the concept of 'fair presentation' and comparing it with 'true and fair view'.

      (3 marks)

   (ii) Explaining the concept of 'substance over form' and its relationship to 'fair presentation'.

      (3 marks)

   (iii) Explaining the circumstances in which non-compliance with the detailed provisions of an IFRS is justified. **(3 marks)**

   (iv) Describing the ASB's current proposals for convergence with IFRS and the reporting issues this will raise for Tattanhoe plc's UK subsidiaries. **(3 marks)**

(b) Identify the ethical issues and actions, from the above scenario, that you should consider arising from the adoption of IFRS and your professional relationship with the finance director.

      (3 marks)

      (15 marks)

4 Darlat Ltd

You are the financial controller of Darlat Ltd which currently prepares financial statements in accordance with UK GAAP. Your finance director has been in discussions with your corporate reporting advisors about whether to move to reporting under IFRS and has forwarded to you the following note received from them:

"There are a number of differences between the UK GAAP and the IFRS recognition and measurement rules. Using information on our files, we have conducted a preliminary review of how your most recent financial statements might change if you had reported under IFRS. Below we show our estimate of the effect on equity at the end of the last year, together with brief notes on the different rules.

	£'000	£'000
Equity as reported under UK GAAP		6,688
Adjustments:		
Amortisation of goodwill acquired in business combination		250
Valuation of property measured under revaluation model	1,200	
Depreciation thereof	(350)	
		850
Development expenditure	180	
Amortisation thereof	(40)	
		140
Equity as reported under IFRS		7,928

Recognition and measurement rules	UK GAAP	IFRS
Goodwill	You, like most UK companies, amortise goodwill over twenty years	Goodwill amortisation is prohibited
Property – revaluation model – basis of valuation	Existing use value, that is taking into account what you use it for	Fair value, that is the open market value taking account of all possible uses
Development expenditure	You, like most UK companies, choose to write off development expenditure as incurred	Recognition as an asset is compulsory when certain conditions are met

We would like to discuss these issues with you at an early date."

Your finance director is aware that those making economic decisions use financial information for various purposes, including for the assessment of financial performance. He is pleased that the introduction of IFRS increases equity, remarking: "if equity increases, then profit must increase both in the year of change and in future years. This will improve our performance. Shouldn't we move to IFRS as soon as possible?"

Requirement

In advance of a meeting with your finance director to discuss his remark, prepare bullet-point notes about the likely effect on performance if Darlat Ltd adopts IFRS. **(10 marks)**

Now go back to the Learning Objectives in the Introduction. If you are satisfied you have achieved these objectives, please tick them off.

Point to note: The whole of the *Conceptual Framework* and *Preface to International Financial Reporting Standards* is examinable. The paragraphs listed below are the key references you should be familiar with.

1 What is financial reporting?

- Financial reporting is the provision of financial information about a reporting entity that is useful to existing and potential investors, lenders and other creditors in making decisions about providing resources to the entity

Concept Frame (OB2)

- Financial statements comprise statement of financial position, statement of comprehensive income, statement of changes in equity, statement of cash flows and notes.

IAS 1 (10)

2 Purpose and use of financial statements

- Users' core need is for information for making economic decisions

Concept Frame (OB2)

- Objective is to provide information on financial position (the entity's economic resources and the claims against it) and about transactions and other events that change those resources and claims

Concept Frame (OB12)

- Financial position:

Concept Frame (OB13)

  - Resources and claims

  - Help identify entity's strengths and weaknesses

  - Liquidity and solvency

- Changes in economic resources and claims:

Concept Frame (OB15-16)

  - Help assess prospects for future cash flows

  - How well have management made efficient and effective use of the resources

- Financial performance reflected by accrual accounting

Concept Frame (OB17)

- Financial performance reflected by past cash flows

Concept Frame (OB20)

3 Qualitative characteristics of useful financial information

- Two fundamental qualitative characteristics are relevance and faithful representation

Concept Frame (QC5)

- Relevance = capable of making a difference to decisions

Concept Frame (QC6)

  - Predictive and confirmatory values

Concept Frame (QC7)

  - Materiality

Concept Frame (QC11)

- Faithful representation

Concept Frame (QC12)

  - Complete, neutral and free from error

- Four enhancing qualitative characteristics

Concept Frame (QC19)

  - Comparability, verifiability, timeliness and understandability

4 Cost constraint on useful financial reporting

- Costs (of preparing and analysing) financial information must be justified by the benefits of reporting it

Concept Frame (QC35)

5 Underlying assumption

- Going concern

Concept Frame (4.1)

6 Elements of financial statements

- **Asset**: A resource controlled by the entity as a result of past events and from which future economic benefits are expected to flow to the entity.

Concept Frame (4.4)

- **Liability**: A present obligation of the entity arising from past events, the settlement of which is expected to lead to the outflow from the entity of resources embodying economic benefits.

Concept Frame (4.4)

- **Equity**: The residual interest in assets less liabilities, that is net assets.

Concept Frame (4.4)

- **Income** (comprising revenue and gains): Increases in economic benefits in the form of asset increases/liability decreases, other than contributions from equity.

Concept Frame (4.25, 4.29)

- **Expenses** (including losses): Decreases in economic benefits in the form of asset decreases/liability increases, other than distributions to equity.

Concept Frame (4.25, 4.33)

7 Recognition

- An asset or a liability should be recognised in financial statements if:

Concept Frame (4.38)

  - It is probable that any future economic benefits associated with the item will flow to or from the entity, and
  - Its cost or value can be measured with reliability

8 Measurement

- Historical cost

Concept Frame (4.55)

- Current cost
- Realisable value
- Present value

9 Capital maintenance

- Financial capital:

Concept Frame (4.57)

  - Monetary
  - Constant purchasing power
- Physical capital

10 IASB

- Objectives of IASB

Preface (6)

- Scope and authority of IFRS

Preface (7-16)

- Due process re IFRS development

Preface (17)

11 Fair presentation

- Financial statements are required to give a fair presentation of the financial position, financial performance and cash flows of an entity

IAS 1 (15)

  In the UK financial statements must present a true and fair view

CA 2006

12 Not-for-profit entities

- Regulated by:

  - Local legislation

  - SORPs

  - IPSAS

- Wording and format of IAS 1 financial statements may not be suitable for not-for-profit entities

IAS 1 (5)

Answers to Interactive questions

Answer to Interactive question 1

	Buckland
Return on capital employed ((100/(300 + 200)) × 100)	20.0%
Gearing ((200/300) × 100)	66.7%
Cash generated from operations (100 + 20 – 5)	£115m
So more than profit	

	Ferrers
Return on capital employed ((200/(500 + 700)) × 100)	16.7%
Gearing ((700/500) × 100)	140.0%
Cash generated from operations (200 + 50 – 60)	£190m
So less than profit	

Ferrers is the larger company in absolute terms, but in relative terms is less profitable, less financially secure and less cash-generative than Buckland.

Answer to Interactive question 2

Key fundamental principles

Professional competence and due care – Do you have the necessary skills and experience to undertake the work?

Professional behaviour – How should you proceed so as not to discredit yourself?

Discussion

Identify relevant facts: Consider the business' policies, procedures and guidelines, accounting standards, best practice, Code of Ethics, applicable laws and regulations. Can you demonstrate your lack of expertise in this area, the potential impact on the organisation and offer alternatives? Can you make reference to the Institute's professional values and disciplinary process?

Identify affected parties: Key affected parties are you and your employer. Other possible affected parties are the human resources, internal audit, external auditors, shareholders and financial backers.

Who would be involved in resolution? Consider not just who should be involved but also for what reason and the timing of their involvement. Have you thought of contacting the Institute for advice and guidance? Do you have a trusted colleague with whom you can discuss your position? At what point will you consider involving the next level of management and human resources?

Possible course of action

Discuss your lack of expertise with your employer and suggest clearly defining the scope of the project and a course of action for addressing this issue, for example employing a person with the necessary expertise.

During the discussion focus on the potential consequences to the business, and you personally of undertaking this project.

Explain that employing a person with the necessary expertise does not remove your obligation to ensure that the work is conducted in accordance with accounting standards, laws and regulations.

If your employer does not agree to the suggested course of action, it may be appropriate to discuss the matter with the next level of management.

If the response from management is not satisfactory it may be necessary to involve human resources, internal audit or the Board.

During the resolution process it may be helpful to document your involvement, the substance of the discussions held, who else was involved, what decisions were made and why.

1 **Has the move towards global accounting standards been successful?**

The move towards global accounting standards has taken great strides in the last decade. International accounting standards themselves have improved, with the elimination of contradictory alternatives and the creation of an open and independent standard setting organisation. This in turn has led to greater acceptance of these standards, particularly in 2005 with the compulsory adoption of IFRS for consolidated financial statements by all quoted companies in the EU. The on-going project with the International Organisation of Securities Commissions will encourage the use of IFRS for cross-border listings.

Since the EU successes there has been further progress on general global convergence. The IASB and the US FASB are working on development of a common conceptual framework. There is also a Memorandum of Understanding between the IASB and FASB in respect of IFRS/US GAAP convergence. This has led to a number of short-term convergence projects between IFRS and US GAAP aimed to reduce differences in accounting practice such as the revised version of IAS 23 *Borrowing Costs,* which brings the IFRS more into line with the US method of capitalising appropriate borrowing costs. Progress has been such that the key aim of removing the requirement for non-US companies to reconcile their IFRS financial statements to US GAAP has been achieved. The Securities and Exchange Commission (the US regulator) has published proposals (in the form of a "roadmap") under which, subject to satisfactory progress being made in a number of areas, it would become compulsory in 2015 or 2016 for US entities to adopt IFRS in place of US GAAP.

However, there is no global system of enforcement, and so it is too early to say if IFRS are being adopted properly.

Some countries with their own highly developed accounting standards see the adoption of IFRS as a backward step, whereas other countries see IFRS as unnecessarily complicated.

There is also the assumption that the globalisation of accounting standards is a good thing. Recent developments in IFRS have focussed on quoted companies in the western world; they may not be suitable for all types and sizes of business organisation, or for all stages of economic development.

2 (a) **Objective of the FRSSE in the UK**

In the UK there is a specific Financial Reporting Standard for Smaller Entities (FRSSE); these entities are defined by maximum size limits.

The stated objective of the FRSSE is to ensure that reporting entities falling within its scope provide information about the financial position, performance and financial adaptability of the entity. This must be information that is useful to users in assessing the stewardship of management and for making economic decisions, recognising that the balance between users' needs in respect of stewardship and economic decision-making for smaller entities is different from that for other reporting entities.

(b) **Content of the FRSSE**

The FRSSE attempts to bring together all that is required for the smaller entities management for accounting purposes. It includes the relevant **accounting requirements and disclosures** from the other accounting standards and UITF Abstracts simplified and modified as appropriate. It is largely based upon the same basic **measurement requirements** as those in other accounting standards although with some simplifications.

However, it dispenses with many of the disclosure and presentation requirements of other standards. Finally, as well as the requirements of accounting standards, the FRSSE also includes the accounting requirements of **companies' legislation** but clearly distinguishes this from the requirements of accounting standards.

(c) **The IASB and SMEs**

The IASB published its IFRS for SMEs in July 2009.

The IASB defines SMEs as entities which do not have public accountability and which publish general purpose financial statements for external users. There are no upper size limits for such entities. An entity has **public accountability** if it has filed, or is in the process of filing, its financial statements with a securities commission or other regulatory organisation for the purpose of issuing any class of financial instruments in a public market or if it holds assets in a fiduciary capacity for a broad group of outsiders, such as a bank, insurance company, securities broker/dealer, pension fund, mutual fund or investment banking entity.

The aim of the IFRS is to reduce the financial reporting burden on SMEs that want to use global standards as well as meeting the needs of users of SME financial statements.

3 (a) **Notes for meeting**

(i) **Fair presentation and true and fair view**

IAS 1 *Presentation of Financial Statements* describes the concept of fair presentation. Fair presentation involves representing faithfully the effect of transactions, other events and conditions in accordance with the definitions and recognition criteria in the *Conceptual Framework*.

This is developed by stating that the application of IFRS, interpretations and additional disclosures will result in fair presentation.

The traditional UK approach required financial statements to comply with the Companies Act (and therefore UK standards) and give a true and fair view. True could be approximated to 'represent faithfully' and fair to 'fair presentation'. IAS 1 links them by stating that compliance with standards will give a fair presentation. As a result there is unlikely to be any difference between the two.

(ii) **Substance over form and fair presentation**

Most transactions are reasonably straightforward and their substance (their commercial effect) is the same as their legal form. In some complex transactions the true substance may not be readily apparent. Their legal form may not adequately express the true commercial effect of such transactions.

Where this is the case, it may not be sufficient to account for them by merely recording their form. The financial statements should represent commercial substance, not just legal form (substance over form). If a transaction gives rise to an asset or liability (as defined in the *Conceptual Framework*), it should be accounted for on this basis even if this is different from its legal form. Applying the definitions of an asset and a liability identifies the appropriate accounting treatment.

The *Conceptual Framework* identifies faithful representation as one of the two fundamental qualitative characteristics of useful financial information. If information is to represent faithfully the transactions it purports to represent, then they should be accounted for in accordance with their substance and economic reality and not merely their legal form. The substance may not be consistent with the legal form of a transaction. An example is a sale and repurchase agreement.

(iii) **Non-compliance with IFRS**

IAS 1 allows non-compliance with a standard (or interpretation) only where management concludes that compliance would be so misleading as to conflict with the objectives of financial statements set out in the *Conceptual Framework*. However this is only where the relevant regulatory framework requires, or does not prohibit, such a departure.

The standard uses the phrase 'where management concludes' which may indicate that there is a margin for those preparing the financial statements to use this exception where they believe it is appropriate. However, IAS 1 talks about this coming about 'in extremely rare circumstances'. To all intents and purposes, these circumstances will never occur.

Inappropriate accounting policies or non-compliance are not rectified by disclosure of the policies adopted or by description in the notes to the financial statements.

The true and fair override is a UK concept and not permitted under IFRSs.

ICAEW

(iv) **Convergence proposals and practical implications**

The ASB accepts that there is no case for maintaining differences between two sets of GAAP, ie between UK accounting standards and IFRS. Adoption, by one method or another, of IFRS within the UK is the long-term goal.

But the IASB has over recent years made a number of short-term fixes to improve its reporting standards while carrying out longer term projects to revise those standards more fundamentally. The ASB was concerned that if UK standards were converged with IFRS too quickly, then further changes would have to be made shortly thereafter.

To avoid companies having to make two changes of accounting policy in a short period, the ASB has concluded that companies not required to change to international standards and choosing to continue using UK GAAP, can make one change, if UK standards are not changed to mirror IFRS until after the longer term set of changes to international standards.

The practical considerations for the UK subsidiaries which do not adopt IFRS are:

–   The need to maintain two sets of financial records to meet group and separate financial statement requirements.

–   Systems requirements to collect accounting and disclosure requirements for both bases of reporting meeting internal and external reporting requirements.

–   Timeframes where the basis of preparation may differ, identifying how management will review performance when the parent's and subsidiaries' reporting differ.

It may be easier for Tattanhoe plc to reconsider whether UK subsidiaries should continue to use UK GAAP.

(b) **Issues and actions**

The Finance Director has a strong personality. He may use his position to dominate. This may result in him exerting influence on those around him, including the financial controller, so they acquiesce to his requirements.

Whilst IFRS narrow down the range of possible alternatives, the adoption of accounting policies still requires judgement and much is left to the discretion of management. It is essential that accounting policy selections generate information that is free from bias and presents faithfully the substance of the transactions.

The financial controller needs to use his professional skills and judgement. It may be appropriate to consult the Code of Ethics, the local district society for confidential support or to take advice from the ethical help lines offered by the ICAEW.

4   **Darlat Ltd**

Notes for meeting with FD
Subject: **Performance measurement under IFRS**
Prepared by: Financial controller
Date: **xx/xx/xx**

•   Comparability is one of the (four) enhancing qualitative characteristics which makes financial statement information useful

•   Changing from one set of accounting rules to another will make the IFRS figures for the current year not comparable with the UK GAAP figures for the previous year

•   Normal comparability rules require restatement of the previous period under IFRS, so the previous period equity will probably increase as well

•   So performance in the current year may not be assessed as having improved

•   Financial statement users have three key measures: cash flow, profitability and gearing

–   Cash flow: cash flows are unaltered by changing recognition/measurement rules for assets and liabilities in the statement of financial position

No performance improvement (no change at all)

    –   Profitability: increase in equity = increase in capital employed, so, other things being equal, ROCE (profit before interest and tax as % of (equity and interest-bearing liabilities)) will go down, not up

- But profit will go up as a result of no goodwill amortisation

- But profit will go down as a result of higher property values – higher depreciation in future years

- It is not clear what effect recognising development expenditure as an asset will have in future years. Depreciation will go up, but perhaps by less than positive effect of capitalisation of expenditure written off under UK GAAP

- Net effect may be performance deterioration

    Gearing: equity goes up, but no change in interest-bearing liabilities. So gearing (interest-bearing liabilities as % of equity) goes down.

- Improvement in performance

CHAPTER 2

Reporting financial performance

Introduction

Examination context

Topic List

1   Overview of material covered in Financial Accounting

2   Profit in financial statements

3   IAS 12 *Income Taxes*

4   IFRS 8 *Operating Segments*

5   IAS 24 *Related Party Disclosures*

6   Other financial and operational information

7   UK GAAP comparison

Summary and Self-test

Technical reference

Answers to Interactive questions

Answers to Self-test

Introduction

Learning objectives

Tick off

- Prepare and present extracts of financial statements in respect of current tax, related party transactions and segmental reporting ☐

- Explain the reasons for disclosure provisions in relation to segment reporting and related party transactions ☐

- Identify and illustrate the main differences between international and UK requirements in relation to segment reporting and related party transactions ☐

- Identify any related ethical issues ☐

- Identify and understand other financial and operating information included in financial statements ☐

Specific syllabus references for this chapter are: 1e, 3a, 3f, 4a and 4c.

Syllabus links

You have already covered IAS 1 *Presentation of Financial Statements,* IAS 8 *Accounting Policies, Changes in Accounting Estimates and Errors* and IFRS 5 *Non-current Assets held for Sale and Discontinued Operations* in the Financial Accounting syllabus. In this chapter we will review these topics briefly as they are an important part of the reporting of financial performance.

You will not have covered the topics of accounting for current tax, segment reporting and related party disclosures before. These will also be relevant at the Advanced Stage where the treatment of tax, in particular, will be developed further.

Examination context

In the examination, candidates may be required to:

- Prepare extracts of financial statements that reflect financial performance

- Interpret the results of an entity produced in accordance with IFRS 8 *Operating Segments*

- Identify related party relationships and explain the disclosure requirements of IAS 24 *Related Party Disclosures*

- Discuss the ethical issues relating to the preparation of segment information and disclosure of related party transactions

- Assess whether financial statements adequately reflect other financial and operating information provided

- Explain the difference between UK GAAP and international requirements, preparing simple calculations to illustrate.

1 Overview of material covered in Financial Accounting

> **Section overview**
>
> This section provides an overview of material covered in Financial Accounting.

1.1 IAS 1 *Presentation of Financial Statements*

Financial statements should present fairly the financial position, financial performance and cash flows of an entity. Management may believe its business is unusual or unique and therefore non-compliance with one or more international standards is essential to provide a fair presentation. However, such non-compliance reduces consistency and comparability of financial information, so international standards limit it to extremely rare circumstances.

The identification of corporate scandals could have the effect of moving financial reporting towards a rules-based approach, with standard setters introducing new rules to block off avenues that have been highlighted. But no set of accounting standards can eliminate the need to exercise judgement and formulate estimates when applying them. Management choices and judgements, from determining the policy for measurement of investment properties to estimating the useful life of major non-current assets, can have a significant effect on earnings, key performance measures and the financial position of an entity. The transparent disclosure of these choices and of the uncertainty surrounding significant estimates is essential if users are to understand the risks faced by that entity.

Accounting standards set out the principles that should be adhered to by management in the preparation of financial statements. The usefulness of the information in financial statements depends entirely on how management applies those principles to the presentation of their business operations. Management may possess information and experience that is both unique and essential in the preparation of the financial statements. It is the integration of this management knowledge with the application of accounting standards that will lead to financial statements which are fairly presented and informative.

- The revised version of IAS 1 published in 2007 made substantial changes to the way statements of financial performance are presented.

- The objective of IAS 1 is to prescribe the basis for the presentation of financial statements to aid **comparability**. IAS 1 prescribes the **minimum content** for inclusion in the financial statements and provides guidance on their presentation. It also provides **suggested formats**, although these are **not prescribed**.

- IAS 1 identifies the purpose of financial statements as being to provide information about the **financial position, financial performance and cash flows** of an entity that is useful to a wide range of users in making economic decisions.

  Such financial statements also show the result of **management stewardship** of the resources of the entity.

- The components of financial statements are:

  - A **statement of financial position**
  - A **statement of comprehensive income** (see below)
  - A **statement of changes in equity**
  - A **statement of cash flows**
  - **Notes** to the financial statements

  These should be clearly identified and distinguished from other information.

- Entities can choose to present items of income and expense recognised in a period in:

  - A single statement of comprehensive income; or

  - Two statements: a statement presenting the components of profit or loss (separate income statement) and a second statement beginning with profit or loss and displaying components of other comprehensive income (statement of comprehensive income).

Point to note: whichever presentation method is adopted, a line item for profit or loss for the period should be presented. In the single statement of comprehensive income it should be presented as a sub-total and in the separate income statement it should be the final total. This is illustrated in the proformas set out below.

- The following general principles must be considered when preparing financial statements:
    - **Fair presentation** and compliance with IFRS
    - **Going concern**
    - **Accrual basis of accounting**
    - **Materiality and aggregation**
    - **Offsetting**
    - Disclosure of **comparative information**
    - **Consistency**

- Financial statements should be prepared **at least annually**.

 ### Interactive question 1: Presentation   [Difficulty level: Exam standard]

An entity supplies seasoned timber to furniture manufacturers. The operating cycle is clearly defined and timber is matured over a three to five year period.

State how the timber inventories would be classified in the statement of financial position and any additional disclosures which would be required.

See **Answer** at the end of this chapter.

The statement of financial position and statement of comprehensive income layouts that follow are consistent with the minimum requirements of IAS 1.

PROFORMA STATEMENT OF FINANCIAL POSITION

XYZ plc – Statement of financial position as at [date]

	£m	£m
ASSETS		
Non-current assets		
Property, plant and equipment		X
Intangibles		X
Investments		X̲
		X
Current assets		
Inventories	X	
Trade and other receivables	X	
Investments	X	
Cash and cash equivalents	X̲	
	X	
Non-current assets held for sale	X̲	
		X̲
Total assets		X̲
EQUITY AND LIABILITIES		
Attributable to owners of the parent		
Ordinary share capital		X
Preference share capital (irredeemable)		X
Share premium account		X
Revaluation surplus		X
Retained earnings		X̲
		X
Non-controlling interest		X̲
Total equity		X

	£m	£m
Non-current liabilities		
Preference share capital (redeemable)	X	
Finance lease liabilities	X	
Borrowings	<u>X</u>	
		X
Current liabilities		
Trade and other payables	X	
Taxation	X	
Provisions	X	
Borrowings	X	
Finance lease liabilities	<u>X</u>	
		<u>X</u>
Total equity and liabilities		<u>X</u>

PROFORMA STATEMENT OF COMPREHENSIVE INCOME

Illustrating the single statement of comprehensive income and classification of expenses by nature

XYZ plc – Statement of comprehensive income for the year ended [date]

Continuing operations	£m	£m
Revenue		X
Other operating income		X
Changes in inventories of finished goods and work in progress		(X)
Work performed by the entity and capitalised		X
Raw material and consumables used		(X)
Employee benefits expense		(X)
Depreciation and amortisation expense		(X)
Impairment of property, plant and equipment		(X)
Other expenses		<u>(X)</u>
Profit/loss from operations		X
Finance costs		(X)
Investment income		X
Share of profit/(losses) of associates		<u>X</u>
Profit before tax		X
Income tax expense		<u>(X)</u>
Profit/loss from continuing operations for the period		X
Discontinued operations		
Profit/(loss) for the period from discontinued operations		<u>(X)</u>
Profit/(loss) for the period		X
Other comprehensive income		
Available-for-sale financial assets:		
Gains/(losses) arising in the period	X	
Reclassification adjustments for gains included in profit or loss	<u>(X)</u>	
		X
Gains on non-current asset revaluations		X
Share of other comprehensive income of associates		<u>X</u>
Other comprehensive income for the period, net of tax		<u>X</u>
Total comprehensive income for the period		<u><u>X</u></u>
Profit attributable to:		
Owners of the parent		X
Non-controlling interest		<u>X</u>
		<u><u>X</u></u>
Total comprehensive income attributable to:		
Owners of the parent		X
Non-controlling interest		<u>X</u>
		<u><u>X</u></u>

PROFORMA INCOME STATEMENT AND STATEMENT OF COMPREHENSIVE INCOME

Illustrating the separate income statement and the statement of comprehensive income, and the classification of expenses by function

XYZ plc – Income statement for the year ended [date]

	£m
Continuing operations	
Revenue	X
Cost of sales	(X)
Gross profit	X
Distribution costs	(X)
Administrative expenses	(X)
Profit from operations	X
Finance costs	(X)
Investment income	X
Share of profit/(losses) of associates	X
Profit before tax	X
Income tax expense	(X)
Profit/(loss) from continuing operations for the period	X
Discontinued operations	
Profit/(loss) for the period from discontinued operations	X
Profit/(loss) for the period	X
Attributable to:	
Owners of the parent	X
Non-controlling interest	X
	X

XYZ plc – Statement of comprehensive income for the year ended [date]

	£m	£m
Profit/(loss) for the period		X
Other comprehensive income		
Available-for-sale financial assets:		
Gains/(losses) arising in the period	X	
Reclassification adjustments for gains included in profit or loss	(X)	
		X
Gains on non-current asset revaluations		X
Share of other comprehensive income of associates		X
Other comprehensive income for the period, net of tax		X
Total comprehensive income for the period		X
Total comprehensive income attributable to:		
Owners of the parent		X
Non-controlling interest		X
		X

Points to note:

1 The sub-total 'profit/loss from operations' is not a current requirement of IAS 1. This Study Manual uses this description as it is used in practice and is not prohibited by IAS 1.

2 Presenting expenses by their nature provides information on how the various costs affect the revenue generation and profit of the entity. Manufacturing entities may find this presentation more appropriate because it highlights, for example, expenditure on raw materials, costs to convert raw materials into finished goods, employee costs and depreciation.

3 The alternative presentation analyses expenses by their function within the entity. This may provide more meaningful identification of expenses. This method is more subjective, however, requiring judgements in the allocation of a particular type of expenses across the different functions.

4   Where expenses are presented by function, additional disclosure is required of total depreciation and total employment costs, because this may be helpful to users in predicting future cash flows.

PROFORMA STATEMENT OF CHANGES IN EQUITY

XYZ plc – Statement of changes in equity for the year ended [date]

	Share capital £'000	Retained earnings £'000	Available-for-sale financial assets £'000	Revaluation surplus £'000	Total £'000	Non-controlling interest £'000	Total equity £'000
Balance at [date]	X	X	X	X	X	X	X
Changes in accounting policy	–	X	–	–	X	X	X
Restated balance	X	X	X	X	X	X	X
Changes in equity during [date]							
Issue of share capital	X	–	–	–	X	–	X
Dividends	–	(X)	–	–	(X)	(X)	(X)
Total comprehensive income for the year	–	X	(X)	X	X	X	X
Transfer to retained earnings	–	X	–	(X)	–	–	–
Balance at [date]	X	X	X	X	X	X	X

(See Financial Accounting Study Manual)

1.2   Context for IAS 1

Recent corporate scandals have increased public concern as to the **adequacy of transparency in financial statements**. Comments that financial statements are difficult to understand and that more explanatory disclosure is required are often made by politicians and in the media. **Accounting standards provide guidance on presentation**, although **no system of principles or rules** can cover all eventualities. The **integrity of management** is therefore essential for the adequate presentation of information in financial statements.

In assessing the **performance or position** of an entity, users should **understand the structure of the information** with which they are presented. The usefulness of financial information presented will depend on the **consistent** preparation and presentation, to ensure **comparability** of information from **one period to the next** and **between different entities**.

As an example, one of the common measures of an entity's liquidity (and one dealt with in more detail in a later chapter) is the current ratio, which expresses current assets as a ratio of current liabilities. If users of financial statements are to make meaningful comparisons between an entity's current ratio from one period to another and between entities in the same period, it is vital that the same basis is used for defining the current assets and the current liabilities. Hence the rules in IAS 1.

1.3   IAS 8 *Accounting Policies, Changes in Accounting Estimates and Errors*

The ability to compare financial statements year on year for an individual entity and between different entities is a fundamental process for investors and businesses alike. Effective comparisons allow an entity to benchmark itself within a particular sector. Useful comparisons could not be undertaken if financial statements were prepared on different bases.

It is also imperative that companies are restricted in their ability to select different ways of treating the same information period on period. Such an ability would allow entities to choose the most beneficial result for any period.

IAS 8 *Accounting Policies, Changes in Accounting Estimates and Errors* provides the guidelines under which accounting policies can be changed and therefore represents the structure that underpins the successful comparison of financial statements.

- The objective of IAS 8 is to enhance **relevance, reliability and comparability** by prescribing both the criteria for selecting and changing accounting policies and the accounting treatment of changes in accounting policies, estimates and of correction of errors.

- **Accounting policies** are the **specific principles, bases, conventions, rules and practices** applied by an entity in preparing and presenting financial statements.

- These are normally developed by reference to the **relevant IFRS** where this is applicable. Otherwise judgement should be applied by reference to specified criteria.

- Accounting policies should be applied consistently from one period to another.

- A change in accounting policy is only allowed:

    – If it is **required** by IFRS or
    – If, in the opinion of management, it results in **reliable and more relevant information**

    Changes should be applied:

    – In accordance with IFRS/Interpretation's **transitional provisions** or
    – **Retrospectively** if there are no transitional provisions or the change is voluntary

- Adoption of a new accounting policy for transactions not previously occurring or which were previously immaterial is not a change of accounting policy.

    Points to note:

    1   The decision to change an accounting policy on the basis that it results in reliable and more relevant information would be made by management. This decision may well be quite subjective and should be scrutinised by the auditors who would need to ensure that the change in policy can be justified appropriately and is not just to improve the position shown by the financial statements. Difficult judgements may well be involved. The key is that a change must not result in misrepresentation of financial performance and position.

    2   Voluntary changes in accounting policies are likely to be relatively uncommon in practice, but may occur where an entity's business operations undergo substantial modification. A substantial change in business operations may mean that an old policy is no longer appropriate as it does not result in relevant information about the new operations.

- **Accounting estimates** are **approximations**, usually based on an assessment of future events. They are the result of **judgements made by management** based on the information available at the time. As a result it is likely that they will need to be adjusted in the future as other information comes to light and circumstances change.

- Changes in accounting estimates should be applied **prospectively**:

    – In the period of change and
    – In future periods if they are affected.

- **Prior period errors** are omissions from, and misstatements in, the entity's financial statements which arise in spite of the fact that reliable information was available at the time and could reasonably have been expected to have been taken into account.

- Such errors should be corrected **retrospectively** in the first set of financial statements authorised for issue after their discovery.

(See Financial Accounting Study Manual.)

Interactive question 2: Accounting policy [Difficulty level: Exam standard]

List the financial reporting and ethical issues you would need to consider when selecting or changing an accounting policy.

See **Answer** at the end of this chapter.

1.4 Context for IAS 8

As stated earlier, the **ability to compare financial statements** year on year for an individual entity and between different entities is a **fundamental need** for investors and businesses alike. Effective comparisons allow an entity to **benchmark** itself within a particular sector. Useful comparisons could not be undertaken if financial statements were prepared on different bases.

IAS 8 provides the guidelines under which accounting policies can be changed and therefore **represents the structure that underpins the successful comparison of financial statements**.

1.5 Discontinued operations and IFRS 5 *Non-current Assets Held for Sale and Discontinued Operations*

- An entity is required to **disclose separately** the activities carried out by a discontinued operation.

- A discontinued operation is a component of an entity that has either been **disposed of or is classified as held for sale** (more detail in Chapter 3).

- A component which is abandoned (that is closed down rather than disposed of) may be treated as a discontinued operation, but only when it ceases to operate.

- A **component** is a group of operations and cash flows which can be clearly distinguished, operationally and for financial reporting purposes, from the rest of the entity.

- The component must also satisfy the following criteria:

  – It represents a **separate major line of business or geographical area of operations**

  – It is part of a **single co-ordinated plan** to dispose of a separate major line of business or geographical area of operations or

  – It is a **subsidiary** acquired exclusively with a view to resale.

- A **single net figure** for discontinued operations should be disclosed in profit or loss.

- An **analysis of this figure** should be provided which may be presented in the **notes** to the financial statements. The analysis must present the component's revenue, expenses, pre-tax profit or loss, the gain or loss on the remeasurement/disposal of the assets and the associated income tax expense.

- The results of the prior period should be **reclassified** as discontinued.

- The disclosure of discontinued operations in the proformas above is in line with Example 11 in the (non-mandatory) *Guidance on Implementing IFRS 5*. (See Financial Accounting Study Manual.)

Worked example: Discontinued operations

An entity has classified a subsidiary as held for sale during the current year. A separate subsidiary is a component of the entity as its operations and cash flows are capable of being separately identified both operationally and for financial reporting purposes. By being classified as held for sale it meets all the criteria of a discontinued activity.

The prior period statement of comprehensive income and note disclosures should be re-presented so that they relate to all operations discontinued by the current year end. But the assets and liabilities of the subsidiary in the prior period statement of financial position are not reclassified as held for sale.

1.6 Context for IFRS 5

An important business issue arises when an entity closes or discontinues a part of its overall business activity. Management will have assessed the impact of the closure on future profitability, but users of financial statements will want to make their own assessment.

IFRS 5 assists users to a certain extent, but can only require an analysis of the contribution, positive or negative, of the discontinued element to the current year's profit or loss, not of the future profit or loss forgone.

The requirement to make disclosures in profit or loss in respect of operations which will continue for the foreseeable future allows users to make relevant future projections of cash flows, financial position and earnings-generating capacity. The past performance of operations which will not continue is then available to users in the analysis required of discontinued operations, which is normally presented in a note rather than in profit or loss.

Point to note:

A held-for-sale component, not just one disposed of, is classified as a discontinued operation, something which takes account of management's intentions. Management can change its mind.

1.7 Not-for-profit entities

There are many different types of not-for-profit entity with a wide variety of different objectives. They can be in the public sector (national and local government, for example) or in the private sector (medical and religious charities, for example). But the common theme across them all is that their key objective is the provision of services for their clients/customers, rather than the creation of profit for their owners.

Financial reporting is governed by local requirements, such as the Companies Act 2006 and the Charities Acts 1993 and 2006 for UK-based charities which are incorporated. The main aim of such regulation is to ensure that the entity accounts properly for the resources entrusted to it. Accounting for the **stewardship** of these resources is much more important than it is in the case of for-profit organisations. Income statements are normally set out in a way which makes clear where resources have come from and how they have been used.

2 Profit in financial statements

Section overview

- There are different views about what constitutes profit
- IAS 1 distinguishes between profit or loss and other comprehensive income
- Reclassification adjustments may become necessary
- A few items are presented separately in the statement of changes in equity

2.1 Introduction

The 'profit' of an entity for the last financial year is:

- A key measure of financial performance, used by analysts in calculating a number of financial performance ratios; and

- The basis on which users of financial statements estimate future profits (and then future cash flows).

But there are many different views about what 'profit' is. 'Profit' has been defined as all net gains:

- Which have been realised; revaluation/remeasurement gains are excluded (this is the traditional view in many countries, including the UK, and was the basis previously adopted by IAS 1); or

- Which are likely to recur in the future; revaluation/remeasurement gains may be included but gains from discontinued operations are excluded, as are one-off gains such as the profit earned by a manufacturing entity on the sale of a freehold property; or

- Except those arising from foreign exchange differences;

and there are many other variants on these themes.

Financial reporting standard setters around the world have therefore struggled to identify a single measure of profit which has near-unanimous support. Instead they have concentrated on improving the presentation and disclosures in financial statements, in order that different users can calculate the (different) profit figures they find most useful.

Recent versions of IAS 1 have required entities to present an amount of profit or loss for each period, but they have left it to the entities themselves to decide how to define which items to include in their profit or loss.

2.2 Revised version of IAS 1

In developing the revised version of IAS 1 the IASB expressed a preference for the single statement of comprehensive income, on the basis that it fits the *Conceptual Framework* better. All changes in equity other than those with owners as owners (share issues and dividend payments) meet the *Conceptual Framework* definitions of income/gains and expenses/losses, so the *Conceptual Framework* does not define profit. Nor does the *Conceptual Framework* provide criteria by which to distinguish those items which should be included and which should be excluded when calculating profit or loss. As there are no clear principles by which to separate income and expenses into two statements (the income statement and the statement of comprehensive income), a single statement was conceptually preferable.

Despite this preference the IASB accepted that there was wide-ranging, deeply seated and vocal support for the two statement approach. So the revised version of IAS 1 allows entities to choose how to present changes in equity other than those with owners as owners (share issues and dividend payments), using either the single statement or the two statement approach.

Under the two statement approach the statement of comprehensive income presents those items which previously were described as being recognised directly in equity. For the purposes of the Financial Reporting syllabus these items are:

*   Revaluation gains (and some losses) on remeasuring property, plant and equipment and intangible assets under the revaluation model; and

*   Differences on remeasuring available-for-sale financial assets to fair value.

The phrase used in IAS 16 *Property, Plant and Equipment* and IAS 39 *Financial Instruments: Recognition and Measurement* to identify where these items should be presented is that they should be "recognised [as income or expense] in other comprehensive income".

The income statement presents all other items of income and expenses. The phrase used across IFRS in general to identify where these items should be presented is that they should be "recognised [as income or expense] in profit or loss".

2.3 Reclassification adjustments

Certain IFRS require remeasurement gains already recognised in other comprehensive income to be reclassified to profit or loss when the related asset is disposed of. This process is known as a reclassification adjustment and in the Financial Reporting syllabus only applies to one type of asset.

As will be seen in a later chapter, IAS 39 *Financial Instruments: Recognition and Measurement* requires a gain or loss arising from a change in the fair value of an available-for-sale financial asset to be recognised in other comprehensive income. It also requires a reclassification adjustment for such a gain or loss when the asset is disposed of, to recognise it in profit or loss.

As such a gain or loss can only increase/decrease equity once, on disposal the double entry in respect of a gain previously recognised in other comprehensive income will be:

		£	£
DR	Other comprehensive income	X	
CR	Profit or loss		X

In the case of a previously recognised loss, the double entry will be:

		£	£
DR	Profit or loss	X	
CR	Other comprehensive income		X

In both cases this transfer is described as a reclassification adjustment from equity to profit or loss.

Point to note:
No such reclassification adjustment is made in respect of previously recognised gains when an item of property, plant and equipment or an intangible asset measured under the revaluation model is disposed of (see below).

2.4 Statement of changes in equity

This statement is effectively a reconciliation between:

- The carrying amount of each component of equity (share capital; reserves; non-controlling interests) at the beginning of the period; and

- The carrying amount of each component of equity at the end of the period.

It presents the changes resulting from:

- Total comprehensive income for the period, with separate presentation of the amounts attributable to the owners of the parent and to the non-controlling interest;

- The effect of adjustments for prior period errors and changes of accounting policy on each component of equity;

- Contributions by owners (share issues) and distributions to them (dividends).

This statement also presents transfers between components of equity. For the purpose of the Financial Reporting syllabus, the main transfers between reserves relate to the revaluation surplus which arises when property, plant and equipment and intangible assets are measured under the revaluation model.

Transfers from the revaluation surplus to retained earnings occur as follows:

- Where an entity chooses to make an annual transfer in respect of excess depreciation (the annual depreciation charge based on the revalued amount less the annual depreciation charge based on historic cost)

- On the disposal of a revalued asset (any revaluation surplus relating to the asset remaining at the date of disposal).

3 IAS 12 *Income Taxes*

Section overview

- Current tax is recognised as an expense (income) in profit or loss and as a liability (asset) in the statement of financial position.

- Adjustments should be made in the current period for tax over/under-charged in respect of prior periods.

- Tax liabilities and assets should be disclosed separately from other liabilities/assets.

- Tax expense (income) should be disclosed in the income statement.

3.1 Introduction

Taxation is a major expense for business entities. In many developed countries taxation accounts for over 30% of corporate profits. This has a direct effect on cash flow and performance measures such as earnings per share and cash flow per share (see Chapters 11 and 12).

Multinational entities use sophisticated tax planning techniques to minimise their tax costs. Tax planning may be through tax effective group structures, industry specific rules, optimisation of capital and revenue structures, and effective planning of acquisitions and disposals. Tax is an important planning consideration in significant business transactions.

With tax being such a significant cost to business, it is essential that an entity's financial statements include relevant information that enables users to understand historical, and predict future, taxation cash flows and liabilities.

IAS 12 deals with two different tax issues:

- **Current tax**

  This is the amount of **income tax payable** by an entity in respect of its **taxable profit** for a period. In the UK, this income tax will take the form of **corporation tax**.

- **Deferred tax**

  This is an **accounting measure** used to match the tax effects of transactions with their accounting impact and thereby produce less distorted results. It is not a tax levied by the government that actually needs to be paid. An example is the calculation of the surplus on the revaluation of a non-current asset; normally no tax is actually payable at the time of the revaluation but deferred tax is calculated so as not to misrepresent to users of the financial statements the amount of the surplus attributable to owners and recognised in other comprehensive income. Deferred tax is not examinable in the Financial Reporting syllabus but will be covered at the Advanced Stage. The effect is that all tax within the Financial Reporting syllabus is recognised in profit or loss.

IAS 12 says little about the basic treatment of current tax. Indeed a number of aspects of presentation are dealt with by IAS 1. In essence, the extent of the tax liability is determined by taxation rules rather than accounting rules.

3.2 Accounting for tax

The basic rule is that when a liability for tax arises it is recognised as an **expense** in profit or loss for the period. It is also recognised as a **liability** to the extent that it remains unpaid.

		£	£
DR	Income tax expense	X	
CR	Cash		X
CR	Current liabilities: taxation		X

3.3 Recognition of current tax liabilities and assets

The income tax due on the profit for any year cannot be finally determined until after the year end when the tax liability has been agreed with the tax authorities, something which takes months and, in some cases, years. So the amount of income tax on profits recognised each year is an estimate. When the tax due is later agreed with the tax authorities, an adjustment to the original estimate will normally be required. This adjustment will be recognised in profit or loss for the accounting period in which the estimate is revised.

IAS 12 requires any **unpaid tax** in respect of the current or **prior periods** to be recognised as a **liability** (resulting in an income tax expense being recognised in profit or loss).

Conversely, any **tax paid** in respect of current or **prior periods** in **excess of** what is due should be recognised as an **asset** (resulting in a reduction in the income tax expense recognised in profit or loss).

Worked example: Current tax

In 20X8 Darton Ltd had taxable profits of £120,000. In the previous year (20X7) income tax on 20X7 profits had been estimated as £30,000.

Calculate tax payable and the charge for 20X8 if the tax due on 20X7 profits was subsequently agreed with the tax authorities as:

(a) £35,000; or
(b) £25,000.

Any under or over payments are not settled until the following year's tax payment is due.

Assume a tax rate of 30%.

Solution

(a)

	£
Tax due on 20X8 profits (£120,000 × 30%)	36,000
Underprovision for 20X7 (£35,000 – £30,000)	5,000
Tax charge and liability	41,000

(b)

	£
Tax due on 20X8 profits (as above)	36,000
Overprovision for 20X7 (£25,000 – £30,000)	(5,000)
Tax charge and liability	31,000

Alternatively, the overprovision could be shown separately as income in profit or loss and as an asset in the statement of financial position. An offset approach like this is, however, most likely.

Taking this a stage further, IAS 12 also requires recognition as an asset of the benefit relating to any tax loss that can be **carried back** to recover current tax of a previous period. This is acceptable because it is probable that the benefit will flow to the entity and it can be reliably measured.

 Worked example: Tax losses carried back

In 20X7 Eramu Ltd paid £50,000 in tax on its profits. In 20X8 the company made tax losses of £24,000. The local tax authority rules allow losses to be carried back to offset against current tax of prior years. The tax rate is 30%.

Show the tax charge and tax liability for 20X8.

Solution

Tax repayment due on tax losses = 30% × £24,000 = £7,200.

The double entry will be:

DR	Tax receivable (statement of financial position)	£7,200
CR	Relief for tax losses (recognised in profit or loss)	£7,200

The tax receivable will be shown as an asset until the repayment is received from the tax authorities.

3.4 Measurement

Measurement of current tax liabilities (assets) for the current and prior periods is very simple. Liabilities (assets) are measured at the **amount expected to be paid to (recovered from) the tax authorities**. The tax rates (and tax laws) used should be those enacted (or substantively enacted) by the end of the reporting period.

3.5 Presentation

In the statement of financial position, **tax assets and liabilities** should be shown separately from other assets and liabilities.

Current tax assets and liabilities can be **offset**, but this should happen only when certain conditions apply.

(a) The entity has a **legally enforceable right** to set off the recognised amounts; **and**

(b) The entity intends to settle the amounts on a **net basis**, or to realise the asset and settle the liability at the same time.

The **tax expense (income)** related to the profit or loss from ordinary activities should be presented in **profit or loss**. An analysis of this figure would be provided in the notes to the financial statements showing the **major components** as follows.

	£
Income tax expense	
Current tax expense	X
Adjustment for current tax of prior periods	X/(X)
	X

Also required is a reconciliation between the actual tax expense (income) and tax notionally payable (receivable) on the accounting profit. This is often presented as a table starting with tax amount calculated as the accounting profit × the normal tax rate; this amount is then adjusted for the tax effect of each type of adjustment, such as tax losses carried back, with the actual expense being the final total. This enables users of financial statements to make judgements about the future, whether, for example, the current period tax charge had been reduced by transactions which will not be repeated in the future.

4 IFRS 8 *Operating Segments*

Section overview

- IFRS 8 only applies to entities whose equity or debt is traded on public markets.

- An entity should identify:

    - Its operating segments, by reference to its internal reporting structure
    - Its reportable segments, using quantitative criteria.

- A measure of profit or loss in respect of each reportable segment should always be disclosed.

- Other disclosures in respect of reportable segments are required in certain circumstances.

- Amounts disclosed are as measured in internal reports, so not necessarily under IFRS.

- Information should also be provided about the entity's products and services, the geographical areas in which it operates and its major customers.

4.1 The issue

The **financial performance and position of large businesses** may be **difficult to analyse** if faced with the overall totals included in the financial statements under IAS 1. This is because such businesses often carry out many **different activities**, which may be in different business sectors and/or operate in **different parts of the world**. These different 'segments' may have very different:

- Rates of profitability
- Rates of growth in the past
- Opportunities for growth in the future
- Degrees of risk associated with their operations.

Some segments may be cyclical, while others may be susceptible to rapid technological change. In some cases segments may suffer from unstable currencies, hyperinflation, low economic growth or political instability.

The ability to predict the future cash flows, earnings-generating capacity and financial position of an entity is hampered when only overall totals are included in financial statements. **Disaggregated information** provides users with a detailed analysis of the financial performance and financial position of the operations of an organisation which can be used as a basis for **economic analysis and decisions**.

Nevertheless, **segment information has its limitations**. Ultimately it is **an entity's management which defines its segments** and therefore **significant judgements** are required. The guidance factors are diverse enough to allow a wide range of different segment definitions. Even broad comparability between reporting entities can be difficult. Management may wish to provide only the absolute minimum information, given its strategic value to competitors and potential market entrants.

4.2 The objective of IFRS 8

IFRS 8 (which converges IFRS with US GAAP by making substantial changes to the way information had to be presented by its predecessor IAS) is solely a disclosure standard, in that it does not contain any recognition or measurement rules but merely requires entities to disclose information to enable users to evaluate the **nature and financial effects** of the:

- **Business activities** in which it engages
- **Economic environments** in which it operates.

4.3 Outline of the requirements

Most IFRSs apply to all entities, but IFRS 8 is an exception, in that it **only applies** to those entities whose **equity or debt is traded in public markets**. Such an entity is then required to:

- Identify its **operating segments** and **which of them are reportable**

- **Always** disclose one item of information **about each reportable segment: a measure of profit or loss**

- **Disclose** other information about each reportable segment **in specific circumstances**

- **Disclose** information about **products and services, geographical areas and major customers**

4.4 Operating segments

Definition

Operating segment: This is a component of an entity:

(a) That engages in business activities from which it may earn revenues and incur expenses (including revenues and expenses relating to transactions with other components of the same entity)

(b) Whose operating results are regularly reviewed by the entity's chief operating decision maker to make decisions about resources to be allocated to the segment and assess its performance, and

(c) For which discrete financial information is available.

Operating segments are identified on **a managerial basis**, ie the way the entity **organises itself internally**. **Little additional guidance** is given to help entities identify their operating segments; reliance is placed on the (unpublicised and unauditable) processes which have led management to structure their activities in the way they have chosen.

The phrase **'chief operating decision maker'** describes **a function, not a person** with a specific title. Often it will refer to the chief executive or the chief operating officer, but it could equally well refer to an executive committee.

Points to note:

- A businesses activity which has yet to earn revenues, such as a start up, is an operating segment if it is separately reported on to the chief operating decision maker

- Not every part of the business is an operating segment; for example, **a central function**, such as a head office, does not earn revenues itself and is therefore **not** generally considered to be **an operating segment.**

- A component is **not excluded** from being an operating segment just **because its sole purpose** is to sell products or services **internally** to other parts of the business. So the different stages in a vertically integrated business may be separate operating segments, if they are reported separately to the chief operating decision maker.

- If the entity has adopted a matrix structure internally (such as where one set of managers is responsible for product/service lines worldwide but another set is responsible for specific geographical areas) and the chief operating decision maker regularly reviews financial information in respect of both sets of managers, the entity shall identify its operating segments by reference to IFRS 8's objective as set out above.

4.5 Aggregation

Two or more operating segments may be **aggregated** if the segments have **similar economic characteristics**, and the segments are similar in *each* of the following respects:

- The **nature of the products or services**
- The **nature of the production process**
- The **type or class of customer** for their products or services
- The **methods used to distribute their products or provide their services**, and
- If applicable, **the nature of the regulatory environment**

4.6 Determining reportable segments

An entity must report separate information about **each operating segment** for which **at least** one of the following reaches a **10% threshold**:

- Its **reported revenue (internal and external)** as a percentage of the **total revenue (internal and external)** of all operating segments, or

- Its **reported profit or loss** as a percentage of the **combined reported profit of all segments not reporting a loss** (or the combined loss of all segments reporting a loss, if greater), or

- Its **assets** as a percentage of the **combined assets of all operating segments**

Point to note:

Operating segments that do not meet **any of the quantitative thresholds** may be reported separately if management believes that information about the segment would be useful to users of the financial statements.

4.6.1 The overall 75% test

Internal sales drop out when consolidated financial statements are produced, so there is then the override that total external revenue of reportable segments must be at least 75% of total external revenue; if the operating segments meeting the 10% test do not add to this total, then other operating segments must be separately reported on until the 75% is reached.

This overall size test is to ensure that all entities present a sufficient level of information regarding their individual activities to ensure that users of the financial statements can make informed economic decisions.

Point to note:

A segment separately reported in the previous period **should continue to be reported separately** even if the thresholds are not met in the current period, where the segment has been identified as being of continuing significance. Equally, where a segment meets the 10% threshold in the current period it should be separately reported **for both the current and the previous period** even if it was not separately reported in the previous period, assuming that it is practicable to do so.

Worked example: Reportable segments

GHI plc, a quoted company, reports six different types of business to its chief executive.

In the most recent financial year, the revenue of these six, as a percentage of total revenue (including that from internal customers), was as follows:

Business	% internal	% external	% total
1	0	40	40
2	0	20	20
3	12	5	17
4	0	9	9
5	0	8	8
6	0	6	6
	12	88	100

Which segments are reportable?

Solution

Business	% internal	% external	% total	
1	0	40	40	Reportable segment because 40% total > 10%
2	0	20	20	Reportable segment because 20% total > 10%
3	12	5	17	Reportable segment because 17% total > 10%
4	0	9	9	Reportable segment (see note)
5	0	8	8	Not a reportable segment (8% total < 10%)
6	0	6	6	Not a reportable segment (6% total < 10%)
	12	88	100	

Note: The external revenue of Businesses 1, 2 and 3 totals 65 percentage points, which is 73.9% of the 88 percentage points of external revenue. Therefore a further operating segment is reportable, under the 75% test.

 Interactive question 3: Reportable segments   [Difficulty level: Exam standard]

BBB plc is an integrated manufacturing company with six operating segments. It has no other activities except those of the six operating segments. It reports segmentally in accordance with the minimum requirements of IFRS 8.

Operating segment	Internal revenue £m	External revenue £m	Total revenue £m	Profit (loss) £m	Assets £m
Ash	25	470	495	155	40
Beech	15	40	55	(25)	35
Conifer	–	200	200	65	285
Daisy	120	110	230	40	60
Elm	25	80	105	(50)	40
Fir	15	100	115	15	40
TOTAL	200	1,000	1,200	200	500

Requirement

Explain whether each of the operating segments is a reportable segment.

See **Answer** at the end of this chapter.

4.7 What has to be reported

The information to be reported has been selected to meet the objective of IFRS 8 as set out above.

4.7.1 General information

The **factors used to identify reportable segments** (such as whether the entity is organised around products/services or geographical areas) and the **types of products and services** from which each reportable segment derives its revenue must be disclosed.

4.7.2 Profit or loss

An entity should always report **a measure of profit or loss** for each reportable segment. Measures of **total assets** and of **total liabilities** should also be disclosed if they are regularly provided to the chief operating decision maker.

IFRS 8 states that the amount of each segment item reported should be **the measure used in internal reporting.**

This may be different from the measurement method used in the published financial statements and required by IFRS.

Points to note:

1 Nowhere in IFRS 8 is 'a measure of profit or loss' defined, other than by the requirement that segment items should be measured in the same way as they are for the regular internal reporting purposes. This means that segment items **do not** have to be recognised and measured in accordance with IFRS; management is permitted to use its own rules provided they are used for internal reporting.

2 Nowhere in IFRS 8 is there any specification of what is meant by 'total assets' and 'total liabilities', so again the entity can decide. Importantly, there is no requirement that the assets and liabilities attributed to an operating segment are those by which the measure of profit or loss is generated; there is nothing to prevent an inconsistency here.

mgt discretion

4.7.3 Other financial information

The other items listed below should be disclosed if they are:

- Included in the measure of profit or loss reviewed by the chief operating decision maker; or

- Regularly reviewed by him/her, even if not included in that measure of profit or loss.

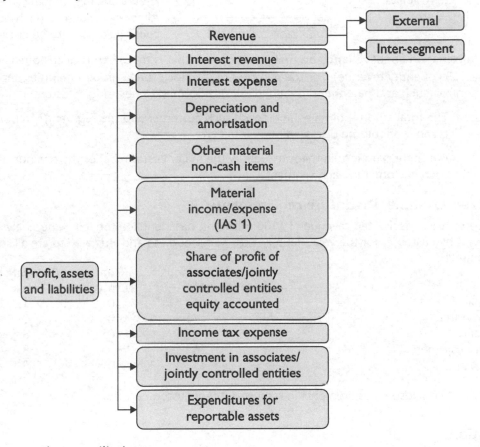

4.7.4 Measurement and reconciliations

The amount for each segment item reported shall be as measured in the reports submitted to the chief operating decision maker. These are not necessarily amounts measured under IFRS. If there are amounts allocated to operating segments (such as in respect of centrally incurred costs), the allocations should be on a reasonable basis.

There should be an explanation of the measurements of segment profit or loss and, where disclosed, assets and liabilities; the minimum disclosure is:

- The basis for accounting for transactions between reportable segments

- The differences, if any, between measurements for segment reporting purposes and measurements for financial statements purposes, such as accounting policies and allocations of centrally incurred costs

- The nature of any changes in measurement methods since the prior period and the effect of such changes on profit or loss

- The nature of asymmetrical allocations, such as a depreciation expense being deducted in arriving at a segment's profit or loss where the assets are not included in total assets.

There should be a **reconciliation** of the reportable segment totals for each of the items disclosed to the entity's figures for the same amounts as presented in the financial statements, eg the total of reportable segment profit or loss to the entity's profit or loss.

4.7.5 Entity-wide disclosures

Certain information should always be disclosed, even if the entity has a single reportable segment. It should be based on the amounts in the financial statements, so **measured on an IFRS basis**. The information required is:

- **External revenue** for each group of products and services (if the reported basis is not products and services).

- **Geographical information**:

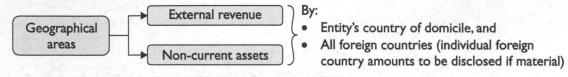

By:
- **Entity's country of domicile, and**
- **All foreign countries (individual foreign country amounts to be disclosed if material)**

- Information about **reliance on major customers** (that is those **external** customers who represent ≥ 10% of entity revenue). For the purposes of this disclosure a group of entities under common control (such as a parent and its subsidiaries) is deemed to be a single customer.

  - The total amount of revenue for each such customer and the segment(s) reporting this revenue should be disclosed.

  - But there is no requirement to identify the major customer(s) or the revenue attributable to each customer in each segment.

Worked example: Disclosure requirements

Majid plc has consolidated revenue of £100 million. It has identified the following analysis of revenue by segment by customer for the year. Rahman Ltd, Mahmood Ltd and Hussain Ltd are all subsidiaries of Jackman Ltd.

	Engineering £'m	Retail £'m	Distribution £'m	Total £'m
Rahman	6	0	1	7
Mahmood	7	0	0	7
Hussain	6	0	6	12
Other customers	26	40	8	74
	45	40	15	100

Identify the disclosure requirements in respect of these customers.

Solution

IFRS 8 requires entities to disclose information about major customers. If a single customer's revenues are 10% or more of Majid plc's revenues, the total amount of revenue from each such customer and the segments in which those revenues are reported must be disclosed. Majid plc need not disclose the identity of a major customer, nor the amount of revenues that each segment reports from that customer. A group of entities under common control should be considered a single customer. Hence Majid plc should disclose that revenues from a single customer are £26 million and that they are reported in the engineering and distribution segments. But Majid plc need not identify the Jackman Group by name, nor the amounts reported in each segment.

4.8 Does segmental reporting provide useful information?

There are some factors which make this reporting very useful, for example the splitting of the totals into segments which represent at least 10% of each one. To explore the extent to which IFRS 8 helps provide useful information consider the three measures that are important to users of financial statements:

Measure	Assistance provided by IFRS 8
Profitability: how profitable is each segment?	Because share capital and borrowings are not normally allocated to segments, no segmental return on capital employed can be calculated.
	But other profitability measures, such as profit as a percentage of revenue (if revenue is reported internally), can be calculated by segment – this is one key potential benefit of IFRS 8
Gearing: how solvent is each segment?	Because share capital and borrowings are not normally allocated to segments, no segmental gearing can be calculated.
Cash flow: how good at creating cash inflows is each segment?	IFRS 8 is silent on this topic but IAS 7 encourages disclosures of each segment's operating, investing and financing cash flows

In addition, comfort can be taken from the facts that:

- **Users** of financial statements **can look at an entity's activities in the same way as management** does when running the businesses ("look through the eyes of management"), the amounts disclosed are as measured for review by management

- The basis of **pricing transfers** between segments must be **disclosed**

- There must be **restatement of comparative figures** when the structure of the internal organisation is changed.

- Revenue is analysed over products and services and over geographical areas

- The reliance on each major customer must be quantified.

But the absence of any definition of profit or loss or of what constitutes segment assets and segment liabilities reduces the objectivity of the amounts disclosed.

Other limitations of IFRS 8 relate to the judgements it requires of management – see below.

4.9 Judgements required

The absence of any definition in IFRS 8 of profit or loss leaves its definition to **management judgement**. So there is some possibility that these figures could be adjusted (perhaps through changes to the basis for allocating centrally incurred costs) to present the picture desired by management, to dress up the profitability of a business segment it is trying to dispose of, for example.

It is also the case that the measurement of items such as segment revenues, segment profit or loss and segment assets/liabilities **may be strongly influenced by management's desire to minimise tax liabilities**. Within entities which operate in a number of countries around the world, management can set the prices at which transactions take place between different segments at any level it wishes. These transfer prices are often set to minimise tax liabilities. Even if these transfer prices are used consistently from period to period, there may well be a distortion, driven by tax planning, of the picture painted of the performance and position of different segments within the entity.

A **Chartered Accountant** involved in producing this type of information should ensure he/she is **not unduly influenced** by non-financial management and that the disclosures do not distort the **fair presentation** of information in the financial statements.

5 IAS 24 *Related Party Disclosures*

Section overview

- Disclosure is required of the nature of any related party relationships and of any transactions between such parties

- There are a number of ways in which one party may be related to another

- The relationship between an entity and its parent and subsidiaries should be disclosed regardless of whether any transactions have taken place between them

- An entity is required to disclose the name of its parent and, if different, that of the ultimate controlling party

- An entity should disclose the pay and other compensation of key management personnel in total together with an analysis of this balance

5.1 Introduction

It is normally assumed that directors of companies attempt to promote the interests of shareholders in their dealings with other entities. As a result **transactions are normally assumed to take place at arm's length values**.

However, companies are made up of a variety of stakeholders with different interests and incentives, which in some cases may lead to **a conflict of interest**. Examples might include:

- Transactions between companies under **common control** (for example a parent and a subsidiary)
- Transactions between the company and its directors

The two parties to the transactions referred to above are said to be related to each other and the transactions between them to be related party transactions.

In these circumstances the normal rules of commercial arrangements **may not** apply and as a result:

- The reported performance of the entity **may** be distorted
- Directors **may** face conflicting incentives.

IAS 24 enhances transparency by requiring **disclosure** to shareholders of these relationships and the transactions stemming from them.

Point to note:

IAS 24 **does not** require any disclosures about whether related party transactions were carried out at prices other than open market prices.

5.2 Objective

The key emphasis of IAS 24 is **appropriate disclosure**. It aims to ensure that an entity's financial statements contain the disclosures necessary to draw attention to the possibility that its position and results may have been affected by the existence of related parties and transactions with them.

Related party transactions are, however, a normal feature of commerce and business, so IAS 24 does not attempt to prevent such relationships or to require any adjustments to the values of related party transactions carried out at non-market prices.

Point to note:

The special rules for entities under the control, joint control or significant influence of government bodies are dealt with in Section 5.9 below.

5.3 Scope

IAS 24 should be applied in:

(a) Identifying **related party relationships** and **transactions**
(b) Identifying **outstanding balances** between an entity and its related parties
(c) Identifying circumstances in which **disclosure** of the items in (a) and (b) is required, and
(d) **Determining the disclosures to be made** about those items

IAS 24 requires disclosure of related party relationships, transactions and outstanding balances in the separate financial statements of:

- A parent (See Chapter 8)
- A venturer in a joint venture
- An investor in an associated entity

Related party transactions and outstanding balances with other entities in a group are disclosed in an **individual entity's financial statements**.

Intra-group related party transactions and outstanding balances **are eliminated on consolidation in the financial statements of the group** and are not disclosed.

Point to note:

On many occasions IAS 24 uses the phrase 'outstanding balances, including commitments', commitments meaning undertakings to do something if a particular event occurs or does not occur in the future. In these notes this phrase had been shortened to 'outstanding balances'.

5.4 Identifying related parties

This depends on a number of key definitions in IAS 24.

Definitions

Related party: A person or entity that is related to the entity preparing its financial statements (the reporting entity).

(a) A person or a close member of that person's family (see definition below) is related to a reporting entity if that person:

    (i) has control or joint control over the reporting entity

    (ii) has significant influence over the reporting entity, or

    (iii) is a member of the key management personnel (see definition below) of the reporting entity or of a parent of the reporting entity.

(b) An entity is related to a reporting entity if any of the following conditions applies:

    (i) The entity and the reporting entity are members of the same group

    (ii) One entity is an associate or joint venture of the other entity (or of a member of the group of which the other entity is a member)

    (iii) Both entities are joint ventures of the same third party

    (iv) One entity is a joint venture of a third entity and the other entity is an associate of the third entity.

    (v) The entity is a post-employment benefit plan for the benefit of employees of either the reporting entity or of an entity related to the reporting entity

    (vi) The entity is controlled or jointly controlled by a person identified in (a) above

    (vii) A person identified in (a) (i) above has significant influence over the entity or is a member of the key management personnel (see definition below) of the entity or of a parent of the entity.

Point to note:

The definitions of a related party treat control and joint control differently from significant influence. So fellow subsidiaries and fellow joint ventures are related parties of each other under definitions (b)(i) and (b)(iii) respectively, but if the same investor has significant influence over two associates, those associates are not related parties of each other.

Close members of the family of a person: Those family members who may be expected to influence, or be influenced by, that person in their dealings with the entity. These include:

(a) that person's children and spouse or domestic partner
(b) children of that person's spouse or domestic partner and
(c) dependants of that person or that person's spouse or domestic partner.

Control: The power to govern the financial and operating policies of an entity so as to obtain benefits from its activities.

Joint control: The contractually agreed sharing of control over an economic activity.

Key management personnel: Those persons having authority and responsibility for planning, directing and controlling the activities of the entity, directly or indirectly, including any director (whether executive or otherwise) of that entity.

Significant influence: The power to participate in the financial and operating policy decisions of an entity, but not to control those policies. Significant influence may be gained by share ownership, statute or agreement.

5.5 Application of substance over form

Under IAS 24 attention should be directed to the **substance** of the relationship rather than focusing on its legal form. For example, the following **are not related parties**:

- Two entities **simply because they have a director** (or other member of key management personnel) **in common**, or because a member of key management personnel of one entity has significant influence over the other entity

- Two venturers **simply because they share joint control over a joint venture**

- Providers of finance, trade unions, public utilities and government departments and agencies which do not fall within the definition of government-related entities (see Section 5.9 below) **simply by virtue of their normal dealings with an entity**

- A customer, supplier, franchisor, distributor, or general agent, with whom an entity transacts a significant volume of business, **simply by virtue of the resulting economic dependence**.

Worked example: Related parties

The following examples illustrate the application of the definition of a related party to practical situations:

(a) Entity H owns 100% of Entity S_1 and 80% of Entity S_2

All three entities are members of the same group, so under definition (b)(i) they must all be treated as related parties in the financial statements of Entity H, Entity S_1 and Entity S_2 and in the consolidated financial statements of H.

(b)　Person A owns 30% of Entity B and Entity C owns 40% of Entity B

　　Entity B is the reporting entity:

　　　　Person A is a related party under definition (a)(ii) and Entity C is a related party under definition (b)(ii)

　　Entity C is the reporting entity:

　　　　Entity B is a related party under definition (b)(ii)

(c)　Person A and Entity B have joint control over Entity C

　　Entity B is the reporting entity:

　　　　Entity C is a related party under definition (b)(ii)

　　Entity C is the reporting entity:

　　　　Person A is a related party under definition (a)(i) and Entity B is a related party under definition (b)(ii)

(d)　Person A is a non-executive director of Entity B

　　Entity B is the reporting entity:

　　　　Person A falls within the definition of Entity B's key management personnel and is a related party under definition (a)(iii)

(e)　Person A owns 70% of Entity B and is a director of Entity C

　　Entity B is the reporting entity:

　　　　Person A is a related party under definition (a)(i) and Entity C is a related party under definition (b)(vii)

　　Entity C is the reporting entity:

　　　　Person A falls within the definition of Entity C's key management personnel and is a related party under definition (b)(iii)

　　　　Entity B is a related party under definition (b)(vi)

Interactive question 4: Related party　　　　　　　[Difficulty level: Intermediate]

Mint is a company that complies with the minimum requirements of IAS 24 *Related Party Disclosures*. The following relationships have been identified.

(1)　Toffee is a separate company, in which one of Mint's junior managers owns 10% of the share capital.

(2)　The daughter of a director of Mint.

(3)　A director of Mint owns 60% of Chocolate, a separate company.

(4)　Miss Butterscotch owns 25% of Mint.

(5)　A director of Mint is also a director of Sugar, a separate company, but is not a shareholder in either company.

(6)　Cream is a company owned by the niece of the finance director of Mint.

Requirement

Identify and explain, which of the above should be disclosed as related parties in Mint's financial statements.

See **Answer** at the end of this chapter.

5.6 Related party transactions

Definition

Related party transaction: A transfer of resources, services or obligations between a reporting entity and a related party, regardless of whether a price is charged.

Note that this definition covers **any transaction that occurs between a reporting entity and a related party**

- It is common practice for a reporting entity's employees to receive goods or services at reduced prices or for free. If the employees fall within the definition of the reporting entity's key management personnel, they will be related parties and the entity should disclose these transactions.

- Even if every transaction with a related party takes place at the full arm's length price, the reporting entity should disclose them.

IAS 24 is based on the principle that **it is the identification of the related party relationship that triggers the disclosure requirements**.

Examples of transactions which should be disclosed include:

- **Transfers of resources for which no charge is made**

  It is common for parent companies not to make a charge for some services, such as for management services provided to a subsidiary. In practice, **it is very difficult to identify transactions for which there is no charge at all**; there is nothing for accounting systems to capture, so there is no easy place to go looking for the relevant information.

- **Transfers of resources for which an artificial charge is made**

  An example of an artificial charge would be where, under instructions from the parent, **sales** between group companies **are at above, or below, open market prices**.

- **Transfers of resources made at full, open market, prices (that is arm's length prices)**

  The reason for including these is that even if in the current year such transfers are made for full consideration, the related party relationship means that in a future year they might not be. Also, **the related party relationship itself is important information to users** in understanding the motivation of the relevant parties in the context of corporate governance.

  Disclosures that related party transactions were made on terms equivalent to those that prevail in arm's length transactions should be made **only if such terms can be substantiated**.

5.7 Disclosures

- **The related party relationship between parent and subsidiaries**.

  This relationship is seen as so important to users of financial statements that **disclosure is always required** irrespective of whether there have been any transactions between the group entities.

  Disclosure is required of the parent's name and, if different, the name of the ultimate controlling party.

  If the financial statements of the parent or ultimate controlling party are not publicly available, the entity is required to identify the next most senior parent in the group that does produce financial statements that are available to the general public.

  Point to note:

  The reason this relationship must be disclosed even if there are no transactions is that the control held by the parent means that there could be such transactions in future periods, if the parent decided this was appropriate.

- **Compensation**, being the consideration in exchange for their services, received by key management personnel in total and for each of the following five categories:

Category	Example
Short-term employee benefits	Salary and holiday pay
Post-employment benefits	Pensions
Other long-term benefits	Long-service awards or sabbatical leave
Termination benefits	Redundancy pay
Share-based payments	Shares and share options

- **Disclosures required only if there have been related party transactions during the period**:
  - The nature of the relationships (but remember this must always be disclosed in respect of a parent)
  - The amount of the transactions
  - The amount of any balances outstanding at the year end
  - The terms and conditions attaching to any outstanding balance (for example, whether security has been provided and what form the payment will take)
  - Details of any guarantees given or received
  - Any provision against any outstanding balances and the expense recognised in the period for bad or doubtful debts due from related parties.

- **Disclosure** of the fact that transactions were on an **arm's length basis**.

  This disclosure may be made only if such terms can be substantiated.

These disclosures should be made separately for different categories of related parties, although items of a similar nature may be disclosed together. Where aggregation results in key information necessary to understand the effect of the transactions on the financial statements being unavailable, separate disclosure should be made.

The different categories for which separate disclosures are required are identified as:

- The **parent**
- Entities with **joint control** or **significant influence** over the entity
- **Subsidiaries**
- **Associates**
- **Joint ventures** in which the entity is a **venturer** (see Chapter 8)
- **Key management personnel** of the entity or its parent
- **Other related parties**.

Although information is required about the nature of related parties, there is no requirement to specifically identify them by name.

5.8 Examples

The following are **examples of transactions that are disclosed** if they are **with a related party**:

- Purchases or sales of goods (finished or unfinished)
- Purchases or sales of property and other assets
- Rendering or receiving of services
- Leases
- Transfers of research and development
- Transfers under licence agreements
- Transfers under finance arrangements
- Provision of guarantees or collateral
- Commitments to do something if a particular event occurs or does not occur in the future
- Settlement of liabilities on behalf of the entity, or by the entity on behalf of another party.

Interactive question 5: Related party disclosures [Difficulty level: Exam standard]

Pinot is a company that complies with the minimum requirements of IAS 24.

Requirements

Explain whether related party relationships exist and what disclosures, if any, would be required by IAS 24 in the current year financial statements of Pinot, in respect of each of the following transactions.

(1) Pinot sells goods on credit to Chablis, which is a company owned by the son of Mr Grigio. Mr Grigio is a director of Pinot. At the year end there was a trade receivable of £100,000 owing from Chablis to Pinot. It was decided to write off £30,000 of this receivable, and make full provision against the remainder. Debt collection costs incurred by Pinot during the year were £4,000.

(2) During the year Pinot purchased goods from Merlot for £600,000, which was deemed to be an arm's length price. Pinot owns 40% of the ordinary share capital of Merlot.

(3) At the year end an amount of £90,000 is due to one of Pinot's distributor companies, Shiraz.

(4) During the year a house owned by Pinot, with a carrying amount of £200,000 and a market value of £450,000, was sold to one of its directors, Mrs Barolo, for £425,000. Pinot guaranteed the loan taken out by Mrs Barolo to purchase the property.

See **Answer** at the end of this chapter.

5.9 Government-related entities

Definitions

Government Government, government agencies and similar bodies whether local, national or international.

Government-related entity: An entity controlled, jointly controlled or significantly influenced by a government.

In environments where government control is pervasive, it can be difficult to identify other government-related entities and the cost of complying with the normal IAS 24 requirements would be greater than the benefits of the increased information being made available.

A reporting entity is therefore exempt from the normal disclosure requirements in respect of related party transactions and outstanding balances with:

- A government which has control, joint control or significant influence over the reporting entity

- Another entity that is a related party because the same government has control, joint control or significant influence over both the reporting entity and the other entity.

Instead the reporting entity should disclose the following:

- The name of the government and the nature of the relationship with the reporting entity (ie control, joint control or significant influence)

- The nature and the amount of each individually significant transaction

- A qualitative or quantitative indication of the extent of all other transactions.

5.10 Judgements required

In practical terms the identification of related parties and the disclosure of transactions with them may not be straightforward. Reasons for this include the following:

- The application of the definitions of a related party can be **subjective** and will involve the use of **judgement**, for example whether someone is a close member of the family of an individual.

- Transactions may be difficult to identify, particularly where **no consideration** has changed hands.

- Directors and key management may be **sensitive** to the disclosure of certain transactions; this increases the risk of deliberate concealment.

- **Quantitative materiality** issues are not necessarily relevant. In many cases the existence of the relationship is the issue rather than the amounts involved.

An accountant preparing financial statements must ensure that **all relevant information is made available to him/her** and that this complies with the requirements of IAS 24, irrespective of any other pressures being applied.

6 Other financial and operational information

Section overview

- Over and above that contained in the financial statements, a large amount of information about a UK company and its directors is available in the directors' report/the operating and financial review.

- Most large companies will include a chairman's report.

6.1 Introduction

Financial statements are normally contained in documents which include other financial and operational information. The extent to which this additional information is required and the form that it takes will depend on **local legislation**. The remainder of this section is based on **UK requirements**.

The information in these other sections should be complementary to the financial statements and consistent with them. Narrative reports are useful as they provide information about:

- An entity's business and markets, together with details of their strategy and objectives

- The current development and performance of the entity

- Details of environmental, employee and social issues

- Forward-looking information about future developments and issues

- Details of resources available to the entity that are not included in the financial statements such as intangible assets

- A description of the risks and uncertainties the business is facing

- Details of financial and non-financial key performance indicators (KPI).

In the examination you will **not** be required to prepare a directors' report or operating and financial review, but you may be provided with extracts from both the financial statements and one of these reports and asked to comment on how well they complement each other. So you need to have an idea of the sort of information provided by these reports.

6.2 Directors' report

The Companies Act 2006 continues the requirement for **a directors' report** (s 415) to be produced for each financial year and **specifies an expanded amount of information which must be included**.

The directors' report is **largely a narrative report**, but certain figures must be included in it. **The purpose of the report is to give the users of accounts a more complete picture of the company's affairs**. In practice the directors' report is often a rather dry and uninformative document, perhaps because it must be verified by the company's external auditors, whereas the chairman's report need not be.

The required content can be summarised as follows.

- The company's **principal activities** during the year

  A **business review**, the purpose of which is set out as being to inform shareholders and help them assess how the directors have performed their statutory duty to promote the success of the company.

- The names of those who were **directors** at any time during the financial year.

- **Employees**

  - Policy in respect of disabled persons, in terms of initial employment, development and promotion

  - Actions taken to introduce, maintain or develop arrangements aimed at providing employees with information on matters of concern to them

- **Other**

  - The difference, if significant, between the book value and market value of land held as non-current assets

  - Political and charitable donations (if they exceed a minimum amount)

  - Details of creditor payments policy (only if a public company)

6.3 Operating and financial review

In the UK, the Operating and Financial Review (OFR) was developed to provide commentary on financial performance and to identify the strategy and development of the business, an area in which stakeholders are becoming increasingly interested.

Guidance on the content of the OFR has been available from the Accounting Standards Board (ASB) since 1993 and is currently in the form of Reporting Statement 1: *Operating and Financial Review*; this is as a **non-compulsory** statement of best practice (rather than as a reporting standard).

Following the revision to the content of the business review in the Directors' Report (see above), the ASB has reassured UK companies that adopting the OFR as described below will fulfil their legal obligations. One acceptable approach is to produce an OFR in line with the Reporting Statement and make cross-references to it in the Directors' Report.

6.3.1 Principles of the OFR

The basic principles of the OFR are as follows.

- It should set out an **analysis of the business** through the eyes of the board of directors

- It should focus primarily on matters relevant to **shareholders** (although other stakeholders are likely to find the information useful)

- The OFR should have a **forward-looking orientation** including trends and factors relevant to the achievement of long-term business objectives

- The OFR should both complement and supplement the financial statements and should **enhance overall corporate disclosure**

- The OFR should be **comprehensive, understandable, balanced, neutral and comparable over time**

- The OFR should focus on those matters the directors consider to have general significance **to the business as a whole.**

6.3.2 Disclosure

The statement does not attempt to provide a template of compulsory headings for an OFR. Rather, it sets out **key content elements** that should be addressed, and leaves directors to determine the precise detail. The nature and content of the OFR are likely to **vary according to different industries, markets and products.**

The key content elements that may be disclosed are:

- **The nature, objectives and strategies of the business**, together with the key performance indicators used to assess progress against these stated objectives.

- **Current and future development and performance**

- Description of the **key resources** available to the entity, including tangible and intangible resources and an explanation of how the resources are managed

- Description of **principal risks and uncertainties** facing the entity (for example strategic, commercial, operational, financial) and the directors' approach to managing risks

- Information about **significant relationships** with stakeholders, other than shareholders, which influence the performance of the business (for example strategic alliances with other entities)

- An analysis of the **financial position** of the entity, including the short and long-term capital structure (for example gearing, maturity profile of debt), treasury policies and objectives, discussion of the cash inflows and outflows during the year and the ability to meet future cash requirements and fund growth

6.3.3 The IASB – *Management Commentary*

Following an extensive period of development the IASB published in December 2010 an IFRS Practice Statement *Management Commentary*. It provides a broad, non-binding framework for the presentation of a narrative relating to financial statements prepared in accordance with IFRS. But it is not an IFRS, so entities applying IFRS are not required to comply with it.

Management commentary is a narrative report that provides a context within which to interpret the financial position, financial performance and cash flows of an entity. It also provides management with an opportunity to explain its objectives and its strategies for achieving those objectives.

6.4 Chairman's report

Most large companies include a chairman's report in their published financial statements. In the UK this is **purely voluntary** as there is no statutory requirement to do so.

The chairman's report is not governed by any regulations and, it could be argued, is often unduly optimistic.

7 UK GAAP comparison

Section overview

- In the UK the presentation of financial statements is dealt with in the Companies Act 2006, FRS 3 *Reporting Financial Performance*, FRS 18 *Accounting Policies* and FRS 28 *Corresponding Amounts*

- In the UK:

  - The presentation of continuing and discontinued operations is dealt with in FRS 3 *Reporting Financial Performance*

  - Segment reporting is dealt with in SSAP 25 *Segmental Reporting*

  - Related party transactions are dealt with in FRS 8 *Related Party Disclosures*

7.1 Presentation of financial statements

7.1.1 Presentation of financial statements

In the UK the presentation of financial statements is primarily dealt with by the following:

- Companies Act 2006
- FRS 3

In the UK the Companies Act sets out balance sheet and profit and loss account formats. In general terms the requirements are similar to those of IAS 1.

The key differences between international and UK formats are as follows:

- **Different terminology** is used.

International terminology	UK terminology
Statement of financial position	Balance sheet
Income statement	Profit and loss account
Revenue	Turnover
Inventories	Stocks
Receivables	Debtors
Payables	Creditors
Non-current assets	Fixed assets
Non-current liabilities	Creditors falling due after more than one year
Current liabilities	Creditors falling due within one year
Retained earnings	Profit and loss account (reserve)
Non-controlling interest	Minority interest

- The profit and loss account formats require less detail than IAS 1, although IAS 1 allows some of the extra detail to be presented in the notes.

- The Companies Act balance sheet formats are **less flexible** than the IAS 1 formats.

  The formats in IAS 1 are contained in the *Guidance on Implementation* and are therefore not mandatory. The Companies Act formats are enshrined in law.

- The UK balance sheet is usually prepared on a **net assets basis**.

  Fixed assets are added to net current assets (current assets less current liabilities) and long-term liabilities are deducted from the result. IAS 1 allows more flexibility in formats.

Other issues are dealt with by FRS 3 as follows:

FRS 3	IAS 1

FRS 3 identifies **two types of exceptional item**:
 	
• So-called **"super exceptionals"** which should be presented **separately on the face of the profit and loss account** after operating profit and before interest:
  – Profit or loss on sale or termination of an operation
  – Costs of a fundamental reorganisation or restructuring that has a material effect on the nature and focus of the reporting entity's operations
  – Profit or loss on disposal of fixed assets
 	
• All other items should be allocated to the appropriate statutory format heading and attributed to continuing or discontinued operations as appropriate. If the item is **sufficiently material** that it is needed to show a true and fair view it must be **disclosed on the face of the profit and loss account**.
	IAS 1 by contrast does not contain the term 'exceptional item' but simply says that material items of income and expense should be disclosed separately.

UK GAAP requires separate presentation of: • The profit and loss account • The **statement of total recognised gains and losses** which includes all the gains and losses occurring during the period.	IAS 1 allows a single statement of comprehensive income which combines both
UK GAAP requires a **note of historical cost profits and losses**.	Not required
FRS 3 requires a **sub-total for operating profit** to be shown in the profit and loss account.	Although this is not prohibited by IAS 1, it is not explicitly required.

Points to note:

FRS 18 *Accounting Policies* only requires a discussion of significant estimation techniques. IAS 1's requirements are more extensive, in that disclosure of estimation techniques used in the application of accounting policies is required.

FRS 28 *Corresponding Amounts* does not specifically require the presentation of comparative amounts for narrative and descriptive information. IAS 1 does so require.

A **statement of total recognised gains and losses** would typically be laid out as follows:	£
Profit for the year (per the profit and loss account)	X
Items taken directly to reserves	
Surplus on revaluation of fixed assets	X
Total recognised gains and losses for the year	X
Prior period adjustments (see later)	(X)
Total gains and losses recognised since last annual report	X

7.1.2 Reporting performance

The issues covered by IAS 8 are dealt with in three UK Standards:

* FRS 3 *Reporting Financial Performance*
* FRS 18 *Accounting Policies*
* FRS 28 *Corresponding Amounts*

UK practice in this area is **very similar** to that required by IAS 8. The following differences however should be noted:

* FRS 3 requires **comparative financial information** to be restated where a **fundamental prior period error** has occurred. This is **more restrictive** than IAS 8 which requires restatement for **material prior period errors**.

* FRS 18 does **not** require the disclosure of impending changes to accounting policies.

7.2 Continuing and discontinued operations

- The basic provision of FRS 3 is **very similar** to that of IFRS 5 in that it requires the separate disclosure of continuing and discontinued activities. There are a number of key differences as follows:

  - Under FRS 3 **detailed analysis** is shown **on the face of the P&L account**. In addition **turnover and operating profit** must be **analysed** between **existing and newly acquired operations**.

  - Under FRS 3 discontinued operations are defined as **fully disposed of or closed down either in the accounting period or within three months of its end**. This will often result in a **later classification** as discontinued as compared to IFRS 5.

- FRS 1 *Cash Flow Statements* **encourages** the separate disclosure of cash flows from discontinued operations. This is **required** rather than encouraged by IFRS 5.

Illustration of a UK profit and loss account

	20X7		20X6 as restated	
	£m	£m	£m	£m
Turnover				
Continuing operations	550			500
Acquisitions	50			
	600			
Discontinued operations	175			190
		775		690
Cost of sales		(620)		(555)
Gross profit		155		135
Net operating expenses		(104)		(83)
Operating profit				
Continuing operations	50		40	
Acquisitions	6			
	56		40	
Discontinued operations	(15)		12	
Less 20X6 provision	10			
		51		52
Profit on sale of properties in continuing operations		9		6
Provision for loss on operations to be discontinued				(30)
Loss on disposal of discontinued operations	(17)			
Less 20X6 provision	20			
		3		
Profit on ordinary activities before interest		63		28
Interest payable		(18)		(15)
Profit on ordinary activities before taxation		45		13
Tax on profit on ordinary activities		(14)		(4)
Profit on ordinary activities after taxation		31		9
Minority interests		(2)		(2)
Profit for the financial year		29		7

Worked example: Profit and loss account

Feelgoode plc's profit and loss account for the year ended 31 December 20X7, with comparatives, is as follows.

	20X7	20X6
	£m	£m
Turnover	200	180
Cost of sales	(60)	(80)
Gross profit	140	100
Distribution costs	(25)	(20)
Administrative expenses	(50)	(45)
Operating profit	65	35

During 20X7 the company sold a material business operation with all activities ceasing on 14 February 20X8. The loss on the sale of the operation amounted to £3m and this is included under administrative expenses. The results of the operation for 20X6 and 20X7 were as follows:

	20X7 £m	20X6 £m
Turnover	22	26
Profit/(loss)	(7)	(6)

In addition, the company acquired a business which contributed £7m to turnover and made an operating profit of £2m.

Prepare the profit and loss account for the year ended 31 December 20X7 complying with the requirements of FRS 3 as far as possible.

Solution

	20X7 £m	20X7 £m	20X6 £m	20X6 £m
Turnover				
Continuing operations				
(200 – 22 – 7)/(180 – 26)		171		154
Acquisitions		7		–
		178		154
Discontinued operations		22		26
		200		180
Cost of sales		(60)		(80)
Gross profit		140		100
Distribution costs		(25)		(20)
Administrative expenses (50 – 3)		(47)		(45)
Operating profit				
Continuing operations* (bal)	73		41	
Acquisitions	2		–	
	75		41	
Discontinued operations	(7)		(6)	
		68		35
Exceptional item		(3)		–
		65		35

* that is 65 + 3 + 7 – 2 = 73; 35 + 6 = 41

7.3 Segment reporting

The UK equivalent standard to IFRS 8 is SSAP 25. In broad terms the principle behind SSAP 25 and IFRS 8 is very similar in that it requires the **disclosure** of segmental information. However the following differences should be noted:

SSAP 25	IFRS 8 comparison
Non-disclosure on the following grounds **is permitted**: • If disclosure would be seriously prejudicial to the interests of the entity • If the entity is not required to disclose turnover, such as for a company classified as small/medium sized under UK company law. • If the entity is the unlisted subsidiary of a listed parent where the parent has prepared segment information	Non-disclosure is **not** permitted.
Requires **disclosures** for both: • Segments identified on the basis of **business** activities • Segments identified on the basis of **geographic** area	IFRS 8 requires **disclosure** about the components of the entity whose **operating results** are regularly **reviewed by the chief operating decision maker** to make decisions about resource allocation and to assess performance
Requires segment information to be prepared in accordance with **accounting policies.**	IFRS 8 requires the amounts reported to be on the same basis as **for internal decision making**

7.4 Related party transactions

The UK standard which deals with this topic is FRS 8. The key requirements of FRS 8 are disclosures of:

- **Information** on related party transactions

- The **name of the party controlling the reporting entity** and, if different, that of the **ultimate controlling party** whether or not any transactions between the reporting entity and those parties have taken place.

In general then, the key requirement, that is the disclosure of related party transactions, is very similar to IAS 24. The following differences however should be noted:

FRS 8	IAS 24 comparison
A parent undertaking is not required to provide related party disclosures in its own financial statements **when those statements are presented with consolidated financial statements of its group.**	No such exemption exists.
Disclosure is not required in the financial statements of wholly owned subsidiary undertakings. These subsidiaries do not have to disclose transactions with entities that are part of the group or investees of the group qualifying as related parties, **provided that the consolidated financial statements in which that subsidiary is included are publicly available.**	No such exemption exists.

Only material related party transactions must be disclosed. In this instance however, materiality should be judged not only in terms of significance to the reporting entity but also **in relation to the other related party** when that party is:	IAS 24 does not deal with materiality (because under IAS 1 disclosure requirements laid down in IFRS do not apply if items are immaterial).
(a) A director, key manager or other individual in a position to influence, or accountable for stewardship of, the reporting entity	IAS 24 has no requirement to judge materiality in relation to the other party.
(b) A member of the close family of any individual mentioned in (a)	
(c) An entity controlled by any individual mentioned in (a) or (b) above.	
The following should be disclosed for a material related party transaction irrespective of whether a price has been charged:	Disclosure requirements differ. (See section 5.7) The name of the related party where a transaction has occurred is not required.
• The **names** of the transacting parties	
• A description of the **relationship**	
• A description of the **transaction**	
• The **amounts** involved	
• **Any other elements** necessary for understanding	
• **Amounts due to/from related parties** at the balance sheet date and allowances for doubtful debts	
• **Amounts written off** in the period in respect of debts due to/from related parties.	

Point to note:

Management compensation disclosures, as well as disclosures on **loans and other transactions involving directors** are included in **Companies Act 2006**, rather than FRS 8.

Summary

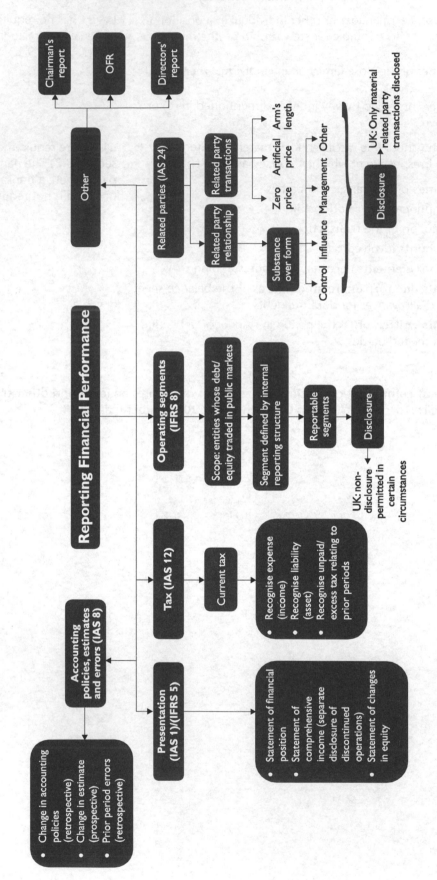

Self-test

Answer the following questions.

1   **Related parties**

   (a)   Discuss the financial reporting and ethical issues associated with related party transactions.

   (b)   Explain whether the following relationships are related party relationships under IAS 24 *Related Party Disclosures.*

      (i)   Albert plc and James plc each have a board containing five directors, four of whom are common. There are no common shareholdings. Are the companies related entities?

      (ii)   James plc has two associated companies, Hector Ltd and Frances Ltd. Is Hector Ltd a related party of Frances Ltd?

      (iii)   Fredrick Pearson is a director of Gambit plc and Frodsham Ltd – are these companies related?

      (iv)   Giprock Ltd controls Jasper plc. Giprock Ltd also exerts influence over Kendal plc. Are Jasper plc and Kendal plc related entities?   **(12 marks)**

2   **Millhouses plc**

Millhouses plc is a multinational business with a 31 December year end operating in several different business sectors.

On 30 June 20X3 Millhouses plc announced the sale of its electronics division. The sale was completed on 30 September 20X3. On 15 December 20X3 the company decided to close down and terminate the operations of the mechanics division and was confident of completion within 12 months. Each division has been disclosed as a separately reportable operating segment in previous financial statements.

Requirements

   (a)   Explain the usefulness of information related to:

      (i)   Segment reporting
      (ii)   Discontinued operations.

   (b)   Identify the presentation requirements of the above transactions in the financial statements of Millhouses plc for the year ended 31 December 20X3.

   (c)   Identify the practical issues relating to accounting for

      (i)   Segment reporting
      (ii)   Discontinued operations.   **(14 marks)**

3   Write a short report which discusses the following issues:

   (a)   What, if any, regulatory requirements relate to the production of an Operating and Financial Review (OFR)?

   (b)   The purpose and typical contents of an OFR

   (c)   The advantages and disadvantages of publishing an OFR from the point of view of the reporting entity.   **(14 marks)**

4 International plc

International plc has produced the following table in respect of its operating segments:

	Revenue from internal sales £m	Revenue from external sales £m	Total revenue £m	Profit or loss £m	Assets £m
Operating segment 1	200	3,400	3,600	80	50
Operating segment 2	600	2,360	2,960	80	50
Operating segment 3		800	800	58	50
Operating segment 4	100	560	660	22	16
Operating segment 5	420	460	880	(40)	14
	1,320	7,580	8,900	200	180
Central costs incurred/assets				(36)	20
Central costs allocated to segments				24	
				(12)	
				188	200

Requirements

(a) Set out the criteria by which International plc should have identified its operating segments

(4 marks)

(b) Explain, with calculations where necessary, which of the five segments is/are reportable segments

(8 marks)

(c) Explain briefly how International plc should have measured the amounts shown in the table

(3 marks)

(d) Identify and explain two areas in which the application of IFRS 8 requires significant amounts of judgement to be exercised by management and explain how a Chartered Accountant should review these judgements

(6 marks)

(21 marks)

Now go back to the Learning Objectives in the Introduction. If you are satisfied you have achieved these objectives, please tick them off.

Technical reference

1 Presentation of financial statements

- Applies to all general purpose financial statements.   IAS 1 (2)
- Content of a complete set of financial statements   IAS 1 (10)
- Links back to much in the *Conceptual Framework*:
    - Fair/faithful presentation   IAS 1 (15)
    - Going concern   IAS 1 (25-26)
    - Accrual basis of accounting   IAS 1 (27-28)
    - Materiality and aggregation   IAS 1 (7 and 29-31)
    - Offsetting   IAS 1 (32-35)
    - Comparative information   IAS 1 (38-44)
    - Consistency of presentation   IAS 1 (45-46)
- Presentation and disclosure rules apply only to material items   IAS 1 (31 and 7)
- Statement of financial position:
    - Layout as in proforma
    - Distinction between current and non-current   IAS 1 (60 and 61)
    - Linked to the operating cycle of the business, not just the next twelve months   IAS 1 (66 and 68-70)
    - Some items should be in the statement, others can be in the notes   IAS 1 (54 and 77-79)
- Statement of comprehensive income:
    - Choice of one statement or two statements   IAS 1 (81)
    - Layout as in proformas
    - Distinction between profit or loss and other comprehensive income   IAS 1 (7 and 84)
    - Some items should be in the statement, others can be in the notes   IAS 1 (82-83 and 97-98)
    - No extraordinary items   IAS 1 (87)
    - Allocate profit for the period between owners of the parent and non-controlling interest   IAS 1 (83)
- Statement of changes in equity: IAS 1 (106-110)
    - Layout as in proforma
    - Revaluation surpluses shown here
    - Dividends declared by the end of the reporting period

2 Accounting policies

- Definition   IAS 8 (5)
- Developed by reference to the relevant Standard where this is applicable   IAS 8 (7)
- Otherwise judgement applied   IAS 8 (10)

- Selection and application should be consistent

IAS 8 (13)

3 Change in accounting policies

- Only allowed if:

  IAS 8 (14)

  - Required by a Standard, or
  - Results in relevant and more reliable information

- Changes should be applied:

  IAS 8 (19-22)

  - In accordance with transitional provisions, or

  - Retrospectively if there are no transitional provisions or the change is voluntary

- Retrospective application is applying a new accounting policy as if that policy had always been applied

  IAS 8 (5)

- If impracticable to determine the period-specific effects:

  IAS 8 (23-27)

  - Apply the new accounting policy from the earliest period for which retrospective application is practicable
  - Disclose this fact

- Disclosures

  IAS 8 (28-29)

4 Changes in accounting estimates

- Definition

  IAS 8 (5)

- Changes relating to assets, liabilities or equity are adjusted in the period of change

  IAS 8 (37)

- All other changes should be applied prospectively:

  IAS 8 (36)

  - In the period of change
  - In the period of change and future periods if both are affected

- Disclosure:

  IAS 8 (39)

  - Nature of change
  - Amount

5 Prior period errors

- Definition

  IAS 8 (5)

- Correct retrospectively in the first set of financial statements authorised for issue after their discovery

  IAS 8 (42)

- Disclose:

  IAS 8 (49)

  - Nature of the prior period error
  - Amount of the correction for each prior period presented
  - Amount of the correction at the beginning of the earliest period presented

- If impracticable to determine the period-specific effects or the cumulative effect of the error:

  - Correct the error from the earliest period/date practicable
  - Disclose this fact

  IAS 8 (43 and 44)

  IAS 8 (49)

6 Discontinued operations

- Definition

  IFRS 5 (31-32)

- Disclosures in profit or loss:

  IFRS 5 (33(a) and 33(A))

  A single amount comprising the total of:

  - The post-tax profit or loss of discontinued operations, and

- The post-tax gain or loss recognised on related assets

- Disclosures in profit or loss or in the notes: IFRS 5 (33(b) (c))

  An analysis of the single amount

- Comparative figures must be restated   IFRS 5 (34)

- Narrative disclosures are also required   IFRS 5 (41)

7 Tax

- Unpaid tax in respect of current or prior periods should be recognised as a   IAS 12 (12)
  liability

- The benefit relating to a tax loss that can be carried back to recover current tax of   IAS 12 (13)
  a previous period should be recognised as an asset

- Tax rates used should be those enacted (or substantively enacted) by the end of   IAS 12 (46)
  the reporting period

- Current tax should be recognised as income or an expense in profit or loss   IAS 12 (58)

- The major components of the tax expense should be disclosed separately: IAS 12 (79)

  - Current tax expense   IAS 12 (80)
  - Adjustments recognised in the period for current tax of prior periods

8 Operating segments

- Designed to enable users to evaluate the nature and financial effects of the   IFRS 8 (1)
  entity's business activities and the economic environments in which the entity
  operates.

- Applies only to entities whose equity or debt is traded on a public market.   IFRS 8 (2)

- Definition of operating segment based around the internal reporting to the chief   IFRS 8 (5)
  operating decision maker

- Can aggregate operating segments if their characteristics are similar   IFRS 8 (12)

- Reportable segments: if any of revenue (internal plus external), profit or loss and IFRS 8 (13)
  assets are 10% or more of entity total

  Report smaller operating segments separately, if this is the only way to reach   IFRS 8 (15)
  75% of external revenue.

- Always disclose a measure of profit or loss for a reportable segment   IFRS 8 (23)

- Other information to be disclosed if regularly reported to chief operating decision IFRS 8 (23)
  maker

- Measurement as per internal reporting – include explanations   IFRS 8 (25 and
                                                                                              27)

- Reconciliations of operating segment totals with entity total   IFRS 8 (28)

- Information about products/services, geographical areas and major customers   IFRS 8 (32-34)

- Otherwise, scope for judgement, for example 'a reasonable basis' for allocations

9 Related party disclosures

- Related party relationships are a normal part of commerce and business   IAS 24 (5)

- Could have an effect on results and financial position   IAS 24 (6)

- Results and financial position may be affected by related party relationships even IAS 24 (7)
  if related party transactions do not occur

- Knowledge of related party transactions, outstanding balances and relationships   IAS 24 (8)
  may affect users view of the financial statements

- Definitions: IAS 24 (9)
    - Related party
    - Related party transaction
    - Close members of the family
    - Control
    - Joint control
    - Key management personnel
    - Significant influence
    - Government
    - Government-related entity

- Disclosures:
    - Relationships between parents and subsidiaries IAS 24 (13)

    - The name of the entity's parent and if different the ultimate controlling entity

    - Key management personnel compensation in total and analysed IAS 24 (17)

    - Where there have been transactions between related parties: IAS 24 (18)
        - Nature of the related party relationship
        - Amount of the transaction
        - Information about outstanding balances, including commitments
        - Provisions for doubtful debts related to outstanding balances
        - Expense recognised during the period in respect of doubtful debts related to debts due from related parties

    - The disclosures required by paragraph 18 should be made separately for specified categories IAS 24 (19)

- Examples of transactions which should be disclosed if they are with a related party IAS 24 (21)

- Disclosures in respect of transactions with a government which has control, joint control or significant influence and with another entity over which the same government has control, etc IAS 24 (26)

Answers to Interactive questions

Answer to Interactive question 1

The cost of the timber inventories would be classified as a current asset as they are realised within the entity's normal operating cycle.

The entity should disclose the amount of inventories to be realised more than twelve months after the end of the reporting period, to assist users in assessing its liquidity and solvency.

Answer to Interactive question 2

Financial reporting and ethical issues

- In most cases there is little choice of accounting policy as IFRS must be complied with.

- Where IFRS does provide a choice, judgement must be exercised.

- Appropriate consideration should be given to users and their needs.

- Accounting policy selected may enhance profitability. An accountant must ensure that IFRS is still being applied and that enhanced profitability is legitimate.

Changes in accounting policy should only be made where IAS 8 criteria are met. An accountant should ensure that changes are not being made purely for creative accounting purposes.

Answer to Interactive question 3

As BBB has both profit making and loss making segments, the results of those in profit and those in loss must be totalled to see which is the greater:

	£m
Profits (155 + 65 + 40 + 15)	275
Losses (25 + 50)	(75)
	200

So the '10% of profit or loss' test must be applied by reference to £275 million.

Segment	Criteria
Ash	Reportable, because it generates more than 10% of total revenue (and profits)
Beech	Not reportable, because it generates less than 10% total revenue, its losses are less than 10% of £275m and its assets less than 10% of total assets
Conifer	Reportable, because it meets one (in fact all the) criteria
Daisy	Reportable, because it meets one (in fact all the) criteria
Elm	Reportable, but only because its losses are more than 10% of £275m
Fir	Not reportable, because it fails all criteria

Check the 75% test is satisfied: (470 + 200 + 110 + 80)/1,000 = 86%

Ash, Conifer, Daisy and Elm are reportable segments.

Answer to Interactive question 4

(1) The junior manager is unlikely to fall within the definition of key management personnel in respect of Mint, so should not be disclosed as a related party. The manager's shareholding in Toffee is therefore irrelevant to Mint.

(2) The director falls within the definition of key management personnel in respect of Mint, so should be disclosed as a related party (definition (a)(iii)). The director's daughter falls within the definition of close members of the family of the director, so should be disclosed as a related party (definition (a)(iii)).

(3) The director falls within the definition of key management personnel in respect of Mint, so should be disclosed as a related party (definition (a)(iii)). Chocolate is under the control of one of Mint's key management personnel, so should be disclosed as a related party (definition (b)(vii)).

(4) With a 25 per cent shareholding Miss Butterscotch is likely to exert significant influence over Mint. (This will depend, however, on who owns the remaining 75 per cent holding.) She should be disclosed as a related party (definition (a)(ii)).

(5) The director falls within the definition of key management personnel in respect of Mint, so should be disclosed as a related party (definition (a)(iii)). IAS 24 is explicit that two entities are not related parties simply because they have a director in common, so Sugar should not be disclosed as a related party.

(6) The niece does not fall within the definition of close members of the family of Mint's finance director, so neither she nor the company she owns should be disclosed as a related party.

Answer to Interactive question 5

(1) Chablis is owned by one of the close members of the family of a member of Pinot's key management personnel, so it is a related party of Pinot. Disclosure should be made of the nature of the relationship, any transactions during the period and the fact that the £100,000 balance has been written off during the period.

There is no requirement to disclose the debt collection costs of £4,000, or the names of Chablis, the director of Pinot or his son.

(2) Merlot is very probably a related party of Pinot because Pinot's 40% shareholding in it appears to provide Pinot with significant influence over Merlot. Despite being an arm's length price, the value of the transaction should be disclosed (aggregated with similar transactions during the year if appropriate).

The company should only disclose that related party transactions were made on terms equivalent to those that prevail in arm's length transactions if these terms can be substantiated.

The nature of the relationship should be disclosed, but no names need to be disclosed.

(3) The distributor is not a related party of Pinot, thus no separate disclosure is required.

(4) Mrs Barolo is a member of the key management personnel of Pinot, so is one of its related parties. The nature of the relationship, details of the amount and nature of the transaction should be disclosed, along with the fact that Pinot is guaranteeing the loan of a related party. Any amount of the sale price still owed to Pinot at the year-end should be disclosed.

1 Related parties

(a) Related party transactions are common in business. When interpreting financial statements users normally presume all transactions have been on an arm's length basis at market prices. In many situations this may be true. However, where other parties influence an entity's operating and financial policies, it may be constrained to act in an unusual way, and the terms and conditions of transactions may not be as they first seem.

Transparent reporting of such transactions is essential so that users can correctly interpret the financial information presented to them. The relationships and transactions with related parties can be difficult to identify and the disclosure of such information depends upon the integrity of management. Many financial statement frauds and misappropriations have involved the use of undisclosed relationships. Financial managers should ensure that procedures are in place to identify the relationships and quantify the related party transactions. They should not succumb to pressure from non-financial management to hide or omit the relevant disclosures.

(b) Note: This question explores the nature of the relationships and attempts to contrast control and the exercise of influence. Two entities which are related parties of a third party are not necessarily related parties of each other.

(i) All five directors of Albert plc are members of its key management personnel and are therefore its related parties. The same is the case for all five directors of James plc. Individually the four common directors do not have significant influence over either Albert plc or James plc, but together, as the clear majority of the board, they can control both of them. There is nothing in IAS 24's definitions of a related party which makes these entities related parties of each other. But IAS 24 requires consideration of the substance of situations, not just their legal form. If the four directors are acting in concert, then in substance they control both entities which are therefore related parties of each other..

(ii) Hector Ltd and Frances Ltd are associates of the same investor. James plc has significant influence over each company, but not control. Hector Ltd and Frances Ltd would not normally be regarded as related parties of each other.

(iii) Gambit plc and Frodsham Ltd have one director in common, but there is no information about shareholdings which would indicate that this director has control over either of them. They would not normally be regarded as related parties of each other.

(iv) Giprock Ltd has control over Jasper plc but only significant influence over Kendal plc. Jasper plc and Kendal plc would not normally treated as related parties of each other.

2 Millhouses plc

(a) **The usefulness of information**

Those making economic decisions in respect of an entity must be able to evaluate the ability of the entity to generate cash and of the certainty and timing of its generation. The reporting of segment and discontinued operations provides information with confirmatory and predictive value.

(i) **Segment reporting**

Most entities supply a variety of products and operate in different geographical areas. These business and geographical sectors present different business risks and opportunities for the entity. It may be difficult to understand the performance and future potential when reviewing the overall totals included within the financial statements. The disaggregating of information about an entity's different activities on the same basis as is used internally by management is relevant to assessing the risks and returns of a diversified or multinational entity.

(ii) **Discontinued operations**

The predictive qualities of information are enhanced when activities of an entity that have ceased or are about to cease are reported separately. Disaggregated information about continuing and discontinued operations improves the ability of users to predict future cash flows, earnings and financial position.

(b) **Identification of presentation requirements for Millhouses plc**

IFRS 5 *Non-current Assets Held for Sale and Discontinued Operations* identifies a discontinued operation as a relatively large component of an entity, such as a reportable segment under IFRS 8 *Operating Segments,* that the entity has disposed of or has classified as held for sale. Disclosures should begin at the time the operations and the associated non-current assets are classified as held for sale. The segment is classified as such when it is highly probable that it will be finally sold within twelve months of classification. This therefore means that the segment may be classified as discontinued for up to twelve months before the disposal actually takes place.

The electronics division was disposed of in the year ended 31 December 20X3. Hence its results should be disclosed as those of a discontinued operation for the year ended 31 December 20X3 and the results for prior periods should be restated for comparability.

No statement of financial position disclosures will be needed with regard to the electronics division because the division was finally disposed of within the current year. There is no reclassification of items in the prior period statement of financial position presented as comparative figures.

The minimum statement of comprehensive income disclosure for the electronics division is a single figure (the net of the after-tax profit or loss of discontinued operations and any after-tax gain or loss on related assets), with disclosure in the notes of revenue, expenses, pre-tax profit or loss and the related tax expense. The result of the division is then described as discontinued in the segmental analysis.

The mechanics division is being closed down and its operations terminated. The related assets will be abandoned because there is no indication that there is anything to be disposed of; so there are no non-current assets to be reclassified as held for sale in the 20X3 financial statements.

Disclosure of the mechanics division as discontinued should be made at the date the related assets are abandoned, that is, at some time in 20X4. The mechanics division operations are part of continuing operations in 20X3.

(c) **Practical issues**

(i) **Segment reporting**

– Scope for management judgement in defining operating segments.
– How to measure amounts for internal reporting.
– Influence of inter-segment pricing policies on segment profit or loss.
– Allocation of shared expenses, assets and liabilities.
– Lack of segment comparability between different entities.

(ii) **Discontinued operations**

– Definition of what constitutes a discontinued operation is not always clear and can involve judgement.

– A component is classified as held for sale if management believe it is 'highly probable' that it will be sold within twelve months of classification. The point of classification can involve judgement and be influenced by management's intentions.

3 **Operating and Financial Review**

(a) Increasingly international companies are including a form of Operating and Financial Review (OFR) within their annual financial statements. However, there is currently **no formal regulatory requirement** internationally to prepare an OFR.

IAS 1 *Presentation of Financial Statements* encourages the preparation and presentation of a management review in the financial statements that would be likely to cover many of the areas typically covered by an OFR. However, this is not mandatory therefore any disclosure is voluntary. In December 2010 the IASB issued an IFRS Practice Statement *Management Commentary* which sets out a broad framework for narrative reporting but this is not an IFRS, so entities applying IFRS are not required to comply with it.

In the UK there is **now a legal requirement** for companies to include a **business review** in their directors' reports. The ASB's *Reporting Statement: Operating and Financial Review* contains everything required by law but this reporting statement has no status except as **a source of guidance**.

(b) The overall purpose of an OFR is that it is to provide **forward-looking information**, addressed to and aimed at shareholders in the company, in order to help them to assess the strategies adopted by the company and the potential for those strategies to succeed. The OFR should both **complement and supplement the financial statements**, it should be comprehensive and understandable, balanced and neutral and comparable over time.

The **key elements** of an OFR will tend to be:

(i) The nature of the business, including a description of the market, competitive and regulatory environment in which the business operates

(ii) The business's objectives and strategies

(iii) The development and performance of the business both in the current financial year and in the future

(iv) The resources, principal risks and uncertainties and relationships that may affect the business's long-term value

(v) The position of the business including a description of the capital structure, treasury policies and objectives and liquidity of the business both currently and in the future

The OFR should also **include information** about:

(i) Environmental matters

(ii) The employees

(iii) Social and community issues

(iv) Details of persons with which the business has contractual arrangements which are essential to the business

(v) Receipts from and returns to shareholders

(vi) Key performance indicators

(c) There are a number of **advantages** to a reporting entity of producing an OFR:

(i) The production of an OFR is often viewed favourably by shareholders as a further means of communication and transparency.

(ii) The investment community could perceive the entity as a progressive and forward looking company.

(iii) If a compulsory OFR were to be introduced at some future date by the IASB, then the reporting entity would already have the structures and systems in place to report the necessary information.

There are, however, **drawbacks** to producing an OFR.

(i) If a genuinely useful OFR is to be produced, then it is likely to require a large amount of management time and therefore be costly to the business.

(ii) There is a risk that users of the financial statements may concentrate only on the rather more user-friendly OFR in preference to the financial statements themselves and therefore not have a clear picture of the position and results of the business.

4   **International plc**

(a) **Criteria**

An operating segment is a component of an entity:

(i)   That engages in business activities from which it may earn revenues and incur expenses (including revenues and expenses relating to transactions with other components of the same entity)

(ii)   Whose operating results are regularly reviewed by the entity's chief operating decision maker to make decisions about resources to be allocated to the segment and assess its performance, and

(iii) For which discrete financial information is available.

The phrase 'chief operating decision maker' describes a function, not a person.

A business activity which has yet to earn revenues, such as a start up, is an operating segment if it is separately reported on to the chief operating decision maker

A component is not excluded from being an operating segment just because its sole purpose is to sell products or services internally to other parts of the business.

(b) **Reportable segments**

Note that:

(i)   In applying the profit or loss test, percentages should be calculated by reference to the greater of the total profit of segments in profit (80 + 80 + 58 + 22 = 240) and the total loss of the segment in loss (40), so £240 million.

(ii)   The £180 million total of operating segment assets should be used when applying the assets test.

Operating segments 1 and 2 are reportable under the revenue test (£3,600m and £2,960m > 10% of £8,900m). (They are also reportable under the other two tests, but it is not necessary to apply them once one test has produced a 10% or more amount.)

Operating segment 3 is reportable under the profit or loss test (£58m > 10% of £240m). (It is also reportable under the assets test but not under the revenue test (£800m < 10% of £8,900m.)

Operating segment 4 is not reportable because all three tests produce figures of less than 10% (£660m on £8,900m, £22m on £240m and £16m on £180m).

Operating segment 5 is reportable under the profit or loss test (£40m loss > 10% of £240m) but not under the other two tests (£880m on £8,900m and £14m on £180m).

The total external revenue attributable to reportable segments is £7,020m (7,580 – 560 Operating segment 4), which is in excess of 75% of total external revenue, so no other segments have to be reported.

Note. Because Operating segment 4 is the only other segment, its revenue, results and assets will be presented separately, perhaps under the heading of "Other".

(c) **Measurement**

The amounts for all items reported for an operating segment should be measured as they are in the reports submitted to the chief operating decision maker for the purposes of making decisions about the resources to be allocated to each operating segment and to assess its performance.

These are not necessarily amounts measured under IFRS.

If there are amounts allocated to operating segments (such as in respect of centrally incurred costs), the allocations should be on a reasonable basis.

(d) **Exercise of judgement**

Two areas in which the application of IFRS 8 requires significant amounts of judgement to be exercised by management are:

(i) Identifying what is 'regularly reported' to the chief operating decision maker

The power and availability of modern IT systems results in almost limitless amounts of information being available to management. Some of it comes in regular management information packs, but some of it comes in ad hoc reports prepared for particular purposes.

The minimum IFRS 8 disclosure is of a measure of profit or loss, with other amounts disclosable only if they are 'regularly reported' to the chief operating decision maker. Judgement is required in deciding what constitutes the information 'regularly reported' and making sure the decision is consistently complied with. It would be unacceptable for amounts which previously were deemed 'regularly reported' subsequently to be classified as "irregularly" reported, and therefore not disclosable, just because they show an operating segment in a poor light.

(ii) Measurement

Measurement should be as in the reports submitted to the chief operating decision maker. But it is possible that several versions of a period report will be submitted, the initial one being the first draft and the subsequent ones after the initial review by the chief operating decision maker. Are closing adjustments to be taken into account when identifying the amounts at which items are measured?

In reviewing these judgements the key duty of a Chartered Accountant is to make sure that they are applied consistently from period to period. Information provided to users of financial statements should be a faithful representation of the transactions and events it purports to represent. This means in part that it should be neutral, ie not presented to achieve a predetermined result. So management should not tailor information to suit its own objectives. The Chartered Accountant should always keep in mind IFRS 8's core principle that users should be able to evaluate the nature and financial effect of an entity's business activities and the economic environments in which it operates. IFRS 8 allows management significant scope as to how to present information, so it is perfectly acceptable for management to make judgements which differ from those that a Chartered Accountant would have made. The critical point is that judgements once made should be applied consistently from period to period and this is where the focus of a Chartered Accountant's review should be.

CHAPTER 3

Non-current assets

Introduction

Examination context

Topic List

1 Property, plant and equipment

2 Intangible assets

3 Impairment

4 Assets and disposal groups held for sale

5 UK GAAP comparison

Summary and Self-test

Technical reference

Answers to Interactive questions

Answers to Self-test

Introduction

Learning objectives

- Prepare and present extracts from financial statements in respect of property, plant and equipment and intangible assets ☐

- Formulate accounting and reporting policies in respect of property, plant and equipment and intangible assets ☐

- Illustrate how different methods of recognising and measuring intangible assets can affect the view presented ☐

- Identify and consider appropriate actions for ethical issues involving non-current assets ☐

- Identify and illustrate the main differences between international and UK requirements in relation to property, plant and equipment and intangible assets and impairment ☐

Specific syllabus references for this chapter are: 1e, 2a, 2b, 3a, 4a and 4c.

Syllabus links

This chapter looks at a range of topics related to the treatment of non-current assets. In Financial Accounting you will have covered IAS 16 *Property, Plant and Equipment.* This is briefly revised. IAS 38 *Intangible Assets* should also be familiar, although it is now examinable at level A (it was examinable at level B in Financial Accounting).

You will also have been introduced to the basic principles of impairment and assets held for sale. This chapter looks in detail at IAS 36 *Impairment of Assets* including the calculation of value in use using discounting, and the concept of cash-generating units.

This chapter also looks at the held-for-sale aspects of IFRS 5, considering the approach adopted for disposal groups as well as individual assets (Discontinued operations were dealt with in Chapter 2). All of these concepts will be relevant to the Advanced Stage.

Examination context

In the examination, candidates may be required to:

- Explain the accounting treatment of property, plant and equipment and intangible assets including the effects of impairments and held-for-sale assets

- Formulate reporting policies for non-current assets

- Prepare financial information so that non-current assets are accounted for correctly in accordance with IFRS

- Interpret financial information and explain the effect of the accounting treatment of non-current assets on financial statements

- Explain and illustrate the difference between the relevant treatment under IFRS and UK GAAP

- Identify and explain any ethical issues

1 Property, plant and equipment

Section overview

This section provides an overview of IAS 16 *Property, Plant and Equipment*, which was covered in full in Financial Accounting, and puts it into a context for Financial Reporting.

1.1 IAS 16 *Property, Plant and Equipment* (PPE)

- PPE are **tangible items** that are held for use in the production or supply of goods or services, for rental to others, or for administrative purposes and **are expected to be used during more than one period.**

- An item of PPE should be recognised if it is **probable that future economic benefits associated with the item will flow to the entity** and the item's cost can be **measured reliably.**

- **Repairs and maintenance expenditure** should **not** be recognised as part of an item of PPE but is recognised in profit or loss as incurred.

- An item of PPE qualifying for recognition should be measured at **cost**. Cost includes **purchase price** (net of discounts), **costs directly attributable to bringing the asset to the location and condition** necessary for use and an initial estimate of **dismantling and site restoration costs** (where there is an **obligation** to so incur such costs).

- Capitalisation of costs ceases **when the item is capable of operating in the manner intended.**

- After initial recognition an item of PPE may be carried under the following models:

  - **Cost model**: initial cost plus subsequent qualifying expenditure less accumulated depreciation and impairment losses.

  - **Revaluation model**: fair value less accumulated depreciation and impairment losses.

    For specialised PPE when no market-based evidence is available, fair value may be estimated using depreciated replacement cost

- Where the revaluation model is adopted it should be applied to an **entire class of PPE** (for example land and buildings, fixtures and fittings and motor vehicles). Revaluations should be carried out on a sufficiently frequent basis that there is no material difference between carrying amount and fair value.

- An **increase in carrying amount** on revaluation should be **recognised in other comprehensive income** (and accumulated in equity under revaluation surplus) except where such an increase reverses an earlier revaluation decrease on the same asset that was recognised in profit or loss.

- A **decrease in carrying amount** on revaluation should be recognised as an **expense in profit or loss** except where such a decrease reverses an earlier revaluation increase on the same asset that was recognised directly in other comprehensive income and is still held in revaluation surplus.

- The **depreciable amount** of an asset (cost less residual value) should be depreciated over its **useful life**. Depreciation should **commence when the asset is in the location and condition necessary for its intended use.**

- Each **significant part** (component) of an item of PPE should be depreciated **separately.**

- Depreciation methods should be reviewed **at each financial year end**. Any changes are a **change in accounting estimate.**

- The **depreciable amount** is **cost less residual value**, or, where an asset has been revalued, the **revalued amount, less residual value.**

- For a revalued asset, IAS 16 allows a **reserve transfer** of the 'excess' depreciation which is recognised in the statement of changes in equity, not in other comprehensive income.

- If an item of PPE suffers an **impairment** in accordance with IAS 36 *Impairment of Assets*, it should be written down to its **recoverable amount**. (See section 3 below.)

- An item of PPE should be **removed** from the statement of financial position (**that is derecognised**) when it is disposed of or when no future economic benefits are expected from its use or disposal (**that is it is abandoned**). The gain or loss is **recognised in profit or loss** in the period in which the derecognition occurs.

Interactive question 1: Revaluation [Difficulty level: Intermediate]

On 1 January 20X2 an asset has a carrying amount of £140 and a remaining useful life of ten years, with a nil residual value. The asset is revalued on that date to £60 and the loss is recognised in profit or loss.

The asset is depreciated straight-line over the next five years, giving a carrying amount of £30 at 31 December 20X6. Then, on 1 January 20X7 when the remaining useful life is the unexpired five years, the asset is revalued to £72.

Requirement

Calculate how much of the revaluation gain on 1 January 20X7 should be recognised in other comprehensive income and how much should be recognised in profit or loss.

Fill in the proforma below.

£

Excess revaluation gain recognised in other comprehensive income
Amount recognised in profit or loss

WORKINGS

See **Answer** at the end of this chapter.

Worked example: Revaluation and depreciation

An entity acquires an item of PPE for £50,000, which is depreciated over 20 years. Three years later, the asset is revalued to £60,000. The useful life has not changed.

Calculate the amount of the annual depreciation expense after the revaluation.

Solution

After revaluation the annual depreciation expense should be based on £60,000 over the remaining 17 years, so £3,529 per annum.

Interactive question 2: Revaluation and depreciation

[Difficulty level: Exam standard]

An entity owns a building which originally cost £200,000. The property is being depreciated over 50 years on a straight-line basis with no residual value. The entity adopts a policy of revaluation for property. The property has so far had three valuations as follows.

At the start of Year 2 – valuation £230,000.
At the start of Year 4 – valuation £260,000.
At the start of Year 6 – valuation £300,000.

Calculate the annual depreciation expense for years one to six, the transfers to revaluation surplus through other comprehensive income in Years 2, 4 and 6 and the transfers from revaluation surplus to retained earnings in the statement of changes in equity in Years 1 to 6.

See **Answer** at the end of this chapter.

Worked example: Commencement of depreciation

An entity with a 31 December year end has acquired at a cost of £500,000 a new item of processing plant which has an expected useful life of ten years and a nil residual value.

The plant was delivered to the entity on 1 January 20X5. The installation and testing by the vendor's employees lasted until 1 April 20X5. The need for the entity's employees to become familiar with operating routines resulted in full production levels not being achieved until 1 July 20X5. On 1 October 20X5 a major problem arose with the quality of the raw materials used as an input to the process, so there was no further output from the plant until 1 January 20X6.

Calculate the depreciation expense for the year ended 31 December 20X5.

Solution

Under IAS 16 an item of PPE should be depreciated from the date it is available for use in the manner intended by management, even if it is not used, or not fully used, from that date. Depreciation should therefore be charged from when installation and testing has been completed, that is from 1 April 20X5. So the 20X5 expense should be £37,500 (£500,000 for nine of the 120 months life).

Interactive question 3: Revaluation

[Difficulty level: Intermediate]

Three years ago an entity acquired an item of highly specialised equipment which is used in a process for which the entity owns the patent. The entity has a policy of not licensing others to use its patents. The item of equipment originally cost £300 and was estimated to have a 15-year life with nil residual value. The item currently has a carrying amount of £240, that is £300 cost, less £60 accumulated depreciation.

The entity's policy is to carry all PPE at revalued amounts, revaluing on a regular three yearly cycle. Since it is highly specialised, there is no market-based evidence for the fair value of this equipment.

The entity has obtained a quotation for a new version of this item. The quotation is for £450 for an item with a useful life of 15 years, but the entity estimates that the service potential, in terms of efficiency of processing, of the item it owns is some 20% less than that of the new item.

What should the carrying amount of the equipment be after the revaluation?

See **Answer** at the end of this chapter.

Worked example: Decommissioning costs

An entity with a 31 December year end completed the building of a power generating facility on 1 January 20X4 at a cost of £400 million. Under the terms of the licence granted by the government, the entity must decommission the power station at the end of its useful life and make good the surrounding environment. The following estimates relate to this decommissioning.

	1 January 20X4	31 December 20X4
Date estimate made		
Amount payable taking account of technological developments	£100m	£105m

Decommissioning costs are payable 35 years after the completion of building of the facility. The discount rate which reflects the risks specific to this liability is 7% per annum.

Show how these transactions and events should be accounted for at 1 January 20X4 and in the year ended 31 December 20X4.

Solution

1 January 20X4

A provision for decommissioning costs should be recognised and the cost added to the carrying amount of the facility. Discounting the £100 million amount payable in 35 years at 7% gives a present value of £9,366,294 (100 million / 1.07^{35}). When this is added to the cost of £400 million, the total cost to be written off over 35 years is £409,366,294, so £11,696,180 per annum.

Year ended 31 December 20X4

The following should be recognised as expenses in profit or loss:

*   A depreciation charge of £11,696,180
*   A finance charge, being unwinding of discount over one year, of £9,366,294 × 7% = £655,641

In the statement of financial position the following carrying amounts should be recognised:

*   A decommissioning provision carried forward of the revised estimate of £105 million payable in 34 years = £10,523,031 (105 million / 1.07^{34})

*   PPE of £397,670,114 (being the £409,366,294 originally capitalised less 20X4 depreciation of £11,696,180) plus the amount by which the decommissioning provision has been revised upward (£10,523,031 less (£9,366,294 at 1 January + £655,641 20X4 finance charge) = £501,096. The carrying amount is therefore £398,171,210.

1.2 Context for IAS 16

Many industries are described as capital intensive. Investment in new machinery may be undertaken for a number of reasons, including the reduction in headcount or labour overhead costs, and the increase in operational efficiency. In industries such as manufacturing and retailing, the cost and associated cash flows of items of property, plant and equipment need to be monitored closely by management and business analysts. It is essential that financial statements communicate capital plans, as these have significant implications for funding and future cash flow.

The distinction between revenue and capital expenditure is not always straightforward and can be judgemental. One of the principal manipulations alleged during the WorldCom scandal was the inappropriate capitalisation of certain expenses. Overstating the carrying amount of non-current assets, either intentionally or unintentionally, leads to the inflation of current earnings. Inflated earnings have consequential effects on key performance indicators such as earnings per share, the debt/equity ratio and return on capital employed. IAS 16 seeks to prevent incorrect capitalisation of expenses by applying rigorously that part of the *Conceptual Framework* definition of an asset which demands that future economic benefits must be attributable to the expense; repairs and maintenance expenditure merely protects the economic benefits anticipated when the asset was originally capitalised.

The prices paid to acquire businesses may be at a significant premium to their reported net asset values, reflecting significant changes in value which are not necessarily reflected in the financial statements. Many observers believe that the usefulness of financial statements is undermined unless the updated values for items of property are reflected in the financial statements. The revaluation of non-current assets such as property can have a significant effect on an entity's financial performance and financial position. This is, however, currently a matter of choice and very few UK entities adopt IAS 16's revaluation model.

The speed with which technology is advancing can have a direct effect on items of property, plant and equipment (PPE), with asset lives shortened to take account of such changes. The useful life of many assets is driven by technological obsolescence rather than being physically worn out. One of the key reporting issues for PPE is the splitting of non-current assets into components to reflect the differing lives of the components or the differing natures of the assets. New technology costs provide specific challenges where property, plant and equipment and intangible assets are closely linked, for example where a machine is preloaded with application software.

1.3 Judgements required

The key judgements with regard to PPE include:

- **Useful lives**: The longer the useful life, the lower the annual depreciation expense but the higher the capital employed. While PPE manufacturers will give guidance as to the maximum operating life of assets, the useful life is more likely to be determined by reference to the threat of new technology and changing patterns of demand for the assets' outputs. When will new PPE make the existing assets an uneconomic way of producing outputs? Over how many years will customers buy the outputs, before they move on to something new?

- **Residual values**: The higher the residual value, the lower the annual depreciation expense but the higher the capital employed. In an era of ever-changing technology, is it prudent to estimate any residual value? Will scrapping/decommissioning costs at the end of the assets' lives exceed any proceeds of disposal?

- **The distinction between capital and revenue**: Does the current expense increase or merely maintain the economic benefits expected from the asset?

It is important that useful lives and residual values are determined by reference to clear and persuasive reasoning and not by motives of wanting to present particular pictures of profit and capital employed. All Chartered Accountants should be very careful about the way they respond to requests from colleagues who do not have financial qualifications to change useful lives and/or residual values.

In terms of the capital/revenue distinction, consider the effect of inappropriately capitalising £10 million of maintenance expense on PPE with a remaining useful life of ten years:

- Expense wholly recognised in profit or loss in current period: current period profit reduced by £10 million, profit for the next ten years not affected

- Expense capitalised and depreciated over ten years: no effect on current period profit, profit for next 10 years reduced, but only by £1 million each year.

An unscrupulous person running a business which was struggling for short-term profits might well be tempted to dress the expense up as leading to increased economic benefits. Current period profits avoid a big hit and future profits are only reduced by a small amount each year.

1.4 Relevance of information to users

1.4.1 Cost/revaluation model

An entity is considering whether to change the measurement model for one class of PPE (remaining average useful life is ten years) from the cost model to the revaluation model. The following projections have been made:

		Cost model £m	Effect of change £m	Revaluation model £m
Statement of financial position				
Property, plant and equipment		100	+50	150
Net current assets		50		50
		150	+50	200
Equity		70	+50	120
Borrowings	(A)	80		80
Capital employed	(B)	150	+50	200
Income statement				
Future annual profit before interest, tax and depreciation		25		25
Future annual depreciation charge		(10)	(5)	(15)
	(C)	15	(5)	10
Return on capital employed	(C) as % (B)	10%		5%
Gearing	(A) as % (B)	53%		40%
Cash generation		25		25

One of the themes which will be taken up in Chapter 11 dealing with ratios and financial analysis is that cash flows and cash generation are not affected by different choices of accounting policies, as is the case here. Accounting policies determine how transactions are allocated to one or more accounting periods and require judgements. The judgements about cash are about when to pay/receive it; once it has left or come into the business, its presentation cannot be affected by any changes of judgement. To that extent cash ratios are said to be more objective than accounting ratios.

As illustrated above, both return on capital employed and gearing are affected by the choice of accounting policy. Nearly all UK entities (over 97% according to one survey) adopt the cost model for PPE. This is probably because they put more emphasis on protecting the apparent profitability of their businesses than on improving their gearing.

It is arguable that resource allocations such as whether to buy or sell shares should be made by reference to up-to-date, rather than historical, values. (One of the things that private equity does when it takes a business private is to increase gearing substantially; one of the reasons private equity firms can do this is that they can raise money on the basis of PPE revaluations which are not reflected in financial statements, in a way that is difficult for listed entities to do.) It is arguable that users of financial statements would be better served by a more wide-spread use of the revaluation model.

1.4.2 Component depreciation

IAS 16 requires each significant component of an item of PPE to be depreciated separately. The reason is that this approach provides more relevant information to users of financial statements.

Worked example: Component depreciation

An entity has acquired an item of PPE for £300,000. It has two components, the structure costing £200,000 and having a useful life of 20 years and the equipment costing £100,000 and having a useful life of five years. The plan is to replace the equipment after every five years at a cost of £100,000.

Explain, with calculations, why the component approach to depreciation provides more useful information.

Solution

- Without component depreciation the expense recognised in profit or loss would be:

    Years 1 to 5, Years 7 to 10, Years 12 to 15 and Years 17 to 20: depreciation of £15,000 (300,000 / 20 years) per year. Total for the 17 years = £255,000

    Plus

    Years 6, 11 and 16: repairs of £100,000 (the replacement cost) plus the £15,000 depreciation charge = £115,000 for 3 years = £345,000

    A total over 20 years of £600,000

- With component depreciation the expense recognised in profit or loss would be:

$$\frac{£200,000}{20\ \text{years}} = £10,000$$

Plus

$$\frac{£100,000}{5\ \text{years}} = £20,000$$

So £30,000 a year for 20 years = a total of £600,000.

Point to note:

After every five years, the carrying amount of the equipment is nil and the replacement expenditure is capitalised.

Most PPE has the same revenue earning capacity each year. Charging the £30,000 component depreciation against it every year results in an even flow of profit.

Without component depreciation the profits in most years would be higher (by £15,000 (30,000 – 15,000)), but in three years would be very much lower (by £85,000 (115,000 – 30,000)). To present such uneven profit flows to users of financial statements does not provide them with relevant information, when the uneven flow is not an economic reality but the result of poor accounting.

2 Intangible assets

Section overview

IAS 38 *Intangible Assets* was covered in Financial Accounting. This section revises the key points you should be familiar with and then goes on to develop a number of issues further.

2.1 IAS 38 *Intangible Assets*

The key points you should remember are as follows:

- An **intangible asset** is an **identifiable non-monetary asset without physical substance**, such as a licence, patent or trademark.

- An intangible asset is **identifiable** if it is **separable** (that is it can be sold, transferred, exchanged, licensed or rented to another party on its own rather than as part of a business) or it arises from **contractual or other legal rights**.

  Employees can never be recognised as an asset; they are not under the control of the employer, are not separable and do not arise from legal rights.

- An intangible asset should be recognised if it is probable that future economic benefits **attributable to the asset** will flow to the entity and the **cost** of the asset can be **measured reliably**.

  The probability of future economic benefits criterion is always satisfied for a separately acquired intangible, because the cost will reflect that probability – the more probable the benefits, the higher the cost.

- At recognition the intangible should be recognised at cost (purchase price plus directly attributable costs). After initial recognition an entity can **choose** between the **cost model** and the **revaluation model**. The revaluation model can only be adopted if an **active market** (as defined) exists for that type of asset.

  - Active markets are rare, but may exist for certain licences and production quotas

  - If the revaluation model is adopted, revaluation surpluses and deficits are accounted for in the same way as those for PPE

- An intangible asset (other than goodwill recognised in the acquiree's financial statements) **acquired as part of a business combination** should initially be recognised **at fair value**.

- Internally generated goodwill should **not** be recognised.

- Expenditure incurred in the **research phase** of an internally generated intangible asset should be **expensed as incurred**.

- Expenditure incurred in the **development phase** of an internally generated intangible asset **should be capitalised** provided **certain tightly defined criteria are met**.

  Expenditure incurred prior to the criteria being met may not be capitalised retrospectively.

- An intangible asset with a **finite useful life** should be **amortised** over its expected useful life, **commencing** when the asset is **available for use** in the manner intended by management.

  Residual values should be assumed to be nil, except in the rare circumstances when an active market exists or there is a commitment by a third party to purchase the asset at the end of its useful life.

- An intangible asset with an **indefinite life** should **not be amortised**, but should be reviewed for **impairment** on an **annual basis**.

  There should also be an annual review of whether the indefinite life assessment is still appropriate.

- On disposal of an intangible asset the gain or loss is recognised in profit or loss.

Common examples of intangible assets are:

- Computer software (other than operating systems which are accounted for under IAS 16)
- Patents and copyrights
- Motion picture films
- Customer lists, customer loyalty, customer/supplier relationships
- Airline landing slots
- Fishing licences
- Import quotas
- Franchises

Interactive question 4: New technology [Difficulty level: Easy]

An entity acquires new technology that will revolutionise its current manufacturing process. The costs are set out below:

	£
List price of the new technology	1,000,000
Discount provided	100,000
Staff training incurred in operating the new process	50,000
Testing of the new manufacturing process	10,000
Losses incurred whilst other parts of the plant stood idle	20,000

What should be capitalised as the cost of this intangible asset?

See **Answer** at the end of this chapter.

Interactive question 5: Cost of intangible [Difficulty level: Intermediate]

An entity acquires technology at a cost of £100,000 on 1 January 20X4. It is available for use straight away and has a useful life of 15 years. Because it will be several years before the technology creates positive net cash flows, the cost had been negotiated on the basis that payment to the supplier would be made on 1 January 20X6. The entity can borrow at 9% per annum and the supplier at 12% per annum.

Show how this transaction should be accounted for at 1 January 20X4 and in the year ended 31 December 20X4.

See **Answer** at the end of this chapter.

Interactive question 6: Internally generated assets   [Difficulty level: Intermediate]

Flintoff Ltd is developing a new production process. Total expenditure incurred to date is £200,000. Of this, £180,000 was incurred before 1 December 20X7 and £20,000 between 1 December 20X7 and 31 December 20X7. Flintoff Ltd can demonstrate that, at 1 December 20X7, the production process met the criteria for recognition as an intangible asset. The recoverable amount of the know-how embodied in the process is estimated to be £100,000.

An advertising campaign has just been completed on behalf of Flintoff Ltd at a cost of £150,000. The go-ahead for this campaign was given on the basis of an assurance from the agency used that it would generate £400,000 additional profit over the next two years.

On 31 December 20X7 Flintoff Ltd acquired the entire share capital of Delgado Ltd for £2.1 million. At the date of acquisition Delgado Ltd's statement of financial position showed the following:

	£
Non-current assets	
Intangibles – goodwill on the acquisition of an unincorporated business	200,000
Property, plant and equipment	600,000
	800,000
Current assets	800,000
	1,600,000
Equity	1,100,000
Current liabilities	500,000
	1,600,000

All assets and liabilities are stated at what Flintoff Ltd regards as their fair values.

A staff training programme has been carried out by Flintoff Ltd at a cost of £250,000, the training consultants having demonstrated to the directors that the additional profits to the business over the next 12 months will be £400,000.

Calculate the amounts which should be recognised as assets in Flintoff Ltd's consolidated statement of financial position at 31 December 20X7.

See **Answer** at the end of this chapter.

C
H
A
P
T
E
R

3

Worked example: Revaluation

Intangible assets are carried by a company under the revaluation model. An intangible with an estimated useful life of nine years was acquired on 1 January 20X6 for £11,250. It was revalued to £13,600 on 31 December 20X6 and a revaluation surplus of £3,600 was correctly recognised on that date. At 31 December 20X7 the asset was revalued at £8,000.

State the accounting treatments required in the 20X7 financial statements.

Solution

Amortisation of £1,700 (£13,600 ÷ the remaining useful life of eight years) should be recognised in profit or loss.

A transfer should be made from revaluation surplus to retained earnings through the statement of changes in equity of the excess depreciation of £450 (1,700 charged less 1,250 (11,250 ÷ 9) based on original cost) and the revaluation surplus reduced to £3,150.

The carrying amount of the intangible is now £11,900 (13,600 – 1,700) but this should be reduced to £8,000.

The revaluation deficit is £3,900, of which £3,150 should be recognised in other comprehensive income (reducing the revaluation surplus to £nil) and the £750 remainder recognised as an expense in profit or loss.

Worked example: Useful lives

1   An entity has acquired a copyright with a remaining legal life of 50 years. Analysis of consumer habits provides evidence that the copyrighted material will generate net cash inflows for only 30 more years.

In this case the copyright should be amortised over its 30 year estimated useful life.

2   An entity has purchased a list of customers who have bought products similar to those sold by the entity. The purchase price was negotiated on the basis that benefits would be generated from the list for two years. The entity plans to extend the useful life of the list by including on it the names of customers attracted to the entity's products by other promotional activity. The extended useful life is expected to be five years.

In this case the customer list should be amortised over two years, because this is the useful life of the asset acquired externally. The extended life results in an internally generated intangible which should not be capitalised.

3   An entity acquired a trademark with a remaining useful life of 10 years with a view to using it to brand products for the indefinite future. The market studies prior to the acquisition supported the view that the trademark will generate profits indefinitely. The procedure for renewing the trademark every twenty years is a mere formality and the cost of doing so is negligible.

In this case the trademark should be regarded as having an indefinite life. It should not be amortised but tested annually for impairment.

Interactive question 7: Amortisation   [Difficulty level: Intermediate]

Ferrers plc successfully bid £330 million for a new generation mobile telephone licence. Professional advisers charged £10 million for their assistance in the bidding for the licence which was for 20 years from 1 January 20X8.

Delays in the construction of the supporting infrastructure meant that the new mobile telephone services were not available to customers until 1 January 20X9.

What is the annual depreciation expense in 20X8 and 20X9 in respect of this licence?

See **Answer** at the end of this chapter.

2.2   Context for IAS 38

Historically, corporate success has been built on physical assets and improving manufacturing efficiency; this is in contrast with leading businesses in the new economy which use ideas and market positions. The most important assets for many businesses are now brands, market positions, knowledge capital and people, although these are rarely recognised in financial statements.

Active strategies have been pursued by some businesses to develop intangible asset management as the core success of the business. One of Coca-Cola's Chief Financial Officers once described the entity's market capitalisation as being the sum of the values of its brand and its management systems. The importance of intangible assets was once highlighted by Bill Gates, Microsoft:

'The law requires circa 40 pages of figures in the annual company report but these figures represent only 3% of the company's value and assets. The remaining 97% are the company's intangible assets'.

In an increasingly fast moving business environment, analysing business performance involves understanding corporate culture, knowledge management systems, product delivery processes, innovation and technological sustainability. Current financial reporting practices are often cited as out of date and unhelpful. The use of historical cost accounting based on past cash flows does not report the strength or value created by modern businesses. This can create challenges for users of financial statements.

It is widely recognised that the quality of employees has a direct effect on future cash flows of an organisation. Indeed, many CEOs describe employees as their most important assets. Cost-based reporting principles mean that it is rare that employee assets appear in corporate statements of financial position. A number of initiatives, such as the Accounting for People Report in the UK, have tried to address the specific issues of accounting for people. Many alternative measurement techniques, including current values, have been suggested, but none has received acceptance by standard setters. As current trends in business management and corporate practice develop, this is an area that standard setters may be forced to revisit.

2.3 Identifiability

That part of the definition of an intangible asset which requires it to be identifiable is of fundamental importance, because an identifiable intangible which has a finite useful life is subject to annual amortisation, whereas an item which is not identifiable is either not recognised at all or, if it is subsumed in goodwill acquired in a business combination, not amortised but subject to annual impairment reviews.

There are few problems in identifying intangibles which meet the identifiability criterion of being separable. To be separable, they should be capable of being disposed of on their own, with the remainder of the business being retained.

Goodwill can only be disposed of as part of the sale of a business, so is not separable.

The other way in which an asset is to be regarded as identifiable is if it arises from contractual or other legal rights and is not separable. An example would be where an entity controls both unique PPE to produce a unique product and the right to manufacture and distribute that product in a particular territory. The unique PPE is worthless without the distribution rights and vice versa, so the distribution rights are non-separable but still identifiable.

Point to note:

It is the lack of identifiability which prevents internally generated goodwill being recognised. It is not separable (see above) and does not arise from contractual or other legal rights.

2.4 Future economic benefits and reliable asset measurement

As already noted an intangible can only be recognised in financial statements if future economic benefits can be attributed to it and the cost of the asset can be measured reliably.

It is these limitations which prevent so many internally generated intangibles being recognised. It is difficult to attribute specific future economic benefits to and/or to measure reliably the cost of expenditure on:

- Brands, mastheads, publishing titles and customer lists developed internally and
- Training, advertising and promotional activities (including mail order catalogues) and relocations and reorganisations.

All of these expenditures are specified by IAS 38 as not being capable of recognition as intangibles. After all, it is impossible to separate expenditure on these from expenditure on developing the business as a whole.

2.5 Separate acquisition

2.5.1 Acquisition as part of a business combination

As noted, the probability of future economic benefits criterion for recognition as an intangible is always met for one separately acquired. An example is an intangible acquired in a business combination, but in this case it is also always the case that the fair value is regarded as being capable of reliable measurement.

- This means that anything acquired as a part of a business combination and **meeting the definition of an intangible asset** should be recognised **separately from goodwill**.

- Goodwill carried in the acquiree's statement of financial position should not be separately recognised by the acquirer because it is not identifiable – it is subsumed in the goodwill acquired in the business combination.

- An intangible asset acquired in a business combination might be separable **but only together with a related item of property, plant and equipment or intangible asset.** In this case the group of assets should be recognised **as a single asset,** for example a publishing title and its related subscriber database.

- An intangible asset may be recognised by the acquirer **that was not recognised by the acquiree,** for example an internally generated brand may be recognised by the acquirer.

  This is because the acquisition provides sufficient evidence that:

  - There will be future economic benefits attributable to it; otherwise, why would the acquirer buy it?

  - The cost can be measured reliably; the acquirer will have built up the total purchase consideration by estimating values (= costs) for each asset.

- IFRS 3 *Business Combinations* also includes a list of items acquired in a business combination which should be recognised separately from goodwill. These are:

  - Market-related intangible assets, for example trademarks
  - Customer-related intangible assets, for example customer lists
  - Artistic-related intangible assets, for example motion picture films
  - Contract-based intangible assets, for example franchise agreements
  - Technology-based intangible assets, for example computer software

- Once all these intangibles have been recognised at fair value, any remaining excess of cost over net assets acquired is recognised as goodwill.

  Goodwill should not be amortised but reviewed annually for impairment.

Worked example: Acquired intangible and goodwill

Newton Ltd has developed internally a branded games console and a number of electronic games which children can play on it. The brand is now highly respected among its target audience and the associated products are regarded as 'must have' games.

On 1 January 20X6 Ashburton plc acquired the whole of Newton Ltd for £10 million. At that date the fair value of the net assets recognised by Newton Ltd was £3 million. Ashburton plc engaged a brand valuation expert who valued Newton Ltd's brand at the acquisition date at £5 million on the basis of a useful life of five years.

The annual impairment test on 31 December 20X6 of the goodwill acquired in the business combination, revealed no impairment.

What amounts should be recognised in Ashburton plc's consolidated financial statements at 31 December 20X6 in respect of the goodwill acquired in the business combination and Newton Ltd's intangible?

Solution

Goodwill should be measured at £2 million (10 million – (3 million + 5 million))

Acquired intangibles should be measured at £4 million (5 million less amortisation of one-fifth)

Amortisation of £1 million should be recognised in profit or loss, reducing earnings.

Note that if the acquired intangible had not been separately recognised, goodwill would have been measured at £7 million (10 million – 3 million) and, assuming no impairment, there would have been no expense recognised in profit or loss in 20X6.

2.5.2 Acquisition by way of government grant

An intangible asset may be acquired free of charge, or for nominal consideration, by way of a government grant. For example, a government may transfer to an entity landing rights, that is the rights to land a specified number of aircraft at a particular airport each day.

A choice of accounting policies is available; the intangible asset (and grant) may be recognised initially either **at fair value** or **at a nominal amount**. (See Chapter 4)

2.6 Non-recognition of internally generated intangibles and relevance of information to users

2.6.1 The issue

As the comments referred to above from Coca-Cola and Microsoft indicate, the non-recognition of internally generated intangibles can result in the assets recognised in financial statements of certain types of businesses being a very small proportion of their total assets. In the case of such a business, which is listed on a stock exchange, its market capitalisation is likely to be at a huge premium to revealed net asset value.

Non-recognition is driven mainly by the inability to measure the cost of the intangible reliably, particularly when it is built up over many years.

IAS 38 is content for acquired intangibles to be recognised, on the basis that their fair value is their cost. This requires the allocation of the total purchase consideration over the different assets by reference to their fair values. Such allocation is bound to be arbitrary, to some extent.

Some then argue that if fair values can be allocated in this way to acquired intangibles, why not allow the same approach for internally generated intangibles? Management which has sufficient expertise to make appropriate fair valuations on an acquisition should be relied on to be able to do the same for internally generated assets. Management are making such valuations all the time, as they decide to refresh their portfolio of brands/products by selling some they own and buying some more.

The argument against is that at least with an acquisition there is a market transaction which identifies reliably the cost of the whole acquired entity, whereas with internally generated assets there is not. But with an acquisition, the allocation to individual assets usually results in there being a residual, recognised as goodwill. Even on an acquisition, there are limits to the accuracy of the fair valuation process.

One of the important considerations in this debate is that IFRS are basically cost-based standards, with fair value being required only for items regularly traded such as current assets or available-for-sale investments. When intangibles are so rarely traded other than through the acquisition of the entity which owns them, to move their measurement from a cost basis to a fair value basis would be a very large step indeed.

2.6.2 Relevance to users

Non-recognition of internally generated intangibles often results in the understatement of capital employed, to such an extent that users of financial statements often prefer to measure profitability on the basis of profit before interest and tax as a percentage of revenue, rather than of capital employed. Recognition in financial statements of such intangibles would enable users to reach a better informed opinion of whether management is doing a good job in generating profit from the intangibles or whether they would be better leveraged by being sold to another management.

Worked example: Internally generated intangible

An entity owns a single brand which it has developed internally over many years. Annual expenditure on maintaining the brand is £2 million, as a result of which management estimates that the brand has an indefinite useful life. Brand valuation experts have recently estimated the fair value of the brand at £20 million.

The entity's statement of financial position presents total assets of £11 million, current liabilities of £4 million, borrowings of £3 million and equity of £4 million. Annual revenue is £30 million and profit before interest and tax is £9 million.

How will users of financial statements currently evaluate the entity and how would that evaluation change if the entity recognised the brand in its statement of financial position?

Solution

Statement of financial position		At present £m	Change £m	Intangible recognised £m
Intangibles		–	+20	20
Other assets		11		11
		11		31
Current liabilities		(4)		(4)
		7		27
Equity		4	+20	24
Borrowings	(A)	3		3
Capital employed	(B)	7		27
Income statement				
Revenue	(C)	30		30
Profit before interest and tax	(D)	9		9
Return on capital employed	(D) as % (B)	129%		33%
Profit as a percentage of revenue	(D) as % (C)	30%		30%
Gearing	(A) as % (B)	43%		11%
Cash generation		9		9

Points to note:

1 The capitalisation of the brand increases assets and equity (the revaluation surplus).
2 As the brand has an indefinite life, there is no amortisation to be recognised in profit or loss.
3 The £2 million annual expenditure on maintaining the brand should remain as an expense.

As always, cash generation is not affected by different accounting policies. In terms of profitability:

- The ROCE calculated by reference to the present statement of financial position is meaningless, because it does not measure the true capital employed in the business (in your mind, reconfigure the 'at present' statement of financial position on the basis that the brand is sold for £20 million cash and see what the capital employed is then)

- The ROCE on the restated basis is meaningful

- Profit as a percentage of revenue is not affected by the choice of accounting policy, which is why this measure of profitability is so commonly used in evaluating service businesses

- The restated gearing is improved, but the measure is not very meaningful. Even today entities other than financial institutions find it hard to borrow if they cannot give tangible assets as security.

3 Impairment

> **Section overview**
>
> - Financial Accounting covered the basic principles of IAS 36 *Impairment of Assets.*
>
>   - An impairment test should be carried out if there are indicators, internal or external, that an asset is impaired, in that its carrying amount exceeds its recoverable amount
>
>   - The recoverable amount of an asset is the higher of its fair value less costs to sell and its value in use
>
>   - Fair value less costs to sell is the amount obtainable from the sale of an asset in an arm's length transaction less disposal costs
>
>   - Value in use is calculated by discounting the future cash flows expected to be derived from the asset to their present value
>
>   - Impairment losses are accounted for in the same way as downward PPE revaluations
>
> - Where it is not possible to estimate the recoverable amount of an individual asset, the comparison should be performed on the basis of the cash-generating unit to which the asset belongs.
>
> - Goodwill and corporate assets which are not directly attributable to a cash-generating unit should be allocated on a reasonable and consistent basis.
>
> - When an impairment loss is recognised for a cash-generating unit the loss should be allocated firstly to goodwill, then to the other assets on a *pro rata* basis. No individual asset should be written down to less than its fair value, less costs to sell.
>
> - An impairment loss recognised for goodwill should not be reversed. Other impairment losses should be reversed in limited circumstances.

3.1 Introduction

US studies have shown that goodwill and other intangible assets constituted over 70% of the purchase consideration in recent business combinations. The continuing emphasis on identifying intangible assets and the mandatory annual impairment testing of goodwill has increased the importance of impairment as a management issue. The impact of recognising impairment losses leads directly to increased volatility in reported earnings.

Impairment testing is designed to ensure that assets are not stated at more than they are worth to a business, with reported values indicating that the assets are generating positive returns. Where asset carrying amounts are not recoverable through the returns generated from them, the underlying assets are impaired and should have their carrying amounts reduced.

Management will often work hard to react to events that give rise to impairments. In some instances this will help to avoid the need to record an impairment loss, by addressing a potential issue before it becomes detrimental to the business. In others, the impairment may have happened before the necessary business improvements can be made, or have even been identified.

One key reporting issue is how to determine an asset's recoverable amount. That determination is a judgemental process within a defined framework carried out by management. This leads to critical asset evaluations being made by those who are judged on their outcome!

Disclosures allow stakeholders to review the key assumptions and the sensitivities of impairment calculations. Where discounted cash flow calculations are used to underpin asset carrying amounts, even small changes in the discount rates or in the timing of cash flows can have significant effects on the calculated amounts.

In recent years interest rates in most developed economies have been at historically low levels. Even relatively modest increases in general interest rates could have a significant impact on the present value of projected cash flows, in addition to the effect on those cash flows of the potential economic slowdown caused by the increased rates. The combination of lower income streams and higher discount rates can have alarming implications for asset measurement.

3.2 Scope

IAS 36 most commonly applies to:

- Assets such as **property, plant and equipment (PPE)** accounted for in accordance with IAS 16 *Property, Plant and Equipment*

- **Intangible assets** accounted for in accordance with IAS 38 *Intangible Assets.*

- **Some financial assets**, namely subsidiaries, associates and joint ventures (see Chapter 8). Impairments of all other financial assets are accounted for in accordance with IAS 39 *Financial Instruments: Recognition and Measurement* (see Chapter 7).

3.3 Indications of impairment

Financial Reporting questions are unlikely to specify directly that you should carry out an impairment test. It is more likely that you will be expected to spot that a scenario contains an indicator of impairment and that an impairment review is therefore necessary.

The basic approach within IAS 36 is that an entity should look for **evidence of impairment at each reporting date.** At a minimum the following **indicators** should be considered:

- **External sources**

    - **Significant decline in the market value of the asset** that is more significant than would normally be expected from passage of time or normal use, for example due to increased competition

    - **Significant changes in the technological, market, legal or economic environment** in which the business operates

    - An increase in market interest rates or market rates of return on investments **likely to affect the discount rate used in the calculation of value in use** (see section 3.7.2)

    - The **carrying amount** of the entity's net assets being **more** than its **market capitalisation**

- **Internal sources**

    - Evidence of **obsolescence or physical damage**
    - Significant changes with an adverse effect on the entity

        - The asset becomes **idle**
        - Plans to **discontinue/restructure the operation** to which the asset belongs
        - Plans to **dispose of an asset** before the previously expected date
        - Reassessing an asset's useful life as **finite rather than indefinite**

    - Internal evidence that asset performance is or will be **worse than expected**

If there is such an indication, the asset's recoverable amount should be estimated, that is an impairment review should be carried out.

When assessing internal factors an entity should compare the **cash flows** associated with an asset, or group of assets, with those **budgeted.** For example cash outflows may exceed budgeted figures due to higher than expected maintenance costs. Cash inflows may be lower than budgeted due to increased competition. Both would indicate potential impairment.

Worked example: Impairment

Poppleford plc acquired a group of assets on the basis that its cash flows over the years 20X5 to 20X9 were budgeted as:

	20X5 £'000	20X6 £'000	20X7 £'000	20X8 £'000	20X9 £'000	Total £'000
Inflows	100	110	120	130	140	600
Outflows	88	98	108	118	128	540
Surplus	12	12	12	12	12	60

As a result of increased competition in the market place, additional amounts will now have to be spent on improving the functionality of the product and on extra promotional activity. The revised budget for cash flows is:

	20X5 £'000	20X6 £'000	20X7 £'000	20X8 £'000	20X9 £'000	Total £'000
Inflows	100	110	120	130	140	600
Outflows	118	125	128	113	115	599
Surplus/(deficit)	(18)	(15)	(8)	17	25	1

Is an impairment review necessary?

Solution

Cash inflow projections are unchanged, but cost increases in the near future result in cash deficits over the next three years. Over the five years the net cash flows are now estimated to be significantly below those originally budgeted, providing internal evidence of the possible impairment of this group of assets. An impairment review is required.

Interactive question 8: Impairment   [Difficulty level: Easy]

A company has three non-current assets, the details of which are as follows:

	Asset 1 £m	Asset 2 £m	Asset 3 £m
Carrying amount	80	120	140
Value in use	150	105	107
Fair value less costs to sell	60	90	110

Requirement

Explain whether any of the three assets is impaired and, if so, calculate the impairment loss.

See **Answer** at the end of this chapter.

Point to note:

It is not always necessary to calculate both fair value less costs to sell and value in use. If either of these amounts **exceeds the asset's carrying amount**, the asset is **not impaired** (therefore it is not necessary to estimate the other amount).

3.4 Annual impairment tests

Annual impairment tests, irrespective of whether there are indications of impairment, are required for:

*   Intangible assets with an indefinite useful life
*   Intangible assets not yet available for use (such as ongoing development work)
*   Goodwill acquired in a business combination.

3.5 Recoverable amount

Assets should be carried at **no more than their recoverable amount**. Where there are indications of impairment an entity should assess the recoverable amount of the asset, or group of assets. Where the **carrying amount exceeds the recoverable amount** the asset is **impaired**.

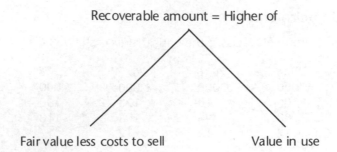

Recoverable amount = Higher of

Fair value less costs to sell   Value in use

3.6 Fair value less costs to sell

Definition

Fair value less costs to sell: is the amount obtainable from the sale of an asset or cash-generating unit in an arm's length transaction between knowledgeable, willing parties, less the costs of disposal.

(We will look at cash-generating units in section 3.9.)

Fair value less costs to sell is determined as follows:

Where there is a **binding sale agreement**	**Price** in the agreement less **incremental costs directly attributable to the disposal** of the asset.
Where there is **no binding sale agreement** but the asset is **traded in an active market**	**Market price (current bid price) less costs of disposal.** Where current bid prices are unavailable, fair value may be based on the price of the most recent transaction.
Where there is **no binding sale agreement or active market**	Based on **best information available** of the amount obtainable in an **arm's length transaction, less costs of disposal.** This should not reflect a forced sale.

Costs of disposal include:

- Legal costs
- Stamp duty and transaction costs
- Costs of removing the asset
- Direct incremental costs to bring an asset into condition for its sale.

Interactive question 9: Measurement   [Difficulty level: Intermediate]

Dartmouth Ltd wishes to estimate the fair value less costs to sell of a group of assets. There is no active market for these assets, so Dartmouth Ltd engages the valuation services of the commercial agents who are reputed to arrange over half the sale transactions carried out each year in such groups of assets. The agents provide the following estimates:

	£
Sale price	900,000
Agents' commission	90,000
Legal costs	50,000
Cost of dismantling the assets so that they can be removed	100,000
Cost of creating access to the group of assets for removal	20,000
Termination costs re staff who would become redundant on the sale	160,000
Cost of retraining staff who would be transferred to new activities	75,000

What is the fair value less costs to sell of this group of assets?

See **Answer** at the end of this chapter.

3.7 Value in use

Definition

Value in use: is the present value of the future cash flows expected to be derived from an asset or cash-generating unit.

The following elements should be reflected in the calculation of an asset's value in use:

- An **estimate of the future cash flows** the entity expects to derive from the asset

- Expectations about **possible variations in the amount or timing** of those future cash flows

- The **time value of money** (represented by the current market risk-free rate of interest)

- The price for bearing the **uncertainty inherent in the asset**

- **Other factors** that market participants would reflect in pricing the future cash flows the entity expects to derive from the asset

In summary, estimating the value in use of an asset involves two steps:

1 **Estimation of the future cash flows** attributable to the asset
2 Application of the **appropriate discount rate** to those future cash flows.

3.7.1 Step 1: Estimation of future cash flows

Future cash flows should include:

- Projected cash inflows from continuing use of the asset

- Projected cash outflows that will be necessarily incurred to generate the cash inflows and that are directly attributable to the asset (or can be allocated on a reasonable basis).

  These include costs of day-to-day servicing as well as allocated overheads.

- Projected cash flows which will be received (or paid) on the disposal of the asset.

These should be based on the amount that the entity expects to receive in an 'arm's length transaction' **using prices prevailing at the date of the estimate for similar assets**. Cash flows should also be adjusted for the effect of **general price inflation and specific price changes**.

Future cash flows **should not include**:

- Cash outflows relating to **obligations already recognised as liabilities**
- The effect of any **future restructuring to which the entity is not yet committed**
- Cash flows from financing activities or income tax receipts and payments.

Points to note:

1 Cash flow projections should be based on **reasonable and supportable assumptions made by management.**

2 Future cash flows should be based on the **most recent financial budgets or forecasts.** These budgets should cover **a maximum period of five years** unless a longer period can be justified.

  Beyond that five year (or longer) limit, detailed cash flow budgets are unreliable, so management should just extrapolate the fifth year using a steady or declining growth rate.

  IAS 36 does permit an increasing growth rate if it can be justified, but notes that this is unlikely, because five years is sufficient time for competitors to enter the market and compete away any super-profits.

3 Future cash flows should be estimated for the asset in its **current condition**. No account should be taken of future restructuring to which the entity is not yet committed or any improvements which may be made to the asset.

Worked example: Impairment

Appleton plc has developed the following cash flow forecast in respect of an asset

	20X5 £'000	20X6 £'000	20X7 £'000	20X8 £'000	20X9 £'000
Net inflows in current state	200	220	240	260	280
Additional inflows when enhanced			60	70	80
Sub-total	200	220	300	330	360
Enhancement outflows			(120)		
Total inflows	200	220	180	330	360

What cash flows should be used in estimating value in use at the end of 20X4 and of 20X7?

Solution

At the end of 20X4 value in use should be estimated by reference to the net inflows in current state, because although management is budgeting for the enhancement outflows, they have not yet occurred. The additional benefits are not attributable to the asset in its end-20X4 state.

At the end of 20X7 and assuming the enhancement outflows have occurred, value in use should be estimated by reference to the total inflows for 20X8 and 20X9, plus any further years now budgeted.

3.7.2   Step 2: Discounting

The cash flows should be **discounted at an appropriate rate**. The discount rate should be a **pre-tax rate** that reflects current market assessments of:

- **The time value of money** and
- The **risks specific to the asset** for which future cash flow estimates **have not been adjusted**.

Point to note:

Risks specific to the asset should be adjusted for, either in estimating the cash flows or in calculating the discount rate, **but not in both**.

The discount rate should be estimated from:

- The **rate implicit in current market transactions for similar assets**, or
- From the **weighted average cost of capital** of a listed entity that has a single asset (or a portfolio of assets) **similar to the asset in question**.

In practice it may be difficult to calculate the asset-specific rate described above as it is dependent on information based on **similar assets**. Where this is the case, an estimate should be made which should take account of the following:

- The entity's **weighted average cost of capital,** for example using the Capital Asset Pricing Model
- The entity's **incremental borrowing rate**
- **Other market borrowing rates**

The discount rate should not be based on the rate applicable to any finance raised to purchase the asset because the future cash flows expected to arise from the asset are not dependent on the way in which the purchase was financed.

Point to note:

Appendix A of IAS 36 contains some examples of discounting calculations.

Interactive question 10: Discounting   [Difficulty level: Exam standard]

An entity has a single manufacturing plant which has a carrying amount of £900,000. A new government elected in the country passes legislation significantly restricting exports of the product produced by the plant. As a result, and for the foreseeable future, the entity's production will be cut by 40%. Cash flow forecasts have been prepared derived from the most recent financial budgets/forecasts for the next five years approved by management (excluding the effects of general price inflation):

Year	1	2	3	4	5
	£'000	£'000	£'000	£'000	£'000
Future cash flows	276	253	188	125	280
					(including disposal proceeds)

If the plant was sold now it would realise £660,000, net of selling costs.

The entity estimates the pre-tax discount rate specific to the plant to be 15%, after excluding the effects of general price inflation.

Requirement

Calculate the recoverable amount of the plant and any impairment loss.

Note: PV factors at 15% are as follows.

Year	PV factor @15%
1	0.86957
2	0.75614
3	0.65752
4	0.57175
5	0.49718

Year	Future cash flows £'000	PV factor @15%	Discounted future cash flows £'000
1			
2			
3			
4			
5			
			£'000
Recoverable amount			
Impairment loss			

See **Answer** at the end of this chapter.

Point to note:

In Interactive question 10 you were provided with the relevant discount factors. In the examination you will be expected to calculate them, as follows.

Year			
1	$1/1.15$	=	0.86957
2	$1/(1.15)^2$	=	0.75614
3	$1/(1.15)^3$	=	0.65752
4	$1/(1.15)^4$	=	0.57175
5	$1/(1.15)^5$	=	0.49718

3.8 Recognising an impairment loss – individual asset

An impairment loss is recognised immediately **in profit or loss** unless the impairment relates to an asset which has been **revalued upwards**.

An impairment loss on an asset held at a revalued amount should be treated as a **revaluation decrease** under the relevant IAS.

In practice this means:

- To the extent that there is a revaluation surplus held in respect of the asset, the impairment loss should be recognised **in other comprehensive income against the revaluation surplus**

- Any excess should be recognised **in profit or loss**.

Interactive question 11: Impairment
[Difficulty level: Intermediate]

An entity has a property that was originally acquired for £500,000. The property was revalued to £800,000 last year, and the £300,000 was recognised in other comprehensive income and held in revaluation surplus in accordance with IAS 16.

The current carrying amount for the property is £750,000.

Due to contamination of the land on which the property stands, the entity has undertaken an impairment review.

The fair value of the property is now estimated to be only £300,000. The value in use of the property is calculated as being £400,000.

Requirement

Determine the relevant treatment of any impairment.

See **Answer** at the end of this chapter.

Following the recognition of an impairment loss, any depreciation charged in respect of the asset in future periods should be based on the revised carrying amount, less any residual value expected, over the remaining useful life of the asset as per IAS 16.

Interactive question 12: Depreciation
[Difficulty level: Easy]

A piece of machinery was originally acquired for £100,000. It was expected to have a useful life of ten years and no residual value. At the start of year six, there was a downturn in demand due to a competitor product entering the market, and this has led to an impairment in the value of the asset. The impairment has been calculated as being £20,000, although it is expected that the asset will continue to have a remaining five-year life.

Requirement

Determine the annual depreciation charge in the remaining years of the asset's life.

See **Answer** at the end of this chapter.

3.9 Cash-generating units

Where it is not possible to estimate the recoverable amount of an individual asset, the entity should estimate the recoverable amount of the **cash-generating unit (CGU)** to which it belongs and performs the impairment test on the CGU.

Definition

A cash-generating unit: is the smallest identifiable group of assets that generates cash inflows that are largely independent of the cash inflows from other assets or groups of assets.

Worked example: Cash-generating units

A bus company has a contract with a local education authority to transport children to and from school. There are ten routes contracted to this particular bus company. One of the routes is making losses because it collects children from remote areas, so the number of children collected is much lower than on highly populated routes. The bus company does not have the ability to withdraw from individual routes. The ten routes are contracted for as a group.

The ten routes should therefore be grouped together as one cash-generating unit.

As we can see from the definition and the worked example above, the identification of a CGU is **a judgemental exercise**. Factors which management should consider include:

- How **management monitors the entity's operations** (for example by product lines, businesses, regions)

- How **management makes decisions about continuing or disposing of the entity's assets and operations**.

Other points to note:

1   If an active market exists for the output produced by a group of assets, this group of assets should be identified as a CGU, even if some or all of the output is used internally.

2   CGUs should be identified consistently from period to period unless a change is justified. Where the composition of a CGU changes, this should be disclosed.

3.9.1   Carrying amount of a CGU

The carrying amount of a CGU is made up of the **carrying amounts of the individual assets that can be directly attributed to it.** Certain assets, however, may contribute to the revenue generating activities of the entity as a whole and it may be difficult to allocate to an individual CGU. Examples include **corporate assets and goodwill.** These should be allocated across the CGUs to which they relate on a **reasonable and consistent basis**.

Point to note:

The procedures to be adopted if corporate assets and goodwill cannot be allocated to individual CGUs falls outside the Financial Reporting syllabus.

The carrying amount of a CGU is normally **not reduced** by recognised liabilities (such as trade payables and provisions which are carried as liabilities in the statement of financial position), because both fair value less costs to sell and value in use are normally determined without consideration of such liabilities.

3.9.2   Allocating goodwill to CGUs

Goodwill does not generate independent cash flows and therefore its recoverable amount as an individual asset cannot be determined. It is therefore **allocated** to each of the acquirer's CGUs that are expected to benefit from the synergies of the combination. The initial allocation of goodwill should be completed **no later than** by the end of the first reporting period commencing after the acquisition date. Each unit to which the goodwill is allocated should:

- Represent the **lowest level** within the entity at which the goodwill is monitored for internal management purposes

- **Not be larger than a reporting segment** determined in accordance with IFRS 8 *Operating Segments* (See Chapter 2).

Goodwill that cannot be allocated to a CGU on a non-arbitrary basis is allocated to the **group of CGUs** to which it relates.

3.9.3   Testing CGUs with goodwill for impairment

A CGU to which goodwill has been allocated should be tested for impairment **annually** (irrespective of whether indicators of impairment are identified). The carrying amount of the unit, including goodwill, should be compared with the recoverable amount . If the carrying amount of the unit exceeds the recoverable amount an impairment loss should be recognised (see 3.10).

The annual impairment test may be performed **at any time during an accounting period, but should be performed at the same time every year.**

Worked example: Allocating goodwill to CGUs

P acquired a wholly owned subsidiary. At the acquisition date P decided that the £60 million goodwill could be allocated on a non-arbitrary basis to the three CGUs within that subsidiary. The allocation was based on the relative carrying amounts of the assets in each CGU:

	CGU_1 £m	CGU_2 £m	CGU_3 £m	Total £m
Carrying amount of acquired assets	140.0	160	180.0	480
Allocation of goodwill	$^{140}/_{480}$ = 17.5	$^{160}/_{480}$ = 20	$^{180}/_{480}$ = 22.5	60
Carrying amount including goodwill	157.5	180	202.5	540

Impairment reviews for each CGU should be carried out using the carrying amounts including goodwill.

3.10 Recognising an impairment loss within a CGU

When an impairment loss is recognised for a CGU, it should be allocated between the assets in the CGU in the following order:

1   To the **goodwill allocated to the CGU**; then

2   To all **other assets in the CGU, on a pro rata basis**, subject to the limitation that no asset may be written down **below its own recoverable amount**

Any remaining amount of the impairment loss should be recognised as a **liability** if required by other IASs, for example IAS 37 *Provisions, Contingent Liabilities and Contingent Assets.*

Worked example: Allocation of impairment loss

A cash-generating unit holds the following assets:

	£'000
Goodwill	20
Patent	40
Property, plant and equipment	60
Total	120

An annual impairment review is required as the cash-generating unit contains goodwill. The most recent review assesses its recoverable amount to be £90,000. An impairment loss of £30,000 has been incurred and has been recognised in profit or loss.

First, the entity reduces the carrying amount of the goodwill. As the impairment loss exceeds the value of goodwill within the cash-generating unit, all goodwill is written off.

The entity then reduces the carrying amount of other assets in the unit on a pro rata basis. Hence the remaining loss of £10,000 should be allocated pro rata between the property, plant and equipment and the patent.

Revised balances should be as follows.

	£'000
Goodwill (20 – 20)	–
Patent (40 – (40/(60 + 40) × (30 – 20)))	36
Property, plant and equipment (60 – (60/(60 + 40) × (30 – 20)))	54
Total	90

Interactive question 13: Impairment of CGU [Difficulty level: Intermediate]

Following on from the worked example in section 3.9.3 above, conditions in the markets in which CGU_2 operates have worsened. At the end of the current reporting period P estimates the recoverable amount of CGU_2 at £170 million. At this date the carrying amount of its assets are as follows:

	£m
Allocated goodwill	20
Patent	10
Property, plant and equipment	115
Inventories	30
Trade receivables	45
Total	220

Requirement

Explain, showing calculations, the impairment loss to be recognised in respect of CGU_2 and the revised carrying amounts of its assets.

See **Answer** at the end of this chapter.

3.11 Goodwill and non-controlling interests

The recoverable amount of a CGU relates to all the assets in or attributable to that CGU, including goodwill. If the CGU is wholly owned, then the allocation of impairment losses is as described above.

If there is a non-controlling interest (NCI) in the CGU (it is a partly-owned subsidiary, for example) **and** at the acquisition date the NCI was measured at its proportionate share of the fair value of the acquiree's net assets, then only the goodwill attributable to the owners of the parent will be recognised. Yet part of the CGU's recoverable amount will relate to the NCI's unrecognised goodwill. In this situation:

- The carrying amount of goodwill allocated to that unit should be notionally **grossed up** to include the goodwill attributable to the NCI.

- Any impairment loss is first recognised against goodwill as per the normal rules (see section 3.10). However, in this case the loss is apportioned between:
    - **Goodwill attributable to the parent**
    - **Goodwill attributable to the NCI.**

Point to note:

Where the NCI is measured at the proportionate share of the acquiree's net assets, the impairment loss allocated against the NCI's goodwill is a **notional amount** which is not actually recognised in profit or loss.

Worked example: At acquisition date NCI measured at share of net assets

On 1 January 20X2 a parent acquired an 80% interest in a subsidiary for £1,600,000, when the identifiable net assets of the subsidiary were £1,500,000. The non-controlling interest was measured at the acquisition date at its share of the net assets. The subsidiary is a cash-generating unit.

At 31 December 20X4, the recoverable amount of the subsidiary was £1,000,000. The carrying amount of the subsidiary's identifiable assets was £1,350,000.

Calculate the impairment loss to be recognised in the year ended 31 December 20X4.

Solution

At 1 January 20X2 the calculation of the goodwill acquired in the business combination was:

	£'000
Consideration transferred	1,600
Non-controlling interest at share of identifiable assets (20% × 1,500)	300
	1,900
Identifiable net assets	1,500
Goodwill	400

At 31 December 20X4 the cash-generating unit consists of the subsidiary's identifiable net assets (carrying amount £1,350,000) and goodwill of £400,000, a total of £1,750,000. Because the non-controlling interest was measured at its share of the net assets at the acquisition date, goodwill should be grossed up to reflect the 20% non-controlling interest.

	Goodwill	Net assets	Total
	£'000	£'000	£'000
Carrying amount	400	1,350	1,750
Unrecognised non-controlling interest (400 × 20/80)	100		100
	500	1,350	1,850
Recoverable amount			(1,000)
Impairment loss			850

The impairment loss should be allocated as follows.

	Goodwill (80%)	Goodwill (NCI)	Identifiable net assets
	£'000	£'000	£'000
Carrying amounts	400	100	1,350
Impairment	(400)	(100)	(350)
	–	–	1,000

The entity recognises an impairment of £750,000 (400,000 + 350,000) in its financial statements, all of it allocated to the owners of the parent.

Note that if the recoverable amount had been £1,400,000, the impairment loss would have been £450,000 (1,850,000 – 1,400,000). As this is less than the grossed-up amount of goodwill, only 80% (360,000) thereof would be allocated against the £400,000 goodwill attributable to the parent, reducing its carrying amount to £40,000. The remaining 20% (90,000) would be allocated to the amount attributable to the non-controlling interest, which is not recognised in the consolidated statement of financial position.

3.12 Reversal of impairment losses

The key points are as follows:

- An entity is required to assess at each period end whether there is any indication that a previously recognised impairment loss has decreased or may no longer exist.

  The indications to be reviewed are the same as for the initial impairment loss, with 'increase' substituted for 'decrease', and so on

- An impairment loss should only be reversed if there has been an increase in the asset's service potential, that is a change in the estimates used to determine the asset's recoverable amount.

- Such a change could result from a change in the discount rate or in the cash flow estimates.

- An asset's recoverable amount may increase simply because time has passed and the discount has unwound as the realisation of cash flows becomes closer; if this is the only reason that the recoverable amount has increased, no impairment reversal is permitted, because the asset's service potential has not increased.

- The reversal of an impairment loss for an asset should only be recognised to the extent that the carrying amount of the asset is revised to the amount it would have been (after subsequent depreciation) if no impairment loss had ever been recognised.

- The recognition of the reversal of the impairment loss should be **consistent with the original treatment of the impairment**, in terms of whether it is recognised in profit or loss or other comprehensive income.

- A reversal of an impairment loss for a CGU should be allocated to the assets of the unit, except goodwill, *pro rata* to the carrying amount of the assets.

Point to note:

An impairment loss recognised for goodwill should not be reversed in a subsequent period.

Worked example: Reversal of impairment

This illustration takes the data from Worked example: Allocation of impairment loss in section 3.10 above where the facts were:

	Initial £'000	Impairment £'000	Revised £'000
Goodwill	20	(20)	–
Patent	40	(4)	36
Property, plant and equipment	60	(6)	54
Total	120	(30)	90

Two years later when the property, plant and equipment and the patent had carrying amounts of £43,200 and £28,800 respectively (a total of £72,000), the recoverable amount was assessed as £90,000.

Calculations show that if the original impairment had not been incurred, the property, plant and equipment would now have been carried at £48,000 and the patent at £32,000 (a total of £80,000).

The impairment on the goodwill should not be reversed. The impairment of the other assets should only be reversed to the extent that they are restored to their pre-impairment amounts less any subsequent depreciation. Hence their maximum amount is £80,000. The amount to be reversed is £8,000 (£80,000 – £72,000). As the original impairment loss was recognised in profit or loss, the reversal should also be recognised in profit or loss.

3.13 Judgements required

Many aspects of the application of IAS 36 require the use of **judgement**. Examples include the following:

- The extent to which indicators suggest that an impairment review is required

- The determination of fair value when there is no binding sale agreement or active market

- Calculation of expected future cash flows (for value in use)

- Selection of an appropriate discount rate which reflects the time value of money and the risks specific to the asset

- The identification of CGUs

- The allocation of goodwill and corporate assets to CGUs

A Chartered Accountant responsible for the preparation of this information would have to ensure that **appropriate decisions** are made based on the information available. Decisions made should **not be biased** in favour of a particular accounting outcome.

3.14 Relevance of information to users

With its emphasis on historical cost, financial reporting is sometimes regarded as adopting an over-prudent approach to the presentation of information. Certainly users of financial statements tend to believe that there are unrecognised profits, rather than unrecognised losses, tucked away in businesses.

IAS 36 supports users by seeking to ensure that non-current and other asset carrying amounts will be, at a minimum, recovered from future operations. This avoids the overstatement of:

- Profit
- Capital employed

which would exist if such assets were carried at above their recoverable amounts.

Properly recognised impairment losses are likely to reduce return on capital employed and increase gearing to more realistic levels, thereby providing useful information to users.

4 Assets and disposal groups held for sale

Section overview

IFRS 5 *Non-current Assets Held for Sale and Discontinued Operations* was covered in Financial Accounting. This section revises the key points you should be familiar with and then goes on to develop a number of issues further.

4.1 Introduction

The key points you should remember are as follows:

- A non-current asset should be derecognised when it is disposed of or abandoned

- A non-current asset should be classified as held for sale when the entity intends to recover its carrying amount principally through sale.

    - Certain criteria should be met, such as that the asset should be available for immediate sale and the sale should be highly probable

    - There should be an expectation that the asset will be sold within one year from the date of classification

- Once classified as held for sale, an asset should no longer be depreciated.

- An asset to be abandoned is not treated as held for sale (its carrying amount is not to be recovered principally through sale) and is still depreciated.

- An asset held for sale is measured at the lower of carrying amount and fair value less costs to sell, with any write down being recognised as an impairment loss.

    - The effect for an asset measured under the cost model is that any loss is recognised immediately, but any gain deferred until actual disposal

    - An asset measured under the revaluation model is remeasured at fair value under IAS 16 immediately before classification, then remeasured at the lower of carrying amount and fair value less costs to sell

    - The effect is that costs to sell are recognised as a loss on reclassification

- Non-current assets held for sale are separately disclosed in the statement of financial position.

- On final disposal any further gain or loss (carrying amount less disposal proceeds) should be recognised as a gain or loss.

Point to note:

If an entity routinely sells items of PPE it has held for rental to others, it should transfer such assets to **inventories** at their carrying amount when they cease to be rented and become held for sale, rather than applying IFRS 5. Sale proceeds should be recognised as revenue under IAS 18 *Revenue*.

Worked example: Asset held for sale (cost model)

An item of PPE was acquired on 1 January 20X6 at a cost of £200,000. A residual value of £20,000 and a useful life of 10 years was assumed for the purposes of depreciation charges.

On 1 January 20X8 the asset was classified as held for sale. Its fair value was estimated at £140,000 and the costs to sell at £5,000.

The asset was sold on 1 July 20X8 for £130,000.

(a)　Show the journal entry to record the classification as held for sale.

(b)　Show the effects on profit or loss of the classification as held for sale and of the disposal.

Solution

(a)　Journal entry to record the classification as held for sale

		£	£
1 January 20X8			
DR	PPE-accumulated depreciation ((200 – 20) × $^{4}/_{10}$)	36,000	
DR	Non-current assets held for sale (140 – 5)	135,000	
DR	Profit or loss (Bal fig)	29,000	
CR	PPE–cost		200,000

(b)　Effect on profit or loss

	£
Impairment loss on classification as held for sale	29,000
Loss on disposal (135 – 130)	5,000

Point to note:

No depreciation is charged in 20X8.

Interactive question 14: Asset held for sale (revaluation model)

[Difficulty level: Intermediate]

An entity carries its land at fair value. One piece of land had a carrying amount of £60,000. On 1 January 20X8 the asset was classified as held for sale, its fair value being estimated at £70,000 and the costs to sell at £2,000. The asset was sold on 30 June 20X8 for £67,000.

Requirement

Describe the accounting entries related to this transaction and show the journal entries needed.

See **Answer** at the end of this chapter.

4.2　Context for IFRS 5

Where the entity does not intend to use a non-current asset as part of its ongoing business but instead intends to sell it, it is not appropriate to classify the asset as PPE as it will not be used to generate economic benefits for the entity in future. In these circumstances IFRS 5 requires the asset to be classified as held for sale.

This separate identification substantially improves the information made available to users as it provides information on the entity's plans and likely future performance.

Many organisations undertake strategic assessments with a view to disposing of non-core assets and exiting from certain business segments. These strategies may take several years to execute and in some cases are postponed as a result of management changes or market conditions. International standards require separate identification of assets held for disposal although stringent criteria apply. Organisations executing a longer term strategy of changes to their business portfolio in a piecemeal manner would not necessarily separately classify these operations as held for sale at the outset of the strategy. This may make the process of predicting future results and cash flows more problematic.

Operations that are closed down rather than being sold are not separately classified until they are closed, as the carrying amount of the assets will principally be recovered through use. This may reduce the predictive quality of information presented in the financial statements, so a narrative explanation of management's future operating intentions will be invaluable for users of the financial statements. A decision to curtail the use of certain assets may be seen as an indicator of impairment and therefore the recoverability of asset carrying amounts should be considered.

4.3 Disposal groups

IFRS 5 also applies to **groups of assets and associated liabilities** which will be disposed of in a single transaction, described as a **disposal group.** (Disposal groups were outside the scope of the Financial Accounting syllabus but are examinable in the Financial Reporting syllabus.)

Definition

Disposal group: A group of assets to be disposed of, by sale or otherwise, together as a group in a single transaction, and liabilities directly associated with those assets that will be transferred in the transaction. The group includes goodwill acquired in a business combination if the group is a cash-generating unit to which goodwill has been allocated in accordance with the requirements of IAS 36 *Impairment of Assets* or if it is an operation within such a cash-generating unit.

Points to note:

1   The definition includes, but is not limited to:

  •   a subsidiary which the parent is committed to selling

  •   a cash-generating unit of the entity, that is a group of assets which generates economic benefits that are largely independent of other activities of the entity.

2   The results of a disposal group should be presented as those of a discontinued operation if the group meets the definition of a component and is a separate major line of business (see Chapter 2).

The normal IAS 36 rules re the allocation of impairment losses apply, so an impairment loss in relation to a **disposal group** recognised on its classification as held for sale should first be allocated against any **goodwill** included in the assets of the disposal group and then against **any other assets within the scope of IFRS 5 on a pro rata basis**. (Inventories and receivables are outside the scope of IFRS 5 and therefore would not be affected.)

Worked example: Allocation of impairment loss

An entity plans to dispose of a group of its assets, which form a disposal group. Immediately before the classification as held for sale the total carrying amount of the disposal group is £22,350. The entity estimates that fair value less costs to sell of the disposal group amounts to £19,500. The impairment of £2,850 (22,350-19,500) should be allocated as follows:

	Carrying amount immediately before classification as held for sale £	Allocated impairment loss £	Carrying amount after allocating impairment loss £
Goodwill	2,250	(2,250)	0
PPE	14,550	(600)	13,950
Inventory	3,300	–	3,300
Receivables	2,250	–	2,250
TOTAL	22,350	2,850	19,500

4.4 Non-current assets or disposal groups acquired for sale

In some circumstances a non-current asset or disposal group may be acquired **exclusively with the view to its subsequent disposal**. The entity should classify the asset or disposal group as held for sale at the date of acquisition only where:

- The condition that it is to be sold **within one year of the acquisition date** is met

- **All other conditions** for recognition as held for sale are met **within a short period of its acquisition** (normally considered to be **three months**).

Points to note:

1   If a new subsidiary is acquired exclusively with a view to its subsequent disposal, it automatically meets the criteria for its results to be presented as discontinued operations.

2   Any other asset or disposal group so acquired should meet the normal IFRS 5 criteria for discontinued operations.

Worked example: Acquired for sale

A Ltd acquired B Ltd on 1 July 20X7. A Ltd intended to sell a number of the properties acquired as part of the acquisition of B Ltd. However, until A Ltd had assessed the properties in detail, it was unable to conclude which properties should be retained and which properties should be sold. A Ltd was confident that any unwanted properties would be sold within twelve months of the acquisition as the market was strong and all the properties were in popular locations.

Solution

Provided that A Ltd makes a decision as to which properties to sell within three months of the acquisition, the properties to be sold should be classified as held for sale from 1 July 20X7. This short period allows for the properties not being ready for immediate sale at the date of acquisition and permits A Ltd thinking time to evaluate which properties it wishes to retain within the business and those which it wishes to sell on.

4.4.1 Business combinations

Normally when an entity acquires another business, the assets and liabilities acquired are measured at **fair value,** in accordance with IFRS 3 *Business Combinations*. (This principle should be familiar from your Financial Accounting studies.) However, if some of the assets or a part of the business (a disposal group) is acquired with a view to its disposal, it should be classified as held for sale and **valued in accordance with IFRS 5, that is at fair value less costs to sell.**

This potentially has implications for the calculation of goodwill arising on acquisition. Where assets or a disposal group are classified as held for sale their carrying amount will be reduced by the amount of costs to sell. **An increased amount of goodwill should therefore be recognised.**

Worked example: Calculation of goodwill

A Ltd acquires 100% of B Ltd for £5.2 million. The fair value of the net assets at the date of acquisition is £4.7 million.

Goodwill would normally be calculated as follows:

	£m
Consideration transferred	5.2
Net assets at fair value at acquisition date	(4.7)
Goodwill	0.5

If we now assume that £500,000 of assets in B Ltd are classified as held for sale at the acquisition date and that costs to sell will amount to £30,000, goodwill would now be calculated as follows:

	£m
Consideration transferred	5.20
Net assets at fair value at acquisition date (4.7-0.03)	(4.67)
Goodwill	0.53

Goodwill in this instance is increased by the amount of the costs to sell.

4.5 Extension of 12 month period to sell

One of the criteria for classification as held for sale is an expectation that the asset, or disposal group, will be sold within one year from the date of classification. If the disposal is not achieved within this time limit, the asset or disposal group should be reclassified as PPE, measured at the date of reclassification at the **lower** of its:

- **Recoverable amount** (determined at the date the decision not to sell is made)

- **Carrying amount at which it would have been recognised if it had never been classified as held for sale** (any adjustments for depreciation etc would be recognised in profit or loss).

But the held-for-sale classification can be continued beyond that time limit if:

- The delay is caused by **events or circumstances beyond the entity's control** and
- There is **sufficient evidence that the entity is still committed to the sale**.

Specific circumstances where this might be the case, together with examples, are listed in Appendix B of IFRS 5 and *Guidance on Implementing IFRS 5*. These can be summarised as follows:

- At the date the entity commits itself to a plan to sell, the entity expects conditions to be imposed by bodies other than the buyer which will extend the period required to complete the sale. An example would be where the competition authorities are expected to launch an investigation which will last more than a year.

- A buyer has made a firm purchase commitment but the buyer or others unexpectedly impose conditions on the transfer which will extend the period required to complete the sale. An example would be where the buyer insists that the seller rectify unexpected structural faults discovered in a building and the work will take more than a year.

- During the initial one-year period, circumstances arise that were previously considered unlikely, such that the non-current asset, or disposal group, is not sold by the end of that period. (An example would be the collapse of market demand.)

 Interactive question 15: Classification   [Difficulty level: Intermediate]

On 30 June 20X4 Lynmouth plc decided to sell a division which manufactures a platform on which to play computerised games. Within weeks Lynmouth plc received a large number of expressions of serious interest from buyers at around the asking price of £300 million, so it expected the sale to be completed in a matter of months. The division met the other IFRS 5 criteria for being classified as held for sale on 1 October 20X4.

Such was the interest in the division that negotiations were still in progress with a shortlist of possible buyers when in March 20X5 a previously unknown foreign supplier caused consternation throughout the industry by announcing the launch of a competitor platform offering increased benefits at a lower price. All potential buyers for Lynmouth plc's platform immediately ceased serious negotiations, despite Lynmouth plc dropping its asking price by 25%.

Over the next six months the industry adjusted to the presence of the new supplier, whose product turned out not to live up to everything claimed in its March announcement. Over this period Lynmouth plc continued talking to those who had been on its shortlist, emphasising that it was prepared to be flexible on the price for its platform.

The sale was completed in December 20X5 at a price of £250 million.

Over what period should the division be classified as held for sale?

See **Answer** at the end of this chapter.

4.6 Changes of plan

If management plans change such that a non-current asset or disposal group **is no longer to be sold**, the asset, or disposal group should be **reclassified** as PPE, measured on the basis described above for reclassifications due to no sale being made within the 12 month time limit.

Where the asset in question is part of a disposal group the remainder of the disposal group may continue to be classified as held for sale provided that the remainder still satisfies the criteria.

Worked example: Change of plan

Bude plc with a 31 December year end decided to sell its Ace division. On 30 June 20X5 all the IFRS 5 criteria for classification as held for sale were met. To improve the prospects of selling the division, the entity included in it an attractive office building. This building had cost £1.2 million on 1 July 20X2 and was being written off over 30 years under the IAS 16 cost model with no residual value. At 30 June 20X5 the fair value less costs to sell of this building and the Ace division's net assets were £1.6 million and £9 million respectively.

By 31 December 20X5 market conditions had improved and interest from potential buyers had increased to the point that Bude plc decided that it could get £9 million net for the Ace division without including the building in it. So on that date, when the building's fair value less costs to sell was £1.7 million, the entity decided to retain it.

What are the accounting requirements at 31 December 20X5?

Solution

This decision to retain the building requires Bude plc to reconfirm that the Ace division still qualifies for classification as held for sale. Given the improvement in market conditions and the level of interest from potential buyers, it would appear that it still qualifies.

The building should be reinstated as a non-current asset in the statement of financial position at 31 December 20X5 on the basis that it had never been classified as held for sale, that is at cost less depreciation. Its carrying amount should be:

£1.2 million cost – (1.2 × 3.5/30 years) = £1.06 million.

It is also necessary to check whether it has been impaired during its held for sale classification. There has been no impairment, as its fair value less costs to sell on reclassification under non-current assets is the higher amount of £1.7 million.

Note that no account needs to be taken of the building's fair value less costs to sell at 30 June 20X5 of £1.6 million; this is in excess of its cost (let alone carrying amount) at that date and so is ignored in respect of PPE measured under IAS 16's cost model.

4.7 Presentation and disclosure

An asset classified as held for sale should be **presented in the statement of financial position separately from other assets**. Typically a separate heading '**non-current assets held for sale**' would be appropriate.

The following disclosures would be necessary:

- The **major classes of assets and liabilities** classified as held for sale shall be separately disclosed either in the statement of financial position or in the notes, except as permitted by the next paragraph. An entity shall present separately any **cumulative income or expense recognised directly in equity** relating to a non-current asset (or disposal group) classified as held for sale.

- If the disposal group is a **newly acquired subsidiary that meets the criteria to be classified as held for sale on acquisition**, disclosure of the major classes of assets and liabilities is not required.

Point to note:

An entity **shall not reclassify** or re-present amounts presented for non-current assets held for sale or for the assets and liabilities of disposal groups classified as held for sale in the statements of financial position for prior periods, to reflect the classification in the statement of financial position for the latest period presented.

The following information should be **disclosed in the notes** in the period, in which a non-current asset (or disposal group) has been either classified as held for sale or sold:

- A **description** of the non-current asset (or disposal group).

- A description of the **facts and circumstances of the sale,** or leading to the expected disposal, and the expected manner and timing of that disposal.

- **The gain or loss** recognised in profit or loss or the caption in the statement of comprehensive income that includes that gain or loss.

- If applicable, **the segment in which the non-current asset (or disposal group) is presented in** accordance with IFRS 8 *Operating Segments*.

If the entity decides to **change the plan** to sell the non-current asset (or disposal group), **a description of the facts and circumstances leading to the decision** and the effect of the decision on the results of operations for the period and any prior periods should be presented.

4.7.1 Previously consolidated subsidiaries

Where a disposal group held for sale constitutes a subsidiary which has previously been consolidated, its assets and liabilities should be **separately** classified as held for sale but should **continue to be consolidated**. The assets figure should include any **goodwill relating to the entity less any costs to sell**. Costs to sell should also be set off against **consolidated retained earnings**.

Worked example: Subsidiary held for sale

Short plc owns a number of subsidiaries, including 100% of Tall Ltd which was acquired some years ago at a cost of £50 million. At the acquisition date Tall Ltd's identifiable net assets were measured at £45 million and goodwill of £5 million was recognised.

After Short plc's consolidated statement of financial position at the 31 December 20X5 year end had been drafted, the finance director passed on the information that as a result of a board decision on 30 December 20X5, the investment in Tall met the criteria for classification as held for sale on that date. The entity expects to be able to sell Tall for net asset value, with disposal costs estimated at £4 million.

The draft statements of financial position of Short plc and its other subsidiaries, of Tall Ltd and of the group at 31 December 20X5 are as follows:

	Short plc + other subsidiaries £m	Tall Ltd £m	Consolidated statement £m
Investment in Tall/goodwill	50	–	5
Other non-current assets	200	90	290
Current assets	100	180	280
	350	270	575
Share capital	40	15	40
Retained earnings (190 + (120 – 45))	190	105	265
Equity	230	120	305
Current liabilities	120	150	270
	350	270	575

Prepare Short plc's revised consolidated statement of financial position at 31 December 20X5.

Solution

The only changes which need to be made to the draft statement of financial position are:

- To present separately Tall Ltd's assets and liabilities as held for sale. As a result of the definition of 'disposal group' in IFRS 5 App A, the assets figure includes the £5 million goodwill relating to Tall Ltd

- To recognise the costs to sell, deducted from the assets' carrying amount and retained earnings.

Revised consolidated statement of financial position at 31 December 20X5

	£m
Other non-current assets (ex-Tall)	200
Current assets (ex-Tall)	100
Assets held for sale (Tall 270 + goodwill 5 – cost to sell 4)	271
	571
Share capital	40
Retained earnings (265 – 4)	261
Equity	301
Current liabilities (ex-Tall)	120
Liabilities associated with assets held for sale (Tall)	150
	571

4.8 Judgements required

IFRS 5 deals with management's intentions, rather than past transactions or events, so the number of judgements involved is perhaps greater than with other IFRS. Taking the conditions for classification as held for sale, for example:

- The asset should be available for immediate sale **in its present condition**.

  It may be clear that an asset on which substantial remedial work is necessary is not available for sale. But what about one which merely needs a general tidying up?

- Management should be **committed** to a plan to sell the asset.

  Is a minute of a board meeting sufficient? After all, decisions can be reversed at a later stage

- There should be an **active programme** to locate a buyer.

  There can be legitimate differences of view about what constitutes an active programme

- The asset should be marketed for sale at **a price that is reasonable** in relation to its current fair value.

  There would be general agreement that an asking price 50% above the current fair value is not reasonable, but what about one 10% above? If that is judged to be reasonable, where is the cut-off point between 10% and 50%?

- The sale should be **expected** to take place within one year from the date of classification.

  Evidence of expectations is notoriously difficult to identify

- It is **unlikely** that significant changes to the plan will be made or that the plan will be withdrawn.

  What evidence is sufficient for the 'unlikelihood' judgement?

So many judgements are involved, and remember that **all** these conditions should be met before the held-for-sale classification is appropriate.

4.9 Relevance of information to users

The combination of the held for sale and the discontinued rules within IFRS 5 result in relevant information being provided to users, in that:

- The main line items presented in the income statement relate to continuing operations, while the assets less liabilities held for sale can be stripped out of capital employed. The result is a return on capital employed relating solely to operations which will continue into the future.

  Point to note:

  As will be seen below UK GAAP has rules in respect of discontinued operations but not in respect of held for sale assets and disposal groups. Under UK GAAP the statement of financial position items to be disposed of are still included within the totals of those to be retained.

- Gearing calculations can also be made by reference to operations which will continue into the future.

But this may be at the expense of faithful representation, in that the financial presentation depends on so many judgements about management intentions.

5 UK GAAP comparison

Section overview

In the UK:

- FRS 15 *Tangible Fixed Assets* deals with property, plant and equipment

- SSAP 13 *Accounting for Research and Development* and FRS 10 *Goodwill and Intangible Assets* deal with intangible assets

- FRS 11 *Impairment of Fixed Assets and Goodwill* deals with impairments

- There is no 'held for sale' concept in the UK

5.1 Property, plant and equipment

FRS 15 *Tangible Fixed Assets*	IAS 16 comparison
The UK approach to revaluation is based around a current value model, which only takes into account current use of the asset (existing use value or EUV).	Revaluations should be to fair value (usually taken as market value). This is generally higher than EUV as it considers alternative uses.
FRS 15 specifies a maximum period of five years between full valuations and an interim valuation every three years.	IAS 16 does not specify a maximum period, instead the timing of revaluations depends on changes in market values.
FRS 15 requires impairment losses to be debited first against any revaluation surplus in respect of the asset unless it reflects a consumption of economic benefits.	IAS 16 does not include such a limitation.
In accordance with FRS 15 the residual values of assets are assessed at the date of acquisition and are not adjusted for expected future price changes. However, residual values should be reviewed at each reporting period and revised to take account of reasonably expected technological changes based on prices prevailing at the date of acquisition.	IAS 16 requires residual values to be reassessed at the end of each reporting period taking into account current price changes. This may affect the depreciation expense.
Annual impairment reviews are required for all assets which are either depreciated over a period of more than 50 years or not depreciated.	IAS 16 does not include such a requirement.

Worked example: Revaluation of property

The following information relates to a property that is currently recorded in the financial statements at cost.

	£
Cost	400,000
Carrying amount	320,000
Open market value	600,000
Existing use value	475,000

Under IAS 16 the revaluation of this property should be recorded as follows:

DR	Non-current asset (600 – 400)	£200,000	
DR	Accumulated depreciation (400 – 320)	£80,000	
CR	Revaluation surplus		£280,000

Under FRS 15 the revaluation of this property should be recorded as follows:

DR	Fixed assets (475 – 400)	£75,000	
DR	Accumulated depreciation	£80,000	
CR	Revaluation reserve		£155,000

Worked example: Residual values

Morley Ltd purchased an item of plant on 1 January 20X6 for £25,000. At that date the residual value was estimated to be £5,000. At 31 December 20X7 the residual value of the asset was reviewed. Taking into account current price changes the residual value was estimated to be £5,500. The total useful life of the asset was estimated at five years and the straight-line method of depreciation was adopted.

Based on IAS 16 the depreciation charges for 20X6 and 20X7 should be as follows:

	£
20X6 (25,000 – 5,000)/5	4,000
20X7 (25,000 – 4,000 – 5,500)/4	3,875

Based on FRS 15 the depreciation charges for 20X6 and 20X7 should be as follows:

	£
20X6 (25,000 – 5,000)/5	4,000
20X7 (as above)	4,000

5.2 Intangible assets

In the UK there are two relevant standards:

SSAP 13 *Accounting for Research and Development*	IAS 38 comparison
The capitalisation of development expenditure which meets certain criteria is **optional**.	IAS 38 **requires** capitalisation where the recognition criteria are met.
The development expenditure recognition criteria under SSAP 13 include a requirement to have a **reasonable expectation of future benefits**.	IAS 38 is more stringent as the requirement is to **demonstrate** future benefits.

FRS 10 *Goodwill and Intangible Assets*	IAS 38 comparison
Only intangibles that can be **sold separately** from the business are recognised under UK GAAP.	IAS 38 also **requires** non-separable assets to be recognised where they arise from contractual or other legal rights.

FRS 10 *Goodwill and Intangible Assets*	IAS 38 comparison
FRS 10 **requires amortisation** of purchased goodwill with a finite useful life.	Under IAS 38 goodwill should not be amortised but instead is tested annually for impairment.
Under FRS 10 there is a presumption that the useful lives of purchased goodwill and intangibles are limited to 20 years, but a longer life, even an indefinite life, can be used if it can be justified.	There is no such presumption under IAS 38.

5.3 Impairment

The UK standard which deals with impairment is FRS 11 *Impairment of Fixed Assets and Goodwill*. The key differences between FRS 11 and IAS 36 are as follows:

FRS 11	IAS 36 comparison
Impairment losses on previously revalued assets are recognised in the profit and loss account **where they relate to a consumption of economic benefits**, for example physical damage or a deterioration in the quality of the service provided by the asset. (This is also a requirement of FRS 15.)	IAS 36 (and IAS 16) **does not include such a requirement**.
Impairment losses are allocated to assets in the following order: • **Goodwill**, then • **Intangible assets**, then • **Tangible assets**	Impairment losses are allocated to assets in the following order: • **Goodwill**, then • **Property, plant and equipment and intangible assets on a pro rata basis**
FRS 11 allows reversals of impairment losses in respect of goodwill in very limited circumstances. FRS 11 allows the reversals in respect of intangible assets other than goodwill in similarly limited circumstances.	Reversals of impairment losses in respect of goodwill are prohibited. There is **no specific prohibition** in respect of intangible assets.
Where cash flows have been used to demonstrate the recoverable amount, **future cash flows should be compared with those forecast for the five subsequent years.** If the actual cash flows are much less than those forecast, the impairment may need to be recalculated. (This process is sometimes referred to as the look back test.)	There is **no equivalent requirement** in IAS 36.

Point to note:

Chapter 8 explains that IFRS 3 contains an explicit option (not in UK GAAP) to measure the non-controlling interest at its fair value (as an alternative to measuring it at its proportionate share of the fair value of the acquiree's net assets). This option demands a different treatment of impairment losses under IAS 36 which is explained in Chapter 8.

Worked example: Recognition of impairment loss within a CGU under UK GAAP and IAS 36

A CGU contains the following assets:

	£'000
Goodwill	24
Patent	48
Tangible fixed assets/property, plant and equipment	72
	144

An impairment review identifies an impairment loss of £40,000.

In accordance with FRS 11 the impairment loss should be allocated as follows:

	£'000
Goodwill (24 – 24)	–
Patent (48 – (40 – 24))	32
Tangible fixed assets	72
	104

In accordance with IAS 36 the impairment loss should be allocated as follows:

	£'000
Goodwill (24 – 24)	–
Patent (48 – (48/(72 + 48) × (40 – 24)))	41.6
Property, plant and equipment (72 – (72/(72 + 48) × (40 – 24)))	62.4
	104.0

5.4 Assets held for sale

IFRS 5 introduces the concept of 'held for sale' (see section 4). There is **no equivalent concept in the UK**. Therefore in the UK an asset is not reclassified when the decision to sell is made and it is depreciated until the time of disposal. A gain or loss is only recognised when the disposal is made.

Under IFRS 5 classification as held for sale results in there being no depreciation charges beyond the date of classification and the asset being measured at that date as the lower of carrying amount and fair value less costs to sell – so a loss may be recognised at that date.

Summary and Self-test

Summary

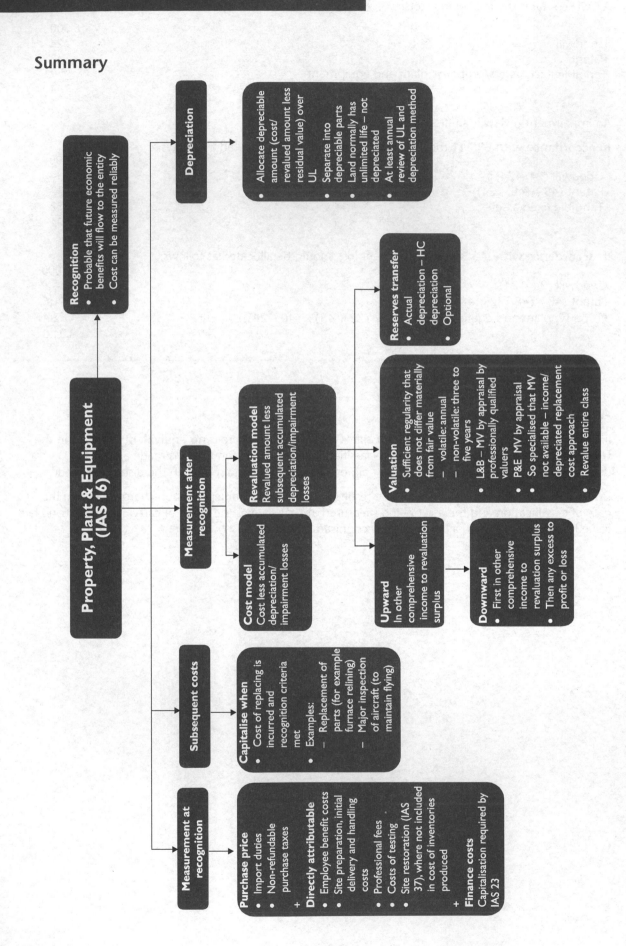

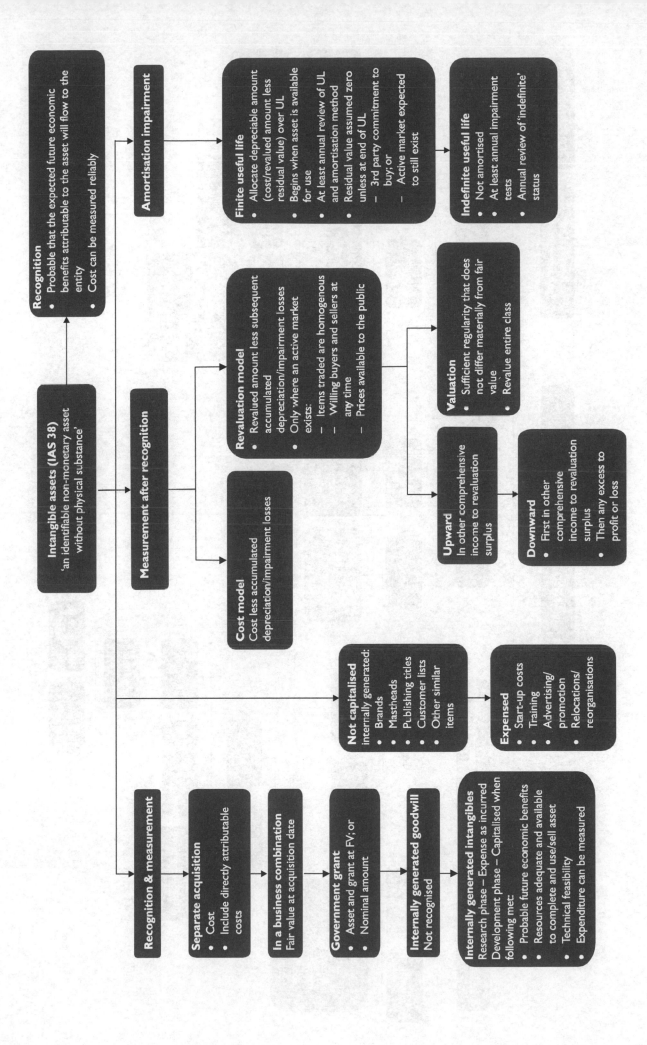

Intangible assets (IAS 38)
'an identifiable non-monetary asset without physical substance'

Recognition
- Probable that the expected future economic benefits attributable to the asset will flow to the entity
- Cost can be measured reliably

Amortisation impairment

Finite useful life
- Allocate depreciable amount (cost/revalued amount less residual value) over UL
- Begins when asset is available for use
- At least annual review of UL and amortisation method
- Residual value assumed zero unless at end of UL
  – 3rd party commitment to buy; or
  – Active market expected to still exist

Indefinite useful life
- Not amortised
- At least annual impairment tests
- Annual review of 'indefinite' status

Measurement after recognition

Revaluation model
- Revalued amount less subsequent accumulated depreciation/impairment losses
- Only where an active market exists:
  – Items traded are homogenous
  – Willing buyers and sellers at any time
  – Prices available to the public

Cost model
Cost less accumulated depreciation/impairment losses

Valuation
- Sufficient regularity that does not differ materially from fair value
- Revalue entire class

Upward
In other comprehensive income to revaluation surplus

Downward
- First in other comprehensive income to revaluation surplus
- Then any excess to profit or loss

Not capitalised
internally generated:
- Brands
- Mastheads
- Publishing titles
- Customer lists
- Other similar items

Expensed
- Start-up costs
- Training
- Advertising/ promotion
- Relocations/ reorganisations

Recognition & measurement

Separate acquisition
- Cost
- Include directly attributable costs

In a business combination
Fair value at acquisition date

Government grant
- Asset and grant at FV; or
- Nominal amount

Internally generated goodwill
Not recognised

Internally generated intangibles
Research phase – Expense as incurred
Development phase – Capitalised when following met:
- Probable future economic benefits
- Resources adequate and available to complete and use/sell asset
- Technical feasibility
- Expenditure can be measured

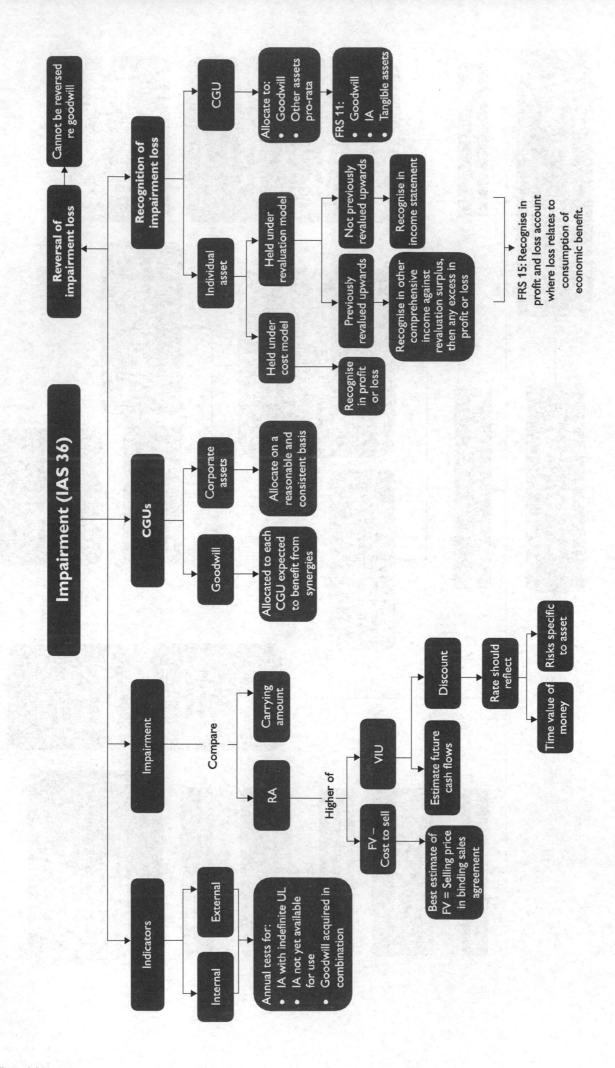

Self-test

Answer the following questions.

1   IAS 38 *Intangible Assets* defines an intangible asset as an <u>**identifiable**</u> non-monetary asset without physical substance. An asset is a resource:

- <u>**Controlled**</u> by an entity as a result of past events, and
- From which <u>**future economic benefits**</u> are expected to flow to the entity.

IAS 38 requires an entity to recognise an intangible asset in its financial statements if it meets the recognition criteria.

Dronfield Ltd is a large company which researches, develops and manufactures pharmaceutical products. The company has in the past prepared its financial statements using UK GAAP and is considering changing to using IFRS. The company invests heavily in the following areas.

(1)   Research into alternative chemically active ingredients that may have therapeutic benefit. The research activities identify chemical compounds that have commercial application possibilities.

(2)   Development of chemical compounds by applying research findings to design new drug therapies. At the end of the development phase each new compound must be successful in a series of regulatory trials before production can commence.

(3)   The investment in marketing and brand development of new pharmaceutical products. This includes the significant launch costs of new drugs and the on-going brand development activities.

(4)   The acquisition, either directly or through business combinations, of pharmaceutical patents and brands at the fully licensed stage.

Requirements

(a)   Discuss the IAS 38 definition of an intangible asset with specific reference to the three terms underlined.   **(3 marks)**

(b)   Explain and justify the required accounting treatment for each of the above four areas by considering the recognition criteria for internally developed and acquired intangible assets.
                                                                                                        (4 marks)

(c)   Outline the key differences between UK GAAP and IFRS in respect of intangible assets other than goodwill.   **(3 marks)**

                                                                                                        (10 marks)

2   Stannington plc is 'knowledge led' and its management has initiated a strategy of investment in areas such as brands, advertising, media, technology, business processes and employee training. The business has few items of property, plant and equipment and the management are concerned that the prior year statement of financial position did not reflect the value of these intangibles. The following events have occurred during the year ended 31 December 20X3.

(1)   On 1 January 20X3 the company acquired a cable television franchise for £10 million. The franchise allows Stannington plc the exclusive right to provide cable television to two million viewers in the Sheffield area for the next 20 years.

A twenty year franchise covering a similar number of viewers in Liverpool was sold by a competitor to a third party on 31 December 20X3 for £30 million. A franchise consultant has provided the management with an independent report that supports an equivalent market value for the Sheffield franchise. The company has measured the franchise rights in its statement of financial position at the valuation of £30 million.

(2)   The company is developing a new production process. In previous years £2 million incurred on the project had been recognised as an expense in profit or loss as research costs. On 1 July 20X3 the company was able to demonstrate that the process met the IAS 38 criteria for recognition as an intangible asset. At 31 December 20X3 the company has recognised the intangible asset at a cost of £4.5 million comprising the following:

	£'000
Research costs from prior years	2,000
Costs incurred in the six months to 30 June 20X3	1,000
Costs incurred in the six months to 31 December 20X3	1,500
	4,500

At the end of 20X3 the development process was nearing completion and a competitor submitted a written offer to acquire the process for £6 million.

(3) On 1 January 20X3 Stannington plc acquired a publishing title for £25 million. The title complemented the company's existing portfolio of four similar publishing titles. During 20X3 £10 million of expenditure was incurred on marketing and promotional activities which management hope has enhanced the value of the publishing portfolio and £2 million has been added to the carrying amount of the acquired publishing title.

The long-term strategic plans for the business show that Stannington plc will invest significantly in the future development of the titles. The management believe this will enhance the value of the titles and that the titles have an indefinite life.

Requirements

(a) Compare the recognition criteria for acquired and internally generated intangible assets.

(4 marks)

(b) Explain the required accounting treatment of the above issues, preparing calculations where appropriate and setting out the presentation requirements. **(12 marks)**

(16 marks)

3 IAS 36 *Impairment of Assets* prescribes the accounting and disclosure for impairment of assets. Volt plc is a large industrial manufacturer. It operates from a single freehold factory. Its accounting policy is that non-current assets, other than land and buildings, are measured subsequent to initial recognition using the cost model in IAS 16 *Property, Plant and Equipment*. Land and buildings are remeasured using the revaluation model of IAS 16, with transfers being made from revaluation surplus to retained earnings when permitted.

Volt plc is considering the accounting treatment of two separate assets for the year ended 31 December 20X5.

(1) A piece of manufacturing equipment was acquired on 1 January 20X4 for £250,000. The useful life was assessed as five years. On 31 December 20X5 the Government published proposed changes in regulations that mean that by 31 December 20X7 the company will have to cease selling certain product lines manufactured on that equipment. At 31 December 20X5 the net sale proceeds of the equipment were estimated at £200,000 and the net cash inflows over the equipment's remaining three year life at £33,000, £22,000 and £7,000 respectively. Volt plc can borrow at 12% pa but estimates that this particular equipment could only be funded at 15% pa.

(2) The company's freehold factory was acquired ten years ago for £2.2 million (of which £200,000 was attributable to the land). Its useful life was estimated at 25 years and the residual value was estimated at £nil. Five years ago the factory was revalued to £2.4 million (land £200,000) and the overall useful life and residual value remained unchanged. The revaluation surplus was recognised in other comprehensive income and held in revaluation surplus. On 31 December 20X5 the management of Volt plc noted that the market value of similar property had declined significantly and the fair value of the factory was now £1.2 million (land £200,000).

Requirements

(a) Explain when a company is required to carry out a review for impairment. **(2 marks)**

(b) Describe, using examples, circumstances that may indicate that a company's assets may have been impaired. **(2 marks)**

(c) Explain, with supporting numerical calculations, the required accounting treatment for Volt plc's manufacturing equipment and freehold factory in 20X5. **(6 marks)**

(10 marks)

4   (a)   East plc organises its activities into four business segments, each comprising a number of companies, and annually reviews each segment to see whether all its constituent parts should be retained. In 20X8 the annual review has focused on Dollar Ltd, a wholly-owned subsidiary within East plc's smallest segment and in respect of which goodwill of £900,000 is carried in East plc's consolidated statement of financial position. Dollar Ltd operates independently of other businesses within the group.

On 31 March 20X8 East plc's board considered a report from Easy Solutions, its external business advisers, which estimated that Dollar Ltd would be very difficult to sell in its current state, but that if it was 'tidied up', it could readily be sold for £10 million. The tidying up needed was identified as:

- A redundancy programme to reduce staffing by 10%

- The transfer to other companies within the East plc group of certain properties owned by Dollar Ltd but which were not related to Dollar Ltd's own activities.

On that day the board decided to proceed with the tidying up and subsequent sale of Dollar Ltd and appointed Easy Solutions to publicise the company's availability and then to handle the sale. Easy Solutions' fee was to be 8% of the sales proceeds.   Following pressure from the director who had been instrumental in the acquisition of Dollar Ltd 12 years previously, the selling price was set at £15 million.

Through the summer the tidying up of Dollar Ltd proceeded, the properties being transferred into other group companies on 20 June 20X8 and the redundancy programme being completed on 30 September 20X8. Easy Solutions reported back to Easy plc's board on a monthly basis, its main theme being that a number of companies wished to acquire Dollar Ltd but could not justify the price being asked. On 18 August 20X8 the board agreed to a reduction in the price to £13 million, and on 15 September, after heated debate, to a further reduction to £10 million. Exclusive negotiations were entered into with one of the potential buyers at this price, the sale of Dollar Ltd for proceeds of £10 million being completed on 28 February 20X9.

Requirement

Prepare notes which explain and justify the date on which Dollar Ltd should be classified as held for sale.   **(5 marks)**

(b)   At the date of classification as held for sale Dollar Ltd's statement of financial position was as follows:

	£'000
Intangibles	1,200
Property, plant and equipment	6,800
Inventory	2,500
Other current assets	1,300
Current liabilities	(1,500)
Equity	10,300

Requirements

(1)   Describe and quantify the entries required in Dollar Ltd's accounting records at the date of classification as held for sale.   **(5 marks)**

(2)   Describe, without quantification, how Dollar Ltd's assets and liabilities should be presented in East plc's consolidated statement of financial position at 31 December 20X8.   **(2 marks)**

(12 marks)

5   Woodhouse plc is a developer and manufacturer of electronic data systems. Its accounting policy is to record non-current assets initially at cost. Subsequent to initial recognition, land and buildings are remeasured at fair value when that value differs materially from carrying amount. Woodhouse plc adopts the policy of transferring the revaluation surplus included in equity to retained earnings as it is realised. Other non-current assets continue to be measured under the cost model.

During the year ended 31 December 20X6 the following events have occurred.

(1)   Demand for the Betax product line has always been susceptible to rapid changes in technology. During the year a major overseas competitor entered the UK Betax market with a low cost alternative. The entry of this competitor has reduced market demand for Woodhouse plc's Betax product.

The Woodhouse plc management team are currently preparing plans to restructure operations and incur capital expenditure in reaction to the changing market conditions. The directors have not yet formally agreed the restructuring and capital expenditure plans, but believe these changes will allow them a more flexible pricing approach, which will improve sales volumes and future revenues from the Betax product line.

The Betax product is manufactured on a single machine. The carrying amount of the asset at 31 December 20X6 is £280,000. A similar machine was recently advertised in a specialist catalogue for a sale price of £300,000. Disposal costs would comprise commission payable to the specialist catalogue of 10% of the gross sale proceeds and dismantling costs of £10,000.

The present value of the cash flows arising from the continuing use and ultimate disposal of the asset has been estimated at £250,000. Management have estimated that their proposals should enhance the use of the asset and increase the present value of the cash flows by £25,000.

The entry of the competitor has reduced the useful life of the machine to four more years. Management believe their restructuring plans will increase this to eight years.

(2)   On 1 January 20X2 Woodhouse plc acquired a freehold manufacturing building. The land element in the purchase price was £500,000 and the building element £2,000,000. The useful life of the building was estimated at 20 years. Since 1 January 20X2 there has been no change to the value of the land. On 31 December 20X3 the building element was revalued to £2,250,000 and the remaining useful life was unchanged. On 31 December 20X6 the open market value of the building element was determined as £1,650,000. The remaining useful life has again remained unchanged.

Requirements

(a)   Describe how fair value less costs to sell and value in use should be calculated so that recoverable amount can be obtained.   **(4 marks)**

(b)   Outline how impairment losses should be recognised in financial statements.   **(3 marks)**

(c)   Explain and justify, with supporting numerical calculations, the accounting treatment for the above issues at 31 December 20X6.   **(7 marks)**

(d)   Calculate the statement of financial position amounts relating to these assets at 31 December 20X7 if no further impairment losses or revaluation surpluses occur during the next year.

(3 marks)
(17 marks)

Now go back to the Learning Objectives in the Introduction. If you are satisfied you have achieved these objectives, please tick them off.

Technical reference

Property, plant and equipment

1 Recognition

- Recognise items of PPE, provided future economic benefits and reliable measurement of cost   IAS 16 (7)

    - Initial costs to acquire or construct   IAS 16 (10)

    - Subsequent costs to add to or replace part of

- Separate into components, with different lives, for example inspections   IAS 16 (13)

2 Measurement at recognition

- At cost   IAS 16 (15)

    - Purchase price   IAS 16 (16)

    - Costs directly attributable to bringing asset into location and condition necessary for it to be capable of working as intended, including testing   IAS 16 (16-17)

    - Costs to dismantle asset and of obligations to restore the site   IAS 16 (16)

- Some costs are excluded because not directly attributable or after the item is capable of working as intended, for example abnormal costs, general overheads, initial losses, internal profits   IAS 16 (19-22)

- Include borrowing costs if asset is an IAS 23 *Borrowing Costs* qualifying asset   IAS 16 (22)

3 Measurement after recognition

- Choice of model: cost or revaluation to fair value   IAS 16 (29-31)

- Frequency of revaluation: to ensure carrying amount not materially different from updated fair value   IAS 16 (31)

    Maximum interval five years?   IAS 16 (34)

- All assets in a single class should be treated in the same way   IAS 16 (36)

4 Accounting for revaluations

- Gain recognised in other comprehensive income and held in revaluation surplus   IAS 16 (39)

    If reverse previous decrease, recognise in profit or loss to extent of that decrease

- Loss recognised in profit or loss   IAS 16 (40)

    If reverse previous increase, recognised in other comprehensive income to extent of the increase still held in revaluation surplus

- Depreciation charge based on revalued amount

- Annual reserve transfer of excess of actual depreciation over historical cost depreciation – made through the statement of changes in equity   IAS 16 (41)

5 Depreciation

- Each significant part of PPE item depreciated separately   IAS 16 (43)

- Charge to profit or loss, unless included in inventory, construction contract   IAS 16 (48)
  or other PPE

- Depreciate depreciable amount (that is cost less residual value (RV)) over   IAS 16 (6)
  estimated useful life (UL)

    - RV is current estimate of disposal proceeds, net of disposal costs, if   IAS 16 (6)
      item already of the age and in the condition expected at the end of
      UL
    - UL is period over which asset expected to be available for use,   IAS 16 (6 and 55)
      commencing with when asset is available for use

- Method should allocate depreciable amount systematically over useful life,   IAS 16 (60-61)
  so as to reflect consumption of future economic benefits

- Annual reviews of RVs, ULs and depreciation methods   IAS 16 (51 and 61)

  Any changes accounted for prospectively   IAS 16 (51 and 61)

6 Derecognition

- Derecognise non-current asset when disposed of or when no future   IAS 16 (67)
  economic benefits expected

  Separate procedures where held for sale – see below

- Proceeds less carrying amount recognised in profit or loss   IAS 16 (68 and 71)

- Revalued assets:

  Reserve transfer with regard to previously recognised gains now realised –   IAS 16 (41)
  made through the statement of changes in equity

7 Disclosures   IAS 16 (73,74 and 77)

- Measurement bases

- Depreciation methods

- Useful lives or depreciation rates

- Gross, accumulated depreciation and net amounts at start and end of
  period

- Additions, disposals, acquisitions through business combinations,
  revaluations, impairments, depreciation, classification as held for sale

- Assets pledged as security for loans and contractual commitments to
  acquire PPE

- For revalued assets, the dates, whether independent valuer used,
  assumptions, reference to active markets/recent transactions, carrying
  amount under historical cost convention, revaluation surplus

Intangible assets

1 Scope and definition

- Scope of IAS 38: excludes what other IFRSs cover, for example goodwill acquired in a business combination (IFRS 3) — IAS 38 (3)

- Intangible asset: an identifiable, non-monetary asset without physical substance — IAS 38 (8)

- Identifiability the key: — IAS 38 (10)

  - Separable – could be sold separately from entity which owns — IAS 38 (12)

  - Arises from contractual or other legal rights. — IAS 38 (12)

- Control is an essential part of the definition of an asset. Many items excluded because not controlled by a business: — IAS 38 (13)

  - Staff (always)

  - Customers (very often).

2 Recognition and initial measurement

- Reliable measurement – the recognition criteria disallow: — IAS 38 (21)

  - Internally generated goodwill — IAS 38 (48)

  - Similar items such as internally generated brands, mastheads and customer lists — IAS 38 (63)

  - Advertising/training — IAS 38 (69)

- Initial measurement at cost — IAS 38 (24)

- Separate acquisition:

  - Future economic benefits are always probable — IAS 38 (25)

  - Cost usually measurable reliably — IAS 38 (26)

  - Cost includes licences, and so on — IAS 38 (27)

- Part of business combination

  - Future economic benefits are always probable — IAS 38 (33)

  - Cost always measurable reliably — IAS 38 (35)

  - Cost = fair value — IAS 38 (33)

  - Includes acquiree's unrecognised intangibles — IAS 38 (34)

- Internally generated: at cost, but:

  - Research expenditure (seeking new knowledge) written off as incurred — IAS 38 (54)

  - Development expenditure (application of research findings) capitalised if it meets stringent conditions as to future economic benefit — IAS 38 (57)

  - Development expenditure includes materials, staff costs and licences but not general overheads — IAS 38 (66 and 67)

  - Only development expenditure incurred after recognition criteria met is to be capitalised. No subsequent capitalisation of earlier expenditure already recognised in profit or loss — IAS 38 (65 and 71)

- Subsequent expenditure almost always written off, because most expenditure relates to maintenance, not enhancement, and is non-separable from that on the business as a whole — IAS 38 (20)

3 Measurement after recognition

- Cost or revaluation models   IAS 38 (72)

  Revaluation only if active market (homogeneous products, always trading, prices available to public)   IAS 38 (75 and 8)

- Useful life:
  - Indefinite – no amortisation, but annual impairment and useful life reviews   IAS 38 (107-109)
  - Finite – annual amortisation, with impairment review if indication of impairment. Residual value almost always nil   IAS 38 (97 and 100)

4 Disclosure

- Disclosures specific to intangibles (otherwise follow IAS 16):

  - Whether useful lives are indefinite or finite (in which case amortisation rates should be disclosed)   IAS 38 (118(a))

  - For intangibles with indefinite useful lives, their carrying amount and the reasons supporting the indefinite life assessment   IAS 38 (122(a))

  - Individual assets material to financial statements as a whole   IAS 38 (122(b))

  - Amount of research and development expenditure recognised as an expense in the period.   IAS 38 (126)

Impairment

1 Indications

- At each reporting date assess whether indication of impairment: IAS 36 (9)

  - If so, estimate recoverable amount (RA)
  - RA is higher of fair value less costs to sell and value in use (present value of future cash flows in use and on disposal).   IAS 36 (6)

- Review both external and internal information for evidence of impairment.   IAS 36 (12)

- Annual tests for intangibles (if indefinite life/not yet in use) and goodwill.   IAS 36 (10)

- Impairment loss where carrying amount exceeds RA.   IAS 36 (59)

2 Fair value less costs to sell

- The way in which fair value is determined depends on whether there is a binding sale agreement and/or an active market   IAS 36 (25-27)

- Examples of disposal costs   IAS 36 (28)

3 Value in use

- Calculation involves the estimation of future cash flows as follows: IAS 36 (39)

  - Cash flows from continuing use
  - Cash flows necessarily incurred to generate cash inflows from continuing use
  - Net cash flows receivable/payable on disposal

- These should reflect the current condition of the asset   IAS 36 (44)

- The discount rate should reflect:

  - The time value of money   IAS 36 (55)
  - Risks specific to the asset for which the future cash flow estimates have not been adjusted.

4 Cash-generating units

- Estimate recoverable amount of CGU if not possible to assess for an individual asset — IAS 36 (66)

- Identification of an asset's CGU involves judgement — IAS 36 (68)

- Goodwill should be allocated to each of the acquirer's CGUs that are expected to benefit — IAS 36 (80)

- Annual impairment review required for any CGU which includes goodwill — IAS 36 (90)

- Corporate assets should be allocated on a reasonable and consistent basis — IAS 36 (102)

5 Impairment losses

- If the asset is held under the cost model, the impairment should be recognised in profit or loss — IAS 36 (60)

- If the asset has been revalued, the impairment loss is treated as a revaluation decrease — IAS 36 (60)

- An impairment loss for a CGU should be allocated: — IAS 36 (104)

  – To goodwill then

  – To all other assets on a *pro-rata* basis

- When a CGU is a non-wholly owned subsidiary AND non-controlling interest measured at acquisition date at share of net assets, notionally gross up goodwill for that part attributable to the non-controlling interest — IAS 36 (Appendix C)

6 Reversals

- An impairment loss recognised for goodwill should not be reversed — IAS 36 (124)

7 Disclosures

- All impairments — IAS 36 (126)

- A material impairment for an individual asset — IAS 36 (130)

- A material impairment for a CGU — IAS 36 (130)

Non-current assets held for sale

1 Classification

- Non-current asset or disposal group should be classified as held for sale when carrying amount to be recovered principally through sale — IFRS 5 (6)

- A disposal group is a group of assets and associated liabilities which will be disposed of — IFRS 5 (4)

- Should be available for immediate sale and sale (within 12 months of classification) should be highly probable — IFRS 5 (7)

- Circumstances where the sale is not made within 12 months but still classified as held for sale — IFRS 5 (9)

- If meet criteria after the end of the reporting period, a non-adjusting event under IAS 10 — IFRS 5 (12)

- An asset which is abandoned should not be classified as held for sale — IFRS 5 (13)

2 Treatment

- Non-current assets or disposal groups should be classified as held for sale at the lower of carrying amount and fair value less costs to sell — IFRS 5 (15)

- Any loss on an asset held under cost model is accounted for under IAS 36 (any gain is recognised on actual disposal) — IFRS 5 (18)

- Different rules if asset previously revalued: — IFRS 5 (18)

    - Revalue before classification, with gain/loss accounted for under IAS 16
    - Costs to sell = impairment loss recognised in profit or loss

- Any subsequent impairment after classification as held for sale recognised in accordance with IFRS 5 (not IAS 36), that is recognised as incurred — IFRS 5 (20)

- Impairment loss in relation to a disposal group should be allocated against goodwill recognised, then against other assets on a *pro-rata* basis — IFRS 5 (23)

- Held for sale assets/assets in disposal group not depreciated or amortised — IFRS 5 (25)

- On ultimate sale any gain or loss recognised in accordance with IAS 16 — IFRS 5 (24)

- A change in management intention may lead to reclassification — IFRS 5 (26)

3 Disclosure

- Assets held for sale/assets in a disposal group should be presented separately in statement of financial position — IFRS 5 (38)

- Other disclosures — IFRS 5 (41)

Answer to Interactive question 1

	£
Excess revaluation gain recognised in other comprehensive income	2
Amount recognised in profit or loss	40

WORKINGS

The revaluation gain on 1 January 20X7 was £42 (72 – 30)

If the previous downward revaluation had not taken place the carrying amount on 31 December 20X6 would have been £70 (£140 less five years' depreciation at £14 each year).

The 'excess' revaluation gain to be recognised in other comprehensive income is £2 (72 – 70).

The amount to be recognised in profit or loss is £40 (70 – 30) or ((72 – 30) – 2)

Answer to Interactive question 2

Annual depreciation charges

Depreciation charges should be calculated by reference to the revalued amounts:

Year 1: $\dfrac{£200,000}{50 \text{ years}} = £4,000$

Year 2: $\dfrac{£230,000}{49 \text{ years}} = £4,694$

Year 3: $\dfrac{£230,000}{49 \text{ years}} = £4,694$

Year 4: $\dfrac{£260,000}{47 \text{ years}} = £5,532$

Year 5: $\dfrac{£260,000}{47 \text{ years}} = £5,532$

Year 6: $\dfrac{£300,000}{45 \text{ years}} = £6,667$

Transfers to revaluation surplus through other comprehensive income

Year 2: Carrying amount of the property is £200,000 – £4,000 = £196,000
Revalued amount is £230,000
Transfer to revaluation surplus is £34,000

Year 4: Carrying amount of the property is £230,000 – (£4,694 × 2) = £220,612
Revalued amount is £260,000
Transfer to revaluation surplus is £39,388

Year 6: Carrying amount of the property is £260,000 – (£5,532 × 2) = £248,936
Revalued amount is £300,000
Transfer to revaluation surplus is £51,064

Transfers from revaluation surplus to retained earnings in the statement of changes in equity

Depreciation, based on the cost of the property, would have been £4,000 per annum (that is $\dfrac{£200,000}{50 \text{ years}}$).

The amounts transferred from the revaluation surplus to retained earnings as the asset is realised through depreciation should be:

Year 1: nil
Year 2: £4,694 – £4,000 = £694
Year 3: £4,694 – £4,000 = £694
Year 4: £5,532 – £4,000 = £1,532
Year 5: £5,532 – £4,000 = £1,532
Year 6: £6,667 – £4,000 = £2,667

Answer to Interactive question 3

When market-based evidence of fair value is not available because of the specialised nature of an item of PPE, IAS 16 allows the use of depreciated replacement cost.

Because the service potential of the equipment owned is less than that of a new item, the gross replacement cost should be estimated as 80% of £450, that is £360. On the basis that the owned item is three years old, depreciation should be 3/15ths of this, which is £72. After revaluation the carrying amount should therefore be £288 (360 – 72).

Answer to Interactive question 4

The following costs should be capitalised

	£
Original cost of the new technology	1,000,000
Less discount provided	(100,000)
Testing of the new manufacturing process	10,000
	910,000

Answer to Interactive question 5

1 January 20X4

The cost of the asset should be reduced for the delay in payment, by reference to the entity's borrowing rate. So the cost is £84,168 (£100,000 / 1.09^2) and a liability to the supplier of the same amount should be recognised.

Year ended 31 December 20X4

The following should be recognised as expenses in profit or loss:

- A depreciation charge of £5,611 $\left(\dfrac{84,168}{15}\right)$

- A finance charge, being unwinding of discount over one year, of £84,168 × 9% = £7,575.

In the statement of financial position the following carrying amounts should be recognised:

- PPE of £78,557 (£84,168 – 5,611)
- A liability to the supplier of £91,743 (84,168 + 7,575).

Answer to Interactive question 6

At the end of 20X7 the production process is recognised as an intangible asset at cost of £20,000. This is the expenditure incurred since the date the capitalisation criteria are met. The £180,000 incurred previously should have been expensed as incurred. It cannot be capitalised retrospectively. At the end of each reporting period any intangible asset that is not yet in use should be tested for impairment. The recoverable amount is £100,000 and no impairment has occurred.

No asset in respect of the advertising campaign should be recognised, because it is not possible to identify the future economic benefits which are attributable solely to this campaign. The whole expenditure is recognised in profit or loss.

Delgado Ltd's property, plant and equipment, current assets and current liabilities should all be measured in the consolidated statement of financial position at their fair values as shown in Delgado Ltd's statement of financial position. In addition, goodwill acquired in the business combination should be measured at £1.2 million, calculated as follows:

	£	£
Consideration transferred		2,100,000
Less: fair values of:		
Property, plant and equipment	600,000	
Current assets	800,000	
Current liabilities	(500,000)	
		(900,000)
		1,200,000

Delgado Ltd's own goodwill asset is subsumed in this goodwill acquired in the business combination, because it is not capable of being separately identified as an intangible asset.

No asset in respect of the staff training programme should be recognised, because staff are not under the control of the employer and when staff leave, the benefits of the training, whatever they may be, also leave. The whole expenditure should be recognised in profit or loss.

Answer to Interactive question 7

Professional fees should be added to the cost of the licence, making the total cost £340 million. In theory the licence is available for use from 1 January 20X8. But this licence intangible is linked to the supporting infrastructure, so depreciation should commence from 1 January 20X9 when the service was first available to customers.

The annual depreciation charge should be calculated on the basis of the 19 remaining years of the licence, so £17.89 million per annum. The depreciation expense is therefore nil in 20X8 and £17.89 million in 20X9.

Answer to Interactive question 8

Asset 1

No impairment has taken place because the current carrying amount (£80 million) is less than the recoverable amount (£150 million).

Asset 2

Impairment has taken place. The recoverable amount is £105 million, which is less than the carrying amount of £120 million and an impairment loss of £15 million should be recognised. The company will continue to use the asset as it is worth more in continued use than it is by sale.

Asset 3

Impairment has taken place. The recoverable amount is £110 million, which is less than the carrying amount of £140 million and an impairment loss of £30 million should be recognised. The company will not continue to use the asset as it is worth more by sale than it is in continued use.

Answer to Interactive question 9

Reorganisation costs such as staff termination and retraining costs following the disposal are not direct costs of disposing of the group of assets. The fair value less costs to sell should be estimated as:

	£
Sale price	900,000
Agents' commission	(90,000)
Legal costs	(50,000)
Cost of dismantling the assets so that they can be removed	(100,000)
Cost of creating access to the group of assets for removal	(20,000)
	640,000

Answer to Interactive question 10

The fair value less costs to sell of the plant is below its carrying amount so it may be impaired. It is now necessary to estimate the value in use in order to determine whether an impairment has occurred and to quantify any impairment loss.

Year	Future cash flows £'000	PV factor at 15%	Discounted future cash flows £'000
1	276	0.86957	240
2	253	0.75614	191
3	188	0.65752	124
4	125	0.57175	71
5	280	0.49718	139
Value in use			765

	£'000
Recoverable amount (higher of value in use and fair value less costs to sell)	765
Impairment loss (900 – 765)	135

Answer to Interactive question 11

The recoverable amount of the property is £400,000 (as £400,000 > £300,000).

An impairment of £350,000 has therefore been incurred, being the difference between the current carrying amount of £750,000 and the recoverable amount of £400,000.

As the property was previously valued upwards, this part of the impairment loss should be set against the revaluation surplus. Consequently, £300,000 (see Point to note) should be recognised in other comprehensive income against the revaluation surplus, reducing it to zero. The remaining loss of £50,000 should be recognised in the profit or loss.

Point to note:

The property has been depreciated since the previous revaluation (the carrying amount is below the revalued amount), so a transfer may have been made from the revaluation surplus to retained earnings for the amount of the revaluation surplus realised through additional depreciation. If so, the amount of the impairment loss recognised against the revaluation surplus should be less (and the amount recognised in profit or loss more) by the amount of the transfer.

Answer to Interactive question 12

At the end of year five, the asset had a carrying amount of £50,000 (£100,000 × 5/10 years). The impairment reduces the carrying amount of the asset to £30,000 (£50,000 less £20,000) which should be depreciated over the remaining life of five years, at £6,000 per annum.

Answer to Interactive question 13

The impairment loss should be measured as CGU_2's recoverable amount less the carrying amount of its assets including allocated goodwill. The loss is therefore £170m – £220m = £50m.

This loss should first be allocated against CGU_2's £20 million goodwill, reducing its carrying amount to £nil. This leaves £30 million to be allocated to other assets on a pro rata basis. No asset should be reduced to below its own recoverable amount, so no loss should be allocated to inventories (already measured at the lower of cost and net realisable value) or trade receivables (already reduced by any provision for uncollectability). The total carrying amount of the remaining assets is £125 million (£10m + £115m), so the £30 million loss should be allocated as £2.4 million (10/125) to the patent and £27.6 million (115/125) to property, plant and equipment. The revised carrying amounts are:

	£m
Goodwill	–
Patent (10 – 2.4)	7.6
Property, plant and equipment (115 – 27.6)	87.4
Inventories	30.0
Trade receivables	45.0
Total	170.0

Answer to Interactive question 14

On 1 January 20X8 the land was revalued to £70,000. The gain of £10,000 should be recognised in other comprehensive income and held in revaluation surplus. The land should then be classified as held for sale and the costs to sell of £2,000 recognised in profit or loss as an impairment loss. The carrying amount should now be £68,000.

Upon sale a further loss of £1,000 should be recognised as a loss on sale, because the sale proceeds are less than the carrying amount. Any balance in revaluation surplus is now realised and should be transferred to retained earnings through the statement of changes in equity.

The journal entries required are as follows:

1 January 20X8

| DR | Non-current assets | £10,000 | |
| CR | Revaluation surplus | | £10,000 |

Revaluation immediately prior to classification as held for sale.

1 January 20X8

DR	Non-current assets held for sale (70 – 2)	£68,000	
DR	Profit or loss	£2,000	
CR	Non-current assets		£70,000

Reclassification of non-current assets held for sale and remeasurement at fair value less costs to sell.

30 June 20X8

DR	Cash	£67,000	
DR	Profit or loss	£1,000	
CR	Non-current assets held for sale		£68,000

Derecognition of non-current asset now sold and recognition of loss on disposal.

30 June 20X8

| DR | Revaluation surplus | £10,000 | |
| CR | Retained earnings | | £10,000 |

Transfer through statement of changes in equity of revaluation surplus now realised.

Answer to Interactive question 15

The division would initially be classified as held for sale on 1 October 20X4. It was initially expected to be sold within the 12 month period from classification as held for sale which is stipulated by IFRS 5. In the event it was not sold until 15 months after the classification date.

The delay was caused by an unexpected event, the intervention of a new competitor. Lynmouth plc appears to have taken all reasonable steps to respond to the changed circumstances, by continuing to talk to potential buyers and by being prepared to reduce its asking price in the light of the increased supply of product into the market.

Because of these actions, the division should be classified as held for sale throughout the October 20X4 – December 20X5 period.

1   (a)   **IAS 38 definitions**

The definition of an intangible asset in IAS 38 *Intangible Assets* (para 8) is consistent with the *Conceptual Framework* asset definition.

The key aspects of the definition are set out below.

Identifiable – an intangible asset should be identifiable so that it can be distinguished from goodwill. Concluding on whether a resource is identifiable is not straightforward.

IAS 38 states that an asset is identifiable when:

- It is separable, that is it is capable of being sold, transferred, rented or exchanged individually or with related items, or

- It arises from contractual or other legal rights, regardless of whether those rights are transferable or separable by the entity from other rights and obligations.

A separable asset is individual and the acquirer does not require other assets to be disposed with it. Examples could be quotas, franchises and licences.

An example of an asset arising from legal rights would be the legal right to operate some plant and equipment in circumstances where the assets cannot generate economic benefits without the transfer of the legal right to do so, and the legal right is of no benefit without the plant and equipment to which it relates.

Control – an entity can demonstrate control of an asset through:

- Being able to obtain future economic benefits from it, and
- Restricting the access of others to those benefits.

This control usually arises from the ability to enforce legal rights in a court of law, for example through the ownership of a patent. However, legal enforceability is not a necessary condition. For example, trade secrets confidentially known to a few people will give access to future benefits and restrict their use by others.

Human resources and market share are examples of intangible resources that fail to meet the control test in the definition of an asset, since they cannot be legally protected or controlled.

Future economic benefits may flow from an increase in revenues or a reduction in costs from the use of the asset. These benefits could arise from the product itself or from the use of the intellectual property as part of the production process.

(b)   **Required accounting treatments**

Dronfield Ltd invests in four key business areas. The intangible resources it develops or acquires would meet the definition of an intangible asset. The issue is whether they meet the recognition criteria and should be included in the statement of financial position.

IAS 38 requires an entity to recognise an intangible asset if future economic benefits are probable and the cost can be measured reliably.

(1)   **Research activities**

Dronfield Ltd's own research activities are planned investigations that try to identify new scientific knowledge. They meet the IAS 38 definition of a research phase of activity.

IAS 38 does not allow the recognition of intangible assets arising from the research phase. An entity cannot demonstrate that it is probable that future economic benefits will be generated. Hence the costs incurred do not meet the recognition criteria and should be recognised as an expense in profit or loss.

(2) **Development activities**

Dronfield Ltd's own development activities apply those research findings to design specific therapies that could be commercially beneficial. This is a development phase because it is further advanced than the research phase.

An intangible asset from the development phase should be recognised if, and only if, the entity can meet a number of stringent conditions. In summary, the entity should be able to demonstrate the following.

- The technical feasibility of completing, and the intention to complete, the asset and the ability to use or sell it (this demonstrates completion of the process that will generate economic benefits).

- How the intangible asset will generate future economic benefits, either through the existence of an external market or its use internally, and the availability of resources to complete it (this demonstrates the generation of economic benefits required by the recognition criteria).

- The ability to measure the development expenditure reliably (recognition criteria requirement).

In practice the criteria severely restrict the ability of entities to recognise development phase costs as assets. Assets should only be recognised from the date that the recognition criteria are met and retrospective recognition of costs previously expensed is not allowed.

The existence of regulatory trials means that costs incurred before the successful outcome of these trials should not be recognised as an asset, because prior to the completion of these trials, technical feasibility cannot be demonstrated. Hence, it is extremely unlikely that any development phase costs should be recognised as an asset by Dronfield Ltd.

(3) **Marketing and brand development costs**

IAS 38 states that internally generated brands and marketing costs should never be recognised as intangible assets.

The standard takes the view that costs of developing market positions and brands cannot be distinguished from the cost of developing the business as a whole. Hence the costs cannot be measured reliably and the recognition criteria cannot be met.

(4) **Acquired intangibles**

IAS 38 states that it is always probable that future economic benefits will arise from acquired intangibles. The basis for this is that if there were no such future benefits, the acquirer would not have bothered to acquire them; the probability that they will arise is adjusted for in the price offered: the greater the probability, the higher the price, and *vice versa.*

IAS 38 also states that the cost of separately acquired intangibles can usually be measured reliably, particularly when the purchase consideration is in the form of cash or other monetary assets. The cost of intangibles acquired through a business combination should also be capable of reliable measurement, for example by reference to the way the acquirer built up the acquisition price. There is a rebuttable presumption of reliable measurement when such intangibles have finite useful lives.

(c) **Key differences between UK GAAP and IFRS with regard to intangibles**

- IFRS 3 requires the recognition of all the acquiree's intangible assets provided they can be reliably measured. (The test that economic benefits are expected to flow to the acquirer is automatically met in a business combination.) IFRS 3 suggests many examples of such intangibles, for example customer contracts, customer relationships and order backlogs. As these are to be recognised separately from goodwill, their carrying amount should go to reduce the carrying amount of goodwill. Under UK GAAP, only intangible assets that can be sold separately from the business are recognised in an acquirer's financial statements. As compared with calculations under UK standards, intangibles will be higher, and goodwill lower, under IFRS 3.

- IAS 38 requires the recognition as assets of all development expenditure meeting the relevant recognition criteria. Under UK GAAP it is an accounting policy choice whether to capitalise or to expense costs that meet the recognition criteria.

- The criteria for recognising development costs are more restrictive under IAS 38 because there is a requirement to demonstrate (rather than have a reasonable expectation of) future benefits.

2 (a) Recognition criteria

Initial or subsequent expenditure on an item should be recognised as an intangible asset if it will give rise to future economic benefits and if its cost or value can be measured reliably.

For acquired intangibles the probability of expected future benefits is reflected in the price paid, so this condition is automatically met. This is the case whether the asset has been purchased separately or as part of a business combination. So the recognition criteria are fully met if the acquiring entity can measure the cost of the intangibles reliably.

IAS 38 outlines the criteria that need to be met for an entity to recognise the costs associated with an internally generated asset (such as technical feasibility, and probable future economic benefits). Costs should only be capitalised from the date that the recognition criteria are met. Costs written off before this point should never be subsequently capitalised. In practice this restricts the capitalisation of costs to the later stages of development when the technical and economic viability of a project is virtually certain. For example, where companies require regulatory approval for developed products, no costs should be recognised as an asset until that approval is successful. This is usually the point at which development is complete.

IAS 38 does not allow the recognition of internally generated goodwill, brands, mastheads, publishing titles and so on, because the costs of individual assets cannot be separated from the development of the business as a whole and then measured reliably. However, such items should be recognised if acquired separately or as part of a business combination. An acquisitive company's statement of financial position would probably identify more intangible assets than a company which has invested in their internal generation.

(b) Accounting treatment

(1) Cable television franchise

The cable television franchise should be recognised at cost of £10 million on 1 January 20X3 provided the management believe cost is reliably measurable. The processes involved in determining whether to acquire the asset should provide sufficient evidence.

The intangible asset should be amortised over its useful life. The rights cover a period of twenty years and so an amortisation expense of £0.5 million per annum should be recognised, such that the carrying amount becomes £9.5 million at the end of the year.

The management have revalued the asset to £30 million at the year end. The revaluation model is allowed by IAS 38 provided

- All assets of the same class are revalued, and
- Fair values can be determined by reference to an active market for the intangible asset.

An active market is one where the items traded in it are homogeneous, willing buyers and sellers can be readily found and prices are available to the public. It is unusual for such a market to exist for many intangible assets and it does not exist for television franchises. The franchises are not homogeneous – they are unique as they cover specific areas and demographics. Also, franchises are not offered at prices available to the public.

As no active market exists the franchise should not be revalued.

(2) New production process

All costs incurred before the production process met the IAS 38 criteria for recognition as an intangible asset should be written off as an expense. Such costs cannot be subsequently capitalised. The asset should be initially stated in the statement of financial position at cost of £1.5 million, the expenditure after 1 July.

The production process is unique and whilst an offer has been received from a competitor that provides a market value, it should continue to be recognised at cost, as the £6 million value is not determined by reference to an active market.

However, as the asset is not ready for use IAS 36 requires an impairment review (that is estimate of recoverable amount) to be made at least annually. The offer from the competitor provides evidence of the recoverable amount and that no impairment has been incurred.

(3) **Publishing title**

The publishing title should be recognised as an asset initially at a cost of £25 million. The usual recognition criteria for intangibles should be applied to any subsequent expenditure, that is it is recognised in profit or loss unless it is probable that the expenditure will lead to future economic benefits and the expenditure can be reliably measured.

The £2 million expenditure does not meet the recognition criteria, as no persuasive evidence is available that future economic benefits are probable. In addition, it is difficult to attribute the expenditure to that asset rather than to the publishing portfolio or business as a whole. It appears that the £2 million is an apportionment of the total amount across the five titles. The £2 million should be recognised in profit or loss and the asset carried at £25 million.

The significant investment in the development of all the titles is powerful evidence that the acquired titles have indefinite lives. There should be no amortisation charges but annual impairment reviews are required, even if there is no indication of any impairment.

3   (a) **Review for impairment**

IAS 36 *Impairment of Assets* requires that a review of impairment, through an estimation of the recoverable amount, should be carried out whenever there is an indication that an asset may be impaired. An entity should assess at the end of each reporting period whether there is any such indication. Where none exists, there is no requirement to estimate recoverable amount. Other standards may include requirements for additional reviews. For example, goodwill arising as a result of a business combination and intangible assets with an indefinite useful life should be reviewed for impairment annually.

(b) **Circumstances which may indicate an impairment**

The circumstances that give rise to impairments generally fall into two categories. First, there are indicators that are asset-specific, such as damage or obsolescence. Second, there are indicators that arise from a change in the environment that the asset operates in, such as through the entrance of a major competitor.

IAS 36 *Impairment of Assets* outlines the indications that an entity should at a minimum consider in assessing whether there is an indication that an asset may be impaired. The indicators may arise from internal or external information. Examples of indicators of impairment include

- Poor economic performance of an asset through operating losses and net cash outflows in the current, previous or future periods

- Plans to discontinue or restructure the operation in which an asset belongs or to dispose of an asset before the previously due date

- Evidence of obsolescence or physical damage

- An increase in market interest rates which could have a material effect on the calculation of the value in use

(c) **Required treatment**

(1) **Manufacturing equipment**

The manufacturing equipment has a carrying amount on 31 December 20X5 of £150,000 (£250,000 less two years of depreciation at £50,000 per annum).

The change to the legal environment is an indicator of possible impairment. The recoverable amount is £200,000, which is the greater of the fair value less costs to sell (£200,000) and the value in use calculated at the rate specific to the asset (£50,000 (W)). The recoverable amount exceeds the carrying amount and no impairment loss should be recognised.

However, if there is no expectation of an alternative use for the equipment after 31 December 20X7, the remaining useful life of the equipment should now be reduced to two years.

WORKING

The calculation of value in use is:

Net inflows	£	Discount factor	£
Year 1	33,000	$(1/1.15)$	28,700
Year 2	22,000	$(1/1.15)^2$	16,640
Year 3	7,000	$(1/1.15)^3$	4,600
			49,940

Say £50,000

(2) **Freehold factory**

The freehold factory was initially recognised at £2.2 million ten years ago. The depreciation expense was £80,000 per annum ((£2.2m – £0.2m)/25 years). Five years later, the carrying amount immediately prior to the revaluation was £1.8 million (£2.2m less five years depreciation at £80,000).

Five years ago the asset was revalued upwards to £2.4 million. The increase of £600,000 was recognised in other comprehensive income and credited to revaluation surplus.

For the last five years depreciation has been £110,000 per annum ((£2.4m – £0.2m)/20 years). In accordance with IAS 16 *Property, Plant and Equipment* some of the surplus was realised as the asset was used, being the difference between depreciation based on the revalued carrying amount and depreciation based on the asset's original cost. The annual transfer from revaluation surplus to retained earnings was made in the statement of changes in equity, not through profit or loss.

The amount realised per annum was £30,000 (£110,000 less £80,000). Each year Volt plc would have made the following adjustment.

DR	Revaluation surplus	£30,000	
CR	Retained earnings		£30,000

On 31 December 20X5, prior to the next revaluation, the following amounts are included in respect of the asset:

- Carrying amount = £1.85 million (£2.4m less five years depreciation at £110,000 pa)

- Revaluation surplus = £450,000 (£600,000 less five years of realisation at £30,000 pa)

The asset is now impaired and should be revalued downwards to £1.2 million. The impairment loss is £650,000, which should be recognised against the revaluation surplus up to the £450,000 revaluation surplus remaining for that asset; the £200,000 remainder should be recognised as an expense in profit or loss. The accounting entry should be:

DR	Other comprehensive income		
	– revaluation surplus	£450,000	
	Profit or loss – impairment expense	£200,000	
	Freehold land and buildings		
	– accumulated depreciation	£550,000	
CR	Freehold land and buildings		
	– cost/valuation		£1,200,000

In future years, the annual depreciation charge should be (£1.2m – £0.2m) ÷ 15 years remaining = £66,667. There should be no annual reserve transfer, as there is no remaining revaluation surplus relating to this asset.

4 (a) As a separate limited company with its own assets and liabilities, Dollar Ltd falls within the definition of a disposal group in IFRS 5 *Non-current Assets held for Sale and Discontinued Operations*. The timing of its classification as such depends on when it meets the classification criteria:

- Availability for immediate sale in its present condition: Dollar Ltd needed 'tidying up', so it does not meet this criterion until the redundancy programme and property transfers have been completed, that is the later of 20 June and 30 September

- Sale highly probable: the tests here are:

  - Management commitment to the sale: on 31 March when the sale decision was taken

  - Active programme to locate buyer: on 31 March when Easy Solutions was appointed

  - Marketed at price which is reasonable in relation to fair value: prices of £15 million and £13 million are not reasonable, so on 15 September when the price was reduced to £10 million

- Expectation of completion of sale within 12 months: expectation from 31 March, when advice was given that the company was 'readily' saleable when tidied up.

The latest of these dates is 30 September, so on that date Dollar Ltd should be classified as a disposal group held for sale.

(b) (1) IFRS 5 requires a disposal group to be measured at the lower of its carrying amount and fair value less costs to sell.

At the date of classification as held for sale the fair value is £10 million and the costs to sell are the 8% fee chargeable by Easy Solutions. So the fair value less costs to sell is £9.2 million.

Dollar Ltd is a separate subsidiary which operates independently of other businesses within the group. It therefore is a cash-generating unit and its carrying amount should include the goodwill carried in respect of it. (As Dollar Ltd is wholly owned, the issue of a notional adjustment to goodwill does not arise.) The carrying amount is the net assets (equity) of £10.3 million plus the goodwill of £0.9 million, so £11.2 million.

The lower of these two amounts is £9.2 million, giving rise to an impairment loss of £2 million. This should be allocated to Dollar Ltd's assets under the IAS 36 *Impairment of Assets* rules, so initially to the £0.9 million goodwill. The £1.1 million remainder should be allocated to other assets, but not so as to reduce any below their own fair value less costs to sell. As inventory and the other current assets will already be measured at the lower of cost and net realisable value, none of the loss should be allocated to them. The loss is allocated:

To intangibles $\qquad$ £1.1 million $\times \left(\dfrac{1,200}{1,200 + 6,800} \right) = £165,000$

To PPE $\qquad$ £1.1 million $\times \left(\dfrac{6,800}{1,200 + 6,800} \right) = £935,000$

In Dollar Ltd's accounting records, intangibles of £1,200,000 should be reduced by £165,000 to £1,035,000 and PPE of £6,800,000 by £935,000 to £5,865,000.

As goodwill is only carried in the consolidated statement of financial position, Dollar Ltd should make no accounting entry in respect of its write off.

(2) In the year end consolidated statement of financial position:

- All of Dollar Ltd's assets (both current and non-current) and the goodwill should be presented as a single line item separately from other assets; this line item is often presented immediately below the sub-total for current assets

- All of Dollar Ltd's liabilities should be presented as a single line item separately from other liabilities; this line item is often presented immediately below the sub-total for current liabilities.

Point to note:

Consideration also needs to be given as to whether the results of Dollar Ltd in 20X8 should be presented as discontinued operations (see Chapter 2) in profit or loss. Dollar Ltd falls within the definition of a 'component', but the issue will be whether it can be regarded as 'a separate major line of business'.

5 (a) **How fair value less costs to sell and value in use are calculated so as to obtain recoverable amount**

Recoverable amount is determined as the higher of an asset's fair value less costs to sell and its value in use.

The best evidence of **fair value less costs to sell** is a binding sale contract in an arm's length transaction. If this is not available, then prices in an active market provide persuasive evidence. Otherwise the price in an arm's length transaction between knowledgeable, willing parties should be estimated. In all cases direct disposal costs should be deducted. Fair value less costs to sell should not reflect a forced sale unless management are compelled to sell immediately.

Value in use is calculated by discounting to their present values the estimated future cash flows expected to arise from the continued use of the asset and its disposal at the end of its useful life.

The cash flow projections should be prepared on reasonable and supportable assumptions that reflect the asset in its current condition and use the best estimate of the future set of economic conditions.

The discount rate used should reflect both the time value of money and the risks specific to the asset(s).

Future cash flows that represent the asset in its current condition should exclude the net benefits of a future restructuring to which the entity is not committed; they should also exclude the benefits from future capital expenditure that will improve or enhance the asset, for example by extending its useful life.

(b) **How impairment losses should be recognised in financial statements**

Where a recoverable amount is less than the carrying amount, the carrying amount should be reduced to recoverable amount, giving rise to an impairment loss.

In the absence of a previous revaluation, the impairment loss should be recognised as an expense in profit or loss.

Where the impairment loss relates to a revalued asset, it should be recognised first in other comprehensive income against any balance on the revaluation surplus relating to that asset. Any excess is recognised in profit or loss.

The remaining balance on the revaluation surplus will be after taking account of any transfers already made to retained earnings of the difference between depreciation on the revalued amount and depreciation on historical cost. Such transfers reflect the fact that some of the revaluation surplus is realised as the asset is used.

(c) **Accounting treatment at 31 December 20X6**

The accounting treatment follows the principles identified above.

(1) Betax machine

The entry of a major competitor into the UK Betax market is an indicator of possible impairment that triggers the need for an impairment test.

The fair value less costs to sell of the machine should be calculated by using the estimated gross sale proceeds and deducting the direct costs of sale, as follows.

	£
Estimated gross sale proceeds	300,000
Less 10% commission	(30,000)
Dismantling costs	(10,000)
	260,000

The value in use should be determined by considering the discounted future cash flows of the asset from its continuing use in its current condition. Whilst management's intentions may bring positive benefits in the future, IAS 36 *Impairment of Assets* prohibits the inclusion of cash flows from uncommitted future restructurings and enhancing capital expenditure. The value in use at 31 December 20X6 is therefore £250,000.

The recoverable amount is the higher of the two amounts, so £260,000. The machine's carrying amount should be adjusted to this amount and an impairment loss of £20,000 recognised in profit or loss.

(2) Freehold manufacturing building

Land normally has an indefinite useful life and is not depreciated. So the land element of the freehold manufacturing building should be measured in the statement of financial position at 31 December 20X6 at its original cost of £500,000.

The building element was initially recognised at cost of £2 million. The annual depreciation charge should have been £100,000 (£2m ÷ 20 years) and the carrying amount immediately before the revaluation on 31 December 20X3 £1,800,000 (£2m less two years' depreciation).

The building element should then have been revalued upwards to £2.25 million and the surplus over carrying amount of £450,000 recognised in other comprehensive income and credited to revaluation surplus.

The depreciation expense should have become £125,000 per annum (£2.25 million ÷ 18 years) and an annual transfer of £25,000 made from the revaluation surplus to retained earnings through the statement of changes in equity. It should have been calculated as the depreciation based on the revalued carrying amount (£125,000) less the depreciation based on historical cost (£100,000).

On 31 December 20X6 the following balances should be included in the statement of financial position.

	£
Carrying amount of the land element of the freehold	500,000
Draft carrying amount of the building element	
(£2.25m less three years' depreciation at £125,000 per annum)	1,875,000
Draft revaluation surplus	
(£450,000 less three years of realisation of £25,000)	375,000

The building element's open market value is now only £1.65 million and an impairment loss of £225,000 should be recognised. As the loss is less than the revaluation surplus on the related asset, the entire loss should be recognised in other comprehensive income and offset against the revaluation surplus, so that its balance becomes £150,000 (375,000 – 225,000).

(d) **Statement of financial position carrying amounts at 31 December 20X7, assuming no further impairment losses or revaluation surpluses**

(1) Betax machine

The annual depreciation expense for the Betax product machine should be based on its useful life in its current condition, so four years. The depreciation expense should be £65,000 per annum (£260,000 ÷ 4) and the carrying amount should be £195,000.

(2) Freehold manufacturing building

The land element of the freehold should remain at £500,000.

For the building element, the depreciation expense should now be £110,000 (£1.65m ÷ 15 years). The amount of revaluation surplus realised per annum should be £10,000 (£110,000 less £100,000).

Carrying amount   = £1,540,000 (£1.65m less £110,000)
Revaluation surplus = £140,000 (£150,000 less £10,000)

CHAPTER 4

Investment properties, government grants and borrowing costs

Introduction

Examination context

Topic List

1 IAS 40 *Investment Property*

2 Government grants

3 IAS 23 *Borrowing Costs*

4 UK GAAP comparison

Summary and Self-test

Technical reference

Answers to Interactive questions

Answers to Self-test

Learning objectives

- Prepare and present extracts of financial statements in respect of investment properties, government grants and borrowing costs

- Formulate accounting and reporting policies in respect of investment property, government grants and borrowing costs

- Illustrate how different methods of recognising and measuring investment properties and borrowing costs can affect the view presented

- Identify and illustrate the main differences between international and UK requirements in relation to investment properties, government grants and borrowing costs

- Identify and consider appropriate actions for ethical issues involving investment properties, government grants and borrowing costs

Specific syllabus references for this chapter are: 1e, 2a, 2b, 3a, 4a and 4c.

Syllabus links

Investment properties, government grants and borrowing costs are introduced for the first time in this paper. Knowledge of IAS 40 *Investment Property,* IAS 20 *Accounting for Government Grants and Disclosure of Government Assistance* and IAS 23 *Borrowing Costs* will also be required at the Advanced Stage.

Examination context

In the examination, candidates may be required to:

- Explain the accounting treatment of investment properties, government grants and borrowing costs

- Draft financial information including investment properties, government grants and borrowing costs

- Interpret results and explain the effect of investment properties, government grants and borrowing costs on financial statements

- Explain and illustrate the difference between the relevant treatment under IFRS and UK GAAP

- Identify and explain any ethical issues

1 IAS 40 *Investment Property*

Section overview

- Investment property is property held to earn income from rentals and/or capital appreciation.

- Owner-occupied property is not investment property.

- Investment property should be initially measured at cost.

- After initial recognition investment property should be recognised under

  - The IAS 16 cost model or
  - The fair value model

- A change in use may change the way the property is classified and measured.

- An investment property should be derecognised when it is disposed of or permanently withdrawn from use.

1.1 Introduction

An entity may own land or a building as **an investment** rather than for use in the business. The land or building may therefore generate cash flows from **rental income, capital appreciation or both** which are largely **independent of those generated by other assets** which the entity holds.

IAS 40 *Investment Property* prescribes the accounting treatment and related disclosure requirements in this situation.

The treatment of **rental income** in the financial statements is largely **uncontroversial** compared with that of the **capital appreciation** of property, which can often involve **complex business processes**. An entity may develop property to **add value** to it to make it more attractive to tenants. Development may be on a **portfolio basis** and carried out by an individual entity or with **other developers**. For example, granting a lease to a blue chip retail tenant in a particular shopping centre can improve the rental yields on property nearby and increase market values. It is not the passage of time alone that creates value.

This commercial environment creates challenges for financial reporting and its interpretation by users. **Market value** is often seen as the most valid measure of investment property. However, short-term issues within the economy and the commercial property market can readily **create volatility**. Recognition of changes in market value **directly in the profit or loss** introduces volatility into an entity's **operating performance** and **earnings per share measure** (see Chapter 9). Because valuation changes result from measurement only, they do not necessarily lead to different cash flows.

It is widely accepted that measuring investment property at a series of out-of-date historical costs is not an appropriate way of evaluating the business objective of commercial property investors – to generate capital gains.

1.2 Investment property

Definition

Investment property is property (land or a building – or part of a building – or both) held (by the owner or by the lessee under a finance lease) to earn rentals or for capital appreciation or both, rather than for:

- Use in the production or supply of goods or services or for administrative purposes or
- Sale in the ordinary course of business.

Point to note:

An entity has the choice as to whether to classify property meeting this definition but held under an operating lease as investment property. If it does, it must also use the fair value measurement model (see section 1.4 below).

IAS 40 lists the following as examples of investment property:

- **Land held for long-term capital appreciation** rather than short-term sale

- **Land held for a currently undetermined future use**

- A building owned by the entity (or held under a finance lease) and leased to a third party under an **operating lease**

- A building which is **vacant but is held to be leased out under an operating lease**

- Property being **constructed or developed for future use as an investment property**.

It also provides examples of items that are **not** investment property and are therefore **outside the scope of IAS 40**. These include the following:

Type of property	Applicable IAS
Property **intended for sale** in the ordinary course of business	IAS 2 *Inventories*
Property being **constructed or developed** on behalf of **third parties**	IAS 11 *Construction Contracts*
Owner-occupied property (see definition below)	IAS 16 *Property, Plant and Equipment*
Property leased to another entity under a **finance lease**	IAS 17 *Leases*

Definition

Owner-occupied property is property held (by the owner or by the lessee under a finance lease) for use in the production or supply of goods or services or for administrative purposes.

Points to note:

1 In some cases it may be possible to treat **part of a property** as an investment property. For example, an entity may use a number of floors of a building as its head office and let out the rest. If these different parts can be **separated**, that is sold separately (or leased separately under a finance lease), the **relevant section** can be treated as an investment property.

2 An entity supplying services such as cleaning and maintenance to the lessee of a property may be regarded as using it in the 'supply of ... services', making the property owner-occupied. But if this supply is insignificant to the arrangements as a whole between lessor and lessee, the classification as investment property will still be appropriate.

3 Where an entity owns property that is leased to, and occupied by, its parent or another subsidiary, the property is treated as an investment property **in the entity's own accounts**. However, the property **does not qualify as investment property** in the **consolidated financial statements** as it is owner-occupied from the group perspective.

Interactive question 1: Identifying investment properties [Difficulty level: Easy]

Explain whether the following should be classified as investment properties:

(1) An entity owns a stately home used for executive training which is no longer required and is now being held for resale.

(2) An entity purchases some land for its investment potential. Planning permission has not been obtained for building construction of any kind.

(3) A new office building used by an insurance entity as its head office was purchased specifically in the centre of a major city in order to exploit its capital gains potential.

See **Answer** at the end of this chapter.

1.3 Initial recognition and measurement

Normal asset recognition conditions apply to investment properties. An investment property should be recognised when:

* It is **probable** that the future economic benefits associated with the investment property will flow to the entity; and

* The cost of the investment property can be **measured reliably**.

An investment property should be initially measured at **cost**.

Cost includes:

* **Purchase price**

* **Directly attributable costs,** for example transaction costs (professional fees, property transfer taxes)

Cost does **not** include:

* Start up costs

* Operating losses incurred before the investment property achieves the planned level of occupancy

* Abnormal amounts of wasted labour, material or other resources incurred in constructing or developing the property

Worked example: Recognition and measurement of investment property

On 30 June 20X4, an entity acquired for £3 million a site on which it planned to build a large office building which it would then let out on a floor-by-floor basis. Construction commenced on 1 September 20X4 and was substantially completed on 30 June 20X5 at a cost of £5 million, at which point tenants could move in.

Due to a misunderstanding, the letting agents only commenced the marketing of the office space on 1 July 20X5, with the first leases being signed by tenants with effect from 1 October 20X5. The building was not fully let until July 20X6.

Solution

The property was developed for future use as an investment property and should be recognised as such from 30 June 20X4 when the land was acquired. The final cost of the asset should be measured at the £8 million costs incurred up to 1 July 20X5 when the offices were ready to be occupied. Costs incurred after this date should be recognised as an expense in profit or loss, even though the entity did not start to receive rentals until 1 October 20X5. Any losses incurred during this 'empty' period and then up to the point the building is fully let are part of the entity's normal business operations and do not form part of the cost of the investment property.

C
H
A
P
T
E
R

4

Point to note:

Where a property held under a lease is classified as an investment property, IAS 17 requires the property to be recognised at the **lower** of:

- **Fair value** and
- The present value of the minimum lease payments

1.4 Measurement after recognition

After initial measurement at cost IAS 40 requires an entity to **choose** between two models:

- The **IAS 16 cost model**
- The **fair value model**

The **policy** chosen should be applied **consistently** to **all of the entity's investment property**.

The policy chosen should be disclosed in financial statements.

Points to note:

Where an entity chooses to **classify** a property held under an **operating lease** as an investment property:

- There is no choice of model. The fair value model must be adopted.

- This classification choice is available separately for each property held under an operating lease. The classification of one property in this way does not make the same classification compulsory for other properties held under operating leases.

- Once this classification choice has been made for the first time, what is compulsory is the use of the fair value model for **all** investment properties.

1.4.1 Cost model

If the cost model is adopted the property should be accounted for **in accordance with IAS 16**.

Investment property should be measured at **cost, less accumulated depreciation and impairment losses**.

Even if this model is adopted, the **fair value** of the investment property should be **disclosed** in financial statements. This allows users to understand the current value of the investment property. This aids comparability between entities adopting the two different measurement approaches.

1.4.2 Fair value model

If the fair value model is adopted, the accounting treatment of investment properties will be as follows:

- **All investment properties** should be **measured at fair value** at the end of **each reporting period** provided fair value can be **measured reliably**.

- **Changes** in fair value, whether gains or losses, should be **recognised in profit or loss for the period in which they arise**.

A consequence of adopting this measurement basis is that no depreciation is ever recognised.

Points to note:

1 IAS 40 **encourages** the assessment of fair value by **independent, appropriately qualified and experienced professionals** but **does not require it**. This allows the potential for **bias**. This may need to be taken into account when **interpreting results,** as the entity's performance ratios will be directly affected by the changes in fair value (see Chapter 11).

2 Financial statements must disclose the methods and significant assumptions applied in measuring fair value, and the extent to which it is based on a valuation by an independent valuer.

Definition

Fair value is the amount for which an asset could be exchanged between knowledgeable, willing parties in an arm's length transaction.

The following points should be noted about this definition:

* Fair value assumes that an arm's length transaction has taken place between 'knowledgeable, willing parties' that is both buyer and seller are **reasonably informed** about the nature and characteristics of the investment property

* A willing buyer is **motivated but not compelled** to buy the asset. A willing seller is neither an **over-eager nor a forced seller**, nor one prepared to hold out for a price not considered **reasonable** in the current market.

Points to note:

1   The fair value of investment property should reflect **market conditions at the end of the reporting period.** Fair value is time specific (since market conditions change), so the valuations should be at the end of the reporting period.

2   The best evidence of fair value is given by **current prices in an active market for similar property in the same location and condition** and subject to similar lease and other contracts. In the absence of this evidence **other factors** may need to be considered.

3   In determining the carrying amount under the fair value model an entity should not **double count assets**. For example, lifts or air conditioning are often an integral part of a building and should be recognised as part of the investment property, rather than recognised separately as plant and equipment.

4   If the fair value of an investment property under construction cannot be reliably determined, the property should be measured at cost. But fair value should be used once construction has finished (or when it can be reliably determined, if earlier).

5   In the rare circumstances where an entity **cannot determine reliably the fair value** of an investment property on a continuing basis, **the cost model in IAS 16** should be applied to that property until it is disposed of. Any other investment properties held by the entity should still be held under the fair value model (assuming their fair value can be measured reliably).

Interactive question 2: Fair value model   [Difficulty level: Easy]

An entity owns two investment properties, A and B. The entity measures its investment properties using the fair value model. Fair values have been assessed as follows:

	31 December	
	20X7	*20X8*
	£m	*£m*
Property A	18	24
Property B	12	10

Requirement

For the year ended 31 December 20X8 show the amounts which should be recognised in the financial statements.

Statement of comprehensive income   £m

Statement of financial position   £m

See **Answer** at the end of this chapter.

1.5 Change in use

An entity may change the way in which it uses its properties. In some instances this should change the way that the property is **classified and measured**. Some examples are provided below.

Evidence of change in use	Accounting treatment
Occupation of an investment property by the entity itself.	The property is now **owner-occupied** and should therefore be recognised as a **property in use by the entity** in accordance with IAS 16. Where the investment property was measured at fair value, its fair value at the date of change of use should be treated as the **deemed cost** for future accounting.
Development of an investment property commences with the intention that on completion of the development works it will be sold by the entity.	The property is to be **sold in the normal course of business** and should therefore be reclassified as **inventory** and accounted for in accordance with IAS 2 *Inventories*. Where the investment property was measured at fair value, its fair value at the date of change in use should be treated as the **deemed cost**.
Development of an investment property commences with the intention that it will be let after completion of the development works.	The property should **continue to be held as an investment property** under IAS 40.
A building that was occupied by the entity is vacated so that it can be let to third parties.	The property is **no longer owner-occupied** and therefore should be **transferred to investment properties** and accounted for in accordance with IAS 40. Where investment properties are measured at fair value the property should be revalued at the date of change of use and any difference should be recognised in other comprehensive income as a revaluation under IAS 16.
A property that was originally held as inventory has now been let to a third party.	The property is no longer held for resale and is instead held to generate future rental income and therefore **should be transferred to investment properties** in accordance with IAS 40. Where investment properties are measured at fair value the property should be revalued at the date of change of use and any difference should be recognised immediately in profit or loss.

Point to note:

Where the **cost model** is used to measure investment properties, a change in classification will **not** normally lead to a change in measurement. The **carrying amount at the date of change** will be used as the initial measurement under the new classification.

Worked example: Change in use

An entity with a 31 December year end purchased an office building, with a useful life of 50 years, for £5.5 million on 1 January 20X1. (The amount attributable to land was negligible). The entity used the building as its head office for five years until 31 December 20X5 when the entity moved its head office to larger premises. The building was reclassified on that date as an investment property and leased out under a 40 year lease.

The fair value of the head office at 31 December 20X5 was £6 million.

Explain the treatment of the office building on the assumption that:

(a) The entity uses the cost model for investment properties
(b) The entity uses the fair value model for investment properties.

Solution

(a) **Cost model**

Until 31 December 20X5 the building should be recognised as property, plant and equipment. At 31 December 20X5 the building has a carrying amount of:

£5.5m × 45/50 years = £4.95 million in accordance with IAS 16.

On 31 December 20X5 the property should be recognised as an investment property at its IAS 16 carrying amount of £4.95 million and should continue to be depreciated over its remaining 45 year life.

(b) **Fair value model**

At 31 December 20X5, the building has a carrying amount of £4.95 million in accordance with IAS 16, as set out above.

On 31 December 20X5 the property should be recognised as an investment property. The property should be revalued to fair value at 31 December 20X5, and any change in value should be recognised in accordance with IAS 16.

The property should therefore be recognised at a carrying amount of £6 million and the difference of £1.05 million (£6 million – £4.95 million) should be recognised in other comprehensive income as a revaluation surplus.

In subsequent periods (unless there is a further change in use) the building should be measured at fair value with any gain or loss recognised directly in profit or loss.

1.6 Disposal

An investment property should be **derecognised** when:

- It is **disposed** of, either through sale or by entering a finance lease, or

- It is **permanently withdrawn from use** and will not generate any future economic benefits, even on its ultimate disposal.

Any gain or loss should normally be determined as the **difference between the net disposal proceeds** (if any) **and the carrying amount of the asset** and recognised directly in **profit or loss** in the period in which the disposal or 'retirement' takes place.

Interactive question 3: Disposal [Difficulty level: Intermediate]

An entity purchased an investment property on 1 January 20X3, for a cost of £3.5 million. The property had a useful life of 50 years, with no residual value and at 31 December 20X5 had a fair value of £4.2 million. On 1 January 20X6 the property was sold for net proceeds of £4 million.

Requirement

Calculate the profit or loss on disposal under both the cost and fair value model.

See **Answer** at the end of this chapter.

1.7 Judgements required

IAS 40 does not set out an explicit preference as to which measurement model should be used for investment properties. The choice of model is a decision that an entity's management makes by considering the most appropriate presentation.

An entity is permitted to change its accounting policy where the revised policy will result in reliable and more relevant information being provided. Any change would be treated in accordance with IAS 8 *Accounting Policies, Changes in Accounting Estimates and Errors.*

IAS 40 does state that it is 'highly unlikely' that a change from the fair value to the cost model would provide a more relevant presentation.

Accounting for investment properties involves a significant level of professional judgement involving:

- Identifying investment property, particularly where an entity supplies services to lessees
- Choosing the appropriate accounting policy
- Obtaining reliable measures of fair value

Point to note:

Entities are required to use the guidance in IAS 40 to develop criteria by which they judge whether or not a property is an investment property, so that judgements can be made consistently, from period to period.

1.8 Relevance of information to users

Users are provided with relevant information by IAS 40's requirement that disclosures are made in financial statements of:

- The measurement model used

- The criteria for judging whether or not a property is an investment property

- The schedule of movements in carrying amount over the year

- The amounts recognised in profit or loss for:

    - Rental income from investment property

    - Direct operating expenses (including repairs and maintenance) arising from investment property that generated rental income during the period

    - Direct operating expenses (including repairs and maintenance) arising from investment property that did not generate rental income during the period.

This last set of information is useful in forecasting future income and expenses.

A key business objective of commercial property owners is to maximise the capital appreciation of their properties by getting other entities to use them. This is a marked contrast to manufacturing companies who acquire items of PPE to use themselves in the generation of profits. Users of financial statements will need information which helps them evaluate the success of property managers in creating capital appreciation, so IAS 40's fair value model will provide highly relevant information. Indeed, investors might well be wary of property companies which adopt the cost model, querying why they depreciate properties when the business objective is capital appreciation.

The requirement that changes in fair value should be recognised in profit or loss does introduce volatility into the earnings reported each year, but sophisticated investors will be unconcerned, understanding that the result of property companies will be as volatile as the property market itself.

This volatility will also affect the gearing measure of solvency, but as property companies typically target very high gearing, it is important that users can calculate the extent to which current property valuations cover borrowings.

2 Government grants

Section overview

- A government grant is one type of government assistance.

- A government grant should only be recognised when there is reasonable assurance that:

  - The entity will comply with the conditions of the grant
  - The entity will receive the grant

- Grants related to income should be recognised over the period in which the associated costs are incurred.

- Grants related to assets may be presented by either:

  - Setting up the grant as deferred income or
  - Netting off the grant from the cost of the asset

- Grants received in the form of non-monetary assets should be recognised at fair value

- Repayment of a grant should be treated as a change in accounting estimate.

2.1 Introduction

It is common for entities to receive government assistance for various purposes. In these terms the reference to 'government' is a **broad concept** including government agencies and similar bodies, whether local, national or international.

Government assistance can take many different forms and there are various motives for governments in providing such aid, including:

- **Geographical** – to stimulate employment in poorer regions
- **Industrial** – to support key industries (such as defence, IT and energy)
- **Inward investment** – to promote investment from overseas
- **New start-ups** – to help infant entities gain a foothold in a market

To ensure that the objective of providing the assistance is met by the recipient entity in its application of such amounts, there are often **a variety of criteria and conditions** attached to their receipt. Conditions, for example, may require a minimum investment to be provided or a minimum level of employment to be sustained over a specified period by the entity.

In a **financial reporting context** it is important to **disclose adequate information** in relation to government assistance, to ensure that **an entity's performance is accurately interpreted**. The identification of government assistance allows **a fair comparison** to be made with other entities in a similar industry that have not received such assistance.

Definition

Government assistance is action by government designed to provide an economic benefit specific to an entity or range of entities qualifying under certain criteria.

Government assistance does not include benefits provided **indirectly** to an entity, for example the provision of infrastructure in development areas.

Government grants are a form of government assistance.

The title of IAS 20 *Accounting for Government Grants and Disclosure of Government Assistance* explains its purpose. However, IAS 20 does not apply to the following situations:

- Government assistance given in the form of 'tax breaks', such as accelerated depreciation allowances and reduced rates of tax

- Government acting as **part-owner** of the entity

Definition

Government grants are assistance by government in the form of transfers of resources to an entity in return for past or future compliance with certain conditions relating to the operating activities of the entity. They exclude those forms of government assistance which cannot reasonably have a value placed upon them and transactions with government which cannot be distinguished from the normal trading transactions of the entity.

Point to note:

Certain forms of government assistance are **excluded** from the above definition and should not be recognised. These include:

- Free technical or marketing advice

- The provision of guarantees

- Transactions with government that cannot be distinguished from the normal trading transactions of the enterprise, for example a government procurement policy that is responsible for a portion of the entity's sales.

2.2 Recognition

A government grant (including a non-monetary grant at fair value) should only be recognised when there is **reasonable assurance** that:

- The entity will **comply with any conditions** attached to the grant
- The entity **will actually receive the grant**

Points to note:

1   Receipt of the grant in itself does not prove that the conditions attached to it have been or will be fulfilled.

2   The manner in which a grant is received does not affect the accounting method adopted, so a grant is accounted for in the same way whether it is received in cash or as a reduction in a liability to the government.

2.3 Measurement

IAS 20 identifies **two methods** which could be used to account for government grants:

- **Capital approach**: recognise the grant outside profit or loss
- **Income approach**: the grant is recognised in profit or loss over one or more periods

IAS 20 requires grants to be recognised under the **income approach**, that is grants should be recognised in profit or loss over the periods in which the entity recognises as expenses the costs which the grants are intended to compensate.

It would be against the accrual principle to recognise grants in profit or loss on a receipts basis, so a **systematic basis of matching** must be used. A receipts basis would only be acceptable if no other basis was available.

It will usually be relatively easy to identify the costs related to a government grant, and thereby the period(s) in which the grant should be recognised in profit or loss.

2.3.1 Depreciating assets

Where grants are received in relation to a depreciating asset, the grant should be recognised over the periods in which the asset is depreciated *and* in the same proportions.

Interactive question 4: Grants for depreciating assets [Difficulty level: Easy]

Arthur Ltd receives a government grant representing 50% of the cost of a depreciating asset which cost £40,000 and has a nil residual value. How should the grant be recognised if Arthur Ltd depreciates the asset:

- Over four years straight line, or
- At 40% reducing balance?

See **Answer** at the end of this chapter.

2.3.2 Non-depreciating assets

In the case of **grants for non-depreciable assets**, certain obligations may need to be fulfilled, in which case the grant should be recognised in profit or loss **over the periods in which the cost of meeting the obligation is incurred**. For example, if a piece of land is granted on condition that a building is erected on it, then the grant should be recognised in profit or loss over the building's life.

2.4 Presentation of grants

2.4.1 Grants related to assets

Grants related to assets are used to acquire or construct specific long term assets.

Government grants related to assets (including non-monetary grants at fair value) should be presented in the statement of financial position either:

- By setting up the grant as deferred income, or
- By deducting the grant in arriving at the carrying amount of the asset (that is netting off).

2.4.2 Deferred income method

The deferred income method sets up the grant as deferred income in the statement of financial position, which is recognised in profit or loss on a systematic and rational basis over the useful life of the asset. Normally this corresponds to the method of depreciation on the related asset.

2.4.3 Netting-off method

The netting-off method deducts the grant in arriving at the carrying amount of the asset to which it relates. The grant is recognised in profit or loss over the life of a depreciable asset by way of a reduced depreciation charge.

Worked example: Grants related to assets

An entity purchased an item of equipment for £50,000 on 1 January 20X5. It will depreciate this machinery on a straight-line basis over its useful life of five years, with a zero residual value. Also on 1 January 20X5, the entity received a government grant of £5,000 to help finance this equipment.

Under the **netting-off method** the grant and the equipment should be presented in the income statement for the year to 31 December 20X5 and in the statement of financial position at that date as follows:

Statement of financial position

	£
Equipment	
Cost (50 – 5)	45,000
Depreciation	(9,000)
Carrying amount	36,000

Income statement

Charge: depreciation	£9,000

Under the **deferred income method** the grant and the equipment should be presented in the income statement for the year to 31 December 20X5 and in the statement of financial position at that date as follows:

Statement of financial position

	£
Equipment	
Cost	50,000
Depreciation	(10,000)
Carrying amount	40,000
Deferred income – non-current	3,000
Deferred income – current (the amount to be recognised in profit or loss in 20X6)	1,000
	4,000

(Total deferred income = 5,000 grant less 1,000 recognised in income statement = 4,000)

Income statement

		£
Charge:	Depreciation	£10,000
Credit:	Deferred income	£1,000

Points to note:

1   There are less likely to be impairment issues if the grant has been deducted from the cost of the asset as this reduces the carrying amount. In addition, the financial statements will be less comparable with those of a similar entity that has not received government assistance.

2   Deferred income (recognised when using the deferred income method) should be split between current and non-current portions for disclosure purposes.

Interactive question 5: Grants related to assets: Deferred income method

[Difficulty level: Easy]

An entity purchased a new item of machinery for £320,000 on 1 January 20X7. It will depreciate this machinery at 25% per annum on the reducing balance basis, as this most closely resembles the pattern of benefits receivable from the asset. Also on 1 January 20X7, a government grant of £160,000 was received to help finance this machinery.

Requirement

Show the amounts to be recognised in profit or loss for the year ended 31 December 20X7 if the entity uses IAS 20's deferred income method for government grants.

See **Answer** at the end of this chapter.

2.4.4   Grants related to income

Government grants related to income are defined as those not related to assets and can be presented in two ways:

*   A credit in profit or loss (either separately, or under a general heading such as 'other income') or
*   A deduction from the related expense.

Treating the grant as a deduction from the related expense (the net treatment) results in the income statement being less comparable with those of similar entities that have not received such grants. This treatment may also lead to the particular category of expenditure being excessively low in one year, or in comparison with other categories of expenditure during that period. Disclosure of grants received will therefore be important to assist comparison and understanding (see section 2.6).

2.5 Other issues

2.5.1 Conditions and compensation

There may be a **series of conditions** attached to a grant. An entity must take care to identify precisely those conditions which give rise to costs which in turn determine the periods over which the grant will be earned. When appropriate, **the grant should be split and the parts allocated on different bases**.

An entity may receive a grant as compensation for expenses or losses which it has **already incurred**. Alternatively, a grant may be given to an entity simply to provide immediate financial support where no future related costs are expected. In cases such as these, the grant should be recognised in profit or loss in the period in which it becomes receivable.

Point to note:

If it is possible that one or more of the conditions attaching to the grant will not be met, a contingent liability should be disclosed. If it turns out that one or more has not been met, then a provision should be recognised for the amount repayable.

2.5.2 Non-monetary government grants

A non-monetary asset may be transferred by government to an entity as a grant, for example a piece of land, or other resources. The **fair value** of such an asset is usually assessed and this is used to account for both the asset and the grant. Alternatively, both may be valued at a nominal amount.

2.5.3 Repayment of government grants

A government grant that becomes repayable should be accounted for as a change in an accounting estimate (see IAS 8 *Accounting Policies, Changes in Accounting Estimates and Errors*).

Repayment of a grant related to income should be applied in the following order:

- Against any **unamortised deferred credit** set up in respect of the grant

- To the extent that the **repayment exceeds any such deferred credit**, or **where no deferred credit exists**, the repayment should be **recognised immediately as an expense**.

Repayment of a grant related to an asset should be recognised by either:

- Increasing the carrying amount of the asset or
- Reducing the deferred income balance by the amount repayable.

The cumulative additional depreciation that would have been recognised to date as an expense in the absence of the grant should be recognised immediately as an expense.

Interactive question 6: Grant recognition   **[Difficulty level: Intermediate]**

Determine if the following grants should be recognised and, if so, the period over which they should be recognised in profit or loss:

(1) A cash grant is available to private child nurseries to spend on toys in urban regeneration areas that qualify for such support. The only condition attaching to the grant is that the money should be spent immediately.

(2) A manufacturing entity receives a grant of £1 million when it creates 50 jobs. £0.5 million is payable when the figure is reached with the remaining £0.5 million payable at the end of four years should the 50 jobs still be in existence. There is reasonable assurance that the employment levels will be maintained when reached.

(3) Free testing equipment is available to new motor emission businesses being set up in a region that qualifies for special government support.

(4) A government department offers a grant in the form of free consulting advice to entities setting-up businesses overseas to help export growth.

See **Answer** at the end of this chapter.

2.6 Disclosure

The disclosure requirements in IAS 20 help a user of the financial statements to understand the extent and effect of government grants on an entity during a particular period.

The following matters should be disclosed:

- The accounting policy adopted for government grants, including the methods of presentation

- The nature and extent of government grants recognised in the financial statements

- An indication of other forms of government assistance from which the entity has directly benefited

- Unfulfilled conditions and other contingencies attaching to government assistance that have been recognised.

2.7 Judgements required

IAS 20 is one of the more straightforward reporting standards. Management judgement is only required in limited circumstances, such as:

- Whether to account for non-monetary grants at fair value or at a nominal amount

- How to deal with a grant to defray the costs of a project if the project involves both capital and revenue expenditure. Some allocation to the different components would be appropriate, because it is likely that the two types of expenditure will be recognised in profit or loss over different periods.

2.8 Relevance of information for users

Users will wish to be aware of any significant amounts of government grants received so that they can:

- Take account of the effect on financial performance and position if further grants are not to be received in future periods

- Compare the financial performance and position of a grant-receiving entity with that of an entity not eligible for grants.

The disclosures required by IAS 20 are very useful in this respect, particularly those in respect of the deferred income method of accounting for capital grants.

3 IAS 23 *Borrowing Costs*

Section overview

- Under IAS 23 certain borrowing costs form part of the cost of a qualifying asset.

- Only the borrowing costs directly attributable to the acquisition/construction/production of the asset should be capitalised.

- If the funds used for the acquisition etc are the general funds of the business, a weighted average borrowing cost should be calculated.

- IAS 23 lays down requirements for the commencement, suspension and cessation of capitalisation of borrowing costs.

3.1 Introduction

If an entity constructs a substantial asset either for use itself or for resale, it is likely that additional funds in the form of loan capital will be required in order to finance the construction. The interest on these additional funds is a cost of the construction of the asset, in the same way that materials and labour are costs of the construction of the asset.

The question is therefore whether these finance costs incurred should be:

- Recognised as an expense in profit or loss, or
- Recognised as part of the cost of the asset carried in the statement of financial position.

Where borrowings have been acquired **specifically to finance the construction of a substantial asset**, a direct cost is incurred that would have been avoided had the construction not taken place. It therefore seems reasonable that the financing cost associated with such borrowings should form **part of the cost of the asset**, as are other costs incurred in the construction process. International standards now **require** this treatment for all "directly attributable" borrowing costs.

Until the IASB issued a revised IAS 23 in 2007, entities had the choice of whether to account for "directly attributable" borrowing costs as part of the cost of the asset or as an expense in profit or loss. The revised IAS 23 removes the option of recognising them as an expense.

The revised standard is now consistent with US GAAP and was developed as part of the convergence project being undertaken with the US FASB. The IASB believes that the new standard will improve financial reporting in three ways:

- The cost of an asset will in future include all costs incurred in getting it ready for use or sale.
- Comparability is enhanced because the choice in previous accounting treatments is removed.
- The revision to IAS 23 achieves convergence in principle with US GAAP.

Point to note:

It is only borrowing costs which should form part of the cost of the asset. Dividends and other costs of equity should not be treated in the same way, but should always be recognised in the statement of changes in equity.

3.2 IAS 23 core principle

Borrowing costs that are directly attributable to the acquisition, construction or production of a qualifying asset form part of the cost of that asset. Other borrowing costs are recognised as an expense.

Definition

A **qualifying asset** is an asset that necessarily takes a substantial period of time to get ready for its intended use or sale.

This could cover:

- Property, plant and equipment
- Investment properties under construction
- Inventories (such as construction of an aeroplane for sale)
- Construction contracts
- Intangible assets

The definition **excludes** an asset which is ready for use or sale at the time it is acquired.

Point to note:

An entity is not required to apply IAS 23 to borrowing costs directly attributable to the acquisition, construction or development of:

- Assets measured at fair value,

- Inventories that are manufactured or produced in large quantities on a repetitive basis even if they take a substantial period of time to get ready for use or sale.

3.3 Borrowing costs to be capitalised

Definition

Borrowing costs are interest and other costs that an entity incurs in connection with the borrowing of funds.

This definition includes:

- Interest expense calculated using the effective interest method as described in IAS 39 *Financial Instruments: Recognition and Measurement* (see Chapter 7)

- Finance charges in respect of finance leases

However, only borrowing costs which are **directly attributable** to the acquisition, construction or production of the qualifying asset should be capitalised; these are the borrowing costs which would have been avoided if the expenditure on the qualifying asset had not been made.

If **funds are borrowed specifically** for the construction:

- The borrowing costs can be readily identified

- If the funds are not all required immediately and some are invested, the borrowing costs capitalised should be reduced by the investment income received on the excess funds.

Worked example: Specific funds

An entity borrowed £1 million at 7.5% in order to finance the construction of a new building which would take 12 months to complete. As stage payments were to be made in respect of the construction costs, surplus funds were invested and during the 12 month period interest income of £35,000 was earned.

Solution

Borrowing costs to be capitalised =   (£1,000,000 × 7.5%) – £35,000
                                    =   £40,000

If the construction is financed out of the **general borrowing** of the entity:

- The amount of borrowing costs that should be capitalised is calculated by reference to the weighted average cost of the general borrowings.

- The weighted average calculation excludes borrowings to finance a specific purpose or building.

If the entity is part of a group and funds are negotiated for the whole group rather than individual entities, then judgement is required as to which borrowings should be used in the calculation of the weighted average cost of (group) borrowings.

Worked example: Weighted average cost

An entity has the following loan finance in place during the year:

£1 million of 6% loan finance
£2 million of 8% loan finance

It constructed a new factory which cost £600,000 and this was funded out of the existing loan finance. The factory took eight months to complete.

What borrowing costs should be capitalised?

Solution

$$\text{Weighted average cost of loans} = \frac{(£1,000,000 \times 6\%) + (£2,000,000 \times 8\%)}{£3,000,000}$$

$$= 7.33\%$$

$$\text{Borrowing costs to be capitalised} = £600,000 \times 7.33\% \times 8/12$$

$$= £29,320$$

The amount of borrowing costs that is capitalised may be **limited** because the total carrying amount of the asset (including borrowing costs) should not exceed the asset's recoverable amount.

3.4 Commencement of capitalisation

Capitalisation should commence when the entity first meets all three of the following conditions:

- It incurs expenditures for the asset
- It incurs borrowing costs
- It undertakes activities that are necessary to prepare the asset for its intended use or sale

Activities necessary to prepare the asset for use or sale include:

- Construction
- Drawing up plans
- Obtaining planning permissions
- Obtaining permissions from utility providers
- Obtaining other consents required

Simply holding an asset for development without any associated activities is not enough to qualify for capitalisation.

3.5 Suspension of capitalisation

If the entity suspends active development of a qualifying asset for an extended period:

- Capitalisation of borrowing costs should be suspended
- Borrowing costs incurred in this period should be recognised as an expense in profit or loss.

However, if the temporary delay is a necessary part of the production or construction process borrowing costs should still be capitalised. Examples include where the maturation of an asset is an essential part of the production process or where there are known natural causes (such as changes in the tide).

Interactive question 7: Commencement of capitalisation [Difficulty level: Easy]

The following events take place:

- An entity buys some land on 1 December.

- Work is undertaken in December and January in preparing a planning application

- Planning permission is obtained on 31 January.

- Payment for the land is deferred until 1 February.

- The entity takes out a loan to cover the cost of the land and the construction of the building on 1 February.

- Due to adverse weather conditions there is a delay in starting the building work for six weeks and work does not commence until 15 March.

When should capitalisation of borrowing costs commence?

See **Answer** at the end of this chapter.

3.6 Cessation of capitalisation

The entity shall cease capitalising borrowing costs when substantially all the activities necessary to get the asset ready for its intended use or sale are complete.

Minor activities such as decoration of a building to a purchaser's specification do not form part of substantial activities, so capitalisation should cease before this work is started.

Point to note:

It is the availability for use or sale which is important, not the actual use or sale. An asset is normally ready for use or sale when its physical construction is complete.

Where an asset is completed in parts:

- Where each part is capable of being used/sold separately while other parts continue to be constructed, the cessation of capitalisation of borrowing costs should be assessed on the completion of each part.

- Where no part is capable of being used/sold separately until all the other parts have been completed, cessation should take place when the last part is completed.

3.7 Disclosure

The entity should disclose:

- The costs which have been capitalised in the current period
- The capitalisation rate used to determine the amount of borrowing costs eligible for capitalisation

3.8 Judgements required

IAS 23 requires some significant judgements on the part of management, particularly in terms of how to define:

- "A substantial period of time to get ready" which is a central part of the definition of a qualifying asset.

- The borrowing costs which are "directly attributable" to work on the qualifying asset. In groups of companies with a central treasury function, it may be that some of the group borrowings are really attributable to activities other than the work on the qualifying asset.

- "Activities necessary to prepare the qualifying asset". This is central to identifying when capitalisation should commence.

- An "extended period" when active development has been suspended and capitalisation should also be suspended.

- When "substantially all the activities necessary … are complete", the point at which capitalisation should cease.

3.9 Relevance of information to users

In evaluating the performance and solvency of different entities users of financial statements want to compare like with like. Reporting standards which allow a choice of accounting policy (such as the previous version of IAS 23) do not serve users well. The revised IAS 23 makes the financial statements of different entities more comparable.

But there is some strength to the argument of those who favour the 'expense as incurred' approach that:

- Entities usually target a particular level of gearing

- The result is that the construction of a qualifying asset is usually financed by both equity and debt

- A reporting standard which excludes the capitalisation of the cost of equity finance is not reflecting the full cost of the asset

- It is therefore better not to capitalise any such costs, rather than just a portion of them.

The effect of capitalisation as compared with recognising borrowing costs as an expense in the period they are incurred is as follows:

- Finance costs in profit or loss will be lower, but capital employed will be higher, as the carrying amount of the asset is increased

- Depreciation charges will be higher as the capitalised borrowings are depreciated as part of the cost of the asset

Unusually, entities which previously recognised all borrowing costs as an expense as incurred and changed their accounting policy to comply with the new IAS 23 were not required to apply the new policy retrospectively. Instead of having to go back to restate all previous periods as if the capitalisation policy had always been applied, entities are required to apply the new standard to qualifying assets for which the commencement date for capitalisation is on or after 1 January 2009, the effective date for the new standard.

Point to note:

The fact that entities changing their accounting policy to comply with the new IAS 23 are applying the new policy prospectively means that their financial statements will remain non-comparable with those of entities which had always adopted the capitalisation policy.

Interactive question 8: Performance measurement [Difficulty level: Intermediate]

Two entities were incorporated on 1 January 20X5 to construct and operate identical plant and equipment (PPE). In each case

- The entity raised £1,000,000 of long-term capital on 1 January 20X5

- Construction commenced on 1 January 20X5 on which date the £800,000 contract price was paid to the contractor

- Construction was completed on 1 October 20X5 on which date the PPE became available for use

- The useful life of the PPE was 5 years, with no residual value

- The profit for the year before PPE depreciation and finance costs was £300,000.

The tax charge for the year for Entity A was £90,000 and that for Entity B was £84,000.

Entity A raised its long-term capital in the form of £1 equity shares issued at par. Entity B raised £200,000 in the form of £1 equity shares issued at par and £800,000 in the form of 10% loans.

Entity B paid its annual interest on 31 December 20X5 and both entities paid a dividend of 10p per equity share on that date.

Requirements

For each entity:

(a) Prepare the income statement for the year ended 31 December 20X5 to the extent possible and calculate its capital employed at 31 December 20X5;

(b) Calculate its return on capital employed and comment on the difference revealed by this performance measure.

See **Answer** at the end of this chapter.

4 UK GAAP comparison

Section overview

- SSAP 19 *Accounting for Investment Properties* deals with investment properties.

- SSAP 4 *Accounting for Government Grants* deals with government grants.

- The capitalisation of borrowing costs is dealt with in FRS 15 *Tangible Fixed Assets*.

4.1 Investment properties

In the UK investment properties are dealt with by SSAP 19. SSAP 19 applies many of the same broad principles; however, the following differences should be noted.

SSAP 19	IAS 40 comparison
Investment property **should be** measured at **open market value**.	A **choice** is allowed between **the cost model and the fair value model.**
All gains and losses should be recognised in the **statement of total recognised gains and losses.** Thus gains and losses are offset in a pool, with the result that there may be an overall net debit balance. The balance, whether credit or debit, is usually presented as the investment property revaluation reserve, to distinguish it from any revaluation reserve in respect of property, plant and equipment.	**If** the fair value model is adopted, **all gains and losses** should be recognised in profit or loss.
The only exception to recognition in the statement of total recognised gains and losses is that where the open market value of an individual property is expected to remain below cost on a **permanent** basis, that deficit should be recognised in profit or loss.	

Worked example: Investment property gains/losses

An entity owns two investment properties and details of their costs and open market values (OMV) are as follows:

	Cost £'000	OMV 1 Jan 20X6 £'000	OMV 31 Dec 20X6 £'000
Property 1	420	500	300
Property 2	580	600	550
	1,000	1,100	850

During the year there was a general downturn in property values, but the value of Property 1 was also affected by the Government's decision not to allow additional flights into the local airport.

Calculate the amounts to be recognised in the statements of financial position at the start and the end of the year and in profit or loss for the year in respect of these properties under:

(a) UK GAAP
(b) IFRS, using the fair value model and assuming fair value is the same as OMV.

Solution

(a) UK GAAP

It appears that the loss in respect of Property 1 is permanent (the Government is unlikely to change its mind) and should be recognised in profit or loss to the extent it exceeds the balance brought forward on investment property revaluation reserve.

	Statement of financial position 1 Jan 20X6		Statement of financial position 31 Dec 20X6	
	Carrying amount £'000	Revaluation reserve £'000	Carrying amount £'000	Revaluation reserve £'000
Property 1	500	80 (500 – 420)	300	–
Property 2	600	20 (600 – 580)	550	(30) (550 – 580)
	1,100	100	850	(30)

Profit and loss account for the year ended 31 Dec 20X6

	£'000
Deficit on investment properties ((500 – 300) – 80 balance on revaluation reserve))	120

(b) IFRS

The statement of financial position should present the same carrying amounts for the two properties as under UK GAAP, but there will be no revaluation surplus, the UK GAAP amount having been recognised in profit or loss at some time in the past.

Income statement for the year ended 31 Dec 20X6

	£'000
Deficit on investment properties ((500 – 300) + (600 – 550))	250

4.2 Government grants

There are **no examinable differences** between IAS 20 and SSAP 4.

4.3 Borrowing costs

FRS 15	IAS 23 comparison
Entities are allowed the **choice** of whether to **capitalise** borrowing costs **or to recognise them as an expense** as incurred.	Capitalisation is required.
The amount capitalised is limited to the finance costs incurred on the expenditure incurred.	The amount capitalised is limited to the borrowing costs on the total related funds less the investment income from any temporary investment of those funds.

Worked example: Borrowing costs to be capitalised

An entity borrowed specifically to finance the construction of a qualifying asset. £800,000 was borrowed at 8% on 1 January 20X6 and construction activity commenced on 1 February. Payments to the contractor were £500,000 on 1 March 20X6 and £300,000 on 1 August 20X6 and the asset became available for use on 31 October 20X6. Interest receivable in 20X6 on the temporary investment of surplus funds was £15,500.

Calculate the borrowing costs to be capitalised during the year under:

(a) UK GAAP
(b) IFRS.

Solution

(a) UK GAAP

The finance costs incurred on the expenditure incurred are:

	£
March to July (500 × 8% × 5/12)	16,667
August to October (800 × 8% × 3/12)	16,000
	32,667

Point to note:

The remainder of the finance costs and all of the investment income should be recognised in profit or loss.

(b) IFRS

	£
Borrowing costs on specific borrowing during period of activity	
February to October (800 × 8% × 9/12)	48,000
Less: investment income on uninvested borrowings	(15,500)
	32,500

Summary and Self-test

Summary

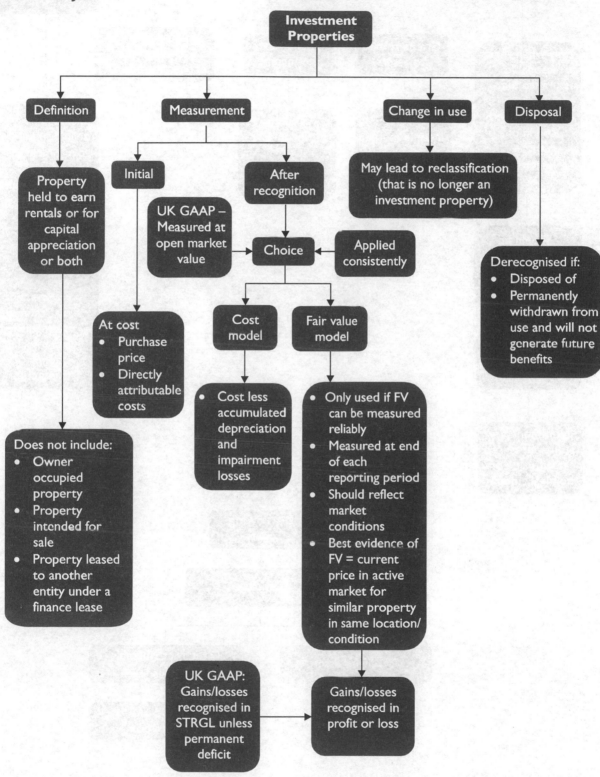

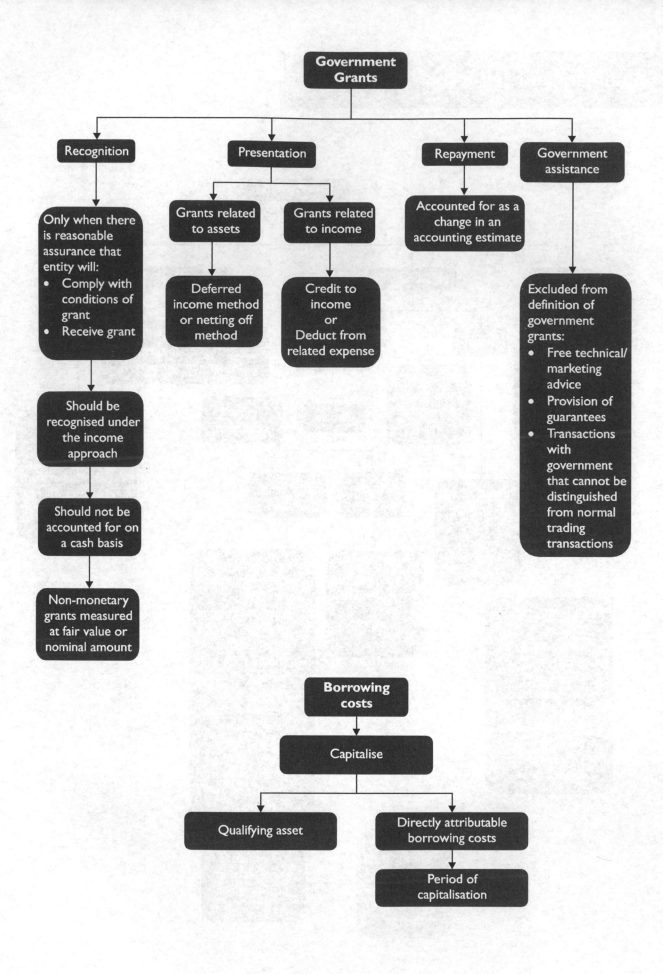

Self-test

Answer the following questions.

1 The Holmesfield Consultancy Company

You have recently been appointed as a technical manager at The Holmesfield Consultancy Company (HCC). HCC provides training and consultancy advice to companies which prepare financial statements using IFRS.

The managing partner of HCC has asked you to prepare the advice to be given to several clients in respect of the accounting requirements for non-current assets for the year ended 31 December 20X3. You have been asked to prepare an internal file note commenting on the recognition, measurement and presentation requirements for each of the following issues:

(1) Apperknowle plc operates in a number of geographical business segments. On 31 December 20X3 the managing director has revalued the following non-current assets.

- All computer equipment in North America using replacement cost.

- All other non-current assets where he believes the market value is substantially above the current carrying amount in the statement of financial position.

Company employees who have the relevant professional qualifications undertook all of the revaluations. The managing partner is uncertain about what advice should be given to Apperknowle plc.

(2) On 1 January 20X3 Unstone plc borrowed £10 million at an interest rate of 6% to fund the construction of a new manufacturing site. Land at a cost of £4 million was acquired on 1 February 20X3 and construction began on 1 June 20X3. Construction was completed on 30 September 20X3 at an additional cost of £6 million. Although the plant was usable from that date, full production did not commence until 1 December 20X3 due to promotional and marketing delays. No investment income was earned on the temporary investment of any unused funds.

(3) Barlow plc constructed a new piece of manufacturing equipment during the year. The costs incurred and capitalised comprise the following.

	£
Cost of supplied parts, excluding VAT	100,000
Recoverable VAT	15,000
Installation and pre-production testing costs	10,000
Start-up losses before full production	25,000

In addition, samples produced during the testing phase were sold for £15,000, which was recognised as revenue.

(4) On 1 January 20X3 Owler plc acquired a new helicopter for £5.2 million. It is expected to have a useful life of eight years and depreciation has been charged for the year on this basis. On 31 December 20X6 it will require a major inspection to obtain a new operating certificate. The expected cost of the inspection is £400,000 and a provision of £100,000 has been created in the 31 December 20X3 financial statements.

(5) On 1 January 20X3 Hilltop plc purchased a new aircraft at a cost of £2 million. The useful life of the aircraft is estimated at 20 years, and a depreciation charge of £100,000 has been recognised in profit or loss.

An aircraft expert has analysed the costs and useful lives of the various aircraft components as follows.

Component	Useful life	Cost
		£'000
Basic aeroplane	20 years	1,200
Engines	8 years	400
Interior	5 years	400
		2,000

(6) On 31 December 20X3 Cowley plc sold a piece of machinery for £1.6 million, net of selling expenses. Cowley plc adopts the IAS 16 *Property, Plant and Equipment* revaluation model accounting policy in respect of the measurement of non-current assets subsequent to initial recognition.

The decision to sell this asset was taken on 18 June 20X3 when its fair value was estimated at £1.6 million and its costs to sell at £50,000, its carrying amount was £1.2 million, and the balance in revaluation surplus in respect of the asset was £0.3 million. Cowley plc has recognised a gain on disposal of the asset of £0.7 million in profit or loss.

(7) On 1 January 20X3 Morris plc entered into a 6-year lease over one of its properties, the lessee agreeing to pay £100,000 per quarter in advance. Morris plc had acquired the property for use as its administrative offices five years earlier for £2 million (the land element costing £200,000), at which time the useful life of the building was estimated at 36 years. Morris plc vacated the property on 1 January 20X3 and its fair value at that date was estimated at £3.9 million. At 31 December 20X3 the property's fair value was estimated at £3.65 million. Morris plc had not previously leased out any properties.

Requirement

Prepare an internal file note that describes and justifies the correct accounting treatment and presentation for each of the above issues.

Note: The preparation of disclosure notes is not required. **(25 marks)**

2   An entity purchased an item of machinery for £500,000 on 1 April 20X5 at which time it received a government grant of 20% of the cost of the machinery. The machinery is being depreciated at 25% per annum on the reducing balance basis.

Show how the machinery and the grant should be presented in the financial statements for the year ended 31 March 20X7 using the deferred income method. **(3 marks)**

3   **Highlife Co**

Highlife Co is a company that builds upmarket holiday resorts. It has sold some of these to third parties and it operates a number of resorts using its own brand.

On 1 July 20X4, Highlife Co borrowed £12 million at an annual interest rate of 10% to finance the purchase of land and development of a resort for its own business.

The asset was built in order to accommodate holidays starting from 1 May 20X5, although it was planned to complete construction by the end of February 20X5 to allow some margin of safety for construction overruns.

Highlife began the construction of the new resort on 1 August 20X4. Construction ceased completely for half a month to accommodate the Christmas and New Year holidays.

The resort was completed on 31 March 20X5, a month behind schedule but in time for the first paying guests. The decoration was completed a few days before the first guests arrived.

Investment income of £100,000 was earned from the temporary investment of borrowings drawn down but not yet applied to finance construction work.

Highlife has also constructed a new head office. The new head office has been financed from the pool of existing borrowings. The cost of the new office block was £2 million. Construction was started on 1 July 20X4 and was scheduled to be completed by 31 March 20X5. In fact, the building was completed on 30 June 20X5 as the company encountered geological complications with the building's foundations. It also suffered a dispute with workers over pay and work conditions which resulted in a strike. This strike caused a halt to construction for two months until it was resolved.

Pool of existing borrowings	Amount	Annual interest rate
	£	%
Bank overdraft	1,000,000	12
Bank loan	2,000,000	9
Debenture	3,000,000	6

All borrowing costs incurred in the year and income receivable from all investments have been recognised in profit or loss in the draft financial statements.

Highlife's year end is 30 June.

Requirements

(a) Explain the circumstances in which borrowing costs should be capitalised, including an explanation of how to deal with periods where no construction is taking place.

(b) Calculate the amounts to be capitalised to increase the carrying amount of the resort and the head office.

(c) Outline the effect of capitalising borrowing costs attributable to qualifying assets, as opposed to recognising them in profit or loss as incurred, on the information provided to users of financial statements.

(20 marks)

Now go back to the Learning Objectives in the Introduction. If you are satisfied you have achieved these objectives, please tick them off.

Investment properties

1 Definition

- Investment property is held to earn rentals or for capital appreciation or both — IAS 40 (5)
- Examples of investment property — IAS 40 (8)
- Examples of items which are not investment property — IAS 40 (9)
- May be possible to treat part of a property as an investment property — IAS 40 (10)

2 Recognition and measurement

- Initially at cost — IAS 40 (20)
- Then using the fair value model or the cost model — IAS 40 (30)
- If the property is held under an operating lease fair value model must be adopted — IAS 40 (34)

3 Cost model

- Cost less accumulated depreciation and impairment losses — IAS 40 (56)

4 Fair value model

- Gain or loss recognised in the profit or loss for the period — IAS 40 (35)
- Fair value should reflect market conditions at the end of the reporting period — IAS 40 (38)
- Best evidence of fair value is current prices in active market for similar property in same location and condition — IAS 40 (45)
- In the absence of current prices in an active market other information considered — IAS 40 (46)
- Assets and liabilities should not be double-counted when determining fair value — IAS 40 (50)
- Where fair value cannot be measured reliably the cost model should be adopted — IAS 40 (53)

5 Changes in use

- A change in use may lead to reclassification — IAS 40 (57)

6 Disposal

- Derecognise when disposed of or permanently withdrawn from use — IAS 40 (66)

7 Disclosure

- All investment properties — IAS 40 (75)
- Investment properties at fair value — IAS 40 (76-78)
- Investment properties at cost — IAS 40 (79)

Government grants

1 Treatment

- Should only be recognised if reasonable assurance that: IAS 20 (7)

    - Entity will comply with conditions

    - Grant will be received

- Manner in which received does not affect accounting method adopted   IAS 20 (9)

- Should be recognised in profit or loss over periods necessary to match with   IAS 20 (12)
  related costs

- Grants should not be accounted for on a cash basis   IAS 20 (16)

- Grants in recognition of specific expenses recognised in profit or loss in same   IAS 20 (17)
  period as expense

- Grants related to depreciable assets usually recognised in proportion to   IAS 20 (17)
  depreciation

- Grants related to non-depreciable assets requiring fulfilment of certain   IAS 20 (18)
  obligations recognised in profit or loss over periods which bear the cost of
  meeting obligations

- Grant received as compensation for expenses already incurred recognised in   IAS 20 (20)
  profit or loss in period in which receivable

- Non-monetary grants should be measured at fair value or at nominal amount   IAS 20 (23)

2 Presentation of grants related to assets

- Can be presented in the statement of financial position by: IAS 20 (24)

    - Setting up the grant as deferred income or

    - Netting it off against the carrying amount of the asset

IAS 20 (29)

3 Presentation of grants related to income

- Either:

    - Recognised in profit or loss separately or under a general heading or

    - Deducted in arriving at the amount of the related expense recognised in
      profit or loss

4 Repayment of government grants

- Accounted for as a change in an accounting estimate   IAS 20 (32)

5 Government assistance

- The following forms of government assistance are excluded from the definition   IAS 20 (34-35)
  of government grants:

    - Assistance which cannot reasonably have a value placed on it

    - Transactions with government which cannot be distinguished from the
      normal trading transactions of the entity

6 Disclosures

- Required disclosures   IAS 20 (39)

IAS 23 *Borrowing Costs*

- Core principle   IAS 23 (1 and 8)
- Qualifying asset   IAS 23 (5 and 7)
- Directly attributable borrowing costs   IAS 23 (10-11)
- Eligible borrowing costs   IAS 23 (12-15)
- Excess of carrying amount over recoverable amount of asset   IAS 23 (16)
- Commencement of capitalisation   IAS 23 (17-19)
- Suspension of capitalisation   IAS 23 (20-21)
- Cessation of capitalisation   IAS 23 (22-25)
- Disclosure   IAS 23 (26)

Answers to Interactive questions

Answer to Interactive question 1

(1) **Stately home**

This is a property held for sale in the ordinary course of business and is not an investment property.

(2) **Land**

This is land held for long-term capital appreciation and therefore is an investment property.

(3) **New head office**

This building is an owner-occupied property and should be dealt with under IAS 16 rather than IAS 40.

Answer to Interactive question 2

	£m
Statement of comprehensive income	
Property A (income) (24 – 18)	6
Property B (charge) (10 – 12)	(2)
	4

	£m
Statement of financial position	
Property A	24
Property B	10
	34

Answer to Interactive question 3

(a) The cost model

	£m
Net proceeds	4.00
Carrying amount 3.5 × 47/50	3.29
Profit on disposal	0.71

(b) The fair value model

	£m
Net proceeds	4.00
Fair value	4.20
Loss on disposal	(0.20)

Answer to Interactive question 4

The grant should be recognised in the same proportion as the depreciation.

(a) **Straight line**

Year	Depreciation expense £	Grant recognised in profit or loss £
1 (40 ÷ 4) and 50% thereof	10,000	5,000
2 (40 ÷ 4) and 50% thereof	10,000	5,000
3 (40 ÷ 4) and 50% thereof	10,000	5,000
4 (40 ÷ 4) and 50% thereof	10,000	5,000

(b) **Reducing balance**

Year	Depreciation expense £	Grant recognised in profit or loss £
1 (40 × 40%) and 50% thereof	16,000	8,000
2 ((40 – 16) × 40%) and 50% thereof	9,600	4,800
3 ((40 – 16 – 9.6) × 40%) and 50% thereof	5,760	2,880
4 (remainder)	8,640	4,320

Answer to Interactive question 5

As the grant is half of the cost of the asset, then the credit in respect of deferred income will be half of the annual depreciation charge.

The depreciation charge for the year ending 31 December 20X7 is £320,000 × 25% = £80,000

The release of deferred income from the grant in 20X7 (50% × depreciation) is 50% × £80,000 = £40,000

Alternative calculation:

Deferred income released £160,000 × 25% = £40,000

Answer to Interactive question 6

(1) **Nursery toys**

This is a cash grant, so it ranks as a government grant which should be recognised. As it is given as immediate financial support to the entity, it should be recognised in profit or loss immediately.

(2) **Job creation**

This is a government grant which should be recognised.

£0.25 million should be recognised in profit or loss for each year from the date the grant becomes receivable (when 50 jobs have been created). This matches the grant with the related costs. Because this does not match the cash receipts, deferred income and a receivable will appear in Years 1 and 3 respectively.

(3) **Testing equipment**

This is a grant of a non-monetary asset. The usual treatment would be to account for both grant and the asset at the fair value of the equipment and recognise the grant in profit or loss over the period the asset is depreciated.

(4) **Consulting advice**

Free technical advice is likely to be a grant which cannot reasonably have a value placed upon it. As a result it should not be recognised.

Answer to Interactive question 7

In this scenario the key dates are as follows:

- Expenditure on the acquisition is incurred on 1 February.

- Borrowing costs start to be incurred from 1 February.

- Activities to prepare the building for intended use/sale (work on planning permission) were carried out during December and January.

The earliest date when all three of these conditions were met is 1 February.

But the six-week inactive period represents an extended period when active development was suspended, so capitalisation of borrowing costs should also be suspended.

Capitalisation of borrowing costs should therefore commence from 15 March.

Answer to Interactive question 8

(a) Income statements for the year ended 31 December 20X5 and capital employed at 31 December 20X5

	Entity A £'000	Entity B £'000
Income statement		
Profit before depreciation and finance costs	300	300
Depreciation (W)	(40)	(43)
Profit before finance costs	260	257
Finance costs (800 × 10% × 3/12)	–	(20)
Profit after finance costs	260	237
Income tax	(90)	(84)
Profit for the year	170	153

	Entity A £'000	Entity B £'000
Capital employed		
Equity shares of £1	1,000	200
Retained earnings:		
(170 profit – (1,000 × 10p dividend)) and		
(153 profit – (200 × 10p dividend))	70	133
Equity	1,070	333
10% loans	–	800
	1,070	1,133

(b) Return on capital employed and comment on performance measure

		Entity A £'000	Entity B £'000
Profit before finance costs	(A)	260	257
Capital employed	(B)	1,070	1,133
Return on capital employed – (A) as % of (B)		24.3%	22.7%

Entity A's performance appears superior, but the difference is entirely driven by the method of financing its PPE. Because no imputed cost of equity is treated as part of the cost of the PPE, its capital employed is lower and its profit before interest and tax is (slightly) higher because there is no borrowing cost component within the depreciation charge.

Care therefore needs to be taken to try to identify any differences in performance which result from different financing choices (and different accounting policies if there are any), rather than from underlying trading.

Point to note:

Another key difference entirely driven by the method of financing is the respective returns on equity. Entity B's return on equity of 45.9% ((153/333) – 1) is substantially higher than Entity A's 15.9% ((170/1,070) – 1).

WORKING

Depreciation

	Entity A £'000	Entity B £'000
Paid to contractor	800	800
Borrowing costs attributable (800 × 10% × 9/12)	–	60
Total cost	800	860
Depreciation (cost ÷ 5 × 3/12)	40	43

Answers to Self-test

1 **The Holmesfield Consultancy Company**

HCC – Internal Memorandum

From: Nigel Smith
Date: 25 February 20X4
Subject: Non-current asset client issues

Introduction

This file note documents the review of seven issues relating to non-current asset accounting.

(1) Apperknowle plc

Under IAS 16 *Property, Plant and Equipment*'s revaluation model accounting policy, non-current assets are to be carried at revalued amount, being fair value at the date of revaluation less any subsequent accumulated depreciation and impairment losses.

However, when an item is revalued, the entire class to which the asset belongs should be revalued.

The fair value of an asset is usually its market value as determined by an appraisal. Professionally qualified valuers normally undertake that appraisal and though the use of internal valuers is not prohibited, it may create concern about the credibility of the valuations.

The client's revaluations are inappropriate for the following reasons.

- Assets cannot be selectively revalued on a geographical basis. All computer equipment should be revalued and to fair value. If fair value is not readily determinable, depreciated replacement cost (not replacement cost) should be used. However, IAS 16 states that this is only appropriate where the assets are specialist and do not change hands frequently, other than in business combinations. This is unlikely with computer equipment.

- In respect of the remaining assets, the revaluation is selective, as it only remeasures assets that are materially below fair value. This is not an appropriate class. All assets of a class should be revalued, so both surpluses and deficits should be recognised.

The client should be advised that classes of assets should be revalued, and not selective groups. Valuation should be at fair, that is market, value. Independent qualified valuers should be used. This prevents the selective revaluation that the client proposes.

If the client wishes to widen the scope of the revaluations, regard should be paid to the on going requirement to revalue the assets whenever carrying amount and fair value differ materially. This would create an ongoing expense.

(2) Unstone plc

IAS 23 *Borrowing Costs* requires the capitalisation as part of the cost of an asset of those borrowing costs that are directly attributable to the acquisition, construction or production of a qualifying asset. A qualifying asset is one which takes a substantial period to be ready for its intended use or sale.

It is often difficult to determine those costs that are directly attributable to the cost of an asset. However, when, as in the present case, an entity borrows funds specifically to fund the asset, the borrowing costs can be readily identified.

The amount eligible for capitalisation is determined as the actual costs incurred during the period less any investment income from the temporary investment of those funds.

The capitalisation of borrowing costs commences at the latest of when borrowing costs are being incurred, when expenditure has been incurred, and when construction activities have started. In this case 1 June 20X3 will be the commencement date.

Capitalisation ceases when substantially all of the activities required to make the asset ready for use/sale have been completed, that is on 30 September 20X3. The actual date it was brought into use is irrelevant.

Borrowing costs of £200,000 ($\frac{4}{12}$ × £10m × 6%) should be added to cost and should be depreciated.

Under IAS 16 depreciation charges should start when the asset is available for use, here for the last three months of the year.

Note:

No investment income was received from the temporary investment of the funds.

(3) **Barlow plc**

The initial measurement of property, plant and equipment should be at cost. Cost includes the purchase price, duties and non-refundable taxes, plus any direct costs of bringing the asset to the condition and location for it to be capable of operating as intended by management.

Barlow plc should exclude the following from cost.

- Recoverable taxes.

- Start-up losses, since costs should only be capitalised to the date when the asset is capable of operating in the manner intended by management. Initial operating losses are incurred after this point.

IAS 16 requires the capitalisation of pre-production testing costs but requires the deduction of the net proceeds of any samples sold when bringing the asset to that location and condition. The proceeds should not be recognised as revenue.

The cost of the asset should be recorded as £95,000 (100,000 + 10,000 – 15,000). The depreciation expense should be calculated on this cost.

(4) **Owler plc**

The treatment proposed by Owler plc was that adopted by many companies prior to the introduction of IAS 37 *Provisions, Contingent Liabilities and Contingent Assets*.

However, the need to undergo a major inspection does not give rise to a legal or constructive obligation at the end of the reporting period. Essentially, it can be avoided by sale of the helicopter. The £100,000 provision should be written back to profit or loss.

IAS 16 requires the expenditure incurred on performing periodic major inspections (to allow the continued use of an asset) to be recognised as the cost of a separate part of that item when incurred. It should then be depreciated over the period until the next inspection. If necessary, the cost of a future inspection may be treated as the cost of inspection included in the cost of the asset on original acquisition.

The £400,000 cost derived from the next inspection should be depreciated over the next four years, that is £100,000 per annum. The £4.8 million remaining balance of cost (5,200 – 400) should be depreciated over eight years, that is £600,000 per annum.

The overall effect is that the carrying amount of the helicopter should be £4.5 million (5,200 – 100 – 600) rather than £4.55 million (5,200 × $\frac{1}{8}$), there is no provision and the expense recognised in profit or loss should be £700,000 (100 + 600) rather than £650,000 (5,200 × $\frac{1}{8}$).

(5) **Hilltop plc**

IAS 16 requires each part of an item of property, plant and equipment with a cost which is significant in relation to the total cost to be depreciated separately, although parts with the same useful life and depreciation method may be grouped.

The depreciation expense for the year should be:

Part (Cost in £'000)	Useful life	Depreciation £'000
Basic aeroplane (1,200)	20 years	60
Engines (400)	8 years	50
Interior (400)	5 years	80
		190

Hence, the depreciation expense should be increased from £100,000 to £190,000. This will reduce reported profits. Hilltop plc should also keep more detailed records of the components of cost.

(6) **Cowley plc**

When a decision is made to dispose of a non-current asset, IFRS 5 *Non-current Assets Held for Sale and Discontinued Activities* requires the asset to be classified as held for sale, with no further depreciation expense being recognised. If the asset is one accounted for under the revaluation model accounting policy, then:

- It should be remeasured to fair value immediately prior to such classification, with any gain or loss being accounted for under IAS 16 in other comprehensive income, taking account of any balance relating to it held in revaluation surplus

- Its carrying amount should then be adjusted to fair value less costs to sell, with the costs to sell being recognised as an impairment loss in profit or loss.

IAS 16 then requires the gain or loss on ultimate disposal to be calculated as the difference between the net disposal proceeds and the (post-revaluation) carrying amount of the asset at the time of disposal. At the same time the balance relating to it in revaluation surplus should be transferred to retained earnings through the statement of changes in equity.

Thus, at 18 June 20X3 this piece of machinery should be revalued to £1.6 million and £400,000 (1.6m – 1.2m) added to the revaluation surplus. The £50,000 estimated costs to sell should be recognised as an expense in profit or loss, reducing the carrying amount of the asset to £1.55 million.

On 31 December the asset was disposed of for £50,000 (1.6m – 1.55m) more than its carrying amount, a gain which should be recognised in profit or loss. (The net effect on profit or loss is £nil, this profit offsetting the previous impairment loss.) The £700,000 held in revaluation surplus should be transferred to retained earnings through the statement of changes in equity. This part of the gain should not be reclassified from other comprehensive income to profit or loss.

The £700,000 gain currently recognised in profit or loss should be cancelled out.

(7) **Morris plc**

On 1 January 20X3 when the property was vacated by Morris plc and leased out, it should be reclassified from property, plant and equipment to investment property and accounted for under IAS 40 *Investment Property*. Because it has not previously leased out any properties, Morris should then adopt as its accounting policy one of the two options permitted under IAS 40.

Under the cost model depreciation should continue to be recognised in respect of the building element of the property's original cost, so (£2 million – £200,000) ÷ 36 = £50,000 for the year. The carrying amount at 31 December 20X3, taking account of the depreciation accumulated over 6 years, should be measured at £1.7 million (£2 million – (6 × £50,000)). The property's period end fair value of £3.65 million should be disclosed by way of note. Rental income of £400,000 should be recognised in profit or loss for the year, together with the £50,000 depreciation expense.

Under the fair value model the property should be remeasured at fair value at 1 January 20X3. At that date the property's carrying amount is £1.75 million (£2 million – (5 × £50,000)) and the surplus of £2.15 million (£3.9 million – £1.75 million) should be recognised as a revaluation surplus under IAS 16, so in other comprehensive income. No depreciation should be recognised under this model but the decrease in fair value over the year of £250,000 (£3.9 million – £3.65 million) should be recognised in profit or loss, along with the rental income of £400,000.

Conclusion

Each issue requires the respective client to adjust its financial statements. Discussions should be undertaken immediately to confirm the facts and brief each client on the potential adjustments and issues.

2   Note that 20X7 is the second year of the asset's ownership, so at 1 April 20X6 the carrying amounts of both the asset and the deferred income will have been reduced to 75% of their initial amounts.

Income statement extract – year ended 31 March 20X7

	£
Depreciation ((£500,000 × 75%) × 25%)	(93,750)
Government grant income ((£100,000 × 75%) × 25%)	18,750

Statement of financial position extract – as at 31 March 20X7

	£
Non-current assets	
Machinery (£500,000 × 75% × 75%)	281,250
Non-current liabilities	
Deferred income (£100,000 × 75% × 75% × 75%)	42,187
Current liabilities	
Deferred income (£100,000 × 75% × 75% × 25%)	14,063

3   **Highlife Co**

(a)   IAS 23 *Borrowing Costs* requires all borrowing costs which are directly attributable to the acquisition, construction or production of a qualifying asset to be capitalised, ie recognised as forming part of the cost of the asset.

The borrowing costs to be capitalised are the costs incurred to finance construction of that particular asset. (This is easiest to demonstrate where a loan has been taken out specifically to finance construction of an asset.) Capitalisation is restricted to periods when construction is actually taking place (see below). The amount to be capitalised is reduced by any interest earned on the temporary investment of surplus funds borrowed to finance construction of a particular asset.

Where there is no clear link between an individual loan and construction of a particular asset (that is where construction is financed from a pool of borrowing to finance the business), the capitalisation rate for determining the borrowing costs to be capitalised should be the weighted average of the borrowing costs applicable to borrowings during the period. (Borrowings made specifically for a qualifying asset and their borrowing costs should be excluded from the calculation.) There is a limit on the amount capitalised, in that it should not exceed the total borrowing costs incurred in the period.

Capitalisation should commence when three conditions are all met: expenditures are incurred for the asset, borrowing costs are incurred and activities necessary to prepare the asset for sale/use are being carried out. 'Activities' include activities such as applying for planning consent, rather than just the physical construction itself. Capitalisation should end when the activities needed to prepare the asset for its intended use or sale are substantially completed.

Capitalisation should be suspended, and any borrowing costs incurred recognised as an expense in profit or loss, during any extended period where development is unexpectedly interrupted. For example, if construction of a project near tidal water is halted because of high tides, borrowing costs incurred in this period would continue to be capitalised, since the occurrence of high tides would have been anticipated during the planning stage of the construction.

(b) **Resort**

Key dates:

Borrowing started	1 July 20X4
Construction started	1 August 20X4
Construction completed	31 March 20X5

The cessation for the Christmas holidays is normal and unavoidable. This would not cause a suspension in borrowing costs. Construction started on 1 August 20X4 and presumably planning consents would have been sought before this, meaning that capitalisation should have started earlier than 1 August 20X4. It is easiest to use the date given for commencement of construction work. Capitalisation should run from 1 August 20X4 to 31 March 20X5 (eight months).

	£
8/12 × 10% × £12 million	800,000
Less: investment income	(100,000)
Net amount capitalised	700,000

Head office

The weighted average cost of borrowings should be calculated as:

$$\frac{(£1m \times 12\%) + (£2m \times 9\%) + (£3m \times 6\%)}{£6m \text{ total pool}} = 8\%$$

Interest per annum on construction project = 8% × £2 million cost of office building = £160,000

However, the two month period when industrial action halted construction should not be capitalised.

The amount to be capitalised: 10/12 × £160,000 = £133,333

(c) **Effect of capitalisation on information provided**

Recognition of borrowing costs in profit and loss as incurred has the effect of writing them off immediately. The effect of capitalisation is that:

- Profitability

  In the period in which capitalisation is made, non-current assets and retained earnings within equity are increased by the amount capitalised. Capital employed (equity + interest-bearing liabilities) is increased (by the increase in equity), so the return on capital employed (ROCE) goes down.

  Point to note:

  Because ROCE is calculated as profit **before interest** and tax as a percentage of capital employed, the profit figure is not changed by the capitalisation of borrowing costs.

  ROCE will also go down in subsequent periods, as the interest capitalised is recognised as part of the depreciation charge on the asset and depreciation is charged in arriving at profit before interest and tax.

  So the effect of capitalisation is to reduce the profitability of Highlife.

- Gearing

  Because equity is increased without any change in interest-bearing liabilities, gearing (interest-bearing liabilities as a percentage of equity) will be reduced and Highlife will appear more solvent.

- Cash flow

  Cash flows are unchanged as a result of a policy of capitalisation, so there is no effect on Highlife's cash flows.

Point to note:

IAS 23 no longer allows a choice of accounting treatment. However, the effect of capitalisation on an entity's financial information may be one factor that management consider when deciding how to finance the purchase or construction of a qualifying asset.

CHAPTER 5

Leases

Introduction

Examination context

Topic List

1　Overview of material covered in Financial Accounting

2　Lessor accounting: finance lease

3　Lessor accounting: operating lease

4　Sale and leaseback transactions

5　Operating lease incentives

6　Judgements required

7　Relevance of information for users

8　UK GAAP comparison

Summary and Self-test

Technical reference

Answers to Interactive questions

Answers to Self-test

Learning objectives

- Prepare and present extracts of financial statements in respect of lessee accounting, lessor accounting and sale and leaseback agreements ☐

- Formulate accounting and reporting policies in respect of different lease transactions ☐

- Illustrate how different methods of recognising and measuring lease transactions can affect the view presented ☐

- Explain and illustrate the main differences between international and UK requirements ☐

- Identify and consider appropriate actions for ethical issues involving lease transactions ☐

Specific syllabus references for this chapter are: 1e, 2a, 2b, 3a, 4a and 4c.

Syllabus links

You have covered the basic accounting treatment of a finance lease and an operating lease from the perspective of a lessee in your Financial Accounting studies. This chapter looks at the remaining aspects of IAS 17 *Leases*: lessor accounting and sale and leaseback transactions. A detailed knowledge of all aspects of IAS 17 will be assumed at the Advanced Stage.

Examination context

In the examination, candidates may be required to:

- Explain lessor accounting and illustrate it by preparing extracts from financial statements

- Explain the accounting treatment of sale and leaseback transactions and illustrate it by preparing extracts from financial statements

- Formulate reporting policies for lease related transactions

- Interpret results including the effects of leasing transactions

- Explain and illustrate the differences between the relevant treatment under IFRS and UK GAAP

- Identify and explain the judgements to be made relating to the classification and treatment of leases and sale and leaseback transactions

1 Overview of material covered in Financial Accounting

Section overview

- This section revises the material covered in Financial Accounting in respect of lessees under IAS 17 *Leases*.

- A lease is an agreement whereby the lessor (legal owner) conveys to the lessee (user) in return for a payment or series of payments **the right to use an asset** for an agreed period of time.

- A finance lease is a lease that **transfers** from lessor to lessee **substantially all the risks and rewards incidental to ownership** of an asset. Title may or may not eventually be transferred.

- An operating lease is a lease **other than a finance lease**.

- The classification of a lease depends on the **substance** of the transaction rather than the form of the contract.

  Classification is made at the **inception of the lease**, not the commencement of the lease term

- There are a number of factors which would normally lead to a lease being classified as a **finance lease**, two of the most important being:

  – The lease term is for the major part of the economic life of the asset

  – At the inception of the lease the present value of the minimum lease payments amounts to at least substantially all of the fair value of the leased asset

- The **land and buildings** elements of a lease of land and buildings should be **assessed separately** for classification purposes.

  The two elements should be measured by reference to their shares of the fair value of the leasehold interests

1.1 Lease accounting

A finance lease and an operating lease should be recognised in the financial statements of the lessee as follows:

Finance lease	Operating lease
Statement of financial position	**Statement of financial position**
An amount **equal to the fair value**, or if lower, the **present value of the minimum lease payments**, determined at the **inception** of the lease, is: • Recognised as a non-current asset • Recognised as a liability	No capitalisation Recognise a prepayment/accrual to the extent the lease payments do not match expense recognised in profit or loss
Income statement	**Income statement**
Recognise a **depreciation charge** Recognise a **finance charge** (allocated using actuarial method or sum of digits method)	Recognise lease payments on a **straight-line basis over the lease term**
Statement of cash flows	**Statement of cash flows**
The **interest** portion is presented within interest paid, usually as an **adjustment to cash generated from operations** under cash flows from **operating activities** The **capital** portion is presented as a separate item under cash flows from **financing activities**	Lease payments are deducted **in computing cash generated from operations** under cash flows from **operating activities**

C
H
A
P
T
E
R

5

Interactive question 1: Finance lease [Difficulty level: Easy]

A company leased an asset on 1 January 20X7. The terms of the finance lease were a non-refundable deposit of £2,000 followed by four annual payments of £2,000 commencing on 31 December 20X7. The fair value of the asset (equivalent to the present value of the minimum lease payments) on 1 January 20X7 was £7,710.

Calculate the interest charge in the income statement and the finance lease liability in the statement of financial position for the year ended 31 December 20X7 using the following methods:

(a) Actuarial method, where the interest rate implicit in the lease is 15%.

(b) Sum of digits method.

(c) Sum of digits method assuming that payments are made annually in advance commencing 1 January 20X7.

(a) **Actuarial method**

£

Income statement (extract)
Finance costs (working)

Statement of financial position (extract)
Non-current liabilities
Finance lease liability (working)

Current liabilities
Finance lease liability (working)

WORKINGS

(b) **Sum of digits method**

£

Income statement (extract)
Finance costs (working)

Statement of financial position (extract)
Non-current liabilities
Finance lease liability (working)

Current liabilities
Finance lease liability (working)

WORKINGS

(c) **Sum of digits method (payments in advance)**

£

Income statement (extract)
Finance costs (working)

Statement of financial position (extract)
Non-current liabilities
Finance lease liability (working)

Current liabilities
Finance lease liability (working)

WORKINGS

See **Answer** at the end of this chapter.

Interactive question 2: Land and buildings [Difficulty level: Intermediate]

On 1 January 20X8 an entity acquired a land and buildings lease with a term of 30 years at an annual rental of £50,000 payable in advance. Other details of the lease were as follows:

*   The useful life of the building was 30 years.

*   The interest rate implicit in the lease was 7.5% and the present value of £50,000 per annum payable in advance over 30 years was £630,000.

*   The fair value of the leasehold interest was £660,000, of which £66,000 is attributable to the land element.

Calculate the amounts to be recognised in the entity's income statement for the year ended 31 December 20X8 and its statement of financial position at that date.

See **Answer** at the end of this chapter.

1.2 Context for IAS 17

Lease finance is a common route to acquiring operating assets. It provides an efficient method of acquiring the use of assets whilst preserving capital resources and can be used for a wide range of short and long-term financing arrangements.

The classification of leases is a particularly sensitive issue for corporate entities. If leases are capitalised in the statement of financial position, an entity's financial gearing will increase and this may have adverse consequences on other key ratios, such as return on capital employed and interest cover. The level of perceived risk may increase, loan covenants may be compromised and an entity's future borrowing capacity may be restricted.

Lease classification issues have featured on accounting standard setters' agendas over many years. Published guidance has revolved around the substance of the transactions rather than their legal form. Nevertheless, opportunities still exist for innovative lease arrangements to be developed that result in financing not being recognised in the statement of financial position. UK studies have revealed that average operating lease commitments are over ten times that of reported finance lease obligations.

2 Lessor accounting: finance lease

Section overview

- The asset subject to the lease is derecognised and the entitlement to receive lease payments is recognised as a receivable.

- The receivable is shown at the net investment in the lease.

- Finance income is added to the receivable, normally being allocated using the actuarial method.

- Lease payments received will represent a reduction in the amount receivable.

- Manufacturer and dealer lessors are treated as a special case.

2.1 Accounting treatment

- In principle, accounting for a finance lease by a lessor is a **mirror image** of the entries made by the lessee.

- In substance the lessor **has transferred the risks and rewards of ownership** of the leased asset to the lessee, so the non-current asset should be **derecognised**.

- Instead, the asset to be recognised in the lessor's books is the **entitlement to receive lease payments from the lessee**. The impact on the financial statements is as follows:

Statement of financial position	Income statement
The **capital sum** receivable is shown as a **financial asset**.	The interest element of the payments made by the lessee is recognised as **finance income** over the lease term.

2.2 Initial recognition

The receivable balance in the lessor's statement of financial position is initially measured at the **net investment in the lease**.

Definition

Net investment in the lease: The gross investment in the lease discounted at the interest rate implicit in the lease.

Gross investment in the lease: The aggregate of:

- The minimum lease payments receivable by the lessor under a finance lease, and
- Any unguaranteed residual value accruing to the lessor.

Minimum lease payments: Payments contractually due from the lessee, including any residual value guaranteed by the lessee or a party related to the lessee.

Unguaranteed residual value: That portion of the residual value of the leased asset, the realisation of which by the lessor is not assured or is guaranteed solely by a party related to the lessor.

Interest rate implicit in the lease: The discount rate that, at the inception of the lease, causes the present value of the gross investment of the lease to be equal to the sum of (i) the fair value of the leased asset and (ii) any initial direct costs of the lessor.

Points to note:

1   The lessor will take the unguaranteed residual value into account in setting the terms of the lease.

2   The definition of the interest rate implicit in the lease is the same as for lessee accounting.

The definition works so as to automatically take account of initial direct costs incurred by the lessor, for example commissions, legal fees and internal costs.

3   Initial direct costs exclude general overheads, for example marketing costs.

Worked example: Gross investment

Wilton Ltd purchased a lorry from Trucks Ltd for £50,000 and leased it to Freight Ltd on a four year lease requiring annual payments in arrears of £13,500. Trucks Ltd has agreed to buy the lorry back at open market value at the end of the lease. Freight Ltd has guaranteed that the value of the lorry after four years will be not less than £6,000. A realistic estimate of its open market value in four years is £9,000.

What is Wilton Ltd's gross investment in the lease at the start of the lease?

Solution

At the start of the lease the 'minimum lease payments' are the rentals due of £54,000 (4 × £13,500) plus the guaranteed residual of £6,000 giving £60,000. Trucks Ltd has agreed to buy the lorry back at an amount estimated at £9,000. £3,000 (£9,000 – 6,000) is the 'unguaranteed residual value', so gross investment in the lease is £63,000.

Point to note:

IAS 17 requires disclosure of the unguaranteed residual values, precisely because they are unguaranteed and may turn out not to be realisable.

2.3   Subsequent measurement

- The receivable is **reduced** by the regular **lease payments**, but **increased** by the **finance income** recognised in profit or loss each period over the lease term.

- The recognition of finance income should be based on a pattern reflecting **a constant periodic rate of return on the lessor's net investment in the finance lease**.

- This normally involves the use of the **actuarial method** which provides the most accurate reflection of the constant rate of return on the net investment.

Point to note:

IAS 17 does not refer to the use of methods of approximation, for example sum of digits, as it does for lessee accounting. Therefore, this method should not be used.

Interactive question 3: Lessor accounting   [Difficulty level: Exam standard]

Snow Ltd leased an asset to Flake Ltd on the following terms:

Lease term	four years
Inception of lease	1 January 20X6
Annual payments in advance	£22,000
Residual value of asset guaranteed by lessee	£10,000
Expected residual value at end of lease	£12,000
Fair value of the asset	£82,966
Initial direct costs incurred by the lessor	£700
Interest rate implicit in the lease	11%

Requirements

(a) Calculate the unguaranteed residual value and the net investment in the lease as at 1 January 20X6.

(b) Prepare extracts from the financial statements of the lessor for the year ended 31 December 20X6 (excluding notes).

Solution

(a) Unguaranteed residual value and net investment in the lease at 1 January 20X6

(b) Financial statement extracts

£

Income statement (extract)
Finance income (working)

Statement of financial position (extract)
Non-current assets
Finance lease receivable (working)

Current assets
Finance lease receivable (working)

WORKING – net investment in finance lease:

See **Answer** at the end of this chapter.

2.4 Finance lease: manufacturer and dealer lessors

2.4.1 Context

- Special consideration is needed of:

    - Manufacturers who lease out assets they have made
    - Dealers who acquire assets to lease to third parties

- The cost of the leased asset to its manufacturer is its manufactured cost, while a dealer would expect to acquire the leased asset at a substantial discount to its retail price. In neither case will cost reflect the asset's fair value.

- Such entities generally offer assets either for outright purchase or for use under arrangements whereby the entities themselves provide a form of financing. Motor dealers commonly do this.

- The issue is whether the manufacturer or dealer should recognise a normal profit at the outset, and, if so, how should that profit be calculated.

2.4.2 Requirements

- Manufacturers and dealers offering finance leases should recognise separately

    - A normal selling profit as if from an outright sale, based on the normal selling price
    - Finance income over the lease term

- The revenue to be recognised at the lease commencement should be measured as the lower of the fair value of the asset and the present value of the minimum lease payments computed at a market interest rate.

- The cost of sale to be recognised at the lease commencement should be measured as the lower of cost of the asset, or its carrying amount if different, less the present value of any unguaranteed residual value.

- Manufacturers/dealers should recognise costs incurred in negotiating and setting up the lease as an expense at the lease commencement, because these costs are mainly related to earning the selling profit.

Point to note:

A market rate of interest should be applied to the minimum lease payments to measure present value. Otherwise the manufacturer/dealer could manipulate an artificially high profit at commencement by quoting an artificially low rate of interest.

Interactive question 4: Dealer   [Difficulty level: Exam standard]

On 1 July 20X6 a dealer sold a car for £26,250, payable either on delivery or by three annual payments in advance. As 0% finance was offered, the annual payment under the lease was £8,750. The dealer purchased the car from the manufacturer for £21,000. A market rate of interest was 8%. The purchaser chose the interest-free option.

Requirement

What amounts should the dealer recognise in profit or loss for the year ending 30 June 20X7 and in its statement of financial position at that date?

See **Answer** at the end of this chapter.

3 Lessor accounting: operating lease

Section overview

- The asset subject to the lease is not derecognised and is depreciated over its useful life.

- Income should be recognised on a straight-line basis over the period of the lease unless there is a more systematic and rational basis.

3.1 Accounting treatment

An asset leased out under an operating lease should be accounted for as follows:

- **Recognised as an asset** of the lessor according to its nature. This is because the risks and rewards of ownership have not been transferred to the lessee.

  For example, an item of PPE should be recognised and depreciated in accordance with IAS 16 *Property, Plant and Equipment*.

- **Impairment reviews** should be conducted in accordance with IAS 36 *Impairment of Assets*.

- Income from an operating lease, excluding charges for services such as insurance and maintenance, should be recognised **on a straight-line basis** over the period of the lease term (even if receipts are not made on this basis). If another **systematic and rational basis** is more representative of the time pattern in which benefit from the leased asset is receivable, this should be used.

- Initial direct costs incurred by lessors in negotiating and arranging an operating lease should be added to the carrying amount of the leased asset and recognised as an expense over the lease term.

  For an asset leased out under an operating lease the lease term is, by definition, shorter than the asset's useful life (if it was the same, the lease would be a finance lease). Initial direct costs relate to a particular lease, so they should be recognised as an expense over the lease term, not the asset's life.

Worked example: Operating lease

An entity acquired a new car with a view to renting it out over two years and then disposing of it. The car cost £20,000 on 1 July 20X7 and the residual value at the end of two years was estimated at £6,000.

On that date the entity rented the car out on a one-year lease and the payments of £1,000 due monthly in advance were all received on time. The cost of negotiating the lease was estimated at £400.

What amounts should be recognised in the entity's statement of financial position at 31 December 20X7 and its income statement for the year ended on that date?

Solution

	£
Statement of financial position – non-current assets	
Cost (20,000 + 400 initial direct costs written off over the lease term)	20,400
Depreciation (((20,000 – 6,000) × 6/24) + (400 × 6/12))	(3,700)
Carrying amount	16,700
Income statement	
Rental receivable (6 × 1,000)	6,000
Depreciation of non-current assets	(3,700)

3.2 Manufacturer and dealer lessors

A lessor who is a manufacturer or dealer **should not recognise any selling profit** on entering into an operating lease because the risks and rewards of ownership have not been transferred to the lessee.

4 Sale and leaseback transactions

Section overview

- A sale and leaseback may result in:
    - A sale and finance leaseback
    - A sale and operating leaseback

- The accounting for a sale and finance leaseback results in any profit being recognised over the lease term.

- The accounting for a sale and operating leaseback depends on the relationship between the sale price and fair value.

4.1 Introduction

Companies can raise finance in a number of different ways. These include short-term measures such as a bank overdraft, medium-term measures such as loans or finance leases and longer-term measures including secured loans.

Another option is a **sale and leaseback transaction**. This is a common feature of certain industries, including retail and hotels. It involves **the original owner of the asset selling it**, typically to a finance house or bank, **and immediately leasing it back**, thereby raising cash and retaining the use of the asset. Such arrangements provide entities with the opportunity to release capital caught up in the business for investment in other opportunities or to return it to shareholders. In essence, an entity acquires cash in exchange for a commitment to make regular lease payments without losing use of the asset.

The sale and leaseback transaction can result in either **a finance lease** or **an operating lease**, as determined by applying the principle of substance over form. As the accounting treatment depends on this categorisation, **this decision is critical**.

4.2 Sale and leaseback as a finance lease

This transaction is essentially a financing arrangement. The seller (who is subsequently the lessee) does not dispose of the risks and rewards of ownership (because the leaseback is through a finance lease) and no profit should be recognised immediately on disposal.

The accounting entries are:

- Derecognise the carrying amount of the asset now sold

- Recognise the sales proceeds

- Calculate the profit on sale as proceeds less carrying amount and recognise it as deferred income

- Recognise the finance lease asset and the associated liability and measure them in the normal way (at the lower of fair value and the present value of the minimum lease payments)

- Amortise the profit on sale as income over the lease term

The effect is to adjust the expense recognised in profit or loss to an amount equal to the depreciation expense before the leaseback transaction.

Point to note:

If the carrying amount exceeds fair value, the asset should be written down to fair value prior to the sale and leaseback and the loss recognised as an impairment loss.

Interactive question 5: Sale and finance leaseback
[Difficulty level: Intermediate]

Frayn plc entered into a sale and finance leaseback arrangement on 1 January 20X1, when:

- The carrying amount of the asset was £70,000
- The sale proceeds were at fair value of £120,000
- The remaining useful life of the asset was five years.

The lease provided for five annual rentals of £30,000 payable in arrears on 31 December of each year. The interest rate implicit in the lease was 8% and the present value of the minimum lease payments was £120,000.

Requirement

Set out the journal entries at the date of disposal and calculate the amounts to be recognised in profit or loss in the year to 31 December 20X1 and in the statement of financial position at that date.

See **Answer** at the end of this chapter.

Because of IAS 36's provisions in respect of impairment testing, any excess of an asset's carrying amount over fair value should be recognised as an impairment loss **before** the sale and finance leaseback transaction is accounted for.

4.3 Sale and leaseback as an operating lease

Some businesses arrange sales and operating leasebacks to give them the capital to build a replacement asset while occupying the original one for a short period of time. For example, a football club might sell its stadium and then lease it back for just one year, using the sale proceeds to fund the construction over that year of its new stadium.

The substance of the transaction is that **a sale has taken place** both in terms of the legal transfer of ownership and because the risks and rewards of ownership are not subsequently substantially reacquired when the leaseback is an operating lease. There is a genuine profit or loss to be recognised.

If the **sale price is at fair value**, the profit or loss measured as proceeds (fair value) less carrying amount should be recognised immediately in profit or loss.

If **the sale is different from fair value** (possibly for one of the reasons set out below), different rules apply.

- If the sale price is below fair value **and future lease payments are at market levels**, any profit or loss shall be recognised immediately.

  Even though lease payments are set at market levels, the sale price might be below fair value because the entity is desperate for cash, and so accepts a low sale price to alleviate its liquidity problems. Under these circumstances it is appropriate that the whole loss on disposal should be immediately recognised.

- If the sale price is below fair value **and** the loss is compensated for by **future lease payments at below market levels**, the loss should be deferred and amortised in proportion to the lease payments over the period for which the asset is expected to be used.

- If the sale price is above fair value, the excess over fair value should be deferred and amortised over the period for which the asset is expected to be used.

The following table summarises these rules.

Sale price at fair value

	Carrying amount equal to fair value	Carrying amount below fair value	Carrying amount above fair value
Profit	No profit	Recognise profit immediately	N/A
Loss	No loss	N/A	Recognise loss immediately

Sale price below fair value

	Carrying amount equal to fair value	Carrying amount below fair value	Carrying amount above fair value
Profit	No profit	Recognise profit immediately	No profit (Note 1)
Loss not compensated for by future lease rentals below market rate	Recognise loss immediately	Recognise loss immediately	(Note 1)
Loss compensated for by future lease rentals below market rate	Defer and amortise loss	Defer and amortise loss	(Note 1)

Sale price above fair value

	Carrying amount equal to fair value	Carrying amount below fair value	Carrying amount above fair value
Profit	Defer and amortise profit	Defer and amortise (sale price less fair value) Recognise immediately (fair value less carrying amount)	Defer and amortise profit (Note 2)
Loss	No loss	No loss	(Note 1)

Note 1

IAS 17 requires the carrying amount of an asset to be written down to fair value where it is subject to a sale and leaseback.

Note 2

Profit is the difference between fair value and sale price because the carrying amount would have been written down to fair value in accordance with IAS 17.

Interactive question 6: Sale and operating leaseback   [Difficulty level: Intermediate]

Six different companies each sell an asset and immediately enter into an operating leaseback for five years. There are different sets of circumstances with respect to each asset for the six companies:

	Carrying amount £	Proceeds generated £	Fair value £
Company (1)	360,000	300,000	400,000
Company (2)	400,000	300,000	360,000
Company (3)	300,000	360,000	400,000
Company (4)	300,000	400,000	360,000
Company (5)	360,000	400,000	300,000
Company (6)	400,000	360,000	300,000

Requirement

Assess the impact of the sale and operating leaseback arrangement on profit or loss for each of the six companies for all years affected by the arrangement.

See **Answer** at the end of this chapter.

5 Operating lease incentives

Section overview

Operating lease incentives should be recognised on a straight-line basis over the lease term.

5.1 Basic issue

Operating lease incentives are dealt with by SIC 15 *Operating Lease – Incentives*.

In negotiating a new or renewed operating lease, the lessor may provide **incentives** for the lessee to enter into the agreement. Examples of such incentives are:

- An up-front payment to the lessee
- The reimbursement of costs of the lessee
- Initial rent-free or reduced rent periods

All incentives for the agreement of a new or renewed operating lease should be **recognised as an integral part of the net amount agreed** for the use of the leased asset, **irrespective of the incentive's nature, form or the timing of payments.**

5.2 Treatment

The lessor	Should normally recognise the aggregate cost of incentives **as a reduction of rental income over the lease term, on a straight-line basis**
The lessee	Should normally recognise the aggregate benefit of incentives **as a reduction of rental expense over the lease term, on a straight-line basis**

Interactive question 7: Operating lease incentives   **[Difficulty level: Easy]**

On 1 January 20X7 Whittaker Ltd entered into an operating lease for a retail unit. Lease payments were £4,000 per month in advance for a period of five years. As an incentive however, Whittaker Ltd was given the first five months as a rent-free period.

Requirement

Calculate the operating lease expense which should be recognised in Whittaker Ltd's income statement for the year ended 31 December 20X7 and any amounts to be recognised in its statement of financial position at that date.

See **Answer** at the end of this chapter.

6 Judgements required

Section overview

This section explains the need for Chartered Accountants to use professional judgement when classifying lease arrangements.

The classification of lease arrangements as operating or finance leases requires professional judgement. IAS 17 sets out qualitative criteria for the classification and management's application of these criteria can have significant effects on the level of reported debt. This may change the perceived risk. Chartered Accountants must use their professional judgement to make the appropriate classifications. They must not be swayed by pressure from non-financial management or for personal gain.

The classification of sale and leaseback arrangements is particularly important. The accounting treatment could involve the recognition of a profit and the derecognition of assets from the statement of financial position. Favourable treatments can significantly improve key performance ratios of an entity. An entity which keeps debt off its statement of financial position by the use of operating leases will have a greater borrowing capacity than a similar entity which classifies a lease as a finance lease, because the former's existing debts appear to be lower.

7 Relevance of information for users

Section overview

This section details IAS 17's requirements regarding lessors' disclosure in their financial statements.

Users are provided with relevant information by IAS 17's requirement that lessors disclose in their financial statements:

- Unearned finance income: useful in the forecasting of future revenue

- Contingent rents recognised as income: these are lease payments which vary (other than with time) and may therefore not be achieved at the same level in the future. Contingent rents are a feature of the retail industry, where the lessor shares in the success (or otherwise) of the lessee by being entitled to a percentage of the lessee's gross revenue (this will be in addition to the fixed amounts of lease payments set down in the lease)

- An analysis of the amounts receivable in both gross and present value terms over specified future periods, such as the one provided by Lloyds Banking Group in its 2010 financial statements:

Receivable in	Gross investment £m	Net investment £m
Not later than one year	1,358	986
Later than one year but not later than five years	2,522	1,965
Later than five years	7,218	5,340
	11,098	8,291
Unearned finance income	(2,603)	
Other adjustments, including expenditure to be incurred on leased assets	(204)	
Carrying amount	8,291	

More generally, the proper recognition of operating and finance leases in financial statements is crucial to the provision of information relevant to decision making. Compared to classification as an operating lease, the initial classification of a lease as a finance lease:

- Increases capital employed, through the recognition of the leased asset

- Increases borrowings through the recognition of the lease liability

- Almost certainly reduces overall profit (or increases loss) in the early years, because the actuarial method of recognising finance charges allocates more interest to the early years of a lease and less to the later. The total of depreciation and interest in the early years will exceed the charge for operating lease rentals.

So return on capital employed falls and gearing rises, results which are usually not attractive to managers but are very relevant to users of financial statements.

Point to note:

As always, overall cash flows do not change as a result of accruals accounting rules, in this case the rules for lease classification. But the presentation of cash flows for each of the two types of lease (see section 1.1 above) is different, so classification as a finance lease improves the cash generated from operations.

8 UK GAAP comparison

Section overview

The UK GAAP equivalent standard to IAS 17 is SSAP 21 *Accounting for Leases and Hire Purchase Contracts.*

8.1 Summary of differences

In broad terms IAS 17 and SSAP 21 are **very similar**. For example:

- They both make the distinction between finance leases and operating leases
- Both focus on the 'risks and rewards' principle
- Interest is calculated and allocated under SSAP 21 in the same way as under IAS 17

SSAP 21	IAS 17
SSAP 21 states that the transfer of risks and rewards of ownership can be **presumed** if at the inception of the lease the present value of the minimum lease payments amounts to **substantially all (normally 90% or more)** of the fair value of the leased asset. There is the **rebuttable presumption** that if:	IAS 17 lists a **number of factors** which would indicate that the risks and rewards of ownership have been transferred, that is that the substance of an arrangement is a finance lease.
• The present value **reaches the 90% level,** the lease is a **finance lease**	
• The present value **does not reach 90%** the lease is an **operating lease**	
This presumption is only overruled (and other factors, such as those in IAS 17) taken into account 'in exceptional circumstances'.	
So the UK standard allows less judgement than IAS 17.	
Under SSAP 21 the lease of **land and buildings is considered as one lease** and is normally treated as an **operating lease**. The non-mandatory Guidance Notes state that this is because a lease is often for only a small part of the useful life of the building. In addition because a lease usually provides for regular rent reviews, the rent is regularly brought up to current market rates. The lease therefore has the characteristics of a provision of a service rather than a financing arrangement.	IAS 17 requires a separate assessment of the **land and buildings elements**, which usually results in the land element being classified as an operating lease.

Worked example: Land and buildings

Under UK GAAP how should the 30 year lease described in Interactive question 2 be accounted for?

Solution

The whole lease should be classified as an operating lease. As the period covered by each annual rental is the same as the financial year, there will be no accrual or prepayment.

So recognise operating lease rentals of £50,000 in the profit and loss account; there is nothing to be presented in the balance sheet.

Point to note:

On the information given, the financial consequences of classification as an operating lease are limited: a level-spread annual expense and nothing in the balance sheet. Compare this with the consequences of classification as a finance lease: the answer to Interactive question 2 shows charges to profit or loss totalling £63,050 (5,000 + 18,900 + 39,150) and borrowings in the statement of financial position of £561,150. So a higher expense (which will in due course come to be lower than £50,000 as the finance charge reduces as a result of capital repayments) and a direct effect on gearing.

UK GAAP	IAS
A lessor should allocate total gross earnings under a finance lease to accounting periods so as to give a constant periodic rate of return on the lessor's **net cash investment** in the lease in the period. The net cash investment is the **net investment** adjusted for other cash flows associated with it, the most important being the tax effects.	Under IAS 17 the allocation should result in a constant periodic rate of return on the lessor's **net investment**, so no account is taken of the other cash flows associated.
Operating lease rental incentives should be spread over the **shorter** of the **lease term** and the period until the **next rent review**.	Any incentives should be spread over the whole lease term.

Summary and Self-test

Summary

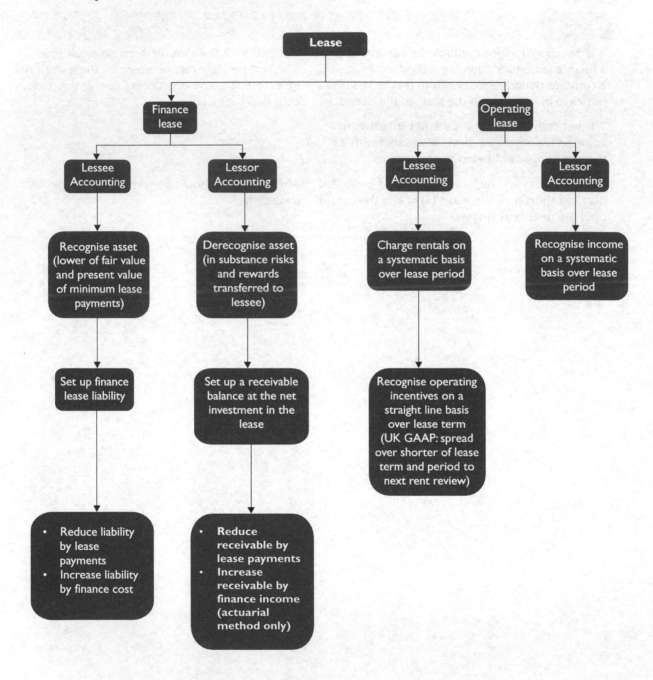

```
                              Lease
                    ┌───────────┴───────────┐
              Finance                    Operating
               lease                       lease
        ┌────────┴────────┐        ┌─────────┴─────────┐
     Lessee            Lessor    Lessee            Lessor
   Accounting        Accounting Accounting       Accounting
        │                 │         │                 │
```

Lessee Accounting (Finance lease)	Lessor Accounting (Finance lease)	Lessee Accounting (Operating lease)	Lessor Accounting (Operating lease)
Recognise asset (lower of fair value and present value of minimum lease payments)	Derecognise asset (in substance risks and rewards transferred to lessee)	Charge rentals on a systematic basis over lease period	Recognise income on a systematic basis over lease period
Set up finance lease liability	Set up a receivable balance at the net investment in the lease	Recognise operating incentives on a straight line basis over lease term (UK GAAP: spread over shorter of lease term and period to next rent review)	
• Reduce liability by lease payments • Increase liability by finance cost	• Reduce receivable by lease payments • Increase receivable by finance income (actuarial method only)		

ICAEW

Self-test

Answer the following questions.

1 **Click**

On 1 January 20X7 Click acquired an asset for its fair value and immediately leased it out to Network for four years under a finance lease with the following lease terms:

Annual payments	£40,000 in advance
Residual value of asset as guaranteed by the lessee	£15,000
Expected residual value at end of lease	£18,000
Fair value of asset	£151,958
Interest rate implicit in the lease	10%
Direct costs incurred by lessor at start of lease	£1,000

Click's policy for similar items of property, plant and equipment is to depreciate them at 40% per annum on a reducing balance basis.

Requirements

(a) Prepare extracts from the financial statements of Click for this leased asset for the year ended 31 December 20X7. **(5 marks)**

(b) Assuming that the lease was classified as an operating lease (perhaps because there were significant restrictions on what the lessee was allowed to do with the asset, but the figures remained the same) show how this operating lease would be presented in the financial statements of Click at 31 December 20X7. **(3 marks)**

(8 marks)

2 **Samways**

Samways Ltd is a company encountering some cash flow difficulties. It owned its factory and office, which had a fair value of £1,600,000. The factory and offices were measured at their depreciated historical cost, giving a carrying amount of £1,200,000.

On 1 January 20X2, Samways entered into a sale and leaseback arrangement with Leviathan plc, a bank and leasing company. At this date, the factory and office were estimated to have a remaining life of 30 years with zero residual value.

Under the terms of the agreement, Leviathan paid Samways an immediate amount of £1,500,000 and Samways signed a non-cancellable agreement on the same date to rent the premises from Leviathan plc for five years at an annual rental of £205,000, payable at the end of each year. At the end of the five year term, Samways had the option to purchase the factory and offices back from Leviathan at a price of £1 million.

Applying the provisions of IAS 17, the rate implicit in this lease was 8% pa and the present value of the lease obligation at 1 January 20X2 was £1,500,000.

Requirement

Show how the above transaction should be presented in the financial statements of Samways Ltd at its year end of 31 December 20X2. You may assume it is acceptable to amortise any deferred gains on a straight line basis. **(8 marks)**

3 **Vader**

Vader builds executive jets which are either sold outright or offered to customers under lease terms. As is common in the aviation industry, many customers choose to acquire aircraft under either operating or finance leases rather than for outright purchase. The useful life of this type of executive jet is typically twenty years. Its residual value after fifteen years is expected to be £400,000.

On 1 July 20X4, Vader completed the manufacture of two executive jets, with registrations G-EDNA and G-BGKY. Each aircraft cost Vader £2.6 million to build. G-EDNA was sold on that date to a customer for cash of £3.2 million. G-BGKY was leased to another customer, Leia Co, under a finance lease with the following terms:

Inception:	1 July 20X4
Primary term:	10 years at an annual rental in arrears of £450,000
Secondary term:	An optional further five years at an annual 'peppercorn' rental of £1
Implicit rate:	8%, which can be considered to be a market rate for this type of lease
Residual value:	The residual value is not guaranteed by the lessee.

Requirements

(a) Explain the factors which led to the lease for aircraft G-BGKY being classified as a finance lease.

(b) Explain how each of the above transactions should be presented in the financial statements of Vader for the year ended 30 June 20X5. **(10 marks)**

4   **Astley**

Astley Co owns a distribution depot which it is considering selling to Newton, a property development company, under a sale and leaseback arrangement. Astley intends moving into newer premises on a different site in approximately three years' time. When Astley moves out, Newton intends demolishing the current buildings and replacing them with flats. The current market value of the premises is approximately £4 million and the current carrying amount of the depot in Astley's statement of financial position is £3.4 million.

The market rental for Astley's depot is estimated to be £350,000 per year and Newton has offered Astley the following two options:

	Option 1	Option 2
Period of leaseback	3 years	3 years
Annual rental payable by Astley	£300,000	£450,000
Purchase price payable by Newton	£3.85 million	£4.3 million

Requirement

Evaluate the impact on Astley's profit or loss of each of the above options. **(6 marks)**

5   **Paradise Stores**

Paradise Stores Ltd has just signed a ten year lease on a retail unit in an ageing shopping complex. Paradise Stores Ltd sells discount goods at the lower end of the market.

It is believed that the shopping complex will be redeveloped within the next ten years, as the land it sits on is located in an increasingly fashionable part of town and has increased in value appreciably. The lease cannot be cancelled by either Paradise Stores or the landlord without the agreement of the other party. Under the lease title to the unit does not pass to the lessee at the end of the lease.

The annual rentals are £30,000 and the unit in the shopping complex on its own is estimated to have a market value of £350,000, although the property agent is clear in her opinion that the value of the shop is principally the value of the land it stands on. The present value of the minimum payments under the lease are estimated to be £210,000.

Requirement

Explain how the above lease should be classified under IAS 17 *Leases* and under SSAP 21 *Accounting for Leases and Hire Purchase Contracts*. Explain how these two standards may suggest different conclusions and outline the advantages of each approach. **(8 marks)**

Now go back to the Learning Objectives in the Introduction. If you are satisfied you have achieved these objectives, please tick them off.

Technical reference

1 Lease classification

- If substantially all of the risks and rewards of ownership are transferred to the lessee, then a lease is a finance lease (Note. 90% rule for UK GAAP.) Factors: IAS 17 (4)

    - Ownership passing at end of term   IAS 17 (10-11)
    - Bargain purchase option
    - Lease term the major part of asset's life
    - Very substantial charges for early cancellation
    - Peppercorn rent in secondary period
    - PV of minimum lease payments substantially all of asset's fair value.   IAS 17 (10(d))

- Otherwise, an operating lease   IAS 17 (4)

- Classify at inception   IAS 17 (13)

- Separate assessment of the land and buildings elements within a single lease (Note. Together, usually as operating lease, for UK GAAP)   IAS 17 (15A)

- Can be a lease even if lessor obliged to provide substantial services.   IAS 17 (3)

2 Lessee accounting – finance lease

- Non-current asset and liability for the asset's fair value (or PV of minimum lease payments, if lower):   IAS 17 (20)

    - Measured at inception of lease   IAS 17 (4)
    - Recognised at commencement of lease term.   IAS 17 (4)

- Depreciate asset over its useful life, or the lease term if shorter and no reasonable certainty that lessee will obtain ownership at end of lease   IAS 17 (27)

- Consider whether IAS 36 impairment procedures needed   IAS 17 (30)

- Debit lease payments to liability, without separating into capital and interest

- Charge lease interest to profit or loss and credit lease liability

- Charge interest so as to produce constant periodic rate of charge on reducing liability – approximations allowed   IAS 17 (25-26)

- Disclosures:

    - Carrying amount of each class of leased assets   IAS 17 (31(a))
    - Liability split between current and non-current   IAS 17 (23)
    - Analysis of total liability over amounts payable in one, two to five and over five years, both gross and net of finance charges allocated to future periods   IAS 17 (31(b))
    - General description of material leasing arrangements   IAS 17 (31(e))
    - Other IAS 16 disclosures re leased PPE assets   IAS 17 (32)

3 Lessee accounting – operating lease

- Recognise lease payments in profit or loss on straight-line basis, unless some other systematic basis is more representative of user's benefit — IAS 17 (33)

- Disclosures:
  - Lease payments recognised as expense in the period — IAS 17 (35(c))
  - Analysis of amounts payable in one, two to five and over five years, even though not recognised in statement of financial position — IAS 17 (35(a))
  - General description of significant leasing arrangements — IAS 17 (35(d))

4 Lessor accounting

Finance lease:

- Recognise a receivable measured at an amount equal to the net investment in the lease — IAS 17 (36)

- Net investment in the lease is the gross investment in the lease discounted at the interest rate implicit in the lease — IAS 17 (4)

- Include initial direct costs incurred but exclude general overheads — IAS 17 (38)

- Recognition of finance income should be based on a pattern reflecting a constant periodic rate of return on the lessor's net investment — IAS 17 (39)

- Special rules for manufacturer/dealer lessors — IAS 17 (42)

- Disclosures — IAS 17 (47)

Operating lease:

- The asset should be recognised in the statement of financial position according to its nature — IAS 17 (49)

- Operating lease income should be recognised on a straight-line basis over the lease term, unless another basis is more appropriate — IAS 17 (50)

- Asset should be depreciated as per other similar assets — IAS 17 (53)

- IAS 36 should be applied to determine whether the asset is impaired — IAS 17 (54)

- Disclosures — IAS 17 (56)

5 Sale and finance leaseback

- Recognise excess sale proceeds as deferred income and amortise over the lease term — IAS 17 (59-60)

6 Sale and operating leaseback

- If the fair value at the time of the sale and leaseback is less than the carrying amount of the asset, the loss (carrying amount – fair value) is recognised immediately — IAS 17 (63)

- Treatment of any profit or loss depends on relationship between sale price and fair value: — IAS 17 (61)
  - Sale price at fair value
  - Sale price below fair value
  - Sale price above fair value

Answers to Interactive questions

Answer to Interactive question 1

(a) Actuarial method

	£
Income statement (extract)	
Finance costs (working)	856
Statement of financial position (extract)	
Non-current liabilities	
Finance lease liability (working)	3,251
Current liabilities	
Finance lease liability (working)	1,315

WORKING

	CR Bal b/f after deposit £	CR Interest accrued at 15% £	DR Payment 31 Dec £	CR Bal c/f 31 Dec £
20X7	(7,710 – 2,000) = 5,710	856	(2,000)	4,566
20X8	4,566	685	(2,000)	3,251

Total lease liability at 31 December 20X7 = £4,566

Capital > 1 year = £3,251   < 1 year (bal fig) = £1,315

(b) Sum of digits method

	£
Income statement (extract)	
Finance costs (working)	916
Statement of financial position (extract)	
Non-current liabilities	
Finance lease liability (working)	3,313
Current liabilities	
Finance lease liability (working)	1,313

WORKING

Total finance charge

	£
Cash paid in total (5 × £2,000)	10,000
Fair value	(7,710)
Total interest	2,290

Sum of digits $= \dfrac{n \times (n+1)}{2}$ where n = number of periods of borrowing

$$= \text{for 4 periods } \dfrac{4 \times 5}{2} = 10$$

Period 1   £2,290 × 4/10 = 916
Period 2   £2,290 × 3/10 = 687

	CR Bal b/f after deposit £	CR Interest accrued at 31 Dec £	DR Payment 31 Dec £	CR Bal c/f 31 Dec £
20X7	(7,710 – 2,000) = 5,710	916	(2,000)	4,626
20X8	4,626	687	(2,000)	3,313

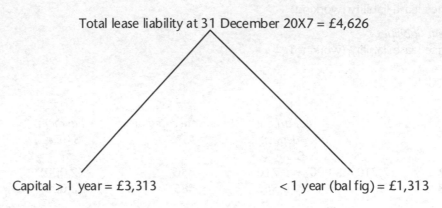

Total lease liability at 31 December 20X7 = £4,626

Capital > 1 year = £3,313   < 1 year (bal fig) = £1,313

(c)   **Sum of digits method (payments in advance)**

	£

Income statement (extract)
Finance costs (working)   1,145

Statement of financial position (extract)
Non-current liabilities
Finance lease liability (working)   2,855

Current liabilities
Finance lease liability (working)   2,000

WORKING

Sum of digits = for 3 periods $\dfrac{3 \times 4}{2} = 6$

Period 1   £2,290 × 3/6 = £1,145
Period 2   £2,290 × 2/6 = £763

	CR Bal b/f after deposit £	DR Payment 1 Jan £	CR Capital remaining 1 Jan £	CR Interest accrued at 31 Dec £	CR Bal c/f 31 Dec £
20X7	(7,710 – 2,000) = 5,710	(2,000)	3,710	1,145	4,855
20X8	4,855	(2,000)	2,855	763	3,618

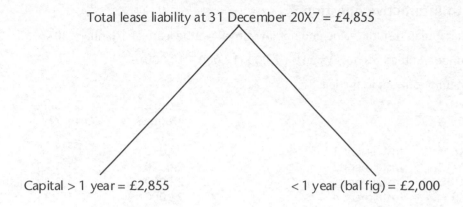

Total lease liability at 31 December 20X7 = £4,855

Capital > 1 year = £2,855   < 1 year (bal fig) = £2,000

Answer to Interactive question 2

The lease extends over the useful life of the building, so the buildings element within the lease should be classified as a finance lease. The useful life of the land is indefinite, so this element should be classified as an operating lease.

The two elements should be measured by reference to the fair value of the leasehold interests, so

- £66,000 (which is 10% of £660,000) is allocated to the land
- £594,000 (the 90% remainder) is allocated to the buildings

The annual rental should be allocated between:

- The land: £5,000 (10% of the £50,000 rental). As the period covered by the rental payment is identical to the financial year, there is no prepayment or accrual to be recognised in the statement of financial position.

- The building: the lower of the £594,000 fair value allocated to the building and the £567,000 (£630,000 × 90%) present value of the minimum lease payments so allocated should be recognised as a non-current asset and as a liability, charging depreciation on the asset and adjusting the liability by £45,000 (90% of the £50,000 annual rental) and by the finance charge at 7.5% of the outstanding amount.

	£
Income statement	
Operating lease rental	5,000
Depreciation (567/30)	18,900
Finance cost (W)	39,150
Statement of financial position	
Property, plant and equipment	
Cost	567,000
Depreciation	(18,900)
	548,100
Non-current liabilities	
Finance lease obligations (W)	516,150
Current liabilities	
Finance lease obligations (W)	45,000

WORKING

	Balance	Lease payment	Balance	Finance cost at 7.5%	Balance
	£	£	£	£	£
20X8	567,000	(45,000)	522,000	39,150	561,150
20X9	561,150	(45,000)	516,150	38,711	554,861

Answer to Interactive question 3

(a) Unguaranteed residual value and net investment in the lease at 1 January 20X6

The unguaranteed residual value is £2,000 (12,000 – 10,000)

The net investment in the lease is

Date		Gross investment £	Discount factor (11%)	Net investment £
1.1.X6	Instalment 1	22,000	1	22,000
1.1.X7	Instalment 2	22,000	1/1.11	19,820
1.1.X8	Instalment 3	22,000	1/1.11⁴	17,856
1.1.X9	Instalment 4	22,000	1/1.11³	16,086
31.12.X9	Guaranteed residual value	10,000	1/1.11⁴	6,587
	Minimum lease payments	98,000		82,349
31.12.X9	Unguaranteed residual value	2,000	1/1.11⁴	1,317
		100,000		83,666

(b) Financial statement extracts

Income statement (extract)

	£
Finance income (working)	6,783

Statement of financial position (extract)

	£
Non-current assets	
Finance lease receivable (working)	46,449
Current assets	
Finance lease receivable (working) (68,449 – 46,449)	22,000

Point to note:

The solution has separated the amount receivable according to the normal non-current/current asset definition. In practice, lessors will usually present their statement of financial position on a liquidity basis and the receivable will be a single figure, with further analysis in the notes.

WORKING – net investment in finance lease:

		£
Year ended 31 December 20X6		
1.1.X6	Net investment	83,666
1.1.X6	Instalment 1 in advance	(22,000)
		61,666
1.1.X6 – 31.12.X6	Interest income at 11%	6,783
Balance at 31.12.X6		68,449
Year ended 31 December 20X7		
1.1.X7	Instalment 2 in advance	(22,000)
Due in more than one year		46,449

Answer to Interactive question 4

	£
Amounts recognised in profit or loss	
Revenue (working)	24,354
Cost of sales	(21,000)
Gross profit	3,354
Finance income (8% × (24,354 – 8,750 balance after first payment))	1,248
Statement of financial position	
Receivable (24,354 – 8,750 first payment + 1,248 finance income)	16,852

WORKING

Present values of amounts receivable in advance

Year	Cash flow	Discount factor	Present value
	£	at 8%	£
20X7	8,750	1/1	8,750
20X8	8,750	1/1.08	8,102
20X9	8,750	$1/1.08^2$	7,502
			24,354

Answer to Interactive question 5

Journal entries at date of disposal

		£	£
DR	Cash	120,000	
CR	Non-current asset (carrying amount)		70,000
	Deferred income (120,000 – 70,000)		50,000
DR	Non-current asset	120,000	
CR	Lease liability		120,000

Income statement

	£
Depreciation (120,000/5)	(24,000)
Interest (120,000 × 8%)	(9,600)
Release of deferred profit (50,000/5)	10,000

Statement of financial position

	£
Non-current assets	
Carrying amount at 1 January 20X1	120,000
Depreciation	(24,000)
Carrying amount at 31 December 20X1	96,000
Non-current liabilities	
Obligations under finance leases (W)	77,568
Deferred income (50,000 × 3/5)	30,000
Current liabilities	
Obligations under finance leases (30,000 – 7,968 (W))	22,032
Deferred income (50,000/5)	10,000

WORKING

	Balance	Finance cost at 8%	Lease payment	Balance
	£	£	£	£
20X1	120,000	9,600	(30,000)	99,600
20X2	99,600	7,968	(30,000)	77,568

Point to note:

The net expense for the year in respect of the asset (excluding the financing cost) is £14,000 (24,000 – 10,000), the same as if the asset had not been sold (70,000/5).

Answer to Interactive question 6

(1) Loss of £60,000 (carrying amount less proceeds = £360,000 – £300,000) should be recognised immediately unless lease rentals are below market rentals in which case it should be deferred and amortised over the five years lease period at £12,000 per year.

(2) A loss of £40,000 based on fair value (carrying amount – fair value = £400,000 – £360,000) should be recognised immediately. The remaining £60,000 of the loss (fair value – proceeds = £360,000 – £300,000) should also be recognised immediately unless the future rentals payable are below market levels, in which case it should be deferred and amortised over the lease term.

(3) The profit of £60,000 (proceeds – carrying amount = £360,000 – £300,000) should be recognised immediately.

(4) A profit of £60,000 based on fair value (fair value – carrying amount = £360,000 – £300,000) should be recognised immediately. The remaining £40,000 of the profit (proceeds – fair value = £400,000 – £360,000) should be deferred and recognised over the five years lease period at £8,000 per year.

(5) A loss of £60,000 based on fair value (carrying amount – fair value = £360,000 – £300,000) should be recognised immediately. The profit of £100,000 (proceeds – fair value = £400,000 – £300,000) should be deferred and recognised over the five years lease period at £20,000 per year.

(6) A loss of £100,000 based on fair value (carrying amount – fair value = £400,000 – £300,000) should be recognised immediately. The profit of £60,000 (proceeds – fair value = £360,000 – £300,000) should be deferred and recognised over the five years lease period at £12,000 per year.

Answer to Interactive question 7

	£
Income statement	
Operating lease rentals (W1)	44,000
Statement of financial position	
Non-current liabilities	
Operating lease liability (W2)	12,000
Current liabilities	
Operating lease liability (W2)	4,000

WORKINGS

(1) *Operating lease rentals*

Total due under lease £240,000 (£4,000 × 12 × 5) – rent free £20,000 (5 × £4,000) = £220,000

Over five years = £44,000 per year

(2) *Operating lease liability*

	£
Income statement charge (W1)	44,000
Paid in year (7 × £4,000)	(28,000)
Liability	16,000
Current liability: amount payable in 20X8 ((12 × £4,000) – 44,000)	4,000
Non-current liability (balance)	12,000

1 **Click**

(a)
	£
Income statement – extract	
Finance income (W2)	11,176
Statement of financial position – extract	
Non-current asset	
Net investment in finance lease (W2)	82,940
Current asset	
Net investment in finance lease (W2) (122,940 – 82,940)	40,000

(b)
	£
Income statement – extract	
Leasing income	40,000
Statement of financial position – extract	
Non-current asset	
Property, plant and equipment (W3)	91,925

The lease income of £40,000 per year should be recognised on a straight line basis, as no other system of recognition seems more appropriate in this case. The expected residual value of £18,000 is above the guaranteed residual value of £15,000; this should not be anticipated but recognised at the end of the lease term.

WORKINGS

(1) **Net investment in finance lease**

	Gross investment £	Discount Factor (10%)	Net investment £
1 Jan X7	40,000	1	40,000
1 Jan X8	40,000	1/1.1	36,360
1 Jan X9	40,000	$1/1.1^{2}$	33,060
1 Jan Y0	40,000	$1/1.1^{3}$	30,050
31 Dec Y0	15,000	$1/1.1^{4}$	10,245
Minimum lease payments	175,000		149,715
Unguaranteed residual	3,000	$1/1.1^{4}$	2,049
	178,000		151,764

Point to note:

Allowance for the initial direct costs will have been made in computing the 10% interest rate implicit in the lease, so they should be ignored in preparing these extracts.

(2) **Statement of financial position and income statement figures**

		£
Year ended 31 Dec 20X7		
1 Jan X7	Net investment (W1)	151,764
1 Jan X7	Instalment	(40,000)
		111,764
31 Dec X7	Interest income (111,764 × 10%)	11,176
Balance at 31 Dec 20X7		122,940
Year ended 31 Dec 20X8		
1 Jan 20X8	Instalment	(40,000)
		82,940

(3) The asset should measured at its fair value plus direct costs. But direct costs should be written off on a straight line basis over the four year lease term (to match revenue from the lease), not the life of the asset.

	At 1 January £	Depreciation on asset @ 40% reducing balance £	At 31 December £	Contract acquisition costs, written off over four years £	Total carrying amount £
20X7	151,958	(60,783)	91,175	750	91,925
20X8	91,175	(36,470)	54,705	500	55,205
20X9	54,705	(21,882)	32,823	250	33,073
20Y0	32,823	(13,129)	19,694	0	19,694

2   Samways

Although the factory and office has a useful life of 30 years and the lease term is only 5 years, a bargain purchase option has been granted to Samways, so this transaction should be accounted for as sale and finance leaseback.

The initial derecognition of the asset should be recorded in accordance with paragraph 59 of IAS 17:

DR	Bank	£1,500,000	
CR	Non-current asset		£1,200,000
CR	Deferred income (over five years)		£300,000

At the same date, the finance lease and associated liability should be recognised and measured at the lower of its fair value and the present value of the minimum lease payments.

Financial statements of Samways Ltd at 31 December 20X2

Statement of financial position (extracts)

	£
Non-current assets	
Assets held under finance leases (£1.5m × 29/30)	1,450,000
Non-current liabilities	
Obligation under finance leases (working)	1,323,200
Deferred income (£0.3m × 3/5)	180,000
Current liabilities	
Obligation under finance leases (working: £205,000 – £113,200)	91,800
Deferred income (£0.3m/5)	60,000

Income statement (extracts)

	£
Depreciation on assets held under finance leases (expense)	50,000
Finance costs (working) (expense)	120,000
Deferred income recognised (£0.3m/5) (income)	60,000

WORKING

	£
Obligation on finance lease	
Inception	1,500,000
Finance costs to 31.12.X2: 8% × £1.5m	120,000
Less: payment made	(205,000)
Closing liability at 31.12.X2	1,415,000
Finance costs to 31.12.X3: 8% × £1.415m	113,200
Less: payment due next year	(205,000)
Closing liability at 31.12.X3	1,323,200

3   **Vader**

(a)   **Classification as finance lease**

Although the aircraft remains Vader's legal property beyond the end of the lease term, the factors which led the lease to be classified as a finance lease are:

- Because the lease includes a secondary term at a peppercorn rental, the expectation should be that the total lease term is 15 years. This is the major part of the asset's useful life, especially as its usefulness may decrease as it becomes older (paragraph 10c IAS 17).

- The present value of the minimum lease payments at the inception of the lease is substantially all the fair value of the leased asset (paragraph 10d IAS 17). The actual present value is calculated as:

	£
Present value of £450,000 per annum in arrears for 10 years at 8% per annum is £450,000 × ((1/1.08) + (1/1.08^2) ... + (1/1.08^{10}))	3,019,500
Fair value at inception = cash selling price	3,200,000
Present value as a percentage of fair value	94.4%

(b)   Financial statements for the year ended 30 June 20X5

G-EDNA

The aircraft has been sold, so this asset should be derecognised by Vader, being replaced by £3.2 million cash. A profit on sale of £600,000 should be recognised in profit or loss.

G-BGKY

The leasing transaction will generate income for Vader in two ways:

1   An initial trading profit.

2   Leasing income from the finance lease granted to the customer.

This aircraft itself should be derecognised by Vader, giving a cost of sales of £2,474,000 (W1) to be set against revenue of £3,019,500 (W2) and a trading profit of £545,500.

Vader should recognise an initial finance lease receivable of £3,145,500 (W3). This receivable should be increased by finance income of 8% thereof (so £251,640) which should be recognised as income in profit or loss. The receivable should be reduced by the £450,000 rental received on the last day of the financial year.

WORKINGS

		£m
(1)	Manufacturing cost	2.600
	Present value of unguaranteed residual value after 15 years (1/1.08^{15} × £0.4m)	(0.126)
		2.474

(2)   Lower of fair value asset (£3.2m) and present value of minimum lease payments (£3.0195m)

(3)   Net investment = £3.0195m + £0.126m = £3.1455m

4   Astley

Option 1

The profit on sale of £450,000 (£3.85 million sales price less £3.4 million carrying amount) should be recognised immediately in profit or loss. This sales price is below the £4 million fair value and the £300,000 annual rental is below the £350,000 market rental, but IAS 17 does not require any adjustment to the profit as calculated above.

This profit should be recognised immediately and the subsequent rentals should be recognised in profit or loss each year at £300,000. This will have the following effect over the three years on profit or loss:

	Year 1 £'000	Year 2 £'000	Year 3 £'000	Total £'000
Profit on derecognition of depot	450	0	0	450
Rental expense recognised	(300)	(300)	(300)	(900)
Total income / (expense)	150	(300)	(300)	(450)

Option 2

This option generates a profit on sale of £900,000 as the £4.3 million sales price is above the £3.4 million carrying amount. This sales price is £300,000 above the £4 million fair value, but this seemingly generous extra consideration appears to be clawed back by Newton planning to charge above market rentals for the following three years.

This excess profit should initially be recognised as deferred income and released to profit or loss over the three years of the leaseback. The profit recognised immediately should be the difference between the £4 million fair value and the £3.4 million carrying amount. The effect on profit or loss will be:

	Year 1 £'000	Year 2 £'000	Year 3 £'000	Total £'000
Profit on derecognition of depot	600	0	0	600
Rentals expense recognised	(450)	(450)	(450)	(1,350)
Deferred income released to profit	100	100	100	300
	(350)	(350)	(350)	(1,050)
Total income / (expense)	250	(350)	(350)	(450)

5   **Paradise Stores**

Under IAS 17 a finance lease is defined as a lease that transfers substantially all the risks and rewards incident to ownership. No numerical guidelines or rules are given but instead preparers need to assess whether the lease is a finance lease by considering:

- If the lease has provision for transfer of ownership from lessor to lessee

- If the lessee has an option to purchase the asset on terms sufficiently advantageous that the option is likely to be exercised

- If the duration of the lease is for a major part of the life of the asset (75% of the life is a common benchmark used in practice, as this is the US GAAP norm)

- If at inception the present value of the lease obligation amounts to substantially all the fair value of the asset.

IAS 17 also requires that when a lease includes both land and buildings elements, there is separate assessment of the two elements, ie one lease for the use of land and another for the use of the building that stands on the land. Given that the rentals charged themselves are rarely split into a rental for land and a rental for the building, this can be a difficult judgemental exercise.

SSAP 21 contains the same definition of a finance lease, but then includes the general rule that this transfer is presumed to have taken place if the present value of the minimum lease payments at inception amounts to substantially all (normally 90%) of the asset's fair value. If the present value is less than 90%, then the lease is presumed to be an operating lease. This general rule is to be over-ridden only in exceptional circumstances.

SSAP 21 does not require disaggregation of a lease for land and buildings into separate elements of a lease for land and a lease for buildings. This has the effect that a number of leases that would otherwise be separated into their finance and operating elements are classified as a single operating lease. This is likely to be preferred by most lessees since it keeps liabilities out of the statement of financial position.

The approach taken by IAS 17 has the following advantages:

- By requiring a number of criteria to be considered, it makes it more difficult for leases to be drawn up in a way that gets round the rules of the standard's requirements, resulting in it being classified as an operating lease when it would more accurately be a finance lease.

- It allows practitioners to more accurately reflect the underlying intention of lease accounting that leases should be accounted for in accordance with substance over form. For example, having a definition of a finance lease that focuses attention on individual numbers (such as whether the present value of the obligation at inception is greater than 90% of fair value) promotes a tendency to favour form over substance because it takes a narrow view of the lease's characteristics. Users of an entity's financial statements are more likely to see them as useful if they believe that each transaction has been prepared in strict compliance with the principle of substance over form.

The UK GAAP approach has the advantage of being less subjective than IAS 17, making it easier to apply in practice. Subjectivity produces different interpretations between different competent accountants. This in turn reduces comparability between entities, which in turn reduces the usefulness of the information provided.

In this example, under UK GAAP the lease should be treated as an operating lease, since the £210,000 present value of the lease obligation at inception is only 60% of the £350,000 fair value of the land and buildings at that date.

Under IAS 17, this lease would not automatically be a finance lease, since title does not transfer to the lessee. However, it would be necessary to disaggregate the lease into its constituent elements of an operating lease for the land and a lease (which could be either operating or finance) for the building that stands on the land. The lease of land is an operating lease since land has an indefinite life and the lease is for the short period of only ten years.

It would be necessary to determine a comparable annual rental for land without buildings in the vicinity of the building, as well as assess the fair value of the building. The figures may be difficult in practice to obtain, causing some unreliability in the classification of the land and building element.

It seems likely here that the building element should be classified as a finance lease because:

- The lease is for substantially all the building's expected remaining useful life.

- The present value of the obligation may well be substantially equal to the fair value of the building; especially as the fair value of the building at the end of the lease is likely to be zero (it is expected to be demolished around that date).

This classification is not clear-cut, however, because not all elements of the lease suggest that it is a finance lease. Difficulties such as this are common when classifying leases under IAS 17.

CHAPTER 6

Revenue and construction contracts

Introduction

Examination context

Topic List

1 Overview of material covered in Financial Accounting

2 IAS 11 *Construction Contracts*

3 UK GAAP comparison

Summary and Self-test

Technical reference

Answers to Interactive questions

Answers to Self-test

Learning objectives

- Account for complex revenue recognition situations

- Define and recognise a construction contract

- Explain the problem involved with accounting for construction contracts

- Recognise contract revenue, costs and profit as the contract progresses

- Account for expected losses on a contract

- Disclose the required information for construction contracts

Specific syllabus references for this chapter are: 1e, 3a, 4a and 4c.

Syllabus links

IAS 18 *Revenue* was covered in your Financial Accounting studies but the principles in IAS 18 are very relevant to Financial Reporting and will also be taken further in the Advanced Stage.

New to your studies is IAS 11 *Construction Contracts*. It builds from the principles in IAS 18 *Revenue* and all areas of the accounting standard are covered in this text. Again this subject could appear at the Advanced Stage.

Examination context

In the examination, candidates may be required to:

- Determine how complex revenue situations should be reported
- Distinguish between revenue from sales and finance income
- Deal with deferred revenue
- Explain the problem involved in accounting for construction contracts
- Explain the principles of the method of dealing with construction contracts outlined in IAS 11
- Prepare income statement extracts for construction contracts
- Prepare statement of financial position extracts for construction contracts

1 Overview of material covered in Financial Accounting

Section overview

This section provides a brief revision of the key areas of IAS 18 *Revenue* covered in the Financial Accounting syllabus, puts it into a context for Financial Reporting and covers some areas in more detail:

- Deferred consideration
- Goods and services provided in one contract
- Faithful representation/substance over form.

1.1 Objective of IAS 18 *Revenue*

The objective of IAS 18 is to ensure that revenue is recognised:

- When it is probable that future economic benefits will flow to the entity; and
- These benefits can be measured reliably.

IAS 18 applies to:

- The sale of goods
- The rendering of services
- Revenue earned from use of the entity's assets

Revenue can be made up of sales turnover, fees, interest, dividends and royalties.

1.2 Criteria for recognising revenue

Revenue from the **sale of goods** should be recognised when the following five criteria have been met:

- The significant risks and rewards of ownership have been transferred from the seller to the buyer.
- The seller no longer has management involvement or effective control over the goods.
- The amount of the revenue can be measured reliably.
- It is probable that economic benefits will be received by the entity.
- The costs incurred, or to be incurred, in relation to the transaction can be measured reliably.

Revenue from the **rendering of services** should be recognised when the following four criteria are met:

- The amount of the revenue can be measured reliably.

- It is probable that economic benefits will be received by the entity.

- The stage of completion of the transaction at the end of the reporting period can be assessed accurately.

- The costs incurred, or to be incurred, in relation to the transaction can be measured reliably.

Point to note:

If these rendering of services criteria are not met, revenue should only be recognised to the extent of costs known to be recoverable from the customer.

Other types of revenue should be recognised as follows:

- Interest on a time basis
- Dividends when the entity has the right to receive payment
- Royalties on an accrual basis

Interactive question 1: Publishing revenue   **[Difficulty level: Easy]**

A magazine publisher launched a new monthly magazine on 1 January 20X7. During January it received £48,000 in annual subscriptions in advance. It has despatched four issues by the year end 31 March 20X7.

What revenue should be recognised for the year ended 31 March 20X7?

Fill in the proforma below.

£

Magazine revenue

Explanation

See **Answer** at the end of this chapter.

Interactive question 2: Advance sales

[Difficulty level: Intermediate]

A DIY store is about to sell a new type of drill. Customer demand is high and the store has taken advance orders for the drill. The selling price of the drill will be £50 and so far two hundred customers have paid an initial 10% deposit on the selling price of the drill. No drills are yet held in inventory.

What amount should be recognised as revenue?

Fill in the proforma below.

£

Revenue

Explanation

See **Answer** at the end of this chapter.

Interactive question 3: Service contract

[Difficulty level: Intermediate]

An entity entered into a contract for the provision of services over a two year period. The total contract price was £150,000 and the entity initially expected to earn a profit of £20,000 on the contract. In the first year costs of £60,000 were incurred and 50% of the work was completed. The contract did not progress as expected and management was not sure of the ultimate outcome but believed that the costs incurred to date would be recovered from the customer.

What revenue should be recognised for the first year of the contract?

Fill in the proforma below.

£

Contract revenue

Explanation

See **Answer** at the end of this chapter.

1.3 Context

Revenue is often the largest single item in the financial statements. US studies have shown that over half of all financial statement frauds and requirements for restatements of previously published financial information involved revenue manipulation. Recent reports of questionable revenue recognition practices have highlighted the need for thorough guidance in this area.

Robust principles for recognition and measurement should be applied. A consistent approach to revenue recognition is essential if financial statements are to present fairly the true economic activity of an entity. One of the main issues is the reporting of revenue within discrete periods, when under a single contract services are provided in the current and future periods. This allocation of revenue has a direct impact on the earnings for each period.

1.4 Deferred consideration

In some sectors of the retail industry it is common practice to provide interest-free credit to customers in order to encourage sales of, for example, furniture and new cars.

Where an extended period of credit is offered, the revenue receivable has two separate elements:

- The fair value of the goods on the date of sale, for example the cash selling price
- Financing income

In order to separate these two elements the future receipts are discounted to present value at an imputed interest rate, identified as either:

- The prevailing rate for lending to a customer with a credit rating similar to that of the customer or
- The rate of interest which discounts the receivable back to the current cash selling price.

The effect on the timing of the revenue recognition is that:

- The fair value of the goods is recognised on delivery of the goods.
- The finance element is recognised over the period that the financing is provided.

Worked example: Deferred consideration

A car retailer sells its new cars by requiring a 20% deposit followed by no further payments until the full balance is due after two years. The price of the cars is calculated using a 10% per annum finance charge.

On 1 January 20X7 a car was sold to a customer for £20,000.

How should the revenue should be recognised in the year ended 31 December 20X7 and what should the carrying amount of the customer receivable be on that date?

Solution

Revenue to be recognised

	£
Sale of goods (£4,000 + £13,223 (W))	17,223
Financing income (£13,223 (W) × 10%)	1,322
Carrying amount of receivable (£13,223 (W) × 1.10)	14,545

WORKING

The deposit is £4,000 (£20,000 × 20%), so the amount receivable in two years is £16,000.

This is discounted at 10% for two years to £13,223 (£16,000 × $1/1.10^2$).

1.5 Goods and services provided in one contract

One marketing tool frequently used is to bundle together into one transaction both goods and services. For example a car dealer may sell new cars with one year's free servicing and insurance.

In such cases:

- The components of the package which could be sold separately should be identified and
- Each should be measured and recognised as if sold separately.

IAS 18 does not specifically state how each component should be measured but general principles require that each component should be:

- Measured at its fair value
- Recognised as revenue only when it meets the recognition criteria.

If the total of the fair values exceeds the overall price of the contract, an appropriate approach would be to apply the same discount percentage to each separate component.

Worked example: Goods and services

A car dealer sells a new car, together with 50 litres of fuel per month for a year and one year's servicing, for £27,000. The fair values of these components are: car £28,000, fuel £1,200 and servicing £800.

How should the £27,000 be recognised as revenue?

Solution

The total fair value of the package is £30,000 (28,000 + 1,200 + 800) but is being sold for £27,000, a discount of £3,000 or 10%.

The discounted fair value of the car should be recognised as revenue upon delivery:

£28,000 × 90% = £25,200

The discounted fair value of the fuel should be recognised as revenue on a straight line basis over the next 12 months:

£1,200 × 90% = £1,080

The discounted fair value of the servicing should be recognised as revenue at the earlier of when the servicing is provided and the end of the year:

£800 × 90% = £720

Interactive question 4: Goods and services   [Difficulty level: Intermediate]

An entity sells an item of equipment to a customer on 1 January 20X7 for £1.5m. Due to the specialised nature of the equipment the entity has agreed to provide free support services for the next two years, despite the cost to the entity of that support being estimated at £120,000 in total. The entity usually earns a gross margin of 20% on such contracts.

How much revenue should the entity recognise for the year ended 30 April 20X7?
Fill in the proforma below.

                                                                                    £

Revenue

WORKINGS

See **Answer** at the end of this chapter.

1.6   Faithful representation/substance over form

The decision about when to recognise revenue on the sale of goods requires consideration of whether the risks and rewards of ownership have been transferred to the buyer, the seller retaining neither management involvement in, nor effective control over, the asset sold.

For the decision to result in faithful representation of the transaction it is critical that the substance of arrangements for the sale of goods is clearly identified and then accounted for. Merely examining the form of arrangements is insufficient. One of the greatest difficulties is establishing whether or not there are arrangements, such as an option, whereby the seller can at a fixed or determinable future date for a fixed or determinable amount repurchase the asset being sold.

In such circumstances, and particularly if the seller retains use of the asset between the sale and repurchase dates, the arrangement is probably in substance a secured loan, not a sale at all.

Worked example: Faithful representation

An entity sold an investment property to a financial institution for £4 million when the fair value of the property was £5 million. Further investigation uncovered an agreement whereby the entity could repurchase the property after one year for £4.32 million.

How should this transaction be accounted for?

Solution

The sale of the property at 20% below fair value is sufficient to cast doubt on whether a real sale has been made. Also, the repurchase price is below fair value at the date of sale and represents a return to the financial institution of 8% ((£4.32m – 4m) as a percentage of £4m) on the amount paid out.

The substance of the arrangement appears to be that the financial institution has granted the entity a one year loan secured on the property, charging interest at 8%.

The transaction should be accounted for by:

- Continuing to recognise the property as an asset
- Crediting the £4 million received to a liability account
- Recognising £0.32m as a finance cost in profit or loss and crediting it to the liability account
- Derecognising the liability when the £4.32 million cash is paid out.

1.7 Judgements required

The key judgements required of management include:

- When do the risks and rewards of ownership of goods pass to the buyer?

- In what circumstances is management involvement in the asset retained?

- How is a decision made as to whether the stage of completion of a service transaction can be measured reliably?

Because revenue has such a direct impact on earnings and because many investors focus on revenue growth as an important measure of performance, management may well be tempted to be very optimistic in its judgements, in order that the amount of revenue recognised is maximised. Chartered Accountants need to be very clear about the need to ensure that there are robust internal policies for the recognition of revenue and that they are applied consistently from one period to another.

1.8 Relevance of information for users

IAS 18 requires only limited information about revenue to be disclosed: the accounting policies for recognition of revenue (including the methods for determining the stage of completion for service transactions) and the amount of revenue from goods, services, interest, royalties and dividends. Accounting policies that are disclosed tend to lack detail.

So users are not very well served, a particular weakness when:

- Revenue has a £1 for £1 effect on profit and therefore the return on capital employed calculation
- Every extra £1 of profit reduces gearing.

2 IAS 11 *Construction Contracts*

Section overview

- The key issue regarding construction contracts is how to recognise revenue and profits over the period of contract activity.

- IAS 11 explains what is meant by a construction contract and the two main types of contract.

- Revenue and costs relating to a contract should be recognised using the stage of completion method, if the outcome of the contract can be measured reliably.

- If it cannot be measured reliably, revenue should only be recognised to the extent of costs recoverable from the customer.

- If it is estimated that a loss will be incurred on a contract, that loss should be recognised immediately.

2.1 Context

In some industries entities will make or build substantial assets for sale, such as aeroplanes or car assembly lines, which will often take a number of years to complete.

The accounting problem is that if a profitable construction contract spans a number of accounting periods:

- When should the profit be recognised?

IAS 11 requires revenue and costs (and therefore profit) to be recognised as contract activity progresses. The measurement of contract activity can require a significant amount of judgement in the assessment of the progress to date, and the ultimate outcome, of the contract. Professional skills and experience are essential in this assessment process. The timing of the recognition of claims, variations and penalties under the contract can also affect revenue and profit significantly.

The negotiation period for contracts can be substantial, starting with an open tender period followed by the selection of a preferred bidder with whom final negotiations are concluded. The costs involved in these negotiations can be significant and their treatment can have an immediate impact on earnings.

The timing of contract receipts is critical to the funding of working capital. There is also the problem that the timing of cash receipts and the recognition of revenue may be different.

2.2 What is a construction contract?

Definition

A **construction contract** is a contract specifically negotiated for the construction of an asset or a combination of assets that are closely interrelated or interdependent in terms of their design, technology and function or their ultimate purpose or use.

IAS 11 applies only to contractors, that is the entities constructing the assets. The customer should account for the asset in accordance with IAS 16 *Property, Plant and Equipment*.

Two distinct types of contract are dealt with by IAS 11:

- Fixed price contracts
- Cost plus contracts

Definition

A **fixed price contract** is a construction contract in which the contractor agrees to a fixed contract price, or a fixed rate per unit of output, which in some cases is subject to cost escalation clauses.

The key characteristics of a fixed price contract are:

- The revenue is fixed or determinable at the start of the contract
- There is therefore a high degree of certainty about the amount of revenue
- But there is less certainty about the costs that will be incurred.

Definition

A **cost plus contract** is a construction contract in which the contractor is reimbursed for allowable or otherwise defined costs, plus a percentage of these costs or a fixed fee.

The key characteristics of a cost plus contract are:

- The contract price is the costs incurred plus an agreed profit margin (or fixed sum)
- There is therefore a high degree of certainty about the profit arising
- But there is less certainty about both revenue and costs.

This distinction becomes very important when deciding the stage at which contract revenues and costs should be recognised (see later in chapter).

2.3 Combining and segmenting construction contracts

Generally IAS 11 requires individual construction contracts to be treated separately. However there are some exceptions, when the substance of the arrangements is that several contracts are really one, or one contract is really several.

2.3.1 Combining contracts

A number of small contracts should be combined into a single larger one if the individual contracts:

- Have been negotiated as one
- Are closely interrelated with an overall profit margin
- Are performed at the same time or consecutively.

2.3.2 Segmenting contracts

If one contract covers a number of individual assets which have been separately tendered for and negotiated, it will be necessary to treat each asset as a separate contract.

2.4 Recognition of contract revenue and contract costs

The objective of IAS 11 is to recognise contract revenue and costs in each accounting period according to the stage of completion of the contract.

Contract revenue and contract costs should only be recognised in profit or loss when the outcome of the contract can be estimated reliably.

2.4.1 Contract revenue

Contract revenue is the total amount of consideration receivable under a contract.

Contract revenue should be built up over the life of the contract as revenue due under the originally agreed contract plus any subsequent changes or variations that have been agreed; all these component parts should be measured at the fair value of the consideration receivable.

In the early stages of a contract the contract revenue will often be an estimate of the final amount as it may be dependent upon future events.

Any variations to the original estimated contract revenue should only form part of contract revenue when:

- It is probable that the customer will approve the cost of the variation and
- The amount can be measured reliably.

2.4.2 Contract costs

Contract costs comprise:

- Those directly related to the specific contract
- An allocation of costs incurred in contract activity in general.

IAS 11 sets out a list of costs which directly relate to a specific contract. These are basically the same sort of variable costs as can be capitalised when plant and equipment is manufactured. More careful judgements of the amounts attributable to a specific contract are needed when allocating costs incurred in contract activity in general, such as:

- Insurance
- Costs of design and technical assistance not directly related to the specific contract
- Construction overheads, such as the costs of payroll administration for construction staff

Overhead costs should be allocated to individual contracts on a systematic basis, based on normal levels of activity.

Points to note:

1   When entities seek contracts with public bodies they incur quite substantial contract negotiation costs. These should be treated in a way quite similar to development expenses under IAS 38 *Intangible Assets*:

   - They should be recognised as an expense up to the time when it first becomes probable that the contract will be won.

   - Negotiation costs subsequent to that time should be included in contract costs.

   - Negotiation costs already expensed cannot subsequently be added to contract costs.

2   Finance costs should be included in contract costs under IAS 23 *Borrowing Costs*.

Interactive question 5: Contract costs   [Difficulty level: Easy]

An entity is involved in a number of construction contracts extending over long periods and has incurred the following costs in respect of construction contracts during the year ended 31 March 20X7.

	£'000
Labour	632
Materials	1,325
Design costs for specific contracts	463
Research costs	321
General administration costs	121
Borrowing costs	56
Selling costs	106

What is the total amount of costs which should be allocated to construction contracts in accordance with IAS 11 in the year ended 31 March 20X7?

Fill in the proforma below.

£

Costs

WORKINGS

See **Answer** at the end of this chapter.

2.4.3 Stage of completion

As a simple example, if a contract is half complete at the year end then half the revenue and half the costs attributable to the contract should be recognised in profit or loss for that year.

C
H
A
P
T
E
R

6

Point to note:

The effect is to recognise half the profit, but IAS 11 consistently talks about recognising revenue and costs.

IAS 11 illustrates three ways in which the stage of completion of a contract can be determined:

- Measurement of costs incurred to date as a proportion of total costs of contract – this is the method commonly adopted.

- Surveys of the work performed, often carried out by an independent valuer.

- Measurement of the proportion of the asset physically complete, for example when the contract is to construct a number of buildings.

Points to note:

1   Cash received from the customer is usually a poor indicator of the stage of completion.

2   Any exam question will contain somewhere within it information about how to measure the stage of completion.

2.5   Estimate of contract outcome is reliable

Contract revenue and costs should only be recognised where the outcome of the contract can be measured reliably.

The criteria to be met for reliability depend upon the type of contract.

The outcome of a **fixed price contract** can be estimated reliably if:

- Total contract revenue can be measured reliably
- It is probable that the economic benefits associated with the contract will be received by the entity
- Contract costs to complete can be measured reliably
- The stage of completion can be measured reliably, and
- Contract costs to date can be identified and measured reliably.

The outcome of a cost plus contract can be estimated reliably if:

- It is probable that the economic benefits associated with the contract will be received by the entity, and
- Total costs can be clearly identified and reliably measured.

Worked example: Cost plus

The following information relates to a cost-plus contract won recently by a business with a 30 June year end. The profit as a percentage of costs has been agreed at 20%.

	20X5 £'000	20X6 £'000
Contract costs incurred to date	100	150

The outcome of the contract can be estimated reliably at both year ends.

What amounts should be recognised as revenue, costs and profit for each of the two financial years?

Solution

The best approach is:

- In the first year, to identify the costs to be recognised in cost of sales, calculate the profit and then insert revenue as the balancing figure.

- In subsequent years, to do the same on a **cumulative** basis and then **deduct** amounts recognised in previous years.

For 20X5 cost of sales is £100,000 and profit £20,000 (20% thereof). So revenue is £120,000.

For 20X6 the amounts to date are cost of sales £150,000, profit £30,000 (20% thereof) and revenue £180,000. Deducting 20X5 amounts gives figures of £50,000, £10,000 and £60,000 respectively.

Interactive question 6: Fixed price contract [Difficulty level: Easy]

The following information relates to a fixed price contract of £500,000 obtained in 20X5 by a business with a 30 June year end.

	20X5 £'000	20X6 £'000	20X7 £'000
Contract costs incurred to date	100	300	410
Estimated costs to complete	300	120	–
Total contract costs – estimated in 20X5 and 20X6, actual in 20X7	400	420	410
Profit – estimated in 20X5 and 20X6, actual in 20X7	100	80	90

The outcome of the contract can be estimated reliably at all three year ends.

Requirement

Calculate the amounts to be recognised in profit or loss for each of the three years.

See **Answer** at the end of this chapter.

2.6 Estimate of contract outcome is not reliable

Where the outcome of the contract cannot be estimated reliably:

- Contract costs should be recognised immediately and

- Contract revenue should only be recognised to the extent that it is probable that the costs are recoverable from the customer.

The effect of this is that:

- No profit is recognised prior to the outcome of the contract being reliably estimated
- A loss is recognised immediately if costs incurred cannot be recovered from the customer.

2.7 Expected losses

When the process of estimating the outcome of a contract results in an overall loss being forecast, the loss should be recognised immediately.

Point to note:

Such a loss should be recognised even if work on the contract has not yet commenced.

Worked example: Expected loss

The following details relate to one of an entity's construction contracts:

	£'000
Estimated contract revenue	400
Contract costs incurred to date	240
Estimated costs to complete	200

How should any expected loss be dealt with?

Solution

On the basis of the estimated costs to complete the contract will be loss-making:

£400,000 – (240,000 + 200,000) = £40,000 loss

This should be recognised in profit or loss immediately.

The revenue should be recognised according to the stage of completion, so:

$$\frac{£400,000 \times 240,000}{(240,000 + 200,000)} = £218,000$$

Cost of sales comes out as the balancing figure

	£'000
Revenue (400 × 240/440)	218
Cost of sales (bal fig)	(258)
Contract loss	(40)

The difference between costs incurred and cost of sales (£240,000 – 258,000 = £18,000) should be recognised as a provision for losses and become part of the gross amounts due from/to customers, as shown in section 2.9.

Point to note:

If the contract is profitable, it is often the case that revenue is the balancing figure; if it is loss-making, then cost is often the balancing figure.

2.8 Judgements required

As noted, accounting for construction contracts requires estimates to be made of how the contracts are likely to turn out once they have been completed. It is very important that consistent approaches are taken to matters such as:

- The combining of contracts into a single contract. If there are two contracts, one profitable, the other loss-making, combining them into a single contract will result in the loss being offset against the profit. Management should be careful not to combine contracts solely to avoid the immediate recognition of the loss on the loss-making contract.

- The estimation of the stage of completion of each contract.

- The costs to be incurred in the future – any understatement will result in an overstatement of the profit recognised in the current period.

- Any additional revenue which will be recovered from the customer as a result of variations to the contract – at the end of the current reporting period there may be uncertainty as to whether the customer will agree that additional amounts are a cost to the customer rather than to the contractor.

Without a consistent approach, there is a risk that estimates may be made to achieve a current period total profit to suit management, rather than one which can be regarded by users of financial statements as a faithful representation of the profit actually earned.

2.9 Relevance of information for users

The timing of cash receipts and the recognition of revenue may be different. IAS 11 requires disclosures to be made of information which is essential as a means of assessing construction contracts in progress and the likely nature of future cash flows. The required disclosures are:

- The contract revenue recognised in the period.

- The methods used to determine that revenue and the stage of completion of contracts in progress.

- The aggregate of the costs incurred and profits less losses recognised to date. These are the cumulative figures for uncompleted contracts.

- The advances received from customers, that is the amounts paid by them in advance of the related work being performed. These show the extent to which customers are financing the business by lending money in advance of work being done on their behalf.

- Retentions, being the amounts held back by customers as security for any remedial work.

- Gross amounts due from customers and due to customers, calculated as:

	£
Costs incurred to date	X
Add: profit recognised	X
Less: losses recognised on contract	(X)
Less: progress billings made	(X)
	X/(X)

If the total is positive, it is the amount due from customers and is recognised as a current asset in the statement of financial position.

If the total is negative, it is the amount due to customers (excess billings) and is recognised as a current liability in the statement of financial position.

These provide information by which users of financial statements can assess the current profitability and make estimates of profitability in the future.

3 UK GAAP comparison

3.1 IAS 18 *Revenue* and UK GAAP

There is no comprehensive UK accounting standard covering revenue. However the main principles of FRS 5 *Reporting the Substance of Transactions* are consistent with IAS 18.

3.2 Construction contracts

	SSAP 9 *Stocks and Long-term Contracts*	IAS 11 *Construction Contracts*
Scope	Service contracts could fall within its scope	Service contracts would not fall within its scope
Statement of financial position amounts	Requires asset representing gross amount from customers to be split between: • Amounts recoverable on contracts (debtors) • Long-term contract balances (stocks)	Just single figure of gross amount from customers needs to be shown
Inequalities in profit generation	Inequalities in profit generation from different stages of a contract should be considered in determining the attributable profit	Not mentioned

Summary and Self-test

Summary

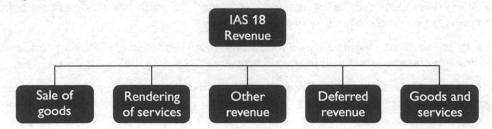

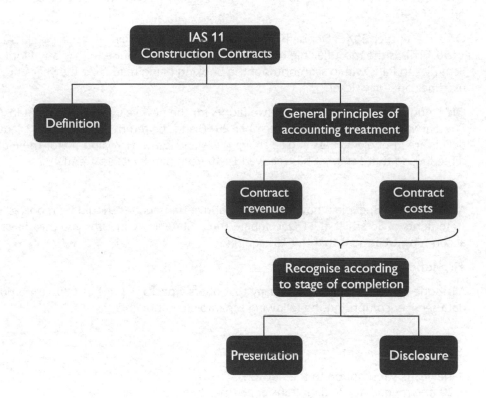

Self-test

Answer the following questions.

1   **Scramjet**

Scramjet is a UK-based airline which has traditionally operated in the low cost sector, but which is trying to attract a greater proportion of business travellers.

The airline sells tickets in different booking classes, each of which has a different set of booking conditions concerning changes, refunds, and so on.

The further in advance flights are paid for and the more restrictive the booking conditions (such as not allowing changes or refunds in any circumstances), the less the flights cost.

At the company's year end of 31 December 20X6, there are a large number of passengers who have paid in advance for their flights. A sample of three passengers below illustrates some of the booking conditions.

Barbara booked flights to and from Reus for travel in August 20X7 in booking class N. This is the most restrictive booking class and does not allow any refunds or changes whatever. If Barbara misses her flight, Scramjet will not provide any refund or move her booking to another flight. On 1 November 20X6, Barbara booked a flight out to Reus and one back a week later, each at a sales price of £40.

On 1 December 20X6, Denise booked a one-way flight to Paris in booking class Y, at a price of £150. This is the most flexible booking class and allows Denise to take any flight operated by Scramjet to Paris within six months of the booking being made. At the year-end, Denise had not used her one-way ticket.

On 7 August 20X6, Dave booked two flights for the new year holiday from Stansted to Prague. The outward flight was on 28 December 20X6 and the return flight was on 3 January 20X7. His tickets are in booking class N (see above for restrictions). He paid £70 for the flight in each direction, so that Scramjet has received £140 from him by its year-end.

Requirement

Applying IAS 18, explain how each of the above transactions should be reported in the financial statements of Scramjet at 31 December 20X6. State any criticisms you may have of the accounting treatment that IAS 18 requires. **(6 marks)**

2   **Airphone**

Airphone is a mobile phone company that offers a package price of £800 for a portable email and data service, comprising the following separable components:

	Fair value £
Handset	300
One year's subscription to the network	100
120 free megabytes of data transfer per month for one year – see below	600
Total fair value of individual components of package	1,000

Payment is due in full upon signing the contract.

The promotion offers 120 free megabytes ('MB') of data transfer per month with unused MB each month being rolled over to the following month. Analysis of similar past promotions shows that on average subscribers use only 1,200 MB over the year with 400 MB used evenly over the first six months and 800 MB used evenly over the second six months. The estimated fair value of free calls from past experience is £0.50 per MB of data.

Requirement

Assuming that a customer signs up for the package above on 1 December 20X6, show how this transaction should be reflected in Airphone's financial statements to 31 December 20X6.

(6 marks)

3 **Henley Co**

Henley Co is an entity that engages in large-scale construction projects. It is summarising costs incurred in its years ended 31 December 20X4 and 31 December 20X5 in respect of a major building construction contract for Astronaut Co.

Negotiations for the contract commenced at the start of August 20X4 and contract preparation and negotiation costs of £170,000 have been incurred up to June 20X5. Negotiations progressed to the point that, on 1 April 20X5, Henley Co judged that it was probable it would be awarded the contract. The contract was signed and building work commenced on 1 July 20X5. The contract was still in progress at the year end.

Costs in the twelve months ended 31 December 20X5 were incurred evenly over the year unless otherwise stated, and were as follows:

- Eight supervisors were employed in the year at a cost of £300,000. Three of these eight were engaged in the contract for Astronaut Co.

- 32 manual workers were employed at a cost of £800,000. 20 of these 32 were engaged on the Astronaut contract.

- Design staff cost £100,000 to employ. These staff split their time approximately evenly throughout the year on four contracts, including the Astronaut contract.

- £50,000 was spent on research and development as part of an ongoing drive to improve efficiency.

- General management costs of £400,000 were incurred.

- £1,200,000 was spent on casual labour on the Astronaut contract.

- Depreciation on construction machinery was £600,000 in the year. 30% of the equipment was allocated to the Astronaut contract.

- It cost £80,000 to move machinery to the Astronaut construction site.

- £120,000 was spent on hire of machinery for the Astronaut contract.

- Henley Co spent £60,000 on public liability insurance. Henley's accounting policy is to apportion this to individual contracts as 10% of depreciation.

- £3,200,000 was spent on materials for the Astronaut contract. Of this, £600,000 remains unused at the year-end and could possibly be used on other contracts.

Requirement

Calculate the amounts which should be classified as contract costs in the year to 31 December 20X5 in respect of the Astronaut contract. **(8 marks)**

4 **Pardew plc**

On 1 April 20X7, Pardew plc, a construction company, began work on a project which was expected to take 18 months to complete. The contract price was agreed at £21 million and total contract costs were estimated to be £16 million. Pardew plc uses independent quantity surveyors to certify the cumulative sales value of construction work at the end of each month. The accounting policy of Pardew is to consider the outcome of contracts to be capable of reliable estimation when they are at least 40% complete.

At 31 December 20X7 amounts relating to the contract were as follows.

	£'000
Certified sales value of work completed	14,700
Invoices raised to customer	13,000
Progress payment received	11,500
Contract costs incurred	12,000
Estimate of additional contract costs to complete	6,000

Requirements

(a) Explain, with calculations where appropriate, how the amounts in respect of this contract should be presented in the income statement and statement of financial position of Pardew plc for the year to 31 December 20X7 if the stage of completion of the contract is calculated by reference to:

    (i) contract costs incurred as a proportion of total estimated contract costs

    (ii) the certified sales value of the work completed as a proportion of the total contract price.

(b) Explain briefly why the two accounting policies result in different amounts in the 20X7 financial statements.

(10 marks)

5 **Prideaux plc**

Prideaux plc (Prideaux), a construction company with a 31 December year end, measures the stage of completion on its contracts by the costs incurred as a proportion of total costs method. During 20X6 Prideaux tendered for the construction of a large building on land owned by the customer. The building would replace one recently demolished and the project was expected to take three years to complete.

In 20X6 Prideaux incurred costs of £0.5 million on preparing its initial quotation, £0.3 million on modifying it once the company had been included on the short list of four tenderers and £0.1 million on finalising it once the contract had been awarded. The contract price was agreed at £40 million and Prideaux estimated its construction costs at £34.2 million. By the end of 20X6 construction costs incurred were £2.8 million, costs to complete were estimated at £31.4 million, progress invoices of £2 million had been raised and the customer had paid £1.5 million.

In 20X7 further construction costs of £10.1 million were incurred and at 31 December 20X7 costs to complete were estimated at £19 million, progress invoices to date totalled £11 million and the customer had paid a total of £8 million.

In 20X8 further construction costs of £15 million were incurred and at 31 December 20X8 costs to complete were estimated at £14 million, progress invoices to date totalled £27 million and the customer had paid a total of £25 million. The 20X8 construction costs included £5 million incurred as a result of problems with the foundations of the final part of the building. Prideaux claimed that because these problems resulted from mistakes made during the demolition of the old building, the contract price should be increased by £6 million. The customer is arguing that the problems resulted from poor materials used by Prideaux and has thrown the £6m claim out.

During 20X9 the project was completed. In the year Prideaux incurred construction costs of £15.5 million and the customer accepted invoices totalling another £19 million. By 31 December 20X9 the customer had settled all these invoices.

Requirement

Calculate, with explanations where appropriate, the amounts in respect of this contract to be presented in the income statement and statement of financial position of Prideaux plc for each of the four years to 31 December 20X9. **(10 marks)**

Now go back to the Learning Objectives in the Introduction. If you are satisfied you have achieved these objectives, please tick them off.

Technical reference

1 IAS 18 *Revenue*

- Revenue recognised when: IAS 18 Objective

    - Probable that future economic benefits will flow to the entity; and

    - These benefits can be measured reliably.

- Apply principle of substance over form.   IAS 18 (13)

- Revenue defined as gross inflows that result in increase in equity.   IAS 18 (7)

    Sales taxes (for example VAT) and amounts collected by agent on behalf of   IAS 18 (8)
    principal are excluded.

- Measured as fair value of consideration – discounted where appropriate.   IAS 18 (9-11)

- Recognition of sale of goods, when buyer has obtained significant   IAS 18 (14)
  risks/rewards of ownership.

- Recognition of rendering of services should take account of stage of   IAS 18 (20)
  completion, if over a long period:

    - Include pro rata costs and consider costs to complete;

    - If overall outcome cannot be estimated reliably, revenue limited to costs   IAS 18 (26)
      recoverable from customer.

- Practical considerations, including 'free' servicing, where revenue deferred to   IAS 18 Appendix A
  cover both cost and reasonable profit.   (all but 9, 10, 13 and
                                                                                           14)

2 IAS 11 *Construction Contracts*

- Definitions   IAS 11 (3)

- Combining and segmenting contracts

    - Standard usually applied to separate contracts   IAS 11 (7)
    - Segmenting construction contracts   IAS 11 (8)
    - Combining construction contracts   IAS 11 (9)

- Contract revenue   IAS 11 (11 – 13)

- Contract costs   IAS 11 (16 – 21)

- Recognition of contract revenue and expenses

    - When outcome estimated reliably recognise by reference to stage of   IAS 11 (22)
      completion

    - Fixed price contract   IAS 11 (23)

    - Cost plus contract   IAS 11 (24)

    - Stage of completion   IAS 11 (25 – 26)

    - Methods of determining stage of completion   IAS 11 (30 – 31)

    - When outcome cannot be estimated reliably   IAS 11 (32)

- Recognition of expected losses   IAS 11 (36 – 37)

- Disclosure   IAS 11 (39 – 44)

Answer to Interactive question 1

Magazine revenue   £16,000

Explanation

Revenue for the magazines should be recognised in the periods in which they are despatched, assuming the items are of similar value in each period. Thus the revenue to be recognised in the year ended 31 March 20X7 is £48,000 × 4/12 = £16,000.

Answer to Interactive question 2

Revenue   £nil

Explanation

Revenue should be recognised when the drills are delivered to the customer. Until then no revenue should be recognised and the deposits should be carried forward as deferred income.

Answer to Interactive question 3

Contract revenue   £60,000

Explanation

If the outcome of a services transaction cannot be estimated reliably, revenue should only be recognised to the extent that expenses incurred are recoverable from the customer.

Answer to Interactive question 4

		£
Revenue –	sale of goods (W)	1,350,000
	sale of services (W)	25,000
Total		1,375,000

WORKINGS

	£
After-sale support (120,000/(100% – 20%))	150,000
Remainder = sale of goods (bal fig)	1,350,000
Total revenue	1,500,000

Revenue for sale of services recognised in the four months to 30 April 20X7 should be £150,000/2 years × 4/12 = £25,000

Answer to Interactive question 5

Costs   £2,476,000

WORKINGS

	£'000
Labour	632
Materials	1,325
Design costs	463
Borrowing costs	56
	2,476

Research costs, general administration costs and selling costs should be recognised as expenses in profit or loss as they are incurred.

Answer to Interactive question 6

The procedure is to identify the costs incurred, to calculate the profit and to insert revenue as the balancing figure.

The amounts relating to this contract which should be recognised in profit or loss for each of the three financial years are:

Stage of completion			Revenue £'000	Cost of sales £'000	Profit £'000
20X5	100/400 = 25%	In 20X5	125	100	25
20X6	300/420 = 71%	Cumulative to end-20X6, then 20X5 amounts deducted	232 (bal fig)	(300 – 100) 200	(57 – 25) 32
20X7	100%	Cumulative to end-20X7, then cumulative previous amounts deducted	<u>143</u> (bal fig)	(410 – 300) <u>110</u>	(90 – 57) <u>33</u>
		Total	500	410	90

1 Scramjet

IAS 18 requires that revenue from rendering of services is recognised by reference to the stage of completion of the transaction at the end of the reporting period. IAS 18 takes an approach which is focused on the income statement rather than the statement of financial position. This means that Scramjet may have taken bookings which are entirely non-refundable but the revenue associated with payments for tickets should be held in the statement of financial position as deferred income until either the flight is taken or the ticket expires.

Barbara

Barbara's flight resulted in Scramjet receiving £80 in November 20X6, which it will be entitled to keep without any further conditions. Both outbound and return flights are after the year-end date and so all this £80 should be recognised as deferred revenue in the statement of financial position, rather than as revenue in the year to 31 December 20X6.

If IAS 18 took an approach more consistent with the IASB's *Conceptual Framework* document, it would have recognised revenue at the same time as recognising the cash asset. This approach is prohibited by IAS 18 however, meaning that IAS 18 itself is inconsistent with the IASB's guiding Framework principles.

Denise

Denise's flight has also not been taken at the year-end and so the £150 received should also be recognised as deferred income in the statement of financial position at 31 December 20X6. The Framework principles for income and asset recognition would also give this same conclusion since Scramjet is not yet unconditionally entitled to the income as it may need to refund the flexible ticket.

Dave

Under IAS 18 revenue for the outbound flight should be recognised as that part of the service has been completed. £70 should thus be recognised in profit or loss and £70 should remain in the statement of financial position as deferred income until Dave's flight back is completed.

2 Airphone

Revenue from the sale of the handset should be recognised when the risks and rewards of ownership pass to the buyer, which will normally be on delivery to the customer.

Access to the network (subscription) and free data transfer represent the rendering of services; the subscription should normally be recognised on a straight-line basis and the free data transfer should be recognised based on past experience as set out in the question.

The bundled package represents a £200 discount (£1,000 total fair value of the individual components less package price of £800). In the absence of any specific discounting strategy, a reasonable basis is to recognise the £200 discount on a pro rata basis.

	Fair value £	%	Discount £	Revenue £
Handset	300	30	60	240
Subscription	100	10	20	80
Free data	600	60	120	480
Total	1,000	100	200	800

The revenue per MB attributable to free data transfer should be calculated by reference to the expected take-up of 1,200 MB, not the contractually allowed take-up of 1,440 MB. The amount is £0.40 per MB (£480/ 1,200 MB).

The total revenue recognised in the current year for this contract should be:

	£
Handset	240.00
Subscription (£80/12)	6.67
Free data transfer (£0.40 × (400/6))	26.67
	273.34

The balance of £526.66 should be recognised as a current liability in the statement of financial position (deferred income).

3 **Henley Co**

Amount incurred from 1 Jan 20X5 to 31 Dec 20X5 on:	Total £'000	Recoverable on Astronaut contract £'000	Basis
Preparation and negotiation (from 1 August 20X4)	170	46.36	3/11 months
Supervision	300	56.25	3/8 × 6/12
Manual labour	800	250	20/32 × 6/12
Design department	100	25	1/4
R&D	50	0	None
General management	400	0	None
Casual labour	1,200	1,200	All
Depreciation	600	90	6/12 × 30%
Moving machinery	80	80	All
Equipment hire	120	120	All
Liability insurance	60	9	10% × depreciation
Materials	3,200	2,600	600 in normal inventory

4 **Pardew plc**

(a) Although contract costs originally estimated at £16 million are now estimated at £18 million (12,000 + 6,000), the contract is still estimated to generate a profit of £3 million (21,000 – 18,000). Contract revenue and expenses should be recognised by the stage of completion method.

(i) Using the contract costs method, the contract is 2/3 (12,000 as a proportion of 18,000) complete, in excess of the 40% cut-off point. So 2/3 of contract revenue and contract profit should be recognised in profit or loss, so £14 million (2/3 × 21,000) and £2 million (2/3 × 3,000) respectively.

In the statement of financial position, gross amounts due from customers should be presented as contract costs incurred plus recognised profits less invoices raised to customers (see below for calculations). Trade receivables should include £1.5 million (13,000 invoiced less 11,500 payments received).

(ii) Using the certified sales value method, the contract is 70% (14,700 as a proportion of 21,000) complete, in excess of the 40% cut-off point. So contract revenue of £14.7 million should be recognised in the income statement, together with cost of sales of £12 million (the costs incurred). A profit of £2.7 million should be recognised.

In the statement of financial position, gross amounts due from customers should be presented in the same way as for the contract costs method (see below for calculations) and trade receivables should include the same £1.5 million.

Income statement

	Contract costs £'000	Work certified £'000
Revenue	14,000	14,700
Cost of sales	(12,000)	(12,000)
Profit	2,000	2,700

Statement of financial position

	Contract costs £'000	Work certified £'000
Gross amount due from customers		
Costs incurred	12,000	12,000
Recognised profits	2,000	2,700
	14,000	14,700
Progress billings	(13,000)	(13,000)
	1,000	1,700
Trade receivables	1,500	1,500

An alternative presentation of profit and cost of sales under the work certified basis would be to calculate cost of sales as a proportion of total expected costs, rather than actual costs incurred to date:

	Work certified £'000
Income statement	
Revenue	14,700
Cost of sales (18m × 0.7)	(12,600)
Profit	2,100
Statement of financial position	
Gross amount due from customers	
Costs incurred	12,000
Recognised profits	2,100
	14,100
Progress billings	(13,000)
	1,100

(b) The contract costs method assumes that the same profit margin is earned on all parts of a construction contract. The certified sales method can, and in this instance does, take account of the margin on certain parts of a contract being higher than on others, perhaps because the customer places a higher value on those parts.

Point to note:

Over the life of the contract, the profit is the same under both methods; it is just its allocation to the reporting periods in which work is done which is different.

5 **Prideaux plc**

Income statement for year to 31 December

	20X6 Note 1 £'000	20X7 Note 2 £'000	20X8 Note 3 £'000	20X9 Note 4 £'000
Revenue	2,900	13,350	10,417	19,333
Cost of sales	(2,900)	(10,100)	(15,667)	(14,833)
Gross profit	–	3,250	(5,250)	4,500
Operating expenses	(800)	–	–	–
Net profit/(loss)	(800)	3,250	(5,250)	4,500

Statement of financial position at 31 December

	20X6 £'000	20X7 £'000	20X8 £'000	20X9 £'000
Costs incurred to date	2,900	13,000	28,000	43,500
Recognised profits less losses	–	3,250	(2,000)	2,500
Recognised cumulative revenue	2,900	16,250	26,000	46,000
Less: progress billings	(2,000)	(11,000)	(27,000)	(46,000)
Gross amount due from customers	900	5,250		–
Gross amount due to customers			1,000	
Trade receivables:				
Progress billings	2,000	11,000	27,000	46,000
Amounts received	(1,500)	(8,000)	(25,000)	(46,000)
	500	3,000	2,000	–

Notes

1   The only tendering costs which can be included in contract costs are those costs incurred after it is probable that the contract will be won. So the £0.5 million and £0.3 million should be recognised as an expense in 20X6.

   Contract costs total £2.9 million (0.1 + 2.8). The contract is only 8.5% (2.9 as a % of (2.9 + 31.4)) complete, too early to be able to estimate its outcome reliably. Contract costs incurred should be recognised as an expense within cost of sales, with revenue of the same amount being recognised (the costs being recoverable from the customer).

2   Contract costs incurred are £13 million (2.9 +10.1). The contract is 40.63% (13 as a % of (13 + 19)) complete, so it is likely that its outcome can be estimated reliably. Cumulatively, 40.63% of the £40 million contract price should be recognised, so £16.25 million (and 16.25 – 2.9 = 13.35 in the year). With cost of sales of £10.1 million (the costs incurred in the year), the profit in the year is £3.25 million (40.63% × the estimated profit of £8 million (40 – 32)).

3   Revenue for variations should only be recognised if it is probable that the customer will approve the variation, so Prideaux should not recognise any benefit from its claim.

   Contract costs incurred are £28 million (13 b/f + 15 in the year). The contract is 2/3 complete (28 as a % of (28 + 14)). But with total revenue still £40 million, an overall loss of £2 million is now estimated; this should be recognised immediately. As the profit to date brought forward is £3.25 million, a loss of £5.25 million should now be recognised. Cumulative revenue should be measured at £26.667 million (40 × 2/3) so £10.417 million (26.667 – 16.25) in the year. Cost of sales for the year is the balancing figure of £15.667 million.

4   Revenue for the year is £19.333 million ((27 billings b/f + 19 billings in the year) – 26.667), cost of sales is £14.833 million ((28 b/f + 15.5 incurred in the year) – 28.667 cost of sales to end-20X8), so profit in the year is £4.5 million, and £2.5 million (4.5 – 2 loss b/f) over the contract as a whole (excluding the £0.8 million tendering costs).

CHAPTER 7

Financial instruments

Introduction

Examination context

Topic List

1   Financial instruments – introduction

2   IAS 32 *Financial Instruments: Presentation*

3   IAS 39 *Financial Instruments: Recognition and Measurement*

4   IFRS 7 *Financial Instruments: Disclosures*

5   Ethical and judgement issues

6   UK GAAP comparison

Summary and Self-test

Technical reference

Answers to Interactive questions

Answers to Self-test

Learning objectives

Tick off

- Prepare and present extracts of financial statements in respect of financial instruments ☐

- Formulate accounting and reporting policies in respect of financial instruments ☐

- Illustrate how different methods of recognising and measuring financial instruments can affect the view presented ☐

- Explain and illustrate the main differences between international and UK requirements ☐

- Identify and consider appropriate actions for ethical issues involving financial instruments ☐

Specific syllabus references for this chapter are: 1e, 2a, 2c, 3a, 4a and 4c.

Syllabus links

Although financial instruments were briefly introduced in the Financial Accounting text, the majority of this chapter is new material. There are three International Financial Reporting Standards relating to this area:

IAS 32 *Financial Instruments: Presentation*
IAS 39 *Financial Instruments: Recognition and Measurement*
IFRS 7 *Financial Instruments: Disclosures*

All areas of IAS 32 are examinable at Financial Reporting but only the more basic areas of IAS 39 and IFRS 7 are examinable at this stage. These two standards will be examined in more detail at the Advanced Stage.

Examination context

In the examination, candidates may be required to:

- Describe the recognition and derecognition criteria for financial instruments

- Calculate the liability and equity elements of compound instruments

- Classify financial instruments and prepare extracts of financial statements for basic financial instruments

- Calculate the carrying amount of a financial asset or liability measured at amortised cost using the effective interest method

- Recognise the correct accounting treatment of a variety of financial instruments

- Recognise and measure impairment losses for simple financial instruments

- Describe the disclosure requirements for financial instruments and their usefulness to users of financial statements

- Identify ethical issues and professional judgements involving financial instruments and the effect this may have on financial performance and financial position

Points to note:

Detailed knowledge of different types of derivatives is not required. Only those types of financial instruments included in this chapter and in the revision questions and answers will be included in examination questions.

Hedge accounting is excluded from the Professional Stage syllabus.

Foreign currency transaction accounting using IAS 21 *The Effects of Changes in Foreign Exchange Rates* is excluded from the syllabus.

1 Financial instruments – introduction

Section overview

- The extensive financial reporting requirements for financial instruments are covered by IAS 32, IAS 39 and IFRS 7.

- A number of common definitions are used in all three standards.

1.1 Introduction

The increasing diversity of businesses and the wider development and availability of financial instruments has increased the use of complex financial transactions by entities in order to reduce their exposure to risks. The existence of financial instruments has a significant effect on the risk profile of organisations. Such instruments can have a significant effect on profits, solvency and cash flow.

Common financial instruments include:

- Cash and timed deposits
- Trade payables and receivables
- Loans payable and receivable
- Debt and equity investments
- Derivatives such as interest rate swaps and foreign exchange contracts
- Redeemable and irredeemable preference shares
- Convertible debt instruments
- Investments in shares issued by other entities

As a result of this widespread use of financial assets and financial liabilities as part of an entity's ordinary activities, International Financial Reporting Standards have been published to deal with:

- Recognition
- Measurement
- Presentation and disclosure.

1.2 Relevant accounting standards

The three relevant accounting standards for financial instruments are:

- IAS 32 *Financial Instruments: Presentation*
- IAS 39 *Financial Instruments: Recognition and Measurement*
- IFRS 7 *Financial Instruments: Disclosures*

The individual standards cannot be studied in isolation. A number of terms and definitions are used across the standards and an understanding of financial instruments requires an understanding of the key concepts in each standard.

1.3 What is a financial instrument?

The definition of a financial instrument is consistent throughout the three accounting standards covering financial instruments. It is introduced in IAS 32.

Definition

A **financial instrument** is any contract that gives rise to a financial asset of one entity and a financial liability or equity instrument of another entity. [IAS 32.11]

Note that a financial instrument has **two parties**. It should be recognised as an **asset** by one party and either a **liability or equity** by the other. The classification of a financial instrument as a financial liability or equity is particularly important as it will have an effect on gearing.

The definitions of financial assets, financial liabilities and equity instruments are necessarily complex. For the Financial Reporting examination it is necessary for you to understand the basic points of each definition and the challenges that these definitions represent for financial reporting.

1.4 What is a financial asset?

Definition

A **financial asset** is any asset that is:

- Cash

- An equity instrument of another entity

- A contractual right:

    - To receive cash or another financial asset from another entity; or

    - To exchange financial assets or financial liabilities with another entity under conditions that are potentially favourable to the entity: or

- A contract that will or may be settled in the entity's own equity instruments and which is:

    - A non-derivative for which the entity is or may be obliged to receive a variable number of the entity's own equity instruments; or

    - A derivative that will or may be settled other than by exchange of a fixed amount of cash or another financial asset for a fixed number of the entity's own equity instruments. For this purpose the entity's own equity instruments do not include instruments that are themselves contracts for the future receipt or delivery of the entity's own equity instruments.   [IAS 32.11]

The key here is that financial assets are cash, a **contractual right** to receive cash or another financial asset (such as shares) or to exchange financial assets or liabilities on favourable terms, or holdings of equity instruments (such as shares).

Derivatives, such as a commodity contract, would be a financial asset if they are 'in the money'. For example, a derivative that allowed you to buy 15,000 tonnes of a commodity for £6,000 today when the spot price is £0.50 per tonne is in the money as you would subsequently be able to sell the 15,000 tonnes for £7,500. Derivatives are discussed later in this chapter.

Assets that have physical substance, such as plant and machinery, are not financial assets and neither are intangible assets, such as patents and brands. These assets generate future economic benefits for an entity although there is no contractual right to receive cash or another financial asset. Examples of financial assets include cash, a trade receivable and equity investments.

Worked example: Financial asset

An entity deposits £20,000 of cash with a bank for a fixed term of three years. The £20,000 is a financial asset of the entity as it has a contractual right to receive the cash in three years' time.

1.5 What is a financial liability?

Definition

A **financial liability** is any liability that is:

- A contractual obligation:

    - To deliver cash or another financial asset to another entity; or

    - To exchange financial assets or financial liabilities with another entity under conditions that are potentially unfavourable to the entity: or

- A contract that will or may be settled in the entity's own equity instruments and which is:

  - A non-derivative for which the entity is or may be obliged to deliver a variable number of the entity's own equity instruments; or

  - A derivative that will or may be settled other than by exchange of a fixed amount of cash or another financial asset for a fixed number of the entity's own equity instruments. For this purpose the entity's own equity instruments do not include instruments that are themselves contracts for the future receipt or delivery of the entity's own equity instruments.   [IAS 32.11]

The key to this definition is that a financial liability is a **contractual obligation** to deliver cash or another financial asset, or a contractual obligation to exchange financial assets or liabilities on potentially unfavourable terms.

This terminology is consistent with the *Conceptual Framework* in which financial liabilities are defined in terms of obligations. Note that the IAS 32 definition requires the obligations to be contractual.

Examples of financial liabilities include trade payables, loans and redeemable preference shares. A bank overdraft is a financial liability as it is repayable in cash and a derivative that is 'out of the money' is also a financial liability. A warranty provision would not be a financial liability because the obligation is to deliver additional goods or services, not cash.

Worked example: Financial liability

In 20X2 an entity entered into a contract that required it to issue shares to the value of £10,000 on 1 January 20X5.

This is a financial liability since the entity is required to settle the contract by issuing a variable number of shares based on a fixed monetary amount.

If the number of shares were fixed, it would not meet the definition of a financial liability and should be presented as an equity instrument.

1.6   What is an equity instrument?

Definition

An **equity instrument** is any contract that evidences a residual interest in the assets of an entity after deducting all of its liabilities.   [IAS 32.11]

In applying all these definitions it is essential to establish whether or not there is in existence a contractual right to receive, or a contractual obligation to deliver, which is enforceable by law.

Worked example: Ordinary shares

Holders of ordinary shares in a company own equity instruments. Although they own the residual interest in a company, they have no **contractual right** to demand any of it to be delivered to them, for example by way of a dividend. Equally, the company has issued an equity instrument, not a financial liability, because the company has no **contractual obligation** to distribute the residual interest.

An entity that invests in the ordinary shares of another entity holds a financial asset, because an equity interest in another entity falls within the definition of a financial asset.

1.7 What is a derivative?

Definition

A **derivative** is a financial instrument or other contract within the scope of IAS 39 with all three of the following characteristics:

- Its value changes in response to the change in a specified interest rate, financial instrument price, commodity price, foreign exchange rate, index of prices or rates, credit rating or credit index, or other variable, provided in the case of a non-financial variable that the variable is not specific to the party to the contract (sometimes called the 'underlying').

- It requires no initial net investment or an initial net investment that is smaller than would be required for other types of contracts that would be expected to have a similar response to changes in market factors; and

- It is settled at a future date.   [IAS 39.9]

The definition is important because derivatives are becoming a common way for companies to manage business risks. Their values are volatile and this is reflected in the accounting treatment because the requirement is that they are always measured at fair value.

Derivatives are often used to hedge risk. IAS 39 includes specific rules for hedge accounting where specific criteria are met. Hedge accounting is outside the Financial Reporting syllabus. You should assume that any derivative does not meet the criteria for hedge accounting.

A derivative **normally** has a notional amount, such as a number of shares or other quantity specified in the contract. For example, a forward currency contract has a quoted amount of currency even though neither the holder nor writer is required to invest or receive the amount at inception of the contract.

However, there are derivatives which do not have a notional amount. For example, a contract sold for £20 that requires the fixed payment of £1,000 if a commodity price increases by 5% is a derivative because:

- Its value changes as the commodity price changes

- It requires a small initial investment in comparison to contracts that would be expected to have a similar response

- It is settled at a future date

In determining whether a derivative exists, the substance of the transaction should be considered. Non-derivative transactions should be aggregated and treated as derivatives when the transactions result, in substance, in derivatives.

Common examples of derivatives include:

Derivative	Description
Forward contracts	Contracts to purchase or sell a specific quantity of a financial instrument, a commodity, or a foreign currency at a specified price determined at the outset, with delivery or settlement at a specified future date. Settlement is at maturity by actual delivery of the item specified in the contract, or by a net cash settlement. An example would be a contract to deliver 20,000 tonnes of gold on 31 December 20X6 for £300 per tonne.
Interest rate swaps and forward rate agreements	Exchange of cash flows as of a specified date or a series of specified dates, based on a notional amount and fixed and floating rates.

Derivative	Description
Options	Contracts that give the purchaser the right, but not the obligation, to buy (call option) or sell (put option) a specified quantity of a particular financial instrument, commodity, or foreign exchange, at a specified price (strike price), during or at a specified period of time. These can be individually written or exchange-traded. The purchaser of the option pays the seller (writer) of the option a fee (premium) to compensate the seller for the risk of being required to sell (call option) or buy (put option) the item under option. For example, a company may purchase an option to sell 5,000 barrels of oil at $50 per barrel on 31 December 20X7.

Worked example: Derivatives

Swapper (ER) Ltd enters into an interest rate swap with Swappee (EE) Ltd that requires ER to pay a fixed rate of 6% and receive a variable rate of three-month LIBOR, reset on a quarterly basis. The fixed and variable amounts are determined based on a £10 million notional amount. The notional amount is not exchanged, but ER pays or receives a net cash amount each quarter based on the difference between 6% and three-month LIBOR, reset quarterly.

The contract meets the definition of a derivative because (i) there is no initial net investment (there is only a small initial cost) (ii) settlements occur at future quarterly dates, and (iii) the underlying variable is LIBOR, which changes over time.

Worked example: Warrants

Holyrood plc issued 5,000 warrants for £3 each. Each warrant gives the holder, Kensington Ltd, the right to acquire one new ordinary share for £20 at anytime during the next five years. At 31 December 20X5 the fair value of each warrant was £9.

Own equity issued, including the issue of options and warrants, falls within the scope of IAS 32. The warrants are a derivative on Holyrood plc's own shares settled by the delivery of a fixed number of shares for a fixed amount of cash.

The £15,000 received on the issue of the warrants should be credited to equity by Holyrood plc. Holyrood plc should not remeasure the warrants for subsequent changes in their fair value because such changes generate gains and losses for the holder, Kensington Ltd, not the issuer.

The warrants are a financial asset for Kensington Ltd.

Interactive question 1: Financial instruments [Difficulty level: Easy]

Identify which of the following are financial instruments, financial assets, financial liabilities, equity instruments or derivatives and for which party.

1   Offertake Ltd sells £5,000 of inventory to Guideprice Ltd on 30 day payment terms.
2   Ashdell Ltd pays £20,000 in advance for a twelve month insurance policy.
3   Tollbar Ltd enters into a contract to sell $400,000 in six months' time for £280,000.
4   Wellbeck Ltd issues 100,000 ordinary shares which are acquired by Keeload Ltd.
5   Cashlow plc borrows £200,000 under a mortgage from Norbert plc.

See **Answer** at the end of this chapter.

2 IAS 32 *Financial Instruments: Presentation*

Section overview

- Financial instruments should be presented as assets, liabilities or equity in the statement of financial position.

- Compound financial instruments should be split between their liability and equity components.

- Interest, dividends, gains and losses should be presented in a manner consistent with the classification of the related financial instrument.

- Financial assets and financial liabilities can only be offset in limited circumstances.

2.1 Objectives and scope of IAS 32

The objective of IAS 32 *Financial Instruments: Presentation* is to enhance a user's understanding of the way in which financial instruments affect an entity's financial performance, financial position and cash flows. IAS 32 sets out the presentation requirements for financial instruments and their related interest or dividends, and specifies the circumstances in which they should be offset. [IAS 32.2]

The principles that underlie the standard are consistent with, and complement, those in IAS 39, which addresses recognition and measurement criteria.

The scope of IAS 32 is that it applies to **all entities** and to all types of financial instruments except where another standard is more specific. Examples of areas which are outside the scope of IAS 32 are:

- Subsidiaries accounted for under IAS 27
- Associates accounted for under IAS 28
- Joint ventures accounted for under IAS 31. [IAS 32.4]

Worked example: Investments in subsidiaries

Greatdane plc acquired 40,000 ordinary shares in Subtime Ltd which represents 80% of its issued ordinary share capital. Whilst these ordinary shares are a financial asset of Greatdane, IAS 32 (and IAS 39) does not apply; the provisions of IAS 27 *Consolidated and Separate Financial Statements* should be applied.

In the separate (company only) financial statements of Greatdane plc, IAS 27 allows a choice of accounting treatment. The investment may be accounted for either at cost or in accordance with IAS 39 (as a financial asset).

In practice most companies account for investments in subsidiaries, associates and jointly controlled entities at cost in their separate financial statements. Therefore, the provisions of IAS 32 (and IAS 39) are generally only applied to minor investments where the investor does not have control, significant influence or joint control.

2.2 Presentation of equity and liabilities

When an entity issues a financial instrument, it should classify it according to the **substance** of the contract under which it has been issued. It should be classified as:

- A financial asset; or
- A financial liability; or
- An equity instrument. [IAS 32.15]

The characteristics of the financial instrument should be considered to ensure that it is appropriately classified. If the financial instrument meets any of the **criteria** set out in the definition of a **financial liability**, then it should be classified as a liability and not as an equity instrument. The classification should be made at the time the financial instrument is issued and not changed subsequently.

The classification is important as it changes the perceived risk of the entity. The classification of an instrument as a financial liability will potentially have an adverse effect on the gearing ratio of a company and may reduce its ability to obtain further debt funding.

Worked example: Equity and liabilities

Preference shares provide the holder with the right to receive an annual dividend (usually of a predetermined and unchanging amount) out of the profits of a company, together with a fixed amount on the ultimate liquidation of the company or at an earlier date if the shares are redeemable. The legal form of the instrument is equity.

In substance the fixed level of dividend is interest and the redemption amount is a repayment of a loan. Because financial reporting focuses on the substance of the transactions, redeemable preference shares should be presented as liabilities.

In practical terms, only irredeemable preference shares are included in equity. They are less common than redeemable preference shares.

Interactive question 2: Liabilities and equity   [Difficulty level: Intermediate]

Moorgate Ltd issued 10,000 preference shares. The preference shares are redeemable only at the option of Moorgate Ltd. A preference share dividend is payable at the same amount per share as any ordinary share dividend declared during that year.

Explain the presentation requirements for Moorgate Ltd's preference shares.

See **Answer** at the end of this chapter.

When a derivative financial instrument gives one party a choice over how it is settled, it is a financial asset or a financial liability unless all of the settlement alternatives would result in it being an equity instrument.   [IAS 32.26]

Worked example: Settlement options

A company has issued a share option that allows it to offer cash in settlement or to issue a variable number of equity shares instead.

This is a financial liability as the derivative has alternative settlement options which are not equity. The share option would be classified as a financial liability even if the choice of settlement as cash or equity shares was at the option of the holder.

2.3   Compound financial instruments

A compound or 'hybrid' financial instrument is one that contains both a **liability component** and an **equity component**. As an example, an issuer of a **convertible bond** has:

- The obligation to pay annual interest and eventually repay the capital – the liability component
- The possibility of issuing equity, should bondholders choose the conversion option – the equity component.

In substance the issue of such a bond is the same as issuing separately a non-convertible bond and an option to purchase shares.

At the date of issue the components of such instruments should be classified separately according to their substance. This is often called 'split' accounting. The amount received on the issue (net of any issue expense) should be allocated between the separate components as follows:

- The fair value of the liability component should be measured at the present value of the periodic interest payments and the eventual capital repayment assuming the bond is redeemed. The present value should be discounted at the market rate for an instrument of comparable credit status and the same cash flows but without the conversion option

- The fair value of the equity component should be measured as the remainder of the net proceeds.

Note that the rate of interest on the convertible will be lower than the rate of interest on the comparable instrument without the convertibility option, because of the value of the option to acquire equity.

The allocation should not be revised for subsequent changes in market interest rates, share prices or other events that have changed the likelihood that the conversion option will be exercised. This is the case even if the terms become so disadvantageous that it is extremely unlikely that the option will be exercised.

Worked example: Convertible bonds

Instead of issuing a 7% loan repayable in ten years' time an entity issues a 5% convertible bond for £50,000 that is repayable in cash in ten years or convertible at that time into 5,000 ordinary shares in the company.

In such a case the company could have issued two separate instruments, a 7% loan repayable in ten years' time and a warrant or option to subscribe for 5,000 ordinary shares on that date.

Note that the cash flows of the instrument are the same regardless of its accounting treatment, but the accounting treatment may affect the user's perception of risk.

Worked example: Compound instruments

A company issued 3,000 convertible 6% ten year bonds at £100 each. The present value of the redemption value and interest payments determined at market yields for an investment without the conversion option was £275,000.

What amounts should be attributed to the liability and equity components?

Solution

	£
Net proceeds on issue (3,000 × £100)	300,000
Fair value of liability component	(275,000)
Equity component	25,000

Therefore the following should be recognised in the statement of financial position:

Liability	£275,000
Equity	£25,000

Note how the treatment of a convertible bond in this way improves a company's gearing as compared to treating the whole £300,000 as debt.

Interactive question 3: Compound financial instruments   [Difficulty level: Exam standard]

On 1 January 20X7 an entity issued 10,000 6% convertible bonds at a par value of £100. Each bond is redeemable at par or convertible into four shares on 31 December 20X8.

Interest is payable annually in arrears. The market rate of interest for similar debt without the conversion option is 8%.

Using the proforma below measure the liability and equity components of these bonds on 1 January 20X7.

Year		Cash flow £	Discount factor	Present value £
20X7				
20X8				
Total liability component				
Net proceeds				
Equity element				

See **Answer** at the end of this chapter.

Subsequently the annual interest expense recognised in profit or loss should be calculated by reference to the interest rate used in the initial measurement of the liability component.

If all or part of the compound financial instrument is eventually converted into equity, the relevant proportion of the carrying amount of the financial liability should be reclassified as equity, being added to the equity amount initially recognised. No gain or loss should be recognised on conversion of the instrument.

Worked example: Compound instruments

In Interactive question 3 the liability component is £964,335. The subsequent accounting for the liability component should be as follows.

Year	Opening balance £	Interest expense (8%) £	Interest paid £	Closing balance £
20X7	964,335	77,147	(60,000)	981,482
20X8	981,482	78,518	(60,000)	1,000,000

Note how the £77,147 interest expense is greater than the £60,000 (6% × 10,000 × £100) interest paid because it includes the amortisation of the discount attributable to the liability element. Only the interest actually paid should be presented in the statement of cash flows.

If on 31 December 20X8 all the bond holders elect to convert into equity, then the £1 million liability should be reclassified to equity, making £1,035,665 in total. The double entry should be:

DR	Financial liability	£1 million	
CR	Equity		£1 million

If none of the bonds are converted to equity, the liability of £1 million will be extinguished by the cash repayment. However, the amount already included in equity of £35,665 should remain there. The double entry should be:

DR	Financial liability	£1 million	
CR	Cash		£1 million

2.4 Interest, dividends, losses and gains

Interest, dividends, losses and gains arising in relation to a financial instrument that is classified as a financial liability should be recognised in profit or loss for the relevant period. [IAS 32.35]

Distributions, such as dividends, paid to holders of a financial instrument classified as equity should be charged directly against equity (as part of the movement on retained earnings in the statement of changes in equity). [IAS 32.35]

The classification will not affect the cash flows which are the same regardless of the presentation.

Interactive question 4: Dividends   [Difficulty level: Intermediate]

Dorehouse Ltd has declared the following dividends during the year:

1   An ordinary dividend of £4 million
2   A £3 million dividend on preference shares redeemable in 20X9.

Explain the presentation requirements for Dorehouse Ltd's dividends in the financial statements for the year.

See **Answer** at the end of this chapter.

When equity shares are issued, the transaction costs should be deducted from equity, net of any related income tax benefit. The transaction costs to be deducted are only those incremental costs attributable to the equity transaction that otherwise would have been avoided.   [IAS 32.35]

Worked example: Issue costs

An entity issued 100,000 new £1 ordinary shares which have a fair value of £2.50 per share for cash.

Professional fees in respect of the share issue were £50,000 and are deductible for tax purposes. The tax rate is 40%. The management of the entity estimates that costs incurred internally for time incurred working on the share issue are £25,000.

How should these transactions be recorded in the financial statements?

Solution

The internal costs should be recognised as an expense in profit or loss as they were not incremental costs; they would have been incurred in any event. The professional fees were directly attributable to the transaction and £30,000 should be deducted from equity (£50,000 net of 40% tax).

The double entry to record this transaction should be:

DR	Cash (£250,000 less £50,000)	£200,000	
DR	Tax liability (£50,000 × 40%)	£20,000	
CR	Share capital		£100,000
CR	Share premium		
	((100,000 × (£2.50 less £1.00)) less £50,000 × 60%)		£120,000

2.5 Offsetting

Financial assets and financial liabilities should generally be presented as separate items in the statement of financial position. However, offset is required if:

- The entity has a legal right of offset, and
- The entity intends to settle on a net basis.   [IAS 32.42]

Worked example: Offsetting

Herdings plc and Intake Ltd trade with each other. Herdings plc has recognised in its financial statements trade receivables of £40,000 and trade payables of £20,000 in respect of Intake Ltd. Herdings plc and Intake Ltd have an informal arrangement to periodically offset balances and settle on a net basis.

Herdings plc should not offset the trade receivables and trade payables as no legal right of offset exists. Whilst its custom and practice is to settle on a net basis, no formal right of setoff exists.

2.6 Treasury shares

It is becoming increasingly popular for companies to reacquire their own shares as an alternative to making dividend distributions and/or as a way to return excess capital to shareholders. Equity instruments reacquired by the entity which issued them are known as treasury shares.

The treatment of these treasury shares is that:

- They should be deducted from equity
- No gain or loss should be recognised in profit or loss on their purchase, sale, issue or cancellation
- Consideration paid or received should be recognised directly in equity

The amount of treasury shares held should be disclosed either in the statement of financial position or in the notes to the financial statements in accordance with IAS 1 *Presentation of Financial Statements*.

Worked example: Treasury shares

An entity entered into a share buyback scheme. It reacquired 10,000 £1 ordinary shares for £2 cash per share. The shares had originally been issued for £1.20 per share.

The entity should record the reacquired shares as a debit entry of £20,000 in equity. The original share capital and share premium amounts of £10,000 and £2,000 remain unchanged.

3 IAS 39 *Financial Instruments: Recognition and Measurement*

Section overview

- Financial instruments should be classified when they are first recognised in financial statements.
- A financial instrument should initially be measured at fair value, usually including transaction costs.
- Subsequent remeasurement depends upon how the financial asset or financial liability was classified.
- Financial assets and liabilities should be remeasured either at fair value or at amortised cost.
- IAS 39 contains detailed requirements regarding the derecognition of financial instruments.
- Financial assets should be reviewed at each reporting date for objective evidence of impairment.
- Reclassification is required/permitted in specified circumstances.

3.1 Introduction

The purpose of IAS 39 is to establish the principles by which financial assets and financial liabilities should be recognised and measured in financial statements. [IAS 39.1]

3.2 Scope of IAS 39

The scope of IAS 39 is consistent with that of IAS 32. However there are a few additional exceptions to its application.

These include rights and obligations under a leasing arrangement accounted for under IAS 17. However, certain elements of leasing do fall within the scope of IAS 39 including:

- A lease receivable recognised by a lessor is subject to the IAS 39 derecognition/impairment provisions
- A finance lease obligation of a lessee is subject to its derecognition provisions. [IAS 39.2]

3.3 Classification of financial assets and financial liabilities

The classification of a financial instrument determines how it should be dealt with in the financial statements. The classification should be made when the instrument is first recognised. The classification is important because it determines how the instrument should be measured and how profits/losses should be presented. The following table summarises the four categories of financial instruments. [IAS 39.9]

Financial assets or liabilities at fair value through profit or loss	Financial assets or financial liabilities held for trading. This classification includes derivative assets and liabilities. This category commonly includes debt and equity securities and loans and receivables acquired with a view to making a short-term profit through a dealer's margin.
Loans and receivables	Financial assets with fixed or determinable payments that are not quoted in an active market and are not held for trading, and which have not been designated as available for sale. These include accounts receivable and loans extended to credit customers where there is no intention to trade them.
Held-to-maturity investments	Financial assets with fixed or determinable payments and fixed maturity for which there is a positive intention and ability to hold to maturity. This classification excludes any investments which meet the definition of loans and receivables or have been designated as available for sale. This classification commonly includes quoted debt securities and quoted redeemable preference shares held as investments. Equity securities should not be classified as held to maturity.
Available-for-sale financial assets	All financial assets that are designated as such or are not classified within any of the three categories above. This category includes all equity securities other than those at fair value through profit or loss. An entity may designate any non-derivative financial asset other than those held for trading in this classification.

Points to note about classification:

1   Financial assets and financial liabilities at fair value through profit or loss:

- IAS 39 also permits the voluntary designation of financial assets and financial liabilities into this category in very limited circumstances where specific criteria are met.   [IAS 39.9]

    – Those criteria are generally only met by financial institutions and other organisations with sophisticated treasury operations.

    – In the Financial Reporting examination you can assume that the financial instrument transactions do **not** meet the criteria for voluntary designation.

- In the examination all financial liabilities other than derivatives should be classified as 'other financial liabilities' (see 3.5.6 below).

- All derivatives in the Financial Reporting examination are classified in this category because hedge accounting is outside the syllabus.

- This is the category for an instrument which is part of a portfolio of financial instruments that are managed together. In this case there should be evidence that the entity has made profits from the turnover of such items in the short-term.   [IAS 39.9]

2   Held-to-maturity investments:

- The held-to-maturity category is an exception and is unlikely to be used in other than limited circumstances. The use of this category is tightly drawn. A positive intention to hold to maturity is a more stringent test than having no present intention to sell. The positive intention and ability to hold such investments to maturity should be reassessed at the end of each reporting period.

- This category cannot be used if an entity has sold (or reclassified – see section 3.9.1 below) held-to-maturity investments in the current or the two preceding financial reporting periods. This 'tainting' rule applies to all entities in the same group.

    The tainting rule does not apply if the sale/reclassification is of an insignificant amount **and** results from a non-recurring isolated event beyond the entity's control that the entity could not have reasonably anticipated.   [IAS 39.9]

- In practice, most entities will categorise financial assets as available for sale rather than as held to maturity.

3 IFRS 9 *Financial Instruments* will replace IAS 39 and is effective for annual periods commencing on or after 1 January 2013. The main changes from IAS 39 in respect of classification are:

- Financial assets should be classified on the basis of both an entity's business model (ie its intentions in acquiring the assets) and the contractual cash flow characteristics of the assets

- Only two measurement categories are available:

  - At amortised cost, which is to be used if the business model is to hold the asset in order to collect the contractual payments of interest and principal on specified dates. Gains and losses should be recognised in profit or loss through the amortisation process and on derecognition.

  - At fair value, which is the default category. Gains and losses should be recognised in profit or loss.

In effect, the available-for-sale and loans and receivables categories have been abolished.

IFRS 9 is currently non-examinable.

Interactive question 5: Classifications   [Difficulty level: Intermediate]

Crimicar Ltd has entered into the following transactions during the year to 31 December 20X2. Identify the classifications that are possible for each financial asset.

1   6,000 shares in Petrolia plc were acquired at £2 each
2   A £10,000 6% loan repayable in 20X4 was made to Totley plc
3   Sold £20,000 of inventory to Fulwood Ltd on 15 December 20X2 on 60 day terms
4   Acquired £20,000 3% Government stock redeemable in 20X9
5   Entered into a forward currency contract to sell $30,000 on 27 January 20X3 for £20,000.

See **Answer** at the end of this chapter.

3.4   Initial recognition and measurement

In general a **financial asset or financial liability** should be:

- **Recognised** when an entity enters into the contractual provisions of the financial instrument
[IAS 39.14]

- Initially **measured** at its fair value

  The general rule is that transaction costs, such as brokers' and professional fees, should be included in the initial carrying amount. The **exception** is that transaction costs for financial instruments classified as at fair value through profit or loss should be recognised as an expense in profit or loss.
[IAS 39.43]

IAS 39 requires the recognition of all financial instruments in the statement of financial position. In the past, derivatives were often not included in statements of financial position because they had a zero initial cost and fair value. Zero initial cost does not now prevent a derivative being recognised in the financial statements.

If an entity has investments in **equity instruments that do not have a quoted price** in an active market and it is not possible to calculate their fair values reliably, they should be measured at cost.

Worked example: Transaction costs

An entity acquires a financial asset for £52. This was the offer price at the time of the transaction. The bid price at that time was £50.

IAS 39 effectively treats the bid-offer spread as a transaction cost. If the financial instrument is classified as at fair value through profit or loss, the transaction cost of £2 is recognised as an expense in profit or loss and the financial asset initially recognised at the bid price of £50. If the financial asset is classified under any other category, the transaction cost should be added to the fair value and the financial asset initially recognised at the offer price (the price actually paid) of £52.

The fair value on initial recognition is normally the transaction price. However, if part of the consideration is given for something other than the financial instrument, then the fair value should be estimated using a valuation technique.

Worked example: Initial fair value

An entity enters into a marketing agreement with another organisation. As part of the agreement the entity makes a two year £5,000 interest free loan. Equivalent loans would normally carry an interest rate of 6%, given the borrower's credit rating. The entity made the loan in anticipation of receiving future marketing and product benefits.

The fair value of the loan can be determined by discounting the future cash flows to present value using the prevailing market interest rate for a similar instrument with a similar credit rating. The present value of the cash flow in two years time at 6% is £4,450 ($£5,000 \times (1/1.06^2)$). On initial recognition of the financial asset the entity should recognise a loss of £550 as follows:

DR	Loan	£4,450	
DR	Loss (finance expense)	£550	
CR	Cash		£5,000

The difference between this initial amount recognised of £4,450 and the final amount received of £5,000 should be treated as interest received and recognised in profit or loss over the two year period.

3.5 Subsequent measurement of financial assets and financial liabilities

After initial recognition at fair value the subsequent measurement of financial assets and the treatment of profits and losses depends upon how they were categorised.

3.5.1 Financial assets and financial liabilities at fair value through profit or loss

At the end of each reporting period:

- The financial asset should be remeasured at fair value without deduction for transaction costs

[IAS 39.46]

- Changes in fair value should be recognised as profits/losses in profit or loss. [IAS 39.55]

Worked example: At fair value through profit or loss

An entity acquired a derivative on 1 May 20X6 for £200 cash. On 31 December 20X6, the next reporting date, the fair value of the derivative was £340. On 31 December 20X7 the derivative's fair value had fallen to £220.

Set out the journal entries to record these transactions.

Solution

On 1 May 20X6:

DR	Derivative financial asset	£200	
CR	Cash		£200

On 31 December 20X6:

DR	Derivative financial asset	£140	
CR	Profit or loss – gain on financial asset (£340 – £200)		£140

On 31 December 20X7:

DR	Profit or loss – loss on financial asset (£340 – £220)	£120	
CR	Derivative financial asset		£120

The use of fair values creates volatility in the statement of financial position and income statement. The changes in fair value recognised in profit or loss directly affect profit measures such as earnings per share. The statement of financial position movements also affect key ratios such as gearing. The cash flows are, as always, the same regardless of the classification and the volatility that this may create. However, the use of fair value will affect key ratios and the perception of risk.

3.5.2 Held-to-maturity investments

A financial asset classified as held to maturity should be measured at **amortised cost** using the **effective interest method**. [IAS 39.46]

Amortised cost is:

- The initial amount recognised for the financial asset
- Less any repayments of the principal sum
- Plus any amortisation.

The amount of amortisation should be calculated by applying the effective interest method to spread the financing cost over the period to maturity (that is the difference between the initial amount recognised for the financial asset and the amount receivable at maturity). The amount amortised in respect of a financial asset should be recognised as income in profit or loss.

Definition

The **effective interest rate** is the rate that exactly discounts estimated future cash payments or receipts through the expected life of the instrument or, when appropriate, a shorter period to the net carrying amount of the financial asset or financial liability. [IAS 39.9]

The use of amortised cost provides predictability to the income recognised in profit or loss and the carrying amount in the statement of financial position. The amortised cost model does not generate the level of volatility inherent in the fair value approach. This is the attractiveness of this classification. However, the requirement to hold to maturity and the tainting rule means that in practice most companies classify as available for sale financial assets that could be classified as held to maturity.

If required, the effective interest rate will be given in the examination. You will not be expected to calculate it.

Worked example: Held to maturity

An entity acquires a zero coupon bond with a nominal value of £20,000 on 1 January 20X6 for £18,900. The bond is quoted in an active market and broker's fees of £500 were incurred in relation to the purchase. The bond is redeemable on 31 December 20X7 at a premium of 10%. The effective interest rate on the bond is 6.49%.

Set out the journals to show the accounting entries for the bond until redemption if it is classified as a held-to-maturity financial asset. The entity has a 31 December year end.

Solution

On 1 January 20X6

DR	Financial asset (£18,900 plus £500)	£19,400	
CR	Cash		£19,400

On 31 December 20X6

| DR | Financial asset (£19,400 × 6.49%) | £1,259 | |
| CR | Interest income | | £1,259 |

On 31 December 20X7

DR	Financial asset ((£19,400+£1,259) × 6.49%)	£1,341	
CR	Interest income		£1,341
DR	Cash	£22,000	
CR	Financial asset		£22,000

3.5.3 Loans and receivables

A financial asset classified as a loan or receivable should be measured at **amortised cost** using the effective interest method. This is the same method as for held-to-maturity financial assets.

Amortisation should be recognised as an income in profit or loss.

Most financial assets that meet this classification are simple receivables and loan transactions. Most companies choose to classify them in this category unless they are held for trading.

Interactive question 6: Loans and receivables   [Difficulty level: Exam standard]

Hallowes plc has agreed to lend a customer £9,500 on 1 January 20X2 subject to the following terms:

- The loan is repaid on 31 December 20X4 in full.
- Three interest payments of £1,000 are paid on 31 December each year.

Hallowes plc incurred £250 of legal fees in agreeing the loan documentation with the customer. The effective rate of interest on the loan is 9.48%.

Demonstrate by journal entries how the loan should be recorded in the financial statements of Hallowes plc for the year ended 31 December 20X2 and subsequent years.

See **Answer** at the end of this chapter.

3.5.4 Available-for-sale financial assets

Available-for-sale assets should be measured at **fair value at the end of each reporting period**.

Any gain arising from an **increase** in fair value should be **recognised in other comprehensive income** and held in equity. Most companies present the unrealised revaluation gains in a separate equity reserve, often called the available-for-sale (AFS) reserve.

Any loss arising from a **decrease** in fair value should also be recognised in other comprehensive income and held in equity. The only exception is that when there is evidence that the asset is impaired (see below), any loss held in equity should be recognised as an expense in profit or loss.

When an AFS financial asset is disposed of, the cumulative gains or losses held in equity should be presented as part of the profit or loss on disposal recognised in profit or loss. This process is known as a reclassification adjustment, the accounting entry being:

- For a cumulative gain:

  | DR | Other comprehensive income |
  | CR | Profit or loss |

- For a cumulative loss:

  | DR | Profit or loss |
  | CR | Other comprehensive income |

Points to note:

- The statement of financial position carrying amount is still subject to volatility arising from the remeasurement to fair value.

- Remeasurement gains/losses are not recognised in profit or loss until disposal and so will not affect earnings until that time.

- One of the key accounting policy choices companies make is whether to classify a financial asset as held to maturity (where it meets the criteria) or available for sale.

Worked example: Held-to-maturity and available-for-sale classifications

An entity acquired a 6% £1,000 par value financial asset for its fair value of £970 at the beginning of Year 1. Interest of 6% was receivable annually in arrears. The financial asset was redeemable at the end of Year 3 at £1,030, a premium of 3% to par value. The financial asset is quoted in an active market and was classified as held to maturity by the entity.

Held-to-maturity financial assets should be measured at amortised cost. The effective interest rate of the financial instrument can be calculated at 8.1%. The rate is higher than the coupon rate, because it amortises the discount on issue and the premium on redemption.

The amortised cost carrying amount should be determined as follows.

Year	Opening balance £	Interest @ 8.1% in profit or loss £	Cash flow £	Closing balance £
1	970	78	(60)	988
2	988	80	(60)	1,008
3	1,008	82	(1,090)	0

If the entity had classified the financial asset as available for sale, the asset should have been measured at fair value at each reporting date. If the fair values of the financial asset at the end of Year 1 and Year 2 were £1,100 and £1,050, the financial asset should have been recognised at the following amounts.

Year	Opening balance £	Interest @ 8.1% in profit or loss £	Cash flow £	Gain/(loss) in other comprehensive income (bal) £	Closing balance – fair value £
1	970	78	(60)	112	1,100
2	1,100	80	(60)	(70)	1,050
3	1,050	82	(1,090)	(42)	0

There is no gain or loss held in equity at the end of Year 3; if there had been, it would have been reclassified to profit or loss.

Note how both the income recognised in profit or loss and the cash flows are the same under the two classifications. The amount recognised in the statement of financial position is different. This will affect statement of financial position ratios.

3.5.5 Summary of treatment of financial assets

Asset	Description	Measurement	Recording of changes
Financial assets at fair value through profit or loss	Financial assets held for the purpose of selling in the short term. This includes derivatives	Fair value	Profit or loss
Available-for-sale financial assets	Non-derivative financial assets available for sale or any such assets not classified in one of the other three categories.		Other comprehensive income, except for interest on assets and impairment losses

Asset	Description	Measurement	Recording of changes
Loans and receivables	Non-derivative financial assets with fixed or determinable payments that are not quoted in an active market, not designated as held for trading and not available for sale	Amortised cost	Profit or loss
Held-to-maturity investments	Intention and ability to hold to maturity and not classified in any of the above categories		

3.5.6 Measurement of financial liabilities

Derivative financial liabilities should be classified as at fair value through profit or loss and measured at fair value. Gains and losses from their movement should be recognised in profit or loss.

Other financial liabilities should be measured at **amortised cost using the effective interest method.**

Interactive question 7: Financial liabilities   [Difficulty level: Exam standard]

Bonds with a nominal value of £200,000 were issued at £157,763 on 1 January 20X1. The coupon rate is 4% while the effective interest rate is 9.5%. Interest is paid annually in arrears. Redemption is at par in five years. Issue costs are immaterial.

Calculate the carrying amount of the bonds in the statement of financial position at 31 December 20X1 and at each subsequent year end until redemption.

Solution

The carrying amount of the bonds at 31 December in the years 20X1 to 20X5 is as follows:

Period end	Amount borrowed £	Interest (at 9.5%) £	Repaid £	Carrying amount £
20X1				
20X2				
20X3				
20X4				
20X5				

See **Answer** at the end of this chapter.

3.6 Determining fair value

Definition

Fair value is the amount for which an asset could be exchanged, or liability settled, between knowledgeable, willing parties in an arm's length transaction.

If there is **an active market** for the financial asset or liability, fair value will be the quoted market price.

The appropriate market price is usually the current bid price for a financial asset held or financial liability to be issued. The asking price should be used for a financial liability held or a financial asset to be acquired.

If there are no bid and asking prices, the price to be used is that at which the latest transaction occurred, assuming there have been no significant changes in fair value since that date.

If there is **no active market** for the financial asset or liability, fair value should be estimated using valuation techniques that use market estimates where possible, and take into account any recent transactions that have taken place between willing parties and the fair value of similar financial instruments.

Where no reliable estimate for unquoted equity shares exists, they should be measured at cost. If a **reliable value subsequently becomes available**, they should be **remeasured to fair value** and classified as held for trading or available for sale.

Worked example: Unquoted equities

Albert plc acquired a small holding of equity shares in Rodney Ltd, a recently incorporated company. Albert plc was unable to determine the fair value of Rodney Ltd's shares as Rodney Ltd had not published any financial information.

Albert plc should account for the equity shares at cost. Unless they are held for trading, they should be classified as available for sale. When Rodney Ltd makes financial information available and a reliable fair value can be measured, the holding should be remeasured at fair value in the financial statements. Management should use the fair value where possible. It would be unethical to apply the cost model by claiming that a reliable fair value was not available when in fact it was.

Worked example: Market values

Neville plc holds 12% of the equity of Unit plc, a quoted entity. These ordinary shares are held for trading and classified as at fair value through profit or loss. Their current quoted market price is £43-£45.

Current market statistics show the average daily trading volume in the last 12 months of 0.4% of the issued share capital. The only other significant investor is Ms A who owns 40% of the issued share capital.

Neville plc's brokers have advised that:

- The 12% holding would be of interest to Ms A because it would give her control of Unit plc
- Others would be interested in the holding as a means of gaining a strategic investment.

The brokers have used a financial model to estimate the value on this basis of the 12% holding at £50 per share.

Despite this valuation each share should be measured at the bid price of £43 per share, because IAS 39 states that a published price is the best estimate of fair value. Neville plc cannot use a different value simply because selling a block of this size may generate a higher per share value.

3.7 Derecognition of financial assets and financial liabilities

3.7.1 Derecognition principles

Definition

Derecognition is the removal of a previously recognised financial asset or financial liability from an entity's statement of financial position.

IAS 39 gives extensive guidance on when a financial instrument should be derecognised, that is removed from the financial statements. A financial asset should generally be derecognised in its entirety but there are circumstances where it is appropriate to derecognise only part of it. Such circumstances are outside the Professional Stage syllabus.

A financial asset should **not** be derecognised where the entity continues to retain the risks and rewards of ownership. This assessment should be carried out by comparing the risks and rewards held by the entity before and after the transfer.

[IAS 39.20]

Derecognition of many financial assets is often straightforward, for example, a trade receivable should be derecognised when an entity collects payment. In more complex cases the substance of the transaction should be considered by reviewing the risks and rewards involved.

Worked example: Derecognition

An entity sold an equity investment classified as available for sale to a bank for £840 and reclassified a £100 gain held in equity to profit or loss. On the same date it entered into a 60 day contract to repurchase the equity investment from the bank for £855 less any dividends received by the bank during the 60 day period.

The existence of the repurchase contract means that the risks and rewards of ownership have not been transferred to the bank. The proceeds of the sale are in substance a secured borrowing. The entity's motivation is probably to recognise in profit or loss (and therefore in earnings) the gain previously recognised in other comprehensive income and held in equity.

The entity should recognise a financial liability of £840. The £100 gain should not be reclassified to profit or loss. The premium on repurchase of £15 should be recognised as a finance cost.

A financial liability should be derecognised when an entity discharges the obligations specified in the contract, or they expire. [IAS 39.39]

3.7.2 Gain or loss on derecognition

When a financial asset or financial liability is derecognised, a gain or loss should be recognised in profit or loss, calculated as the difference between the carrying amount of the asset/liability and the consideration received/paid. [IAS 39.26, 39.41]

In addition any cumulative gain or loss previously recognised in other comprehensive income and still held in equity in respect of an available-for-sale financial asset should now be reclassified into profit or loss. [IAS 39.55(b)]

Worked example: Gain or loss on disposal

An entity classified a financial asset as available for sale. The current carrying amount is £200 and cumulative gains recognised in other comprehensive income and held in equity (in an AFS reserve) relating to the financial asset are £50.

If the entity disposes of the asset for £320, the gain recognised in profit or loss should be £170, being:

- The difference between the proceeds and the carrying amount of £120 (£320 less £200); plus
- The gains of £50 held in equity.

The journal to record the disposal would be:

DR	Cash	£320	
DR	Other comprehensive income – AFS reserve	£50	
CR	Financial asset		£200
CR	Profit or loss – gain on disposal		£170

Interactive question 8: Disposal of financial assets [Difficulty level: Easy]

A company purchased a portfolio of financial assets for £30,000 on 1 July 20X6. On 31 December 20X6, the next financial year end, the portfolio had a fair value of £34,000. On 16 May 20X7 one quarter of the portfolio of financial assets was sold for £10,000.

Requirement

Calculate the amount recognised in profit or loss on disposal on the alternative bases that the financial assets were initially classified as:

(a) held for trading
(b) available for sale.

Fill in the proforma below.

Held for trading

	£
Proceeds	
Carrying amount	

Available for sale

	£
Proceeds	
Carrying amount	
Reclassification of cumulative gain held in equity	

See **Answer** at the end of this chapter.

3.8 Impairment of financial assets

An entity is required to consider whether financial assets are impaired (carried at more than their recoverable amount) at the end of each reporting period.

Impairment is where an event has occurred, after initial recognition, which has a detrimental effect on the future cash flows of the financial asset. No account is taken of losses that are expected to arise as a result of future events.   [IAS 39.58 – 59]

The most common impairment of a financial asset occurs where a trade receivable is unpaid due to liquidity problems on the part of the customer.

Worked example: Impairment of trade receivables

Trade receivables are most commonly classified as loans and receivables and accounted for using the amortised cost model. In most cases no effective interest rate is used as the period to payment is short.

If an entity has a receivable due of £50,000 and the customer is not expected to pay, then impairment has occurred and an impairment loss of £50,000 should be recognised in profit or loss.

The decline in fair value to below cost is not necessarily evidence of impairment. It is possible in the short term for available-for-sale financial assets to be carried at below cost with a cumulative loss held in the AFS reserve in equity. However, a significant or prolonged decline in the fair value of an equity investment below its cost is objective evidence of impairment.   [IAS 39.60, 39.61]

Worked example: Impairment of an investment

An equity instrument was acquired for £2,000 a number of years ago and classified as available for sale. At 31 December 20X4 the cumulative loss recognised in other comprehensive income and held in equity was £100 and the financial asset was carried at a fair value of £1,900.

At 31 December 20X5 the issuer of the equity was in severe financial difficulty and the instrument's fair value had fallen to £1,600. £400 should be recognised as a loss in profit or loss. This amount includes the £100 loss previously recognised in other comprehensive income and held in equity, which should now be reclassified to profit or loss.

When a financial asset carried at amortised cost is impaired, the asset should be reduced to the recoverable amount which is the present value of the expected future cash flows discounted at the original effective interest rate. The impairment loss should be recognised in profit or loss.   [IAS 39.63]

Worked example: Impairment of a loan

On 1 January 20X4 Palace plc granted a loan of £1,000 at 7% pa. Interest was payable annually in arrears and the loan was repayable at a premium on 31 December 20X6. The effective interest rate was 8%.

The borrower paid the interest due on 31 December 20X4 but by then was in such financial difficulty that Palace plc granted a concession: no further annual interest would be payable and the principal would be repaid on 31 December 20X8 at £1,100. On 31 December 20X4 the amortised cost carrying amount of the loan was £1,010.

The financial difficulty of, and granting of a concession to, the borrower are both objective evidence of impairment. The recoverable amount should be calculated as £809 by discounting the £1,100 agreed repayment at the original effective interest rate of 8% over a four-year period. An impairment loss of £201 (£1,010 – 809) should be recognised at 31 December 20X4.

In 20X5 interest income of £65 (8% × £809) should be recognised in profit or loss and the carrying amount of the loan should be increased to £874. This process is repeated in 20X6 to 20X8, at which point the loan will be carried at the £1,100 repayable.

3.9 Reclassification of financial assets

There are few circumstances in which a classification should or may be changed. So the classification of financial instruments at initial recognition is important.

3.9.1 Reclassification is required

Reclassification as available-for-sale is **required** for held-to-maturity investments in the following circumstances:

- If an entity sells more than an insignificant amount of such investments (see section 3.3 above), reclassification of all remaining held-to-maturity investments held by the entity is **required** (this is the 'tainting' rule)

- If as a result of a change in intention or ability it is no longer appropriate to classify an investment as held to maturity, reclassification of that investment is **required**

In both cases the difference (whether profit or loss) between the carrying amount as a held-to-maturity investment at reclassification and its then fair value as an available-for-sale financial asset should be recognised in other comprehensive income and reclassified to profit or loss when the asset(s) is sold.

[IAS 39.51 – 54].

Worked example: Held to maturity and tainting

An entity with a 31 December reporting date acquired 1,000 6% preference shares that are quoted in an active market and are redeemable in 20X9. The shares were classified as held to maturity. In May 20X3, following a period of trading losses, 800 of the preference shares were sold to generate working capital.

Because a significant portion of investments classified as held to maturity have been sold, the tainting rule will apply and the remaining 200 preference shares, together with any other investments currently classified as held to maturity, should be reclassified as available for sale. No financial assets acquired in the period up to 1 January 20X6 should be classified as held to maturity.

Worked example: Held to maturity and reclassification

In 20X7 an entity acquired 5,000 7% redeemable preference shares that are quoted in an active market. The shares were classified as held to maturity. As a result of a strategic review in December 20X9, management decided that it would be prepared to sell these shares, should an attractive offer be made for them. At 31 December 20X9 the amortised cost of these shares was £98,000 and their fair value £99,000.

Because there is now no positive intention to hold the shares to maturity, they should be reclassified as available for sale. They should be remeasured at their fair value of £99,000 and the £1,000 gain recognised in other comprehensive income and held in an available-for-sale reserve.

If these shares are more than an insignificant amount of the total held-to-maturity investments owned by the entity, then the tainting rule comes into play and all other such investments should be reclassified in the same manner.

3.9.2 Reclassification is permitted

Reclassification as loans and receivables is **permitted** for a financial asset which meets the definition of loans and receivables (eg it is unquoted) and is:

- A financial asset initially acquired for trading purposes (and therefore classified as at fair value through profit or loss) but no longer held for these purposes; or

- A financial asset initially classified as available for sale.

In both cases, reclassification is only permitted if the entity has the intention and ability to hold the asset for the foreseeable future or until maturity.

Point to note:

This intention/ability is similar, but not identical, to that for held-to-maturity investments.

In both cases, the new carrying amount is measured as the fair value at reclassification. If the asset was initially acquired for trading, amounts already recognised in profit or loss should not be reversed. If the asset was initially classified as available for sale, amounts already recognised in other comprehensive income should be amortised to profit or loss over the remaining life of the investment. [IAS 39.50 – 50F].

3.9.3 Reclassification never permitted

Equity investments and derivatives should never be reclassified. (Equity investments can be reclassified in rare circumstances, but this is beyond the scope of the Financial Reporting syllabus.)

No financial instrument should ever be reclassified **into** the fair value through profit or loss category.

[IAS 39.50 – 50F]

Worked example: Trading securities

An entity acquired a range of equity investments. The entity classified the investments as at fair value through profit or loss because it intended to trade the items for the purpose of realising a profit. The entity ceased trading in the investments and decided to hold the remainder as part of its long-term investment portfolio. The portfolio was supplemented by the acquisition of a number of further investments.

Because the investments already owned are equity, they should not be reclassified out of fair value through profit or loss even though they will no longer be traded. Subsequently acquired investments should be classified as available for sale, because there is no intention to trade them.

4 IFRS 7 *Financial Instruments: Disclosures*

Section overview

- The disclosures required by IFRS 7 are extensive.

- They are designed to show the significance of financial instruments for the entity's financial position and performance.

- They should indicate the nature and extent of risks arising from financial instruments to which the entity is exposed during the period and at the reporting date, and how the entity manages those risks.

4.1 The risks associated with financial instruments

The use of financial instruments by entities continues to be widespread and the risk associated with such instruments can be significant. As financial instruments become more complex and commonplace, clear and full disclosure becomes increasingly important. Financial instruments may or may not be recognised in an entity's financial statements, depending upon their nature. However, an entity's exposure to risk associated with unrecognised instruments may still be significant, and therefore disclosure is even more important.

The disclosure of information about financial instruments held by an entity is essential as an entity increases the use of such instruments, for example entities operating in the financial services sector. Over the last decade entities have changed the way in which they use financial instruments and manage their exposure to risk. As a result a fundamental review of what information should be disclosed by entities in relation to their financial instruments was undertaken by the IASB.

4.2 Objectives of IFRS 7

Information concerning an entity's exposure to risk and how the entity manages that risk continues to be important when assessing an entity's financial position and performance. The IASB issued IFRS 7 because it felt that existing standards needed to be improved to ensure that disclosures made in this area provided greater transparency of information, to allow users to better assess the risks that an entity is exposed to.

The objective of IFRS 7 is to require entities to provide disclosures in their financial statements which enable users to evaluate:

- The **significance of financial instruments** for the entity's financial position and performance, and

- The **nature and extent of risks** arising from financial instruments to which the entity is exposed during the period and at the reporting date, and how the entity manages those risks.

4.3 Assessing financial performance and financial position

As set out above, one of the overall objectives of IFRS 7 is to ensure that users of financial statements can adequately evaluate the significance that financial instruments have in the assessment of financial position and performance of an entity. To meet this objective IFRS 7 sets out detailed disclosure requirements in relation to both the statement of financial position and the statement of comprehensive income. [IFRS 7.7]

Either in the statement of financial position or in the notes the carrying amounts of **each of the following categories** should be disclosed:

- Held-to-maturity investments
- Loans and receivables
- Available-for-sale financial assets
- Financial assets and financial liabilities at fair value through profit or loss, showing separately:
    - Those designated as such upon initial recognition
    - Those classified as held for trading

- Financial liabilities measured at amortised cost [IFRS 7.8-11]

The fair values of each class of financial instrument should also be disclosed. [IFRS 7.25]

Worked example: Extract from financial statements of Marks and Spencer Group plc 2010

Book and fair values of financial instruments

	2010		2009	
	Carrying value £m	*Fair value* £m	*Carrying value* £m	*Fair value* £m
Fixed rate bond debt	(2,183.9)	(2,107.7)	(2,018.5)	(1,616.6)

Disclosure requirements in relation to interest income and expense for financial assets and liabilities not measured at fair value, gains and losses on each category of financial instrument and impairment losses for financial assets, highlight the effect of financial instrument transactions in the statement of comprehensive income. [IFRS 7.20]

The disclosure of the net gains or losses on financial assets and liabilities by class complements the disclosures made in the statement of financial position.

Worked example: Extract from the financial statements of Barclays plc 2010

	2010 £m	2009 £m	2008 £m
Net trading income	8,078	7,001	1,339
Net gain from disposal of available for sale assets	1,027	349	212
Dividend income	116	6	196
Net gain/(loss) from financial instruments designated at fair value	274	(208)	33
Other investment income/(losses)	60	(91)	239
Net investment income	1,477	56	680
Total	9,555	7,057	2,019

4.4 Nature and extent of risks arising from financial instruments

An entity should fully explain the accounting policies that have been applied in recognising and measuring its financial instruments. [IFRS 7.21]

Worked example: Extract from the annual report and accounts of Rolls-Royce 2010

Financial instruments

IAS 39 *Financial Instruments: Recognition and Measurement* requires the classification of financial instruments into separate categories for which the accounting requirements are different. The Group has classified its financial instruments as follows:

- Short-term investments are classified as available for sale, if designated upon initial recognition.

- Short-term deposits (principally comprising funds held with banks and other financial institutions), trade receivables and short-term investments not designated as available for sale are classified as loans and receivables.

- Borrowings, trade payables, certain risk and revenue sharing partnerships and C Shares are classified as other liabilities.

- Derivatives, comprising foreign exchange contracts, interest rate swaps and commodity swaps are classified as held for trading.'

The accounting policy shows that Rolls-Royce does not use the held-to-maturity category.

Disclosures should be made to ensure that the nature and extent of risks arising from the use of financial instruments can be assessed by users of the financial statements. The specific disclosures required focus on how the risks arising from financial instruments are managed by an entity. These disclosures are both qualitative and quantitative in nature. [IFRS 7.31, 7.32]

The qualitative disclosures focus on the exposure to risk, how the risk arises as well as an entity's policy on managing those risks, including its processes for monitoring such information. [IFRS 7.33]

Quantitative disclosures are included to ensure that users understand the potential impact that risks from financial instruments may have on an entity's financial position and performance in a period. Quantitative information should be consistent with internal management information. The quantitative information should be split between the different risks, generally being credit risk, liquidity risk and market risk. [IFRS 7.34]

Definitions

Credit risk is the risk that one party to a financial instrument will cause a financial loss for the other party by failing to discharge an obligation.

Liquidity risk is the risk that an entity will encounter difficulty in meeting obligations associated with financial liabilities that are settled by delivering cash or another financial asset.

Market risk is the risk that the fair value or future cash flows of a financial instrument will fluctuate because of changes in market prices. [IFRS 7 App A]

Worked example: Extract from the financial statements of Centrica plc 2010

Liquidity

Cash forecasts identifying the Group's liquidity requirements are produced regularly and are stress-tested for different scenarios, including, but not limited to, reasonably possible increases or decreases in commodity prices and the potential cash implications of a credit rating downgrade.

Interest rate risk management

In the normal course of business the Group borrows to finance its operations. The Group is exposed to interest rate risk because the fair value of fixed rate borrowings and the cash flows associated with floating rate borrowings will fluctuate with changes in interest rates. The Group's policy is to manage the interest rate risk on long-term borrowings by ensuring the exposure to floating interest rates remains within a 30% to 70% range, including the impact of interest rate derivatives. A sensitivity analysis that is intended to illustrate the sensitivity of the Group's financial position and performance to changes in interest rates is provided below …

A sensitivity analysis, along with an explanation of how such an analysis was determined and whether it is consistent with the method used in the previous period, should be provided to help explain the exposure to market risk. Market risk is assessed by considering how much currency and interest rates may fluctuate over a period. [IFRS 7.40, 7.41]

These disclosures are often made in the Operating and Financial Review.

Worked example: Extract from the financial statements of GlaxoSmithKline plc 2010

'Interest rate sensitivity

The table below shows the Group's sensitivity to interest rates on its floating rate Sterling, US dollar and Euro financial instruments…GSK has considered movements in these interest rates over the last three years and concluded that a 2% increase is a reasonable benchmark… A 2% movement in interest rates is not deemed to have a material effect on equity.

	2010 Increase/(decrease) in income £m	2009 Increase/(decrease) in income £m
2% increase in Sterling interest rates	29	(2)
2% increase in US dollar interest rates	(18)	38
2% increase in Euro interest rates	37	18

These interest rates could not be decreased by 2% as they are currently less than 1.0%.'

5 Ethical and judgement issues

Section overview

The application of accounting standards to financial instruments requires significant judgement.

The failure to report transactions involving financial instruments appropriately has contributed to a number of recent accounting scandals. The complexity of many financial instruments presents challenges for financial reporting. This is evidenced by the length of the accounting standards and the detailed application guidance.

Even the application of the accounting standards to the simple financial instruments in this chapter requires significant judgements to be made by management. These include:

- Determining fair values using other valuation mechanisms where market values are not readily available.

- Determining whether financial instruments are financial liabilities or equity.

- Classifying financial assets within the four categories in an appropriate manner and ensuring those decisions are appropriately documented at the time.

- Ensuring qualitative disclosures of treasury policies are consistent with the actual transactions undertaken.

Worked example: Ethics and judgement

An entity acquires equity shares in another company representing 3% of the ordinary share capital. The Managing Director (MD) has requested that the ordinary shares be classified as available for sale. However, he has sent a private note to the Finance Director (FD) which says, 'We will trade these ordinary shares as we normally do, create some documentation to cover this up and indicate that we have acquired them for the long-term rather than being held for trading'.

The motivation of the MD is eliminate the volatility in profit or loss by classifying them as available for sale. This is unethical. The FD should not be influenced by the MD. He should explain the situation to the MD, follow the guidance in the ICAEW Code of Ethics and act with integrity.

6 UK GAAP comparison

6.1 IAS 32 and FRS 25 *Financial Instruments: Presentation*

There are no examinable differences.

6.2 IAS 39 and FRS 26 *Financial Instruments: Recognition and Measurement*

There are no examinable differences.

6.3 IFRS 7 and FRS 29 *Financial Instruments: Disclosures*

There are no examinable differences.

Summary and Self-test

Summary

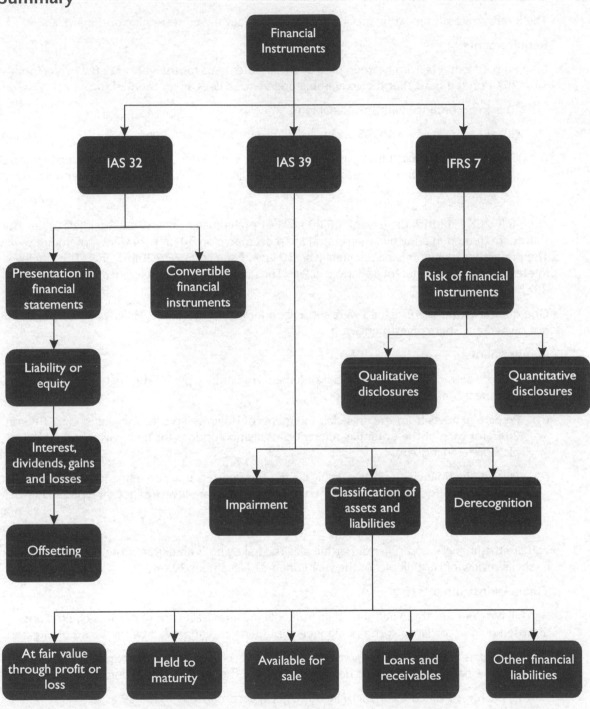

Self-test

Answer the following questions.

1   On 1 January 20X4 Maroon plc issued 100,000 £1 6% convertible redeemable preference shares. Issue costs of £5,000 were incurred and the preference shares are redeemable at par for cash on 31 December 20X8 or are convertible into 20,000 new £1 ordinary shares at that time. The preference dividend is paid on 31 December each year.

The interest rate on similar financial instruments without the convertibility option is 8%.

Requirements

(a) Prepare extracts from Maroon plc's financial statements for the year ended 31 December 20X4 on the basis that the convertible preference shares are accounted for:

    (i)   In accordance with their legal form

    (ii) In accordance with IAS 32 *Financial Instruments: Presentation.*   **(6 marks)**

(b) Comment on the usefulness of the presentation requirements of IAS 32 in understanding the nature of the preference shares and how its requirements affect the view presented. **(4 marks)**

                                                                                          (10 marks)

2   On 1 July 20X4 Lindrick plc issued 100,000 6% £1 preference shares at par, their fair value. The shares are quoted in an active market and are redeemable on 30 June 20X8 at a premium of 4%. The preference dividend is paid annually on 30 June. Issue costs were immaterial. The effective interest rate on the preference shares is 6.9%. The fair value of one preference share on 30 June 20X5 is 95p.

One quarter of the shares issued were subscribed for by Hollinwell plc. Hollinwell plc has previously not owned any share investments.

Requirements

(a) Prepare extracts from the financial statements of Lindrick plc for the year ended 30 June 20X5 in respect of the preference shares   **(4 marks)**

(b) Prepare extracts from the financial statements of Hollinwell plc for the year ended 30 June 20X5 for each of the potential different classification options for the investment in Lindrick plc's preference shares   **(10 marks)**

(c) Discuss the financial reporting, ethical and other matters that the management of Hollinwell plc should consider when classifying the preference share investment as a type of financial asset.   **(5 marks)**

                                                                                          (19 marks)

3   You are the financial controller of Harthill plc. The following is an extract from the operating and financial review of Harthill plc for the year ended 31 December 20X4.

'Financial instruments

Harthill plc does not trade in financial instruments. All financial instruments are acquired and disposed of in accordance with risk management guidelines approved by the board of directors.

Financial assets are derecognised when the rights to receive benefits have expired or been transferred. Financial liabilities are derecognised when the obligation is extinguished.

Harthill plc has classified its financial instruments in accordance with IAS 39 as follows:

Non-derivative financial assets

Unquoted loans made for investment purposes and trade receivables are classified as loans and receivables.

Equity and non-equity investments (other than unquoted loans, interests in subsidiaries, associates and joint ventures) are classified as available for sale.

The held-to-maturity classification is not used by Harthill plc as the directors' policies include criteria for monitoring and disposing of any investments and there is no positive intention to hold any investment to maturity.

Non-derivative financial liabilities

Borrowings, the liability component of convertible instruments and trade payables are classified as other liabilities.

Derivatives

Derivatives, comprising foreign exchange contracts, interest rate swaps and commodity options are classified as held for trading'.

The following events have occurred during the year ended 31 December 20X5:

(1) Harthill plc reacquired 25,000 of its own £1 ordinary shares for £30,000 cash on 1 June 20X5. The shares had been issued at a premium of 10% many years ago.

(2) Harthill plc acquired 60% of the issued ordinary share capital of Loftdrop Ltd on 13 March 20X5 for £400,000 cash. Professional fees of £3,000 were incurred. The fair value of the 60% holding has been estimated at £440,000 at 31 December 20X5.

(3) Harthill plc acquired 20,000 shares in Rapport plc on 1 June 20X5. The shares are quoted and the share price at the time was £23-£25. Broker fees were immaterial. Rapport plc shares are quoted as £30-£32 at 31 December 20X5.

(4) Harthill plc acquired an interest rate swap for £200,000 on 1 December 20X5. It was sold on 31 December 20X5 for £225,000. A member of the treasury staff has told you; 'We bought it as we had a tip that we could make a quick profit on swaps in the current market.'

(5) Harthill plc had acquired an equity security in 20X1. At 31 December 20X4 the fair value of the equity was £300,000 and the cumulative gain held in the available-for-sale reserve in equity in respect of the investment was £270,000. On 27 December 20X5 the equity security was sold for £320,000. You recall signing a payment to acquire a similar equity security on 4 January 20X6 for £325,000. Further investigation reveals that the equity security was reacquired from the same party that it was originally sold to. The market value at the time of repurchase was £315,000.

Requirements

(a) Explain the required accounting treatment for these events in Harthill plc's financial statements for the year ended 31 December 20X5. **(15 marks)**

(b) Discuss the ethical issues identified as part of your review and the actions you should consider. **(3 marks)**

(18 marks)

4 Bolehill Ltd made an advance to Hilltop Ltd of £100,000 on 1 June 20X2. Bolehill Ltd incurred professional fees of £5,000 on agreeing the terms and the time cost of Bolehill Ltd's treasury team in negotiating the loan was estimated at £3,000. The key features of the loan agreement were as follows:

(1) The term of the loan was four years

(2) Four repayments of capital and interest of £30,000 were due on 31 May 20X3 and each year thereafter

(3) The effective interest rate was calculated by the Bolehill Ltd treasury department at 7%

Hilltop Ltd made the first repayment on 31 May 20X3 but failed to make the repayment on 31 May 20X4. Bolehill Ltd agreed to forgive the non-payment and to reschedule the repayments by accepting two further repayments of £45,000 per annum on 31 May 20X5 and 31 May 20X6.

The following is an extract from the accounting policy of Bolehill Ltd:

'Advances made to third parties are classified under IAS 39 as loans and receivables'

Requirement

Explain, using extracts from financial statements, the financial reporting treatment for the loan in the financial statements of Bolehill Ltd for the year ended 31 May 20X3 and subsequent years.

(12 marks)

5   Ancotes Ltd issued 20,000 warrants for £4 each on 15 February 20X6. Each warrant gives the holder the right to subscribe for one new ordinary share in Ancotes Ltd on 15 February 20X9 for £22 each. Ancotes Ltd incurred £3,000 of professional fees in issuing the warrants. The professional fees are deductible for tax purposes at a rate of 30%.

Ladybarn Ltd subscribed for 15,000 of the warrants. It incurred £500 of broker fees in acquiring the warrants.

The warrants have a fair value of £5.50 each at 31 December 20X6.

Requirement

Explain, using extracts from financial statements, the financial reporting treatment for the warrants in the financial statements of Ancotes Ltd and Ladybarn Ltd for the year ended 31 December 20X6.

(8 marks)

Now go back to the Learning Objectives in the Introduction. If you are satisfied you have achieved these objectives, please tick them off.

IAS 32 *Financial Instruments: Presentation*

1 Presentation of equity and liabilities

- Classification as financial asset, financial liability or equity instrument   IAS 32 (15 – 16)
- Definitions   IAS 32 (11)
- Contractual obligation and substance of instrument   IAS 32 (17 – 18)
- Settlement options   IAS 32 (26 – 27)
- Treasury shares   IAS 32 (33 – 34)
- Interest, dividends, losses and gains   IAS 32 (35 – 36)
- Offsetting   IAS 32 (42)

2 Compound instruments

- Recognising liability and equity elements   IAS 32 (28)
- Example of convertible bonds   IAS 32 (29 – 30)
- Calculation of liability and equity elements   IAS 32 (31 – 32)

IAS 39 *Financial Instruments: Recognition and Measurement*

1 Definitions   IAS 39 (9)

- Four categories of financial instruments
- Amortised cost and effective interest method

2 Recognition

- Initial recognition   IAS 39 (14)
- Derecognition   IAS 39 (17)
- Transfer of financial asset   IAS 39 (18 – 20)
- Profit or loss on derecognition   IAS 39 (26 – 28)

3 Measurement

- Initial measurement of financial assets and financial liabilities   IAS 39 (43)
- Subsequent measurement of financial assets   IAS 39 (45 – 46)
- Subsequent measurement of financial liabilities   IAS 39 (47)
- Determining fair value   IAS 39 (48 – 49)

4 Treatment of gains and losses

- Financial assets/liabilities at fair value   IAS 39 (55)

  Reclassification adjustments re available-for-sale financial assets
- Financial assets/liabilities at amortised cost   IAS 39 (56)
- Treatment of impairment   IAS 39 (58)

CHAPTER

7

5 Impairment of financial assets

- Financial assets carried at amortised cost   IAS 39 (63)

- Financial assets carried at cost   IAS 39 (66)

- Available-for-sale financial assets   IAS 39 (67)

6 Reclassifications   IAS 39 (50 – 54)

IFRS 7 *Financial Instruments: Disclosures*

1 Statement of financial position disclosures   IFRS 7 (8)

2 Statement of comprehensive income and equity   IFRS 7 (20)

3 Nature and extent of risks arising from financial instruments

- Purpose of disclosures   IFRS 7 (31 – 32)

- Qualitative disclosures   IFRS 7 (33)

- Quantitative disclosures   IFRS 7 (34)

Answer to Interactive question 1

1   The inventory is not a financial instrument as it is a physical asset. Guideprice Ltd should recognise a trade payable in its financial statements; this is a financial liability because there is a contractual obligation to pay the amount in cash. Conversely, Offertake Ltd records a trade receivable for £5,000, which is a financial asset as it has the contractual right to receive cash.

2   Ashdell Ltd has paid for services in advance. The £20,000 should be recorded as a prepayment. The future economic benefit is the right to receive insurance services rather than cash, ordinary shares or another financial asset. Therefore, prepayments are not financial instruments.

3   Tollbar Ltd has entered into a forward currency contract. The contract is a derivative financial instrument as it is linked to an underlying variable (the $/£ exchange rate), which requires no initial investment and is due for settlement in six months time. At inception it will have no value so is neither an asset nor liability.

4   The ordinary shares are an equity instrument of Wellbeck Ltd as they give the holder a residual interest in the assets of Wellbeck Ltd after deducting the liabilities. The ordinary shares are a financial asset of Keeload Ltd.

5   Cashlow plc has entered into a mortgage. The contractual obligation to repay £200,000 to Norbert plc is a financial liability. Norbert plc has a financial asset as it has the contractual right to receive £200,000 cash.

Answer to Interactive question 2

Preference shares redeemable at the issuer's option are classified as equity because there is no obligation to transfer financial assets (for example cash) at some future time. However, if Moorgate Ltd notifies the holders of an intention to redeem the preference shares at some future time, then an obligation arises and the preference shares should be reclassified as financial liabilities.

The rights attaching to the shares should be considered, to establish the substance of the instruments for classification. The dividends are not contractual obligations as they are only paid when ordinary share dividends are declared. In substance they are at the discretion of Moorgate Ltd and this confirms the classification as equity.

Answer to Interactive question 3

Year	Cash flow £	Discount factor	Present value £
20X7	60,000	1/1.08	55,556
20X8	1,060,000	$1/1.08^2$	908,779
Total liability component			964,335
Total proceeds 10,000 × £100			1,000,000
Equity element			35,665

Answer to Interactive question 4

Dividends payable should be classified according to the underlying financial instrument:

•   Dividends payable on ordinary shares (an equity instrument) should be charged directly against equity. Dorehouse Ltd's £4 million ordinary dividend should be recognised in the statement of changes in equity.

•   Dividends payable on redeemable preference shares (a financial liability) should be recognised as an expense in profit or loss. Dorehouse Ltd's £3 million preference dividend should be recognised in profit or loss. The dividend may be presented as part of the finance cost or as a separate line item.

Answer to Interactive question 5

All these financial instruments should be classified as 'at fair value through profit or loss' if they are held for trading. However, the held-for-trading category requires the asset to have been acquired with a view to short-term profit or be part of a portfolio that is managed together, where profits have been made from the turnover of such items.

1   Purchase of 6,000 shares in Petrolia. Unless held for trading, these equity shares should be classified as available for sale.

2   £10,000 6% loan repayable in 20X4. Provided it is not quoted in an active market, this loan would most commonly be classified under loans and receivables, because it has a fixed date for repayment. It could alternatively be classified as available for sale.

3   Sale of inventory on 60 day terms. The sale of the inventory creates a trade receivable from Fulwood Ltd. This would most commonly be classified under loans and receivables as it has a fixed date for repayment and the balance is not quoted in an active market. It could alternatively be classified as available for sale.

4   Purchase of £20,000 3% Government stock redeemable in 20X9. Government stocks are quoted in an active market, so the loans and receivables category is not available. This stock has a fixed date for repayment, so it could be classified as held to maturity if there is a positive intention and ability to hold it until its redemption in 20X9. It is more likely that it would be classified as available for sale.

5   A forward currency contract to sell $30,000. This is a derivative contract and should be classified as held for trading and thus as at fair value through profit or loss.

Answer to Interactive question 6

1 January 20X2

| DR | Loan (£9,500 + £250) | £9,750 | |
| CR | Cash | | £9,750 |

31 December 20X2

DR	Cash	£1,000	
CR	Interest income (£9,750 × 9.48%)		£924
CR	Loan (bal fig)		£76

Note: loan balance is now £9,674 (£9,750 – £76)

31 December 20X3

DR	Cash	£1,000	
CR	Interest income (£9,674 × 9.48%)		£917
CR	Loan (bal fig)		£83

Note: loan balance is now £9,591 (£9,674 – £83)

31 December 20X4

DR	Cash (£9,500 + £1,000)	£10,500	
CR	Interest income (£9,591 × 9.48%)		£909
CR	Loan (bal fig)		£9,591

Answer to Interactive question 7

The carrying amount of the bonds at 31 December in the years 20X1 to 20X5 is as follows:

Period end	Amount borrowed £	Interest (at 9.5%) £	Repaid (4% × £200,000) £	Carrying amount £
20X1	157,763	14,988	(8,000)	164,751
20X2	164,751	15,651	(8,000)	172,402
20X3	172,402	16,378	(8,000)	180,780
20X4	180,780	17,174	(8,000)	189,954
20X5	189,954	18,046	(8,000)	200,000

Answer to Interactive question 8

Held for trading

	£
Proceeds	10,000
Carrying amount (£34,000 × 1/4)	(8,500)
	1,500

Available for sale

	£
Proceeds	10,000
Carrying amount (£34,000 ×1/4)	(8,500)
Reclassification of cumulative gain held in equity ((£34,000 − £30,000) × 1/4)	1,000
	2,500

Note: The total amount recognised in profit or loss over the whole period that the financial instrument is held will be the same. The available-for-sale classification recognises the whole amount in profit or loss on derecognition whereas the held-for-trading classification recognises it each year as the fair value changes and then any final amount on derecognition.

1 (a) **Extracts from financial statements for the year ended 31 December 20X4**

	(i) Legal Form	(ii) IAS 32
Income statement		
Finance cost (W2)	–	7,361
Statement of changes in equity		
Dividends paid	6,000	–
Statement of financial position		
Non-current liabilities		
Borrowings (W2)	–	93,376
Equity		
Equity element of convertible debt (W1)	–	2,985
Convertible Preference Shares (100,000-5,000)	95,000	–
Statement of cash flows		
Cash flows from operating activities		
Interest paid	–	(6,000)
Dividends paid	(6,000)	–
Cash flows from financing activities		
Proceeds from issue of convertible, redeemable preference shares	95,000	95,000

Note: IAS 7 *Statement of Cash Flows* allows flexibility in the presentation of interest paid and dividends paid.

WORKINGS

(1) Splitting the liability and equity components on initial recognition

Payments	Amount	Discount factor (Note)	Present value
	£		£
20X4	6,000	0.9259	5,556
20X5	6,000	0.8573	5,144
20X6	6,000	0.7938	4,763
20X7	6,000	0.7350	4,410
20X8	106,000	0.68058	72,142
Liability component			92,015
Equity component (Bal fig)			2,985
Total (£100,000 less £5,000)			95,000

Note: The discount factors are calculated using the $1/(1+r)^n$ formula.

(2) Calculating the liability carrying amount at year end

	£
Liability at 1 January 20X4	92,015
Interest expense at 8% (8% × 92,015)	7,361
Cash paid	(6,000)
Liability at 31 December 20X4	93,376

(b) The legal form of the preference shares is equity. They are a type of share capital. If the transaction is accounted for in accordance with its legal form, the preference shares are included in equity and the dividends are presented as part of the movement in equity.

The substance of redeemable preference shares is that they are debt as there is a contractual obligation to make repayments of interest and capital. These terms meet the definition of a financial liability.

However, the convertibility option means that the preference shares also have an equity component. The same effect could have been achieved by issuing warrants and redeemable preference shares separately.

The requirements of IAS 32 reflect the substance of the transaction, focusing on the economic reality that in effect two financial instruments have been issued. These preference shares are a compound financial instrument and split accounting should be applied.

The requirements of IAS 32 will increase the amount of borrowings in the financial statements compared with if the preference shares had been accounted for in accordance with their legal form. As a result gearing will be higher and it may be more difficult for Maroon plc to obtain further borrowing.

Should the legal form be accounted for, the preference share dividend should be recognised in the statement of changes in equity. Under IAS 32 the amount should be recognised as an expense in profit or loss. The IAS 32 expense is higher than the dividend paid as it includes · the amortisation of the discount of the liability. Earnings under IAS 32 will be lower than under the legal form.

The cash flows are the same in both sets of circumstances, although they will be categorised differently as interest and dividends paid. However, users of financial statements may perceive a different level of risk.

Point to note:

Convertible bonds are another type of compound financial instrument. Their legal form is debt. For convertible bonds, gearing would be higher if the legal form was applied.

2 (a) **Lindrick plc**

Extracts of financial statements for the year ended 30 June 20X5

	£
Income statement	
Finance cost (W)	6,900
Statement of financial position	
Non-current liabilities	
Borrowings (W)	100,900
Statement of cash flows	
Cash flows from operating activities	
Interest paid	(6,000)
Cash flows from financing activities	
Proceeds from preference share issue	100,000

WORKING

	£
Initial amount recognised	100,000
Finance cost (6.9% × 100,000)	6,900
Amount paid	(6,000)
	100,900

(b) **Hollinwell plc**

The classification options for the investment in Lindrick plc's quoted redeemable preference shares are:

- At fair value through profit or loss (FVTPL), on the basis that the shares are held for trading

- Held to maturity (HTM), on the basis that Hollinwell plc has the positive intention and ability to hold them until maturity

- Available for sale (AFS) – a category open to all types of financial asset.

Because the shares are quoted, classification under loans and receivables is not an option.

Extracts of financial statements for the year ended 30 June 20X5

	(i) FVTPL (W1) £	(ii) HTM (W2) £	(iii) AFS (W3) £
Income statement			
Finance income	250	1,725	1,725
Statement of financial position			
Non-current assets			
Financial assets	23,750	25,225	23,750
Equity			
Available for sale reserve	–	–	(1,475)
Statement of cash flows			
Cash flows from operating activities			
Interest received	1,500	1,500	1,500
Cash flows from financing activities			
Financial investment	(25,000)	(25,000)	(25,000)

WORKINGS

(1) Fair value through profit or loss

	£	£
Interest received (6% × 100,000 × 25%)		1,500
Initial amount recognised (100,000 × 25%)	25,000	
Fair value at year end (25% × 100,000 × 0.95)	(23,750)	
Reduction in fair value		(1,250)
Amount recognised in profit or loss		250

(2) Held to maturity

	£	£
Initial amount recognised (100,000 × 25%)		25,000
Interest income in profit or loss (6.9% × 25,000)	1,725	
Interest received	(1,500)	
		225
Carrying amount at 30 June 20X5		25,225

(3) Available for sale

	£	£
Initial amount recognised (100,000 × 25%)		25,000
Interest income in profit or loss (6.9% × 25,000)	1,725	
Interest received (6%)	(1,500)	
Fair value change in equity (Bal fig)	(1,475)	
		(1,250)
Fair value at year end (25% × 100,000 × 0.95)		23,750

Notes

1 The held-to-maturity carrying amount is greater than the current fair value. The discounted cash flows still equal the carrying amount, so provided Hollinwell plc believes that the future cash flows will be received on time, no impairment should be recognised.

2 The AFS reserve has a debit balance on it. If Hollinwell plc believes that the financial asset is impaired, then this should be reclassified out of other comprehensive income into profit or loss.

(c) A preference share investment could be classified into any one of the three categories in (b).

Unless the investment has been acquired to make a short-term profit, it is unlikely that it would be classified as at fair value through profit or loss, because no similar investments are held and there is no recent evidence of short-term profit taking.

The preference shares would most likely be classified as held to maturity (HTM) or available for sale (AFS). However, this designation should be made at the time of initial recognition and it would be best practice to document this at the time.

The HTM designation requires a positive intention and ability to hold the investments until maturity. The management should think carefully before using this category since:

- A positive intention to hold is far more onerous than a current intention not to sell

- Any significant sales of preference shares would incur the 'tainting rules' that would preclude the use of this classification for the current and two succeeding financial years

However, this category is often favoured by management as it is a cost based model. Its effects are predictable and do not introduce volatility from the use of fair values.

The AFS classification is commonly used by companies for such investments. It does not have the onerous requirements and penalties associated with the HTM classification. Moreover, fair value changes are recognised in other comprehensive income and held in equity and have no effect on earnings. However, there may be some volatility in the statement of financial position from the use of fair values.

3   (a)   The required accounting treatment of the issues is:

(1)   Shares that are reacquired are described as treasury shares by IAS 32 *Financial Instruments: Presentation.* IAS 32 requires them to be deducted directly from equity and no gain or loss to be recognised. The cost of the buyback should be shown as a debit balance in equity. The required journal entry is:

DR	Shares repurchased (equity)	£30,000	
CR	Cash		£30,000

(2)   The financial instruments standards do not apply where an equity investment gives one entity control over another. Harthill plc has acquired 60% of the ordinary capital of Loftdrop Ltd and has control. Consolidated financial statements should be prepared.

IAS 27 *Consolidated and Separate Financial Statements* gives the preparer a choice in respect of the separate (individual) financial statements of Harthill plc. Harthill plc may use the cost model or apply the provisions of IAS 39.

Most companies use the cost model as it is easier to apply and investors are usually not really interested in separate financial statements. The £3,000 professional fees should be written off to profit or loss and the journal entry should be:

DR	Investment	£400,000	
CR	Cash		£400,000

Alternatively Harthill plc could adopt IAS 39 and account for it as an available-for-sale (AFS) financial asset. The professional fees should be added to the cost of the investment (AFS transaction costs should be included in the initial measurement) but at 31 December 20X5 the financial asset should be remeasured to fair value of £440,000 and the movement in fair value of £37,000 (440,000 less 403,000) should be recognised in other comprehensive income.

DR	Financial asset	£37,000	
CR	Other comprehensive income (AFS reserve)		£37,000

(3)   Harthill plc's published accounting policy is to classify equity investments as available-for-sale financial assets. There is no indication that they are held for trading and so this classification is appropriate.

Available-for-sale assets should be initially recognised at fair value including transaction costs. Broker fees were immaterial but the £2 bid-offer spread should be treated as a transaction cost. The asset should initially be measured at £500,000 (20,000 × £25).

At 31 December 20X5 the financial asset should be remeasured to fair value. The fair value should be measured by reference to the bid (exit) price as £600,000 (20,000 × £30) and the movement in fair value of £100,000 (600,000 less 500,000) should be recognised in other comprehensive income.

The required journal entries are:

DR	Financial asset (SFP)	£500,000	
CR	Cash (SFP)		£500,000
DR	Financial asset (SFP)	£100,000	
CR	Other comprehensive income (AFS reserve)		£100,000

(4) Interest rate swaps are derivatives and should be classified as at fair value through profit or loss. The derivative should be recognised at cost of £200,000 and the profit on derecognition of £25,000 (225,000 – 200,000) should be recognised in profit or loss.

The required journal entries are:

DR	Derivative asset (SFP)	£200,000	
CR	Cash (SFP)		£200,000
DR	Cash (SFP)	£225,000	
CR	Derivative asset (SFP)		£200,000
CR	Profit or loss – profit on derecognition (I/S)		£25,000

(5) The substance of the transaction looks unusual. It appears to be a sale and repurchase agreement. The motivation appears to be to reclassify the gain from the AFS reserve in equity to profit or loss in 20X5. The substance and legal form of the transaction appear to differ because:

- The security is repurchased shortly after the year end
- The repurchase price is not the market price
- The repurchase is from the same party that it was originally sold to

The equity security should not be derecognised. Harthill plc still bears the risks and rewards of ownership. No profit on disposal should be recognised. The accounting treatment should be:

- The proceeds should be treated as borrowings

- The premium on repurchase in 20X6 of £5,000 (325,000 less 320,000) should be recognised as a finance cost

The journal required is:

DR	Cash	£320,000	
CR	Borrowings		£320,000

(b) There appear to be a number of ethical issues that need investigating including:

- Whether the derivative trading transaction is consistent with company policy as it is clearly a trading transaction that was speculative

- Whether the sale and repurchase transaction is also consistent with company policy. It appears to have been motivated by a wish to manipulate earnings

You should consider discussing the matters with management.

4   Per the disclosed accounting policy the advance to Hilltop Ltd should be classified as a 'loan and receivable' and measured at amortised cost.

The loan should be initially recognised at fair value including transaction costs. Transaction costs are those directly attributable costs incurred specifically as part of acquiring the financial asset. Apportioned internal costs, such as treasury team time, would have been incurred anyway and should not be included in transaction costs. The loan should be measured on initial recognition at £105,000 (£100,000 plus £5,000 professional costs).

Amortised cost is:

- The initial amount recognised for the financial asset (£105,000)
- Plus any amortisation
- Less any repayments

Amortisation should be calculated by applying the effective interest rate (7%) to the carrying amount at the start of the accounting period.

At the end of each year, Bolehill Ltd is required to determine whether any objective evidence of impairment exists. The failure of Hilltop Ltd to make the required payment on 31 May 20X4 and the new terms granted are objective evidence of impairment.

The impairment should be calculated by comparing the amortised cost at that date with the present value of the agreed future cash flows discounted at the original effective interest rate. This impairment loss should be recognised in profit or loss. Subsequent interest income should be calculated by applying the original effective interest rate to the revised carrying amount.

Bolehill Ltd

Extracts of financial statements for the years ended 31 May

	20X3 (W1) £	20X4 (W1) £	20X5 (W3) £	20X6 (W3) £
Income statement				
Treasury team expenses	(3,000)			
Impairment expense (W2)	–	(6,754)	–	–
Finance income (W1) and (W3)	7,350	5,765	5,695	2,944
Statement of financial position				
Non-current assets				
Financial assets (W5)	58,115	42,056	0	0
Current assets				
Financial assets (W5)	24,235	39,305	42,056	0
Statement of cash flows				
Cash flows from operating activities				
Treasury team expenses	(3,000)			
Interest received (W4)	7,350	0	5,695	2,944
Cash flows from financing activities				
Loan advance	(105,000)	–	–	–
Repayment of advance (W4)	22,650	0	39,305	42,056

WORKINGS

(1) Amortised cost

Year ending 31 May	Opening balance £	Finance income @ 7% £	Receipts £	Closing balance £
20X3	105,000	7,350	(30,000)	82,350
20X4	82,350	5,765	0	88,115

(2) Impairment expense

Year ending 31 May	Future cash flow £	DF @ 7%	Present value £
20X5	45,000	0.93458	42,056
20X6	45,000	0.87344	39,305
			81,361
Current carrying amount (W1)			88,115
Impairment loss			6,754

(3) Revised amortised cost

Year ending 31 May	Opening balance	Finance income @ 7%	Receipts	Closing balance
	£	£	£	£
20X5	81,361	5,695	(45,000)	42,056
20X6	42,056	2,944	(45,000)	0

(4) Cash is received at year end and is treated first of all as a repayment of interest. The remaining amount received is then treated as a repayment of capital.

(5) Split of receivable

	Current	Non-current (Bal fig)	Total
	£	£	£
20X3 (30,000 due in 12 months – 5,765 (W1))	24,235	58,115	82,350
20X4 (45,000 due in 12 months – 5,695 (W3))	39,305	42,056	81,361

5   **Extracts of financial statements for the year ended 31 December 20X6**

	Ancotes Ltd £	Ladybarn Ltd £
Income statement		
Operating expenses	–	(500)
Finance income	–	22,500
Statement of financial position		
Non-current assets		
Financial asset	–	82,500
Equity		
Share warrants issued	77,900	–
Statement of cash flows		
Cash flows from investing activities		
Financial asset acquired	–	(60,000)
Cash flows from financing activities		
Net proceeds from share warrant issue	77,900	–

Explanation

The warrants are a derivative on Ancotes Ltd's own shares settled by the delivery of a fixed number of shares for a fixed amount of cash. They are an equity instrument and the proceeds should be credited directly to equity.

The directly attributable transaction costs should be deducted from the proceeds, net of the tax benefit. The net proceeds from issuing the warrants are:

	£
Gross proceeds (20,000 × £4)	80,000
Transaction costs	(3,000)
Tax benefit (3,000 × 30%)	900
	77,900

Ancotes Ltd should not recognise subsequent changes in the fair value of the warrants because they generate gains and losses for the holder, not the issuer.

The warrants are a derivative. Ladybarn Ltd should classify as them as held for trading and account for them as at fair value through profit or loss. As a result:

- The financial asset should initially be recognised at a fair value of £60,000 (15,000 × £4)

- The £500 transaction costs should be recognised as an expense in profit or loss

- The financial asset should be remeasured at the year end to its fair value of £82,500 (15,000 × £5.50)

- The movement in the fair value of £22,500 (82,500 – 60,000) should be recognised as finance income in profit or loss

CHAPTER 8

Group financial statements

Introduction

Examination context

Topic List

1 Overview of material covered in Financial Accounting

2 Control

3 Measurement of non-controlling interest

4 Adjustment to consideration, fair values and goodwill

5 Disposal of investment in associate

6 Joint ventures

7 Jointly controlled operations

8 Jointly controlled assets

9 Jointly controlled entities

10 Other areas of IAS 31

11 Judgements required and relevance of information for users

12 UK GAAP comparison

Summary and Self-test

Technical reference

Answers to Interactive questions

Answers to Self-test

Learning objectives

- Determine the circumstances when an investment is a subsidiary, even if less than 50% of the voting rights are owned ☐

- Understand the effect of potential shares on a shareholding ☐

- Recognise a special purpose entity and determine its accounting treatment ☐

- Account for advanced consolidation adjustments ☐

- Recognise and explain what is meant by a joint venture ☐

- Recognise that there are three forms of joint venture ☐

- Account for a jointly controlled entity using proportionate consolidation or the equity method ☐

Specific syllabus references for this chapter are: 3b, 3c, 3d and 4a.

Syllabus links

You have already covered most aspects of preparing consolidated financial statements in the Financial Accounting syllabus. In this chapter we will review the key topics briefly, as you will need to thoroughly understand these basics.

You will not have covered the more advanced areas of consolidated financial statements and the accounting for joint ventures which will be covered in this chapter. This will also be relevant at the Advanced Stage.

Examination context

In the examination, candidates may be required to:

- Assess the status of investments in complex situations

- Deal with losses of a subsidiary and the non-controlling interest effect

- Explain the two methods of measuring the non-controlling interest at acquisition and prepare financial information by the two methods

- Deal with adjustments after the acquisition date

- Explain the treatment of joint ventures

- Prepare extracts of consolidated financial statements including joint ventures

- Compare the different treatments of joint ventures in consolidated financial statements

1 Overview of material covered in Financial Accounting

Section overview

This section revises the key areas of consolidated financial statements covered in Financial Accounting and puts it into context for Financial Reporting.

1.1 Business combinations

A business combination is a transaction or other event in which an **acquirer** obtains control of one or more **businesses**.

All business combinations should be accounted for by applying the **acquisition method**:

- **Identifying the acquirer**

- Determining the **acquisition date**

- Recognising, and measuring at fair value, the **identifiable assets acquired**, the **liabilities assumed** and any **non-controlling interest** in the acquiree

- Recognising and measuring **goodwill** or a gain from a bargain purchase.

Costs directly attributable to the acquisition process (such as legal and professional fees) should be recognised as an expense in profit or loss.

The costs of issuing debt or equity should be deducted from the liability/equity.

Goodwill acquired in a business combination (or a gain on a bargain purchase) should be measured as:

	£	£
Consideration transferred		
Fair value of assets given, liabilities assumed and equity instruments issued		X
Non-controlling interest at the acquisition date		X
		X
Less: Fair value of tangible assets	X	
Fair value of intangible assets	X	
Fair value of assets	X	
Fair value of liabilities, including contingent liabilities	(X)	
Fair value of net assets		(X)
Goodwill (gain from a bargain purchase)		X/(X)

Point to note:

Because the goodwill calculation at Financial Reporting is more complex than it was at Financial Accounting, it is helpful to insert a sub-total of the consideration transferred and the non-controlling interest.

1.2 Basic principles of consolidated financial statements

A group is made up of a **parent** and its **subsidiaries.**

A parent/subsidiary relationship exists where one company has **control** over another company. Control normally exists where the parent owns over 50% of the equity shares of another company.

The purpose of consolidated financial statements is to show the group as a **single economic entity** – this reflects the **economic substance** of the combination.

Consolidated financial statements take account of **control and ownership**.

The fact that the parent **controls** the subsidiary leads to:

- All of the assets and liabilities of the subsidiary being included in the consolidated statement of financial position (CSFP)

- All of the income and expenses of the subsidiary being included in the consolidated statement of comprehensive income – in this chapter income and expenses will normally be restricted to those included in the consolidated separate income statement (CIS)

Even though it controls the subsidiary, in many cases the parent will not own all of the shares in the subsidiary – there will be a **non-controlling interest**. The **ownership position** is reflected by:

- Inclusion of a non-controlling interest in the CSFP
- Inclusion of a non-controlling interest in the CIS

Consolidated statement of financial position (CSFP)

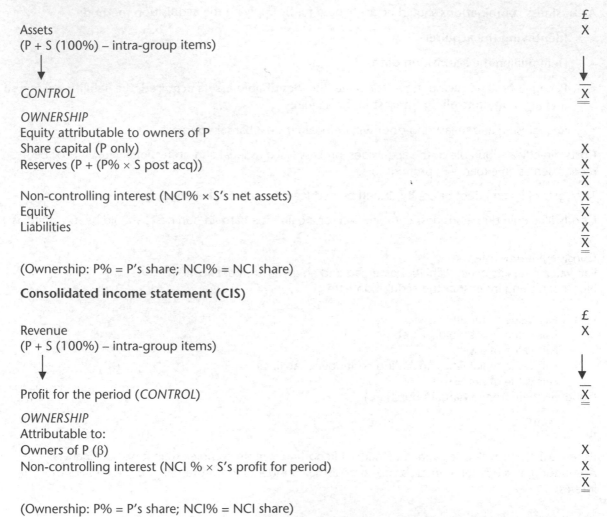

```
                                                              £
Assets                                                        X
(P + S (100%) – intra-group items)

                   ↓                                          ↓
CONTROL                                                       X

OWNERSHIP
Equity attributable to owners of P
Share capital (P only)                                        X
Reserves (P + (P% × S post acq))                             X
                                                              X

Non-controlling interest (NCI% × S's net assets)             X
Equity                                                        X
Liabilities                                                   X
                                                              X

(Ownership: P% = P's share; NCI% = NCI share)
```

Consolidated income statement (CIS)

```
                                                              £
Revenue                                                       X
(P + S (100%) – intra-group items)

                   ↓                                          ↓
Profit for the period (CONTROL)                               X

OWNERSHIP
Attributable to:
Owners of P (β)                                               X
Non-controlling interest (NCI % × S's profit for period)     X
                                                              X

(Ownership: P% = P's share; NCI% = NCI share)
```

1.3 Consolidated statement of financial position – techniques

The main consolidated statement of financial position techniques:

- **Assets and liabilities**

  - Include all of Parent (P) and Subsidiary (S)
  - Exclude any intra-group balances such as current accounts in receivables and payables

- **Fair values**

  - Net assets at acquisition are measured at fair value
  - IFRS 3 *Business Combinations* gives guidance on measuring fair values
  - Include net assets at fair value in the current CSFP
  - If fair value adjustments relate to depreciable assets, adjust accumulated depreciation

- **Goodwill acquired in a business combination**

  Treated as an intangible asset in the CSFP, with no annual amortisation charges but with annual review for impairment (see Chapter 3 on intangible assets)

- **Bargain purchase in a business combination**

  Where the fair value of consideration is less than the fair value of net assets acquired

  - Reassess the identification and measurement of the net assets acquired and the measurement of the consideration transferred
  - Recognise any remaining balance as a gain in the CIS in period of acquisition

- **Unrealised intra-group profit on inventory**

  - Reduce consolidated inventory by the amount of the unrealised profit (PURP)
  - If P sells to S, reduce group retained earnings by entire PURP
  - If S sells to P, reduce group retained earnings/NCI by relevant shares

- **Equity attributable to owners of P**

  - All of P's share capital and reserves and P's share of S's post acquisition reserves
  - Adjust retained earnings for any accumulated impairments of goodwill, PURP, etc

- **Non-controlling interest presented within equity**

  Calculate as:

  - NCI share of S's period end net assets; **or**
  - NCI share of S's net assets at acquisition + share of S's post acquisition retained earnings and other reserves (similar to equity accounting for an associate)

- **Mid-year acquisition**

  Reserves at acquisition are opening reserves plus profit earned up to the date of acquisition (assume that S's profits accrue evenly unless told otherwise)

1.4 Consolidated statement of financial position – standard workings

(1) Establish group structure

(2) Set out **net assets of S (one for each subsidiary)**

	At period end £	At acquisition £	Post-acquisition £
Share capital	X	X	–
Retained earnings	X	X	X
Fair value adjustments	X	X	(X)
Contingent liabilities	(X)	(X)	–
	X	X	X

(3) Calculate **goodwill**

	£
Consideration transferred	X
Plus: NCI at acquisition	X
	X
Less: net assets at acquisition (see W2)	(X)
Carrying amount before impairment	X
Impairment to date	(X)
Balance c/f	X

(4)   Calculate **NCI**

	£
Share of net assets at period end (see W2)	X
Or (similar to an associate)	
Share at acquisition (see W2)	X
Share of post acquisition retained earnings and other reserves (see W2)	X
	X

(5)   Calculate **retained earnings**

	£
P Ltd (100%)	X
S Ltd (share of post-acquisition retained earnings (see W2))	X
Goodwill impairment to date (see W3)	(X)
	X

Interactive question 1: Consolidated statement of financial position

[Difficulty level: Easy]

The summarised statements of financial position of Close Ltd and Steele Ltd as at 31 December 20X9 were as follows.

	Close Ltd		Steele Ltd	
	£	£	£	£
ASSETS				
Non-current assets				
Property, plant and equipment		80,000		58,200
Investments		84,000		–
		164,000		58,200
Current assets				
Inventories	18,000		12,000	
Trade and other receivables	62,700		21,100	
Investments	–		2,500	
Cash and cash equivalents	10,000		3,000	
Current account – Close Ltd	–		3,200	
		90,700		41,800
Total assets		254,700		100,000
EQUITY AND LIABILITIES				
Equity attributable to owners				
Ordinary share capital (£1 shares)		120,000		60,000
Share premium account		18,000		–
Revaluation surplus		23,000		16,000
Retained earnings		56,000		13,000
		217,000		89,000
Current liabilities				
Trade and other payables	35,000		11,000	
Current account – Steele Ltd	2,700		–	
		37,700		11,000
Total equity and liabilities		254,700		100,000

The following information is relevant.

(1)   On 1 January 20X7 Close Ltd acquired 48,000 shares in Steele Ltd for £84,000 cash when the retained earnings of Steele Ltd were £8,000 and the balance on the revaluation surplus was £16,000.

(2)   The inventories of Close Ltd include £4,000 of goods invoiced by Steele Ltd at cost plus 25%.

(3)   A cheque for £500 from Close Ltd to Steele Ltd, sent before 31 December 20X9, was not received by the latter company until January 20Y0.

(4)   An impairment review at 31 December 20X9 revealed that a further impairment loss of £500 should be recognised in respect of the goodwill acquired in the business combination with Steele Ltd. By 1 January 20X9 this goodwill had already suffered impairments totalling £1,700.

Requirement

Prepare the consolidated statement of financial position of Close Ltd and its subsidiary Steele Ltd as at 31 December 20X9.

Fill in the proforma below.

Close Ltd – Consolidated statement of financial position as at 31 December 20X9

	£	£
ASSETS		
Non-current assets		
Property, plant and equipment		
Intangibles		
Current assets		
Inventories		
Trade and other receivables		
Investments		
Cash and cash equivalents		
Total assets		
EQUITY AND LIABILITIES		
Attributable to owners of Close Ltd		
Ordinary share capital		
Share premium account		
Revaluation surplus		
Retained earnings		
Non-controlling interest		
Equity		
Current liabilities		
Trade and other payables		
Total equity and liabilities		

See **Answer** at the end of this chapter.

1.5 Consolidated income statement – techniques

The main consolidated income statement techniques are:

- **Income and expenses**

    – Generally include all of P and all of S (see below for intra-group trading)
    – Exclude any dividend income from S

- **Intra-group sales**

    – Deduct amount of intra-group sales from both revenue and cost of sales
    – Add amount of unrealised profit to seller's cost of sales

- **Impairment of goodwill**

    Add current year impairment loss to consolidated expenses

- **Non-controlling interest**

    NCI's share of S's profit after tax (and after any unrealised profit if S sold goods to P)

- **Mid-year acquisition**

    Time apportion S's profit and deduct any intra-group items

1.6 Consolidated income statement – standard workings

1 Establish group structure

2 Prepare consolidation schedule

	P £	S £	Adj £	Consol £
Revenue	X	X	(X)	X
C of S – Per question	(X)	(X)	X	(X)
– PURP (seller's books)	(X)	(X)		(X)
Exps – Per question	(X)	(X)		(X)
– Goodwill impairment				(X)
Tax – Per question	(X)	(X)		(X)
Profit		X		X

May need workings for items such as PURP and goodwill impairment

3 Calculate NCI

			£
S profit for period × NCI%	NCI% ×	X =	X

1.7 Consolidated statement of changes in equity

Given below is a proforma for a typical consolidated statement of changes in equity (CSCE):

	Attributable to owners of P			Non-controlling interest	Total
	Share capital £	Retained earnings £	Total £	£	£
Brought forward	X	X	X	X	X
Total comprehensive income for the period	–	X	X	X	X
Dividends paid	–	(X)	(X)	(X)	(X)
Carried forward	X	X	X	X	X

The main consolidated statement of changes in equity techniques are:

- **Share capital**

  P only, including new shares issued during the period

- **Retained earnings**

  P plus post-acquisition share of S

- **Dividends**

  - P's dividends in P's retained earnings column
  - NCI's share of S's dividends in non-controlling column

- **Non-controlling interest**

  - NCI's share of S's net assets b/f
    If S acquired during the year, the b/f figure is zero. Insert additional line for the NCI's share of net assets at acquisition date
  - Non-controlling interest's share of S's total comprehensive income for period
  - Non-controlling interest's dividend (see above)

Interactive question 2: Consolidated statement of comprehensive income and consolidated statement of changes in equity [Difficulty level: Intermediate]

The following summarised statements of comprehensive income have been prepared for the year ended 30 June 20X5 for Higg plc and its subsidiary Topp Ltd.

	Higg plc £	Higg plc £	Topp Ltd £
Revenue		647,200	296,800
Cost of sales		(427,700)	(194,100)
Gross profit		219,500	102,700
Operating costs		(106,300)	(42,300)
Profit from operations		113,200	60,400
Investment income			
Dividends from Topp Ltd	7,000		–
Dividends from quoted investments	3,000		2,000
Interest from Topp Ltd	1,600		–
		11,600	
Finance cost		–	(8,000)
Profit before tax		124,800	54,400
Tax		(58,300)	(27,300)
Profit and total comprehensive income for the period		66,500	27,100

The following information is relevant.

(1) Higg plc acquired 70% of the £100,000 issued ordinary shares of Topp Ltd for £95,000 on 1 July 20X1 when retained earnings of Topp Ltd were £13,200. On the same date Higg plc acquired 20% of the 8% loan stock of Topp Ltd. The total loan stock issued at par is £100,000.

(2) The revenue of Higg plc includes sales to Topp Ltd of £36,000, all invoiced at cost plus 25%. On 30 June 20X5 the inventory of Topp Ltd included £9,000 in respect of such goods.

(3) Three years ago a goodwill impairment loss of £5,910 was recognised in profit or loss. A further impairment loss of £1,970 needs to be recognised in the current year.

(4) Higg plc paid an ordinary dividend of £20,000. Topp Ltd paid an ordinary dividend of £10,000.

(5) The retained earnings of Higg plc and Topp Ltd as at 1 July 20X4 were £72,400 and £29,600 respectively. The share capital of Higg plc comprises 500,000 £1 ordinary shares.

Requirement

Prepare the consolidated income statement and consolidated statement of changes in equity for the year ended 30 June 20X5.

Fill in the proforma below.

Higg plc – Consolidated statement of comprehensive income for the year ended 30 June 20X5

	£
Revenue	
Cost of sales	
Gross profit	
Operating costs	
Profit from operations	
Finance cost	
Investment income	
Profit before tax	
Tax	
Profit and total comprehensive income for the period	

Attributable to:
Owners of Higg plc
Non-controlling interest

Consolidated statement of changes in equity for the year ended 30 June 20X5

	Attributable to owners of Higg plc			Non-controlling interest £	Total £
	Share capital £	Retained earnings £	Total £		
Balance brought forward					
Total comprehensive income for the period					
Dividends paid					
Balance carried forward					

See **Answer** at the end of this chapter.

1.8 Associates

An associate is an entity over which the group has **significant influence, but not control.**

A holding of 20% or more is presumed to give significant influence, but there are other ways in which it can be gained.

The associate is not part of the group, because the group comprises only the parent and the subsidiaries.

Associates should be accounted for by the **equity method** of accounting.

- **Statement of financial position**

  - Carrying amount

	£
Cost of investment (in P's books)	X
Add: P's share of post acquisition retained profits and other reserves (see W2)	X
Carrying amount before impairment	X
Less impairment losses	(X)
	X

  Points to note:

  1 When the investment is bought, the associate's net assets should be measured at fair value. If an associate's asset has a fair value in excess of its carrying amount, the cost of the investment should be reduced as that excess is consumed, eg through additional depreciation.

  2 Goodwill in relation to the investment is not separately presented. But any bargain purchase should be recognised in profit or loss when the investment is bought.

  3 It is the total carrying amount, not just any goodwill component, which is subject to impairment tests. So the whole amount of any impairment loss is capable of reversal if the recoverable amount of the investment in A increases

  4 Any long-term loan made by the investor to the associate should be included in this amount

  5 Trading balances with associate should not be cancelled against each other

  - CSFP Standard working 2

    - Prepare net assets working for A, in the same way as for a subsidiary

  - **Consolidated reserves**

    - Include P's share of A's post acquisition reserves
    - Deduct any cumulative impairment of investment in A

- **Consolidated income statement**
    - A's profit for the period
        - Include P's share of A's profit for the period, time-apportioned if acquired in current period
        - Adjust for any fair value excess now consumed
        - Deduct any current period impairment of investment from P's share of A's profit
    - Dividends
        - Do not include any dividends from A
    - Unrealised profit is only adjusted for P's percentage holding in A

        Adjust earnings of the seller. If P sold to A, increase P's cost of sales; if A sold to P, reduce A's profit for the period

Worked example: Fair value adjustment in associate

On 1 January 20X1 Gamma plc acquired 25% of the equity of Delta Ltd for £500,000 when the carrying amount of Delta Ltd's net assets was £1.6 million. Carrying amounts of individual assets approximated to their fair value with the exception that the fair value of a machine exceeded its carrying amount by £50,000. On 1 January 20X1 this machine had a remaining useful life of five years. Delta Ltd did not adjust its carrying amount to fair value. At 31 December 20X1 Delta Ltd's financial statements presented net assets of £2.2 million.

Calculate the carrying amount of Gamma plc's investment in Delta Ltd in Gamma plc's consolidated statement of financial position at 31 December 20X1.

Solution

	£'000	£'000
Cost of investment		500
Add: Share of post-acquisition retained earnings – 25% of (2,200 – 1,600)	150	
Less: Depreciation of fair value excess (50/5)	(10)	
		140
		640

Interactive question 3: Associate – statement of financial position

[Difficulty level: Easy]

The draft statements of financial position of three companies as at 31 December 20X9 are set out below.

	Haley plc £	Socrates Ltd £	Aristotle Ltd £
Property, plant and equipment	300,000	100,000	160,000
Investments at cost			
18,000 shares in Socrates Ltd	75,000	–	–
18,000 shares in Aristotle Ltd	30,000	–	–
Current assets	345,000	160,000	80,000
	750,000	260,000	240,000
Ordinary shares of £1 each	250,000	30,000	60,000
Retained earnings	400,000	180,000	100,000
Equity	650,000	210,000	160,000
Current liabilities	100,000	50,000	80,000
	750,000	260,000	240,000

The retained earnings of Socrates Ltd and Aristotle Ltd when the investments were acquired eight years ago were £70,000 and £30,000 respectively.

Impairment reviews to date have resulted in the need for the following impairment losses to be recognised in respect of Haley plc's investments.

	£
Socrates Ltd	12,000
Aristotle Ltd	2,400

Requirement

Prepare the consolidated statement of financial position as at 31 December 20X9.

Fill in the proforma below.

Haley plc

Consolidated statement of financial position as at 31 December 20X9

	£
ASSETS	
Non-current assets	
Property, plant and equipment	
Intangibles	
Investment in associates	
Current assets	
Total assets	
EQUITY AND LIABILITIES	
Attributable to owners of Haley plc	
Ordinary share capital	
Retained earnings	
Non-controlling interest	
Equity	
Current liabilities	
Total equity and liabilities	

See **Answer** at the end of this chapter.

 Interactive question 4: Associate – income statement　　　　[Difficulty level: Intermediate]

Corfu Ltd holds 80% of the ordinary share capital of Zante Ltd (acquired on 1 February 20X9) and 30% of the ordinary share capital of Paxos Ltd (acquired on 1 July 20X8).

The draft income statements for the year ended 30 June 20X9, are set out below.

	Corfu Ltd	Zante Ltd	Paxos Ltd
	£'000	£'000	£'000
Revenue	12,614	6,160	8,640
Cost of sales and expenses	(11,318)	(5,524)	(7,614)
Trading profit	1,296	636	1,026
Dividends receivable from Zante Ltd	171	–	–
Profit before tax	1,467	636	1,026
Tax	(621)	(275)	(432)
Profit for the period	846	361	594

Included in the inventory of Paxos Ltd at 30 June 20X9 was £150,000 for goods purchased from Corfu Ltd in May 20X9, which the latter company had invoiced at cost plus 25%. These were the only goods Corfu Ltd sold to Paxos Ltd but it did make sales of £50,000 to Zante Ltd during the year. None of these goods remained in Zante Ltd's inventory at the year end.

Requirement

Prepare a consolidated income statement for Corfu Ltd for the year ended 30 June 20X9.

Fill in the proforma below.

Corfu Ltd

Consolidated income statement for the year ended 30 June 20X9

£'000

Revenue
Cost of sales and expenses
Share of profit of associates
Profit before tax
Tax
Profit for the period

Attributable to:
Owners of Corfu Ltd
Non-controlling interest

See **Answer** at the end of this chapter.

Interactive question 5: Associate – impairment   [Difficulty level: Exam standard]

On 1 January 20X4 Keen plc paid £760,000 to acquire 35% of the ordinary share capital of Guest Ltd, with a view to sharing in its profitable future. Since 1 January 20X4 Keen plc has had the power to appoint two out of the five directors. The fair value and carrying amount of the net assets recognised by Guest Ltd at that date was £2 million.

In the year ended 31 December 20X4 Guest Ltd incurred losses of £400,000 and at the period end the present value of its future cash flows was estimated by Guest Ltd's directors at £1.7 million. At 31 December 20X4 a competitor offered Keen plc £550,000 (plus reimbursement of any selling expenses incurred) for its interest in Guest Ltd.

Requirement

Explain whether Keen plc should carry out an impairment test in respect of its investment in Guest Ltd at 31 December 20X4 and for this investment calculate the amount to be recognised by Keen plc in its consolidated financial statements in respect of profit or loss for the year and carrying amount at the period end.

See **Answer** at the end of this chapter.

1.9   Disposal of subsidiary

As in Financial Accounting, only **disposals of the total holding** in a subsidiary are within the Financial Reporting syllabus.

When a group disposes of all of a subsidiary this should be recognised in both:

*   The parent's separate financial statements
*   The consolidated financial statements

In the **parent's separate financial statements** the **profit or loss on disposal** should be calculated as:

	£
Sales proceeds	X
Less: carrying amount (cost in P's own statement of financial position)	(X)
Profit or loss on disposal	X

In the **consolidated financial statements** the **profit or loss on disposal** should be calculated as:

			£	£
Sales proceeds				X
Less:	Carrying amount of goodwill at date of disposal:			
	Consideration transferred at acquisition date		X	
	Non-controlling interest at acquisition date		X	
			X	
	Net assets at acquisition date		(X)	
	Goodwill at acquisition date		X	
	Impairment to date		(X)	
	Goodwill at disposal			(X)
	Carrying amount of net assets at date of disposal (W)			(X)
Add back:	Non-controlling interest in net assets at date of disposal			X
Profit/(loss) on disposal				X

WORKING

Carrying amount of net assets

	£
Net assets b/f	X
Profit/(loss) for current period to date of disposal	X/(X)
Dividends paid in current period prior to date of disposal	(X)
Net assets at date of disposal	X

Point to note: There are other methods of setting out this calculation.

Other effects of disposal:

- S is not a subsidiary at period end, so not in CSFP
- Include in CIS the profits and non-controlling interest up to date of disposal

Worked example: Disposal of subsidiary

Alpha plc acquired 80% of the equity of Beta Ltd for £1.9 million when the fair value of Beta Ltd's net assets was £1.2 million. By 1 January 20X1 Alpha plc had recognised impairment losses of £200,000 in respect of the goodwill acquired in the business combination with Beta Ltd. At 1 January 20X1 Beta Ltd's net assets were £1.4 million. Beta Ltd's profits for the year ended 31 December 20X1 were £240,000, accruing evenly over the year. On 30 June 20X1 Alpha plc sold its holding in Beta Ltd for £3 million.

Calculate the profit or loss on disposal to be recognised in Alpha plc's consolidated profit or loss for the year ended 31 December 20X1.

Solution

			£'000	£'000
Sales proceeds				3,000
Less:	Carrying amount of goodwill at date of disposal:			
	Consideration transferred at acquisition date		1,900	
	Non-controlling interest at acquisition date (20% × 1,200)		240	
			2,140	
	Net assets at acquisition date		(1,200)	
	Goodwill at acquisition date		940	
	Impairment to date		(200)	
	Goodwill at disposal			(740)
	Carrying amount of net assets at date of disposal (W)			(1,520)
Add back:	Non-controlling interest in net assets at date of disposal			
	(20% × 1,520 net assets)			304
Profit on disposal				1,044

WORKING

Net assets at disposal

	£'000
Net assets b/f	1,400
Profit for current period to date of disposal (240 × 6/12)	120
	1,520

1.10 Context

Entities, whether multinational or national, may have complex group structures. These structures are usually driven by the legal, taxation and regulatory requirements within the countries in which the entities operate. Investors are interested in the financial performance and financial position of a group of entities as this represents the business activities controlled by the entity in which they have invested. The combination of all of the legal entities within a group shows the substance of their investment.

The requirement to include subsidiaries in consolidated financial statements is based around the concept of control. Control needs to be distinguished from management or trusteeship. The decision as to whether an entity has joint control over a joint venture or significant influence over an associate rather than control over a subsidiary can be difficult where confidential agreements exist between shareholders concerning vetoes and options.

A non-controlling stake, leading to associate status, may be acquired in a business whose viability and success will play an integral part in an entity's own success. For example, where an entity uses distributors or agents in foreign countries, it may wish to take an equity stake in them. This strengthens the relationship between the parties and allows a level of influence and communication that is greater than could be obtained through a contractual agreement alone. Alternatively, a non-controlling stake may be the initial stage of a larger plan to obtain control of the target entity. The investor is able to gain board representation and strengthen its business relationships with the target. If the relationship is successful, further investment can be facilitated. The advantage of such a process is that the investor can evaluate closely the strategic fit of the investment and develop stronger post-merger integration plans. This approach is common in high technology and developing industries where small, newly established entities require capital funding. Capital is provided with a view to using or exploiting the technology at a later stage. In addition the investing entities often provide non-financial assistance such as management services, logistics and knowledge transfer.

Business combinations are becoming increasingly complex. Structures are carefully modelled to ensure that transactions optimise post acquisition earnings as well as meeting corporate strategic objectives. Goodwill acquired in a business combination can be significant and any loss in its value may lead to significant impairment losses being recognised in the group's profit or loss. This will introduce volatility into earnings and highlights poorly performing acquisitions.

Current accounting requirements emphasise the importance of disaggregating goodwill into identifiable intangible assets. This reflects the move towards a knowledge-based economy where intangible assets, such as brands, are key business assets. They represent an increasingly important economic business resource. Amortisation of intangible assets with a short life may therefore reduce earnings in the short term.

As an example of the sums involved, Vodafone plc's 2007 financial statements recognised goodwill of £40,567 million (after recognising in profit or loss an impairment loss in the year of £11,600 million) and other intangible assets of £15,705 million. These represented 60% and 23% respectively of 2007 equity of £67,293 million.

2 Control

Section overview

- Control over another entity is the key to whether it is a subsidiary.
- It is not necessary to own over 50% of the voting rights to have control.
- Potential shares should in some circumstances be considered.
- A special purpose entity controlled by another entity should be consolidated by that entity.
- A subsidiary should no longer be consolidated when control of that subsidiary is lost.
- The non-controlling interest should bear its share of losses accumulated in subsidiaries.
- Control may be achieved by successive share purchases.

2.1 Business combinations and control

A business combination is a transaction or other event in which an **acquirer** obtains control over one or more **businesses**.

The key words here are **control** and **business**.

Definition

Control is the power to govern the financial and operating policies of an entity so as to obtain benefits from its activities.

In your Financial Accounting studies, control was assumed if the parent (P) owned more than 50% of the equity shares of the subsidiary (S), or to be more specific more than 50% of the voting rights. However:

- If P owns more than 50% of the voting rights of S, then control over S is presumed to exist

- If P owns more than 50% of the voting rights of S but P decides that it does not have control of S, then P should demonstrate that this is not the case in order to avoid having to consolidate S.

Definition

Business: An integrated set of activities and assets capable of being conducted and managed for the purpose of providing:

(a) A return in the form of dividends; or
(b) Lower costs or other economic benefits directly to investors or other owners.

A business generally consists of inputs, processes applied to those inputs, and resulting outputs that are, or will be, used to generate revenues. If goodwill is present in a transferred set of activities and assets, the transferred set is presumed to be a business.

The important point to understand is that it is the acquisition of activities which is accounted for under IFRS 3. If it is just some assets, and perhaps liabilities, which are acquired, then the consideration is allocated according to other IFRS (eg IAS 16 in the case of property, plant or equipment) across what has been acquired; no goodwill should be recognised.

2.1.1 Business combinations involving entities under common control

- It may be that the same party controls two entities which are then subject to a business combination as a result of which the party still controls both entities.

  For example Ms A, an individual, owns directly the whole of the share capital of two separate entities, B Ltd and C Ltd. Ms A decides to reorganise her affairs by selling her shareholding in C Ltd to B Ltd. The acquisition of C Ltd by B Ltd is a business combination, but Ms A controls both entities, before and after the combination.

  Alternatively, it might be A plc which controls the two entities which are therefore its direct subsidiaries and are consolidated into the A plc consolidated financial statements. If B Ltd buys C Ltd, A plc still controls C Ltd through its control of B Ltd, so it has control over both entities, both before and after the combination.

- The scope of IFRS 3 specifically excludes such business combinations and there is at present no guidance in IFRS on how these combinations should be accounted for.

2.2 Control with less than 50% of the voting rights

IAS 27 *Consolidated and Separate Financial Statements* sets out four circumstances where control exists, even though P has less than 50% of the voting rights in S:

- P has the power over more than 50% of the voting rights through the existence of an agreement with other investors. For example P may own 40% of the voting rights but shareholders owning a total of 21% between them agree not to vote on resolutions. P owns 40% of the 79% of voting rights which could be exercised and therefore controls S.

- P has the power to govern the financial and operating policies of S either by agreement or through statute.

- P has the power to appoint or remove the majority of the board of directors (or equivalent body) of S and that body controls S.

- P has the power to cast the majority of votes at a meeting of the board of directors (or equivalent body) of S and that body controls S.

There is no further guidance in IFRS on these points; therefore the **substance** of the situation should be considered in any such case.

2.3 Potential voting rights

In determining whether control exists potential voting rights stemming from financial instruments such as convertible debt, warrants and options should be taken into account, but only when the instruments giving rise to them are **currently exercisable or convertible**, that is:

- During the conversion period for convertible debt
- During the exercise period for warrants and options.

In such cases the entitlement to these extra voting rights provides the **power** to govern the policies of another entity, ie to control it, even before the instruments are exercised or converted.

Point to note:

Potential voting rights should only be taken into account when determining whether control exists. If it does exist, the attribution of profits or losses between the owners of the parent and the non-controlling interest is still based upon entitlements **excluding** potential voting rights.

Interactive question 6: Potential voting rights [Difficulty level: Easy]

A owns 38% of the voting shares of C. A also owns warrants in C which will allow A to acquire a further 14% of the voting shares of C in three years' time.

Requirement

Explain whether A has control of C.

See **Answer** at the end of this chapter.

2.4 Special purpose entities

Definition

A **special purpose entity (SPE)** is another entity which has been created to 'accomplish a narrow and well-defined objective' (SIC 12 *Consolidation – Special Purpose Entities*).

An SPE is often set up as a trust or a partnership (rather than as a company) in order to effect a lease or to provide securitisation of financial assets for example.

If an entity has **control** over an SPE, then the SPE should be consolidated as part of the consolidated financial statements.

SIC 12 sets out the circumstances in which the **substance of the arrangement** is that the SPE is under the control of the entity which arranged its creation:

- The activities of the SPE are conducted on behalf of the entity, with the entity obtaining benefits from the SPE's operations; or

- The entity has the decision-making powers which lead to obtaining the majority of the benefits of the SPE's operations; or

- The entity has the right to the majority of the benefits of the SPE and as a result may also be exposed to the majority of the risks associated with the SPE's activities; or

- The entity retains the majority of the residual ownership risks related to the SPE or its assets.

In each case the substance of the SPE and its relationship with the entity which arranged its creation should be considered.

In its 2009 financial statements British Land plc reported that at "31 March 2009 £2.1 billion (2008: £3.0 billion) of outstanding debt had been issued, by ring-fenced, special purpose subsidiaries, with no recourse to other companies or assets in the Group". Taking account of the factors listed above these entities are regarded as being controlled by British Land and have to be consolidated, but the company is keen to point out that other Group assets are not at risk for these debts, because the subsidiaries have been set up in a way to seal (ring fence) them from the rest of the Group.

2.5 Loss of control

A parent should only cease to consolidate an entity as a subsidiary when it loses control of that entity.

It is only then that the entity no longer meets the definition of a subsidiary.

A parent **loses control** of an entity when it loses the power to govern the financial and operating policies, so as to obtain benefits from its activities.

Control can be lost by:

- A direct disposal of shares in the subsidiary

- A deemed disposal (a subsidiary makes a rights issue and the parent does not take up its allocation, for example)

- Where the subsidiary becomes subject to control of a government, court, administrator or regulator

- As a result of a contractual agreement.

Only the direct disposal of all the shares held in a subsidiary is within the Financial Reporting syllabus.

2.6 Losses in a subsidiary

When profits are earned by a partly owned subsidiary, they are allocated between the parent and the non-controlling interest in proportion to their holdings. Any losses incurred by such a subsidiary should be treated in the same way:

Debit   Non-controlling interest with their share of loss for the year
Debit   Consolidated retained earnings with group share of loss for the year

However if a subsidiary is making **continuing losses** year after year, the debits to the non-controlling interest account could come to exceed the credit for the non-controlling interest's share in the equity in the subsidiary, leading to a net debit balance.

This net deficit should be recognised as a reduction in the total non-controlling interest presented in equity. This can lead to the total non-controlling interest having a debit (negative) balance in the CSFP.

2.7 Control achieved in stages (step acquisitions)

On the acquisition date (the date the acquirer obtains control) the acquirer should recognise the acquiree's identifiable net assets and any goodwill acquired (or bargain purchase) in the business combination.

An acquirer which gained control after purchasing shares on different dates should:

- Remeasure equity held immediately before control is gained at its fair value at the acquisition date.
- Recognise the gain or loss on remeasurement in profit or loss.

When calculating the goodwill acquired in the business combination, the acquisition date fair value of the previously held equity is added to the consideration transferred at the acquisition date and the non-controlling interest at that date.

Points to note:

1   One of the consequences of the previously held equity being remeasured at its fair value is that any gains previously recognised in other comprehensive income and still held in equity should be accounted for under the relevant IFRS:

*   If the previously held equity was classified as an available-for-sale financial asset, any gains in respect of it which had previously been recognised in other comprehensive income should now be reclassified from other comprehensive income to profit or loss (IAS 39)

*   If the previously held equity was classified as an investment in an equity-accounted associate and a share of the associate's revaluation surpluses in respect of property, plant and equipment had been recognised, these surpluses should now be transferred within reserves, from the revaluation surplus to retained earnings in the statement of changes in equity (IAS 16).

2   Once control has been obtained, no remeasurement gain or loss is recognised on any subsequent increase in the ownership percentage. Instead, the difference between the consideration transferred and the reduction in non-controlling interests should be reported in **equity**.

Worked example: Control in stages – previous holding an AFS investment

Bath Ltd has 1 million shares in issue. Bristol plc acquired 50,000 shares in Bath Ltd on 1 January 20X6 for £100,000. These shares were classified as available-for-sale financial assets and on 31 December 20X8 their carrying amount was £230,000 and increases in fair value of £130,000 had been recognised in other comprehensive income and were held in equity. On 1 June 20X9 when the fair value of Bath Ltd's net assets was £4 million, Bristol plc acquired another 650,000 shares in Bath Ltd for £3.9 million. On 1 June 20X9 the fair value of the 50,000 shares already held was £250,000.

Show the journal entry required in respect of the 50,000 shareholding on 1 June 20X9 and calculate the goodwill acquired in the business combination on that date.

Solution

Journal entry

		£'000	£'000
DR	Investment in Bath Ltd (250,000 – 230,000)	20	
DR	Other comprehensive income and AFS reserve	130	
CR	Profit or loss		150

To recognise the gain on the remeasurement of the shareholding in Bath Ltd immediately prior to control being obtained.

Calculation of goodwill in respect of 70% (5% + 65%) holding in Bath Ltd

	£'000
Consideration transferred	3,900
Non-controlling interest (30% × £4 million)	1,200
Acquisition-date fair value of previously held equity	250
	5,350
Net assets acquired	(4,000)
Goodwill	1,350

Point to note:

If the size of Bristol plc's previously held equity had resulted in Bath Ltd being an associate of Bristol plc, it would have been the carrying amount of that investment under the equity method which would have been remeasured.

Interactive question 7: Control in stages – previous holding equity accounted

[Difficulty level: Exam standard]

On 31 December 20X7 when the fair value of Feeder Ltd's net assets was £460,000 Lawn plc acquired 40,000 of Feeder Ltd's 100,000 equity shares. The consideration given was shares in Lawn plc valued at £200,000.

Lawn plc acquired a further 30,000 shares in Feeder Ltd on 31 December 20X8 when the fair value of Feeder Ltd's net assets was £510,000, the increase being:

(a)   £20,000 in respect of a revaluation surplus on freehold land
(b)   £30,000 in respect of retained earnings.

The consideration given was shares in Lawn plc valued at £216,000. On 31 December 20X8 the fair value of the shares in Feeder Ltd previously held by Lawn plc was £236,000.

Requirement

Calculate the gain or loss on the remeasurement of Lawn plc's previously held equity investment in Feeder Ltd on 31 December 20X8 and the goodwill acquired in this business combination.

See **Answer** at the end of this chapter.

3   Measurement of non-controlling interest

Section overview

*   IFRS 3 allows two methods of measuring the non-controlling interest (NCI) at the acquisition date:

    –   At the NCI's share of the acquiree's net assets
    –   At its fair value.

*   The fair value method results in the NCI's share of goodwill being recognised.

    So there is then no need for any notional grossing up of goodwill for IAS 36 impairment testing.

3.1   Measurement of non-controlling interest at acquisition date

*   The traditional method of measuring the NCI at the acquisition date is to measure it at the NCI's share of the acquiree's net assets. This is the method dealt with in Financial Accounting and used in all the consolidated financial statements examples and questions up to this point in this Study Manual.

    This method results in goodwill being in effect the difference between the cost of the parent's investment and its share of the net assets acquired. The rationale is that the market transaction which is the business combination has only provided evidence of the amount of the parent entity's goodwill; there has been no market transaction to provide evidence of the amount of goodwill attributable to the NCI.

    This method is the one adopted in the UK, and by international standards prior to 2007.

*   The alternative approach works on the basis that the goodwill attributable to the NCI can be calculated from the estimate of the fair value of the NCI itself. It is an approach which is consistent with the rest of IFRS 3 which requires the consideration transferred, the previously held equity (if any), and the assets acquired and the liabilities acquired all to be measured at fair value.

    This method was the one adopted in the US by the FASB.

    The fair value method usually results in a higher amount for the NCI; the difference between this and the amount as traditionally measured is added to the goodwill acquired in the business combination and is the goodwill attributable to the NCI at the acquisition date.

Point to note:

The choice of method is available for each business combination separately. The choice in respect of one combination is **not binding** for subsequent combinations.

Worked example: Measurement of NCI (1)

The consideration transferred by National plc when it acquired 800,000 of the 1,000,000 £1 equity shares of Locale Ltd was £25 million. At the acquisition date Locale Ltd's retained earnings were £20 million and the fair value of the 200,000 equity shares in Locale Ltd not acquired was £5 million.

Calculate the goodwill acquired in the business combination on the basis that the NCI in Locale Ltd is measured at:

(a)   Its share of net assets
(b)   Fair value

Solution

	NCI at share of net assets £'000	NCI at fair value £'000
Consideration transferred	25,000	25,000
NCI – 20% × £21 million/fair value	4,200	5,000
	29,200	30,000
Net assets acquired (£1 million + £20 million)	(21,000)	(21,000)
Goodwill acquired in business combination	8,200	9,000

The only difference between the results of the two methods at the acquisition date is that the NCI and goodwill are higher by £0.8 million, the amount by which the fair value of the NCI exceeds its share of the acquired net assets.

Point to note:

There is always likely to be a difference between the fair values per share of an equity holding which provides control over another entity and a holding which does not, because buyers are prepared to pay a higher price per share if they end up gaining control of the other entity. This higher price is sometimes referred to as the 'control premium'. In the above example:

*   The controlling interest is valued at £31.25 per share (25,000/800)
*   The NCI is valued at £25.00 per share (5,000/200)

3.2   Subsequent measurement of NCI in statement of financial position

If the NCI was measured at the acquisition date at fair value, then the carrying amount at the end of each subsequent reporting period should take that fair value into account. This is best achieved by adapting the standard consolidated working 4 along the lines of equity accounting for associates, as follows:

Consolidation working (4) – Non-controlling interest

	£
Fair value of NCI at acquisition date	X
Share of post acquisition profits and other reserves	
(NCI% × post acquisition (W2))	X
	X

Point to note:

It is to cope with the subsequent measurement of an NCI measured at the acquisition date at fair value that the standard working 4 was extended in section 1.4 above along the lines of an associate.

Worked example: Measurement of NCI (2)

Continuing with the immediately preceding worked example, Locale Ltd's retained earnings three years later were £23 million.

Calculate the carrying amount of the non-controlling interest three years later on the basis that at acquisition it was measured at:

(a) Its share of net assets
(b) Fair value

Solution

Consolidation working (2) – Net assets of Locale Ltd

	Column 1 At period end £'000	Column 2 At acquisition £'000	Column 3 Post-acquisition £'000
Share capital	1,000	1,000	–
Retained earnings	23,000	20,000	3,000
	24,000	21,000	3,000

Consolidation working (4) – Non-controlling interest

	NCI at share of net assets £'000	NCI at fair value £'000
NCI at acquisition date – share of net assets (20% × Column 2(W2))/fair value	4,200	5,000
Share of post acquisition profits – (20% × post acquisition Column 3(W2))	600	600
	4,800	5,600

Point to note:

If the NCI was measured at the acquisition date at its share of net assets, it can subsequently be measured at X% × working 2 Column 1. These learning materials use the alternative calculation set out above because it is effective for both methods of measuring the NCI at the acquisition date and it is more efficient to use a single method.

Interactive question 8: Subsequent measurement of NCI   [Difficulty level: Exam standard]

On 1 January 20X8 Foot plc acquired 75,000 equity shares in Belt Ltd for £750,000. Belt Ltd's issued equity share capital was 100,000 £1 shares and at 1 January 20X8 the fair value and the carrying amount of its net assets was £600,000. On the same date the fair value of the equity shares in Belt Ltd not acquired by Foot plc was estimated at £175,000.

On 31 December 20X8 the summarised statements of financial position of the two entities were as follows:

	Foot plc £	Belt Ltd £
ASSETS		
Non-current assets		
Property, plant and equipment	150,000	500,000
Investments	750,000	–
	900,000	500,000
Current assets	1,700,000	680,000
Total assets	2,600,000	1,180,000

	Foot plc £	Belt Ltd £
ASSETS		
EQUITY AND LIABILITIES		
Equity		
Ordinary share capital (£1 shares)	500,000	100,000
Retained earnings	1,500,000	880,000
	2,000,000	980,000
Current liabilities	600,000	200,000
Total equity and liabilities	2,600,000	1,180,000

Requirement

Prepare the consolidated statement of financial position of Foot plc and its subsidiary Belt Ltd as at 31 December 20X8 on the basis that at acquisition the non-controlling interest was measured at:

(a) Its share of net assets;

(b) Fair value.

See **Answer** at the end of this chapter.

3.3 Non-controlling interests and disposals

If a subsidiary is disposed of and on acquisition some goodwill was attributed to the NCI as a result of it being measured at fair value, the calculation of the parent's profit or loss on disposal should allow for some of the carrying amount of goodwill at the disposal date being attributable to the NCI. This can be achieved by measuring the carrying amount of the NCI at the date of disposal per the adjusted standard consolidated working 4 set out in section 3.2.

Interactive question 9: NCI and disposal [Difficulty level: Exam standard]

On 1 January 20X5 Foot plc acquired 75% of the equity shares in Cone Ltd for £800,000. At that date the fair value and carrying amount of Cone Ltd's net assets was £640,000. On the same date the fair value of the equity shares in Cone Ltd not acquired by Foot plc was estimated at £180,000. At 31 December 20X7 the fair value and carrying amount of the net assets recognised by Cone Ltd was £900,000 and Cone Ltd's profit for the year ended 31 December 20X8 was £400,000.

Foot plc disposed of its interest in Cone Ltd for £1.35 million on 30 September 20X8.

Requirement

Calculate the profit or loss on disposal to be recognised in Foot plc's consolidated profit or loss for the year ended 31 December 20X8 on the basis that at acquisition the non-controlling interest was measured at:

(a) Its share of net assets

(b) Fair value

See **Answer** at the end of this chapter.

3.4 Non-controlling interests and impairment of goodwill

Accounting for impairment losses under IAS 36 *Impairment of Assets* is dealt with in Chapter 3, assuming that at the acquisition date the NCI is measured at its **share of the fair value of the acquiree's net assets**. Chapter 3 explains that if there is a NCI in the CGU (it is a partly-owned subsidiary, for example) **and** at the acquisition date the NCI was measured on this basis, then only the goodwill attributable to the owners of the parent will be recognised. Yet part of the CGU's recoverable amount relates to the NCI's unrecognised goodwill. Chapter 3 explains that in this situation the requirements of IAS 36 are:

• The carrying amount of goodwill allocated to that unit should be **notionally grossed up** to include the goodwill attributable to the NCI.

- Any impairment loss should first be recognised against goodwill as per the normal rules and apportioned between:

  - **Goodwill attributable to the parent**
  - **Goodwill attributable to the NCI**

Because goodwill is only **notionally** grossed up, the impairment loss allocated against the NCI's goodwill is not actually recognised in profit or loss.

If the alternative accounting policy of **measuring the NCI at the acquisition date at its fair value** is adopted:

- No grossing up is necessary, because the goodwill attributable to the CGU already includes the amount attributable to the NCI

- The whole of the impairment loss should be recognised in profit or loss

- The relevant proportion of the impairment loss should be allocated to the NCI, rather than all of it being allocated to the owners of the parent.

Points to note:

IAS 36 *Impairment of Assets* states explicitly that any impairment loss should be allocated on the same basis as that on which profit or loss is allocated. This may lead to an allocation to the NCI of a goodwill impairment loss in excess of the goodwill element previously carried within the NCI.

The allocation in partly owned subsidiaries of impairment losses in excess of the carrying amount of goodwill is outside the scope of the Financial Reporting examination.

Worked example: Impairment loss less than goodwill

Continuing with the information in the answer to Interactive question 8, the carrying amount of Belt Ltd's net assets (equity) at 31 December 20X8 was £980,000. Its recoverable amount was estimated at £1,200,000. The other key carrying amounts at 31 December 20X8 were:

	Share of net assets £	Fair value £
Measurement of NCI at acquisition		
Intangibles (goodwill in respect of Belt Ltd)	300,000	325,000
Equity		
Attributable to owners of Foot plc	2,285,000	2,285,000
Non-controlling interest (W4)	245,000	270,000
Total equity	2,530,000	2,555,000

Calculate the impairment loss, its allocation to the owners of Foot plc and Belt Ltd and revised key carrying amounts on the basis that at acquisition the non-controlling interest in Belt Ltd was measured at:

(a) Its share of net assets
(b) Fair value

Solution

If the NCI was measured at its share of net assets, then the goodwill attributable to Belt Ltd should be notionally grossed up, but only Foot plc's share of any goodwill impairment loss should be recognised.

The impairment loss in each case is as follows:

	Share of net assets £	Fair value £
Measurement of NCI at acquisition		
Belt Ltd's net assets	980,000	980,000
Goodwill (300 × 100/75 and 325)	400,000	325,000
	1,380,000	1,305,000
Recoverable amount	1,200,000	1,200,000
Impairment loss – all allocated against goodwill	180,000	105,000

Attributable to owners of Foot plc (75%)	135,000	78,750
Non-controlling interest (0%/25%)	–	26,250
	135,000	105,000

The revised key carrying amounts are as follows:

	Share of net assets £	Fair value £
Measurement of NCI at acquisition		
Intangibles (300 – 135) and (325 – 105)	165,000	220,000
Equity		
Attributable to owners of Foot plc (2,285 – 135 and 78.75)	2,150,000	2,206,250
Non-controlling interest (245) and (270 – 26.25)	245,000	243,750
Total equity	2,395,000	2,450,000

Point to note:

Using the information in the answer to Interactive question 8, standard consolidated working 4 at 31 December 20X8 would appear as follows:

Consolidated working (4) – Non-controlling interest

	Share of net assets £	Fair value £
Share of net assets/fair value of NCI at acquisition date	150,000	175,000
Share of post acquisition profits and other reserves		
(25% × 380,000)	95,000	95,000
	245,000	270,000
Share of goodwill impairment to date	–	(26,250)
	245,000	243,750

Interactive question 10: NCI and impairment   [Difficulty level: Exam standard]

On 1 January 20X5 Foot plc acquired 60% of the equity shares in Belding Ltd for £900,000 and elected to measure the non-controlling interest at acquisition at fair value. At that date the fair value and carrying amount of Belding Ltd's net assets was £850,000. On the same date the fair value of the equity shares in Belding Ltd not acquired by Foot plc was estimated at £430,000. At 31 December 20X7 the fair value and carrying amount of the net assets recognised by Belding Ltd was £1.1 million and Foot plc estimated Belding Ltd's recoverable amount at £1.3 million.

Requirement

Calculate the amounts of impairment loss attributable to the owners of Foot plc and to the non-controlling interest in Belding Ltd for the year ended 31 December 20X7 and the carrying amount of the non-controlling interest at that date.

See **Answer** at the end of this chapter.

4 Adjustment to consideration, fair values and goodwill

Section overview

- The consideration given for an acquisition may not all be issued at the acquisition date; some may be deferred until a later date.

- The amount of the consideration may not be fixed at the acquisition date; some may be contingent on future events.

  Subsequent adjustments to contingent consideration are normally recognised in profit or loss.

- Fair values at acquisition date should be attributed to all the identifiable net assets acquired, including intangibles and contingent liabilities not recognised by the acquiree.

- Fair values for the identifiable net assets acquired which are finalised within the measurement period (a maximum of 12 months after the acquisition date) should be related back to the acquisition date, potentially with an effect on the goodwill amount.

  The effects of finalisation after the end of the measurement period should **not** be related back but recognised in profit or loss.

- Special rules for acquired contingent liabilities.

4.1 Deferred consideration

Part of the consideration for an acquisition may not pass to the acquiree's shareholders at the acquisition date but be deferred until a later date.

Deferred consideration should be measured at its **fair value at the acquisition date.** The fair value depends on the form of the deferred consideration.

Where the deferred consideration is in the form of **equity shares**:

- Its fair value should be measured at the acquisition date

- The deferred amount should be recognised as part of equity, under a separate heading such as 'shares to be issued'.

Where the deferred consideration is payable in cash:

A **liability** should be recognised at the **present value** of the amount payable.

Points to note:

1   The market price of shares at the date the consideration is recognised is regarded as the present value of all the future benefits arising from those shares, so no adjustment should subsequently be made for any change in the market price over the period until any deferred consideration in the form of equity shares is issued.

2   As with other present value measurements, the increase in the liability for deferred consideration over the period until it is issued should be recognised in profit or loss as a finance cost.

Worked example: Deferred consideration

The acquisition date for Winter plc's purchase of the whole of the share capital in Summer Ltd was 1 July 20X5. The consideration comprised 1,000,000 shares in Winter plc to be issued on 1 July 20X5, £10 million in cash payable on 1 July 20X5, 200,000 shares in Winter plc to be issued on 1 January 20X6 and £5 million in cash payable on 1 July 20X6.

The market price of one Winter plc share was 450p on 1 July 20X5, 475p on 1 January 20X6 and 480p on 1 July 20X6. A discount rate of 7% was appropriate.

What is the total consideration for this acquisition?

Solution

	£m
1,000,000 shares issued on 1 July 20X5 at 450p	4.50
200,000 shares to be issued on 1 January 20X6 at 450p	0.90
Cash payable on 1 July 20X5	10.00
Cash payable on 1 July 20X6 – £5m/1.07	4.67
	20.07

4.2 Contingent consideration

Definition

Contingent consideration is an obligation of the acquirer to transfer additional consideration to the former owners of the acquiree if specified future events occur or conditions are met.

The acquiree's shareholders may have a different view from the acquirer as to the value of the acquiree.

- The acquiree may be the subject of a legal action which the acquiree's shareholders believe will be settled at no cost, but is believed by the acquirer to be likely to result in an expensive settlement

- The two parties may have different views about the likely future profitability of the acquiree's business

In such cases it is often agreed that additional consideration may become due, depending on how the future turns out (the settlement of the legal actions at a cost lower than that expected by the acquirer and future earnings being higher than the acquirer expected). Such consideration is 'contingent' on those future events/conditions.

Contingent consideration agreements result in the acquirer being under a legal obligation at the acquisition date to transfer additional consideration, should the future turn out in specified ways. IFRS 3 therefore requires contingent consideration to be recognised as part of the consideration transferred and measured at its fair value at the acquisition date.

Point to note:

Estimates of the amount of additional consideration and of the likelihood of it being issued are both taken into account in estimating this fair value.

As with deferred consideration

- If the contingent consideration is to be in shares, the amount should be measured by reference to the market price at the acquisition date.

- If the contingent consideration is to be in cash, the amount should be **discounted to its present value** at the acquisition date.

It may turn out that the amount of the contingent consideration actually transferred is different from the original estimate of fair value. In terms of the examples given above, the legal action may be settled at no cost to the acquiree and the acquiree's profits may be higher than the acquirer expected.

IFRS 3 treats such subsequent adjustments to the **quantity** of the contingent consideration in ways familiar from IAS 10 *Events after the Reporting Period*:

- If (and this will be very rare) the adjustments result from additional information becoming available about conditions at the acquisition date, they should be related back to the acquisition date, provided the adjustments are made within the measurement period (see below).

- If (and this will be common) the adjustments result from events occurring after the acquisition date, they are treated as changes in accounting estimates; they should be accounted for prospectively and the effect usually recognised in profit or loss. This will be the treatment required for the additional consideration due after the legal action was settled/the earnings being higher than expected.

Worked example: Contingent consideration

On 1 January 20X7 A acquired 100% of the shares of B when the fair value of B's net assets was £25 million. The consideration was 4 million shares in A issued at 1 January 20X7 when their market value was £6 per share and a cash payment of £6 million on 1 January 20X9 if the cumulative profits of B exceeded a certain amount by that date. At 1 January 20X7 the probability of B hitting that earnings target was such that the fair value of the possible cash payment was £2 million. A discount rate of 8% was used in measuring this fair value.

At 31 December 20X7 the probability that B would exceed the required profit level was the same as at the acquisition date. At 31 December 20X8 it was clear that B had exceeded that profit target.

Show calculations of the amounts to be recognised in the statements of financial position and in profit or loss for the two years ended 31 December 20X8.

Solution

The contingent consideration should be recognised at the acquisition date. It should be increased each year by the unwinding of the discount at 8% and any increase in ultimate settlement recognised in profit or loss.

		£'000
Statement of financial position at 31 December 20X7		
Non-current assets – goodwill		
Consideration transferred	– current 4 million × £6	24,000
	– contingent at fair value	2,000
		26,000
Net assets acquired		(25,000)
Goodwill		1,000
Non-current liabilities – deferred consideration – £2 million × 1.08		2,160
Profit or loss for year ended 31 December 20X7		
Finance cost – unwinding of discount – £2 million × 8%		160
Statement of financial position at 31 December 20X8		
Non-current assets – goodwill (unchanged)		1,000
Current liabilities – deferred consideration – amount payable on 1 January 20X9		6,000
Profit or loss for year ended 31 December 20X8		
Finance cost – unwinding of discount – £2.16 million × 8%		172.8
Additional consideration for acquisition – £6 million – (2.16 + 0.1728 million)		3,667.2

Interactive question 11: Contingent consideration   [Difficulty level: Exam standard]

Autumn plc acquired 100% of Spring Ltd on 1 January 20X5 when the fair value of Spring Ltd's identifiable assets net of liabilities assumed was £20 million.

The consideration was:

- Eight million shares in Autumn plc issued on 1 January 20X5 when the market price of Autumn plc's shares was 350p.

- A further payment of cash on 31 December 20X6:

  - £700,000 if Spring Ltd's profits for the year then ended were no less than £2 million or
  - £1,750,000 if Spring Ltd's profits for the year then ended were no less than £3 million.

At 1 January 20X5 the fair value of the contingent consideration was £100,000.

At 31 December 20X5 the fair value of the contingent consideration was £1.2 million.

A discount rate of 10% was used in measuring these fair values.

At 31 December 20X6 Spring Ltd's 20X6 profits per draft financial statements were £3.5 million.

Requirement

Show calculations of the amounts to be recognised in the statements of financial position and in profit or loss for the two years ended 31 December 20X6.

See **Answer** at the end of this chapter.

4.3 Fair values of acquired net assets at acquisition date

The presumption in IFRS 3 is that:

- An acquirer reviews carefully the value of the net assets to be acquired as part of the process of deciding how much to offer for the acquiree.

- The purchase consideration is the result of a transaction between a willing buyer and a willing seller in an arm's length transaction, so it is at fair value.

- This fair value can reliably be allocated across the identifiable assets and liabilities assumed.

IFRS includes specific advice in respect of:

- Operating leases An intangible asset (or a liability) should be recognised for any operating lease which has terms favourable (or unfavourable) relative to market rates

- Items acquired in a business combination which meet the IAS 38 *Intangible Assets'* definition of an intangible asset (ie they are identifiable because they either are separable or arise from legal/contractual rights). Remember that under IAS 38 both the probability of economic benefits and reliable measurement recognition criterion are always considered to be satisfied for intangibles acquired in a business combination. So the intangibles should be recognised.

It is usually the case that:

- Many intangibles acquired in a business combination will not have been recognised in the acquiree's financial statements, because they were internally generated.

- Such intangibles are still not recognised in the acquiree's subsequent financial statements

so adjustments for them should be made in preparing the consolidated financial statements.

Point to note:

Fair value adjustments may also require adjustments to depreciation and amortisation.

Worked example: Fair value adjustments

On 1 July 20X5 Brown plc acquired 80% of White Ltd for £16 million, the non-controlling interest being measured at its share of the net assets acquired. At the acquisition date the fair value of the net assets recognised in White Ltd's financial statements was £10 million.

The details of assets identified by Brown plc but not recognised by White Ltd were as follows:

- An order/production backlog with a fair value of £2 million and an estimated useful life of two years

- Trade marks with a fair value of £1 million. These are renewable without time limit at negligible cost.

White Ltd has not disposed of any of these unrecognised assets and made a profit of £5 million in the year ended 31 December 20X5.

What amounts in respect of White Ltd should be recognised in Brown plc's consolidated statement of financial position at 31 December 20X5?

Solution

Brown plc consolidated statement of financial position at 31 December 20X5

In respect of White Ltd:	£m
Intangibles (1.5 (W1) + 1.0 (W1) + 5.6 (W2))	8.1
Other net assets (15 (W1) – 1.5 (W1) – 1.0 (W1))	12.5
Retained earnings (80% × 2.0 (W1))	1.6
Non-controlling interest (20% × 15.0 (W1))	3.0

Point to note:

As White Ltd is not wholly owned, the non-controlling interest is allocated its share of the fair value adjustments.

WORKINGS

(1) *Net assets*

	At period end £m	At acquisition £m	Post acquisition £m
Recognised net assets at acquisition	10.0	10.0	–
Fair value adjustments – order/ production backlog (6 months amortisation to period end)	1.5	2.0	(0.5)
Trade marks (assumed to have indefinite lives)	1.0	1.0	–
Post acquisition profits (5 × 6/12)	2.5	–	2.5
	15.0	13.0	2.0

(2) *Goodwill*

	£m
Consideration transferred	16.0
Non-controlling interest (20% × 13 (W1))	2.6
	18.6
Net assets acquired (W1)	(13.0)
	5.6

Interactive question 12: Fair value adjustments [Difficulty level: Exam standard]

On 1 January 20X5 Crawford plc acquired 60% of Delamere Ltd for £25 million, the non-controlling interest being measured at its share of the net assets acquired. At the acquisition date the carrying amount of the net assets recognised in Delamere Ltd's financial statements was £18 million. The carrying amounts of these assets and liabilities were close approximations to their fair values, with the exception that the plant and equipment had a carrying amount of £5 million and a remaining useful life of five years, but a fair value of £4 million.

Part of Crawford plc's rationale for acquiring Delamere Ltd was to kick-start new activities by gaining access to Delamere Ltd's customers and outstanding contracts. Crawford plc identified assets which were not recognised by Delamere Ltd at the acquisition date, as follows:

- Customer lists in the form of a database of information about customer preferences and purchasing history. Delamere Ltd has always traded with its customers on the basis that such information would remain confidential to Delamere Ltd. Crawford plc estimated the fair value of this list at £6 million and its remaining useful life at four years.

- Customer supply contracts with an average remaining life of two years and a fair value of £5 million.

Delamere Ltd has not disposed of any of these unrecognised assets.

Requirements

Calculate the carrying amounts in respect of Delamere Ltd in Crawford plc's consolidated statement of financial position at 31 December 20X5 for goodwill, other intangible assets and plant and equipment.

Calculate the consolidation adjustments required when preparing Crawford plc's consolidated income statement for the year ended 31 December 20X5.

See **Answer** at the end of this chapter.

4.4 Adjustments to provisional accounting for business combinations and the measurement period

It may be that the process of determining the fair value of acquired net assets has not been finally completed by the end of the first reporting period after the acquisition date. There is a high chance of this in respect of an acquisition made in the last month of a financial year.

IFRS 3's requirements are:

- At the first year end the acquisition should be accounted for using provisional fair values.

- Adjustments to provisional values as a result of the finalisation of fair values within the **measurement period** should be recognised **as from the acquisition date** as long as the financial statements at the first year end stated that the fair values then used were provisional.

- Adjustments due to finalisation of fair values after the end of the measurement period are changes in estimates and should be recognised prospectively in profit or loss in the period in which they are made.

Point to note:

The measurement period ends as soon as the acquirer has obtained all the relevant information or has learnt that more information is not available. But it shall not exceed one year from the acquisition date.

4.4.1 Adjustments within the measurement period

Because these adjustments are recognised as from the acquisition date:

- The amount provisionally recognised for goodwill may need to be adjusted.

- The **prior period amounts** presented as comparative figures should be **restated** for any effect of the adjustments.

Worked example: Adjustments within the measurement period

Lindland plc acquired 75% of Waterlink Ltd on 1 July 20X7, the non-controlling interest being measured at its share of the net assets acquired. There were difficulties in estimating the fair value of certain plant and equipment with a remaining useful life of ten years, and a provisional fair value of £8 million was used in preparing Lindland plc's consolidated financial statements for the year ended 31 December 20X7. On this basis goodwill acquired in the business combination was measured at £4 million. The consolidated financial statements were approved for publication on 25 February 20X8.

On 1 April 20X8 the fair value of the plant and equipment was finalised at £7.2 million.

How should the effects of the finalisation of this fair value be recognised in Lindland plc's consolidated financial statements for the year ended 31 December 20X8, including comparative figures?

Solution

The downwards adjustment to the fair value of the plant and equipment was identified within 12 months of the acquisition date and is recognised as from the acquisition date.

	£'000

Consolidated statement of financial position at 31 December 20X8

The cost of the plant and equipment should be measured at the finalised fair value	7,200
The accumulated depreciation should be measured at 1.5 years/10 years thereof	(1,080)
The carrying amount of the plant and equipment should be measured at	6,120
Goodwill should be measured at £4,000 plus 75% of (£8,000 less £7,200)	4,600

Consolidated income statement for year ended 31 December 20X8

Depreciation on the plant and equipment should be measured at £7,200 × 1/10	720

The comparative figures for 20X7 should be restated to recognise the finalised fair value

	£'000	£'000
Consolidated statement of financial position at 31 December 20X7		
The cost of the plant and equipment should be measured at the finalised fair value		7,200
The accumulated depreciation should be measured at 0.5 years/10 years thereof		(360)
The carrying amount of the plant and equipment should be measured at		6,840
Goodwill should be measured at £4,000 plus 75% of (£8,000 less £7,200)		4,600
Non-controlling interest as previously measured should be reduced as follows:		
Original carrying amount of plant and equipment in 20X7 financial		
statements (£8,000 – 0.5/10 thereof)	7,600	
Adjusted carrying amount (as above)	(6,840)	
Reduction	760	
25% thereof		190

Consolidated income statement for year ended 31 December 20X7

Depreciation on the plant and equipment as previously measured should	
be reduced by (£8,000 less £7,200) × 0.5/10	40
Attributable to:	
Owners of Lindland plc (75%)	30
Non-controlling interest	10

4.4.2 Adjustments after the end of the measurement period

Because these should be recognised in profit or loss prospectively in the period in which they are made:

- No change should be made to the amounts initially recognised. The adjustment should be recognised prospectively from the date the fair value is finalised.

- There is no restatement of goodwill or of the prior period amounts.

Worked example: Adjustments after the end of the measurement period

The facts are as in the previous worked example, except that the fair value of the equipment was finalised on 1 October 20X8.

How should the effect of the finalisation of this fair value be recognised in Lindland plc's consolidated financial statements for the year ended 31 December 20X8, including comparative figures?

Solution

The downwards adjustment to the fair value of the plant and equipment was not identified within 12 months of the acquisition date and should be recognised prospectively from 1 October 20X8.

The carrying amount at 1 October 20X8 based on the provisional fair value is £7 million (8,000 less 1.25/10 thereof). It should really have been £6.3 million (7,200 less 1.25/10 thereof).

No information is given about its recoverable amount, so no impairment test can be made. Future depreciation charges should be calculated by reference to the £7 million carrying amount at 1 October 20X8 and the remaining useful life. The annual charge should be £0.8 million (7,000 ÷ 8.75) which is the same amount as the charge calculated by reference to the provisional fair value.

Points to note:

1   The effect is that the £0.7 million (7,000 – 6,300) "overvaluation" is recognised as an expense over the remaining useful life of 8.75 years.

2   Where there is no impairment loss to be recognised at the date of finalisation, the shortcut is to continue to charge depreciation by reference to the provisional fair value.

	£'000
Consolidated statement of financial position at 31 December 20X8	
The cost of the plant and equipment should be measured at the provisional fair value	8,000
The accumulated depreciation should be measured at 1.5 years/10 years thereof	(1,200)
The carrying amount of the plant and equipment should be measured at	6,800
Goodwill should be measured at £4,000	4,000
Consolidated income statement for year ended 31 December 20X8	
Depreciation on the plant and equipment should be measured at £8,000 × 1/10	800

Financial statements for the year ended 31 December 20X7

No adjustments are made.

4.5   Adjustments to contingent liabilities

Under IAS 37 *Provisions, Contingent Liabilities and Contingent Assets* a contingent liability is defined as:

* A possible obligation arising from past events; or

* A present obligation arising from past events which is not recognised because either an outflow of resources in settlement is not probable or the obligation cannot be measured reliably.

IFRS 3 applies a special recognition principle to contingent liabilities. A contingent liability should be recognised at the acquisition date if it is:

* A present obligation arising from past events; and
* Its fair value can be measured reliably.

So contrary to IAS 37 possible obligations should not be recognised and present obligations **should** be recognised even if an outflow of resources in settlement is not probable.

Contingent liabilities should initially be measured at their fair value at the acquisition date. Subsequently they should be measured at the **higher** of (i) the amount initially recognised (less any amortisation) and (ii) the amount required by IAS 37 (which would be the full amount of the liability if an outflow of resources is now probable or nil if an outflow is possible but not probable).

If a liability is finally recognised for the contingency, then the carrying amount of the contingent liability should be released to profit or loss, to offset the cost of the liability.

Worked example: Acquired contingent liabilities

On 1 July 20X6 Perfect plc acquired 100% of Simple Ltd, when the carrying amount of Simple Ltd's net assets was £2 million. The only adjustment needed to this amount was the recognition of contingent liabilities with a fair value of £150,000 in respect of legal proceedings.

On 1 December 20X7 the legal proceedings were settled with Simple Ltd's liability being set at £200,000. Simple Ltd recognised this liability in its 31 December 20X7 financial statements which showed the carrying amount of its net assets at £2.5 million.

How should these events be dealt with in the working papers for Perfect plc's consolidated financial statements for the year ended 31 December 20X7?

Solution

The finalisation of the amount payable was not made within the measurement period, so there is no need for an analysis of whether the additional amount should be recognised as an adjustment to the fair value at the acquisition date. (In practice, it is often difficult to decide whether adjustments like this are fair value adjustments or post-acquisition events.)

Simple Ltd's net assets at 31 December 20X7 are after deduction of the whole £200,000 cost of the settlement, so the adjustment needed is to reduce this cost by the amount provided for on acquisition. This can be achieved in the net assets working:

	At period end £'000	At acquisition £'000	Post-acquisition £'000
Net assets	2,500	2,000	500
Contingent liabilities	–	(150)	150
	2,500	1,850	650

4.6 Adjustments to correct accounting errors

One of the ways in which Financial Reporting makes greater demands than Financial Accounting is that you may well be presented with draft financial statements together with descriptions of certain transactions and events and explanations of how they have been (incorrectly) accounted for. Sometimes, no accounting may yet have taken place. You will then be asked:

- To explain how these transactions/events should have been accounted for under IFRS – this requires application of those IFRS dealt with in other chapters which are relevant to the situations described.

- To correct the draft financial statements.

In consolidated financial statements it will be important to consider whether there is any effect on the non-controlling interest.

One approach to making such corrections is to:

- Reverse all the incorrect accounting entries made
- Make the correct accounting entries.

Interactive question 13: Correcting errors　　　　　　　　　[Difficulty level: Easy]

A 70% owned subsidiary has accounted for a new lease of plant and equipment as a finance lease with effect from 1 January 20X8 and has recognised the following in its income statement for the year ended 31 December 20X8.

	£
Depreciation on non-current asset held under finance lease	40,000
Finance cost in respect of finance lease	50,000

Further investigation reveals that the lease should have been classified as an operating lease. The lease payments are £75,000 in advance each year.

Requirements

What adjustments should be made in respect of this lease when preparing the parent's consolidated income statement for the year ended 31 December 20X8?

Explain the adjustments to be made in preparing the parent's consolidated statement of financial position at 31 December 20X8.

See **Answer** at the end of this chapter.

Interactive question 14: Closing adjustments

[Difficulty level: Easy]

The following issues have been identified in the preparation of Sydney plc's consolidated financial statements.

* Brisbane Ltd, a 70% owned subsidiary, has discovered that its closing inventory has been overstated by £200,000.

* Sydney plc's inventory includes £280,000 of goods acquired from Perth Ltd. Sydney plc owns 30% of Perth Ltd which sells goods at a mark up of 40% on cost. No adjustment for unrealised profit has been made.

* Melbourne Ltd's inventory includes £260,000 of goods acquired from Sydney plc. Sydney plc owns 25% of Melbourne Ltd and sells goods at a mark up of 30% on cost. No adjustment for unrealised profit has been made.

Requirement

Identify and quantify the adjustments to be made in preparing Sydney plc's consolidated financial statements.

See **Answer** at the end of this chapter.

5 Disposal of investment in associate

Section overview

Disposal of a holding in an associate is dealt with in the same way as the disposal of a holding in a subsidiary.

When the whole of a shareholding in an associate is disposed of, the **profit or loss on disposal** in the **parent's separate financial statements** should be calculated as for a subsidiary disposed of, ie sale proceeds less the carrying amount in the parent's financial statements.

In the **consolidated financial statements** the **profit or loss on disposal** should be calculated as:

	£	£
Sales proceeds		X
Less: Cost of investment	X	
Share of associate's post acquisition retained profits and other reserves (net assets at disposal – net assets at acquisition)	X	
Carrying amount before impairment	X	
Impairment to date	(X)	
Carrying amount at date of disposal		(X)
Profit/(loss)		X/(X)

The other effects of disposal are also similar to those of the disposal of a subsidiary:

* There is no holding in the associate at the end of the reporting period, so there is no investment to recognise in the consolidated statement of financial position

* The associate's after tax earnings should be included in consolidated profit or loss up to the date of disposal.

Worked example: Disposal of associate

In 20X6 Complex plc paid £200,000 cash to acquire 30% of Wild Ltd, when the fair value and the carrying amount of Wild Ltd's net assets were £500,000.

At 1 December 20X8 Wild Ltd's net assets were £600,000. Up to 31 December 20X7 Complex plc had recognised in its consolidated financial statements impairment losses of £10,000 in respect of its investment in Wild Ltd. No impairment was considered necessary in Complex plc's individual financial statements and it measures the investment in Wild Ltd at cost in its individual financial statements.

On 1 December 20X8 Complex plc sold its holding in Wild Ltd for £224,000.

Calculate the profit or loss on disposal in the separate financial statements of Complex plc and in its consolidated financial statements for the year ending 31 December 20X8.

Solution

	£'000	£'000
Separate financial statements of Complex plc		
Sales proceeds		224
Less: carrying amount		(200)
Profit on disposal		24
Consolidated financial statements of Complex plc		
Sales proceeds		224
Less: Cost of investment	200	
Share of associate's post acquisition retained profits and other reserves (30% of (600,000 – 500,000))	30	
Carrying amount before impairment	230	
Impairment to date	(10)	
Carrying amount at date of disposal		(200)
Profit on disposal		4

6 Joint ventures

Section overview

- IAS 31 *Interests in Joint Ventures* defines joint ventures.
- IAS 31 recognises three broad types of joint venture

    - Jointly controlled operations

    - Jointly controlled assets

    - Jointly controlled entities – the only type where a separate legal entity is set up to operate the joint venture.

6.1 What is a joint venture?

Definition

A **joint venture** is a contractual arrangement whereby two or more parties (venturers) undertake an economic activity that is subject to joint control.

The key characteristics of a joint venture are that:

- The venturers have a contractual agreement between themselves
- The agreement results in them having **joint control** over the shared activities.

Definitions

A **venturer** is a party to a joint venture and has joint control over that joint venture.

Joint control is the contractually agreed sharing of control over an economic activity, and exists only when the strategic, financial and operating decisions relating to the activity require the unanimous consent of the parties sharing control (the venturers).

An **investor** in a joint venture is a party to a joint venture and does not have joint control over that joint venture.

Worked example: Joint venturers and investors

An entity is established to build a sports stadium for a customer. Once the stadium is built, the entity will be wound up.

Eight contractors invest in the equity of the entity. Contractors 1 to 5 own 14% each and Contractors 6 to 8 own 10% each. There is a contractual arrangement whereby all strategic, financial and operating decisions are taken unanimously by Contractors 1, 2, 3 and 8.

Do these arrangements give rise to a joint venture? If so, who are the venturers and who are the investors?

Solution

The contractual agreement provides for joint control. The contractors who are parties to the contractual agreement are Contractors 1, 2, 3 and 8. Between them they own 52% ((3 × 14%) + 10%) of the entity, so they have joint control over it. There is a joint venture as far as they are concerned and they are venturers.

The other contractors are not involved in the contractual arrangement and therefore are only investors in the joint venture.

A contractual arrangement will usually be in writing either as a formal document or in the form of minutes from a meeting. It will normally cover the purpose of the joint venture, its expected duration, any financial reporting requirements, appointments to the managing committee, voting rights, capital contributions, procedures for running the day to day operations and how expenses and income are to be shared.

6.2 Context

Entities often operate together as strategic alliances to overcome commercial barriers and share risks. These alliances are often contractually structured as joint ventures. The objective of a joint venture may be to carry out a one-off project, to focus on one area of operations or to develop new products jointly for a new market. The joint venture focuses on the partners' complementary skills and resources. The creation of synergies amongst the venture partners creates value for each. Joint venture arrangements provide the opportunity for organisations to obtain a critical mass and more competitive pricing.

There are many factors critical to the success of joint ventures, the most important being the relationship between the venturers. It is essential that all contractual terms and arrangements are agreed in advance including the process for resolving disputes. An exit strategy should be developed and the terms for dissolution agreed between the venturers at the outset. It is particularly important that the agreement identifies the party which will at dissolution retain any proprietary knowledge held within the joint venture.

The different joint venture structures available provide challenges for financial reporting. The unique risks of joint venture arrangements need to be readily apparent to users of financial statements, since their financial and operational risks may be substantially different from those of other members of the reporting group.

6.3 Scope of IAS 31 *Interests in Joint Ventures*

IAS 31 does not apply in the following circumstances:

- Where the venturer is a venture capital organisation, or
- Where the joint venture is owned by a mutual fund or unit trust, and

under IAS 39 *Financial Instruments: Recognition and Measurement* the investment is at fair value through profit or loss or a financial asset held for trading.

6.4 Forms of joint venture

IAS 31 identifies, and deals with, three broad types of joint venture:

- Jointly controlled operations
- Jointly controlled assets
- Jointly controlled entities

7 Jointly controlled operations

Section overview

- This section explains what is meant by a jointly controlled operation.
- It deals with how jointly controlled operations should be accounted for.

7.1 What is a jointly controlled operation?

A jointly controlled operation is where:

- No separate entity is set up
- The parties to the transaction share the activities that are to be carried out
- The contractual arrangement will normally set out how revenue and expenses are to be shared

In such an operation the venturers will:

- Pool their resources
- Provide their own expertise
- Use their own property, plant and equipment
- Incur their own expenses
- Be responsible for raising their own finance

The **substance** of this type of joint venture is that each venturer is carrying on its own activities as a separate part of its own business and the accounting procedures reflect this.

7.2 Accounting for jointly controlled operations

Each venturer should recognise the following amounts **in its own individual entity financial statements**:

- Its share of income from the operations
- The expenses that it incurs relating to the operation
- Its property, plant and equipment that it uses to carry out the activities of the operation
- Any other of its assets involved in the operation
- Any liabilities that the venturer has an obligation to meet.

At the end of each accounting period it will be necessary to produce a memorandum income statement for the joint venture combining all the income and expenses of all the venturers, so that a calculation can be made of the profit entitlements of each venturer. Each venturer should then recognise a receivable (additional profit due to the venturer) or a payable (excess profit payable to the other venturers).

No additional adjustments are required when preparing the consolidated financial statements because all of the above will already have been recognised in the venturer's own financial statements.

Worked example: Jointly controlled operations

An office building is being constructed by A Ltd and B Ltd under a contractual agreement which results in the activity being classified as a jointly controlled operation. Each party is to record its own transactions and to be entitled to a half share in the profits.

At the end of the accounting period, the following information is recorded in accounting records of the two companies.

	A Ltd £	B Ltd £
Amount invoiced to and cash received from customers	300,000	500,000
Costs incurred and paid	280,000	420,000

How should A Ltd account for this joint venture?

Solution

The memorandum income statement for the joint venture and the calculation of A Ltd's share should be:

	A Ltd £	B Ltd £	Total £	A Ltd's share (50%)
Revenue	300,000	500,000	800,000	400,000
Expenses	(280,000)	(420,000)	(700,000)	(350,000)
	20,000	80,000	100,000	50,000
Due to A Ltd	30,000	(30,000)	0	
Share (50:50)	50,000	50,000	100,000	

A Ltd should record a receivable due from B Ltd of £30,000. In addition, it should amend its financial statements to record in full its share of the revenue and expenses as follows:

DR	Receivables – B Ltd	£30,000	
DR	Expenses (350,000 – 280,000)	£70,000	
CR	Revenue (400,000 – 300,000)		£100,000

8 Jointly controlled assets

Section overview

- This section explains what is meant by jointly controlled assets.
- It deals with how jointly controlled assets should be accounted for.

8.1 What are jointly controlled assets?

A joint venture uses jointly controlled assets when:

- No separate entity is set up
- The assets may be jointly owned
- The venturers use the assets as an extension of their own activities
- The assets are used to generate benefits to be shared by each of the venturers
- Each venturer will normally bear an agreed share of the expenses incurred

The most important point is that the assets are **jointly controlled**.

A common use of the arrangement for jointly controlled assets is by oil production companies that jointly control and operate an oil pipeline. The benefit of such an arrangement is that only one pipeline is needed, with each venturer using the pipeline to transport its own supply of oil and in return paying a proportion of the running costs.

8.2 Accounting for jointly controlled assets

As with jointly controlled operations the **substance** of the venture is that the venturers are essentially using the assets as part of their normal operating activities.

A venturer should recognise in its **own financial statements**:

- Its share of the jointly controlled assets
- Any liabilities that the venturer has an obligation to meet
- Its share of any liabilities that are jointly incurred
- Expenses incurred by the venturer
- Its share of expenses incurred jointly
- Its share of any revenue

The accounting is similar to that for jointly controlled operations, except that each venturer should record its share of the jointly controlled assets and of any financing raised to fund the assets.

No additional adjustments are required when preparing the consolidated financial statements because all of the above will already have been recognised in the venturer's own financial statements.

9 Jointly controlled entities

Section overview

- Jointly controlled entities are separate legal entities, so they should prepare their own financial statements.

- In the consolidated statements of the venturer the results and position of the jointly controlled entity should be included using either proportionate consolidation or the equity method of accounting.

- Proportionate consolidation results in the venturer's share of the assets, liabilities, income and expenses of the jointly controlled entity being included with the venturer's own or shown separately on a line by line basis.

- Under proportionate consolidation goodwill on acquisition of a jointly controlled entity should be calculated and appropriately included in the consolidated financial statements.

- The equity method of accounting is the same as that used under IAS 28 *Investments in Associates*.

9.1 What is a jointly controlled entity?

The key identifying factor for a jointly controlled entity is that in this type of joint venture arrangement a **separate legal entity** is set up, with the ownership of that entity being shared by the venturers.

This separate entity may be a:

- Company or
- Partnership

As a separate legal entity the jointly controlled entity can enter into contracts and raise finance in its own name. It will maintain its own accounting records and prepare its own financial statements.

The jointly controlled entity will own its own assets, incur its own liabilities, incur its own expenses and earn its own income.

Normally each joint venturer will be entitled to a pre-determined share of the profits made by the entity.

9.2 Accounting for jointly controlled entities

IAS 31 requires each venturer in a jointly controlled entity to recognise in its **consolidated financial statements** its share of the entity by either:

- Proportionate consolidation, or
- The equity method of accounting.

Although allowing the use of the equity method of accounting, IAS 31 states that proportionate consolidation better reflects the substance and economic reality of the venturer's interest, that is control over its share of future economic benefits.

Point to note:

The share of the jointly controlled entity's post acquisition retained earnings which is recognised in consolidated retained earnings is the same, whichever method is used.

9.3 Proportionate consolidation

Definition

Proportionate consolidation is a method of accounting whereby a venturer's share of each of the assets, liabilities, income and expenses of a jointly controlled entity is combined line by line with similar items in the venturer's financial statements or reported as separate line items in the venturer's financial statements.

As you can see from the definition, there are two methods for presenting proportionate consolidation:

(1) By adding the relevant proportion of the jointly controlled entity's assets, liabilities, income and expenses on a line by line basis to those of the venturer – this results in a single figure for each line.

(2) By splitting each line of the financial statements between the amount which relates to the venturer and that which represents the proportion of the jointly controlled entity.

Proportionate consolidation reflects the existence of **joint control** by only recognising the venturer's share.

Proportionate consolidation also provides **useful information** to users of the venturer's financial statements as the assets and liabilities are separately identified (particularly with the second method of presentation).

Using this method the consolidated statement of financial position combines controlled items (owned by the parent and subsidiaries) with jointly controlled items (the share of those owned by the joint venture). Those who judge that it is inappropriate to combine different items in this way use the equity method of accounting.

9.4 Equity method of accounting

You have used the equity method of accounting when accounting for associates under IAS 28.

Under the equity method:

- The investment in the jointly controlled entity is initially recorded at cost.

- There are adjustments each period for the venturer's share of the retained profits or losses of the jointly controlled entity for the current period. Profits are added to the investment and losses deducted.

- In the venturer's consolidated **statement of financial position** the investment in the jointly controlled entity is shown as a single line figure as part of non-current assets.

- In the venturer's consolidated **income statement** there is a single line for the share of the jointly controlled entity's results.

9.5 Goodwill

When the interest in the jointly controlled entity is acquired, there should be a comparison of:

- The proportion acquired of the fair value of the identifiable assets acquired and liabilities assumed of the jointly controlled entity, and

- The fair value of the consideration given.

Any excess of consideration over assets less liabilities at fair value represents goodwill.

The accounting treatment of goodwill will depend upon which accounting method is used:

- **Proportionate consolidation** – goodwill on acquisition is separately presented alongside any goodwill on acquisition of subsidiaries and is subject to annual impairment testing.

- **Equity method** – goodwill on acquisition is subsumed in the carrying amount of the jointly controlled entity in the statement of financial position – the total investment should be tested for impairment when appropriate.

Worked example: Jointly controlled entity

AB controls a number of subsidiaries and therefore prepares consolidated financial statements.

AB is also a venturer in JV, a jointly controlled entity in which AB owns 25%. AB acquired its share of JV at a cost of £1 million on the creation of JV. At that time JV had net assets of £4 million. Hence, no goodwill was recognised.

A summarised draft statement of financial position of the AB Group (AB and its subsidiaries, but not its interest in JV), and JV is as follows:

	AB Group £m	JV £m
Non-current assets		
Property, plant and equipment	60	20
Intangibles	30	8
Investment in JV	1	0
Current assets		
Inventories	50	16
Other	80	24
Current liabilities	(90)	(36)
Equity	131	32

	£m
The equity in AB Group plus JV can be calculated as:	
AB Group	131
JV post-acquisition ((32 – 4) × 25%)	7
	138

Requirement

Using the following three methods prepare the AB Group consolidated statement of financial position including JV.

- (a) Proportionate consolidation – line by line
- (b) Proportionate consolidation – JV share shown separately
- (c) Equity method

Solution

(a) **Proportionate consolidation – line by line**

	£m
Non-current assets	
Property, plant and equipment (60 + (25% × 20))	65
Intangibles (30 + (25% × 8))	32
Current assets	
Inventories (50 + (25% × 16))	54
Other (80 + (25% × 24))	86
Current liabilities (90 + (25% × 36))	(99)
Equity	138

(b) **Proportionate consolidation – share shown separately**

			£m	£m
Non-current assets				
Property, plant and equipment	– own		60	
	– JV		5	
				65
Intangibles	– own		30	
	– JV		2	
				32
Current assets				
Inventories	– own		50	
	– JV		4	
				54
Other	– own		80	
	– JV		6	
				86
Current liabilities	– own		(90)	
	– JV		(9)	
				(99)
Equity				138

(c) **Equity method of accounting**

	£m
Non-current assets	
Property, plant and equipment – own	60
Intangibles – own	30
Investment in JV (cost £1m plus 25% x increase in retained reserves [£28m])	8
Current assets	
Inventories – own	50
Other – own	80
Current liabilities – own	(90)
Equity	138

Note how the different methods result in a significantly different presentation of the financial position of AB, even though equity is the same under all three methods.

10 Other areas of IAS 31

Section overview

- Adjustments have to be made for sales and purchases between the venturer and the joint venture.

- Adjustments may be required for receivables and payables balances between the venturer and the joint venture.

- SIC 13 deals with the treatment of profits on non-monetary items paid as capital for the joint venture.

10.1 Transactions between a venturer and the joint venture

In all three types of joint venture adjustments similar to those in respect of associates are required where there are sales or purchases between the venturer and the joint venture. An adjustment is required for any **profit** on the transaction that is internal to the entity.

If a venturer sells an asset to the joint venture at a profit and the asset is still held by the joint venture:

- The proportion of the asset that is consolidated includes an element of profit recorded by the venturer.

- This should be removed as it is unrealised profit.

- What remains is only the profit that relates to the share of the asset relating to the other venturers.

Where a venturer purchases assets from the joint venture the venturer's share of the profit made by the joint venture should not be recognised until the asset is sold to a third party.

Where a loss is made on a transaction between the venturer and joint venture, it should be recognised immediately if it represents a reduction in realisable value of current assets or an impairment loss.

10.2 Receivables and payables

If there are receivables or payables outstanding between a joint venture and the venturer the treatment should be in accordance with IAS 27 or IAS 28.

If proportionate consolidation is used:

The share of the receivables or payables consolidated should be eliminated.

If equity accounting is used:

Outstanding balances between the venturer and the joint venture should not be eliminated.

10.3 Non-monetary contributions by venturers

SIC 13 *Jointly Controlled Entities – Non-monetary Contributions by Venturers* deals with the situation where a venturer's capital paid into the joint venture is in the form of a non-monetary asset:

- Provided that the risks and rewards of ownership have passed to the joint venture
- The venturer should only recognise gains and losses attributable to the other venturers.

Interactive question 15: Jointly controlled entity   [Difficulty level: Intermediate]

Bodmas plc acquired 30% of the equity capital of a joint venture entity, Matrix Ltd, in 20X2 when the reserves of Matrix were £120 million. It is currently preparing its financial statements for the year ending 31 December 20X5.

The summary statements of financial position for Bodmas and Matrix at 31 December 20X5 were as follows.

	Bodmas plc £m	Matrix Ltd £m
Property, plant and equipment	820	320
Investment in Matrix	100	–
Current assets	240	160
Loan to Matrix	60	–
	1,220	480
Share capital (£1 shares)	780	100
Retained earnings	440	320
Loan from Bodmas	–	60
	1,220	480

Requirement

Prepare the summarised consolidated statement of financial position of Bodmas plc at 31 December 20X5 using the proportionate consolidation, separate line method in accordance with IAS 31 *Interests in Joint Ventures*.

Fill in the proforma below.

Consolidated statement of financial position

	£m	£m
Goodwill		
Property, plant and equipment		
Group		
JV		
Current assets		
Group		
JV		
Loan to JV		
Share capital		
Retained earnings		

See **Answer** at the end of this chapter.

11 Judgements required and relevance of information for users

Section overview

- Judgements have to be made in a number of difficult areas.
- Different decisions lead to different presentations in the financial statements.
- Users of financial statements should ensure they examine all disclosures carefully.

11.1 Judgements required

Judgements have to be made in the following difficult areas:

- Does an interest carrying less than 50% of the voting rights in another entity together with other entitlements result in control over that other entity? If it does, the other entity is a subsidiary.

- Does an interest in another entity result in significant influence over that entity? If it does, the other entity is an associate.

- The estimation of fair values at acquisition date, particularly in respect of:

    - **Intangibles not recognised by the acquiree**

        There are difficulties in identifying some of the intangibles illustrated by IFRS 3, let alone measuring their fair values.

    - **Contingent liabilities**

        Does any further information becoming available after the acquisition date provide evidence of the fair value at that date or of post acquisition events?

    - **Contingent consideration**

        How should the probability of this extra consideration becoming due be measured?

- How to present the share owned of a jointly controlled entity?

Different decisions will lead to very different presentations in the financial statements. Care must be taken to ensure that the result is a fair representation of the underlying activities and financial position, not the achievement of a presentation to suit management.

11.2 Relevance of information for users

Many users of financial statements will be making economic decisions about whether to hold shares in the parent company. They will be aware that such a holding exposes them to the risks and rewards of all the activities carried out by entities within the parent's group, so consolidated financial statements which present all these activities as those of a single economic entity provide the right kind of information.

It is the case however that an unprofitable (and/or almost insolvent) subsidiary can be masked by the profits (and solvency) of the rest of the group, even if there are no guarantees from the parent to support that subsidiary. To that extent, consolidated information can be misleading.

The judgement as to whether an entity is a subsidiary or an associate can be critical to the presentation of information in the financial statements. The borrowings of a subsidiary are consolidated while those of an associate are not, so the return on capital employed and gearing will be affected by the classification. The judgement will also have an effect on cash flow information. Cash flows of a subsidiary are consolidated, while those of an associate are limited to dividends received.

Different presentations also result from the judgement as to whether to account for jointly controlled entities by proportionate consolidation (share of borrowings consolidated) or by equity accounting (share of borrowings not consolidated).

Users must therefore be careful to study all the disclosures available, for example those about associates in the notes to the financial statements, where summaries of associates' assets, liabilities, revenue and profit and information about shareholdings of above and below 20% which are not and are, respectively, treated as associates. Another key disclosure (required by IAS 7 *Statement of Cash Flows*) is of any significant cash and cash equivalent balances that are not available for use by the group, perhaps as a result of exchange control or other legal regulations.

12 UK GAAP comparison

Section overview

In the UK:

- Consolidations are dealt with in FRS 6 *Acquisitions and Mergers*, FRS 7 *Fair Values in Acquisition Accounting*, FRS 10 *Goodwill and Intangible Assets* and FRS 2 *Accounting for Subsidiary Undertakings*.

- Associates and joint ventures are dealt with in FRS 9 *Associates and Joint Ventures*.

12.1 Consolidated financial statements

UK requirements	IFRS
Merger accounting (a method of consolidating a subsidiary) **is required** where certain criteria are met (FRS 6).	**Merger accounting is not allowed.** IFRS 3 requires **all** business combinations to be accounted for using the **acquisition method**.
Minority interest is always measured at its share of net assets (FRS 6).	IFRS 3 allows non-controlling interest to be measured at fair value or its share of net assets.
Specific guidance is given on fair value measurement (FRS 7).	IFRS 3 provides **less detailed** guidance on fair value measurement.
Only separable intangible assets are required to be recognised (FRS 10), so assets arising from contractual or other legal rights are not recognised unless they are separable.	Intangible assets recognised under a business combination include **separable assets and assets arising from contractual or other legal rights (regardless of whether these rights are transferable or separable)**, that is more intangibles are recognised under IFRS.
Acquisition-related costs are added to the cost of the investment in the subsidiary and affect goodwill (FRS 7).	Acquisition-related costs are recognised as an expense in profit or loss as incurred.
A reasonable estimate of the fair value of the amounts payable as contingent consideration (discounted where appropriate) is added to the cost of the investment at the acquisition date. **All subsequent adjustments** to the amount of contingent consideration are **related back** to the acquisition date, increasing or decreasing goodwill (FRS 7).	At the acquisition date the fair value of contingent consideration (taking account of both discounting and the amount likely to be paid) is recognised as part of the consideration transferred. If subsequent adjustments to this fair value occur *within* the measurement period ***and*** are as a result of additional information about facts or circumstances at the acquisition date, those adjustments are related back to the acquisition date, increasing or decreasing goodwill. However, if subsequent adjustments to this fair value occur either: (i) *within* the measurement period, but are **not** as a result of additional information about facts or circumstances at the acquisition date; or (ii) are *outside* the measurement period, they are **not related back** to the acquisition date but are recognised as an expense in profit or loss. They do not increase or decrease goodwill.

UK requirements	IFRS
Goodwill is **usually amortised over its estimated useful economic life**. There is a rebuttable presumption that this is not more than 20 years (FRS 10).	IFRS 3 **prohibits amortisation** and requires annual impairment reviews.
Negative goodwill is recognised as a separate item within goodwill. Negative goodwill up to the fair values of the non-monetary assets acquired should be recognised in the profit and loss account in the periods in which the non-monetary assets are recovered, whether through depreciation or sale. Any negative goodwill in excess of the fair values of the non-monetary assets acquired should be recognised in the profit and loss account in the periods expected to be benefited (FRS 10).	IFRS 3 requires **immediate recognition as a gain in profit or loss.**
A subsidiary should be excluded from consolidation if severe long-term restrictions prevent the parent exercising control (FRS 2).	No such exemption on this basis exists under IAS 27 (although control may be lost as a result of the restrictions, such that the entity should no longer be classified as a subsidiary).
The existence of potential voting rights is not considered in assessing control (FRS 2).	Under IAS 27 the existence of potential voting rights should be considered in assessing control.
Minority interest should be presented separately from shareholders' funds (FRS 2).	Under IAS 27 non-controlling interest is a separate component of equity.

Worked example: UK GAAP and IFRS

On 31 December 20X7 Magnate plc acquired 90% of the equity of Tycoon Ltd for a cash payment of £5 million. At that date the fair value of the 10% of the equity not acquired was £380,000.

Magnate plc incurred external professional fees in respect of this acquisition of £250,000 and estimated that the amount chargeable to the business combination in respect of the staff who worked on it was £200,000.

At 31 December 20X7 the carrying amount of the net assets recognised by Tycoon Ltd was £2.8 million, which approximated to their fair value. In addition Magnate plc identified the following:

- A trademark developed by Tycoon Ltd which at the acquisition date had a fair value of £400,000 and a useful life of 4 years

- A set of processes legally registered by Tycoon Ltd with the local regulator on terms which prohibit its transfer to any other party. At the acquisition date this set had a fair value of £300,000 and a useful life of 5 years.

Magnate plc adopts the following accounting policies:

- To measure the non-controlling interest at the acquisition date at fair value, where this is permitted.

- To amortise goodwill over 20 years, where amortisation is permitted.

On 31 December 20X9 the carrying amount of Tycoon Ltd's recognised net assets was £4.2 million and the recoverable amount of Tycoon Ltd, a separate cash-generating unit, was £6.3 million.

Calculate under UK GAAP and IFRS:

(a) The goodwill acquired in the business combination on 31 December 20X7.
(b) Any impairment loss to be recognised at 31 December 20X9.
(c) The carrying amount of the minority/non-controlling interest at 31 December 20X9.

Solution

(a) The goodwill acquired in the business combination on 31 December 20X7

	UK GAAP £'000	IFRS £'000
Cost of investment/consideration transferred	5,000	5,000
External acquisition costs (Note 1)	250	–
Non-controlling interest at fair value	–	380
	5,250	5,380
Net assets recognised by Tycoon Ltd (UK = 90% × 2,800)	(2,520)	(2,800)
Trademark (Note 2) (UK = 90% × 400)	(360)	(400)
Set of processes (Note 3)	–	(300)
Goodwill (Note 4)	2,370	1,880

Notes

(1) Both UK GAAP and IFRS require internal acquisition costs to be recognised as an expense as incurred.

UK GAAP requires external costs to be added to the cost of the investment in the subsidiary, but IFRS require them to be recognised as an expense as incurred.

(2) Both UK GAAP and IFRS require the recognition of the trademark as an acquired intangible, because it is separable.

(3) UK GAAP prohibits the recognition of the set of processes as an acquired intangible, because it is not separable. IFRS requires its recognition because it arises from legal rights.

(4) UK GAAP requires the amortisation of goodwill, while IFRS prohibits it. Both require goodwill to be tested for impairment.

(b) Any impairment loss to be recognised at 31 December 20X9

	UK GAAP £'000	IFRS £'000
Net assets recognised by Tycoon Ltd	4,200	4,200
Trademark (initial amount less 2 out of 4 years)	200	200
Set of processes (initial amount less 2 out of 5 years)	–	180
	4,400	4,580
Goodwill (UK = initial amount less 2 out of 20 years)	2,133	1,880
	6,533	6,460
Recoverable amount	6,300	6,300
Impairment loss – allocated against goodwill	233	160

(c) The carrying amount of the minority/non-controlling interest at 31 December 20X9.

UK GAAP: 10% of Tycoon Ltd's net assets of (4,200 + 200) = £440,000.

	£'000
IFRS	
Fair value at acquisition date	380
Share of post acquisition earnings (10% × (4,580 – 2,800 – 400 – 300))	108
	488
Less: 10% × £0.16m goodwill impairment loss	(16)
	472

12.2 Associates and joint ventures

FRS 9	IFRS
The investor's share of the associate's operating results, exceptional items, interest, profit before tax and tax should be separately disclosed.	IAS 28 merely requires the investor's share of the profit or loss of an associate to be disclosed. IAS 1's illustrative format for the income statement discloses the after tax amount in arriving at pre tax profits.
If the share of an associate's losses exceeds the investment in the associate, the investor should recognise its share of the excess as a liability.	Under IAS 28 such a liability should only be recognised where the investor has a legal or constructive obligation to make the loss good.
The gross equity method should be used for joint ventures. It is the same as equity accounting for associates, except that: • In the profit and loss account disclose the investor's share of the turnover of its joint venture. In the segmental analysis the revenue of the joint venture is shown separately. • In the balance sheet disclose the investor's share of gross assets and liabilities underlying the net equity amount.	IAS 31's tacitly preferred treatment – proportionate consolidation. There are two alternative methods of proportionate consolidation permitted: • On a line-by-line basis add the venturer's share of the JV's assets, liabilities, income and expenses to its own. • On a line-by-line basis show the venturer's share of the JV's assets, liabilities, income and expenses on a separate line next to its own. The effect on equity is the same; it is only the presentation that differs.
No alternative method is allowed by FRS 9 for joint ventures. The gross equity method is required.	The equity method is permitted as an alternative.

ICAEW

Summary

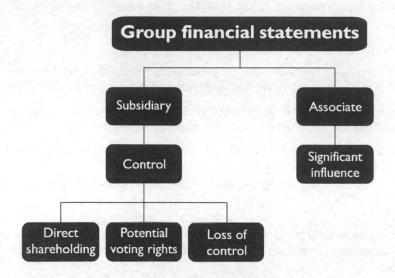

Group financial statements

- Subsidiary
  - Control
    - Direct shareholding
    - Potential voting rights
    - Loss of control
- Associate
  - Significant influence

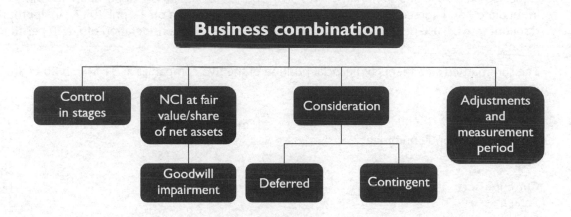

Business combination

- Control in stages
- NCI at fair value/share of net assets
  - Goodwill impairment
- Consideration
  - Deferred
  - Contingent
- Adjustments and measurement period

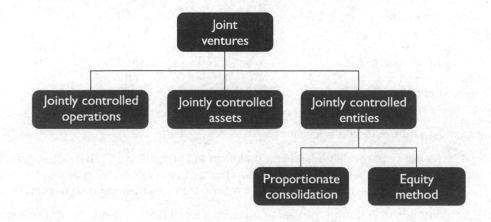

Joint ventures

- Jointly controlled operations
- Jointly controlled assets
- Jointly controlled entities
  - Proportionate consolidation
  - Equity method

Self-test

Answer the following questions.

1 **Emma plc**

Emma plc, a company with a number of subsidiary companies, acquired 18,000 'A' shares in Leaner Ltd for a cash payment of £55,000. The share capital of Leaner Ltd is made up of:

Equity voting A shares   30,000
Equity non-voting B shares   42,000

All of Leaner's equity shares are entitled to the same dividend rights; however during the year to 31 December 20X7 Leaner made substantial losses and did not pay any dividends.

Emma has always classified its investment in Leaner as a non-current asset available-for-sale investment in its consolidated financial statements on the basis that:

(i)   It is only entitled to 25% (18,000/(30,000 + 42,000)) of any dividends that Leaner may pay
(ii) It does not have any directors on the board of Leaner
(iii) It does not exert any influence over the operating policies or management of Leaner.

Requirement

Comment on the accounting treatment of Leaner by Emma's directors, suggesting a reason why they have adopted it, and state how the investment should be accounted for.   **(6 marks)**

2 **H plc**

H plc acquired 75% of S's ordinary shares on 1 April 20X6. H paid £4.20 per share in cash immediately and agreed to pay a further amount of £110 million on 1 April 20X7. An appropriate discount rate is 10% per annum. H has only recorded the cash consideration of £4.20 per share in its books.

The summarised statements of financial position of the two companies at 31 March 20X7 are shown below:

	H £m	H £m	S £m	S £m
Property, plant and equipment		425		380
Investment in S		315		–
		740		380
Current assets		160		110
Total assets		900		490
Equity and liabilities				
Ordinary shares of £1 each		320		100
Share premium		100		50
Revaluation surplus		60		0
Retained earnings				
– 1 April 20X6	150		160	
– year to 31 March 20X7	210	360	90	250
Equity		840		400
Current liabilities		60		90
Total equity and liabilities		900		490

The following information is relevant:

(1) H has a policy of revaluing land and buildings to fair value. At the date of acquisition S's land and buildings had a fair value £26 million higher than their carrying amount and at 31 March 20X7 this had increased by a further £8 million (ignore any additional depreciation).

(2) S sold goods to H during the year at a profit of £8 million, one-quarter of these goods were still in the inventory of H at 31 March 20X7.

(3) An impairment test at 31 March 20X7 resulted in the need to recognise an impairment loss of £25 million in respect of goodwill. No other assets were impaired.

(4) In February 20X7 it was discovered that an error had been made in valuation of S's inventory at the acquisition date, in that it had been undervalued by £4 million at the acquisition. All this inventory had been sold by 31 March 20X7.

(5) H plc decided to measure the non-controlling interest at the acquisition date at its share of the net assets acquired.

Requirements

Calculate the following amounts for the consolidated statement of financial position of H at 31 March 20X7:

(a) Goodwill
(b) Non-controlling interest
(c) The equity attributable to the owners of H plc.

(12 marks)

Note: Show your workings.

3 **High Five**

High Five Group has an agreement with Jake Ltd to jointly fund Park Ltd on a 50:50 basis. There is a contractual agreement between High Five and Jake under which all the strategic and operational decisions require the consent of both of them.

Park Ltd's statement of financial position at 31 December 20X7 was as follows:

	£'000
Property, plant and equipment	500
Bank and cash	50
	550
Capital at 1 Jan 20X7	
High Five	240
Jake	240
	480
Profit for year	70
	550

Requirements

(a) Discuss the advantages and disadvantages of using proportionate consolidation to account for joint ventures, in terms of the information provided to users of financial statements.

(4 marks)

(b) Explain how the investment in Park Ltd should be dealt with in the financial statements of High Five at 31 December 20X7 using proportionate consolidation. **(3 marks)**

(7 marks)

4 **Red Air**

Red Air and Stripe Air operate flights through mainland Europe. Both are a member of the Flying Team alliance, meaning that customers on connecting flights that start with one airline and connect to a flight operated by another Flying Team member are able to through-check their luggage to their final destination.

A number of Flying Team flights fly to Stressville airport, which has a poor record for baggage handling.

To remedy this, on 1 January 20X5, Red Air and Stripe Air each agreed to contribute £3 million to buy and install a baggage handling system at Stressville airport for their exclusive use. The two airlines signed an agreement whereby all the strategic financial and operating decisions would require the consent of both parties. Each airline agreed to share ongoing costs and any revenues *pro rata* to their initial contribution. All invoicing would be done by Red Air, which has an office in Stressville. Each airline employed its own on-site supervisor. The baggage handling hardware has an expected life of ten years and nil residual value.

No legal entity was set up and in law the system belongs to Red Air which also is the employer of all the baggage handlers who operate the system. Day to day operating decisions are made by whichever supervisor is on duty at the time any decision needs to be made.

The cash paid or received by Red Air and Stripe Air in the year ended 31 December 20X5 has been:

	Red Air £'000	Stripe Air £'000
Costs of purchasing the system	(2,600)	(2,600)
Costs of installing system	(800)	0
Employment costs: baggage handlers	(320)	0
Employment costs: supervisors	(60)	(75)
Income from handling other airlines' baggage	124	0

Requirement

Explain, with calculations, how Red Air and Stripe Air should account for the above operations.

(9 marks)

5   **Piaf**

Piaf Co is an international brewing concern. It bought 80% of McKenny's distillery for £10 million on 1 August 20X5. At that date, estimates were made of McKenny's specialist non-current assets and long-term inventory value.

At the time of the acquisition, the net assets of McKenny were measured at the following provisional amounts:

	£'000
Property, plant and equipment	8,400
Long-term inventory	2,200
Other net assets	600
Total net assets	11,200

Subsequently, the finalised fair values at the acquisition date were determined as:

	£'000
Property, plant and equipment	8,160
Long-term inventory	2,600
Other net assets	600
Total net assets	11,360

The property, plant and equipment is estimated to have a 20 year useful life from the date of Piaf's acquisition. None of the long-term inventory has yet been sold. Both Piaf and McKenny have a year-end of 30 September. There was no evidence of impairment of the goodwill acquired in the business combination by any of the dates below.

Piaf decided to measure the non-controlling interest at the acquisition date at its share of the net assets acquired.

Assume that, where necessary, Piaf stated that the fair values were provisional in its financial statements.

Requirements

Explain, with calculations, the impact on the consolidated financial statements, including comparatives, if the finalised fair values were determined on each of these dates:

(a)   1 September 20X5
(b)   1 July 20X6
(c)   1 September 20X6.

(15 marks)

6   **Brentford plc**

In its year ending 31 December 20X5 Brentford plc made two acquisitions:

(i)   On 1 January 20X5 Brentford plc acquired 60,000 of the 100,000 issued equity shares in Crystal Ltd. The consideration comprised £3 million cash payable on the acquisition date and £530,000 cash payable on 31 December 20X5. On 1 January 20X5 the carrying amount of Crystal Ltd's net assets was £4.75 million, which approximated to fair value.

Brentford plc chose to measure the non-controlling interest in Crystal Ltd at the acquisition date at its fair value of £2 million. Brentford plc uses a discount rate of 6% per annum for liabilities which are legally enforceable.

In the year to 31 December 20X5 Crystal Ltd earned a loss of £600,000 and paid no dividends. At the period end the recoverable amount of Crystal Ltd was estimated at £4.7 million.

(ii) On 31 December 20X2 Brentford plc had acquired 200,000 of the 2,000,000 issued equity shares in Fulham Ltd for £500,000. These shares were classified as available-for-sale financial assets and on 31 December 20X4 their carrying amount was £610,000, increases in fair value having been recognised in other comprehensive income and held in equity. On 31 December 20X5 Brentford plc acquired a further 1,400,000 shares in Fulham Ltd for £5.6 million. On that date the fair value of Fulham Ltd's net assets was £7 million and the fair value of the 200,000 shares already owned by Brentford plc was £640,000.

Brentford plc chose to measure the non-controlling interest in Fulham Ltd at the acquisition date at its share of Fulham Ltd's net assets.

Requirements

To the extent the above information allows, calculate the amounts in respect of these two acquisitions which should be recognised in the consolidated financial statements of Brentford plc for the year ending 31 December 20X5. **(12 marks)**

Now, go back to the Learning Objectives in the Introduction. If you are satisfied you have achieved these objectives, please tick them off.

IFRS 3 *Business Combinations*

Basics

- Definitions: control, acquisition date, goodwill.   IFRS 3 (App A)

- Acquisition method: acquirer, acquisition date, recognition and measurement of identifiable assets acquired, liabilities assumed and non-controlling interest.   IFRS 3 (5)

Recognition and measurement

- Recognise separately from goodwill the identifiable assets acquired, liabilities assumed and non-controlling interest   IFRS 3 (10)

  - May or may not have been recognised in the acquiree's own financial statements   IFRS 3 (13)

  - Contingent liabilities recognised if a present obligation and fair value can be measured reliably   IFRS 3 (23)

- Measure identifiable assets acquired and liabilities assumed at fair value   IFRS 3 (18)

- Measure any non-controlling interest either at fair value or share of net assets   IFRS 3 (19)

  Separate choice for each acquisition

Goodwill

- Recognised as at the acquisition date as the excess of: IFRS 3 (32)

  - Consideration transferred plus non-controlling interest plus acquirer's previously held interest in acquiree

    over

  - net of acquisition date amounts of identifiable assets acquired and liabilities assumed

Bargain purchase

- Reassess identification and measurement of the net assets acquired, the non-controlling interest, previously held equity in acquiree and consideration transferred.   IFRS 3 (36)

- Any remaining amount recognised in profit or loss at the acquisition date.   IFRS 3 (34)

Consideration transferred

- Measure at fair value at acquisition date   IFRS 3 (37)

  - Include fair value of contingent consideration   IFRS 3 (39)

  - Exclude acquisition-related costs   IFRS 3 (53)

Business combination achieved in stages

- Remeasure previously held equity interest at fair value   IFRS 3 (42)

  Recognise any gain or loss in profit or loss

Measurement period

- Cannot exceed one year from acquisition date

  IFRS 3 (45)

- Retrospectively adjust at the acquisition date the effects on recognition and measurement of information becoming available about facts and circumstances at the acquisition date

  IFRS 3 (46–49)

  Retrospective adjustments may affect measurement of goodwill

Subsequent measurement and accounting

- Contingent liabilities measured at the higher of the amount under IAS 37 and the amount initially recognised

  IFRS 3 (56)

- Contingent consideration: changes to cash payable resulting from events after the acquisition date recognised in profit or loss

  IFRS 3 (58)

Disclosures

- Business combinations effected in the accounting period or after its finish but before financial statements authorised for issue (in the latter case, by way of note).

  IFRS 3 (59)

- Financial effects of adjustments in current period which relate to combinations occurring in the current or previous periods.

  IFRS 3 (61)

IAS 27 *Consolidated and Separate Financial Statements*

- Definitions: control, parent, subsidiary.

  IAS 27 (4)

- Control through:

  IAS 27 (13)

  - P holds more than half of the voting rights in S

  - P holds a majority of voting rights in S, through an agreement with others

  - P has power to govern the financial and operating policies of S under statute or agreement

  - P has power to appoint or remove the majority of S's top management

  - P has power to cast the majority of votes at board meetings

Basic rule

- Parent should prepare CFS to include all subsidiaries as if single economic entity.

  IAS 27 (9)

- No control if 'subsidiary' in legal reorganisation and so on.

  IAS 27 (32)

Exception

- No need for CFS if wholly owned or all non-controlling shareholders have been informed of and none have objected to the plan that CFS need not be prepared.

  IAS 27 (10)

- If new subsidiary meets held for sale criteria at acquisition date, account for it under IFRS 5.

  IAS 27 (12)

Procedures

- Accounting dates of group companies to be no more than three months apart.

  IAS 27 (22 – 23)

- Uniform accounting policies across group or adjustments to underlying values.

  IAS 27 (24 – 25)

- Bring in share of new subsidiary's income and expenses:

  IAS 27 (26)

  - From date of acquisition, on acquisition

- To date of disposal, on disposal

- Non-controlling interest shown as a separate figure:

  - In the statement of financial position, within total equity but separately from the parent shareholders' equity — IAS 27 (27)

  - In the statement of comprehensive income, the share of profit or loss and of other comprehensive income — IAS 27 (28)

Parent's separate financial statements

- Account for subsidiary at cost/under IAS 39 and recognise dividends in profit or loss. — IAS 27 (38 and 38A)

Disclosures

- Details where own more than 50% but do not consolidate, and *vice-versa*. — IAS 27 (41)

Key areas of consolidations

- Potential voting rights — IAS 27 (14 – 15)

- Loss of control — IAS 27 (32)

- Subsidiary losses and non-controlling interest — IAS 27 (28)

- Measurement of non-controlling interest at acquisition date – implications for impairment testing — IFRS 3 (19)

- Contingent consideration — IFRS 3 (39 and 58)

IAS 28 *Investments in Associates*

Definitions

- The investor has significant influence, but not control. — IAS 28 (2)

- Significant influence is the power to participate in financial and operating policy decisions of the investee, but is not control over those policies (if the investor had control, then under IAS 27 the investee would be its subsidiary).

- Presumptions with regard to less than 20%, 20% or more. — IAS 28 (6)

- Can be an associate, even if the subsidiary of another investor.

- No significant influence if 'associate' in legal reorganisation and so on — IAS 28 (10)

Equity method

- In statement of financial position: non-current asset = cost plus share of post-acquisition share in A's net assets. — IAS 28 (38, 11 and 39)

- In income statement: share of A's post-tax profits less any impairment loss. — IAS 28 (11 and 38)

- In other comprehensive income: share of A's changes. — IAS 28 (39)

- Use cost/under IAS 39 to account in investor's separate financial statements. — IAS 28 (35)

Disclosures

- Fair value of associate where there are published price quotations. — IAS 28 (37)

- Summarised financial statements of the associate.

- Reasons why 20% presumptions overcome, if that be the case.

- The investment to be shown as a non-current asset in the statement of financial position, at cost plus/minus share of post acquisition change in associate's net assets plus long-term financing less impairment losses. — IAS 28 (38)

- The investor's share of the associate's:
  - After-tax profits
  - Discontinued operations
  - Other comprehensive income   IAS 28 (39)
  - Contingent liabilities   IAS 28 (40)

IAS 31 *Interests in Joint Ventures*

- Definitions   IAS 31 (3)
- Three forms of joint venture   IAS 31 (7)
- Contractual arrangement to form a joint venture   IAS 31 (9 – 12)
- Jointly controlled operations   IAS 31 (13 – 17)
- Jointly controlled assets   IAS 31 (18 – 23)
- Jointly controlled entities
  - What a jointly controlled entity is   IAS 31 (24 – 29)
  - Proportionate consolidation   IAS 31 (30 – 37)
  - Equity method   IAS 31 (38 – 41)
- Transactions between a venturer and a joint venture   IAS 31 (48 – 49)
- Disclosures   IAS 31 (54 – 57)

CHAPTER

8

Answer to Interactive question 1

Close Ltd Consolidated statement of financial position as at 31 December 20X9

	£	£
ASSETS		
Non-current assets		
Property, plant and equipment (80,000 + 58,200)		138,200
Intangibles (W3)		14,600
		152,800
Current assets		
Inventories (18,000 + 12,000 – 800)	29,200	
Trade and other receivables (62,700 + 21,100)	83,800	
Investments	2,500	
Cash and cash equivalents (10,000 + 3,000 + 500)	13,500	
		129,000
Total assets		281,800
EQUITY AND LIABILITIES		
Attributable to owners of Close Ltd		
Ordinary share capital		120,000
Share premium account		18,000
Revaluation surplus		23,000
Retained earnings (W5)		57,160
		218,160
Non-controlling interest (W4)		17,640
Equity		235,800
Current liabilities		
Trade and other payables (35,000 + 11,000)		46,000
Total equity and liabilities		281,800

WORKINGS

(1) **Group structure**

Close Ltd

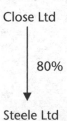

80%

Steele Ltd

(2) **Net assets of Steele Ltd**

	At period end £	£	At acquisition £	Post-acquisition £
Share capital		60,000	60,000	–
Revaluation surplus		16,000	16,000	–
Retained earnings				
Per question	13,000			
Less PURP (4,000 × 25∕125)	(800)			
		12,200	8,000	4,200
		88,200	84,000	

(3) **Goodwill**

	£
Consideration transferred	84,000
Non-controlling interest at the acquisition date (20% × 84,000 (W2))	16,800
	100,800
Less net assets acquired	(84,000)
	16,800
Impairment to date (500 + 1,700)	(2,200)
Balance c/f	14,600

(4) **Non-controlling interest**

	£
Share of net assets (20% × 88,200 (W2))	17,640
Or	
At acquisition (20% × 84,000 (W2))	16,800
Share of post-acquisition retained earnings (20% × 4,200 (W2))	840
	17,640

(5) **Retained earnings**

	£
Close Ltd	56,000
Steele Ltd (80% × 4,200 (W2))	3,360
Less goodwill impairment to date (W3)	(2,200)
	57,160

Answer to Interactive question 2

Higg plc – Consolidated statement of comprehensive income for the year ended 30 June 20X5

	£
Revenue (W2)	908,000
Cost of sales (W2)	(587,600)
Gross profit	320,400
Operating costs (W2)	(150,570)
Profit from operations	169,830
Finance cost (W2)	(6,400)
Investment income (W2)	5,000
Profit before tax	168,430
Tax (W2)	(85,600)
Profit and total comprehensive income for the period	82,830

Attributable to:	
Owners of Higg plc (β)	74,700
Non-controlling interest (W3)	8,130
	82,830

Consolidated statement of changes in equity for the year ended 30 June 20X5

	Attributable to owners of Higg plc			Non-controlling interest £	Total £
	Share capital £	Retained earnings £	Total £		
Balance brought forward (W4), (W6)	500,000	77,970	577,970	38,880	616,850
Total comprehensive income for the period	–	74,700	74,700	8,130	82,830
Dividends paid (W5)	–	(20,000)	(20,000)	(3,000)	(23,000)
Balance carried forward	500,000	132,670	632,670	44,010	676,680

WORKINGS

(1) **Group structure**

Higg plc

$\downarrow$ 70%

Topp Ltd

(2) **Consolidation schedule**

	Higg plc £	Topp Ltd £	Adj £	Consol £
Revenue	647,200	296,800	(36,000)	908,000
C of S				
Per question	(427,700)	(194,100)	36,000	
PURP (25/125 × 9,000)	(1,800)			(587,600)
Op costs				
Per question	(106,300)	(42,300)		
Impairment of goodwill	(1,970)			(150,570)
Inv income				
Div from quoted investments	3,000	2,000		5,000
Interest received	1,600		(1,600)	–
Finance cost		(8,000)	1,600	(6,400)
Tax	(58,300)	(27,300)		(85,600)
Profit for the period		27,100		

(3) **Non-controlling interest**

30% × 27,100 = £8,130

(4) **Retained earnings b/f**

	£
Group	
Higg plc	72,400
Topp Ltd (70% × (29,600 – 13,200))	11,480
Less: goodwill impaired to 1 July 20X4	(5,910)
	77,970

(5) **Inter-company dividends and interest**

	£
Paid by Topp Ltd	
Dividends	10,000
Interest	8,000
Received by Higg plc	
Dividends (70% × 10,000)	7,000
Interest (20% × 8,000)	1,600
Dividends paid to NCI (30% × 10,000)	3,000

(6) **Non-controlling interest b/f**

	£
Share capital	100,000
Retained earnings	29,600
	129,600

£129,600 × 30% = 38,880

Answer to Interactive question 3

Haley plc

Consolidated statement of financial position as at 31 December 20X9

	£
ASSETS	
Non-current assets	
Property, plant and equipment (300,000 + 100,000)	400,000
Intangibles (W3)	3,000
Investment in associates (W6)	48,600
	451,600
Current assets (345,000 + 160,000)	505,000
Total assets	956,600
EQUITY AND LIABILITIES	
Attributable to owners of Haley plc	
Ordinary share capital	250,000
Retained earnings (W5)	472,600
	722,600
Non-controlling interest (W4)	84,000
Equity	806,600
Current liabilities (100,000 + 50,000)	150,000
Total equity and liabilities	956,600

WORKINGS

(1) **Group structure**

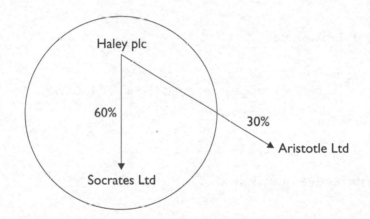

(2) **Net assets**

Socrates Ltd

	At period end £	At acquisition £	Post-acquisition £
Share capital	30,000	30,000	–
Retained earnings	180,000	70,000	110,000
	210,000	100,000	

Aristotle Ltd

	At period end £	At acquisition £	Post-acquisition £
Share capital	60,000	60,000	–
Retained earnings	100,000	30,000	70,000
	160,000	90,000	

(3) **Goodwill**

	Socrates Ltd £
Consideration transferred	75,000
Non-controlling interest at the acquisition date (40% × 100,000 (W2))	40,000
	115,000
Less: net assets acquired	(100,000)
	15,000
Impairment to date	(12,000)
Balance c/f	3,000

(4) **Non-controlling interest**

	£
Socrates Ltd (40% × 210 (W2))	84,000
Or	
At acquisition (40% × 100 (W2))	40,000
Share of post acquisition retained earnings (40% × 110 (W2))	44,000
	84,000

(5) **Retained earnings**

	£
Haley plc	400,000
Socrates Ltd (60% × 110,000 (W2))	66,000
Aristotle Ltd (30% × 70,000 (W2))	21,000
Less: impairment to date (12,000 + 2,400)	(14,400)
	472,600

(6) **Investments in associates**

	£
Cost of investment in Aristotle Ltd	30,000
Share of post acquisition change in net assets (30% × 70,000 (W2))	21,000
	51,000
Impairment to date	(2,400)
	48,600

Answer to Interactive question 4

Corfu Ltd

Consolidated income statement for the year ended 30 June 20X9

	£'000
Revenue (W2)	15,131
Cost of sales and expenses (W2)	(13,579)
	1,552
Share of profit of associates (30% × 594)	178
Profit before tax	1,730
Tax (W2)	(736)
Profit for the period	994
Attributable to:	
Owners of Corfu Ltd (β)	964
Non-controlling interest (W3)	30
	994

WORKINGS

(1) **Group structure**

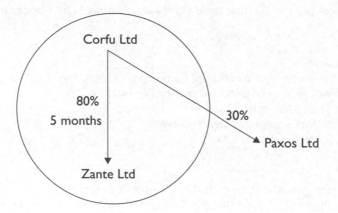

(2) **Consolidation schedule**

	Corfu Ltd £'000	Zante Ltd 5◀2 £'000	Adj £'000	Consol £'000
Revenue	12,614	2,567	(50)	15,131
C of S				
Per question	(11,318)	(2,302)	50	(13,579)
PURP re Paxos' inventory (30% × (150,000 × 25◀25))	(9)			
Tax	(621)	(115)		(736)
		150		

(3) **Non-controlling interest**

Zante Ltd (20% × 150,000 (W2)) = £30,000

Answer to Interactive question 5

Keen plc acquired its interest in Guest Ltd in order to share in its profitable future, but Guest Ltd has under-performed, incurring losses of £400,000 in the year. Under IAS 36 *Impairment of Assets* economic performance worse than expected is internal evidence indicating that the asset may have been impaired and an impairment review should be carried out.

The carrying amount of the investment at the period end should initially be measured at £760,000 cost less £140,000 (35% of £400,000) share of losses incurred, so £620,000.

The recoverable amount of this investment is the higher of the value in use and fair value less costs to sell. Value in use should be estimated at Keen plc's 35% share of the £1.7 million estimated present value of future cash flows, so £595,000. Fair value less costs to sell should be estimated at the £550,000 net offered by the competitor. The recoverable amount is £595,000 and an impairment loss of £25,000 (£620,000 – £595,000) should be recognised by Keen plc.

The amount to be recognised in profit or loss is a loss of £165,000 (£140,000 + £25,000) and the carrying amount of the investment at the period end should be measured at the recoverable amount of £595,000.

Answer to Interactive question 6

The terms of the warrants do not yet allow A to acquire additional voting rights, so these potential voting rights should not be taken into account. The voting rights A controls in C is its current holding of 38%, so A does not have control of C.

Answer to Interactive question 7

The holding of 40,000 out of Feeder Ltd's 100,000 shares gave Lawn plc significant influence over Feeder Ltd, so Lawn plc should have used equity accounting. The remeasurement gain should be calculated as:

	£'000
Cost of 40,000 shares	200
Share of revaluation surplus over period of ownership (40% × 20)	8
Share of retained earnings over period of ownership (40% × 30)	12
Carrying amount at 31 December 20X8	220
Acquisition-date fair value of previously held equity	236
Gain to be recognised in profit or loss	16

Point to note:

The revaluation gain should not be reclassified to profit or loss, because it would not be so reclassified if there had been a disposal of the interest in Feeder Ltd. It should, however, be transferred to retained earnings in the statement of changes in equity.

Goodwill acquired in the business combination

	£'000
Consideration transferred at acquisition date	216
Non-controlling interest (30% × 510)	153
Acquisition-date fair value of previously held equity	236
	605
Net assets acquired	(510)
Goodwill	95

Answer to Interactive question 8

Foot plc – Consolidated statement of financial position as at 31 December 20X8

Measurement of NCI at acquisition	Share of net assets £	Fair value £
ASSETS		
Non-current assets		
Property, plant and equipment (150,000 + 500,000)	650,000	650,000
Intangibles (W3)	300,000	325,000
	950,000	975,000
Current assets (1,700,000 + 680,000)	2,380,000	2,380,000
Total assets	3,330,000	3,355,000
EQUITY AND LIABILITIES		
Attributable to owners of Foot plc		
Ordinary share capital (£1 shares)	500,000	500,000
Retained earnings (W5)	1,785,000	1,785,000
	2,285,000	2,285,000
Non-controlling interest (W4)	245,000	270,000
Equity	2,530,000	2,555,000
Current liabilities (600,000 + 200,000)	800,000	800,000
Total equity and liabilities	3,330,000	3,355,000

WORKINGS

(1) **Group structure**

Foot plc

↓ 75%

Belt Ltd

(2) Net assets of Belt Ltd

	At period end £	Acquisition date £	Post-acquisition £
Share capital	100,000	100,000	–
Retained earnings	880,000	500,000	380,000
	980,000	600,000	380,000

(3) Goodwill

		Share of net assets £	Fair value £
Measurement of NCI at acquisition			
Consideration transferred		750,000	750,000
NCI at the acquisition date – 25% × 600,000/at fair value		150,000	175,000
		900,000	925,000
Less: net assets acquired		(600,000)	(600,000)
		300,000	325,000

(4) Non-controlling interest

		Share of net assets £	Fair value £
Measurement of NCI at acquisition			
Share of net assets – 25% × 600,000 (W2)/fair value		150,000	175,000
Share of post acquisition profits – 25% × 380,000 (W2)		95,000	95,000
		245,000	270,000

(5) Retained earnings

	£
Foot plc	1,500,000
Belt Ltd (75% × 380,000 (W2))	285,000
	1,785,000

Answer to Interactive question 9

	NCI at acquisition at share of net assets		NCI at acquisition at fair value	
	£'000	£'000	£'000	£'000
Sales proceeds		1,350		1,350
Less: Carrying amount of goodwill at date of disposal:				
Consideration transferred at acquisition date	800		800	
Non-controlling interest at acquisition date (25% × 640 and fair value)	160		180	
	960		980	
Net assets at acquisition date	(640)		(640)	
Goodwill at acquisition date		(320)		(340)
Carrying amount of net assets at date of disposal (W1)		(1,200)		(1,200)
Add back: NCI in net assets at date of disposal (W2)		300		320
Profit/(loss) on disposal		130		130

WORKINGS

(1) Net assets at date of disposal

Net assets b/f		900		900
Profit for current period to date of disposal (400 × 9/12)		300		300
		1,200		1,200

(2) Non-controlling interest at date of disposal

(25% × 1,200 (W1)) and (180 fair value + (25% × (1,200 – 640 increase in net assets)))		300		320

Answer to Interactive question 10

Impairment loss

	£'000
Goodwill acquired in the business combination	
Consideration transferred	900
Non-controlling interest at fair value	430
	1,330
Fair value of net assets acquired	850
Goodwill	480
Fair value of net assets at 31 December 20X7	1,100
	1,580
Recoverable amount	1,300
Impairment loss	280

Attributable to:	£'000
Owners of Foot plc (60%)	168
Non-controlling interest (40%)	112
	280

Carrying amount of non-controlling interest

	£'000
Fair value at acquisition	430
Share of post-acquisition profits (40% × (1,100 – 850))	100
	530
Share of impairment loss	(112)
	418

Answer to Interactive question 11

	£'000
Statement of financial position at 31 December 20X5	
Non-current assets – goodwill	
Consideration transferred – current 8 million × £3.50	28,000
– contingent at fair value at acquisition date	100
	28,100
Net assets acquired	(20,000)
Goodwill	8,100
Current liabilities – deferred consideration at fair value at period end	1,200
Profit or loss for year ended 31 December 20X5	
Finance cost – unwinding of discount – £100,000 × 10%	10
Additional consideration for acquisition – (£1.2 million – (100,000 + 10,000))	1,090
Statement of financial position at 31 December 20X6	
Non-current assets – goodwill	8,100
Profit or loss for year ended 31 December 20X6	
Finance cost – unwinding of discount – £1.2 million × 10%	120
Additional consideration for acquisition – (£1.75 million paid – (1.2 + 0.12 million))	430

Note that the contingent consideration of £1.75 million was settled in cash on 31 December 20X6 so there is no liability to be recognised at the end of 20X6.

Answer to Interactive question 12

Fair value adjustments are required in respect of the plant and equipment and the customer supply contracts.

The customer lists should not be recognised as intangible assets. Because the information is confidential to Delamere Ltd, the lists are not a separable asset (they cannot be sold by Delamere Ltd) and they do not result from contractual or legal rights. Therefore they do not meet the IAS 38 definition of an intangible asset.

Crawford plc Consolidated statement of financial position at 31 December 20X5

	£m
Goodwill (W)	11.8
Other intangible assets (£5m less 50% amortisation)	2.5
Plant and equipment (£4 million less 20% amortisation)	3.2

Adjustments for Crawford plc consolidated income statement for the year ended 31 December 20X5

	£m
Decrease operating expenses by reduction in depreciation of plant and equipment ((£5m – £4m) × 20%)	0.2
Increase operating expenses by amortisation of other intangibles (£5m × 50%)	(2.5)

WORKING

Goodwill	£m	£m
Consideration transferred		25.0
Non-controlling interest at the acquisition date (40% × 22m per below)		8.8
		33.8
Recognised by Delamere Ltd	18.0	
Fair value adjustment to plant and equipment (5 – 4)	(1.0)	
Recognition of intangible	5.0	
		(22.0)
		11.8

Point to note:

The net increase in operating expenses is £2.3 million. 60% of this reduction in profit is attributed to the owners of Crawford plc (so £1.38m) and 40% (£0.92m) to the non-controlling interest.

Answer to Interactive question 13

Consolidated income statement

	£
Reverse incorrect entries, so increase profits (40,000 + 50,000)	90,000
Make correct entry for operating lease – reduce profits	(75,000)
Net increase in profits	15,000
Allocation:	
Owners of the parent – 70%	10,500
Non-controlling interest – 30%	4,500

Consolidated statement of financial position

- Derecognise the non-current asset's cost and accumulated depreciation (this is the first year of the lease, so the depreciation is £40,000).

- Derecognise the non-current liability and the current liability in respect of the finance lease.

- Increase retained earnings and non-controlling interest by £10,500 and £4,500 respectively.

Point to note:

There is no accrual or prepayment to be recognised in the statement of financial position in respect of the operating lease because the annual payment is due in advance on the first day of each accounting period.

Answer to Interactive question 14

Brisbane Ltd

In the statement of financial position reduce inventory by the £200,000 overstatement and reduce retained earnings by £140,000 (70%) and non-controlling interest by £60,000 (30%).

In the income statement increase cost of sales by £200,000 and reduce the profit attributable to owners of Sydney plc by £140,000 and that attributable to the non-controlling interest by £60,000.

Perth Ltd

In the statement of financial position reduce inventory by the amount of the unrealised profit earned by Perth Ltd which is attributable to Sydney plc, so 30% × (40/140 × £280,000) = £24,000 and reduce retained earnings by the same amount.

In the income statement reduce the share of Perth Ltd's earnings presented as profits of associates by Sydney plc's £24,000 share of the unrealised profit and reduce the profit attributable to owners of Sydney plc by the same amount.

Melbourne Ltd

In the statement of financial position reduce retained earnings by Sydney plc's share of the unrealised profit earned on sales to Melbourne Ltd, so 25% × (30/130 × £260,000) = £15,000 and reduce the investment in Melbourne Ltd by the same amount.

In the income statement increase cost of sales by the £15,000 PURP and reduce the profit attributable to owners of Sydney plc by the same amount.

Answer to Interactive question 15

Consolidated statement of financial position as at 31 December 20X5

	£m	£m
Goodwill (W1)		34
Property, plant and equipment		
Group	820	
JV (320 x 30%)	96	
		916
Current assets		
Group	240	
JV (160 x 30%)	48	
		288
Loan to JV (Note)		42
		1,280
Share capital (£1 shares)		780
Retained earnings (W2)		500
		1,280

WORKINGS

(1) Goodwill

	£m
Cost of investment	100
Share of net assets (30% x (100 + 120))	(66)
Goodwill	34

(2) Retained earnings

	£m
Group	440
JV post acquisition (320 – 120) × 30%	60
	500

Note: The loan of £42 million is the proportion of the loan that relates to the other venturers (ie 70% × £60m).

Answers to Self-test

1   Emma plc

Emma's interest in Leaner amounts to 60% (18,000/30,000) of the voting rights, as against 25% of any dividends paid.

The approach taken by Emma to its investment in Leaner is based on the view that although a 25% interest should normally be accounted for as an associate under IAS 28 *Investments in Associates*, Emma does not exert any significant influence over Leaner. Hence it can rebut the presumption of associate status.

IAS 27 *Consolidated and Separate Financial Statements* bases the treatment of an investment in another entity around control rather than ownership. Emma can control Leaner by virtue of holding the majority of the voting rights in the company. Leaner is thus a subsidiary and should be consolidated in full in Emma's consolidated financial statements, from the date of acquisition.

Emma's directors may have been motivated by a desire to avoid consolidation of Leaner's losses. These losses may indicate that the value of the investment in Leaner may be overstated. A test for impairment, as required by IAS 36 *Impairment of Assets*, may reveal that the recoverable amount of the investment has fallen below £55,000, thus requiring a write down in Emma's financial statements.

2   H plc

(a) Goodwill in S

	£m	£m
Consideration transferred		
100m shares × 75% × £4.20		315
Deferred consideration; £110m × $^1/_{1.10}$		100
		415
Non-controlling interest – share of net assets		
25% × £340m (see below)		85
		500
Share of the net assets acquired at fair value		
Carrying amount of net assets at 1 April 20X6:		
Ordinary shares	100	
Share premium	50	
Retained earnings	160	
	310	
Fair valuation adjustment to inventory	4	
Revaluation of land at the date of acquisition	26	
Fair value of the net assets at acquisition		(340)
Goodwill		160
Impairment charge given in question		(25)
Carrying amount at 31 March 20X7		135

The present value of the deferred consideration should be used in the goodwill calculation. The £10 million discount should be recognised as a finance cost in profit or loss in the year ended 31 March 20X7.

The land and buildings should be measured at their acquisition date fair value. The £8 million gain arising subsequently should be treated as a normal revaluation and recognised in other comprehensive income and held in the revaluation surplus as part of equity. (See below.)

The adjustment to inventory values should be made against the initially recognised amounts because the under-valuation was a result of an error (errors should always be corrected retrospectively, even if identified after the end of the measurement period). This adjustment increases post-acquisition cost of sales and reduces post-acquisition earnings.

(b) **Non-controlling interest in S's net assets**

	£m	£m
Share of net assets at the acquisition date (as above)		85
Share of post-acquisition total comprehensive income:		
S unadjusted profit (per question)	90	
Less: PURP ('/₄ x £8m)	(2)	
Less: increase in cost of sales to correct inventory error	(4)	
Adjusted profit	84	
Revaluation surplus re land and buildings	8	
	92	
Share (25%)		23
		108

No adjustment to inventory is required at the year end because it has all been sold.

(c) **Consolidated equity**

	£m
Ordinary shares of £1 each	320
Share premium	100
Revaluation surplus (60 + (75% x 8))	66
Retained earnings ((H 360 – 10 finance cost – 25 impairment) + S (75% x 84))	388
	874

3   **High Five**

(a) Proportionate consolidation is the tacitly preferred treatment under IAS 31; the investor's share of its joint venture assets, liabilities, income and expenses is presented within each line item in the financial statements. Under the equity accounting permitted as an alternative the net investment and the share of earnings are the only two amounts presented.

Advantages of proportionate consolidation to users

(1) This method treats the investment as if the investor had direct control of its share of the assets and results of the joint venture, which is very close to the reality of the situation, even though in fact it shares control of the entire venture.

(2) This method clearly shows the size of an investor's interest in a joint venture and any related liabilities. The financing and structure of the venture is also shown in relation to the rest of the group.

(3) This method is the one required for joint ventures which consist of a sharing of assets or operations other than through the creation of a separate legal entity, so assists consistency of presentation.

This information helps users to judge past performance and assess future prospects.

Disadvantages of proportionate consolidation to users

(1) It may not be made clear (and it may not be possible to make clear) those assets and liabilities which are fully controlled by the investor and those which are not. This will muddy the waters around the consolidated results and confuse users of financial statements.

(2) What does 50% of an asset such as an item of machinery mean? Taking fractions of items and adding them into the consolidated financial statements may only confuse users.

(b) Treatment of Park Ltd

Each venturer should present in its consolidated statement of financial position:

	£
50% of property, plant and equipment	250,000
50% of bank and cash	25,000
	275,000

The consolidated income statement of each venturer should include 50% of the profit earned, so £35,000 broken down into a share of revenues and costs as appropriate.

4   **Red Air**

The agreement that all strategic financial and operating decisions require the consent of both Red Air and Stripe Air results in them having joint control and their shared activities should be accounted for as joint ventures under IAS 31 *Interests in Joint Ventures*. There are two operations within this scenario, each of which is governed by IAS 31. The baggage handling system is a jointly controlled asset and the operation of it is a joint operation.

The cost of acquiring (2 × £2.6 million) and installing (£800,000) the baggage handling system should be presented in both Red Air and Stripe Air's financial statements, at 50% of the £6 million total cost. Red Air is owed money by Stripe Air in respect of the installation.

Each company's statement of financial position should therefore present a non-current asset of £2.7 million (£3 million minus one year's 10% depreciation).

The expenses and income should be presented in each company's books in accordance with the agreement. Both companies bring their own experience and staff to the activities. Therefore each company should recognise the expense of employing a supervisor in its own books. (IAS 31 states that each venturer shall recognise any expenses it has incurred in respect of its interest in a jointly controlled asset.)

The income and expenditure of the joint operation is:

	£'000
Baggage handlers	(320)
Depreciation	(600)
Income from rental	124
Result	(796)

Both Red Air and Stripe Air should present 50% of each of the above amounts as income and expenditure in their financial statements. The total amount due to Red Air from Stripe Air is:

	Paid by Red Air £'000	Red Air's share £'000	Due (to)/ from Stripe Air £'000
Installation	(800)	(400)	400
Baggage handlers	(320)	(160)	160
Supervisors	(60)	(60)	0
Income	124	62	(62)
Net total			498

Each company should present its payments for supervisors as its own expense.

5   **Piaf**

(a)   **If determined on 1 September 20X5**

Because fair values were finalised before the first year-end after the acquisition, they should be used in the consolidated statement of financial position (CSFP) as follows:

	30.9.X5 £'000
Goodwill ((£10m consideration + (20% × £11.36m NCI)) – £11.36m)	912
Property, plant and equipment (8.16m – ((8.16m ÷ 20) × 2/12))	8,092
Long-term inventory	2,600

The non-controlling interest should be measured at 20% of McKenny's net assets at 30 September 20X5.

A depreciation expense in respect of McKenny's assets of £68,000 ((8.16m ÷ 20) × 2/12) should be recognised in the consolidated income statement (CIS).

There should be no effect on the comparative figures to 30 September 20X4, because McKenny was not a subsidiary at 30 September 20X4.

(b) **If determined on 1 July 20X6**

Fair values were finalised after the first year-end after the acquisition but within the measurement period (within 12 months of the acquisition date). The finalised amounts should therefore be used retrospectively in the consolidated financial statements to 30 September 20X6 and retrospective adjustment made to the amounts at 30 September 20X5. The CSFP at 30 September 20X6 should include:

	30.9.X6 £'000
Goodwill (as in (a) above)	912
Property, plant and equipment (8.16m – ((8.16m ÷ 20) × 14/12))	7,684
Long-term inventory	2,600

The non-controlling interest should be measured at 20% of McKenny's net assets at 30 September 20X6.

A depreciation expense in respect of McKenny's assets of £408,000 (8.16m ÷ 20) should be recognised in the CIS.

The comparative figures at 30 September 20X5 should be the same amounts as in (a) above.

(c) **If determined on 1 September 20X6**

Fair values were finalised after the end of the measurement period, being more than twelve months after the acquisition. The adjustments should be applied prospectively from the date of determination.

Goodwill should remain at its initially recognised amount. As there is no indication of impairment the carrying amount of non-current assets should be depreciated over their estimated remaining useful life. The carrying amount of inventory should remain at its initially recognised amount (the uplift in value should be recognised as part of the profit when the inventory is eventually sold).

The CSFP at 30 September 20X6 should include:

	30.9.X6 £'000
Goodwill ((£10m consideration + (20% × £11.2m NCI)) – £11.2m)	1,040
Property, plant and equipment (8.4m – ((8.4m ÷ 20) × 14/12))	7,910
Long-term inventory	2,200

A depreciation expense in respect of McKenny's assets of £420,000 (8.4m ÷ 20) should be recognised in the CIS.

Point to note:

Calculated by reference to the adjusted amounts, goodwill should have been £912,000. This may indicate that an impairment test would show that the recoverable amount of goodwill is below the carrying amount of £1,040,000, in which case an impairment loss should be recognised.

Financial statements for year ended 30 September 20X5

As the adjustments should be applied prospectively only, the previously published amounts for 30 September 20X5, based on provisional values, should remain without any adjustments. The comparative CSFP at 30 September 20X5 should include:

	30.9.X5 £'000
Goodwill ((£10m consideration + (20% × £11.2m NCI)) – £11.2m)	1,040
Property, plant and equipment (8.4m – ((8.4m ÷ 20) × 2/12))	8,330
Long-term inventory	2,200

A depreciation expense in respect of McKenny's assets of £70,000 ((8.4m ÷ 20) × 2/12) should be recognised in the comparative CIS.

6   **Brentford plc**

(a) **Acquisition of Crystal Ltd**

At the acquisition date Brentford plc should measure goodwill acquired in the business combination with Crystal Ltd as:

	£'000
Consideration transferred:	
Cash payable at acquisition date	3,000
Cash payable on 31 December 20X5	
(present value of £0.53m at 6% for one year)	500
	3,500
Non-controlling interest at fair value	2,000
	5,500
Net assets acquired	(4,750)
Goodwill	750

At the period end the net assets attributable to Crystal Ltd are £4.9 million, being £4.75 million at the acquisition date plus £750,000 goodwill less £600,000 loss incurred. Its recoverable amount has been estimated at £4.7 million, so an impairment loss of £200,000 should be recognised.

At the period end goodwill should be remeasured at £550,000 (750,000 – 200,000 impairment).

The profit or loss for the year should include the following:

- Crystal Ltd's loss for the year of £600,000 plus the impairment loss of £200,000, so £800,000

- A finance cost of £30,000 being the unwinding of the discount on the deferred consideration (500,000 × 6%).

The amount attributable to the owners of Brentford plc should include a loss of £510,000 ((60% × 800,000) + 30,000)

The amount attributable to the non-controlling interest should include a loss of £320,000 (40% × 800,000)

At the period end Brentford plc should measure the non-controlling interest at:

	£'000
Fair value at acquisition date	2,000
Share of post acquisition loss and impairment loss (see above)	(320)
	1,680

There is no liability for deferred consideration; it was payable on the last day of the period.

(b) **Acquisition of Fulham Ltd**

Consolidated statement of financial position at 31 December 20X5

Brentford plc should recognise goodwill acquired in the business combination with Fulham Ltd, measured as:

	£'000
Consideration transferred	
Cash payable at acquisition date	5,600
Non-controlling interest at share of net assets (20% × 7,000)	1,400
Acquisition date fair value of previously held equity	640
	7,640
Net assets acquired	(7,000)
Goodwill	640

As the acquisition was on the last day of the reporting period Brentford plc should recognise the non-controlling interest at £1.4 million (see above).

Consolidated statement of comprehensive income for the year ended 31 December 20X5

Brentford plc should recognise in profit or loss the gain on remeasurement of the previously held equity at fair value, calculated as:

	£'000
Gain arising in the period (640,000 fair value – 610,000 carrying amount)	30
Reclassification to profit or loss of gains arising in previous periods (610,000 carrying amount – 500,000 cost)	110
	140

Brentford plc should recognise in other comprehensive income:

	£'000
Reclassification to profit or loss of gains arising in previous periods	(110)

CHAPTER 9

Earnings per share and distributable profits

Introduction

Examination context

Topic List

1 Context for IAS 33 *Earnings per Share*

2 Basic EPS – earnings calculations

3 Basic EPS – number of shares

4 Diluted EPS

5 Other measures of EPS

6 Judgements required

7 Relevance of information for users

8 Distributable profits

9 UK GAAP comparison

Summary and Self-test

Technical reference

Answers to Interactive questions

Answers to Self-test

Learning objectives

- Calculate basic earnings per share

- Calculate diluted earnings per share

- Define and calculate the distributable profits of an entity and allocations of distributable profit

Specific syllabus references for this chapter are: 1e, 3e, 4a and 4b.

Syllabus links

You will have already seen how to prepare an income statement according to IAS 1 and how to calculate the profit for the period. In this chapter we will look at how that profit is used in order to calculate a key performance indicator, earnings per share. This is an important figure that should be disclosed because it is useful when interpreting financial statements. For Financial Reporting we consider the basic calculations for earnings per share and this will then be taken further at the Advanced Stage.

Examination context

In the examination, candidates may be required to:

- Calculate basic earnings per share where there has been an issue for cash, a rights issue or a bonus issue

- Calculate diluted earnings per share

- Explain the purpose of presenting diluted earnings per share

- Comment on and indicate how earnings per share could be altered by differing accounting policies

- Use earnings per share as part of an assessment of financial performance of an entity

- Disclose the information required by IAS 33 for earnings per share

1 Context for IAS 33 *Earnings per Share*

Section overview

- This section sets the context within which IAS 33 needs to be considered.

- Basic earnings per share is calculated as the profit or loss attributable to the ordinary equity holders divided by the number of shares in issue.

- IAS 33 is only mandatory for listed entities.

Context

One of the most commonly used performance measures worldwide is basic earnings per share (EPS), which is calculated as the profit or loss attributable to the ordinary equity holders divided by the number of shares in issue.

In addition to being an important independent measure, it also is a component in the price earnings (P/E) ratio which often forms a pivotal role in the valuation of businesses. A meaningful comparison between entities, or against a benchmark figure, can only be made where entities measure their EPS figure on a consistent basis. IAS 33 prescribes what that consistent basis should be.

Standard EPS calculations assist in comparisons which are meaningful across entities, but they take account of all income and expenses that have been reported during the period, whether or not they are likely to recur in the future. These calculations provide a historical performance measure and do not purport to provide a measure of future performance. So entities frequently present alternative forms of EPS, based on income and expenses which have been adjusted to exclude non-recurring items; entities generally refer to the adjusted profit figure as 'maintainable earnings'. Industry or market standard EPS figures are also often reported. Both of these additional performance measures are claimed to provide a more realistic measure of the entity's performance in future periods.

The standard EPS figure may not be maintainable where there are convertible instruments already in issue which on conversion will lead to an increase in the number of shares in issue in the future. Investors should therefore be made aware of any such instruments and of the effect they would have had on EPS had they been converted into equity shares during the period. IAS 33 therefore requires a second EPS figure to be presented, which is the diluted EPS figure.

Compliance with IAS 33 is mandatory for:

- The separate financial statements of entities whose ordinary shares are publicly traded or are in the process of being issued in public markets

- The consolidated financial statements for groups whose parent has shares similarly traded/being issued.

Other entities need not present EPS (because their shares are not traded, there is no readily available market price which can be used to calculate the P/E ratio), but if they do voluntarily, they should comply with IAS 33.

IAS 33 requires the EPS to be presented in the income statement.

2 Basic EPS – earnings calculations

Section overview

- The calculation for basic EPS is earnings divided by the number of shares in issue.

- The earnings to be used in the basic EPS calculation are the profit or loss attributable to the ordinary equity holders.

- Profits disclosed in the income statement need adjustment for dividends on irredeemable preference shares.

2.1 Calculation

The calculation for basic EPS is profit or loss divided by the number of shares in issue.

The fully worded calculation is:

$$\frac{\text{Profit/(loss) attributable to ordinary equity holders of the parent}}{\text{Weighted average number of ordinary shares outstanding during the period}}$$

Shares are usually included in the weighted average number of shares from the date any consideration for them is receivable by the issuer. This is generally the date of their issue.

Point to note:

The need for a weighted average number of shares is explained in section 3 below.

2.2 Calculating earnings

The earnings figure to be used is the profit or loss attributable to **the ordinary equity holders**. The income statement presents the profit attributable to the **owners** of the entity. Usually this will be the amount attributable to ordinary equity holders, but in some cases a deduction should be made for the amount attributable to preference equity holders.

Whether such a deduction is needed depends upon the type of preference share:

- Redeemable preference shares should be classified as liabilities and the finance charge relating to them (both dividend and any premium on redemption adjustment) should already have been recognised in profit or loss as part of finance charges. No adjustment is needed.

- Irredeemable preference shares should be classified as equity and the dividend should be deducted in the statement of changes in equity. An adjustment is needed; the dividend should be deducted from the profit figure taken from the income statement to arrive at the profit attributable to the ordinary equity holders.

Interactive question 1: Dividend on irredeemable preference shares

[Difficulty level: Easy]

	£m
Profit for the period	2,177
Attributable to:	
Owners of the parent	1,897
Non-controlling interests	280
	2,177
Dividends presented in statement of changes in equity	
On irredeemable preference shares	400
On ordinary shares	600

The weighted average number of ordinary shares in issue is 6,241 million.

Requirement

Calculate the basic EPS.

Fill in the proforma below.

	£m
Profit attributable to owners of the parent	
Less: dividend on irredeemable preference shares	
Profit attributable to ordinary equity holders of the parent	
EPS =	

See **Answer** at the end of this chapter.

2.2.1 Cumulative dividends on irredeemable preference shares

If the dividends on such shares are cumulative, any dividend not paid in the current year (due, for example, to lack of distributable profits) will be payable in subsequent years when distributable profits become available. All such arrears need to be paid off before any ordinary share dividend is paid.

The **treatment of such cumulative dividends** for EPS purposes is as follows.

- If the dividend is not paid in the year, then it should still be deducted from profit.
- When the arrears of dividend is subsequently paid, it should be excluded from the EPS calculation.

Interactive question 2: Cumulative dividend on irredeemable preference shares
[Difficulty level: Intermediate]

	£m
Profit for the period	88

Attributable to:

	£m
Owners of the parent	82
Non-controlling interest	6
	88

Dividends presented in statement of changes in equity

	£m
On irredeemable preference shares (Note)	20
On ordinary shares	5

Note:

This figure includes £15m in respect of arrears of cumulative dividend not paid in previous years due to lack of distributable profits.

The weighted average number of ordinary shares is 1,200 million.

Requirement

Calculate the basic EPS.

Fill in the proforma below.

	£m
Profit	
Less: dividend on irredeemable preference shares	
Profit attributable to ordinary equity holders of the parent	
EPS =	

See **Answer** at the end of this chapter.

3 Basic EPS – number of shares

Section overview

- If shares are issued for cash at full market price, the weighted average number of shares should be calculated by weighting the shares on a time basis.

- If a bonus issue is made, the bonus shares should be treated as always having been in issue.

- A rights issue should be treated as a mixture of a bonus issue and an issue for cash at full market price.

- The bonus element of a rights issue should be adjusted for using a fraction involving the theoretical ex-rights price (TERP).

3.1 Calculating the weighted average number of ordinary shares

If no additional shares have been issued during the year, there are no complications; the number of shares in issue at the start (or end) of the period is used.

If additional shares **have been issued** during the current period, the calculation of the weighted average number of shares depends upon whether:

- The resources of the entity have increased, for example an issue of shares for cash at full market price

- The resources of the entity have not changed, for example a bonus issue

3.2 Issue of shares for cash at full market price

Where shares are issued during the period for cash at full market price, the cash received is an **increase in the resources** of the entity. These additional resources will only have been available to increase earnings (the numerator in the EPS fraction) for part of the period, so the additional shares should only be included in the shares in issue (the denominator of the fraction) for part of the period. The number of new shares is 'weighted' for the proportion of the period they have been in issue.

Point to note:

An issue of shares in an acquisition at market value is equivalent to an issue of shares for cash in these calculations.

The weighted average number of shares is calculated as follows.

- Start with the number of shares in issue **at the start of the year** and time-apportion it for the period **up to** the date the new shares were issued.

- Take the number of shares in issue **after** the new shares were issued and time-apportion it for the period **after** the date of issue.

- The total of these two is the weighted average number of shares in issue over the year.

Worked example: Issue of shares for cash at full market price

X plc has 10 million ordinary shares in issue at 1 January 20X4. Its accounting year end is 31 December. During 20X4 the following events occur:

1 April 20X4   2 million shares are issued to acquire a subsidiary
1 October 20X4   2 million shares are issued at full market price

What is the weighted average number of ordinary shares outstanding during the period?

Solution

The weighted average number of ordinary shares is calculated as follows.

		Weighted Av (million)
January to March	10 million x 3/12 =	2.5
April to September	12 million x 6/12 =	6.0
October to December	14 million x 3/12 =	3.5
		12.0

3.3 Bonus issue

When a bonus issue is made:

- Additional shares are issued to the ordinary equity holders in proportion to their current shareholding, for example one new share for each five shares already owned

- No cash is received for these shares

- Reserves are capitalised by a debit to share premium/retained earnings

In this case the issuing entity has not received any additional resources to help increase earnings. Each shareholder has more shares, but still has the same proportionate interest in the entity. As an example, a shareholder owning 100,000 shares out of the 1 million in issue has a 10% interest. If the entity makes a 1 for 2 bonus issue, the shareholder will own 150,000 shares out of the 1.5 million now in issue, still a 10% interest.

For a bonus issue the treatment for the weighted average number of shares is to assume that the **shares have always been in issue**. This means that they should be treated as having been issued at the start of the earliest period for which results are reported, usually the start of the year presented as the comparative figures.

Worked example: Bonus issue

X plc has 10m ordinary shares in issue at 1 January 20X3. Its accounting year end is 31 December.

Earnings:

	£m
20X4	13
20X3	10

Two million bonus shares are issued on 1 October 20X4.

What basic EPS amount was presented in the 20X3 financial statements and what two basic EPS amounts should be presented in the 20X4 financial statements?

Solution

20X3 financial statements: EPS (£10m/10m shares)   100p

20X4 financial statements:

Basic EPS for both years should be calculated as if the bonus shares had always been in issue.

Basic EPS for 20X4 (£13m/(10+2)m)	108.3p
Basic EPS for 20X3 (£10m/(10+2)m)	83.3p

Point to note:

An alternative adjustment to the 20X3 basic EPS as originally stated would be to multiply it by (shares before bonus/shares after bonus), so 100p x (10m/12m) = 83.3p

Interactive question 3: Bonus issue
[Difficulty level: Intermediate]

At 1 January 20X4 and 1 January 20X5 X plc had in issue 20 million ordinary shares.

During 20X5 the following events took place.

31 May 20X5	Issue of 6 million shares for cash at full market price
30 September 20X5	Bonus issue of 1 for 2

Earnings for the year ended 31 December 20X4 were £6m and for the year ended 31 December 20X5 were £8m.

Requirements

(a) Calculate the basic EPS originally reported in 20X4.
(b) Calculate the basic EPS reported in 20X5 including comparative.

See **Answer** at the end of this chapter.

3.4 Rights issue

A rights issue is:

- An issue of shares for cash to the existing ordinary equity holders in proportion to their current shareholdings.

- At a discount to the current market price.

Because the issue price is below the market price, a rights issue is in effect a combination of **an issue at full value and a bonus issue.**

In order to calculate the basic EPS number of shares when there has been a rights issue, an adjustment for the bonus element is required:

$$\text{Adjustment} = \frac{\text{Pre-rights issue price of shares}}{\text{Theoretical ex-rights price (TERP)}}$$

The pre-rights issue price of the shares is the market price immediately before the rights issue is announced. The TERP is the theoretical price at which the shares would trade after the rights issue and takes into account the diluting effect of the bonus element in the rights issue.

The adjustment is used to increase the number of shares in issue **prior to** the rights issue for the bonus element.

Point to note:

The TERP is used because the market price at which the shares trade after the rights issue takes account of other factors; for example, it will go up above the TERP if investors interpret the rights issue as a positive sign for the development of the issuing company, and go down below it if they interpret it as a negative sign.

Worked example: TERP

A 1 for 3 rights issue is made at 132p when the market price is 220p

What is the TERP?

Solution

	No.	Price	Total
		p	p
Pre-rights issue holding	3	220	660
Rights share	1	132	132
	4		792

TERP (792/4) = 198p

Point to note:

To prove that a rights issue is a combination of an issue at full market price and a bonus issue, consider the effect if instead of this rights issue, an issue of 1 for 8 had been made at the full market price of 220p, followed immediately by a 1 for 9 bonus:

	No.	Price p	Total p
Initial holding	8	220	1,760
Issue at full market price	1	220	220
Revised holding	9		1,980
Bonus issue	1	N/A	0
Revised holding	10		1,980

Theoretical price (1,980/10) = 198p

Worked example: Rights issue

The following information is available for an entity.

	£'000
Earnings	
20X2	1,000
20X3	1,300
20X4	1,500

Number of shares in issue at 1 January 20X2: 800,000
Rights issue: 1 for 4 at £5 each on 1 April 20X3 when the market value was £7
What are the basic EPS amounts for each of the three years **after** adjustment for the rights issue?

Solution

Computation of theoretical ex-rights price (TERP):

	No.	Price p	Total p
Pre-rights issue holding	4	700	2,800
Rights share	1	500	500
	5		3,300

Therefore TERP = $\dfrac{3,300}{5}$ = 660p

Computation of bonus adjustment factor:

Adjustment = $\dfrac{\text{Value of shares before rights}}{\text{TERP}}$ = $\dfrac{700p}{660p}$

Computation of EPS:
20X2
Earnings £1m/(800,000 shares × (700/660)) = 117.9p
20X3
Earnings = £1.3 million

	Total
Weighted average shares	
1 Jan – 31 Mar 800,000 × 700/660 × 3/12	212,121
1 Apr – 31 Dec 800,000 × ((4+1) /4) × 9/12	750,000
	962,121

Basic EPS $\dfrac{£1.3m}{962,121}$ = 135.1p

20X4 Basic EPS $\dfrac{£1.5m}{(800,000 \times (4+1)/4)}$ = 150.0p

---

Interactive question 4: Rights issue [Difficulty level: Intermediate]

At 1 January 20X8 and 1 January 20X9 Box plc had in issue ten million ordinary shares. On 30 June 20X9 Box plc made a 1 for 4 rights issue at £2.40 per share. At that date the market price before the issue was announced was £3.20 per share. The earnings of the company were £4m for 20X8 and £4.8m for 20X9.

Requirement

Calculate the reported basic EPS for 20X9 (including the comparative).

See **Answer** at the end of this chapter.

4 Diluted EPS

Section overview

- Diluted EPS recognises the effect of additional shares that the entity is committed to issuing in future.
- An adjustment may be needed to the earnings figure used in the basic EPS calculation.
- An adjustment is always needed to the weighted number of shares used in the basic EPS calculation.
- If a future issue of shares would appear to increase basic EPS, no diluted EPS is presented.

4.1 Potential ordinary shares and dilution

At the end of the reporting period an entity may have a **commitment to issue more shares** in future, as a result of having previously issued:

- Convertible debt: on conversion into ordinary shares the debt is derecognised and additional equity shares recognised

- Convertible preference shares: on conversion into ordinary shares the preference shares are derecognised and additional shares recognised

- Warrants to subscribe for ordinary shares.

The securities/contracts giving rights to ordinary shares are known as potential ordinary shares.

If potential ordinary shares are converted in the future, there could be a **dilutive effect** on basic EPS due to the increase in shares in issue. **Diluted EPS**, ie the EPS if all dilutive potential ordinary shares had been converted, should be presented in the income statement.

Potential ordinary shares are dilutive if on conversion the percentage increase (if any) in earnings (for example through interest on convertible loan stock no longer being payable) would be less than the percentage increase in the number of shares in issue.

Points to note:

1 The only diluted EPS calculations which fall within the Financial Reporting syllabus are those relating to convertible debt (including convertible, redeemable preference shares).

2 The conversion terms may be such that on conversion the percentage increase in earnings would be greater than the percentage increase in the number of shares, thereby leading to an **increase in basic EPS**. Such arrangements are said to be anti-dilutive and are left out of account when calculating diluted EPS.

3 Conversion is deemed to have taken place at the start of the period, or the date on which the potential ordinary shares were issued, if later. So for an entity preparing financial statements for the year ended 31 December 20X8, convertible debt issued at any time in 20X7 or earlier is deemed to have been converted on 1 January 20X8, but such debt issued on 30 June 20X8 is deemed to have been converted on that date.

4.2 Convertible debt

An entity which has issued convertible debt will be paying interest on that debt. If the debt were converted into ordinary shares, the interest would no longer be payable.

Interest usually attracts tax relief, so the effect of conversion on earnings will be to increase it by the saved interest, net of the tax relief no longer given.

There is the complication that when the convertible debt was originally issued, the proceeds would have been split between the equity component and the liability component (see Chapter 7).

- The finance cost to be added back to profit or loss is calculated as the carrying amount of the liability component **at the start of the period** multiplied by **the effective interest rate** (which takes account of the issue costs of the convertible).

- You should assume that the whole of this finance cost attracted tax relief, unless told differently.

- The number of shares to be issued on conversion is calculated by reference to the conversion terms and the nominal value in issue.

Worked example: Convertible debt

On 1 January 20X7 an entity had in issue five million £1 ordinary shares and £4 million of 6% convertible redeemable loan stock.

The convertible redeemable loan stock can be converted at any time after 31 December 20X9 and the conversion terms are 30 ordinary shares for every £100 of loan stock.

The liability component of the convertible loan stock was carried in the statement of financial position on 1 January 20X7 at £3.6 million and the effective interest rate is 8%. The company pays tax at the rate of 25%.

The profit attributable to the ordinary equity holders for the year ended 31 December 20X7 is £1.2 million.

What amounts for basic EPS and diluted EPS should be presented for the year ended 31 December 20X7?

Solution

Basic EPS = £1.2m/5m = 24 pence

Diluted EPS

	£
Earnings for basic EPS	1,200,000
Finance cost saved on conversion, net of tax (£3,600,000 x 8% × (100 – 25)%)	216,000
Earnings for diluted EPS	1,416,000
Shares for basic EPS	5,000,000
Additional shares on conversion ((£4,000,000/£100) x 30)	1,200,000
Shares for diluted EPS	6,200,000

Diluted EPS $\left(\dfrac{£1,416,000}{6,200,000}\right)$ = 22.8 pence

The calculation of diluted EPS when there are convertible redeemable preference shares is the same, except that it is unlikely that any tax relief would be given for these dividends, so the full amount of the dividends should be added back to earnings for basic EPS.

Where there are differing conversion terms at different dates, the terms to be used for this calculation are those which result in the **largest** number of additional shares being issued.

Interactive question 5: Conversion terms   [Difficulty level: Intermediate]

On 1 January 20X4 an entity had in issue four million £1 ordinary shares and £5 million of 7% convertible redeemable loan stock, on which the conversion terms were:

- On 31 December 20X7: 40 ordinary shares for each £125 of loan stock
- On 31 December 20X8: 40 ordinary shares for each £130 of loan stock
- On 31 December 20X9: 40 ordinary shares for each £135 of loan stock

The liability component of the convertible redeemable loan stock was carried in the statement of financial position on 1 January 20X4 at £4.8 million and the effective interest rate 8.5%. The company pays tax at the rate of 20%.

The profit attributable to the ordinary equity holders for the year ended 31 December 20X4 was £1 million.

Requirement

Calculate the basic and diluted EPS for the year ended 31 December 20X4.

See **Answer** at the end of this chapter.

4.3 Presentation of EPS

IAS 33 requires entities to:

- Present in **the statement of comprehensive income** both basic and diluted EPS based on profit or loss from **continuing operations**.

- Present in **the statement of comprehensive income** both basic and diluted EPS based on the profit or loss attributable to ordinary equity holders (which includes the profit or loss from **discontinued operations** but excludes gains/losses recognised in other comprehensive income).

- Present basic and diluted EPS with equal prominence for current year and comparative.

- Present a loss per share if a loss is made.

Point to note:

If an entity presents the components of profit or loss in a separate income statement, then all the EPS amounts referred to above should be presented in that separate statement.

5 Other measures of EPS

Section overview

An entity may present measures of EPS in addition to those required by IAS 33.

An entity may choose to present other measures of EPS **in addition to** the basic and diluted versions required by IAS 33. Such measures usually exclude what the management regards as one-off, non-recurring items, resulting (in management's view at least) in a measure which is more typical of the business' future performance.

Such measures should:

- Use the same denominator (weighted average number of shares) as is used in the calculations required by IAS 33

- Show both basic and diluted EPS on the chosen basis

- Be presented in the notes, not in the statement of comprehensive income

- Be accompanied by a reconciliation of the figures used for the numerators with a line item in the statement of comprehensive income (so it is easy to see what adjustments have been made to earnings).

6 Judgements required

Section overview

- Few judgements are required in the calculation of the weighted average number of shares.
- Any judgements relate to the earnings figure used.

IAS 33 is explicit about its focus being on the calculation of the weighted average number of shares in issue; as a result of its detailed rules, few judgements are required in arriving at this number.

All the judgements required of management relate to the earnings figure used, because that is dependent on the accounting policies adopted by management and the accounting estimates made in line with those policies. So all the judgements relating to all IFRS have an impact on the earnings figure.

7 Relevance of information for users

Section overview

The basic and diluted EPS are:

- Often regarded as critical measures of performance in their own right
- The foundation of many business valuation techniques

So users of financial statements benefit from the tight rules laid down for the calculation of the weighted average number of shares in issue.

Users can make reliable predictions of future EPS figures by taking their own estimates of future earnings and then using the following detailed information which should be disclosed in the financial statements:

- Amounts used as the numerator for both basic and diluted calculations and a reconciliation of those amounts with the reported profit or loss attributable to the parent entity for the period

- The weighted average number of ordinary shares used as the denominator in both calculations

- A reconciliation of the weighted average number of shares used in the basic EPS calculation to that used for diluted EPS – individual adjustments should be separately identified.

IAS 33 is of no help in evaluating solvency (gearing) or cash flows; its contribution is solely to measures of profitability.

8 Distributable profits

Section overview

- Distributable profits are calculated by reference to the individual entity, not the consolidated group.
- The rule for private companies is that distributable profits are net accumulated realised profits.
- Public companies also have to deduct any net unrealised losses.
- ICAEW/ICAS have issued technical releases in order to provide guidance on distributable profits.

8.1 Introduction

Distributable profits are the profits that under the Companies Act 2006 an entity is legally entitled to **distribute to its equity holders**. The rules are slightly different for private companies (Ltd) and public companies (plc).

For entities within a group, the calculation is made for each entity separately, not for the consolidated group.

Point to note:

In a group it is the parent company which pays the dividends to group shareholders, so it is important that there are sufficient distributable profits in the parent company. If the parent does not trade but acts solely as an investment holding company, its only income, and only source of distributable profits, will be dividends passed up by its subsidiaries. An important part of year-end planning will be to make sure that sufficient dividends are passed up before the year end.

8.2 Rule for private companies

Distributable profits are measured as accumulated realised profits less accumulated realised losses.

Point to note:

It is the accumulated position which is important, not the profits/losses arising in a particular year.

Generally this equates to the **retained earnings balance** determined under **generally accepted accounting principles**. There is specific guidance in the Companies Act 2006 that:

- A provision is a realised loss

- A revaluation surplus is an unrealised profit

- Any additional depreciation on revalued non-current assets can be added back to profits for determining distributable amounts

- When a revalued asset is disposed of, the unrealised surplus or loss on revaluation becomes a realised profit or loss

8.2.1 The effect of revaluations

When a revaluation of non-current assets takes place:

- Gains are unrealised unless they reverse a loss previously treated as realised

- Losses are realised except where the loss

  - Offsets a previous surplus on the same asset, or

  - Arises on a revaluation of all non-current assets, or

  - Arises on a revaluation of some non-current assets where the directors consider that the assets not revalued are worth at least their book value

8.3 Additional rules for public companies

Over and above the rule for private companies there is an additional restriction for public companies; they may not make a distribution if this reduces its net assets below the total of **called-up share capital and undistributable reserves**.

Undistributable reserves are:

- Share premium account

- Net unrealised profits

- Any other reserve specified by law or the company's constitution to be unrealised (for example a capital redemption reserve)

One way of calculating the distributable profits of a public company is:

	£
Distributable profits per rule for private companies	X
Less: any excess of unrealised losses over unrealised profits	(X)
Distributable profits per rule for public companies	X

Worked example: Distributable profits

The summarised draft statement of financial position of a company at 31 March 20X0 was as follows.

	£'000
Non-current assets	
Land and buildings	1,500
Plant and machinery	60
Fixtures	15
	1,575
Net current assets	925
	2,500
Share capital	1,600
Retained earnings	900
	2,500

An independent professional valuation undertaken on 31 March 20X0 showed valuations of £1.4 million and £50,000 for the land and buildings and plant and machinery respectively, which the directors decided to incorporate into the company's accounting records from 1 April 20X0. They considered the value of fixtures was not less than £15,000.

Requirements

Calculate the maximum amount of distributable profit for the year ended 31 March 20X0 assuming the company is:

(a) A private company
(b) A public company.

Solution

	(a) Private company £'000	(b) Public company £'000
Accumulated realised profits less accumulated realised losses	900	900
Less: net unrealised losses (1,500 + 60 – 1,400 – 50)	N/A	(110)
	900	790

The £110,000 downward revaluation is treated as unrealised because the directors have reassessed the values of all non-current assets. This unrealised loss should be taken into account for the public company calculation, but not for the private company calculation.

Interactive question 6: Distributable profits
[Difficulty level: Intermediate]

Haver Ltd is a rapidly-expanding company which was incorporated two years ago to benefit from limited liability, issuing 10,000 £1 shares for £5 per share.

On 1 January 20X2 the company revalued its non-current assets to improve its statement of financial position, and thus help it to raise finance, giving a revaluation surplus of £400,000. The remaining useful life of these assets at the date of revaluation was 25 years.

At 1 January 20X2 retained earnings brought forward were £80,000 and profits for the year ended 31 December 20X2 were £40,000.

The directors, who are also equity holders, are considering taking dividends for the first time but are unsure how much they may distribute.

Requirements

(a) Explain the calculation of and calculate the distributable profits for Haver Ltd at 1 January 20X2.

(b) Explain the calculation of and calculate the distributable profits for Haver Ltd at 31 December 20X2.

(c) Explain how the revaluation surplus should be treated if in the future the assets are sold.

Fill in the proforma below.

Solution

(a)

(b)

(c)

See **Answer** at the end of this chapter.

8.4 Relevant accounts

For the purposes of calculating their distributable profits, entities should use the amounts shown in the 'relevant accounts', normally their last annual accounts.

If distributable profits shown in the last annual accounts are insufficient to justify a proposed distribution, then more recent interim accounts should also be used. The requirements as to their preparation are:

- For private companies: they should be sufficient to determine the legality of distribution
- For public companies: they should be properly prepared under the Companies Act 2006.

8.5 ICAEW/ICAS Technical Release 01/08 – realised profits

As we have seen above, distributable profits are based upon generally accepted accounting practice and legal rules from the Companies Act.

The concept of realised profit is intended to be dynamic, changing with the development of generally accepted accounting principles. The ICAEW and ICAS have issued a number of technical releases over the years to assist practitioners in identifying realised profits. These have been consolidated into Technical Release 01/08 which deals with the accounting standards in issue at 1 August 2007. TR 01/08 is based on the Companies Act 1985 provisions, but is relevant to the Financial Reporting syllabus because the distributable profit provisions in the 2006 Act are the same as those in the 1985 Act.

The purpose of TR 01/08 is stated as 'to identify, interpret and apply the principles relating to the determination of realised profits and losses for the purposes of making distributions'.

8.5.1 Principles of realisation

FRS 18 *Accounting Policies* states that it is generally accepted that profits shall be treated as realised when realised in the form of cash or of other assets the ultimate cash realisation of which can be assessed with reasonable certainty. According to TR 01/08 this definition catches profits and losses arising from changes in fair values recognised in accordance with accounting standards, to the extent they are readily convertible into cash. More specifically:

- Many fair value adjustments relating to financial instruments will meet the test of being readily convertible into cash.

- Unquoted equity investments are not readily convertible into cash (there is no market), so fair value adjustments will be unrealised.

- Investment properties are not readily convertible to cash and therefore fair value adjustments will be unrealised.

- Profits or losses on available-for-sale financial assets should be tested for convertibility to cash, even though these profits and losses are recognised in other comprehensive income. If the asset is viewed to be readily convertible to cash, then profit/loss will be treated as realised.

- Losses arising from fair value accounting will be treated as realised losses where profits on the same asset or liability would have been treated as realised profits.

9 UK GAAP comparison

9.1 IAS 33 and FRS 22

There are no examinable differences between IAS 33 *Earnings per Share* and FRS 22 *Earnings per Share*.

Summary and Self-test

Summary

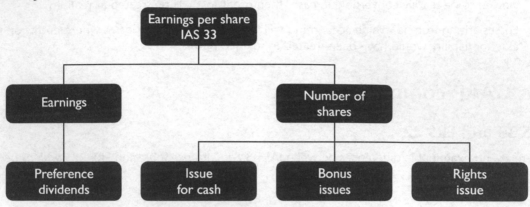

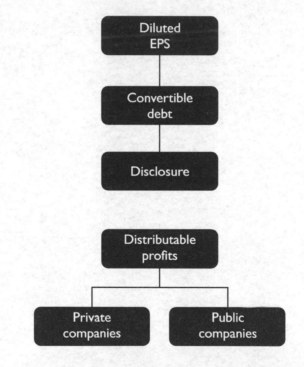

Self-test

Answer the following questions.

1 **Lemon plc**

Lemon plc prepares its financial statements to 30 September each year. On 1 October 20X6 Lemon had ten million 50 pence shares in issue and on 1 April 20X7 made a 1 for 5 rights issue at a price of £1.20 per share. The market price of a Lemon share immediately before the rights issue was announced was £1.50. Earnings for the year ended 30 September 20X7 were £4,697,000.

Lemon plc also has in issue £3,200,000 of 6% convertible redeemable loan stock with the following terms of conversion for every £100 of loan stock:

Conversion at 30 September 20X8 108 shares
Conversion at 30 September 20X9 104 shares

The liability component of the convertible redeemable loan stock was carried in the statement of financial position on 1 October 20X6 at £3 million and the effective interest rate is 9%.

Lemon plc pays tax at a rate of 30%.

Requirements

(a) Calculate basic and diluted EPS for the year ended 30 September 20X7.

(b) Explain to a holder of Lemon plc shares both the usefulness and limitations of the diluted EPS figure. **(10 marks)**

2 **Denton plc**

At the start of its financial year ended 31 December 20X5, Denton plc had ten million ordinary shares in issue. On 30 April it issued three million shares in consideration for the acquisition of a majority holding in another entity. On 31 August it went through a share reconstruction by consolidating the shares in issue, on the basis of one new share for two old shares.

Requirement

Calculate the weighted average number of shares to be used in the basic earnings per share calculation for Denton plc for the year ended 31 December 20X5. State the impact of the share consolidation on the EPS of the previous year to be disclosed in the current year's financial statements. **(4 marks)**

3 **Silvers plc**

Silvers plc had 20 million ordinary shares in issue throughout its financial year ended 31 December 20X4. In that year, it reported profit attributable to the ordinary equity holders of £10 million. Basic EPS of 50p was therefore presented in the financial statements at 31 December 20X4.

On 1 August 20X5, Silvers made a 1 for 4 rights issue at £5 per share. This was the only change to the ordinary share capital in the year. The cum-rights price (that is price immediately before the rights issue was announced) was 600p. A profit of £14 million was reported as the profit attributable to the ordinary equity holders for the year ended 31 December 20X5.

Requirement

Calculate basic EPS for the year ended 31 December 20X5 and the basic EPS for the year ended 31 December 20X4, as restated in the 31 December 20X5 financial statements. **(6 marks)**

4 **Mitchell Bros plc**

Mitchell Bros plc had 14 million ordinary shares in issue on 1 January 20X4 and 20X5. In its financial years ended 31 December 20X5 it issued further shares as follows:

- On 1 April, four million shares in consideration for the majority holding in another entity; and

- On 1 July a rights issue of 1 for 6 at a price of £15 per share. The market price of Mitchell Bros shares immediately prior to the rights issue had been £20 per share.

A profit of £17 million attributable to the ordinary equity holders was reported for 20X5 and £14 million for 20X4.

The shares issued on the acquisition were issued at their full fair value.

Requirement

Calculate basic EPS for the year ended 31 December 20X5 and the basic EPS for the year ended 31 December 20X4, as restated in the 31 December 20X5 financial statements. **(6 marks)**

5 Boulton plc

Boulton plc had 3,600,000 ordinary shares in issue on 1 January 20X6. Its draft profit for the year ended 31 December 20X6 was £2,700,000, before considering the transactions below. In the previous year, Boulton plc reported a basic EPS of 80p.

On 1 April 20X6, Boulton plc issued 500,000 7% £10 convertible bonds at a discount to par of 5%. On 31 March 20X9 they can be either redeemed for cash at their par value or converted into ordinary shares at the rate of two new ordinary shares for each £10 bond. The proceeds of the convertible bond issue have been credited to non-current liabilities. Interest is payable annually in arrears on 31 March; interest has been accrued for the period to 31 December 20X6 and debited to finance costs. Boulton plc's advisors have calculated that the effective rate of interest on the bond is 9% per annum and that the effective rate of interest on an equivalent bond without the option to convert to ordinary shares would be 11% per annum.

On 1 July 20X6, the company made a rights issue at a price of £9.50 per share on the basis of one new share for every five shares previously held. The share price immediately prior to the rights issue being announced was £12.50 per share. The net cash received was correctly recorded in cash, capital and share premium account.

Requirements

(a) Explain how the convertible bond should be recognised on issue.

(b) Prepare journals to correct the accounting treatment of the convertible bond in the statement of financial position and income statement for the year ended 31 December 20X6.

(c) Calculate the revised profit for the year ended 31 December 20X6 after making any adjustments to profit deemed necessary.

(d) Calculate basic EPS for the year ended 31 December 20X6.

(e) Calculate the restated EPS for the year ended 31 December 20X5 as it should be disclosed in the financial statements to 31 December 20X6.

(f) Calculate diluted EPS for the year ended 31 December 20X6.

(14 marks)

Note:

Ignore taxation.

6 Totnes Group

The Totnes Group comprises Totnes plc and its 100% owned subsidiary, Holne Ltd. An analysis of the equity of Totnes plc, of Holne Ltd and of the group at 31 December 20X7 shows:

	Totnes plc £'000	Holne Ltd £'000	Totnes Group £'000
Share capital – 50p ordinary shares	100,000	40,000	100,000
Share premium	120,000	–	120,000
Revaluation surplus (Note 1)	25,000	20,000	45,000
Available-for-sale-reserve (Note 2)	(15,000)	35,000	20,000
Retained earnings (Note 3)	345,000	105,000	450,000
	575,000	200,000	735,000

Notes

(1)   The revaluation surplus relates to property, plant and equipment

(2)   The available-for-sale reserve relates to equities traded on a recognised exchange

(3)   Retained earnings comprise

	Totnes plc £'000	Holne Ltd £'000	Totnes Group £'000
Brought forward:			
Cumulative losses on investment properties	(40,000)	(15,000)	(55,000)
Other	235,000	90,000	325,000
	195,000	75,000	270,000
In the year:			
Gains on investment properties	10,000	5,000	15,000
Other	140,000	25,000	165,000
	150,000	30,000	180,000
Carried forward:			
Cumulative losses on investment properties	(30,000)	(10,000)	(40,000)
Other	375,000	115,000	490,000
	345,000	105,000	450,000

Requirement

Explain and calculate the maximum dividends per share which Totnes plc and Holne Ltd could pay at 31 December 20X7.   **(8 marks)**

Now go back to the Learning Objectives in the Introduction. If you are satisfied you have achieved these, please tick them off.

Technical reference

1 Earnings per share – calculation of earnings

- Basic EPS   IAS 33 (10)
- After preference dividends   IAS 33 (12 - 13)
- Cumulative preference dividends   IAS 33 (14)

2 Earnings per share – number of shares

- Weighted average number of shares   IAS 33 (19 – 20)
- Issue of shares for cash   IAS 33 (21 – 22)
- Bonus issue   IAS 33 (28)
- Rights issue   IAS 33 App A (A2)

3 Diluted earnings per share

- Adjustments required   IAS 33 (30 – 32)
- Adjustment to earnings   IAS 33 (33)
- Adjustment to number of shares   IAS 33 (36)
- Convertible debt terms – use that which gives greatest number of shares   IAS 33 (39)

4 Other

- Presentation   IAS 33 (66 – 69)
- Disclosure   IAS 33 (70)
- Additional EPS calculations   IAS 33 (73)

Answer to Interactive question 1

	£m
Profit attributable to owners of the parent	1,897
Less dividend on irredeemable preference shares	(400)
Profit attributable to ordinary equity holders of the parent	1,497

$$EPS = \frac{1,497}{6,241} = 24p \text{ per share}$$

Answer to Interactive question 2

	£m
Profit attributable to owners of the parent	82
Less one year's dividend on irredeemable preference shares (20 – 15)	(5)
Profit attributable to ordinary equity holders of the parent	77

$$EPS = \frac{77}{1,200} = 6.4p \text{ per share}$$

Answer to Interactive question 3

(a)   EPS originally reported in 20X4 (£6m/20m) = 30p

(b)   EPS reported in 20X5

The bonus issue is treated as having been issued at the start of 20X4 (the earliest reported period).

The adjusted weighted average number of shares for 20X4 is (20m x (2+1)/2) = 30m

The restated 20X4 EPS is (£6m /30m) = 20p

EPS for 20X5

Weighted average shares:

As the bonus issue came **after** the issue for cash at full market price, the 6 million new shares rank for the bonus issue.

	Weighted Av (million)
1 January – 31 May 20m x (2+1)/2 x 5/12	12.50
1 June – 31 December (20m + 6m) x ((2+1)/2) x 7/12 =	22.75
	35.25

EPS (£8m/35.25m) = 22.7p

Answer to Interactive question 4

Computation of theoretical ex-rights price (TERP).

	No	£
Pre-rights issue holding	4 @ 3.20	12.80
Rights share	1 @ 2.40	2.40
	5	15.20

$$TERP = \frac{£15.20}{5} = £3.04$$

Computation of bonus adjustment factor:

$$Adjustment = \frac{\text{Value of shares before rights}}{TERP} = \frac{320p}{304p}$$

Computation of basic EPS:

$$20X8 \text{ EPS} = \frac{£4m}{\left(10m \text{ shares} \times \left(\frac{320}{304}\right)\right)} = 38.0p$$

20X9 Earnings = £4.8 million

		Total
Weighted average shares		
1 Jan – 30 June	10m × 320/304 x 6/12	5,263,158
1 July – 31 Dec	10m × ((4+1) /4) x 6/12	6,250,000
		11,513,158

$$\text{EPS} = \frac{£4.8m}{11,513,158} = 41.7p$$

Answer to Interactive question 5

Basic EPS = £1m/4m = 25 pence

Diluted EPS

The **largest** number of additional shares is:

- (£5m/125) × 40 = 1,600,000
- (£5m/130) × 40 = 1,538,462
- (£5m/135) × 40 = 1,481,481

So 1,600,000.

	£
Earnings for basic EPS	1,000,000
Finance cost saved on conversion, net of tax (£4,800,000 × 8.5% × (100 – 20)%)	326,400
Earnings for diluted EPS	1,326,400
Shares for basic EPS	4,000,000
Additional shares on conversion	1,600,000
Shares for diluted EPS	5,600,000

$$\text{Diluted EPS} = \left(\frac{£1,326,400}{5,600,000}\right) = 23.7 \text{ pence}$$

Answer to Interactive question 6

(a) **Distributable profits at 1 January 20X2**

As Haver Ltd is a private limited company the profits available for distribution are defined as accumulated realised profits less accumulated realised losses. This is usually the balance on retained earnings, so £80,000.

Haver Ltd also has a share premium account of £40,000 (10,000 × (£5 - £1)) and a current revaluation surplus of £400,000, both of which are non-distributable.

(b) **Distributable profits at 31 December 20X2**

The £80,000 balance at the start of the year is increased by the £40,000 profits earned during the year, to £120,000.

The additional depreciation in the year on non-current assets is £16,000 (£400,000/25) and this is added, making total distributable profits of £136,000.

(c) **Revaluation surplus**

Each year Haver Ltd should transfer the extra £16,000 depreciation to retained earnings from the revaluation surplus.

Any revaluation surplus remaining when these assets are finally sold would then be realised and should be transferred to retained earnings in the statement of changes in equity.

ICAEW

1   **Lemon plc**

(a)   Basic EPS $= \dfrac{£4,697,000}{11,172,414}$ (W2)

$= 42.0 \text{ p}$

Diluted EPS $= \dfrac{£4,886,000 \text{ (W3)}}{14,628,414 \text{ (W4)}}$

$= 33.4 \text{ p}$

WORKINGS

(1)   *Theoretical ex-rights price*

	No.	Price	Total
Pre-rights	5	150p	750p
Rights	1	120p	120p
	6		870p

Theoretical ex-rights price = 870p/6 = 145p

Rights fraction = 150/145

(2)   *Weighted average number of shares in issue for year ending 30 September 20X7*

Date	Narrative	Shares	Time	Fraction	Weighted average
Oct 20X6 – March 20X7	B/F	10,000,000	$^6/_{12}$	150/145 (W1)	5,172,414
April – Sept 20X7	Rights issue				
	(10m × 6/5)	12,000,000	$^6/_{12}$		6,000,000
					11,172,414

(3)   *Earnings for diluted EPS*

Earnings for basic EPS	4,697,000
Add post tax interest saved (3,000,000 × 9%) × (1 – 0.30)	189,000
Earnings for diluted EPS	4,886,000

(4)   *Number of shares for diluted EPS*

Always use the largest number of shares per unit of convertible in this calculation.

	Number
Weighted average number of shares for basic EPS	11,172,414
Convertible loan 3,200,000/100 × 108	3,456,000
	14,628,414

(b)   **Historical information** presented in financial statements, is **not on its own particularly useful** for making economic decisions. **Forecasts** and projections for the future can be much more useful for **decision making**.

The **diluted** earnings per share figure provides limited **information about the future to current holders of shares**. Where financial instruments have been issued by a company which will potentially dilute the earnings in the future, the diluted EPS figure shows how the current earnings of the company would be diluted, or shared out, amongst the additional equity holders as well as the current equity holders. This gives the current equity holders an idea of the effect that these dilutive financial instruments may have on their shareholding in future.

However, there are **limitations** to the use of these figures. The most basic limitation is that the diluted EPS is based upon the **current earnings** figure which **may not be relevant in future years**. What is more important is the level of earnings at the time conversion actually takes place. Also, the calculation for **convertible loan stock assumes that all holders will convert** to ordinary shares rather than having their loan stock redeemed. Whether they will or not depends on the share price at the conversion date: is it more valuable to convert into shares or to wait for the redemption proceeds and reinvest them elsewhere?

2   **Denton plc**

The three million new shares issued at the time of the acquisition should be weighted from the date of issue, but the share consolidation should be related back to the start of the financial year (and to the start of any previous years presented as comparative figures).

The calculation of the weighted average number of shares in issue is as follows:

Date	No shares 000	Time	Bonus fraction	Weighted average
1 Jan 20X5	10,000	4/12	1/2	1,666,667
30 Apr 20X5	3,000			
	13,000	4/12	1/2	2,166,667
31 Aug 20X5	(6,500)			
	6,500	4/12		2,166,666
Weighted average				6,000,000

The previous year's EPS should be doubled by 2/1 (being the reciprocal of the bonus fraction above). In this example, the bonus fraction is less than 1, as it represents a share consolidation rather than an increase in the number of shares in issue.

3   **Silvers plc**

Earnings per share for 20X5 = $\dfrac{£14,000,000}{22,485,633}$ = 62.26p

Date	No shares 000	Time	Bonus fraction	Weighted average
1 Jan 20X5	20,000	7/12	(W) 600/580	12,068,966
1 Aug 20X5	5,000			
	25,000	5/12	–	10,416,667
Weighted average				22,485,633

WORKING

Calculation of theoretical ex-rights price (TERP) and bonus element.

	No	Price p	Total p
Pre-rights holding	4	600	2,400
Rights share	1	500	500
Post-rights holding	5		2,900

TERP = $\dfrac{2,900p}{5}$ = 580p

Future earnings are expected to be diluted to 580/600 compared to the pre-rights earnings. The number of shares prior to the rights issue should therefore be restated by the reciprocal of the expected future dilution of earnings, that is 600/580.

The previous year's reported EPS of 50p should be restated to 50p x (580/600) = 48.33p. This is the same as if the previous year's number of ordinary shares had been restated to 600/580 of the previous figure.

4 Mitchell Bros plc

The issue at full market price does not contain any bonus element (that is it is not expected to reduce/ dilute the future earnings potential of each share). It is therefore simply time apportioned.

The rights issue is priced below market price, which will dilute the future earnings potential of each ordinary share. There will need to be a retrospective adjustment to EPS to allow for this. This is achieved by calculating the bonus fraction and retrospectively increasing the number of ordinary shares prior to the rights issue occurring.

The calculation of the weighted average number of shares in issue is as follows:

Date	No shares 000	Time	Bonus fraction	Weighted average
1 Jan 20X5	14,000	3/12	(W) 20/19.29	3,628,823
1 Apr 20X5	4,000			
	18,000	3/12	(W) 20/19.29	4,665,630
1 July 20X5	3,000			
	21,000	6/12		10,500,000
Weighted average				18,794,453

The basic EPS for 20X5 is therefore £17 million / 18,794,453 = 90.45p.

The previous year's EPS should have been reported in the 20X4 financial statements as £14 million / 14 million = 100p per share. This should be restated as 100p x 19.29/ 20 = 96.45p.

WORKING

Calculation of theoretical ex-rights price (TERP) and bonus element.

	No	Price £	Total £
Pre-rights holding	6	20	120
Rights share	1	15	15
Post-rights holding	7		135

TERP = £135/ 7 = £19.29

The bonus element of this issue is therefore 20/ 19.29. This means that future EPS is expected to be 19.29/20 of the amount before the rights issue at below market price.

5 Boulton plc

(a) The convertible bond is a compound financial instrument per IAS 32 *Financial Instruments: Presentation*, in that it has both equity and liability components. It should be accounted for using 'split accounting'. The components should be measured and presented separately at the time of issue.

The liability component should be measured first, at the present value of the capital and interest payments. The discount rate used should be the effective interest rate for an instrument with the same terms and conditions except for the convertibility, so 11%.

	Cash flow £'000	Discount Factor @ 11%	Present value £'000
31 March X7	350	1/1.11	315
31 March X8	350	$1/1.11^2$	284
31 March X9	5,350	$1/1.11^3$	3,912
			4,511

The liability component should be measured at £4,511,000. The equity component should be calculated as the residual amount and measured at £239,000 ((£5m x 0.95) less £4.511m).

(b) The interest expense for the nine months the convertible bonds have been in issue should be calculated as 11% of the liability component, so £372,158 (£4.511m x 11% x 9/12). The accrued interest payable is £262,500 (£5m x 7% x 9/12). The carrying amount of the bonds at the period end and the interest expense for the period should be increased by the difference of £109,658.

The journals to correct the accounting treatment are therefore:

DR	Non-current liabilities	£239,000	
CR	Equity		£239,000
DR	Interest expense	£109,658	
CR	Non-current liabilities		£109,658

(c)

	£
Profit as currently drafted	2,700,000
Less additional interest on convertible bond	(109,658)
Revised profit	2,590,342

(d) Basic earnings = £2,590,342

The calculation of the weighted average number of shares in issue is as follows:

Date	No shares 000	Time	Bonus fraction	Weighted average
1 Jan	3,600	6/12	(W) 12.5/12	1,875,000
1 July (1 for 5)	720			
	4,320	6/12		2,160,000
				4,035,000

The basic EPS for 20X6 is therefore £2,590,342/ 4,035,000 = 64.2p

WORKING

Calculation of theoretical ex-rights price (TERP) and bonus element.

	No	Price £	Total £
Pre-rights holding	5	12.50	62.50
Rights share	1	9.50	9.50
Post-rights holding	6		72.00

TERP = £72/6 = £12.

(e) The 20X5 EPS of 80p should be restated by the reciprocal of the bonus fraction.

80p x 12/12.50 = 76.8p.

(f) Ignoring tax, if the convertibles had been converted on the date they were issued:

- Finance costs recognised as an expense in profit or loss would have been lower by £372,158.

- The weighted average number of shares in issue would have been increased by 750,000 (500,000 x 2 x 9/12).

The overall effect is as follows:

	Earnings	Number of shares
For basic EPS calculation	2,590,342	4,035,000
Re convertible bonds	372,158	750,000
	2,962,500	4,785,000

The diluted EPS is therefore $\dfrac{£2,962,500}{4,785,000}$ = 61.9p

6   Totnes Group

Distributable profits are calculated by reference to entity, not group, financial statements. So the calculation for Totnes plc is based on its own financial statements, not those of the group. They are calculated on a cumulative basis, not on the results of the current financial year.

To be distributable, profits should be realised.

The revaluation surplus relating to property, plant and equipment contains surpluses in respect of non-current assets still recognised in the statement of financial position; these are unrealised and therefore non-distributable (as are the balances on share capital and share premium).

The available-for-sale reserves relate to fair value adjustments in respect of equities traded on a recognised exchange. Such equities meet the test of being readily convertible into cash, so fair value adjustments to them are treated as realised.

Investment properties do not meet the test of being readily convertible into cash, so profits/losses arising from adjustment to their fair values are unrealised, even though they have been recognised in profit or loss. Any profits would be non-distributable.

Distributable profits for Holne Ltd, a private company, are accumulated realised profits less accumulated realised losses; for Totnes plc, a public company, they are accumulated realised profits less accumulated realised losses, less net unrealised losses.

The calculation of the maximum dividends per share is as follows.

	£'000	Totnes plc £'000	Holne Ltd £'000
Other retained earnings carried forward		375,000	115,000
Available-for-sale reserves		(15,000)	35,000
		360,000	150,000
Unrealised losses on investment properties	(30,000)		
Unrealised profits on property, plant and equipment	25,000		
Net unrealised losses		(5,000)	–
Distributable profits		355,000	150,000
Number of shares in issue (100,000 and 40,000 × 2)		200,000	80,000
Maximum dividend (distributable profits ÷ number of shares)		177.5p	187.5p

CHAPTER 10

Other standards

Introduction

Examination context

Topic List

1   IAS 2 *Inventories*

2   IAS 7 *Statement of Cash Flows*

3   IAS 10 *Events After the Reporting Period*

4   IAS 37 *Provisions, Contingent Liabilities and Contingent Assets*

5   UK GAAP comparison

Summary and Self-test

Technical reference

Answers to Interactive questions

Answers to Self-test

Introduction

Learning objectives

- Measure inventories in accordance with IFRS

- Prepare the statements of cash flow of an individual entity and a group of entities

- Distinguish between an adjusting event after the reporting period and a non-adjusting event after the reporting period

- Recognise and measure a provision

- Identify the circumstances in which a contingency is disclosed

Specific syllabus references for this chapter are: 1e, 3a, 4a and 4c.

Syllabus links

This chapter revisits the following accounting standards which were examined in the Financial Accounting paper:

- IAS 2 *Inventories*
- IAS 7 *Statement of Cash Flows*
- IAS 10 *Events After the Reporting Period*
- IAS 37 *Provisions, Contingent Liabilities and Contingent Assets*

There are only two minor areas of new knowledge covered:

- The treatment of the joint venture in the statement of cash flows
- The discounting of provisions

A detailed understanding of these standards will also be expected at the Advanced Stage.

Examination context

In the examination, candidates may be required to:

- Assess the impact of the accounting policy selected for inventories on the financial statements
- Interpret information presented in a statement of cash flows
- Explain and apply the treatment of events after the reporting period
- Advise on the appropriate treatment of provisions, contingent liabilities and contingent assets

1 IAS 2 *Inventories*

Section overview

This section provides an overview of IAS 2 *Inventories* which was covered in full in Financial Accounting and puts it into a context for Financial Reporting.

1.1 Review of material covered in Financial Accounting

1.1.1 Valuation of inventories

Inventories shall be measured at the **lower of**:

- Cost
- Net realisable value

taking each item of inventory separately (in practice each group/category of items separately).

1.1.2 Allowable costs per IAS 2

The **cost** of inventories shall comprise all of the **costs of purchase, costs of conversion** and **other costs** incurred in bringing the inventories to their **present location and condition**.

- Costs of conversion include a **systematic allocation** of fixed and variable production overheads incurred in converting materials into finished goods.

  The allocation of fixed production overheads is based on **normal capacity** (average over a number of seasons under normal circumstances). In periods of abnormally high production fixed overhead **unit allocations are reduced** to avoid measuring inventories above cost.

- **Other costs** can include costs such as the non-production overheads of designing a product for a specific customer.

  Cost of inventory **excludes** costs of storing finished goods and selling them.

Interactive question 1: Production overheads [Difficulty level: Easy]

Manufacturer Ltd has budgeted as follows for the year to 31 December 20X8:

Production in units	25,000 per month
Indirect production overhead recovery rate	£3 per unit

During the year overhead costs were in line with budget but production was disrupted by technical difficulties. Production levels were therefore as follows:

Jan-May	25,000 units per month
June	15,000 units
July	40,000 units
August-December	25,000 units per month

Requirement

Calculate the amount of indirect production overheads which should be recognised in cost of inventories.

See **Answer** at the end of this chapter.

1.1.3 Determining cost – items not interchangeable

IAS 2 requires specific identification of individual costs for items that are not ordinarily interchangeable.

Estimation techniques may be used for convenience if the results **approximate to actual costs**. Examples of estimation methods include:

- **Standard cost**: Cost is based on **normal** levels of materials and supplies, labour efficiency and capacity utilisation. Standard costs should be regularly reviewed and revised where necessary.

- **Retail method**: Cost is determined by reducing the sales value of the inventory by the appropriate percentage gross margin. The percentage used takes into consideration inventory which has been marked down to below its original selling price. Often used in the retail industry for measuring inventories of rapidly changing items that have similar margins.

1.1.4 Determining cost – interchangeable items

If various batches of inventories have been manufactured or purchased at different prices, it may be impossible to determine precisely which items are still held at the year end and therefore what the actual cost of the goods was. In such circumstances, the following cost formulas should be used as estimation techniques:

- **FIFO** (first in, first out)

  Assumption: the quantities in hand represent the latest purchases or production

  OR

- **Weighted average cost**

  Total cost divided by the total number purchased/produced. The unit cost is recalculated on a periodic basis or as each additional shipment is received.

The use of the LIFO (last in first out) method is **not** permitted.

An entity should use the same cost formula for all inventories having a similar nature and use to the entity.

1.1.5 Net realisable value

Net realisable value (NRV) is the estimated selling price in the ordinary course of business less:

- Estimated costs of completion, and
- Estimated costs necessary to make the sale (for example marketing, selling and distribution costs).

NRV is based on:

- The contracted price, rather than ordinary selling price, if the inventory is held to meet a firm contract

- The selling price in the specific market in which the inventory is intended to be sold

  For example, if the selling prices are £40 in the domestic market and £25 in the overseas market, NRV for inventory held for sale overseas should be based on £25. Costs to sell may also be higher overseas, for example higher transport costs.

Point to note:

Fair value (which is the price between knowledgeable willing parties in an arm's length transaction) is not used as the basis for measuring inventory. Fair value takes account of prices in the market as a whole, whereas, as noted above, the estimated selling price in the ordinary course of business takes account of prices in the particular market in which the inventory is intended to be sold.

Interactive question 2: Measurement   [Difficulty level: Easy]

Production Ltd provides the following information about the standard cost of its inventories at 31 December 20X7:

	Product X £	Product Y £	Product Z £
Manufacturing cost	120	320	235
Selling price	180	360	270
Sales commission	(18)	(36)	(40)
Other selling costs	(20)	(10)	(25)

Calculate the carrying amount of inventories at 31 December 20X7.

See **Answer** at the end of this chapter.

1.2 Context

Inventories are often the most significant current assets carried in an entity's statement of financial position. Entities generally try to minimise the amount of capital invested in the operating cycle, and therefore in inventories, while still being in a position to meet customer demand. The industry in which entities operate is a crucial factor; manufacturers concentrate on the whole production cycle from raw materials through work in progress to finished goods, but retailers may principally be concerned with fashions in consumer demand, trying to predict, influence and capitalise on changing trends. Other factors influencing inventory levels are:

* Purchasing economies of scale, supply and demand economics
* The need to hold buffer stocks to cope with unpredicted changes in demand
* Building up inventories in advance of the launch of new products.

Inventory buying policies have a direct impact on cash management within a business as well as on obsolescence risk. Obsolescence risk depends on the products an entity sells and increases when they are based on the latest technology, fashion, seasonal demand or perishability. Inventories are the core to many businesses, so decisions driving inventory buying and holding policies will be fundamental to the success of those businesses.

1.3 Judgements required

IAS 2 sets out basic principles and application guidance for inventory measurement, but detailed application still requires significant judgements on the part of management in the following areas:

* The use of cost formulas
* The identification of estimated selling prices in the ordinary course of business
* Estimation of costs to complete and selling costs
* The grouping of different items of inventory when applying the lower of cost and NRV rule.

It is important that clear policies and procedures are established in these areas and that they are applied consistently from period to period. In certain business segments obsolescence risk can change from period to period as market demand patterns change, so it is particularly important that estimates of obsolescence are based upon external market factors, rather than on any desire to arrive at inventory levels which result in a desired profit level.

1.4 Relevance of information for users

Users of financial statements will be aware of the effect on profit of the measurement of inventories: £1 more inventory results in £1 more profit, with consequential beneficial effects on return on capital employed and gearing. Users will study carefully the information which IAS 2 requires to be disclosed, particularly:

- The **accounting policies** adopted in measuring inventories including the cost formulas used
- The total carrying amount of inventories **in classifications appropriate to the entity**
- The amount of inventories **recognised as an expense** during the period
- The amount of any **write-down to NRV** recognised as an expense in the period

No disclosure is required of how reporting entities assess their obsolescence risk, a shortcoming which is not helpful to users.

2 IAS 7 *Statement of Cash Flows*

Section overview

This section provides an overview of IAS 7 *Statement of Cash Flows* which was covered in detail in Financial Accounting and puts it into a context for Financial Reporting.

2.1 Review of material covered in Financial Accounting

The level of knowledge in respect of the preparation of statements of cash flows in the Financial Reporting examination is the same as for the Financial Accounting examination. However, the key in Financial Reporting is to be able to analyse and interpret a consolidated statement of cash flows and Chapter 11 looks at this in more detail. It is unlikely that you will have to prepare a full statement of cash flows but you may well have to prepare extracts from one.

2.1.1 Preparation of the statement of cash flows

The statement of cash flows provides historical information about the **changes in cash and cash equivalents**.

Definitions

Cash: Comprises cash on hand and demand deposits.

Cash equivalents: Short-term highly liquid investments that are readily convertible into known amounts of cash and which are subject to an insignificant risk of changes in value.

Cash flows are categorised under three headings:

- **Operating** activities
- **Investing** activities
- **Financing** activities

Cash flows from interest and dividends received and paid should be disclosed separately, but an entity can choose under which of the three headings to present them, as long as classification is consistent from one period to another.

Cash flows from taxes on income should be disclosed separately under the operating activities heading, unless they specifically relate to items presented under the other two headings.

Cash flows in respect of finance leases should be separated into their interest and capital components.

There are **two** methods for presenting cash flows from **operating activities**:

- The indirect method
- The direct method

Point to note:

IAS 7 'encourages' entities to use the direct method, but few UK companies do so.

Illustration of a statement of cash flows using the indirect method

	31 December 20X8	
	£'000	£'000
Cash flows from operating activities		
Cash generated from operations (see below)	2,550	
Interest paid	(270)	
Income taxes paid	(900)	
Net cash from operating activities		1,380
Cash flows from investing activities		
Purchase of property, plant and equipment	(900)	
Proceeds from sale of property, plant and equipment	20	
Interest received	200	
Dividends received	200	
Net cash used in investing activities		(480)
Cash flows from financing activities		
Proceeds from issue of share capital	250	
Proceeds from issue of long-term borrowings	250	
Payments of finance lease liabilities	(90)	
Dividends paid	(1,200)	
Net cash used in financing activities		(790)
Net increase in cash and cash equivalents		110
Cash and cash equivalents at beginning of period		120
Cash and cash equivalents at end of period		230

Reconciliation of profit before tax to cash generated from operations for the year ended 31 December 20X8.

	£'000
Profit before tax	3,390
Finance cost	400
Investment income	(500)
Depreciation charge	450
Increase in trade and other receivables	(500)
Decrease in inventories	1,050
Decrease in trade payables	(1,740)
Cash generated from operations	2,550

Using the **direct method** cash flows from operating activities are calculated as follows:

	£
Cash flows from operating activities	
Cash receipts from customers	X
Cash paid to suppliers and employees	(X)
Cash generated from operations	X

Interactive question 3: Statement of cash flows   [Difficulty level: Intermediate]

Precipitate Ltd statement of financial position at 30 April 20X7

	20X7		20X6	
	£'000	£'000	£'000	£'000
Non-current assets (Note)		491		643
Current assets				
Inventories	773		591	
Trade receivables	792		598	
Bank	133		117	
		1,698		1,306
		2,189		1,949

	20X7 £'000	£'000	20X6 £'000	£'000
Equity				
Share capital		820		720
Retained earnings		259		71
		1,079		791
Non-current liabilities				
9% debentures		416		555
Current liabilities				
Bank	297		162	
Trade payables	286		401	
Income tax	111		40	
		694		603
		2,189		1,949

Note: Non-current assets

	£'000
Freehold land	
At cost 30 April 20X6	455
At cost 30 April 20X7	340

Land originally costing £235,000 was sold during the year for £425,000.

Plant and equipment

	Cost £'000	Depreciation £'000
On 30 April 20X6	282	94
Additions at cost	53	–
Disposals (proceeds £99,000)	(109)	(25)
Charge for the year	–	6
On 30 April 20X7	226	75

Income statement for the year ended 30 April 20X7

	£'000
Revenue	2,930
Operating expenses	(2,806)
Profit from operations	124
Profit on sale of non-current assets	205
	329
Finance costs	(39)
Profit before tax	290
Income taxes	(102)
Profit for the period	188

Requirement

Prepare the statement of cash flows using the indirect method for the year ended 30 April 20X7.

See **Answer** at the end of this chapter.

2.1.2 Consolidated statement of cash flows

The consolidated statement of cash flows should disclose only those flows to/from parties outside the group. This is achieved by applying the single entity techniques with some additional adjustments.

Dividends in respect of non-controlling interest and associates

The cash flows to be disclosed are those in respect of dividends paid to the non-controlling interest (NCI) and received from associates, rather than the share of earnings presented in the statement of comprehensive income. The reconciliation schedule supporting the indirect method commences with the profit before tax, which:

- Includes associates on an earnings basis. So a deduction should be made for those earnings (addition if a loss) in the reconciliation and the dividends received should be presented as a separate item under cash flows from investing activities

- Is before the attribution of profit/loss to the NCI. No adjustment is necessary in the reconciliation, but the dividend paid to the NCI should be presented as a separate item under cash flows from financing activities.

Interactive question 4: Statement of cash flows [Difficulty level: Intermediate]

Consolidated statement of comprehensive income (extract)

	£'000
Year ended 31 December 20X7	
Profit from operations	98
Share of profit of associates	22
Profit before tax	120
Income tax expense	(40)
Profit for year	80

Profit attributable to:	
Owners of the parent	60
Non-controlling interest	20
	80

Consolidated statement of financial position (extracts) as at 31 December

	20X7 £'000	20X6 £'000
Investments in associates	150	144
Non-controlling interest	408	400

Calculate the dividends paid to the non-controlling interest and received from associates during 20X7.

See **Answer** at the end of this chapter.

Subsidiaries/associates acquired/disposed of

Payments (receipts) of cash to acquire (dispose of) an interest in a subsidiary or an associate should be presented under cash flow from investing activities.

Only consideration in the form of cash should be included. Any consideration in the form of shares or loan stock (quite often the case in the acquisition of a subsidiary) should be excluded, although in the case of a subsidiary the notes should disclose:

*   The **total purchase/disposal consideration** (including how much was discharged by cash and cash equivalents)

*   The **assets, liabilities, and cash and cash equivalents acquired/disposed of**.

Point to note:

In the case of a subsidiary acquired or disposed of, the cash flow should be reduced by the cash and cash equivalents held by the subsidiary at the date of acquisition/disposal. So if a subsidiary holding £100,000 in cash is acquired for £2.8 million, the cash outflow to be presented under investing activities is £2.7 million, the amount by which consolidated cash and cash equivalents has been reduced.

Illustration: Consolidated statement of cash flows – investing activities

This section presents the cash flows relating to investing activities, including the disposal of a subsidiary and the acquisition of an investment in an associate, for the year ended 31 December 20X5.

	£'000
Cash flows from investing activities	
Interest received	2,329
Dividends received from associate	10,000
Disposal of subsidiary (Note)	6,700
Proceeds on disposal of property, plant and equipment	8,342
Purchases of property, plant and equipment	(18,700)
Acquisition of investment in an associate	(29,567)
Net cash used in investing activities	(20,896)

Note: Disposal of subsidiary

On 31 October 20X5 the Group sold its subsidiary Remit Limited. The net assets of Remit Limited at the date of disposal were as follows:

	£'000
Property, plant and equipment	9,125
Inventories	876
Trade receivables	10,133
Cash and cash equivalents	1,300
Income tax liability	(4,246)
Trade payables	(12,554)
Attributable goodwill	1,500
	6,134
Gain on disposal	7,897
Total consideration	14,031

Satisfied by:

	£'000
Cash	8,000
Deferred consideration	6,031
	14,031

Net cash inflow arising on disposal:

Cash consideration	8,000
Cash and cash equivalents disposed of	(1,300)
Net cash flow	6,700

When a subsidiary is acquired (disposed of), consolidated assets and liabilities other than cash are increased (decreased) by the subsidiary's assets at the date of acquisition (disposal). The adjustments needed to compute cash flows are:

- Acquisition: calculate the change in each asset and liability in the normal way, then **reduce** it by new subsidiary's amount at the acquisition date

- Disposal: calculate the change in each asset and liability in the normal way, then **increase** it by old subsidiary's amount at the acquisition date.

One of the liabilities to be adjusted for in this way is the NCI at the acquisition/disposal date.

Interactive question 5: Acquisition of subsidiary (1)　　　　[Difficulty level: Intermediate]

Newton plc acquired 100% of Abbott Ltd by issuing 500,000 £1 shares at an agreed value of £3.00 and £400,000 in cash. At the date of acquisition Abbott Ltd's net assets included cash and cash equivalents of £60,000 and property, plant and equipment of £500,000.

At its next year end Newton plc's consolidated statement of financial position included property, plant and equipment with a carrying amount of £1,400,000 (comparative figure: £800,000). There were no disposals of property, plant and equipment in the year and the depreciation expense was £50,000.

Requirement

Calculate the amounts to be disclosed under cash flows from investing activities.

See **Answer** at the end of this chapter.

Interactive question 6: Acquisition of a subsidiary (2)　　　　[Difficulty level: Intermediate]

Note to financial statements

Acquisition of subsidiary

On 1 September 20X5, the Group acquired 80% of the issued share capital of BB Limited. The consideration was cash of £2 million and 300,000 ordinary shares with a fair value of £3 each. At the acquisition date the fair values of the assets and liabilities acquired were:

	1 September 20X5
	£'000
Property, plant and equipment	8,050
Inventories	3,550
Trade receivables	5,300
Bank and cash balances	1,300
Trade payables	(17,100)
	1,100

At the acquisition date the non-controlling interest was measured at its share of these fair values.

Requirement

Prepare the supporting note to the consolidated statement of cash flows for the acquisition of the subsidiary.

See **Answer** at the end of this chapter.

2.2 Joint ventures

Joint ventures were covered in Chapter 8.

A joint venture accounted for under the equity method should be reported in the consolidated statement of cash flows in the same way as an associate is.

Where the joint venture has been accounted for under the **proportionate consolidation method** the consolidated statement of cash flows should report the **group share of the Joint venture's cash flows in each relevant line item**.

2.3 Context

Cash flow information is integral to investment and credit decisions. Corporations involved in reporting scandals often boasted strong earnings growth but poor cash flows. As a result their stock prices had often fallen dramatically even before the announcement of alleged accounting scandals; many analysts attributed this to a period of continuous significant cash outflows.

Modern performance measures such as free cash flow, cash value added and cash flow return on investment are increasingly used as benchmarks of business performance. Each is derived from the statement of cash flows and they are used in close correlation with earnings related measures.

Businesses can manipulate cash flows in the short–term by running down inventories, tightening credit control policies or delaying payments. Each of these has potentially detrimental effects on business relationships and the supply chain. They are not long-term solutions.

2.4 Judgements required

A maxim often quoted is that 'earnings are an opinion; cash flows are fact'. After all, the cash and cash equivalents at the end of each reporting period are a question of fact, and therefore the change in them over a year is a matter of fact and not subject to any estimation techniques.

The key judgement involved in the preparation of statements of cash flows is in the definition of cash and cash equivalents. Other than that, there are no significant judgements to be made in adjusting the amounts in the statement of comprehensive income, the statement of changes in equity and the statement of financial position to arrive at the cash flow figures.

2.5 Relevance of information for users

The statement of cash flows provides the important information needed by users as to how good the entity is at generating cash. The analysis of cash flows under the three headings of operating, investing and financing activities enables users to make assessments of the success of the business in generating cash (through operating activities), in laying the foundations of future cash generation (investing activities) and in funding the overall activities of the entity in an efficient way (financing activities). The disclosure, required by IAS 7, of the components of cash and cash equivalents and a reconciliation of the statement of cash flows amount to the relevant statement of financial position items gives a useful insight into what management regards as the cash balances it needs to manage.

The information provided is therefore essential to making projections as to cash generation in the future. It also helps users assess whether the entity is suffering such net cash outflows as to raise questions as to its future solvency.

3   IAS 10 *Events After the Reporting Period*

 Section overview

This section provides an overview of IAS 10 *Events after the Reporting Period* which was covered in full in Financial Accounting and puts it into a context for Financial Reporting.

3.1   Review of material covered in Financial Accounting

 Definition

Events after the reporting period: events, both favourable and unfavourable, which occur between the end of the reporting period and the date on which the financial statements are **authorised for issue**.

There are two types of events after the reporting period:

- **Adjusting events after the reporting period** which provide evidence of conditions which existed at the end of the reporting period.

- **Non-adjusting events after the reporting period** are those that are indicative of conditions that arose after the reporting period.

3.1.1   Accounting treatment

Adjusting events after the reporting period – an entity should **adjust the amounts recognised** in its financial statements.

Non-adjusting events after the reporting period – an entity should **not adjust** the amounts recognised in its financial statements

Dividends declared on equity instruments **after the reporting period** should not be recognised as a liability at the end of the reporting period because no obligation exists at that date.

An entity **should not prepare its financial statements on a going concern basis** if management determines after the reporting period either that it intends to liquidate the entity or to cease trading, or that it has no realistic alternative but to do so.

3.1.2   Disclosure

An entity should disclose the date when the financial statements were **authorised for issue** and who gave the authorisation.

If non-adjusting events after the reporting period are **material**, non-disclosure could influence the decisions of users taken on the basis of the financial statements. Accordingly, the following should be disclosed for each **material category** of non-adjusting event after the reporting period:

- The **nature** of the event; and
- An estimate of its **financial effect**, or statement that such an estimate cannot be made.

Interactive question 7: Building defects
[Difficulty level: Intermediate]

A routine inspection of an entity's main freehold building two weeks after its year end of 30 June 20X8 revealed substantial cracks in the walls. A more detailed review was immediately undertaken by specialist professionals, who reported that there were major problems with the foundations. In their view these problems must have arisen several years ago, even though the visible evidence had only now come to light.

Requirement

Explain how this event should be dealt with in the financial statements for the year ended 30 June 20X8.

See **Answer** at the end of this chapter.

Interactive question 8: Inventories
[Difficulty level: Easy]

At its year end of 30 June 20X8 an entity held in inventories 4,000 units of a particular product line at a cost of £550 each. The product had been selling well, at £750 each with selling costs of £100 each.

Early in its new financial year the entity learnt that competitor action was such that it could only sell its product for £605, with selling costs unchanged.

Requirement

Explain how this event should be dealt with in the financial statements for the year ended 30 June 20X8.

See **Answer** at the end of this chapter.

3.2 Context and relevance of information for users

Financial statements are, by their very nature, prepared to a specific historical date. The process of preparing them can lead to a significant amount of time passing between the end of the reporting period and the publication date. Regardless of how quickly the financial statements are published, there will be a period of time before publication, during which further events and transactions will take place.

Events that take place after the reporting period often provide further information on the financial position at the end of the reporting period. It is therefore reasonable that such information should be reflected in the financial statements.

Events may also arise prior to the publication of the financial statements that do not provide information on the financial position at the end of the reporting period but do have an impact on the operations of the entity in future periods. Where non-disclosure of such events is likely to influence the economic decisions of users of the financial statements, an explanation of the events should be included in the financial statements. For example, the sale of a significant operation after the year end could be key information for a user who is basing future earnings, cash flow and solvency forecasts on the financial statements.

IAS 10's requirement to disclose not just the nature but the financial effect of events occurring after the reporting period provides information which users should evaluate carefully.

4 IAS 37 *Provisions, Contingent Liabilities and Contingent Assets*

Section overview

This section provides an overview of IAS 37 *Provisions, Contingent Liabilities and Contingent Assets* which was covered in full in Financial Accounting and puts it into a context for Financial Reporting.

4.1 Review of material covered in Financial Accounting

4.1.1 Provisions

Definition

A **provision** is a liability of uncertain timing or amount.

A provision should be recognised when:

- An entity has a present obligation as a result of a past event
- It is probable that an outflow of economic resources will be required to settle the obligation
- A reliable estimate can be made of the amount of the obligation

An obligation can be:

- **Legal** or
- **Constructive**

Definitions

A **legal obligation** is an obligation which derives from a contract, legislation or other operation of law.

A **constructive obligation** is an obligation that derives from an entity's actions where:

- By an established pattern of past practice, published policies or a sufficiently specific current statement, the entity has indicated to other parties that it will accept certain responsibilities; and

- As a result, the entity has created a valid expectation on the part of those other parties that it will discharge those responsibilities.

The amount recognised should be the **best estimate** of the expenditure required to settle the obligation at the end of the reporting period. The effect is that it should be re-estimated each year until settlement.

Points to note:

1   A provision should only be used for the expenditure for which it was originally set up. Using it to cover some other event would reduce information, by masking the separate effects of different events.

2   A provision for work to be carried out in the future should be reduced by changes in technology expected to be in place before the work is carried out, but only when there is expert, independent evidence to support this expectation.

3   Gains expected to arise on future disposals of assets should not be taken into account in measuring a provision, but accounted for when the assets are actually derecognised.

4   Any reimbursement, such as the proceeds of an insurance claim, should be recognised only when receipt is virtually certain. The amount should not exceed the provision and should be presented separately as an asset, not netted off against the liability. (In the income statement the provision less the reimbursement may be presented as the net expense.)

Specific types of expenditure should be dealt with as follows:

Future operating losses	Provisions should **not** be recognised for future operating losses – there has been no past event.
Onerous contracts (a contract in which unavoidable costs of completing the contract exceed the benefits expected to be received)	The **present obligation** under the contract should be recognised – the past event was the signing of the contract.

Restructuring costs	A provision should only be recognised when the entity has a **constructive obligation** to restructure: • It has a **detailed formal plan** to restructure • It has **raised valid expectations** in those affected that it will carry out the restructuring, either by starting to implement the plan or announcing its main features to those affected A restructuring provision should only include **direct expenditures** arising from the restructuring and which are: • Necessarily entailed by the restructuring and • Not associated with the ongoing activities of the entity So staff retraining and relocation costs should not be included in the provision.
Decommissioning and other environment restoration costs	A provision should only be recognised **from the date on which the obligating event occurs**. Taking a mining business as an example, obligations for future restoration costs incurred as a result of installing extraction equipment should be provided for at the time of installation, but obligations for similar costs resulting from extraction activities which take place in future periods should be provided for in those future periods, not in the current period.

Interactive question 9: Onerous contract [Difficulty level: Intermediate]

You have a contract to buy 300 metres of silk from India Co each month for £18 per metre. From each metre of silk you make one silk dress. You also incur labour and other direct variable costs of £16 per dress.

Usually you can sell each dress for £40 but in late July 20X8 the market price falls to £28. You are considering ceasing production since you think that the market may not improve.

If you decide to cancel the silk purchase contract without two months' notice, you must pay a cancellation penalty of £2,400 for each of the next two months.

Requirements

(a) Is there a present obligation at 31 July 20X8?

(b) What amounts should be recognised in respect of the contract in your financial statements for the period ending 31 July 20X8?

See **Answer** at the end of this chapter.

4.1.2 Contingent liabilities

Definition

A **contingent liability** is:

• A possible obligation that arises from past events and whose existence will be confirmed only by the occurrence or non-occurrence of one or more uncertain future events not wholly within the control of the entity or

• A present obligation that arises from past events but is not recognised because:

– It is not probable that an outflow of resources embodying economic benefits will be required to settle the obligation or

– The amount of the obligation cannot be measured with sufficient reliability.

An entity should **not** recognise a contingent liability.

A contingent liability is **disclosed** unless the possibility of an outflow of economic benefit is **remote**.

The following disclosures are required:

*   **Nature** of the contingent liability
*   Estimate of its **financial effect**
*   Indication with regard to any **uncertainties**
*   Possibility of **re-imbursement**

4.1.3 Decision tree

The following diagram summarises the treatment of provisions and contingent liabilities.

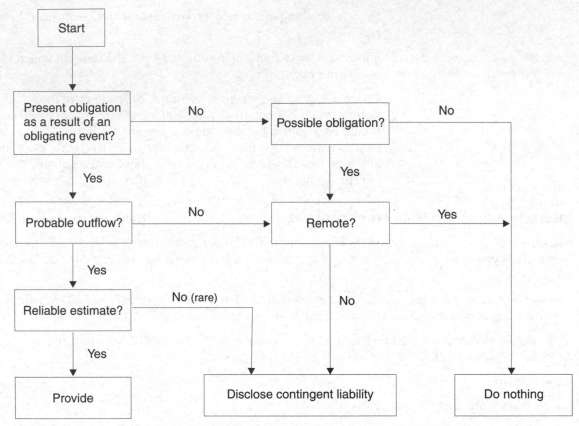

Interactive question 10: Recognition and measurement   [Difficulty level: Intermediate]

(1) Conditional Ltd issued a one year guarantee for faulty workmanship on a single item of specialist equipment that it delivered to a customer. At the company's year end, the company is being sued by the customer for refusing to replace or repair the item of equipment within the guarantee period. Conditional believes the fault is not covered by the guarantee, but instead has arisen because the customer did not follow the operating instructions.

The company's lawyer has advised Conditional that it is more likely than not that the company will be found liable. This would result in the company being forced to replace or repair the equipment plus pay court costs and damages amounting to approximately £20,000.

Based on past experience with similar items of equipment, the company estimates that there is a 70% chance that the central core would need to be replaced, which would cost £80,000, and a 30% chance that the repair would only cost about £30,000.

(2) The company also manufactures small items of equipment which it sells via a retail network. The company sold 15,000 items of this type this year, which also carry a one year guarantee against failure. Based on past experience, 5% of items sold are returned for repair or replacement. In each case, one third of the items returned can be repaired at a cost of £100, while the remaining two-thirds are scrapped and replaced. The manufacturing cost of a replacement item is £300.

Requirement

Discuss the accounting treatment of the above situations.

See **Answer** at the end of this chapter.

4.1.4 Contingent assets

Definition

Contingent asset: A probable asset that arises from past events and whose existence will be confirmed only by the occurrence or non-occurrence of one or more uncertain future events not wholly within the control of the entity.

A contingent asset should **not** be recognised. When the realisation of profit is virtually certain, the asset is no longer contingent and should be recognised.

A contingent asset is **disclosed where an inflow of economic benefit is probable**.

The following should be disclosed:

- Description of the **nature** of the contingent asset
- Estimate of the **financial effect**.

4.2 Discounting

Where the effect of the **time value of money** on the measurement of provisions **is material**, provisions should be **discounted**. By doing so provisions are recognised at the present value of expenditures expected to be required to settle the obligation.

Over the period between the recognition of a provision and its ultimate settlement, the provision should be increased each year by the discount rate. The increase should be recognised as a finance cost in profit or loss, not as a further expense under the line item where the original provision was charged.

Points to note:

1   The entity's average borrowing rate **should not** be used as the discount rate. The discount rate should be pre-tax and reflect current market rates of the time value of money and the risks specific to the liability.

2   The discount rate should not be risk-adjusted if the cash flows already take account of this.

This is relevant when risk is being incorporated directly in cash flows (for example a potential outflow may be increased to reflect its greater risk). When this has been done, adding a risk premium to the discount rate would be double-counting the risk effect.

3   Disclosure should be made of the **increase during the period in the discounted amount** arising from the passage of time and the **effect of any change** in the discount rate.

Worked example: Discounting

A company has a present obligation at 31 December 20X6, which it expects to settle in three years' time for £100,000. The rate which reflects the time value of money and the risks specific to the liability is 10%.

At what amount should the provision be measured at 31 December 20X6? How much should be recognised as a finance charge in each of the three years ending 31 December 20X7, 20X8 and 20X9? What accounting entry is required to record the finance charge in the year ending 31 December 20X7?

Solution

The provision should be measured at its present value at 31 December 20X6, that is £100,000/(1.1)^3 = £75,131.

The finance charge in each of the three years is calculated as:

	Balance b/f £	Finance cost @ 10% £	Balance c/f 31 Dec £
20X7	75,131	7,513	82,644
20X8	82,644	8,264	90,908
20X9	90,908	9,092	100,000

The accounting entry to record the finance charge in 20X7 is:

DR	Finance costs in profit or loss	£7,513	
CR	Provisions		£7,513

Interactive question 11: Discounting
[Difficulty level: Intermediate]

At 31 December 20X8 a company has an obligation in respect of costs that will be payable in ten years' time arising from the restoration of land subject to quarrying and which satisfies the criteria for a provision as set out in IAS 37. The costs in ten years' time are estimated at £1.2m.

Some asset disposals are anticipated that should help defray some of the anticipated costs and they are estimated at £0.2m in ten years' time. It is possible that new site-cleaning technology might reduce the anticipated costs to £1m. The relevant discount rate has been assessed as 9%.

Requirement

Calculate the finance cost to be recognised as an expense in the year ended 31 December 20X9.

See **Answer** at the end of this chapter.

4.3 Context

Business analysts and investors see earnings as a key performance measure. In addition, management may have substantial proportions of their remuneration based on earnings performance or share price movements which can be heavily dependent on financial results. The manipulation of earnings is a significant financial reporting issue given the pressure on management to deliver 'the numbers'.

Prior to the introduction of accounting rules the manipulation of provisions was a common method of managing earnings. US studies at that time showed that provision (or reserve) accounting was present in over 25% of the cases of earnings manipulation. As an example, the Xerox Corporation once paid a $10 million fine and restated three years of financial statements after being charged by the Securities and Exchange Commission with flattering its results by releasing almost $500 million of excess provisions, originally established for some other purpose, to income, without making full disclosures of these releases.

The manipulation of provisions was undertaken for a wide range of reasons, such as to smooth earnings, to meet the expectations of lenders and to enhance business valuations, including public offerings. A practice common in the UK in the 1980s and 1990s was to set aside provisions for future costs, often those associated with a fundamental restructuring, which were known to be excessive. The unused amounts were then released, to the benefit of future earnings. In some cases where there was a change in senior management, the need to restructure and the associated provisions were placed at the door of past mismanagement, while the new management claimed the credit for the improved future earnings, some of which arose only as a result of the write-back of the excess provisions they themselves had set up.

4.4 Judgements required

The application of the principles of IAS 37 in setting up and revising the amounts of provisions requires a great deal of estimation and judgement on the part of management. This is an area where it is vital that clear and comprehensive policies and procedures are laid down and then applied consistently from one period to another.

Even then, the carrying amounts of provisions are estimates of the effect of uncertain future events, so it is entirely legitimate for different people to take different views. The important objective is to make estimates which are neutral in terms of the information provided, rather than designed to achieve a pre-determined profit or net asset figure. The integrity of management as a factor in financial statement preparation can never be overlooked.

4.5 Relevance of information for users

The key principle underlying IAS 37 is that an entity is required to recognise provisions on the basis of its obligations, rather than its management's intentions. This requirement has improved the usefulness of information in financial statements, which should provide a more faithful representation of the entity's activities during the reporting period. Of course, the IAS is dealing with matters which are by their nature uncertain, so users of financial statements should study carefully the disclosures in respect of:

- The movements in provisions over the year, which should include any amounts previously provided which are written back as no longer being needed

- The nature of each class of obligation and the expected timing of outflows in respect of it. This timing information will be very useful in making cash flow projections

- An indication of the uncertainties as to the amounts and timings of outflows, together with the assumptions (in respect of the benefits of future new technology, for example) used

These extensive disclosures and explanations surrounding the uncertainties and estimates used in assessing provisions allow users to focus on the creation, use and reversal to profit or loss of provisions. They should then be able to make calculations of past return on capital employed and gearing and projections of these measures into the future which can sensibly be used as a basis for making economic decisions.

5 UK GAAP comparison

Section overview

In the UK cash flow statements are dealt with in FRS 1 *Cash Flow Statements*.

5.1 Statement of cash flows

The key differences are as follows:

UK GAAP	IAS 7
Scope: certain entities **exempt**	Applies to **all entities**
Shows change in **cash** which includes deposits repayable on demand	Shows change in **cash and cash equivalents**, a wider category
In effect cash equivalents are dealt with under 'management of liquid resources'	
Nine headings in the statement	**Three** headings in the statement
Operating activities Dividends from JVs and associates Returns on investments and servicing of finance Taxation	Operating activities

UK GAAP	IAS 7
Capital expenditure and financial investment Acquisitions and disposals	Investing activities
Equity dividends Management of liquid resources Financing	Financing activities
Specific requirements as to where certain items should appear, eg interest paid should be under returns on investments and servicing of finance	More flexibility as to where these items are presented; interest paid can be under any of the three headings

5.2 Other standards

There are **no examinable differences** between international and UK GAAP in respect of:

- Inventories
- Events after the reporting period
- Provisions and contingencies

Summary and Self-test

Summary

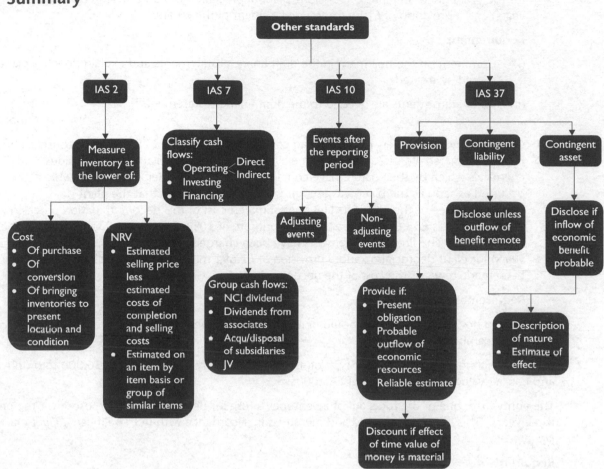

Self-test

Answer the following questions.

1   (a)   On 1 July 20X8 an item of plant which cost of £30 million became available for use. The plant had an estimated life of eight years with no residual value, but its engine would need replacing after four years at an estimated cost of £10 million. The draft financial statements for the year ended 30 June 20X9 include plant depreciation of £3.75 million (£30 million/8 years) and a provision of £10m for the replacement of the engine.

Requirement

(i)   Comment on the treatment in the draft financial statements and explain how the plant should be treated.

(ii)   What adjustments are needed to the draft financial statements?

(6 marks)

(b)   On 1 January 20X7 a new plant that had cost another company £25 million to construct and had an estimated life of 20 years became available for use. The plant uses hazardous chemicals which by their nature have contaminated the plant itself, something which occurred as soon as the plant was used. It is a legal requirement that the plant is decontaminated at the end of its life. The estimated cost of this decontamination process in 20 years' time is £53.82 million and a discount rate of 10% per annum is appropriate to the risks involved. The financial statements have been charged with £1.25 million (£25 million/20 years) for plant depreciation and a provision of £2.691 million (£53.82 million/20 years) has been made towards the cost of the decontamination.

Requirement

Explain how this transaction should be treated in the financial statements for the year ended 31 December 20X7.

(12 marks)

2   An entity manufactures a particular type of machine tool, each of which costs £36,000 to produce and has fair value less costs to sell of £45,000.

The entity takes one of the tools out of inventories to use for demonstration purposes over the next three years. This item is reclassified and measured in accordance with IAS 16 *Property, Plant and Equipment*.

Requirement

Assuming the tool has a nil residual value at the end of the three years, calculate its carrying amount as part of property, plant and equipment one year later.

(2 marks)

3   A production line results in two outputs, Product 1 and Product 2. Parts of the production process give rise to indirect costs specifically identifiable with only one of these products, although other costs are not separately identifiable.

Budgeted cost information for the most recent month is as follows:

	Total £	Product 1 £	Product 2 £
Direct costs	300,000	140,000	160,000
Indirect production overheads			
Identifiable	82,000	37,000	45,000
Other	50,000		
	432,000		
Budgeted output: units		690	900

The entity has a policy which allocates indirect costs which are not specifically identifiable to an individual product by reference to relative selling prices. This results in 60% being allocated to Product 1 and 40% to Product 2.

During the month, costs were incurred in line with the budget, but due to a temporary defect in the manufacturing process, only 675 units of Product 2 could be taken into inventory. The remainder had to be scrapped, for zero proceeds.

Requirement

Using the information above, calculate the amount to be recognised as inventory and the amount to be recognised as an expense in profit or loss for Product 1 and Product 2. **(6 marks)**

4 In mid-January 20X5, there was widespread press coverage in respect of contamination of rivers and surrounding countryside which had occurred over the last eight months. The source of the press coverage was a lawsuit launched by a group of activists, claiming damages from a wide range of organisations.

An entity, which has a 31 December 20X4 accounting year end, manufactured some of the plant which led to the contamination and has been named in the lawsuit as a defendant. The entity's legal advisers have reported that in their opinion there is only a small chance, in the 15% - 20% range, of the suit against it succeeding, but that if it did, the amounts payable would be substantial.

In February 20X5, the same entity agreed an out-of-court settlement of £30,000 with a former senior employee who on 1 November 20X4 had started proceedings to sue for unfair dismissal. The entity's legal advisers had advised that the chances of the former employee winning were small but that the disruption likely to be caused would be substantial. The entity therefore agreed to settle to minimise nuisance value. The entity continued to assert that the dismissal had been fair. The settlement was final and on a 'no fault' basis.

Requirement

Explain how, if at all, these two matters will be reported in the financial statements for the year ending 31 December 20X4. Assume the financial statements were authorised by the directors in April 20X5. **(4 marks)**

5 On 1 January 20X5, an entity entered into a 20 year lease for land and buildings. The lease payments were £910,000 annually in advance, of which £546,000 related to the land. The land is classified as being held under an operating lease. £364,000 related to buildings held under a finance lease.

A finance charge in respect of finance leases of £50,000 was recognised in profit or loss in 20X5. The lease for the building is the entity's only finance lease. The entity treats interest paid as relating to its operating activities.

Requirement

Show how the lease payments should be reported in the statement of cash flows for the years ended 31 December 20X5 and 31 December 20X6. **(4 marks)**

6 **Love Co**

On 1 October 20X5, Love Co bought 100% of a new subsidiary, Day Co.

At this date, the statement of financial position of Day Co disclosed the following:

	1 October 20X5 £'000
Property, plant and equipment	275
Inventory	14
Receivables	26
Prepayments	8
Short-term investments	0
Cash	0
Equity	179
Trade payables	78
Provisions	21
Overdraft	45

The consolidated income statement of the Love Co group for the year ended 31 December 20X5 included the following figures:

Profit before tax	£163,000
Depreciation on property, plant and equipment	£245,000

There were no issues nor redemptions of shares in the year.

Due to a government scheme to promote the activities the Love Co Group is involved in, neither company pays any tax.

The statements of financial position of the Love Co group of companies at 31 December 20X5 and 31 December 20X4 included the following net assets:

	20X5 £'000	20X4 £'000
ASSETS		
Goodwill	141	0
Property, plant and equipment	1,550	1,100
Inventory	172	170
Receivables	104	74
Prepayments	22	16
Short-term investments	30	60
Cash	0	28
EQUITY AND LIABILITIES		
Equity	851	688
Trade payables	720	512
Provisions	208	178
Overdraft	240	70

Love Co acquired its interest in Day Co by paying cash of £320,000.

The short-term investments comprise government bonds approaching their maturity date (which the company considers to be subject to only an insignificant chance of change in value) and investments in shares in other companies. The split was:

	20X5 £'000	20X4 £'000
Government bonds	10	24
Shares	20	36
	30	60

Requirement

So far as the information above allows, prepare the group statement of cash flows and supporting notes for Love Co for the year ended 31 December 20X5 under each of IFRS and UK GAAP. Comparative figures are not required. **(20 marks)**

7 **Saver Co**

Saver Co has a number of subsidiaries and a 40% interest in the ordinary voting shares of Bettabuys Co. Saver Co treats that interest as an investment in an associate under IAS 28.

The group statement of financial position of the Saver Co group showed the following:

	20X6 £'000	20X5 £'000
Investment in associate	1,436	1,380

The group income statement showed a share of profit of associates of £220,000.

Requirement

Assuming that Saver Co prepares its group statement of cash flows using the indirect method of IAS 7, show how its investment in Bettabuys Co will be shown in the group statement of cash flows for the year ended 31 December 20X6. State in which ways, if any, the solution would be different under UK GAAP. **(4 marks)**

Now go back to the Learning Objectives in the Introduction. If you are satisfied you have achieved these objectives, please tick them off.

1 Inventories

- Measurement but not recognition   IAS 2 (1)

- Inventories should be measured at the lower of cost and net realisable value   IAS 2 (9)

- Cost = expenditure incurred in bringing the items to their present location and   IAS 2 (10)
  condition, so the cost of purchase and the cost of conversion

  Fixed costs included by reference to normal levels of activity   IAS 2 (13)

- Cost formulae: FIFO or weighted average   IAS 2 (25)

  Use same formula for all inventories with similar nature

- Net realisable value takes costs to complete into account, as well as selling costs   IAS 2 (6)

- Disclosures include accounting policies, carrying amounts and amounts   IAS 2 (36 and 38)
  recognised as an expense

2 Statement of cash flows

- Objective of the statement of cash flows

  - The statement of cash flows should show the historical changes in cash and
    cash equivalents

  - Cash comprises cash on hand and demand deposits   IAS 7 (6)

  - Cash equivalents are short-term, highly liquid investments that are readily   IAS 7 (6)
    convertible to known amounts of cash and which are subject to an
    insignificant risk of changes in value

- Presentation of a statement of cash flows   Appendix A

  - Cash flows should be classified by operating, investing and financing   IAS 7 (10)
    activities

  - Cash flows from operating activities are primarily derived from the principal   IAS 7 (13-14)
    revenue-producing activities of the entity

  - Cash flows from investing activities are those related to the acquisition or   IAS 7 (16)
    disposal of any property, plant and equipment, intangible assets or trade
    investments together with returns received in cash from investments (that is
    dividends and interest)

- Financing activities include: IAS 7 (17)

  - Cash proceeds from issuing shares

  - Cash proceeds from issuing debentures, loans, notes, bonds, mortgages and
    other short or long-term borrowings

  - Cash repayments of amounts borrowed

  - Dividends paid to shareholders

  - Principal repayments of amounts borrowed under finance leases

- Cash flows from operating activities

  There are two methods of presentation allowed:

  - Direct method   IAS 7 (19)

  - Indirect method   IAS 7 (20)

- Non-cash transactions

  The statement of cash flows does not record non-cash transactions

  IAS 7 (43)

- Disclosures

  - Components of cash and cash equivalents

    IAS 7 (45)

  - Reconciliation of the amounts in the statement of cash flows with the equivalent balance in the statement of financial position

  - Information (together with a commentary) which may be relevant to the users

    IAS 7 (50)

Provisions and contingencies

1 Recognition

- Provisions are liabilities of uncertain timing or amount

  IAS 37 (10)

- A provision is recognised when conditions are met

  IAS 37 (14)

- A useful decision tree in Appendix B

  IAS 37 (App B)

2 Measurement and use

- Measure at best estimate of expenditure required to settle obligation at the end of the reporting period

  IAS 37 (36)

- Discount where material

  IAS 37 (45)

- No account taken of gains from expected disposal of assets

  IAS 37 (51)

- Treat reimbursements as separate assets, recognised only where virtually certain, and only up to amount of provision

  IAS 37 (53)

  Expense recognised in profit or loss may be shown net of reimbursement

  IAS 37 (54)

- Review provisions at each reporting date and adjust to current best estimate

  IAS 37 (59)

- Use a provision only for the expenditures for which it was created

  IAS 37 (61)

3 Specific applications

- Do not provide for future operating losses

  IAS 37 (63)

- Provide for unavoidable costs of meeting onerous contracts

  IAS 37 (66)

- Provide for restructuring only where legal or constructive obligation exists at the end of the reporting period, and provision should only comprise costs:

  IAS 37 (72 & 80)

  - Necessarily entailed by restructuring and

  - Not associated with ongoing activities

- No obligation arises on sale of an operation until there is a binding sale agreement

  IAS 37 (78)

- A useful set of examples is given in Appendix C

  IAS 37 (App C)

4 Contingent liabilities and assets

- Definitions

  IAS 37 (10)

- Do not recognise contingent liabilities but disclose unless possibility of outflow is remote

  IAS 37 (27 & 86)

- Do not recognise contingent assets but disclose where inflow is probable

  IAS 37 (31 & 89)

Events After The Reporting Period

- Definitions of adjusting and non-adjusting events

  IAS 10 (3)

- Financial statements should be adjusted for:

  - Adjusting events

    IAS 10 (8)

  - Non-adjusting events that indicate that going concern assumption is not appropriate

    IAS 10 (14)

- Disclosure

  - Material non-adjusting events

    IAS 10 (21)

  - Proposed equity dividends not declared by the end of the reporting period

    IAS 10 (12)

  - Date on which financial statements authorised for issue

    IAS 10 (17)

Answer to Interactive question 1

		£
June	15,000 units actual production × £3 recovery rate	45,000
July	25,000 units (as budgeted) × £3	75,000
10 other months	25,000 units × £3 × 10	750,000
		870,000

Point to note:

The under-recovery of £30,000 (900,000 – 870,000) should be recognised as an expense in profit or loss.

Answer to Interactive question 2

	Product X £	Product Y £	Product Z £
Cost	120	320	235
NRV	142	314	205
Lower of cost and NRV	120	314	205
Total carrying amount (120 + 314 + 205)	639		

Answer to Interactive question 3

Precipitate Ltd
Statement of cash flows for the year ended 30 April 20X7

	£'000	£'000
Cash flows from operating activities		
Cash used in operations (Note 1)	(361)	
Interest paid	(39)	
Income taxes paid (111 – 40 – 102)	(31)	
Net cash used in operating activities		(431)
Cash flows from investing activities		
Purchase of property, plant and equipment		
(340 – 455 + 235 + 53 plant)	(173)	
Proceeds from sale of property, plant and equipment (425 + 99)	524	
Net cash from investing activities		351
Cash flows from financing activities		
Proceeds from issue of ordinary share capital (820 – 720)	100	
Repurchase of debentures (416 – 555)	(139)	
Net cash used in financing activities		(39)
Net decrease in cash and cash equivalents		(119)
Cash and cash equivalents at beginning of period (Note 2)		(45)
Cash and cash equivalents at end of period (Note 2)		(164)

Notes:

(1) Reconciliation of profit before tax to cash used in operations for the year ended 30 April 20X7

	£'000
Profit before tax	290
Interest payable	39
Profit on sale of property, plant and equipment	(205)
Depreciation charge	6
Increase in trade and other receivables (792 – 598)	(194)
Increase in inventories (773 – 591)	(182)
Decrease in trade payables (401 – 286)	(115)
Cash used in operations	(361)

(2) Cash and cash equivalents

	20X7	20X6
	£'000	£'000
Bank deposits	133	117
Bank overdrafts	(297)	(162)
	(164)	(45)

Answer to Interactive question 4

The dividend paid to the non-controlling interest is £12,000 (400 balance b/f + 20 profit for the year – 408 balance c/f).

The dividend received from associates is £16,000 (144 asset b/f + 22 earnings for the year – 150 asset c/f).

Answer to Interactive question 5

	£'000
Cash flows from investing activities	
Acquisition of subsidiary (400 – 60)	(340)
Purchase of property, plant and equipment (1,400 + 50 – 800 – 500)	(150)

Answer to Interactive question 6

	£'000
Net assets acquired	
Property, plant and equipment	8,050
Inventories	3,550
Trade receivables	5,300
Bank and cash balances	1,300
Trade payables	(17,100)
	1,100
Non-controlling interest (20% × 1,100)	(220)
	880
Goodwill (bal fig)	2,020
Consideration (2,000 + (300 × £3))	2,900
Cash and cash equivalents	(1,300)
Non-cash consideration (300 × £3)	(900)
Net cash flow	700

Answer to Interactive question 7

The cracks in the walls are clear evidence of a change in the building's condition.

The specialist professionals have provided their opinion that the problems must have arisen several years ago (not since the year end), thus providing evidence as to the building's condition at the end of the reporting period.

The draft financial statements should be adjusted to take account of this change in condition. A full impairment review under IAS 36 *Impairment of Assets* should be carried out and any impairment loss should be recognised in the June 20X8 financial statements.

Point to note:

It is highly likely that expenditure on repairs will be needed in the 30 June 20X9 financial year to rectify the damage and that the cost may be significant. But no provision for these repairs should be recognised at 30 June 20X8. There is a past event (the faults now identified) but at the end of the reporting period there is no obligation to incur the expenditure on repairs; so no provision should be recognised.

Answer to Interactive question 8

The reduction in selling price is evidence of the inventory's net realisable value at the end of the reporting period. It is therefore an adjusting event.

The net realisable value of the inventory is (£605 – £100) × 4,000 = £2,020,000.

The inventory is currently measured at a cost of £550 × 4,000 = £2,200,000, so it should be written down to the lower amount.

Answer to Interactive question 9

(a) The contract having been signed, there is a present obligation arising out of past events to pay the unavoidable costs under the contract.

(b)

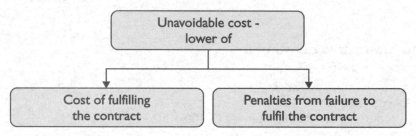

Cost of fulfilling the contract	Penalties from failure to fulfil the contract
Take deliveries of silk and scrap it	Stop silk deliveries and pay penalties
Costs (300m × £18 × 2 months) £(10,800)	Penalties (£2,400 × 2 months) £(4,800)

Take deliveries of silk and make and sell dresses

Revenue (300m × £28 × 2 months)	£16,800
Costs (300m × (£18 + £16)) × 2 months	£(20,400)
Loss	(£3,600)

Therefore the unavoidable cost is £3,600.

This should be recognised as a provision in the statement of financial position and as an expense in profit or loss.

Disclosure notes will give a brief description of the circumstances and of the obligation as well as an indication of the uncertainties about the timing of payments, amounts and assumptions.

Answer to Interactive question 10

(1) At the end of the reporting period, Conditional disputes liability (and therefore whether a present obligation exists).

However, the lawyer's advice is that it is more likely than not that Conditional will be found liable. A present obligation should be assumed to exist (IAS 37 paras 15–16).

Given that a single obligation is being measured, a provision is made for the outflow of the most likely outcome (IAS 37 para 40).

Consequently a provision should be recognised for £20,000 court costs and damages + £80,000 repair costs = £100,000.

(2) A present obligation exists at the end of the reporting period based on historical evidence of items being repaired under the guarantee agreement.

Here, a large population of items is involved. A provision should therefore be recognised for the expected value of the outflow:

	£
$15,000 \times 5\% \times 1/3 \times £100$	25,000
$15,000 \times 5\% \times 2/3 \times £300$	150,000
	175,000

Answer to Interactive question 11

Measurement of the amount payable in ten years' time:

- Anticipated asset disposals: these should not be used to reduce the amount payable

- Possible site-cleaning technology: this is said to be 'new' and there is no expert, independent evidence to support its likely availability. It should not be used to reduce the amount payable

The amount to be provided for is therefore £1.2m. This will arise after ten years and the relevant discount rate is 9%. The finance cost to be recognised in the year ended 31 December 20X9 is:

		£
Provision at 31 December 20X9	$£1.2m/1.09^9$	552,513
Provision at 31 December 20X8	$£1.2m/1.09^{10}$	506,893
Increase = finance cost		45,620

1   (a)   No obligation to replace the engine exists until a contract for its replacement has been signed. In the interim the company may decide to sell the plant rather than replace the engine. So it is inappropriate to recognise a provision for its replacement. Also, the £3.75m depreciation charge includes an element in respect of the engine, so a provision would result in double-counting.

Under IAS 16 the plant should be treated as an asset with two separate components (the engine and the remainder) with different useful lives. The engine (cost £10m) should be depreciated over four years, while the remainder of the machine (cost £20m) should be depreciated over eight years.

Depreciation charge		*Cost*
		£'000
Engine	Depreciated over four years. The charge is £2,500,000 per annum	10,000
The rest	Depreciated over eight years. The charge is £2,500,000 per annum	20,000
Total	Total annual depreciation charge £5,000,000	30,000

If the engine is replaced in four years' time, the cost and accumulated depreciation of the existing engine should be derecognised and the cost of the new engine should be recognised as an asset and depreciated over its working life.

The adjustments required to the draft financial statements are:

Income statement

Depreciation charge – increase by £1,250,000 (5m – 3.75m)
Cost of provisions – decrease by £10,000,000.

Statement of financial position

Carrying amount of plant – decrease by £1,250,000
Provisions – decrease by £10,000,000

(b)   The obligation to clean up the contamination existed in full from the day that the plant was brought into use. Therefore rather than being accrued incrementally over the life of the plant, the provision should be recognised in full immediately, but at the present value of the future obligation. Over the next twenty years the present value should be increased as the discount unwinds, using the "money rate" discount rate. Care needs to be taken not to mix mutually incompatible assumptions about estimates and discount rate, such as mixing an estimated cash outflow in "real" terms and yet discounting it at a "money" discount rate. This should be reported by increasing the provision and recognising the increase as a finance cost in profit or loss.

On initial recognition, the cost of the plant should include the present value of the decontamination. This is calculated as £53.82 million $\div (1.1)^{20}$ = £8 million.

Statement of financial position

	£'000
Plant (a non-current asset)	
1 Jan 20X7: cost (£25m + £8m)	33,000
Depreciation (£33m/20 years)	(1,650)
31 Dec 20X7: carrying amount	31,350

Provision (a non-current liability)	
1 Jan 20X7	8,000
Finance cost @ 10%	800
31 Dec 20X7	8,800

Income statement

	£'000
Depreciation charge	1,650
Finance cost	800

2   Carrying amount is cost of £36,000 (being lower than fair value less costs to sell) less depreciation of £12,000 (£36,000 / 3 years) = £24,000

3   The cost of 690 units of Product 1 (recognised in inventory) is calculated as:

£140,000 + £37,000 + (60% × £50,000) = £207,000.

The cost per unit of Product 1 is therefore £207,000/ 690 = £300 each.

The total cost attributable to Product 2 is:

£160,000 + £45,000 + (40% × £50,000) = £225,000.

The cost per unit of Product 2 is therefore £225,000 / 900 = £250.

The allocation of the cost for Product 2 is therefore:

£250 × 675 = £168,750 as inventories

£250 × 225 = £56,250 as an expense recognised in profit or loss.

The indirect costs not specifically identifiable with either product which are allocated to the scrapped Product 2 cannot be recovered into the cost of Product 1.

4   The lawsuit and press coverage for the environmental damage provide evidence of conditions which existed at 31 December 20X4. In light of the legal advice received, no provision should be recognised since it is not probable that the entity will be required to pay damages under the action. Disclosure is required as the lawsuit provides further evidence of an uncertainty (the contingent liability) which existed at the end of the reporting period.

The lawsuit for unfair dismissal has been settled after the year-end, although it was in progress at the year end. Although it appeared that there was no obligating event at the year end, it was settled in the post year-end period as if an obligating event did exist. The most appropriate accounting treatment is therefore to recognise a provision at the year end in accordance with IAS 37, measuring it at the amount the lawsuit was settled for in February 20X5.

5

	20X5	20X6
	£	£
Cash flows from operating activities		
Operating lease payments	(546,000)	(546,000)
Interest paid (see below)	–	(50,000)
Cash flows from financing activities		
Payments under finance leases	(364,000)	(314,000)

Point to note:

The payments are made in advance, so there is no interest in the January 20X5 payment.

6 **Love Co**

Under IAS 7

Statement of cash flows for the year ended 31 December 20X5

	£'000	£'000
Cash flows from operating activities		
Profit before tax		163
Depreciation		245
Decrease in inventory (172 – 170 – 14)		12
Increase in receivables (104 – 74 – 26)		(4)
Decrease in prepayments (22 – 16 – 8)		2
Increase in trade payables (720 – 512 – 78)		130
Increase in provisions (208 – 178 – 21)		9
Cash generated from operations		557
Cash flows from investing activities		
Cash paid for property, plant and equipment		
(1,550 – 1,100 + 245 – 275)	(420)	
Cash paid to acquire subsidiary (320 + 45)	(365)	
Cash received on sale of shares (36 – 20)	16	
Net cash used in investing activities		(769)
Decrease in cash and cash equivalents		(212)
Cash and cash equivalents at 31 December 20X4 (Note 1)		(18)
Cash and cash equivalents at 31 December 20X5 (Note 1)		(230)

Note

(1) **Analysis of cash and cash equivalents**

	20X5 £'000	20X4 £'000	Change £'000
Cash and bank balances	0	28	(28)
Overdrafts	(240)	(70)	(170)
Government bonds	10	24	(14)
Total cash and cash equivalents	(230)	(18)	(212)

(2) **Acquisition of subsidiary**

On 1 October 20X5, the group acquired 100% of the issued share capital of Day Co for cash consideration of £320,000. The net assets acquired were:

	£'000
Property, plant and equipment	275
Inventory	14
Receivables	26
Prepayments	8
Trade payables	(78)
Provisions	(21)
Overdraft	(45)
Goodwill (balance)	141
Net assets acquired	320

Satisfied by:

Cash paid	320

Point to note:

There are no financing activities. Love has no long-term borrowings and the profit for the year accounts for the whole of the change in equity.

Under UK GAAP

Statement of cash flows for the year ended 31 December 20X5

Reconciliation of operating profit to net cash inflow from operating activities

	£'000	£'000
Operating profit		163
Depreciation		245
Decrease in inventory (172 – 170 – 14)		12
Increase in receivables (104 – 74 – 26)		(4)
Decrease in prepayments (22 – 16 – 8)		2
Increase in trade payables (720 – 512 – 78)		130
Increase in provisions (208 – 178 – 21)		9
Net cash inflow from operating activities		557

Capital expenditure and financial investment

		£'000
Cash paid for property, plant and equipment (as per IFRS)		(420)

Acquisitions and disposals

Cash paid to acquire subsidiary (320 + 45)		(365)

Management of liquid resources

	£'000	
Cash received on sale of shares (36 – 20)	16	
Cash received on sale of bonds	14	

Net cash from management of liquid resources		30

Decrease in cash		(198)
Cash 31 December 20X4 (Note 1)		(42)
Cash 31 December 20X5 (Note 1)		(240)

Notes

(1) **Analysis of cash**

	20X5 £'000	20X4 £'000	Change £'000
Cash and bank balances	0	28	(28)
Overdrafts	(240)	(70)	(170)
Total cash	(240)	(42)	(198)

(2) The same as under IAS 7

7 **Saver Co**

Cash flows from operating activities

	£'000
Profit before tax	X
Share of profit of associate	(220)
Net cash from operating activities	X

Cash flows from investing activities

Dividends received from associate (1,380 + 220 – 1,436)	164

Under UK GAAP, the same figures would apply, except that the dividend received from associate of £164,000 would be classified under a separate heading 'Dividends from joint ventures and associates'.

CHAPTER 11

Financial statement analysis: introduction and ratios

Introduction

Examination context

Topic List

1 Users and user focus

2 Accounting ratios and relationships

3 Statements of cash flows and their interpretation

4 Performance measurement – not-for-profit organisations

Summary and Self-test

Technical reference

Answers to Interactive questions

Answers to Self-test

There are three chapters that cover financial statement analysis and interpretation. The first chapter covers the basic calculation and meaning of ratios. The second chapter develops interpretation skills by considering the factors that influence financial statement analysis and more advanced analysis techniques. The third chapter covers relevant exam techniques.

Learning objectives

Tick off

- On completion of this chapter you should be able to:

  - Identify the needs of different users of financial information ☐

  - Calculate and interpret accounting ratios, using appropriate figures, to measure performance, short-term liquidity, long-term solvency and efficiency ☐

  - Calculate and interpret investors' ratios ☐

  - Interpret statements of cash flows and calculate and interpret cash flow ratios ☐

- In Chapter 12 you will consolidate these objectives and after completing that chapter you should be able to:

  - Take account of economic and business factors and the reporting requirements of business events ☐

  - Take account of accounting factors, such as non-current asset revaluation ☐

  - Interpret non-financial performance measures ☐

  - Identify and resolve the ethical issues associated with financial statement analysis ☐

  - Calculate and interpret other common financial ratios used by financial analysts ☐

  - Be aware of the limitations of ratios ☐

Specific syllabus references for this chapter are: 2b and 4b.

Syllabus links

The performance measurement section of the Business and Finance module covered measures of profitability, liquidity, solvency, efficiency and working capital management. In the Accounting and Financial Accounting modules and the previous Financial Reporting chapters, you have covered the preparation of financial statements and extracts thereof. This and the following chapter on the analysis and interpretation of financial statements draws on all this content and uses it in a more complex way, because it is not practicable to analyse and interpret financial statements without understanding:

(1) The basis on which they are prepared
(2) The underlying objectives of their preparation
(3) The purpose of financial reporting generally.

The next two chapters will use that knowledge to develop your skills of financial statement analysis. The skills of analysis are also important at Advanced Stage particularly in the advanced case study (ACS). It is essential that you can interpret and analyse financial information. These chapters are important to your preparation for all the Advanced Stage examinations in addition to the Financial Reporting module.

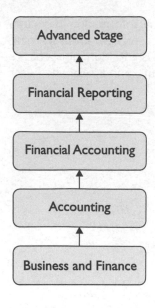

Examination context

The analysis and interpretation of financial statements is a significant portion of the Financial Reporting examination and will account for approximately 30% of the total marks across two or more questions. You may be required to interpret extracts from financial statements or to comment on how chosen accounting policies and/or their application affect the interpretation of the information.

Although you may be required to calculate ratios in the exam, this part of any question would only carry a small number of marks. It is possible that some questions will present ratios in pre-calculated form, while others may present some but require others to be calculated. More marks will be available for showing that you can interpret ratios, which will only come from understanding the way they are calculated and their limitations. Consider, for example, a business raising a large loan in the last two weeks of its accounting period; ratios, such as gearing, which use amounts presented in the statement of financial position will be meaningful, but interest cover will not, since the historic interest charge will not be representative of future charges.

You must also use the contextual (that is background) information given in the question to think through the relevance of ratios; trying to make sense of the trade receivables collection period in an industry where revenue is predominantly in cash would not be sensible. Equally, 'business events' such as the acquisition or disposal of subsidiaries and the closing down of a major division can substantially distort what ratios seem at face value to indicate. Wherever possible, the effects of such events need to be stripped out, so that the focus can be on amounts likely to recur in the future. In practice, many analysts spend a lot of time 'cleaning' the figures found in financial statements solely in order to establish maintainable/core figures that can then be used as the basis for projecting future results.

In the assessment, candidates may be required to:

- Select and calculate relevant indicators, including ratios (for example, stock market ratios), trends and interrelationships, to analyse a single entity's or group's financial position, performance and changes in financial position

- Identify the choice of accounting treatments adopted in financial statements and other financial information and assess how they affect the view presented

- Identify and compare significant features in the information supplied for a given entity or entities, including inconsistencies between the results of analysis and the information supplied

- Specify any additional information required for a meaningful analysis

- Draw conclusions and make inferences from an analysis which takes account of significant features in the information supplied, and which allows for the limitations of the information supplied and the analytical methods used, economic conditions and the business's circumstances

- Recognise the ethical and professional issues for a professional accountant undertaking work in and giving advice on accounting and financial reporting; explain the relevance and importance of these issues and evaluate the relative merits of different standpoints taken in debate

- Identify financial and operational information in documents containing audited financial statements (for example, reports on operations by management or those responsible for governance, financial summaries and highlights) that could be relevant to the legal entity or consolidated financial statements, and assess whether those financial statements adequately reflect that information

1 Users and user focus

> **Section overview**
>
> - Different groups of users of financial statements will have different information needs.
> - The focus of an investigation of a business will be different for each user group.

1.1 Information needs

External users and their information needs are covered in detail in the Financial Accounting module. The following table summarises the main groups of users of financial statements and the information they need.

Users	Need information to:
Present and potential investors	Make investment decisions, therefore need information on: • Risk and return on investment • Ability of entity to pay dividends
Employees	• Assess their employer's stability and profitability • Assess their employer's ability to provide remuneration, employment opportunities and retirement and other benefits
Lenders	Assess whether loans will be repaid, and related interest will be paid, when due
Suppliers and other trade creditors	Assess the likelihood of being paid when due
Customers	• Assess whether the entity will continue in existence – important where customers have a long-term involvement with, or are dependent on, the entity, for example where there are product warranties or where specialist parts may be needed • Assess whether business practices are ethical
Governments and their agencies	• Assess allocation of resources and, therefore, activities of entities • Assist in regulating activities • Assess taxation • Provide a basis for national statistics
The public	Assess trends and recent developments in the entity's prosperity and its activities – important where the entity makes a substantial contribution to a local economy, for example by providing employment and using local suppliers

An entity's management also needs to understand and interpret financial information, both as a basis for making management decisions and also to help in understanding how external users might react to the information in the financial statements.

1.2 User focus

The primary focus of users of the financial statements differs according to their interests. For example:

- Customers and suppliers are most interested in current liquidity, but also focus on overall pre-tax profitability and net worth of the business in their evaluation of likely future liquidity

- Lenders focus on liquidity, longer-term solvency and ability to service and repay debts

- Shareholders' main concern is with risk and return. They therefore focus mainly on gearing and dividend cover to measure the risk, and on post-tax returns and the overall net worth of the business to measure return. However, they are also interested in solvency, as they will be the first to lose out in the event that the company runs into financial difficulties. Finally, shareholders are interested in liquidity as this affects the security of their dividends.

1.3 Financial position and performance

Different users usually require different information. However, there is overlap, as all potential users are interested in the financial performance and financial position of the company as a whole.

The next section examines how accounting ratios can be used to help assess financial performance and position. The additional perspective provided by analysis of the statement of cash flows is covered later in this chapter.

2 Accounting ratios and relationships

Section overview

- Ratios are commonly classified into different groups according to the focus of the investigation.

- Ratios can help in assessing performance, short-term liquidity, long-term solvency, efficiency and investor returns.

2.1 Introduction to ratios

Accounting ratios help to summarise and present financial information in a more understandable form. They assist in assessing the performance of a business by identifying significant relationships between different figures. The phrase 'accounting ratios' is used loosely, to cover the outcome of different types of calculation; some ratios measure one amount as a ratio of another (such as 2:1) whereas others measure it as a percentage of the other (such as 200%).

Ratios are of no use in isolation. To be useful, a basis for comparison is needed, such as:

- Previous years
- Other companies
- Industry averages
- Budgeted or forecast-vs-actual

Ratios do not provide answers but help to focus attention on important areas, therefore minimising the chance of failing to identify a significant trend or weakness.

Ratios divide into the following main areas:

- Performance
- Short-term liquidity
- Long-term solvency
- Efficiency (asset and working capital)
- Investors' (or stock market) ratios

2.1.1 Which figures to use?

Many accounting ratios are calculated using one figure from the income statement (which covers a period of time, usually a year) and one from the statement of financial position (which is a snapshot at a point in time, usually the year end). The result may be distorted if the statement of financial position (snapshot) amounts are not typical of the amounts throughout the period covered by the income statement.

Consider a toy retailer with a 31 December year end: over half its annual sales may well be made in the three months leading up to Christmas, while its inventory levels at 31 December will probably be at their lowest point throughout the year, and certainly much lower than at their highest point which might be sometime in October in the run up to Christmas. To calculate a relationship between cost of sales for 12 months and the 31 December level of inventories and then use it as a measure of management's efficiency in managing inventory levels (as does the inventory turnover ratio in section 2.5.2 below) runs the risk of a major distortion. The calculation should really be done using the income statement amount and the average inventory holding throughout the year, calculating the average every month or more frequently.

But monthly statement of financial position amounts are not made available to financial statement users. Sometimes half-yearly (or quarterly) statements of financial position are published, in which case they may well result in useful averages. But averaging the amounts at the current year end and the previous year end may well be no better than just using current year end amounts, since the result may only be to average two unrepresentative amounts.

Simplifications have to be made for the Professional Stage examination, so any ratios presented in a question will be based on non-averaged year end amounts only and calculations of additional ratios required by a question should also be made on this basis. But it is always worth noting that one of the limitations of ratio analysis is that it is based on published, and therefore incomplete, data.

2.2 Performance

2.2.1 Significance

Performance ratios measure the rate of return earned on capital employed, and analyse this into profit margins and use of assets. These ratios are frequently used as the basis for assessing management effectiveness in utilising the resources under their control.

2.2.2 Key ratios

Return on capital employed (ROCE)

This measures the overall efficiency of a company in employing the resources available to it, that is its capital employed.

$$\frac{\text{Return}}{\text{Capital employed}} \times 100 \qquad \left(\begin{array}{l}\text{Source}:\text{IS} \\ \text{Source}:\text{SFP}\end{array}\right)$$

where: Return = profit before interest and tax (PBIT) + associates' post-tax earnings

Capital employed = equity + net debt, where net debt = interest-bearing debt (non-current and current) minus cash and cash equivalents.

Remember that:

- Equity includes irredeemable preference shares and the non-controlling interests
- Net debt includes redeemable preference shares

Many different versions of this ratio are used in practice (this one is slightly more sophisticated than the version used in Business and Finance), but all are based upon the same idea: identify the long-term resources available to a company's management and then measure the financial return earned on those resources.

In the version used in this Study Manual, the total resources available to a company are the amounts owed to shareholders who receive dividends, plus the amounts owed to those who provide finance only on the condition that they receive interest in return. So interest bearing-debt, both long-term and short-term (for example bank overdrafts), are included but trade payables (which are an interest-free source of finance) are not. But to cope with companies which move from one month to another between positive and overdrawn bank balances, holdings of cash and cash equivalents (but not any other 'cash' current assets which management does not describe as cash equivalents) are netted off, to arrive at 'net debt'.

The return is the amount earned before deducting any payments to those who provide the capital employed. So it is the profits before both dividends and interest payable (and, for the purpose of the Financial Reporting syllabus, before the addition of dividend and interest receivable). Because interest is tax-deductible, the profit figure is also before taxation. The PBIT (profit before interest and tax) tag is well-established within the UK, so this term is used in ratio calculations although in the income statement layout used in this Study Manual the description given to this figure is 'profit/(loss) from operations'.

To allow valid comparisons to be made with other companies, the return must also include the earnings from investments in associates, because some groups carry out large parts of their activities through associates, rather than the parent or subsidiaries.

Strictly speaking, it is the associates' pre-tax earnings which should be included, but under IAS 28 only the post-tax amount is shown. In practice, some users adjust this figure using an estimated tax rate for the associates to establish a pre-tax return.

Like profit, capital employed is affected by the accounting policies chosen by a company. For example, a company that revalues its PPE will have higher capital employed than one which does not. The depreciation expense will be higher and profits will be reduced as a result of the policy. The accounting adjustments will reduce ROCE.

Return on shareholders' funds (ROSF)

This measures how effectively a company is employing funds that parent company shareholders have provided.

$$\frac{\text{Profit attributable to owners of parent}}{\text{Equity minus non-controlling interest}} \qquad \left(\begin{array}{l} \text{Source : IS} \\ \text{Source : SFP} \end{array} \right)$$

It is the return on the funds provided by the parent company's shareholders that is being analysed here, so it is their equity which goes on the bottom of the fraction. This is the equity used in the ROCE calculation minus the non-controlling interest.

The return is the profit for the year attributable to those shareholders.

Analysis usually focuses on ROCE, as opposed to ROSF, because the issue is management's ability to generate return from overall resources rather than how those resources are financed.

Worked example: Calculating ROCE and ROSF

Consider two companies without subsidiaries in the same industry with different capital structures:

		Company 1 £m	Company 2 £m
Statement of financial position			
Equity	(A)	80	20
Loans at 10%		20	80
Capital employed	(B)	100	100
Income statement			
PBIT	(C)	20	20
Loan interest at 10%		(2)	(8)
Profit before tax		18	12
Tax at 30%		(5)	(4)
Profit after tax (for owners)	(D)	13	8

Solution

		Company 1 %	Company 2 %
ROCE	(C) as % of (B)	20	20
ROSF	(D) as % of (A)	16	40

ROCE is the same, so the companies are equally good in generating profits. But with different capital structures, ROSF is very different.

If it wished, Company 1 could achieve the same capital structure (and therefore the same ROSF) by borrowing £60m and using it to repay shareholders.

It is often easier to change capital structures than to change a company's ability to generate profits. Hence the focus on ROCE.

Note that Company 2 has much higher gearing and lower interest cover (these ratios are covered later in this chapter).

Interactive question 1: ROCE and ROSF [Difficulty level: Easy]

Name five considerations that you should consider when drawing conclusions from ROCE and ROSF calculations.

-
-
-
-
-

See **Answer** at the end of this chapter.

Gross profit percentage/margin

This measures the margin earned by a company on revenue, before taking account of overhead costs.

$$\frac{\text{Gross profits}}{\text{Revenue}} \times 100 \qquad \left(\begin{array}{l}\text{Source:IS}\\\text{Source:IS}\end{array}\right)$$

Interactive question 2: Gross profit percentage [Difficulty level: Easy]

List four possible reasons for changes in the year on year gross profit percentage.

-
-
-
-

See **Answer** at the end of this chapter.

Operating cost percentage

This measures the relationship of overheads (fixed and variable, which usually comprise distribution costs and administrative expenses) to revenue.

$$\frac{\text{Operating costs/overheads}}{\text{Revenue}} \times 100 \qquad \left(\begin{array}{l}\text{Source:IS}\\\text{Source:IS}\end{array}\right)$$

Ideally this should be broken into variable overheads (expected to change with revenue) and fixed overheads. However, such information is not usually published in financial statements.

Interactive question 3: Operating cost percentage [Difficulty level: Easy]

List two considerations that could account for changes in the operating cost percentage.

-
-

See **Answer** at the end of this chapter.

Operating profit margin/net margin

This shows the profit margin after all operating expenses.

$$\frac{\text{PBIT}}{\text{Revenue}} \times 100 \text{ or } \frac{\text{Profit from operations}}{\text{Revenue}} \times 100 \qquad \left(\begin{array}{l}\text{Source:IS}\\\text{Source:IS}\end{array}\right)$$

2.2.3 Commentary

ROCE measures the return achieved by management from assets that they control, before payments to providers of financing for those assets, (lenders and shareholders).

For companies without associates, ROCE can be further subdivided into net profit margin and asset turnover (use of assets).

Net profit margin $\times$ Net asset turnover $=$ ROCE

$$\frac{PBIT}{Revenue} \times \frac{Revenue}{Capital\ employed} = \frac{PBIT}{Capital\ employed}$$

This subdivision is useful when comparing a company's performance from one period to another. While ROCE might be identical for the two periods, there might be compensating changes in the two components, that is an improvement in margin might be offset by a deterioration in asset utilisation. The subdivision might be equally useful when comparing the performance of two companies in the same period.

Although associates' earnings are omitted, it will probably be worth making this subdivision even for groups with earnings from associates, unless those earnings are very substantial indeed.

Net profit margin is often seen as a measure of quality of profits. A high profit margin indicates a high profit on each unit sold. This ratio can be used as a measure of the risk in the business, since a high margin business may remain profitable after a fall in margin while a low margin business may not.

Worked example: Net profit margin

Two companies with a revenue of £200 have net profit margins of 30% and 4%. If each company discounts their sale prices by 5%, compute revised net profit margins.

Company 1	Base £	5% price discount £	Revised £
Revenue	200	(10)	190
Costs	(140)		(140)
Profit	60	(10)	50
Net profit margin	30%		26%

Company 2	Base £	5% price discount £	Revised £
Revenue	200	(10)	190
Costs	(192)		(192)
Profit	8	(10)	(2)
Net profit margin	4%		–1%

By contrast, net asset turnover (considered further under efficiency ratios in section 2.5.2 below) is often seen as a quantitative measure, indicating how intensively the management is using the assets.

A trade-off often exists between margin and net asset turnover. Low margin businesses, for example food retailers, usually have high asset turnover. Conversely, capital-intensive manufacturing industries usually have relatively low asset turnover but higher margins, for example electrical equipment manufacturers.

Gross profit is useful for comparing the profitability of different companies in the same sector but less useful across different types of business, as the split of costs between cost of sales and other expense headings varies widely according to the nature of the business. Even within companies competing within the same industry distortions can be caused if companies allocate individual costs to different cost headings.

Particular care must be taken when calculating, and then considering the implications of, these ratios if the company concerned is presenting both continuing and discontinued operations. In the income statement layout used in this Study Manual, the amounts for revenue, gross profit, operating costs and profit from operations all relate to continuing operations only. Although amounts relating to the discontinued operations' revenue, total costs and profit from operations are made available in the notes, it is probably not worth adding them back in to the continuing operations' amounts, for the simple reason that the results of continuing operations form the most appropriate base on which to project future performance.

2.3 Short-term liquidity

2.3.1 Significance

Short-term liquidity ratios are used to assess a company's ability to meet payments when due. In practice, information contained in the statement of cash flows is often more useful when analysing liquidity.

2.3.2 Key ratios

Current ratio

This measures the adequacy of current assets to cover current liabilities.

$$\frac{\text{Current assets}}{\text{Current liabilities}} \text{ (usually expressed as X:1)} \qquad \left(\begin{array}{l}\text{Source: SFP}\\\text{Source: SFP}\end{array}\right)$$

Quick (acid test or liquidity) ratio

Inventories, often rather slow moving, are eliminated from current assets, giving a better measure of short-term liquidity. This is appropriate for those types of business that take significant time to convert inventories into cash, such as an aircraft manufacturer.

$$\frac{\text{Current assets – inventories}}{\text{Current liabilities}} \text{ (usually expressed as X:1)} \qquad \left(\begin{array}{l}\text{Source: SFP}\\\text{Source: SFP}\end{array}\right)$$

Interactive question 4: Current and quick ratios [Difficulty level: Easy]

Suggest a conclusion that may be drawn from high and low current and quick ratios.

-
-

What factors should be considered when investigating changes in short-term liquidity ratios?

-
-

See **Answer** at the end of this chapter.

2.3.3 Commentary

The current ratio is of limited use as some current assets, for example inventories, may not be readily convertible into cash, other than at a large discount. Hence, this ratio may not indicate whether or not the company can pay its debts as they fall due.

As the quick ratio omits inventories, this is a better indicator of liquidity but is subject to distortions. For example retailers have few trade receivables and utilise cash from sales quickly, but finance their inventories from trade payables. Hence, their quick ratios are usually low, but this is in itself no cause for concern.

A high current or quick ratio may be due to a company having excessive amounts of cash or short-term investments. Though these resources are highly liquid, the trade-off for this liquidity is usually a low return. Hence, companies with excessive cash balances may benefit from using them to repay longer-term debt or invest in non-current assets to improve their overall returns.

Therefore, both the current and quick ratios should be treated with caution and should be read in conjunction with other information, such as efficiency ratios and cash flow information.

In the statement of financial position layout used in this Study Manual, any non-current assets held for sale will be presented immediately below the sub-total for current assets. In classifying them as held for sale, the company is intending to realise them for cash, so it will usually be appropriate to combine this amount with current assets when calculating both the current and quick ratios.

2.4 Long-term solvency

2.4.1 Significance

Gearing ratios examine the financing structure of a business. They indicate to shareholders and lenders the degree of risk attached to the company and the sensitivity of earnings and dividends to changes in profitability level.

2.4.2 Key ratios

Gearing ratio

Gearing measures the relationship between a company's borrowings and its risk capital.

$$\frac{\text{Net debt (per ROCE)}}{\text{Equity (per ROCE)}} \times 100 \qquad \left(\frac{\text{Source: SFP}}{\text{Source: SFP}}\right)$$

Alternatively, the ratio may be computed as follows:

$$\frac{\text{Net debt}}{\text{Net debt + equity}} \times 100$$

Worked example: Gearing

The following are the summarised statements of financial position for two companies. Calculate the gearing ratios and comment upon each.

	Company 1 £m	Company 2 £m
Non-current assets	7	18
Inventory	3	3
Trade receivables	4	3
Cash	1	2
	15	26
Equity	10	10
Trade payables	3	4
Borrowings	2	12
	15	26

Solution

	Company 1	Company 2
Gearing $= \dfrac{\text{Net debt}}{\text{Equity}}$	$10\% \left(\dfrac{(2-1)}{10}\right)$	$100\% \left(\dfrac{(12-2)}{10}\right)$

Both companies have the same equity amount. Company 1 is lower risk as its borrowings are lower relative to equity. This is because interest on borrowings and capital repayments of debt **must** be paid, with potentially serious repercussions if they are not. Dividend payments on equity instruments are an optional cash outflow for a business.

Company 2 has a high level of financial risk. If the borrowings were secured on the non-current assets, then the assets available to shareholders in the event of a winding up are limited.

Interactive question 5: Gearing

[Difficulty level: Easy]

When drawing conclusions from gearing ratios suggest two matters that should be considered.

-
-

See **Answer** at the end of this chapter.

Interest cover

$$\frac{\text{Profit before interest payable (ie PBIT + investment income)}}{\text{Interest payable}} \qquad \left(\begin{matrix}\text{Source:IS}\\\text{Source:IS}\end{matrix}\right)$$

In calculating this ratio, it is standard practice to add back into interest any interest capitalised during the period.

2.4.3 Commentary

Many different measures of gearing are used in practice, so it is especially important that the ratios used are defined.

Note that under IAS 32 *Financial Instruments: Presentation* redeemable preference shares should be included in liabilities (non-current or current, depending on when they fall due for redemption), while the dividends on these shares should be included in the finance cost/interest payable.

It is also the case that IAS 32 requires compound financial instruments, such as convertible loans, to be split into their components for accounting purposes. This process allocates some of such loans to equity.

Points to note:

- Interest on debt capital generally must be paid irrespective of whether profits are earned – this may cause a liquidity crisis if a company is unable to meet its debt capital obligations.

- Loan capital is usually secured on assets, most commonly non-current assets – these should be suitable for the purpose (not fast-depreciating or subject to rapid changes in demand and price).

High gearing usually indicates increased risk for shareholders as, if profits fall, debts will still need to be financed, leaving much smaller profits available to shareholders. Highly geared businesses are therefore more exposed to insolvency in an economic downturn. However, returns to shareholders will grow proportionately more in highly geared businesses where profits are growing.

The gearing ratio is significantly affected by accounting policies adopted, particularly the revaluation of PPE. An upward revaluation will increase equity and capital employed. Consequently it will reduce gearing.

Worked example: Impact of gearing on earnings

A company has an annual profit before interest of £200. Its interest on non-current debt is fixed at £100 per annum.

Consider the effects on net profits if the profits before interest were to decrease or increase by £100 per annum.

	(1) £	(2) £	(3) £
Profit before interest	200	100	300
Interest on non-current debt	(100)	(100)	(100)
Profit available to shareholders (earnings)	100	–	200
Compared to situation (1):			
Change in profits before interest		–50%	+50%
Change in earnings		–100%	+100%

Low gearing provides scope to increase borrowings when potentially profitable projects are available. Low-geared companies will usually be able to borrow more easily and cheaply than already highly-geared companies.

However, gearing can be too low. Equity finance is often more expensive in the long run than debt finance, because equity is usually seen as being more risky. Therefore an ungeared company may benefit from adjusting its financing to include some (usually cheaper) debt, thus reducing its overall cost of capital.

Gearing is also significant to lenders as they are likely to charge higher interest, and be less willing to lend, to companies which are already highly geared, due to the increased default risk.

Interest payments are allowable for tax purposes, whereas dividends are not. This is another attraction of debt.

Interest cover indicates the ability of a company to pay interest out of profits generated. Relatively low interest cover indicates that a company may have difficulty financing the running costs of its debts if its profits fall, and also indicates to shareholders that their dividends are at risk, as interest must be paid first, even if profits fall.

2.5 Efficiency

2.5.1 Significance

Asset turnover and the working capital ratios are important indicators of management's effectiveness in running the business efficiently, as for a given level of activity it is most profitable to minimise the level of overall capital employed and the working capital employed in the business.

2.5.2 Key ratios

Net asset turnover

This measures the efficiency of revenue generation in relation to the overall resources of the business. As the amount of net assets equals the amount of capital employed and as capital employed is used in the ROCE calculation, it is easiest to calculate net asset turnover as:

$$\frac{\text{Revenue}}{\text{Capital employed}} \qquad \left(\begin{array}{l}\text{Source: IS}\\\text{Source: SFP}\end{array}\right)$$

Note that net asset turnover can be further subdivided by separating out the non-current asset element to give non-current asset turnover:

$$\frac{\text{Revenue}}{\text{Non-current assets}} \qquad \left(\begin{array}{l}\text{Source: IS}\\\text{Source: SFP}\end{array}\right)$$

This relates the revenue to the non-current assets employed in producing that revenue.

Asset turnover is sometimes known as 'sweating the assets'. It is a reference to management's ability to maximise the output from each pound (£) of capital that the company uses within the business.

Inventory turnover

The inventory turnover ratio measures the efficiency of managing inventory levels relative to demand. A business needs inventory to meet the needs of customers, but inventories are not generating revenues until they are physically sold, and tie up capital during this period. Like all management decisions, a delicate path has to be followed between keeping too much or too little inventory.

$$\frac{\text{Cost of sales}}{\text{Inventories}} \qquad \left(\begin{array}{l}\text{Source: IS}\\\text{Source: SFP}\end{array}\right)$$

(= number of times inventories are turned over each year – usually the higher the better.)

or

$$\frac{\text{Inventories}}{\text{Cost of sales}} \times 365$$

(= number of days on average that an item is in inventories before it is sold – usually the lower the better.)

Ideally the three components of inventories should be considered separately:

- Raw material to volume of purchases
- WIP to cost of production
- Finished goods to cost of sales

Interactive question 6: Inventory turnover
[Difficulty level: Easy]

State two implications of high and low inventory turnover rates.

-
-

Remember – the inventory turnover rate can be affected by seasonality. The year end inventory position may not reflect the average level of inventory.

See **Answer** at the end of this chapter.

Trade receivables collection period

This measures in days the period of credit taken by the company's customers.

$$\frac{\text{Trade receivables}}{\text{Revenue}} \times 365 \qquad \left(\frac{\text{Source: SFP}}{\text{Source: IS}} \right)$$

To obtain a full picture of receivables collection, it is best to exclude from the revenue figure any cash sales, since they do not generate receivables. This may be difficult, because published financial statements do not distinguish between cash and credit sales. Strictly speaking, VAT should be removed from receivables (revenue excludes VAT), but such adjustments are rarely made in practice.

Interactive question 7: Trade receivables collection period
[Difficulty level: Easy]

Suggest three matters that a change in the ratio could indicate.

-
-
-

Remember – the year end receivables may not be representative of the average over the year.

See **Answer** at the end of this chapter.

Trade payables payment period

This measures the number of days' credit taken by the company from suppliers.

$$\frac{\text{Trade payables}}{\text{Credit purchases}} \times 365 \qquad \left(\frac{\text{Source: IS}}{\text{Source: SFP}} \right)$$

This should be broadly similar to the trade receivables collection period, where a business makes most sales and most purchases on credit. If no figures are available for credit purchases, use cost of sales.

Interactive question 8: Trade payables payment period [Difficulty level: Easy]

Suggest two matters that a high and increasing trade payables payment period may indicate.

-

-

Remember – the year end payables may not be representative of the average over the year.

See **Answer** at the end of this chapter.

Working capital cycle/cash operating cycle

These last three ratios are often brought together in the working capital cycle (alternatively the cash operating cycle), calculated as inventory days plus trade receivables collection period minus trade payables payment period.

Any increase in the total working capital cycle may indicate inefficient management of the components of working capital.

2.5.3 Commentary

Net asset turnover enables useful comparisons to be made between businesses in terms of the extent to which they work their assets hard in the generation of revenue.

Inventory turnover, trade receivables collection period and trade payables payment period give an indication of whether a business is able to generate cash as fast as it uses it. They also provide useful comparisons between businesses, for example on effectiveness in collecting debts and controlling inventory levels.

Efficiency ratios are often an indicator of looming liquidity problems or loss of management control. For example, an increase in the trade receivables collection period may indicate loss of credit control. Declining inventory turnover may suggest poor buying decisions or misjudgement of the market. An increasing trade payables payment period suggests that the company may be having difficulty paying its suppliers; if they withdraw credit, a collapse may be precipitated by the lack of new supplies.

If an expanding business has a positive working capital cycle, it will need to fund this extra capital requirement, from retained earnings, an equity issue or increased borrowings. If a business has a negative working capital cycle, its suppliers are effectively providing funding on an interest-free basis.

As with all ratios, care is needed in interpreting efficiency ratios. For example, an increasing trade payables payment period may indicate that the company is making better use of its available credit facilities by taking trade credit where available. Therefore, efficiency ratios should be considered together with solvency and cash flow information.

2.6 Non-current asset analysis

Analysts of financial statements use the information provided to understand future performance. For capital-intensive companies it is essential that they understand the capital expenditure policies and efficiency of non-current assets.

2.6.1 Capital expenditure to depreciation

$$\frac{\text{Capital expenditure (additions)}}{\text{Depreciation}}$$

This ratio highlights whether a company is expanding its non-current assets. A ratio below one would indicate that it is not even maintaining its operating capacity. A ratio in excess of one would indicate that the company is expanding operating capacity. But PPE price changes should be taken into account: if they are rising, a ratio of more than one may still indicate a reduction in capacity, unless significant operating efficiencies are being generated from the new assets.

This ratio should include all additions, including those acquired under finance leases. The ratio is of limited benefit where the entity leases operating facilities and classifies those leases as operating leases.

It is often helpful to review this ratio over a number of years to identify trends. In the short-term capital expenditure can be discretionary.

2.6.2 Ageing of non-current assets

$$\frac{\text{Accumulated depreciation}}{\text{Gross carrying amount of non - current assets}}$$

This ratio identifies the proportion of the useful life of PPE that has expired. It should be calculated for each class of PPE. It helps identify:

- Assets that are nearing the end of their useful life that may be operating less efficiently or may require significant maintenance; and

- The need to invest in new PPE in the near term.

Obviously both of these ratios are influenced by the depreciation policies adopted by management.

Worked example: Capital expenditure

The following is an extract from the financial statements of Raport Ltd for the year ended 31 December 20X4.

Note 1	Plant and Equipment £'000
Cost	
At 1 January 20X4	2,757
Additions	137
Disposals	(94)
At 31 December 20X4	2,800
Accumulated depreciation	
At 1 January 20X4	1,922
Depreciation	302
Disposals	(60)
At 31 December 20X4	2,164
Carrying amount 1 January 20X4	835
Carrying amount 31 December 20X4	636

Note 2	20X4 £'000	20X3 £'000
Profit from operations is stated after charging		
Depreciation	302	289
Loss on disposal of plant and equipment	25	32

Requirement

Provide an analysis of the plant and equipment of Raport Ltd.

Solution

- Capital expenditure represents 45% $\left(\dfrac{137}{302} \times 100\%\right)$ of the depreciation expense for the year. This suggests that management is not maintaining capacity.

- Accumulated depreciation represents 77% $\left(\dfrac{2,164}{2,800} \times 100\%\right)$ of the cost of the assets.

This has increased from 70% $\left(\dfrac{1,922}{2,757} \times 100\%\right)$ in the previous year.

This confirms that plant and equipment is ageing without replacement. On average the plant and equipment is entering the last quarter of its useful life. This could indicate that the plant is becoming less efficient.

- The accounting policies should be reviewed, because the losses on disposal could indicate that depreciation rates are too low and that useful lives have been overestimated. This would confirm that the plant and equipment is aged and raise further concerns about its renewal and efficiency.

2.7 Investors' ratios

2.7.1 Significance

Different investors' ratios (also known as stock market ratios) help different investors:

- Price/earnings ratio will be important to those investors looking for capital growth.

- Dividend yield, dividend cover and dividends per share will be important to those investors seeking income.

Because all economic decisions relate to the future, not the past, investors should ideally use forecast information. In practice only historic figures are usually available from financial statements, but investment analysts devote substantial amounts of time to making estimates of future earnings and dividends which they publish to their clients.

Investors' ratios are only meaningful for quoted companies as they usually relate, directly or indirectly, to the share price.

2.7.2 Key ratios

Dividend yield

$$\frac{\text{Dividend per share}}{\text{Current market price per share}} \times 100$$

The market price per share is a forward-looking value, since a buyer of a share buys into the future, not past, performance of the company. So the most up-to-date amount for the dividend per share needs to be used; using information in financial statements, the total dividend will be the interim for the year recognised in the statement of changes in equity plus the final for the year disclosed in the notes to the accounts.

Dividend yield may be more influenced by dividend policy than by financial performance. A high yield based on recent dividends and the current share price may come about because the share price has fallen in anticipation of a future dividend cut. Rapidly growing companies may exhibit low yields based on historic dividends, especially if the current share price reflects anticipated future growth, because such companies often retain cash in the business, through low dividends, to finance that growth.

Dividend cover

$$\frac{\text{Earnings per share}}{\text{Dividend per share}}$$

A quoted company is required by IAS 33 *Earnings Per Share* to disclose an amount for its earnings per share (EPS). In the examination you may be required to calculate EPS and use it in ratio analysis.

The dividend cover ratio shows the extent to which a current dividend is covered by current earnings. It is an indication of how secure dividends are, because a dividend cover of less than one indicates that the company is relying to some extent on its retained profits, a policy that is not sustainable in the long term.

Price/earnings (P/E) ratio

$$\frac{\text{Current market price per share}}{\text{Earnings per share}}$$

The P/E ratio is used to indicate whether shares appear expensive or cheap in terms of how many years of current earnings investors are prepared to pay for. The P/E ratio is often used to compare companies within a sector, and is published widely in the financial press for this purpose.

A high P/E ratio calculated on historic earnings usually indicates that investors expect significant future earnings growth and hence are prepared to pay a large multiple of historic earnings. (Remember that the share price takes into account market expectations of *future* profits, whereas EPS is based on *past* levels of profit.) Low P/E ratios often indicate that investors consider growth prospects to be poor.

Net asset value

$$\frac{\text{Net assets (equity attributable to owners of parent company)}}{\text{Number of ordinary shares in issue}}$$

This calculation results in an approximation to the amount shareholders would receive if the company were put into liquidation and all the assets were realised for, and all the liabilities were paid off at, their statement of financial position amounts. In theory it is the amount below which the share price should never fall, because if it did, someone would acquire all the shares, liquidate the company and take a profit through distributions totalling the net asset value.

But the statement of financial position does not measure non-current assets at realisable value (many would sell for less than their carrying amount but some, such as freehold and leasehold properties, might realise more) and additional liabilities, such as staff redundancy payments and liquidation fees, would need to be recognised. But there might be cash inflows on liquidation relating to items such as intangible assets, which can be sold but were not recognised in the statement of financial position because they did not meet the recognition requirements.

So net asset value is only an approximation to true liquidation values, but it is still widely regarded as a solid underpinning to the share price.

2.8 Other indicators

Ratios are a key tool of analysis but other sources of information and comparisons are also available.

2.8.1 Absolute comparisons

Absolute comparisons can provide information without computing ratios, for example comparing statement of financial position or income statement amounts between this year and last and identifying changes.

Such comparisons may help to explain changes in ratios; if, for example, the statement of financial position shows that new shares have been issued to repay borrowings or finance new investment, this may explain a change in gearing and ROCE.

2.8.2 Background information

Background information supplied about the nature of the business may help to explain changes or trends, for example you may be told that the business has made an acquisition, disposal or entered a new market. The type of business itself has a major impact on the information presented in the financial statements.

2.8.3 Cash flow information

The statement of cash flows provides information as to how a business has generated and used cash so that users can obtain a fuller picture of liquidity and changes in financial position. Interpretation of cash flow information is covered in the next section.

Interactive question 9: Calculations

[Difficulty level: Intermediate]

Now try this comprehensive example to practise the calculation of various ratios that could be required in the examination.

JG Ltd Group

Summarised consolidated statement of financial position at 31 December 20X1

	£	£
Non-current assets		2,600
Current assets		
Inventories	600	
Trade receivables	900	
Investments	40	
Cash and cash equivalents	60	
		1,600
		4,200
Equity		
Ordinary share capital (£1)		1,000
Retained earnings		650
Attributable to owners of JG Ltd		1,650
Non-controlling interest		150
Equity		1,800
Non-current liabilities		
Borrowings	1,400	
Redeemable preference shares	200	
		1,600
Current liabilities		
Trade payables	750	
Bank overdraft	50	
		800
		4,200

Summarised consolidated income statement for the year ended 31 December 20X1

	£	£
Revenue		6,000
Cost of sales		(4,000)
Gross profit		2,000
Operating expenses		(1,660)
Profit from operations		340
Interest on borrowings	(74)	
Preference share dividend	(10)	
		(84)
Income from investments		5
Profit before tax		261
Tax		(106)
Profit after tax		155
Attributable to:		
Owners of JG Ltd		140
Non-controlling interest		15
		155

Requirement

Calculate the ratios applicable to JG Ltd.

Solution

(a) Return on capital employed (ROCE)

$$\frac{\text{Profit before interest and tax}}{\text{Capital employed}} \times 100 \quad =$$

(b) Return on shareholders' funds (ROSF)

$$\frac{\text{Profit attributable to owners of parent company}}{\text{Equity} - \text{non-controlling interest}} \quad =$$

(c) Gross profit %

$$\frac{\text{GP}}{\text{Revenue}} \times 100 \quad =$$

(d) Net profit margin

$$\frac{\text{Profit before interest and tax}}{\text{Revenue}} \times 100 \quad =$$

(e) Net asset turnover

$$\frac{\text{Revenue}}{\text{Capital employed}} \quad =$$

(f) Proof of ROCE   = Net profit margin   × Net asset turnover

ROCE   =   ×

(g) Non-current asset turnover

$$\frac{\text{Revenue}}{\text{Non-current assets}} \quad =$$

(h) Current ratio

$$\frac{\text{Current assets}}{\text{Current liabilities}} \quad =$$

(i) Quick ratio

$$\frac{\text{Current assets less inventories}}{\text{Current liabilities}} \quad =$$

(j) Inventory turnover

$$\frac{\text{Cost of sales}}{\text{Inventories}} \quad =$$

(k) Inventory days

$$\frac{\text{Inventories}}{\text{Cost of sales}} \times 365 \quad =$$

(l) Trade receivables collection period

$$\frac{\text{Trade receivables}}{\text{Revenue}} \times 365 \quad =$$

(m) Trade payables payment period

$$\frac{\text{Trade payables}}{\text{Cost of sales}} \times 365 \quad =$$

(n) **Gearing**

$$\frac{\text{Net debt}}{\text{Equity}} \times 100 \qquad\qquad =$$

(o) **Interest cover**

$$\frac{\text{PBIT} + \text{Investment income}}{\text{Interest payable}} \qquad\qquad =$$

See **Answer** at the end of this chapter.

3 Statements of cash flows and their interpretation

Section overview

- The analysis of the statement of cash flows is essential to an understanding of business performance and liquidity of individual companies and groups.

- Cash flow ratios provide crucial information as a part of financial statement analysis.

The ratios examined so far relate to information presented in the statement of financial position and income statement. The statement of cash flows provides valuable additional information, which facilitates more in-depth analysis of the financial statements.

You will not be asked to prepare a full statement of cash flows in the Financial Reporting examination, but you may be required to prepare extracts from one. However, you could be asked to analyse and interpret the information contained in a full statement of cash flows.

The importance of the statement of cash flows lies in the fact that businesses fail through lack of cash, not lack of profits:

- A profitable but expanding business is likely to find that its inventories and trade receivables rise more quickly than its trade payables (which provide interest-free finance). Without adequate financing for its working capital, such a business may find itself unable to pay its debts as they fall due.

- An unprofitable but contracting business may still generate cash. If, for example, an income statement is weighed down with depreciation charges on non-current assets but the business is not investing in any new non-current assets, capital expenditure will be less than book depreciation.

IAS 7 *Statement of Cash Flows* therefore requires the provision of information about changes in the cash and cash equivalents of an entity, as a basis for the assessment of the entity's ability to generate cash inflows in the future and its needs to use such cash flows. Cash flow information, when taken with the rest of the financial statements assists the assessment of:

- Changes in net assets
- Financial structure
- Ability to affect timing and amount of cash flows

Cash flow information also facilitates comparisons between entities, because it is unaffected by different accounting policies – to this extent it is often regarded as more objective than accrual-based information.

3.1 Types of cash flow

3.1.1 Operating activities

Operating cash flows may be compared with profit from operations. The extent to which profits are matched by strong cash flows is an indication of the quality of profit from operations, in that while profit from operations represents the earnings surplus available for dividend distribution, operating cash flows represents the cash surplus generated from trading, which the company can then use for other purposes.

However, caution is required where there are significant non-current assets, because depreciation is included in operating profit, but not operating cash flow. Depreciation could therefore be excluded from operating profit for comparison with cash flows, as the cash flows for non-current asset replacement are presented under investing, not operating, activities.

If operating cash flows are significantly lower than profit from operations, this may indicate that the company is in danger of running out of cash and encountering liquidity problems. In such cases, particular attention needs to be paid to the liquidity and efficiency ratios.

Significant operating cash outflows are unsustainable in the long run. If operating cash flow is negative, this needs to be investigated. Possible reasons include:

- Building up inventory levels due to expansion of the business, which tends to increase cash paid to suppliers but does not produce profit from operations because costs are included in inventories.

- Declining revenue or reduced margins.

Rapid expansion of a business is often associated with operating cash outflows. In the short term, this need not be a problem provided that sufficient finance is available.

Payments to service debt finance are non-discretionary, in that the terms of loan agreements usually require finance to be serviced, even if the business is not profitable.

If operating cash flows are insufficient to cover the interest cash flows, the company is likely to be in serious financial trouble, unless there is an identifiable non-recurring cause for the shortfall or new equity finance is forthcoming, for example to reduce interest-bearing debts.

Taxation cash flows are also non-discretionary. They tend to lag behind tax charges recognised in the income statement. In growing businesses, tax cash outflows will often be smaller than tax charges.

Point to note:

Cash payments to manufacture or acquire, and cash receipts on the sale of, assets held for rental to others are cash flows from operating (not investing) activities.

3.1.2 Investing activities

This heading in the statement of cash flows includes cash flows relating to property, plant and equipment. In the short-term, these cash flows are discretionary, in that the business will normally survive even if property, plant and equipment expenditure is delayed for some months, or even years.

Significant cash outflows indicate property, plant and equipment additions, which should lead to the maintenance or enhancement of operating cash flows in the long term. However, such investment must be financed, either from operating cash flows or from new financing.

Net outflows on property, plant and equipment replacement can also be compared with the depreciation expense in the income statement. A significant shortfall of capital spend compared to depreciation may indicate that the company is not replacing its property, plant and equipment as they wear out, or might suggest that depreciation rates are wrongly estimated.

3.1.3 Financing activities

Financing cash flows show how the company is raising finance (by debt or shares) and what finance it is repaying.

The reasons underlying financing cash flows need to be analysed. For example, inflows may be to finance additions to property, plant and equipment to expand the business or renew assets. New share finance may be used to repay debt, thus reducing future interest costs. Alternatively, new financing may be necessary to keep the company afloat if it is suffering significant operating and interest cash outflows. This last situation is unsustainable in the long term, as the company will eventually become insolvent.

3.1.4 Equity dividends paid

Equity dividends paid are, in theory, a discretionary cash flow. However, companies are often under significant investor pressure to maintain dividends even where their profits and cash flows are falling. Equity dividends paid should be compared to the cash flows available to pay them. If a company is paying out a significant amount of the available cash as dividends, it may not be retaining sufficient funds to finance future investment or the repayment of debt.

It is common policy amongst private equity companies, who own a number of well known companies, both in the UK and overseas, to not pay dividends and focus instead on debt minimisation.

3.2 Cash flow ratios

Traditional ratios are based on information in the income statement and statement of financial position. Some of these can be adapted to produce equivalent ratios based on cash flow.

3.2.1 Cash return on capital employed

$$\frac{\text{Cash return (see below)}}{\text{Capital employed}} \times 100 \qquad \left(\frac{\text{Source: SCF}}{\text{Source: SFP}}\right)$$

Cash return is computed as:

Cash generated from operations	X
Interest received (from investing activities)	X
Dividends received (from investing activities)	X
	X

Capital employed is the same as that used in ROCE.

The cash return is an approximate cash flow equivalent to profit before interest payable. As capital expenditure is excluded from the cash return, care is needed in comparing cash ROCE to traditional ROCE which takes account of depreciation of non-current assets.

3.2.2 Cash from operations/profit from operations

$$\frac{\text{Cash generated from operations}}{\text{Profit from operations}} \times 100 \qquad \left(\frac{\text{Source: SCF}}{\text{Source: IS}}\right)$$

This measures the quality of the profit from operations. Many profitable companies have to allocate a large proportion of the cash they generate from operations to finance the investment in additional working capital. To that extent, the profit from operations can be regarded as of poor quality, since it is not realised in a form which can be used either to finance the acquisitions of non-current assets or to pay back borrowings and/or pay dividends.

So the higher the resulting percentage, the higher the quality of the profits from operations.

3.2.3 Cash interest cover

$$\frac{\text{Cash return (as in 3.2.1)}}{\text{Interest paid}} \qquad \left(\frac{\text{Source: SCF}}{\text{Source: IS}}\right)$$

This is the equivalent of interest cover calculated based on the income statement. Capital expenditure is normally excluded on the basis that management has some discretion over its timing and amount. Caution is therefore needed in comparing cash interest cover with traditional interest cover, as profit from operations is reduced by depreciation. Cash interest cover will therefore tend to be slightly higher.

3.2.4 Investors' ratios

Cash flow per share

$$\frac{\text{Cash flow for ordinary shareholders (= cash return (as in 3.2.1) – interest paid – tax paid)}}{\text{Number of ordinary shares}} \quad \begin{pmatrix} \text{Source: SCF} \\ \text{Source: SFP} \end{pmatrix}$$

This is the cash flow equivalent of earnings per share. It is common practice to exclude capital expenditure from this measure, because of the discretion over the timing of such expenditure. Therefore caution needs to be exercised in comparing cash flow per share with traditional EPS, as earnings do take account of depreciation.

Cash dividend cover

$$\frac{\text{Cash flow for ordinary shareholders (as above)}}{\text{Equity dividends paid}}$$

This is the cash flow equivalent of dividend cover based on earnings. Similar comments apply regarding exclusion of capital expenditure as are noted under cash flow per share.

Interactive question 10: Calculation of cash flow ratios

[Difficulty level: Intermediate]

The following is a statement of cash flows for a company.

	Year ended 31 March 20X6	
	£'000	£'000
Cash flows from operating activities		
Cash generated from operations (Note)		12,970
Interest paid		(360)
Tax paid		(4,510)
Net cash from operating activities		8,100
Cash flows from investing activities		
Purchase of property, plant and equipment	(80)	
Dividends received	20	
Proceeds on sale of property, plant and equipment	810	
Net cash from investing activities		750
Cash flows from financing activities		
Dividends paid	(4,500)	
Borrowings	(1,000)	
Net cash used in financing activities		(5,500)
Change in cash and cash equivalents		3,350
Cash and cash equivalents brought forward		2,300
Cash and cash equivalents carried forward		5,650

Note:

	£'000
Reconciliation of profit before tax to cash generated from operations	
Profit before tax	8,410
Finance cost	340
Amortisation	560
Depreciation	2,640
Loss on disposal of property, plant and equipment	160
Decrease in inventories	570
Decrease in receivables	340
(Decrease) in trade payables	(50)
Cash generated from operations	12,970

The profit from operations for 20X6 is £8,750,000 and the capital employed at 31 March 20X6 was £28,900,000. There were 15 million ordinary shares in issue throughout the year.

Requirement

Calculate the cash flow ratios listed below for 20X6.

Solution

(a) **Cash return**

Cash generated from operations	=
Interest received	=
Dividends received	=

(b) **Cash return on capital employed**

$$\frac{\text{Cash return (from above)}}{\text{Capital employed}} \times 100 \qquad =$$

(c) **Cash from operations/profit from operations**

$$\frac{\text{Cash generated from operations}}{\text{Profit from operations}} \times 100 \qquad =$$

(d) **Cash interest cover**

$$\frac{\text{Cash return}}{\text{Interest paid}} \qquad =$$

(e) **Cash flow per share**

$$\frac{\text{Cash flow for ordinary shareholders}}{\text{Number of ordinary shares}} \qquad =$$

(f) **Cash dividend cover**

$$\frac{\text{Cash flow for ordinary shareholders}}{\text{Equity dividends paid}} \qquad =$$

See **Answer** at the end of this chapter.

4 Performance measurement – not-for-profit organisations

Section overview

- Analysis tools need to be modified to fit the different objectives of not-for-profit organisations (NFPOs)

- Profit and profitability cannot be the measure of how well NFPOs satisfy their customers

- NFPOs should be just as efficient and effective as for-profit entities.

4.1 Different objectives of NFPOs

By definition, NFPOs have objectives which are different from those of for-profit entities. Examples are:

- Minimising homelessness – local authorities
- Improving members' terms and conditions of employment – trade unions
- Maximising exam grades – educational establishments
- Minimising hunger – famine relief charities

Because NFPOs are not aiming to make a profit, performance measures such as ROCE which relate the profit earned to the resources used are not relevant. Performance measures must be designed around the objectives of the NFPO and the way they are structured.

4.2 Different performance measures

Because the objectives of NFPOs are so diverse, it is not possible to work with a single ratio or set of ratios, in the way it is possible for organisations which are focused on profit-making. But two key principles can be borne in mind in devising specific measures:

- How successful has the entity been in achieving its objectives?

  Using the examples given above, has the ratio of the homeless to those with homes fallen, have the monetary rewards for members been increased, has the proportion of top grades increased, has the proportion of hungry people in a country fallen?

- How economical has the entity been in achieving its objectives?

  This could be measured by relating the output (fall in the homeless ratio) to the input (number of person hours required of staff to achieve this output).

  The second principle is very important because in theory it ought to be possible to abolish homelessness or to ensure all students achieve top grades if limitless resources are thrown at the objective. But nowhere are resources limitless, so the economical use of resources is very important.

  This emphasises the importance of the concept of **stewardship** in the evaluation of performance of the management of an NFPO. Taking a charity as an example, all its funding may come from the voluntary donations of members of the public. Management is entrusted with these donations on the assumption that it will use them wisely and for the purposes for which the donations were raised. Management must therefore account to its donors for the stewardship of the donations received.

4.3 Efficiency and effectiveness

The differences between an NFPO and a for-profit entity only relate to what their objectives are. There need be no difference in the way they achieve these objectives, so there is no reason why an NFPO should be less efficient and effective in the use of its resources.

This is particularly important when for so many NFPOs employee costs are such a high proportion of total costs, up to 75% in some cases.

So measurement of employee units of input per unit of output are almost always important. Examples would be the staff/student ratio and the staff/top grade ratio in an educational establishment. In the case of a charity giving consumer advice, the measurement might be the average number of telephone calls handled per hour. In a medical environment it might be the average number of initial screenings per day.

ICAEW

Summary

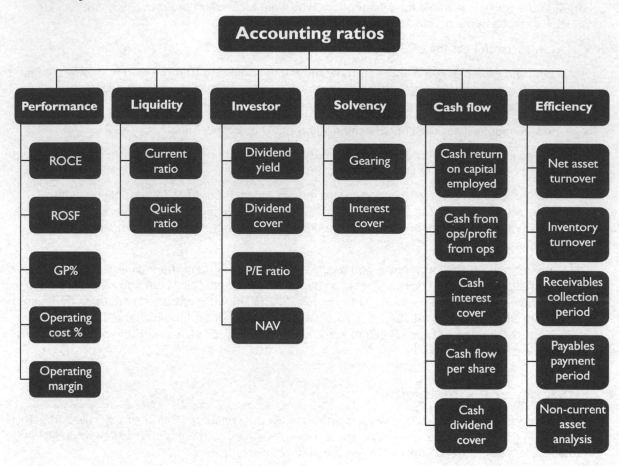

Self-test

Answer the following questions

1   The following extracts have been taken from the financial statements of Wild Swan Ltd, a manufacturing company.

Statements of financial position as at 31 December

	20X3		20X2	
	£'000	£'000	£'000	£'000
ASSETS				
Non-current assets				
Property, plant and equipment		4,465		2,819
Current assets				
Inventories	1,172		1,002	
Trade and other receivables	2,261		1,657	
Cash and cash equivalents	386		3	
		3,819		2,662
Total assets		8,284		5,481
EQUITY AND LIABILITIES				
Ordinary share capital		522		354
Preference share capital (irredeemable – 8%)		150		150
Revaluation surplus		1,857		–
Retained earnings		2,084		2,094
Equity		4,613		2,598
Non-current liabilities				
Borrowings		105		–
Current liabilities				
Trade and other payables	1,941		1,638	
Taxation	183		62	
Bank overdraft	1,442		1,183	
		3,566		2,883
Total equity and liabilities		8,284		5,481

Statements of comprehensive income for year ended 31 December

	20X3	20X2
	£'000	£'000
Revenue	24,267	21,958
Cost of sales	(20,935)	(19,262)
Gross profit	3,332	2,696
Net operating expenses	(2,604)	(2,027)
Profit from operations	728	669
Net finance cost payable	(67)	(56)
Profit before tax	661	613
Taxation	(203)	(163)
Profit for the year	458	450
Other comprehensive income for the year		
Revaluation of property, plant and equipment	1,857	–
Total comprehensive income for the year	2,315	450

Statements of changes in equity for the year ended 31 December

	20X3 £'000	20X2 £'000
Balance brought forward	2,598	2,400
Total comprehensive income for the year	2,315	450
Issue of ordinary shares	168	–
Final dividends on ordinary shares	(300)	(180)
Interim dividends on ordinary shares	(156)	(60)
Dividends on irredeemable preference shares	(12)	(12)
Balance carried forward	4,613	2,598

Statement of cash flows for the year ended 31 December 20X3

	£'000	£'000
Cash flows from operating activities		
Cash generated from operations		1,208
Interest paid		(67)
Tax paid		(82)
Net cash from operating activities		1,059
Cash flows from investing activities		
Purchases of non-current assets	(1,410)	
Proceeds on sale of property, plant and equipment	670	
Net cash used in investing activities		(740)
Cash flows from financing activities		
Dividends paid	(468)	
Proceeds from borrowings	105	
Issue of shares	168	
Net cash used in financing activities		(195)
Net change in cash and cash equivalents		124
Cash and cash equivalents brought forward (3 – 1,183)		(1,180)
Cash and cash equivalents carried forward (386 – 1,442)		(1,056)

Reconciliation of profit before tax to cash generated from operations

	£'000
Profit before tax	661
Depreciation charge	965
Profit on disposal of property, plant and equipment	(14)
Finance cost	67
Increase in inventories	(170)
Increase in trade and other receivables	(604)
Increase in trade and other payables	303
Cash generated from operations	1,208

Key ratios

	20X3	20X2
Gross profit percentage	13.7%	12.3%
Net margin	3.0%	3.0%
Net asset turnover	4.2 times	5.8 times
Trade receivables collection period	34 days	28 days
Interest cover	10.9	11.9
Current ratio	1.1	0.9
Quick ratio	0.7	0.6

Cash flow ratios (20X3 only)

Cash return on capital	22.1%
Cash interest cover	18 times

Requirements

(a) Calculate return on capital employed and gearing (net debt/equity) for both years.

(b) Comment on the financial performance and position and on the statement of cash flows of Wild Swan Ltd in the light of the above information. **(25 marks)**

2 **Statement of changes in equity for the year ended 31 December 20X4**

Attributable to the owners of Reapson plc	Revaluation surplus £m	Retained earnings £m	Total £m
Balance brought forward	–	800.00	800.00
Total comprehensive income for the year	350.00	222.90	572.90
Transfer between reserves	(17.50)	17.50	–
Dividends on ordinary shares	–	(81.75)	(81.75)
Balance carried forward	332.50	958.65	1,291.15

As well as revaluing property, plant and equipment during the year (incurring significant additional depreciation charges) Reapson plc also incurred £40 million of costs relating to the closure of a division.

Reapson plc has £272.5 million of 50p ordinary shares in issue. The market price per share is 586p.

Requirement

Explain the following statistics from a financial journal referring to Reapson plc and relate them to the above information.

(a)	Dividend per share			= 15p
(b)	Earnings per share	$= \dfrac{\text{Profit before ordinary dividends}}{\text{No of ordinary shares in issue}}$	$= \dfrac{222.9}{545}$	= 40.9p
(c)	Dividend cover	$= \dfrac{\text{EPS}}{\text{Dividend per share}}$	$= \dfrac{40.9}{15}$	= 2.7
(d)	Dividend yield	$= \dfrac{\text{Dividend per share}}{\text{Current market price per share}}$	$= \dfrac{15}{586}$	= 2.6%
(e)	Price/earnings ratio	$= \dfrac{\text{Current market price per share}}{\text{EPS}}$	$= \dfrac{586}{40.9}$	= 14.3

(10 marks)

Now go back to the Learning Objectives in the Introduction. If you are satisfied you have achieved these objectives, please tick them off.

Technical reference

1 Users and user focus

- Users need information on financial performance, financial position and changes in financial position.

- Primary focus depends on user, for example:

  - Management: overall profitability and use of assets
  - Lenders: solvency
  - Shareholders: investor returns.

- All users are interested in liquidity and cash flow.

2 Accounting ratios and relationships

- Use year end statement of financial position data without averaging, but note the limitations of this approach.

- Performance: measure rate of return on resources and utilisation of assets. Include:

  - Return on capital employed (ROCE): return as percentage of capital employed, where:

    - Return = PBIT + associates' post-tax earnings
    - Capital employed = equity + net debt, where net debt = interest-bearing debt (non-current and current) – cash and cash equivalents

  - Return on shareholders' funds (ROSF): return as percentage of parent company shareholders' funds, where:

    - Return = net profit for the period (so after tax and non-controlling interest)
    - Shareholders' funds = equity – non-controlling interest

  - Gross margin/gross profit percentage: gross profit as percentage of revenue

  - Operating cost percentage: operating costs as percentage of revenue

  - Net margin/operating margin: PBIT as percentage of revenue

  - Net asset turnover: revenue ÷ capital employed

  - Non-current asset turnover: revenue ÷ non-current assets.

- Short-term liquidity: assess ability to meet short-term financial commitments. Include:

  - Current ratio: current assets ÷ current liabilities
  - Quick/liquidity/acid test ratio: (current assets – inventories) ÷ current liabilities.

- Long-term solvency: assess financing structure and degree of risk. Include:

  - Gearing ratio: net debt as percentage of equity
  - Interest cover: (PBIT + investment income) ÷ interest payable

- Efficiency: assess working capital management. Include:

  - Net asset turnover: as above
  - Non-current asset turnover: as above
  - Inventory turnover: cost of sales ÷ inventories
  - Trade receivables collection period: (trade receivables x 365) ÷ revenue
  - Payables payment period: (trade payables x 365) ÷ credit purchases or cost of sales.

- Efficiency: assess non-current assets. Include:

  - Capex to depreciation: additions to non-current assets ÷ depreciation
  - Asset ageing: accumulated depreciation ÷ gross carrying amount of non-current assets

- Investors' (or stock market) ratios: look at investor returns. Include:

  - Dividend yield: dividend per share (most recent interim + final) as percentage of current market price

  - Dividend cover: earnings per share ÷ dividend per share or net profit for the period ÷ total ordinary dividends

  - Price/earnings ratio: current market price per share ÷ earnings per share or total market value ÷ profit for the period

  - Net asset value: net assets ÷ number of ordinary shares in issue, where net assets = equity attributable to owners.

3 Statements of cash flows and their interpretation

- Statement of cash flows offers a basis for assessment of entity's ability to generate cash and need to use it.

- Analyses changes in cash and cash equivalents (as defined).

- Headings:

  - Operating activities, to include interest and tax paid

  - Investing activities, to include interest and dividends received

  - Financing activities, to include dividends paid

- Use in cash flow ratios, such as:

  - Cash return on capital employed, where:

    - Cash return =

cash generated from operations	X
Plus	
interest received	X
Plus	
dividends received	X
	X̲

    - Capital employed = as for ROCE

  - Cash from operations/profit from operations: $\dfrac{\text{Cash generated from operations}}{\text{Profit from operations}} \times 100$

  - Cash interest cover: cash return (as above) ÷ interest paid

  - Cash flow per share: cash flow for ordinary shareholders ÷ number of ordinary shares, where:

  - Cash flow for ordinary shareholders = cash return (as above) − interest paid − tax paid

  - Cash dividend cover: cash flow for ordinary shareholders (as above) ÷ ordinary dividends paid.

Answers to Interactive questions

Answer to Interactive question 1

When drawing conclusions from ROCE/ROSF consider:

- Target return on capital (company or shareholder)

- Real interest rates

- Age of plant

- Leased/owned assets

- Upward revaluations of non-current assets, which increase capital employed, increase depreciation charges and reduce ROCE/ROSF

Answer to Interactive question 2

Variations between years may be attributable to:

- Change in sales prices
- Change in sales mix
- Change in purchase/production costs
- Inventory obsolescence

Answer to Interactive question 3

May change because of:

- Change in the amount of sales – investigate whether due to price or volume changes
- Non-recurring costs

Answer to Interactive question 4

Low and high ratios could suggest:

- Liquidity problems (low ratio)
- Poor use of shareholder/company funds (high ratio)

Two possible factors to investigate would be:

- Constituent components of ratio: inventory obsolescence (in case of current ratio), recoverability of receivables (in case of both ratios)

- Manipulation – if company has positive cash balances and a ratio greater than 1:1, payment of current liabilities such as trade payables just prior to the year end will improve ratio

Answer to Interactive question 5

When drawing conclusions from gearing ratios consider:

- Upward revaluations of non-current assets increase shareholders' funds and decrease gearing
- Whether carrying amounts of non-current assets are likely to be volatile

Answer to Interactive question 6

- High inventory turnover rate – may be efficient but the risk of running out of inventory is increased.
- Low inventory turnover rate – inefficient use of resources and potential obsolescence problems.

Answer to Interactive question 7

A change in the ratio may indicate:

- Bad debt/collection problems
- Change in nature of customer base (new customer is big but is a slow payer)
- Change in settlement terms

Answer to Interactive question 8

- High figure may indicate liquidity problems
- Potential appointment of receiver by aggrieved suppliers

Answer to Interactive question 9

(a) Return on capital employed (ROCE)

$$\frac{\text{Profit before interest and tax}}{\text{Capital employed}} \times 100 \qquad = \frac{340}{1,800 + 1,600 + 50 - 60} \times 100 = 10\%$$

(b) Return on shareholders' funds (ROSF)

$$\frac{\text{Profit attributable to owners of parent company}}{\text{Equity} - \text{non-controlling interest}} \qquad = \frac{140}{1,800 - 150} \times 100 = 8.5\%$$

(c) Gross profit %

$$\frac{\text{GP}}{\text{Revenue}} \times 100 \qquad = \frac{2,000}{6,000} \times 100 = 33.33\%$$

(d) Net profit margin

$$\frac{\text{Profit before interest and tax}}{\text{Revenue}} \times 100 \qquad = \frac{340}{6,000} \times 100 = 5.7\%$$

(e) Net asset turnover

$$\frac{\text{Revenue}}{\text{Capital employed}} \qquad = \frac{6,000}{1,800 + 1,600 + 50 - 60} = 1.8 \text{ times}$$

(f) Proof of ROCE

ROCE $\qquad$ = Net profit margin × Net asset turnover

$\qquad$ = 5.7% × 1.8 times

(g) Non-current asset turnover

$$\frac{\text{Revenue}}{\text{Non-current assets}} \qquad = \frac{6,000}{2,600} = 2.3 \text{ times}$$

(h) Current ratio

$$\frac{\text{Current assets}}{\text{Current liabilities}} \qquad = \frac{1,600}{800} = 2 \text{ times}$$

(i) Quick ratio

$$\frac{\text{Current assets less inventories}}{\text{Current liabilities}} \qquad = \frac{1,600 - 600}{800} = 1.25 \text{ times}$$

(j) Inventory turnover

$$\frac{\text{Cost of sales}}{\text{Inventories}} \qquad = \frac{4,000}{600} = 6.66 \text{ times}$$

(k) **Inventory days**

$$\frac{\text{Inventories}}{\text{Cost of sales}} \times 365 \qquad = \frac{600}{4,000} \times 365 = 55 \text{ days}$$

(l) **Trade receivables collection period**

$$\frac{\text{Trade receivables}}{\text{Revenue}} \times 365 \qquad = \frac{900}{6,000} \times 365 = 55 \text{ days}$$

(m) **Trade payables payment period**

$$\frac{\text{Trade payables}}{\text{Cost of sales}} \times 365 \qquad = \frac{750}{4,000} \times 365 = 68 \text{ days}$$

(n) **Gearing**

$$\frac{\text{Net debt}}{\text{Equity}} \times 100 \qquad = \frac{1,600 + 50 - 60}{1,800} \times 100 = 88.3\%$$

(o) **Interest cover**

$$\frac{\text{PBIT} + \text{Investment income}}{\text{Interest payable}} \qquad = \frac{340 + 5}{84} = 4.1 \text{ times}$$

Answer to Interactive question 10

(a) **Cash return**

	£'000
Cash generated from operations	12,970
Interest received	–
Dividends received	20
	12,990

(b) **Cash return on capital employed**

$$\frac{\text{Cash return (from above)}}{\text{Capital employed}} \times 100 \qquad = \frac{12,990}{28,900} \times 100 = 44.9\%$$

(c) **Cash from operations/profit from operations**

$$\frac{\text{Cash generated from operations}}{\text{Profit from operations}} \times 100 \qquad = \frac{12,970}{8,750} \times 100 = 148\%$$

(d) **Cash interest cover**

$$\frac{\text{Cash return}}{\text{Interest paid}} \qquad = \frac{12,990}{360} = 36 \text{ times}$$

(e) **Cash flow per share**

$$\frac{\text{Cash flow for ordinary shareholders}}{\text{Number of ordinary shares}} \qquad = \frac{(12,990 - 360 - 4,510)}{15,000} = 54\text{p per share}$$

(f) **Cash dividend cover**

$$\frac{\text{Cash flow for ordinary shareholders}}{\text{Equity dividends paid}} \qquad = \frac{(12,990 - 360 - 4,510)}{4,500} = 1.8 \text{ times}$$

Answers to Self-test

1 (a) Calculation of ratios ⠀⠀⠀⠀⠀⠀⠀⠀⠀**20X3** ⠀⠀⠀⠀⠀⠀⠀⠀⠀**20X2**

$$\text{ROCE} = \frac{\text{Profit before interest and tax}}{\text{Capital employed}} \qquad \frac{728}{4{,}613 + 105 + 1{,}442 - 386} = 12.6\% \qquad \frac{669}{2{,}598 + 1{,}183 - 3} = 17.7\%$$

$$\text{Gearing} = \frac{\text{Net debt}}{\text{Equity}} \qquad \frac{105 + 1{,}442 - 386}{4{,}613} = 25.2\% \qquad \frac{1{,}183 - 3}{2{,}598} = 45.4\%$$

(b) Commentary on financial performance and position

Profitability

The overall profitability of the company has remained stable, with a constant net margin and a slightly increased gross margin offset by increased overhead costs. Revenue growth of 10.5% has been achieved without an adverse effect on the net margin.

The drop in ROCE from 17.7% to 12.6% is due to the asset revaluation in 20X3. If the revaluation surplus is removed, the comparison between the years is much more valid.

Asset turnover and ROCE may be artificially high due to the company's plant being old and therefore heavily depreciated. This is suggested by the large depreciation charge on plant (as a percentage of carrying amount). Alternatively, this together with the major investment in replacing assets could indicate that plant has a relatively short life.

Liquidity and working capital management

For a manufacturer the trade receivables collection period appears satisfactory, though it has increased by six days compared with 20X2. This may be due to the increased sales volume, possibly encouraged by easier credit terms.

The current and quick ratios both appear low, though they have improved compared with 20X2. This appears to be due mainly to the large and increasing bank overdraft and to trade payables, which have increased by 18% compared with revenue growth of 10.5%.

Seasonal factors may have distorted the liquidity position, for example because the business has built up inventory to meet a sales peak shortly after the year end. This would tend to increase trade payables and overdrafts. Interest expense amounts to only 6% of the average overdraft, which suggests that the year end balance is high relative to the year as a whole.

The decision to hold large amounts of cash, when the company has a bank overdraft equating to 25% of net assets, appears to lack business logic, unless the amounts for some reason cannot be set off against each other.

Long-term solvency

The company made a share issue for £168,000 in the year. It has very little non-current debt, having issued only £105,000 in 20X3 and having none in issue in 20X2, but it does have significant overdrafts. Although the gearing ratio of 25.2% appears acceptable, it has been reduced by the asset revaluation.

Even if the debt was issued just prior to the year end (and therefore would not have had much effect on the amount of interest charged), the group has high interest cover and could finance more non-current debt. If the business does need debt financing on an ongoing basis (rather than as a result of seasonal factors), it would probably be cheaper to obtain this via long-term loans, rather than maintaining a large overdraft. This would also improve the company's short-term liquidity position.

Cash flow analysis

Operating cash inflows of £1,208,000 compare favourably with operating profits of £728,000. If non-current asset replacement cash flows are deducted, the resulting net operating cash inflow falls to £468,000. This is still more than adequate to finance taxation, interest and preference dividends, leaving £307,000 available for more discretionary use.

£468,000 was paid out in equity dividends, representing 147% of available cash flows before financing (468 as a percentage of (1,059 - 740)).The excess was funded by the share issue/borrowings. This level of dividends places an unnecessary strain on the company's cash position and, if maintained, may lead to insufficient reinvestment to maintain operations.

The net debt of £1,161,000 (105 + 1,442 - 386) equates to 25.2% of the £4,613,000 equity. This is unlikely to threaten long-term solvency but the company would nevertheless benefit from reducing its overdraft in favour of less costly forms of finance.

The cash flow ratios given help analyse the cash amount of

- Return on capital employed
- Interest cover

These cash flow ratios eliminate non-cash items such as accruals from the traditional ratios.

The cash return on capital employed (cash ROCE) for 20X3 shows a greater return on net assets than the traditional ROCE. In other words, the net assets generate more cash than profit. This is because the quality of profits is good (net cash inflow is greater than operating profit). Care should be taken in comparing these two ratios. Traditional ROCE includes depreciation, whereas cash ROCE excludes it, as it is non cash. Depreciation is £965,000, which if taken into account, more than counteracts this advantage.

Cash interest cover of 18 (1,208 ÷ 67) in 20X3 again compares favourably with the traditional interest cover of 10.9 (728 ÷ 67). Cash interest cover would be expected to be slightly higher as it is also based on net cash flow from operating activities. Interest paid and payable in 20X3 both amount to £67,000 so there are no opening/closing accruals to consider.

Overall it would appear that Wild Swan Ltd has plenty of cash to cover its interest payments at the current time. Interest payable will increase next year if the borrowings were made just before the year end. Given the carrying amount of the debentures of £105,000 at 31 December 20X3 the interest payable next year should not dent either the interest cover or cash interest cover sufficiently to cause concern.

2 (a) **Dividend – 15p per share**

This should be the cash amount of total dividends paid per share (in pence) in the most recent financial year. It ties in with the information provided as it is the total dividend per the statement of changes in equity divided by the number of shares in issue, that is

$$\frac{£81.75m}{2 \times 272.5m} = 15p \text{ per share}$$

This is the absolute amount of the per share dividend paid out by the company. To be of any real meaning, it should be related to some other amount – see below.

(b) **Earnings per share**

This is the measure of the amount earned by the company on behalf of each ordinary share. Its amount is not influenced by the dividend distribution policy of the company, being a measure of earning capacity.

(c) **Dividend cover**

This gives an indication of the security of the dividend flow from the company, measured by reference to its current year profits. (In practice a company can cover dividends out of retained earnings.) If dividend cover is high, then the company is likely to be able to maintain the level of dividend payments even if earnings fall.

Dividend cover is calculated as earnings per share divided by net dividends per share. The impact of the exceptional closure costs (£40m) and the increase in depreciation resulting from the current year revaluation (£17.5m reserve transfer) has been to reduce earnings by £57.5m. If these are added back, the earnings per share would become

$$\frac{£222.9m + £57.5m}{545m} = 51.4p$$

Revised dividend cover would therefore be

$$\frac{51.4p}{15p} = 3.4 \text{ times}$$

(d) **Dividend yield**

This gives an indication of the income return that an investor might expect on his or her shares. Because it is based on dividends, it too reflects distribution policy rather than earnings and performance.

The investor could use this to compare with returns on alternative investments.

(e) **Price/earnings ratio**

This is a way of measuring how highly investors value the earnings a company produces. It is therefore not affected by dividend policy.

Investors will pay more for shares now if they expect earnings to rise in the future, as these earnings will be reflected in future dividends and/or capital appreciation.

Using the adjusted EPS figure calculated above the ratio would be:

$$\text{P/E ratio} = \frac{\text{Market price per share}}{\text{Earnings per share}} = \frac{586p}{51.4p} = 11.4 \text{ times}$$

CHAPTER 12

Financial statement analysis: interpretation

Introduction

Examination context

Topic List

1 Economic events

2 Business issues

3 Accounting choices

4 Ethical issues

5 Industry analysis

6 Non-financial performance measures

7 Advanced earnings measures

8 Limitations of ratios and financial statement analysis

Summary and Self-test

Answers to Interactive questions

Answers to Self-test

Learning objectives

You should complete Chapter 11 before you work through this chapter.

In Chapter 12 you will consolidate the learning objectives from Chapter 11 and after completing this chapter you should be able to:

- Take account of economic and business factors and the reporting requirements of business events ☐

- Take account of accounting factors, such as non-current asset revaluation ☐

- Interpret non-financial performance measures ☐

- Identify and resolve the ethical issues associated with financial statement analysis ☐

- Calculate and interpret other common financial ratios used by financial analysts ☐

- Be aware of the limitations of ratios ☐

Specific syllabus references for this chapter are: 2b, 4b, 4d, 4e and 4f.

Syllabus links

This chapter will draw on the base of reporting knowledge that you have developed in the Financial Accounting and Financial Reporting modules. It will build upon the information introduced in Chapter 11 of this text. Chapter 13 will provide you with a suggested approach to analysis questions in the Financial Reporting examination.

Business analysis is an important aspect of the Advanced Stage technical integration and case study exams. Financial statement analysis skills are an integral part of business analysis. The skills that you develop in this chapter are fundamental to your success at Advanced Stage.

Examination context

The analysis and interpretation of financial statements is a significant portion of the Financial Reporting examination and will account for approximately 30% of the total marks across two or more questions. You may be required to interpret extracts from financial statements or to comment on how chosen accounting policies or their application affect the interpretation of the information.

Questions will provide extracts from financial statements including accounting policy notes, disclosure notes and background contextual information. Candidates will be expected to utilise this detailed information in providing a financial statement analysis of the entity. The questions will test your development of higher level skills including your analysis, judgement and evaluation skills.

In the assessment, candidates may be required to:

- Select and calculate relevant indicators, including ratios (for example stock market ratios), trends and interrelationships, to analyse a single entity's or group's financial position, performance and changes in financial position

- Identify the choice of accounting treatments adopted in financial statements and other financial information and assess how they affect the view presented

- Identify and compare significant features in the information supplied for a given entity or entities, including inconsistencies between the results of analysis and the information supplied

- Specify any additional information required for a meaningful analysis

- Draw conclusions and make inferences from an analysis which takes account of significant features in the information supplied, and which allows for the limitations of the information supplied and the analytical methods used, economic conditions and the business's circumstances

- Recognise the ethical and professional issues for a professional accountant undertaking work in and giving advice on accounting and financial reporting; explain the relevance and importance of these issues and evaluate the relative merits of different standpoints taken in debate

- Identify financial and operational information in documents containing financial statements (for example reports on operations by management or those responsible for governance, financial summaries and highlights) that could be relevant to the legal entity or consolidated financial statements, and assess whether those financial statements adequately reflect that information

1 Economic events

Section overview

Economic factors can have a pervasive effect on company performance and should be considered when analysing financial statements.

The economic environment that an entity operates in will have a direct effect on its financial performance and financial position. The economic environment can influence management's strategy but in any event will influence the business performance.

Examples of economic factors that should be considered when analysing financial statements could include:

- **State of the economy**

    If the economy that a company operates in is depressed then it will have an adverse effect on the ratios of a business. When considering economic events it is important to consider the different geographical markets that a company operates in. These may provide different rates of growth, operating margins, future prospects and risks. Some businesses are more closely linked to economic activity than others, especially if they involve discretionary spending, such as holidays, eating out in restaurants and so on.

- **Interest rates and foreign exchange rates**

    Increases in interest rates may have adverse effects on consumer demand particularly if the company is involved in supplying products that are discretionary purchases or in industries, such as home improvements, that are sensitive to such movements. Highly geared companies are most at risk if interest rates increase or if there is an economic downturn; their debt still needs to be serviced, whereas un-geared companies are less exposed. Changes in foreign exchange rates will have a direct effect on import and export prices with direct effects on competitiveness.

- **Government policies**

    Fiscal policy can have a direct effect on performance. For example, the use of trade quotas and import taxes can affect the markets in which a company operates. The availability of government export assistance or a change in levels of public spending can affect the outlook for a company.

- **Rates of inflation**

    Inflation can have an effect on the comparability of financial statements year on year. It can be difficult to isolate changes due to inflationary aspects from genuine changes in performance.

In analysing the effect of these matters on financial statements, the disclosures required by IFRS 8 *Operating Segments* are widely regarded as necessary to meet the needs of users.

2 Business issues

Section overview

The nature of the industry in which the company operates and management's actions have a direct relationship with business performance, position and cash flow.

The information in financial statements is shaped to a large extent by the nature of the business and management's actions in running it. These factors influence trends in the business and cause ratios to change over time or differ between companies.

Examples of business factors influencing ratios are set out below.

- **Type of business**

    This affects the nature of the assets employed and the returns earned. For example, a retailer may have higher asset turnover but lower margins than a manufacturer and a services business may have very little property, plant and equipment (so low capital employed and high ROCE) while a manufacturer may have lots of property, plant and equipment (so high capital employed and low ROCE).

- **Quality of management**

  Better managed businesses are likely to be more profitable (and have improved working capital management) than businesses where management is weak. Where management is seen as high quality then this can have a favourable effect.

- **Market conditions**

  If a market sector is depressed, this is likely to affect companies adversely and make most or all of their ratios appear worse. Diverse conglomerates may operate in a number of different business sectors, each of which is affected by different market risks and opportunities.

- **Management actions**

  These will be reflected in changes in ratios. For example price discounting to increase market share is likely to reduce margins but increase asset turnover; withdrawing from unprofitable market sectors is likely to reduce revenue but increase profit margins.

- **Changes in the business**

  If the business diversifies into wholly new areas, this is likely to change the resource structure and thus impact on key ratios. An acquisition near the year end will mean that capital employed will include all the assets acquired but profits from the acquisition will only be included in the income statement for a small part of the year, thus tending to depress ROCE. But this can be adjusted for, because IFRS 3 *Business Combinations* requires acquirers to disclose by way of note, total revenue and profit as if all business combinations had taken place on the first day of the accounting period.

Worked example: Acquisition during year

A group's revenue for the current period was £10 million (previous year £8 million) and its period end trade receivables were £1.6 million (previous year £900,000). During the year a new subsidiary was acquired which carried trade receivables of £300,000 at the acquisition date.

At first sight there appears to be a very disproportionate increase in trade receivables, up by almost 78% ((1,600/900) – 1) when revenue is up by 25%. But if the previous year receivables are increased by the acquired receivables of £300,000, the increase in receivables is 25% ((1,600/1,200) – 1), matching the revenue increase.

Points to note:

1 The acquisition renders the period end trade receivables collection period non-comparable with that for the previous period.

2 The consolidated statement of cash flows will present the trade receivables component in the working capital adjustments as the amount **after** the acquired receivables have been added on to the group's opening balance.

3 IFRS 3 requires disclosure in respect of each acquisition of the amounts recognised at the acquisition date for each class of assets and liabilities and the acquiree's revenue and profit or loss recognised in consolidated profit or loss for the year. In addition, there should be disclosure of the consolidated revenue and profit or loss as if the acquisition date for all acquisitions had been the first day of the accounting period. This allows users to understand the impact of the acquired entity on the financial performance and financial position as evidenced in the consolidated financial statements.

Worked example: Impact of type of business

Set out below are example ratios for two quoted companies:

		Heavy manufacturing	Advertising and media
Return on capital employed	$\left(\dfrac{\text{PBIT}}{\text{Capital employed}}\right)$	13.9%	36.6%
Net margin	$\left(\dfrac{\text{PBIT}}{\text{Revenue}}\right)$	13.2%	3.1%
Net asset turnover	$\left(\dfrac{\text{Revenue}}{\text{Capital employed}}\right)$	1.05 times	11.8 times
Current ratio	$\left(\dfrac{\text{Current assets}}{\text{Current liabilities}}\right)$	1.35:1	0.84:1
Quick ratio	$\left(\dfrac{\text{Current assets} - \text{inventories}}{\text{Current liabilities}}\right)$	0.96:1	0.78:1
Gearing	$\left(\dfrac{\text{Net debt}}{\text{Equity}}\right)$	38.4%	104.1%
Interest cover	$\left(\dfrac{\text{PBIT} + \text{investment income}}{\text{Interest payable}}\right)$	4.1 times	5.9 times
Inventory turnover	$\left(\dfrac{\text{Cost of sales}}{\text{Inventories}}\right)$	4.5 times	58.8 times
Trade receivables collection period	$\left(\dfrac{\text{Trade receivables}}{\text{Revenue}} \times 365\right)$	63 days	30 days

This illustration shows that very different types of business can have markedly different ratios. A heavy manufacturing company has substantial property, plant and equipment and work in progress and earns a relatively high margin. An advertising and media company generates a very high ROCE, mainly because its asset base, as reflected in the financial statements, is small. Most of the 'assets' of such a business are represented by its staff, the value of whom is not recognised in the statement of financial position.

In analysing the effect of business matters on financial statements, the segment disclosures required by IFRS 8 *Operating Segments* provide important information that allows the user to make informed judgements about the entity's products and services.

One of the complications in analysing financial statements arises from the way IFRSs are structured:

- IAS 1 *Presentation of Financial Statements* sets down the requirements for the format of financial statements, containing provisions as to their presentation, structure and content; but

- The recognition, measurement and disclosure of specific transactions and events are all dealt with in other IFRSs.

So preparers of financial statements must consider the possible application of several different IFRS when deciding how to present certain business transactions and business events and users must be aware that details about particular transactions or events may appear in several different parts of the financial statements.

Interactive question 1: The effect of business issues on financial reporting
[Difficulty level: Intermediate]

A listed company operating in the electronics manufacturing sector has decided that due to cost pressures it will downsize its UK based operations. A number of manufacturing facilities will close and the activities will be outsourced to South East Asian countries.

Requirement

Identify six IFRSs that may need to be considered and briefly give examples of why.

Solution

-
-
-
-
-
-

See **Answer** at the end of this chapter.

3 Accounting choices

Section overview

- IFRSs include scope for choices in accounting treatment.
- Management make estimates on judgemental matters such as inventory obsolescence that can have a significant effect on the view given.

3.1 Accounting policy choices

The scope for making choices in accounting treatment has been narrowed significantly in recent years due to the development of more prescriptive accounting standards.

Nevertheless, significant choices still exist in a number of areas, for example:

- **Asset revaluation**

    Revaluation of property, plant and equipment is particularly significant because it affects the total amounts recognised as depreciation expense in profit or loss over the life of an asset. Some analysts neutralise the problems created by revalued assets through the use of EBITDA (see section 7 below) as a performance measure. Revaluation also has a significant impact on gearing and ROCE. If assets are revalued upwards, this increases equity and total net assets but does not alter debt. Therefore, the gearing ratio will fall. Asset revaluations also increase capital employed without a pound (£) for pound (£) effect on profits, so the ROCE will fall. Because depreciation is based on the revalued amount, it will rise, further depressing ROCE.

- **Cost or fair value model for measurement of investment property**

    Where the cost model is used, the asset should be depreciated over its useful life. This produces a systematic expense in profit or loss. The use of the fair value model potentially introduces volatility into profit or loss and capital employed. Key ratios such as ROCE will be more difficult to predict if the fair value model is adopted.

- **Classification of financial assets**

    Financial assets can be classified in up to four different ways. The classification affects their measurement in the statement of financial performance and the presentation of the gains or losses. This will have a direct effect on profit and capital employed.

The disclosure of accounting policies within the financial statements allows users to understand those policies and adjust financial statements to a different basis, if desired.

Interactive question 2: Asset revaluation
[Difficulty level: Easy]

On 1 January 20X1, Tiger Ltd bought for £120,000 an item of plant with an estimated useful life of 20 years and no residual value. Tiger Ltd depreciates its property, plant and equipment on a straight line basis. Tiger Ltd's year end is 31 December.

On 31 December 20X3, the asset was carried in the statement of financial position as follows:

	£'000
Non-current asset at cost	120
Accumulated depreciation (3 × (120,000 ÷ 20))	(18)
	102

Situation A

The asset continues to be depreciated as previously at £6,000 per annum, down to a carrying amount at 31 December 20X6 of £84,000.

On 1 January 20X7, the asset is sold for £127,000, resulting in a profit of £43,000.

Situation B

On 1 January 20X4, the asset is revalued to £136,000, resulting in a gain of £34,000. The total useful life remains unchanged. Depreciation will therefore be £8,000 per annum, that is £136,000 divided by the remaining life of 17 years.

On 1 January 20X7, the asset is sold for £127,000, resulting in a reported profit on disposal of £15,000.

Requirement

Ignoring the provisions of IFRS 5 summarise the impact on reported results and net assets of each of the above situations for the years 20X4 to 20X7 inclusive.

Solution

Situation A – Asset is not revalued

	20X4 £'000	20X5 £'000	20X6 £'000	20X7 £'000
Income statement				
Profit from operations				
Includes depreciation of				
Profit on disposal of property, plant and equipment	_____	_____	_____	_____
Total impact on reported profit for 20X4 to 20X7				
Statement of financial position				
Carrying amount of asset at year end (included in capital employed)	_____	_____	_____	_____

Situation B – Asset is revalued

	20X4 £'000	20X5 £'000	20X6 £'000	20X7 £'000
Income statement				
Profit from operations				
Includes depreciation of				
Profit on disposal of property, plant and equipment	_____	_____	_____	_____
Total impact on reported profit for 20X4 to 20X7				
Statement of comprehensive income				
Gain on revaluation of property, plant and equipment	_____	_____	_____	_____
Gain is not reported as part of profit				
Therefore not included in earnings for any year				

	20X4 £'000	20X5 £'000	20X6 £'000	20X7 £'000
Statement of financial position Carrying amount of asset at year end (included in capital employed)	——	——	——	——

Summary

	Situation A No revaluation £'000	Situation B Revaluation £'000
Aggregate impact on earnings (20X4 to 20X7)	——	——

See **Answer** at the end of this chapter.

3.2 Judgements and estimates

Even though accounting standards set out detailed requirements in many areas of accounting, management still needs to exercise judgement and make significant estimates in preparing the financial statements.

Examples of judgements and estimates required of management include:

Financial statement area	Judgement or estimation required
Property, plant and equipment	• Depreciation methods • Residual values • Useful lives • Revaluations/impairments
Intangible assets	• Allocation of consideration in a business combination • Future cash flows for impairment tests • Amortisation periods
Inventories	• Inclusion of overheads and the normal level of activity • Inventory valuation methods
Lease transactions	• Classification as an operating or finance lease • Method of allocating finance charges
Provisions	• Probability of outflow of economic benefits • Measurement of liabilities
Construction contracts	• Estimates of future costs • Estimation of stage of completion
Trade receivables	• Collectability and impairment
Segment analysis	• Allocation of common costs to segments • Setting of transfer prices between segments

The increasing use of cash flow analysis by users of financial statements is often attributed to the issues surrounding the inappropriate exercise of judgement in the application of accounting policies.

In certain areas business analysts adjust financial statements to aid comparability to facilitate better comparison. These adjustments are often termed 'coping mechanisms'.

For example, some analysts convert operating leases into finance leases in the statement of financial position using the 'Rule of 8'. This involves multiplying the operating lease expense in the income statement by a factor (8 being the most commonly used), and adding this to debt in the statement of financial position.

This is because there is often a fine dividing line between finance and operating leases. Some leases are sold by lessors on the basis that they will qualify as operating leases, and thus keep gearing low. The Rule of 8 adjustment nullifies such an approach, and increases comparability between companies using these different types of lease.

4 Ethical issues

Section overview

Ethical issues can arise in the preparation of financial statements. Management may be motivated to improve the presentation of financial information.

The preparation of financial statements requires a great deal of professional judgement, honesty and integrity. Therefore, Chartered Accountants should employ a degree of healthy scepticism when reviewing financial statements and any analysis provided by management.

The financial statements and the associated ratio analysis could be affected by pressure on the preparers of those financial statements to improve the financial performance, financial position or both. Managers of organisations may try to improve the appearance of the financial information to:

- Increase their level of bonus pay or other reward benefits

- Deliver specific targets such as EPS growth to meet investors' expectations

- Reduce the risk of corporate insolvency, such as by avoiding a breach of loan covenants

- Avoid regulatory interference, for example, where high profit margins are obtained

- Improve the appearance of all or part of the business prior to an initial public offering (IPO) or disposal, so that an enhanced valuation is obtained

- Understate revenues and overstate expenses to reduce tax liabilities

Users of financial statements must be wary of the use of devices which improve short-term financial position and financial performance. Such inappropriate practices can be broadly summarised into three areas:

- **Window dressing of the year end financial position**

  Examples may include:

  - Agreeing with customers that receivables are paid on shorter terms around year end, so that the trade receivables collection period is reduced and operating cash flows are enhanced

  - Modifying the supplier payment cycle by delaying payments normally made in the last month of the current year until the first month of the following year; this will improve the cash position

  - Offering incentives to distributors to buy just before year end rather than just after.

- **Exercise of judgement in applying accounting standards**

  Examples may include:
  - Unreasonable cash flow estimates used in justifying the carrying amount of assets subject to impairment tests

  - Reducing the percentage of outstanding receivables for which full provision is made

  - Reducing the obsolescence provisions in respect of slow-moving inventories

  - Extending useful lives of property, plant and equipment to reduce the depreciation charge.

- **Inappropriate transaction recording**

  Examples may include:
  - Additional revenue can be pushed through in the last weeks of the accounting period, only for returns to be accepted and credit notes issued in the next accounting period

  - Intentionally failing to correct a number of accounting errors which individually are immaterial but are material when taken together

  - Deferring revenue expenses, such as repairs and maintenance, into future periods.

Actions such as these will not make any difference to financial performance over time, because all they do is to shift profit to an earlier period at the expense of the immediately following period. Financial position can be improved by measures such as these only in the short-term. But there may well be short-term benefits to management if these improvements keep the business within its banking covenants or if performance bonuses are to be paid to management if certain profit levels are achieved.

Interactive question 3: Changing payment dates [Difficulty level: Intermediate]

A company prepares a budget for the months of December 20X5 and January 20X6 and the position at 31 December 20X5 which include the following:

	£'000
Supplier payments in each of December 20X5 and January 20X6	300
Current assets at 31 December 20X5	
Trade receivables	700
Cash	400
	1,100
Inventories	500
	1,600
Current liabilities at 31 December 20X5	1,000

Requirement

Calculate the current and quick ratios under the following options:

Option 1   Per the budget

Option 2   Per the budget, except that the supplier payments budgeted for December 20X5 are made in January 20X6

Option 3   Per the budget, except that the supplier payments budgeted for January 20X6 are made in December 20X5

Solution

	Current ratio	Quick ratio
Option 1	_____	_____
Option 2	_____	_____
Option 3	_____	_____

See **Answer** at the end of this chapter.

Finance managers who are part of the team preparing the financial statements for publication must be careful to withstand any pressures from their non-finance colleagues to indulge in reporting practices which dress up short-term performance and position. Financial managers must be conscious of their obligations under the ethical guidelines of the professional bodies of which they are members and in extreme cases may find it useful to seek confidential guidance from district society ethical counsellors and the ICAEW ethics department which is maintained for members. For members of ICAEW guidance can be found in the Code of Ethics.

Interactive question 4: Ethical pressures [Difficulty level: Exam standard]

You are the financial controller of Haddock plc. A new Managing Director (MD) with a strong domineering character has recently been appointed by Haddock plc. She has decided to launch an aggressive acquisition strategy and a target company has been identified. You have drafted a report for Haddock plc's management team that identifies several material fair value adjustments which would increase the carrying amount of the acquired assets if the acquisition occurs. The MD has demanded that you revise your report on the fair value adjustments so that the carrying amounts of the acquired assets are materially reduced rather than increased.

Requirement

Identify the motivations of the MD and discuss the actions that you should consider.

Solution

Motivations

-
-
-
-

Actions to consider

-
-
-
-

See **Answer** at the end of this chapter.

5 Industry analysis

Section overview

Industry-specific performance measures can be extremely useful when analysing financial statements.

Introduction

Some industries are assessed using specific performance measures that take into consideration their specific natures. This is often the case with industries that are relatively young and growing rapidly, for which the traditional finance based performance criteria do not show the full operational performance.

Many professional analysts use non-financial performance measures when valuing companies for merger and acquisition (M&A) purposes. The M&A industry uses sophisticated tools that combine a variety of figures, both financial and non-financial in nature, when advising clients on the appropriate price to pay for a company.

Specific industries

Mobile phone operators often quote their growth in subscriber numbers and the average spend per customer per year. This is because such companies have high fixed costs, such as the cost of the communications licence and the maintenance of the mobile mast network, and so increases in customers have an accelerating effect on profits.

Satellite television companies similarly are keen to quote increases in their customer base.

Worked example: Sky TV

Sky TV's results for the six months to 31 December 2010 showed net customer growth of 236,000, an increase in the total customer base of some 2% - the total was just over 10 million. But there was a big change in the sales mix, with a net 558,000 customers switching to Sky+HD, bringing the total to 3,497,000. Churn was 9.5%, compared to 9.6% for a year earlier. Average revenue per customer was £541, up 10% on a year earlier. Overall, revenue was up by 15%, operating profit by 19% and EPS by 32%.

The 'churn' rate quoted above is the percentage of customers who cancel their subscriptions. It is closely monitored by industry analysts, to see whether the growth in subscribers is being offset by existing customers leaving the industry.

Service companies with a finite number of places to offer, such as airlines and hotels, will quote their seat/bed occupancy rates. This is viewed by industry analysts as a measure of the individual success of the company, and is compared to both industry averages, as well as competitors.

Retailers are often assessed on sales per square metre of floor space. Such information can be used by external users to compare the performance of retailers operating within the same industry, and also internally by management to identify poorly performing stores operated by the organisation.

Retailers will also quote 'like-for-like' sales. This is the growth in sales revenues, after stripping out the impact of new stores that have opened during the year. The reason for this is that they can demonstrate to users that they are increasing revenues both organically from existing outlets as well as by expanding their operations.

Worked example: J Sainsbury plc

Extract from J Sainsbury plc preliminary results for the 52 weeks to 19 March 2011:

'Total sales (inc VAT, ex fuel) up 4.9 per cent, like-for-like sales (inc VAT, ex fuel) up 2.3 per cent'

Worked example: Professional service companies

Some of the specific performance measures used in professional service companies include:

- Fees per partner (or director)

- Chargeability percentage of staff – this could be calculated as the total hours billed to clients divided by the total number of available hours

- Employee turnover – this could be calculated as the number of voluntary resignations and terminations, divided by the total number of employees at the beginning of the period

- Average fee recovery per hour – this could be calculated as the total fee income divided by the number of hours incurred

- Days of unbilled inventory

6 Non-financial performance measures

Section overview

Non-financial performance measures can often be as important as financial performance measures in analysing financial statements.

Profit-seeking entities

Company performance can be measured in terms of volume growth as well as financial growth. Some companies will therefore present non-financial information in the form of the growth in the level of sales in terms of units. Therefore an oil company might quote barrels of oil produced, a games console company the units sold at launch. This is especially important if the price for the product is erratic, such as oil or raw materials.

Market share is also an important benchmark of success within an industry. This can be used as a benchmark of the success of an individual product line, or used as the basis to increase other types of revenues.

Worked example: Market shares

A web traffic analysis firm reported that in April 2011 Microsoft had a 56% share of the web browser market, down from 60% twelve months earlier. In the same month Mozilla Firefox had a 22% share, followed by Google's Chrome at 12% and Apple's Safari at 7%.

Other interested parties can also make use of the financial statements. For example, there may be information relating to the number of employees working at an entity. Such information can be used to assess employment prospects, as a company that is increasing its number of staff probably has greater appeal to prospective employees. Staff efficiency can also be calculated by calculating the average revenue per employee.

However, as with all performance measures, care must be taken to make sure the information means what it says. For example, a company might outsource a significant number of its functions, such as HR, IT, payroll, after sales service and so on. Thus it would appear to have a relatively low employee base compared to a competitor who operated such functions in-house. Comparability would be distorted.

Not-for-profit entities

Not all entities are profit-seeking. Schools, hospitals, charities and so on may all have objectives that are not financially based. However, they may be assessed by interested parties and present information alongside their financial statements.

Institution	Performance measure
Hospital	Speed at attending to patients, success rates for certain types of operation, length of waiting lists
School	Exam pass rates, attendance records of pupils, average class sizes
Charity	Percentage of income spent on administrative expenses, speed of distribution of income

7 Advanced earnings measures

Section overview

Users often adjust the reported profits figures for comparison to other companies.

Some users of financial statements adjust the reported profits figures to calculate what they perceive as maintainable levels of performance.

EBIT

EBIT stands for earnings before interest and tax, but also adjusts for non-recurring expenses and income to arrive at a final figure. What constitutes a non-recurring item is itself a subjective decision and different users will produce different figures. If a company presents reorganisation costs as an exceptional item in profit or loss once, then it is likely to be seen as non-recurring. However, if the company incurred reorganisation costs in three years out of five, should such costs be seen as recurring or non-recurring?

EBITDA

EBITDA is EBIT *plus* the addition of depreciation and amortisation costs recognised in profit or loss. The rationale for this calculation is that EBITDA removes the subjective figures for depreciation and amortisation. Many users of financial statements are cautious about relying on figures that are based solely on management judgements and vary from company to company. The lack of consistency in figures such as depreciation from company to company distorts comparability.

Some supporters of EBITDA also claim that it is an effective representation of normalised/underlying cash flows.

Point to note:

Although the ratio is initially calculated on the basis of the most recent income statement, some analysts adjust for "non-recurring items" to arrive at an amount on which to base future projections.

EBITDAR

EBITDAR adds back operating lease **rental** costs to the EBITDA figure. Certain user groups view operating leases as a form of finance which is not recognised in the statement of financial position. By adding back operating lease rentals, consistency is achieved between companies, whether they use finance or operating leases.

The EBITDAR figure is sometimes used when calculating valuations of companies for acquisition purposes. It is often used in conjunction with the 'Rule of 8' adjustment discussed earlier.

Worked example: Calculate EBIT, EBITDA and EBITDAR

Fin plc and Op plc operate in the same industry and are of similar size. Both have entered into a number of significant lease arrangements to obtain the use of key operating assets. Under IAS 17 *Leases* Fin plc's leases are finance leases, while Op plc's are operating leases. The following amounts have been extracted from the income statements of Fin plc and Op plc.

	Fin plc £'000	Op plc £'000
Gross profit	300	300
Depreciation of leased assets	(60)	–
Operating lease rentals	–	(80)
Other operating expenses	(100)	(100)
Operating profit	140	120
Finance lease interest expense	(20)	–
Other interest expense	(30)	(30)
Profit before taxation	90	90

The profitability measures can be calculated as follows:

	£'000	£'000
EBIT	140	120
EBITDA (140 + 60)/120	200	120
EBITDAR (140 + 60)/(120 + 80)	200	200

This simple example demonstrates the objective of calculating EBITDAR to facilitate comparison where operating leases are significant.

EBITDA/Interest

This is a variant of the interest cover ratio calculated in Chapter 11. It uses EBITDA instead of operating profit on the grounds that EBITDA is a closer approximation to maintainable cash flows generated from operations.

Total Debt/EBITDA

This ratio looks at how difficult a company finds it to service its debt commitments from operations. This figure is often used as the basis of a lending covenant by a bank to a company. The higher the ratio, the higher the perceived risk of default on the loan.

8 Limitations of ratios and financial statement analysis

Section overview

Summary of the limitations of ratios and financial statement analysis.

Financial statement analysis is based upon the information in financial statements. As such ratio analysis is subject to the same limitations as the financial statements themselves.

- Ratios are not definitive measures. They provide clues to the financial statement analysis but qualitative information is invariably required to prepare an informed analysis.

- Ratios calculated on the basis of published, and therefore incomplete, data are of limited use. This limitation is particularly acute for those ratios which link statement of financial position and income statement figures. A period end statement of financial position may well not be at all representative of the average financial position of the business throughout the period covered by the income statement.

- Ratios use historic data, which may not be predictive, as it ignores future actions by management and changes in the business environment.

- Ratios may be distorted by differences in accounting policies between entities and over time.

- Ratios are based on figures from the financial statements. If there is financial information that is not captured within the financial statements (such as changes to the company reputation), then this will be ignored.

- Comparisons between different types of business are difficult because of differing resource structures and market characteristics. However, it may be possible to make indirect comparisons between businesses in different sectors, by comparing each to its own sector averages.

- Window dressing and creative practices can have an adverse effect on the conclusions drawn from the interpretation of financial information.

- Price changes can have a significant effect on time based analysis across a number of years.

Summary and Self-test

Summary

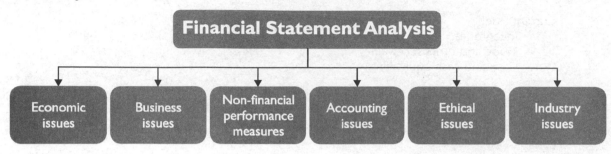

Self-test

Answer the following questions.

1 Verona

Verona plc is a parent company. The Verona plc group includes two manufacturers of kitchen appliances. One of these companies, Nice Ltd, serves the North of England and Scotland. The other company, Sienna Ltd, serves the Midlands, Wales and Southern England. Each of the two companies manufactures an identical range of products.

Verona plc has a quarterly reporting system. Each group member is required to submit an abbreviated set of financial statements to head office. This must be accompanied by a set of ratios specified by the board of Verona plc. All manufacturing companies, including Nice Ltd and Sienna Ltd, are required to calculate the following ratios for each quarter:

- Return on capital employed
- Trade receivables collection period
- Trade payables payment period
- Inventory turnover (based upon average inventories)

The financial statements for the three months (that is 89 days) ended 30 April 20X3, submitted to the parent company, were as shown below.

Income statements for the quarter ended 30 April 20X3

	Nice Ltd		Sienna Ltd	
	£'000	£'000	£'000	£'000
Revenue		3,000		4,400
Opening inventories	455		684	
Purchases	1,500		2,100	
	1,955		2,784	
Closing inventories	(539)		(849)	
Cost of materials	1,416		1,935	
Wages and salaries	700		960	
Depreciation	128		83	
Cost of sales		(2,244)		(2,978)
Gross profit		756		1,422
Marketing	450		570	
Administration	147		238	
Loan interest	10		–	
Overdraft interest	–		5	
		(607)		(813)
Profit for the period		149		609

Statements of financial position at 30 April 20X3

	Nice Ltd		Sienna Ltd	
	£'000	£'000	£'000	£'000
ASSETS				
Non-current assets				
Property		2,000		1,300
Plant and equipment		1,700		1,100
		3,700		2,400
Current assets				
Inventories	539		849	
Trade and other receivables	1,422		1,731	
Cash and cash equivalents	71		–	
		2,032		2,580
Total assets		5,732		4,980
EQUITY AND LIABILITIES				
Equity				
Ordinary share capital		1,745		479
Revaluation surplus		700		–
Retained earnings		2,049		3,309
Equity		4,494		3,788
Non-current liabilities				
Borrowings		800		–
		5,294		3,788
Current liabilities				
Trade and other payables	438		1,062	
Overdraft	–		130	
		438		1,192
Total equity and liabilities		5,732		4,980

The managing director of Nice Ltd feels that it is unfair to compare the two companies on the basis of the figures shown above, even though they have been calculated in accordance with the group's standardised accounting policies. The reasons he puts forward are as follows.

- Verona plc is in the process of revaluing all land and buildings belonging to group members. Nice Ltd's properties were revalued up by £700,000 on 1 February 20X3 and this revaluation was incorporated into the company's financial statements. The valuers have not yet visited Sienna Ltd and that company's property is carried at cost less depreciation.

  The Verona group depreciates property on a quarterly basis, calculated at a rate of 4% per annum.

- Nice Ltd's new production line costing £600,000 became available for use during the final week of the period under review. The cost of purchase was borrowed from a bank and is included in the figures for non-current borrowings.

  The managing director of Nice Ltd believes the effect of the purchase of this machine should be removed as it happened so close to the period end.

  The Verona group depreciates machinery at a rate of 25% of cost per annum.

- Nice Ltd supplied the Verona group's hotel division with goods to the value of £300,000 in October 20X2. This amount is still outstanding and has been included in Nice Ltd's trade receivables figure. Nice Ltd has been told that this balance will not be paid until the hotel division has sufficient liquid funds.

- Nice Ltd purchased £400,000 of its materials, at normal trade prices, from a fellow member of the Verona group. This supplier had liquidity problems and the group's corporate treasurer ordered Nice Ltd to pay for the goods as soon as they were delivered.

Requirements

(a) Calculate the ratios required by the Verona group for both Nice Ltd and Sienna Ltd for the quarter, using the figures in the financial statements submitted to the holding company.

(b) Explain briefly which company's ratio appears the stronger in each case.

(c) Explain how the information in the notes above has affected Nice Ltd's return on capital employed, trade receivables collection period and trade payables payment period.

(d) Explain how the calculation of the ratios should be adjusted to provide a fairer basis for comparing Nice Ltd with Sienna Ltd. **(18 marks)**

2 Brass Ltd

You are the financial accountant of Brass Ltd, a company which operates a brewery and also owns and operates a chain of hotels and public houses. Your managing director has obtained a copy of the latest financial statements of Alliance Breweries Ltd, a competitor, and has gained the impression that, although the two companies are of a similar overall size, Alliance's performance is rather better than that of Brass Ltd.

He is also concerned about his company's ability to repay a £20 million loan. The income statements and statements of financial position of the two companies for the year to 31 December 20X2 and extracts from the notes are set out below.

Income statements

	Brass Ltd		Alliance Breweries Ltd	
	£'000	£'000	£'000	£'000
Revenue		157,930		143,100
Cost of sales		(57,400)		(56,500)
Gross profit		100,530		86,600
Distribution costs	27,565		21,502	
Administrative expenses (Note 1)	53,720		29,975	
		(81,285)		(51,477)
Profit from operations		19,245		35,123
Finance cost		(2,000)		–
Profit before tax		17,245		35,123
Tax		(5,690)		(11,590)
Profit for the year		11,555		23,533

Statements of financial position

	Brass Ltd		Alliance Breweries Ltd	
	£'000	£'000	£'000	£'000
ASSETS				
Non-current assets				
Property, plant and equipment (Note 3)		71,253		69,570
Intangibles (Note 2)		–		3,930
		71,253		73,500
Current assets				
Inventories	7,120		4,102	
Trade and other receivables	28,033		22,738	
Cash and cash equivalents	5,102		–	
		40,255		26,840
Total assets		111,508		100,340
EQUITY AND LIABILITIES				
Equity				
Ordinary share capital		30,000		50,000
Revaluation surplus		15,253		–
Retained earnings		16,775		32,080
		62,028		82,080
Non-current liabilities (10% loan)		20,000		–
Current liabilities (Note 4)		29,480		18,260
Total equity and liabilities		111,508		100,340

Notes:

(1) Administrative expenses

These include the following:

	Brass Ltd £'000	Alliance Breweries Ltd £'000
Directors' remuneration	2,753	1,204
Advertising and promotion	10,361	2,662

(2) Intangible assets – Alliance Breweries Ltd

Intangible assets include brand names and trade marks purchased from Odlingtons Breweries Ltd in 20X0, which are being amortised over their useful lives.

(3) Brass Ltd – Property, plant and equipment

	Freehold land and buildings £'000	Motor vehicles £'000	Plant and machinery £'000	Total £'000
Cost or valuation 1 January 20X2	113,712	655	3,397	117,764
Additions	3,150	125	523	3,798
Cost or valuation 31 December 20X2	116,862	780	3,920	121,562
Provision for depreciation 1 January 20X2	(43,239)	(272)	(2,548)	(46,059)
Charge for year	(3,506)	(156)	(588)	(4,250)
Provision for depreciation 31 December 20X2	(46,745)	(428)	(3,136)	(50,309)
Carrying amount 31 December 20X2	70,117	352	784	71,253

The company's freehold land and buildings were revalued during 20X0 by the directors.

Alliance Breweries Ltd – Property, plant and equipment

	Freehold brewery £'000	Freehold hotels and public houses £'000	Motor vehicles £'000	Plant and machinery £'000	Total £'000
Cost 1 January 20X2	5,278	80,251	874	5,612	92,015
Additions	–	8,920	79	489	9,488
Cost 31 December 20X2	5,278	89,171	953	6,101	101,503
Provision for depreciation 1 January 20X2	(2,771)	(23,291)	(477)	(3,838)	(30,377)
Charge for year	(96)	(490)	(238)	(732)	(1,556)
Provision for depreciation 31 December 20X2	(2,867)	(23,781)	(715)	(4,570)	(31,933)
Carrying amount 31 December 20X2	2,411	65,390	238	1,531	69,570

(4) Current liabilities

	Brass Ltd £'000	Alliance Breweries Ltd £'000
Trade payables	23,919	7,875
Taxation	5,561	10,235
Bank overdraft	–	150
	29,480	18,260

(5) Non-current liabilities

The 10% loan is redeemable in June 20X4.

(6) **Accounting policies**

Both companies have similar accounting policies apart from depreciation where the policies are as follows:

Brass Ltd – Depreciation

Depreciation is provided by the company to recognise in profit or loss the cost of property, plant and equipment on a straight line basis over the anticipated life of the assets as follows.

	%
Freehold buildings	4
Motor vehicles	20
Plant and equipment	10–33

Freehold land is not depreciated.

Leasehold property is amortised over the term of the lease.

Alliance Breweries Ltd – Depreciation

Property, plant and equipment are depreciated over their useful lives as follows.

	%
Motor vehicles	25
Plant and equipment	10–25
Freehold land	NIL
Freehold buildings	1

The following ratios have been calculated for Brass Ltd for the year ended 31 December 20X2.

(1) $\text{ROCE} = \dfrac{\text{Profit before interest and tax}}{\text{Capital employed}}\%$ $\qquad \dfrac{19,245}{62,028 + 20,000 - 5,102} = 25\%$

(2) $\text{Asset turnover} = \dfrac{\text{Revenue}}{\text{Capital employed}}$ $\qquad \dfrac{157,930}{62,028 + 20,000 - 5,102} = 2.05$

(3) $\text{Net profit margin} = \dfrac{\text{Profit before interest and tax}}{\text{Revenue}}\%$ $\qquad \dfrac{19,245}{157,930} = 12.2\%$

(4) $\text{Gross profit percentage} = \dfrac{\text{Gross profit}}{\text{Revenue}}\%$ $\qquad \dfrac{100,530}{157,930} = 63.7\%$

(5) $\text{Current ratio} = \dfrac{\text{Current assets}}{\text{Current liabilities}}$ $\qquad \dfrac{40,255}{29,480} = 1.37$

(6) $\text{Quick ratio} = \dfrac{\text{Current assets} - \text{inventories}}{\text{Current liabilities}}$ $\qquad \dfrac{33,135}{29,480} = 1.12$

(7) $\text{Trade receivables collection period} = \dfrac{\text{Trade receivables}}{\text{Revenue}}$ $\qquad \dfrac{28,033}{157,930} \times 365 = 65 \text{ days}$

(8) $\text{Inventory turnover} = \dfrac{\text{Cost of sales}}{\text{Inventory}}$ $\qquad \dfrac{57,400}{7,120} = 8.1$

Requirements

(a) Prepare a report to the managing director comparing the profitability and liquidity of Brass Ltd with Alliance Breweries Ltd, using the ratios given for Brass Ltd and appropriate accounting ratios for Alliance Breweries Ltd and suggest possible reasons for the differences between the results of the two companies.

(b) State briefly what adjustments would be necessary to the financial statements of the companies for a more relevant comparison of their relative performance.

(20 marks)

3 Caithness plc

Caithness plc, a parent company, requires sets of management information, including key ratios, from all of its subsidiaries. The most recent sets of information for two of its subsidiaries, Sutherland Ltd and Argyll Ltd, two manufacturing companies, show the following.

	Sutherland Ltd	Argyll Ltd
Return on capital employed (ROCE)	5%	13%
Gross profit percentage	30%	35%
Net margin	13%	10%
Current ratio	2.5:1	3:1
Quick ratio	1.8:1	2.7:1
Trade receivables collection period	60 days	45 days
Trade payables payment period	40 days	50 days
Inventory turnover	60 days	20 days
Gearing (debt/equity)	55%	100%
Interest cover	4 times	2 times
Cash return on capital employed (cash ROCE)	7%	8%

Additional information

(1) Each company is treated as a mainly autonomous unit, although they share an accounting function and Caithness plc does determine the dividend policy of the two subsidiaries. Companies in the group must use the same accounting policies.

(2) It is group policy to record all assets at cost less accumulated depreciation and impairment losses. However, Sutherland Ltd has revalued its freehold property and included the results in the recent management information above.

(3) Argyll Ltd has recently leased a specialised item of plant and machinery. In the management information above the lease rentals have been recognised as an expense in profit or loss, but the managing director has said that this is a finance lease and the group directors are aware that the year end published financial statements will need to reflect this.

(4) Sutherland Ltd and Argyll Ltd trade with other companies in the group. At the instigation of Argyll Ltd, Sutherland Ltd has supplied one of the other companies in the group with goods with a selling price of £200,000. These are no longer in group inventories but Sutherland Ltd has been told that the goods will not be paid for until the liquidity problems of the other company are resolved.

Requirements

(a) Comment on the relative financial performance and position of Sutherland Ltd and Argyll Ltd from the above information. **(12 marks)**

(b) Identify what further information you would find useful to help with your commentary in (a), providing reasons. **(5 marks)**

(c) It transpires that the managing director of Argyll Ltd, who was previously head of the accounting function for both companies, was aware, at the time of preparing the above information, that Caithness plc is considering selling its stake in one of these companies and that Caithness plc intends to use the information to help it in making its decision.

Comment on the information above in the light of this and set out any additional information which would help you to form a view on the situation. **(3 marks)**

(20 marks)

4 Trendsetters Ltd

Trendsetters Ltd is a long-established chain of provincial fashion boutiques, offering mid-price clothing to a target customer base of late teens/early twenties. However, over the past eighteen months, the company appears to have lost its knack of spotting which trends from the catwalk shows will succeed on the high street. As a result, the company has had to close a number of its stores just before its year end of 31 December 20X2.

You have been provided with the following information for the years ended 31 December 20X1 and 20X2.

Statement of cash flows for the year ended 31 December

	20X2 £'000	20X1 £'000
Cash flows from operating activities		
Cash generated from operations	869	882
Interest paid	(165)	(102)
Tax paid	(13)	(49)
Net cash from operating activities	691	731
Cash flows from investing activities		
Dividends received	–	55
Proceeds from sales of investments	32	–
Proceeds from sale of property, plant and equipment	1,609	12
Net cash generated from investing activities	1,641	67
Cash flows from financing activities		
Dividends paid	–	(110)
Borrowings taken out	500	100
Net cash generated from/(used in) financing activities	500	(10)
Net change in cash and cash equivalents	2,832	788
Cash and cash equivalents brought forward	910	122
Cash and cash equivalents carried forward	3,742	910

Reconciliation of profit before tax to cash generated from operations

	20X2 £'000	20X1 £'000
Profit before tax	2,293	162
Investment income	–	(55)
Finance cost	165	102
Depreciation charge	262	369
Loss on disposal of investments	101	–
Profit on disposal of property, plant and equipment	(1,502)	(2)
Increase in inventories	(709)	(201)
Increase/decrease in trade and other receivables	(468)	256
Increase in trade and other payables	727	251
Cash generated from operations	869	882

Extracts from the income statement and statement of financial position for the same period were as follows.

	20X2 £'000	20X1 £'000
Revenue	2,201	3,102
EQUITY AND LIABILITIES		
Equity		
Ordinary share capital	100	100
Retained earnings	7,052	4,772
	7,152	4,872
Long-term liabilities		
Borrowings	1,500	1,000
Current liabilities		
Trade and other payables	1,056	329
	9,708	6,201

Requirements

(a) Comment on the above information, calculating three cash flow ratios to assist you in your analysis. **(15 marks)**

(b) You have now learnt that the financial controller of Trendsetters Ltd has been put under severe pressure by his operational directors to improve the figures for the current year.

Discuss how this pressure might have influenced both the above information and other areas of the financial statements, and suggest what actions the financial controller should consider in responding to these pressures. **(5 marks)**

(20 marks)

Now, go back to the Learning Objectives in the Introduction. If you are satisfied you have achieved these objectives, please tick them off.

Answer to Interactive question 1

Decisions to dispose of a group company or to close down a business activity within the group result in restructurings. The decision to restructure a major part of the business will require consideration of:

- IAS 7 *Statement of Cash Flows'* requirements as to disclosure within investing activities of the cash flows resulting from disposals.

- IAS 10 *Events After the Reporting Period's* requirements as to events occurring after the end of the reporting period, whether they are adjusting events (that is, confirmation of the carrying amounts of assets/liabilities) or non-adjusting events (for example, the disclosure of a decision to restructure).

- IFRS 8 *Operating Segments'* requirements as to segment reporting – a disposal could well affect the segments which are reportable.

- IFRS 5 *Non-current Assets Held for Sale and Discontinued Operations'* requirements – a decision to restructure a major part of the business is likely to lead to disclosures of both discontinued operations in the income statement and non-current assets held for sale in the statement of financial position.

- IAS 36 *Impairment of Assets'* requirements as to impairment of assets – impairment will almost certainly result from a restructuring decision.

- IAS 37 *Provisions, Contingent Liabilities and Contingent Assets'* requirements as to provisions – liabilities which previously were only contingent may well now require recognition and provisions for restructuring costs may need to be recognised.

Other standards such as IAS 2 *Inventories* may also be relevant. Any surplus or excess inventory may require disposal at below cost. In addition, the presentation of these events may need the consideration of IAS 1 *Presentation of Financial Statements*.

Answer to Interactive question 2

Situation A – Asset is not revalued

	20X4 £'000	20X5 £'000	20X6 £'000	20X7 £'000
Income statement				
Profit from operations				
Includes depreciation of	(6)	(6)	(6)	–
Profit on disposal of property, plant and equipment	–	–	–	43

Total impact on reported profit for 20X4 to 20X7 = £25,000 = proceeds of £127,000 less carrying amount of £102,000 at 1 January 20X4

	20X4 £'000	20X5 £'000	20X6 £'000	20X7 £'000
Statement of financial position				
Carrying amount of asset at year end (included in capital employed)	96	90	84	–

Situation B – Asset is revalued

	20X4 £'000	20X5 £'000	20X6 £'000	20X7 £'000
Income statement				
Profit from operations				
Includes depreciation of	(8)	(8)	(8)	–
Profit on disposal of property, plant and equipment	–	–	–	15

Total impact on reported profit for 20X4 to 20X7 = £(9,000)

	20X4 £'000	20X5 £'000	20X6 £'000	20X7 £'000
Statement of comprehensive income				
Gain on revaluation of property, plant and equipment	34	–	–	–

Gain is not reported as part of profit
Therefore not included in earnings for any year

	20X4 £'000	20X5 £'000	20X6 £'000	20X7 £'000
Statement of financial position				
Carrying amount of asset at year end (included in capital employed)	128	120	112	–

Summary

	Situation A No revaluation £'000	Situation B Revaluation £'000
Aggregate impact on earnings (20X4 to 20X7)	25	(9)

Answer to Interactive question 3

		Current ratio	Quick ratio
Option 1	(1,600 ÷ 1,000) and (1,100 ÷ 1,000)	1.60:1	1.10:1
Option 2	((1,600 + 300) ÷ (1,000 + 300)) and ((1,100 + 300) ÷ (1,000 + 300))	1.46:1	1.08:1
Option 3	((1,600 – 300) ÷ (1,000 – 300)) and ((1,100 – 300) ÷ (1,000 – 300))	1.86:1	1.14:1

Answer to Interactive question 4

Motivations

- The new Managing Director (MD) is motivated to try to maximise the post-acquisition earnings from the target company. This will help to increase EPS and the acquisition may be perceived as more successful.

- If asset carrying amounts are reduced at the date of acquisition, then goodwill will be increased by the same amount. Goodwill is not amortised and assuming no impairment occurs in the immediate post-acquisition period, the effect on earnings from increasing goodwill will be nil.

- By reducing the asset carrying amounts, the depreciation and amortisation expense related to non-current assets will be reduced in the post-acquisition period, as will inventory amounts charged to cost of sales. If asset carrying amounts were increased, the opposite would occur and post-acquisition earnings would be adversely affected.

- Accounting standards such as IFRS 3 are clear in the determination and treatment of the fair values of the acquired assets, liabilities and contingent liabilities. However, judgement is still required in determining fair values. It is essential that an unbiased approach be used in applying the judgement necessary.

Actions to consider

- The MD should be made aware of the issues involved, including the potential professional and legal issues. The requirements of the relevant accounting standards should be explained to her.

- It may be appropriate to discuss and explain the situation to other members of the board of directors and to seek their opinions. They may be able to add support.

- If the MD continues to try to dominate and exert influence on the contents of the report, then it would be appropriate to consult the ICAEW ethical handbook, the local district society support member and/or the confidential ethics help line.

- The approach of the MD may raise concerns about her ethical approach to business in areas other than financial reporting. It is important to remain alert to other potential areas of inappropriate practice. Ultimately the domineering approach of the MD may lead to the conclusion that alternative employment should be sought.

1 Verona

(a) Ratios using figures from the financial statements

	Nice Ltd	Sienna Ltd

Return on capital employed (ROCE)

$$\frac{\text{Profit before interest and tax}}{\text{Capital employed}} \times 100 \qquad \frac{149 + 10}{4,494 + 800 - 71} \times 100 = 3\% \qquad \frac{609 + 5}{3,788 + 130} \times 100 = 16\%$$

Trade receivables collection period

$$\frac{\text{Trade receivables}}{\text{Revenue}} \times 89 \qquad \frac{1,422}{3,000} \times 89 = 42 \text{ days} \qquad \frac{1,731}{4,400} \times 89 = 35 \text{ days}$$

Trade payables payment period

$$\frac{\text{Trade payables}}{\text{Purchases}} \times 89 \qquad \frac{438}{1,500} \times 89 = 26 \text{ days} \qquad \frac{1,062}{2,100} \times 89 = 45 \text{ days}$$

Inventory turnover

$$\frac{\text{Cost of materials}}{\text{Average inventory}} \qquad \frac{1,416}{(455 + 539)/2} = 2.8 \text{ times} \qquad \frac{1,935}{(684 + 849)/2} = 2.5 \text{ times}$$

(b) **Comparison of the two companies**

(i) **ROCE**

The managers of Nice Ltd are generating a far smaller return on the resources under their control than are the managers of Sienna Ltd. Sienna Ltd has produced a greater percentage return for each pound invested in the company than has Nice Ltd. This suggests that Sienna Ltd is using its net assets more effectively than Nice Ltd.

(ii) **Trade receivables collection period**

Generally, the management of any company will try to obtain payment from credit customers as soon as possible. Sienna Ltd again out-performs Nice Ltd by receiving cash from customers seven days sooner on average.

(iii) **Trade payables payment period**

In this case companies usually prefer to put off paying creditors for as long as possible to aid cash flow. Sienna Ltd has successfully managed to pay creditors an average of nineteen days later than Nice Ltd.

(iv) **Inventory turnover**

As a further means of improving cash flow, companies try to turn over inventory as quickly as possible, avoiding working capital being tied up in slow-moving lines. Here, Nice Ltd is performing approximately 10% better than Sienna Ltd.

(c) **Effect of information on Nice Ltd's ratios**

ROCE

This will be affected by the revaluation and the purchase of new machinery.

The revaluation will have had a two-fold effect on ROCE. It will increase capital employed by £700,000 and reduce profit before interest and tax by additional depreciation of £7,000 (700,000 × 4% × 3 ÷ 12).

Overall this will have reduced ROCE.

The purchase of the machinery will also have reduced ROCE due to capital employed increasing. The depreciation charge for just the last week of the period will not be sufficiently large as to distort comparisons.

Trade receivables collection period

The £300,000 receivable at some point in the future has artificially increased both trade receivables and the related collection period.

Trade payables payment period

The £400,000 will have been included in purchases used in the calculation of the trade payables payment period but as it was paid immediately it will not have been included in trade payables. The payment period will appear lower than it otherwise would have been.

(d) **Adjusted ratios**

For ratio analysis to be meaningful, it is important to compare like with like. The managing director of Nice Ltd has good reason to feel that the ratio analysis carried out on the two sets of adjusted accounts results in misleading figures.

The group is intending to revalue the property of all group members. Until such time as figures are available for all the companies, an adjustment should be made to exclude revaluations from the ratios. Revaluation of property can result in a marked change in ROCE (as well as other asset-based ratios). The additional depreciation charge should also be added back to net profit.

The trade receivables collection period is normally used to analyse trade receivable payment profiles. Debts due from group companies, especially the holding company, may be subject to constraints outside the control of the receiving company, as in this case. As the holding company can dictate when the debt is paid, the directors of Nice Ltd should not be held answerable for this. Trade receivables should be reduced by the £300,000.

The trade payables payment period should be calculated based on the ratio of trade payables to credit purchases. As the payment was made as soon as the goods were delivered, this amount should be treated as a cash purchase and excluded from the calculation.

2   Brass Ltd

(a) **REPORT**

To: B Brewster. Managing Director
From: C Counter. Financial Accountant
Date: 9 June 20X3
Subject: Comparative analysis of results with Alliance Breweries Ltd

I set out below my comments on the profitability and liquidity of Brass Ltd compared with those of our competitor, Alliance Breweries Ltd (Alliance). Equivalent accounting ratios to those already calculated for Brass Ltd have been calculated for Alliance and are set out in the Appendix.

Profitability

The fundamental profitability ratio 'return on capital employed' (ROCE) for Brass Ltd is 25% and for Alliance 42.7%. It does therefore at first sight appear that Alliance has a better overall performance. Further analysis throws light on the reasons for this performance differential.

The return on capital employed can be subdivided into its two components: asset turnover and net profit margin.

The asset turnovers of Brass Ltd and Alliance are fairly similar (2.05 and 1.74 respectively). This ratio indicates how well a business is utilising its assets. Brass Ltd appears to be making slightly better use of its assets, that is generating more revenue per pound of assets. This comparison assumes that the assets of the two businesses are comparable and, in particular, that the property, plant and equipment are comparable.

The major reason for the differing ROCE of the two companies would seem to be their different net profit margins. The net profit margin of Brass Ltd is 12.2% whilst that of Alliance is 24.5%. This is despite the fact that Brass Ltd has the better gross profit margin of 63.7%

compared with 60.5% for Alliance. Since both companies operate in the same business, the gross profit percentage should be fairly similar and in fact the cost of sales figures are very similar. Brass Ltd appears to be able to sell its beer at higher prices. Possible reasons for this might include the following:

- A greater proportion of premium beer sales, such as real ale and more expensive lagers
- A greater proportion of higher added value goods, such as meals and accommodation
- A greater proportion of sales to the free trade at a higher margin (indicated by higher receivables)
- A better reputation and more long standing customer base

This favourable differential in the gross profit percentage is more than negated by Brass Ltd's substantially higher overheads which cause our company to have a considerably inferior net profit margin.

Reasons for the differences in administrative and distribution costs include the following:

- Low depreciation (1%) of freehold hotels and public houses by Alliance (see below)
- Higher expenditure on advertising and promotion to establish the brands of Brass Ltd
- Directors of the two businesses earning substantially different salaries

In conclusion, Brass Ltd should be the more profitable business because of its higher gross margin. Overheads need to be carefully reviewed and reduced so that this is reflected in the net profit.

In particular, we must carefully review our advertising and promotion expenditure in comparison with Alliance. Currently Alliance spends considerably less than Brass Ltd because it has invested a substantial amount in the acquisition of well established brands.

Liquidity

Brass Ltd has a current ratio of 1.4 and a quick ratio of 1.1, whereas Alliance has a current ratio of 1.5 and a quick ratio of 1.2. This would suggest that Alliance has slightly better liquidity; however, the figures may not be strictly comparable due to the different trading strategies.

Brass Ltd has inventory turnover of 8.1 compared with 13.8 for Alliance. This suggests that either Brass Ltd is overstocked or possibly that we hold a greater number of inventory lines. This greater range of products may account to some extent for our higher prices and gross margin. In either case, a serious review of stockholding policy is necessary to remedy any deficiency and to optimise the strategy.

The trade receivables collection period for Brass Ltd stands at 65 days, about a week slower than Alliance at 58 days. This is probably due to our higher proportion of customers buying on credit.

Brass Ltd has a £20 million loan in issue which is due for repayment in 18 months. As you are aware, that is why we are accumulating our cash balance which currently stands at £5,102,000. Hopefully, by the redemption date, we will have sufficient cash to redeem the debt.

In summary, the liquidity positions of the two companies appear fairly similar except that Brass Ltd has to be able to generate sufficient funds to repay its debenture in 18 months. To facilitate this the company needs to reduce its inventory levels so that the inventory turnover ratio is closer to that of Alliance, and also to improve credit control to reduce the trade receivables collection period. Improved cost control, as mentioned above under profitability, should also have positive benefits.

(b) **Adjustments required to the financial statements of the two companies for a more relevant comparison of their relative performance**

    (i) **Depreciation of freehold buildings**

        The freehold buildings of Alliance Breweries Ltd are being depreciated over 100 years as opposed to our 25 years. This has a significant impact on the depreciation charge and therefore on profit. We should review our depreciation policy for buildings.

    (ii) **Revaluation of land and buildings**

        Either eliminate the revaluation and associated depreciation from the Brass Ltd accounts, or revalue the land and buildings of Alliance Breweries on a similar basis. Either adjustment would have the effect of improving the ROCE of Brass Ltd relative to that of Alliance.

    (iii) **Intangibles**

        Write off the intangibles and associated amortisation from the accounts of Alliance. This would have the effect of reducing the ROCE of Alliance.

The net effect of the three adjustments would be to improve the ROCE of Brass Ltd relative to that of Alliance Breweries Ltd.

Appendix – Ratio analysis for Alliance Breweries Ltd

(1) ROCE $= \dfrac{\text{Profit before interest and tax}}{\text{Capital employed}}$ $\dfrac{35,123}{82,080 + 150} = 42.7\%$

(2) Asset turnover $= \dfrac{\text{Revenue}}{\text{Capital employed}}$ $\dfrac{143,100}{82,080 + 150} = 1.74$

(3) Net profit margin $= \dfrac{\text{Profit before interest and tax}}{\text{Revenue}}\%$ $\dfrac{35,123}{143,100} = 24.5\%$

(4) Gross profit percentage $= \dfrac{\text{Gross profit}}{\text{Revenue}}\%$ $\dfrac{86,600}{143,100} = 60.5\%$

(5) Current ratio $= \dfrac{\text{Current assets}}{\text{Current liabilities}}$ $\dfrac{26,840}{18,260} = 1.47$

(6) Quick ratio $= \dfrac{\text{Current assets – inventories}}{\text{Current liabilities}}$ $\dfrac{22,738}{18,260} = 1.25$

(7) Trade receivables collection period $= \dfrac{\text{Trade receivables}}{\text{Revenue}} \times 365$ $\dfrac{22,738}{143,100} \times 365 \text{ days} = 58 \text{ days}$

(8) Inventory turnover $= \dfrac{\text{Cost of sales}}{\text{Inventory}}$ $\dfrac{56,500}{4,102} = 13.8$

3   Caithness plc

(a) **Commentary on relative financial performance and position**

Manufacturing companies tend to have a lower return on their capital employed (ROCE) than non-manufacturing, due to their higher capital base.

However, Sutherland Ltd's ROCE is significantly lower than that of Argyll Ltd. The revaluation of Sutherland Ltd's freehold property will be a factor if it resulted in an uplift of asset values. This would:

- Increase the depreciation charge and reduce the return

- Increase capital employed

However, Argyll Ltd's ROCE will probably decrease once the finance lease has been properly accounted for; property, plant and equipment will probably increase capital employed by a greater relative amount than the replacement of lease rentals by depreciation will increase profit. (The finance cost element of a finance lease is presented within finance charges, below the profit before interest and tax.)

Although the gross profit percentage of Sutherland Ltd is less than that of Argyll Ltd

- The net margin is higher – indicating overhead costs are higher in Argyll Ltd
- But Argyll Ltd's rental costs with regard to the finance lease are recognised at present in profit or loss.

The current and quick ratios look healthy as they are all well in excess of 1:1.

Sutherland Ltd appears to hold more inventories than Argyll Ltd. This is evident from:

- The higher number of days in inventories
- The fall from the current to the quick ratio for Sutherland Ltd is greater than for Argyll Ltd

Sutherland Ltd has more money invested in working capital than Argyll Ltd. This is evident from:

- A higher trade receivables collection period (although this is artificially high as another group company accounts for £200,000)
- A lower trade payables payment period
- A higher inventory turnover period – though Argyll Ltd's inventory looks very low for a manufacturing company

Argyll Ltd has a higher gearing ratio than Sutherland Ltd and, probably as a consequence of this, a lower interest cover. Both these ratios will worsen once the finance lease is correctly accounted for.

Argyll Ltd could have raised some finance in the year, though this might be unlikely given Argyll Ltd has leased equipment recently.

Cash ROCE relates operating cash flow to the same capital as in ROCE.

It would appear that Sutherland Ltd is more efficient than Argyll Ltd at turning operating profits into cash, as cash ROCE is higher than ROCE for Sutherland Ltd and lower for Argyll Ltd.

However, it is not clear what the effect of the finance lease capitalisation will be on Argyll Ltd's cash ROCE. The cash generated from operations (the numerator in the calculation) will rise as the lease payments are added back, but so will capital employed (the denominator). The effect on cash ROCE depends on the relative changes in each.

Short-term liquidity may be more of an issue for Sutherland Ltd, given its higher working capital ratios.

The effect of dividend policy also needs to be considered as this could affect a number of ratios.

(b) **Further information needed with reasons**

- The particular manufacturing sector in which the group operates – would help to provide sector comparatives.
- Comparatives for the same period in the previous year – would help to provide a benchmark for each company.
- Actual statements of comprehensive income and of financial position for each company – to judge the effect of the revaluation, the finance lease, and the £200,000 receivable. Specific amounts would be needed for the revaluation and the finance lease.
- Cash flow information to establish
  - Whether Sutherland Ltd may have short-term liquidity problems from high working capital ratios
  - Whether Argyll Ltd has raised any finance in the year.
- Details of any dividend distribution.

Point to note:

Marks awarded for any other valid comment.

(c) **Commentary in the light of the managing director's knowledge**

Certain facts regarding the managing director of Argyll Ltd now appear to be suspicious.

- He was previously the head of the (combined) accounts department and may still be in a position to exert influence.

- Once Argyll Ltd's lease has been reclassified, its ROCE will decrease but its gross profit percentage and net margin will increase. Although at the moment its ROCE and gross profit percentage compare favourably with Sutherland Ltd, its net profit percentage does not. It is the managing director who is pushing for this adjustment; in the light of what is now known, the validity of this lease classification should be questioned.

- Sutherland Ltd appears to be taking longer to collect its debts than Argyll Ltd – this is in part because of the inter-group sale arranged at the instigation of Argyll Ltd.

The following information would be useful to confirm the legitimacy of items listed under Additional information (2) to (4).

- The reasons behind the revaluation.

- The details of the lease to establish whether it really is finance or operating in nature.

- Whether the inter-group sale really was to the benefit of Sutherland Ltd (for example sale made at a profit) or a transaction engineered by Argyll Ltd's managing director.

- Whether the managing director of Argyll Ltd has any other motive to improve Argyll Ltd's figures (shareholding, bonus, and so on).

4 **Trendsetters Ltd**

(a) **Cash flow ratios**

	20X2	20X1
Cash return on capital employed		
$\dfrac{\text{Cash return}}{\text{Capital employed}} \times 100$	$\dfrac{869}{7,152+1,500-3,742}$	$\dfrac{882+55}{4,872+1,000-910}$
	$=\dfrac{869}{4,910}=17.7\%$	$=\dfrac{937}{4,962}=18.9\%$
$\dfrac{\text{Cash from operations}}{\text{Profit from operations}} \times 100$	$\dfrac{869}{2,293+165}$	$\dfrac{882}{162+102-55}$
	$=35.4\%$	$=422\%$
Cash interest cover		
$\dfrac{\text{Cash return}}{\text{Interest paid}}$	$\dfrac{869}{165}=5.3\text{ times}$	$\dfrac{882+55}{102}=9.2\text{ times}$

Commentary

- The slight fall in the cash return on capital employed from 18.9% to 17.7% shows that the company's efficiency is falling. This is confirmed by a more dramatic fall in the net asset turnover from 0.63 (3,102/(4,872 + 1,000 – 910)) to 0.45 (2,201/(7,152 + 1,500 – 3,742)).

- Although on the face of it the company has made a much higher profit before tax in 20X2 (£2,293,000) compared to 20X1 (£162,000), this 20X2 profit before tax a one-off includes £1,502,000 profit on disposal of PPE.

- This is further illustrated by the decline in the ratio of cash from operations to profit from operations which has fallen from 422% to 35.4%. The quality of Trendsetters Ltd's profits is clearly falling.

- Cash interest cover has fallen from 9.2 to 5.3. This is partly because the cash return has fallen slightly (from £937,000 to £869,000) but mainly because of the increase in interest paid from £102,000 in 20X1 to £165,000 in 20X2.

- Interest paid has increased by 62% over the year, yet borrowings have increased by only 50%. It may be that the company is now having to pay higher interest rates to compensate lenders for increased risk, perhaps due to shorter-term or unsecured borrowings.

- The disposal of stores, which has led to a profit of £1,502,000 (presumably because of low carrying amounts and properties held for some years) may indicate the presence of a well thought out restructuring plan which could save the company. However, this seems unlikely as the company's interpretation of fashion trends is likely to be equally well or badly received whatever the location of its stores.

- The sale of the stores therefore looks to be a short-term measure to boost the company's cash resources. Whether this will help the company in 20X3 and beyond depends on how the proceeds of sale are utilised. If the proceeds are used to acquire a more successful chain of stores or more up-to-date expertise, the company's real profitability could improve.

- Other factors indicate similar short-termism.

    - Long-term investments have been sold, boosting cash in 20X2 by £32,000 but at the expense of dividends received of £55,000. This sale also made a loss of £101,000, indicating that the original investments were bought when stock markets were higher.

    - The statement of cash flows shows that trade and other payables have risen very substantially during 20X2 (and by a lesser amount in 20X1). This indicates either an inability to pay suppliers (the cash injection from the sale of stores was close to the year end and opening cash only £122,000) or an unwillingness to do so. Pressing suppliers for extended credit terms could lead to a loss of goodwill and ultimately a refusal to supply.

- No dividends were paid in 20X2, indicating that the company's cash resources were low.

- Inventories have increased significantly over the year. This may indicate the holding of obsolete inventories which should be written down.

- Overall, the company appears to be struggling to survive long term, despite the substantial cash balances, and investors should be looking for a change in leadership of the design department to take the company forward with a smaller number of stores.

(b) **Pressure to improve the figures**

There are several short-term devices which improve short-term performance and/or position, many of which could have been used at Trendsetters Ltd.

- A company could 'window-dress' its cash position by taking out borrowings just before the year end, which it then repays early in the next accounting period.

- The sale of assets (as here, with the disposal of stores) just before the year end will improve the cash position in the short term but the impact of selling any profit-generating assets will not have a detrimental effect on profits until the following year.

- Borrowings taken out close to the year end will not impact on interest payable and profit until the following period.

- In areas where management have to make judgments, for example the level of inventory, the recoverability of receivables or the level of impairments in respect of tangible or intangible assets, it is always possible for an unscrupulous manager to justify lower write-offs than are really needed.

- The timing of payments to suppliers can improve the trade payables payment period.

- Sales may be made in the last few weeks of the year, but no provision made for returns (a provision which should be made in Trendsetters Ltd if it allows customers to return for refunds, as many fashion stores do).

Actions

In response to such pressures, the financial controller should

- Consider his own professional position and the ethics of the situation

- Outline the issues to the operational directors and propose solutions that comply with laws and standards

- Contact the ethical help lines maintained by the professional bodies.

CHAPTER 13

Financial statement analysis examination techniques

Introduction

Examination context

Topic List

1 Financial statement analysis

2 Financial reporting complications in analysing financial statements

3 Disaggregation of information

4 Approach to examination questions

5 Examination question – Lydford plc

6 Initial review

7 Structuring the answer

8 Mark plans and model answers

9 Examiners' suggestions to improve your answer

Summary and Self-test

Answers to Interactive questions

Answers to Self-test

Introduction

Financial statement analysis is an important technique that Chartered Accountants have to apply at all stages of their careers. This chapter extends the interpretation skills developed in Chapters 11 and 12 to examination situations. It will help you to understand the key aspects of analysis that you may have to address in examinations, how you should approach the examination questions and allow you to develop important skills that are essential to further success at Advanced Stage. You should have completed Chapters 11 and 12 before you work through this chapter.

Learning objectives

Tick off

After completing this chapter you should be able to:

- Explain, in non-technical language and with suitable examples, the application of IFRS, UK GAAP and other accounting and disclosure requirements to information provided in single entity and consolidated financial statements ☐

- Select and calculate relevant indicators, including ratios (for example, stock market ratios), trends and interrelationships, to analyse a single entity's or group's financial position, performance and changes in financial position ☐

- Identify the choice of accounting treatments adopted in financial statements and other financial information and assess how they affect the view presented ☐

- Identify and compare significant features in the information supplied for a given entity or entities, including inconsistencies between the results of analysis and the information supplied ☐

- Specify any additional information required for a meaningful analysis ☐

- Draw conclusions and make inferences from an analysis which takes account of significant features in the information supplied, and which allows for the limitations of the information supplied and the analytical methods used, economic conditions and the business's circumstances. ☐

Syllabus links

In the Financial Accounting and Financial Reporting modules you have developed knowledge and application skills relating to accounting standards and the preparation of financial statements. These sessions on financial statement analysis allow you to use those skills in interpreting and understanding the information produced from the application of accounting standards within financial statements and to make decisions on what further investigation may be necessary.

As you progress to Advanced Stage, you will develop these skills further by:

- Applying financial statement analysis techniques to questions across a range of areas such as financial reporting, assurance and taxation, that are integrated into one question

- Using financial statement analysis with other techniques such as strategic analysis in preparing for the advanced case study examination.

Examination context

The analysis and interpretation of financial statements is a significant portion of the Financial Reporting examination and will account for approximately 30% of the total marks usually across two or more questions.

It is almost certain that each examination will include an individual question that requires you to analyse the extracts from the financial statements and additional information for an organisation. You may also be required to comment on how chosen accounting policies or their application affect the interpretation of the information.

Questions will provide extracts from financial statements including accounting policy notes, disclosure notes and background contextual information. Candidates will be expected to use this detailed information in providing a financial statement analysis of the entity. The questions will test your development of higher level skills including your analysis, judgement and evaluation skills.

The Financial Reporting financial statement analysis questions focus around three core areas, profitability, liquidity (and cash flow) and financial position. In each examination you should expect to need to review one or more of these areas.

In the assessment, candidates may be required to:

- Select and calculate relevant indicators, including ratios (for example, stock market ratios), trends and inter-relationships, to analyse a single entity's or group's financial position, performance and changes in financial position

- Identify the choice of accounting treatments adopted in financial statements and other financial information and assess how they affect the view presented

- Identify and compare significant features in the information supplied for a given entity or entities, including inconsistencies between the results of analysis and the information supplied

- Specify any additional information required for a meaningful analysis

- Draw conclusions and make inferences from an analysis which takes account of significant features in the information supplied, and which allows for the limitations of the information supplied and the analytical methods used, economic conditions and the business's circumstances

- Recognise the ethical and professional issues for a professional accountant undertaking work in and giving advice on accounting and financial reporting; explain the relevance and importance of these issues and evaluate the relative merits of different standpoints taken in debate

- Identify financial and operational information in documents containing audited financial statements (for example, reports on operations by management or those responsible for governance, financial summaries and highlights) that could be relevant to the legal entity or consolidated financial statements, and assess whether those financial statements adequately reflect that information

1 Financial statement analysis

Section overview

Financial statement analysis is the review and explanation of the financial state of a business.

Financial statement analysis is the review and explanation of the financial state of a business. This is achieved by considering the published financial statements, the accompanying notes and additional information (such as financial and non-financial performance indicators).

The review can range from a high-level overview considering a small number of key aspects of the whole business through to a detailed analytical review of a business activity. In the Financial Reporting examination the analysis required lies somewhere in between the two. In examination questions, you will be provided with extracts from the financial statements, some prepared ratios and additional comments and information.

The information provided will be far less than that which is contained in the full set of financial statements or other information available within the public domain. However, it will be relevant to the context of the question, such as when a business event has occurred.

Common business events that may occur in financial statement analysis questions include:

- Business restructurings
- Reorganisations
- Mergers and acquisitions
- Sale or demerger
- Refinancing
- Outsourcing
- Strategy changes
- Competitors entering and leaving markets
- Regulatory changes
- Contractual terms re-negotiated
- Market, legal and environmental changes

These business events will influence the relevant financial information provided in the examination question.

2 Financial reporting complications in analysing financial statements

Section overview

This section describes some of the financial reporting complications students may come across in analysing financial statements.

One of the complications in analysing financial statements arises from the way IFRSs are structured:

- IAS 1 *Presentation of Financial Statements* sets down the requirements for the format of financial statements, containing requirements as to their presentation, structure and content; but

- The recognition, measurement and disclosure of specific transactions and events are all dealt with in other IFRSs.

So preparers of financial statements must consider the possible application of several different IFRSs when deciding how to present certain transactions and events and users must be aware that details about particular transactions or events may appear in several different parts of the financial statements.

2.1 Overriding requirement for disclosures

In considering which IFRS will be relevant in different circumstances, it is necessary to remember the overriding requirement in IAS 1, that in addition to disclosure of the specific items listed within the standard, there shall be disclosure of:

- Additional line items, when such a presentation is relevant to an understanding of an entity's financial position

- The nature and amounts of material items of income and expense (often described as exceptional items)

- Key assumptions about the future, and other sources of estimation uncertainty, that have a significant risk of causing a material adjustment to the carrying amounts of assets and liabilities within the next financial year

So IAS 1 should result in more detailed sub-classification of assets and liabilities in the statement of financial position or the notes thereto, disclosure of 'exceptional' items, usually in the notes, and coverage of the key measurement uncertainties being faced by management, usually in the notes.

2.2 Specific events

When a specific business event has occurred, the consequences of that event may be covered by more than one accounting standard and details may be spread throughout the financial information provided.

Worked example: Identifying relevant financial reporting information

Analysis of the consolidated financial statements of a group is made more difficult by changes to the make up of the group and/or to the activities of group companies.

Decisions to dispose of a group company or to close down a business activity within the group both result in restructurings.

Requirement

Identify both the IFRS that may require disclosure of relevant financial information when a restructuring occurs and the nature of the information required.

Solution

The decision to restructure a major part of the business will require consideration of:

- IAS 7 *Statement of Cash Flows'* requirements as to disclosure within investing activities of the cash flows resulting from disposals

- IAS 10 *Events After the Reporting Period*'s requirements as to events occurring after the end of the reporting period, whether they are adjusting events (for example, confirmation of the carrying amounts of assets/liabilities) or non-adjusting events (for example the disclosure of a decision to restructure)

- IFRS 8 *Operating Segments'* requirements as to segment reporting – a disposal could well affect the segments which are reportable

- IFRS 5 *Non-Current Assets Held for Sale and Discontinued Operations'* requirements – a decision to restructure a major part of the business is likely to lead to disclosures of both discontinued operations in the income statement and non-current assets held for sale in the statement of financial position

- IAS 36 *Impairment of Assets'* requirements as to impairment of assets – impairment will almost certainly result from a restructuring decision

- IAS 37 *Provisions, Contingent Liabilities and Contingent Assets'* requirements as to provisions – liabilities which previously were only contingent may well now require recognition

- IAS 24 *Related Party Disclosures'* requirements if the restructuring involves part of the business being sold to a related party such as management.

Interactive question 1: Acquisition of a business   [Difficulty level: Easy]

An acquisition of another company or business is also a major business event. Identify six IFRSs that may require disclosure of relevant information and the nature of the information required.

Solution

-
-
-
-
-
-

See **Answer** at the end of this chapter.

3 Disaggregation of information

Section overview

IAS 1, IFRS 5 and IFRS 8 provide valuable information to users who are analysing financial statements.

The information presented in financial statements is highly aggregated. Where a business is large and complex, disaggregation of data helps to facilitate analysis. However, whilst management has access to internal management accounting information, external users must rely on the more limited disaggregation of data provided as a result of the requirements of accounting standards, in particular IAS 1, IFRS 5 and IFRS 8. Disaggregated information provided in examination questions is highly useful and should be analysed carefully, because it often provides additional information which explains the key events.

3.1 IAS 1 and IFRS 5

IAS 1 *Presentation of Financial Statements* requires:

- Identification of 'exceptional' items
- The statement of comprehensive income
- Reconciliations of all movements in equity.

The disclosure of 'exceptional' items is important in identifying trends and understanding the reasons for fluctuations in performance, while the statement of comprehensive income identifies the impact of gains and losses, in relation to property, plant and equipment revaluations in particular, which have not been recognised in profit or loss. The reconciliations allow users of financial statements to separate out changes in equity (and therefore capital employed) which may have occurred late in the accounting period and therefore distort ROCE calculations.

IFRS 5 *Non-current Assets Held for Sale and Discontinued Operations* requires the separation of the results of continuing operations from those of discontinued operations. This allows projections into the future to be based on continuing operations only. These projections can be combined with adjustments for 'exceptional' items to allow users to determine underlying (core) profitability.

3.2 IFRS 8

IFRS 8 *Operating Segments* requires certain businesses to identify their operating segments and then to make additional disclosures, about segment profit or loss at a minimum.

This allows analysis of the profitability of different segments, which may well have different risk/reward characteristics. However, there is a great deal of scope for management judgements in the preparation of segment information, particularly in the allocation of expenses and assets to segments (there is no requirement for segmental assets to be those which are used to earn the segmental profit). So it is possible for the figures to be adjusted to present a picture which suits management objectives; an example could be an artificial reduction in the profitability of a particular segment so as not to reveal to competitors how much profit there is to be made in it.

Solvency and investors' ratios cannot normally be applied in a meaningful way on a segmental basis as major companies and groups are often financed as a whole. Therefore it is difficult to apportion debt, equity finance and profit or loss between segments without making significant arbitrary judgements and allocations.

If a user is aware that different markets (geographical or business) are growing at different rates, then a segment report can assist in projections of future revenues and profits for the business as a whole.

4 Approach to examination questions

Section overview

The best way to approach an examination question will be demonstrated using a question provided by the examiners.

In helping you to develop an approach to financial statement analysis, we will base our discussions around the question Lydford plc. Lydford plc is a sample question that was produced by the examination team when the syllabus was first introduced to demonstrate the style of a common financial statement analysis examination question. This chapter will lead you through the Lydford plc question. You will be able to develop a range of skills that should help you in the real examination.

You need to focus particularly on the requirements of the question and the sort of answer which provides valuable analysis that would generate you a good mark in the examination.

As you read the question you should bear in mind the common weaknesses of candidates' answers. From answers to financial statement analysis examination questions over the years, the examiners have identified the following seven common weaknesses.

- **'Scattergun' approach**

    Candidates fail to focus their financial statement analysis on the specific circumstances of the company in the question. Answers often provide a range of short, limited value statements across the full range of financial ratios rather than those relevant to the company.

- **'Boiler plate' answers**

    Candidates often restate facts from the question without applying them to the specific context of the question. They often state that an absolute amount or ratio has changed without including anything by way of explanation of that change.

- **Lacking reader focus**

    The answers are not focused on the reader's requirements. They do not specifically address the information requirements of the addressee of the report. They are often writer, not reader, focused.

- **Quality versus quantity**

    Candidates often prepare several pages of poor quality analysis rather than shorter, focused answers. Quantity is not a replacement for quality. Such answers often do not link related points or ratios together and hence do not gain many marks.

- **Ignore additional information**

    The examiner provides additional information, such as industry data, in addition to the financial statement extracts. Candidates often fail to use this information in formulating answers, although such information will often provide the benchmark information that is needed to make an informed assessment of the company.

- **Big picture**

  Candidates often dwell on movements in insignificant numbers rather than focusing on the big picture.

- **Communication skills**

  Candidates are often unable to explain their findings in a coherent manner that is unambiguous and readily understandable. Too few answers are structured in a professional manner.

The approach that follows is designed so that your answer will not repeat these common failings.

5 Examination question – Lydford plc

Section overview

The sample question – read it carefully.

Read the following examination question

Lydford plc is a listed parent of a group of chemical manufacturing companies operating in several different business sectors. The group's operations, management structure and internal financial reporting are organised into business segments and this is the basis used for reporting in accordance with IFRS 8 *Operating Segments*.

A fund manager for an institutional investor who holds 10% of the ordinary share capital in Lydford plc has approached you because she is concerned about the performance of senior management and would like to propose a resolution at the forthcoming Annual General Meeting for a change of directors. She has provided you with an article that appeared in the May 20X6 edition of *Industrial Chemistry*, a highly regarded trade magazine with a reputation for reporting exclusive breaking news articles. The following is an extract from that article.

'Lydford in business reorganisation

Interesting challenges lie ahead for Lydford plc. In common with many other global catalysed synthesis players, the rising price of oil has forced a strategic review of its operations. Negotiations are at an advanced stage with a number of interested parties to establish a preferred bidder to acquire Lydford's Monomer division. Lydford will then look to concentrate on the Electronics and Organics markets. It is estimated that 25% of Lydford's Monomer division output is sold to the Electronics and Organics divisions. It has always been difficult to understand the effect of this on financial performance, as transfer pricing details offered by the company are vague. Other revenue transactions between its three operating divisions are insignificant. Lydford has declined to comment on the potential disposal or the long-term outlook for its three divisions.'

She has also provided you with the following extracts from the financial statements and some additional information.

Lydford plc – Income statement for the year ended 31 March 20X6

	Year ended 31 March 20X6 £'000	Year ended 31 March 20X5 £'000
Revenue	40,910	39,260
Cost of sales	(23,490)	(24,440)
Gross profit	17,420	14,820
Operating expenses	(9,730)	(9,200)
Profit from operations	7,690	5,620
Finance costs	(1,660)	(1,070)
Profit before tax	6,030	4,550
Income tax expense	(2,010)	(1,770)
Profit for the period	4,020	2,780

Additional information

	20X6	20X5
Return on capital employed (ROCE)	21.1%	17.6%
Chemical sector – ROCE	22.1%	21.9%
Chemical sector – PE ratio	16.1 times	14.0 times
Cash return on capital employed	28.7%	26.4%
Cash flow per share	68.1p	56.2p
Cash dividend cover	3.4 times	2.8 times
Gearing (net debt/equity)	63.0%	57.0%
Non-current asset turnover	1.57 times	1.81 times
Dividend per share	18p	20p
Earnings per share	40.2p	27.8p
Market share price (at 31 March)	620p	580p

Segment information

The information regularly provided to the chief operating decision maker includes the following.

	Year ended 31 March 20X6 £'000	Year ended 31 March 20X5 £'000
Segment revenue		
Organics	23,640	21,030
Electronics	5,520	5,090
Monomers	15,810	16,080
Less: Inter-segment sales	(4,060)	(2,940)
	40,910	39,260
Segment profit from operations		
Organics	5,300	3,910
Electronics	1,550	910
Monomers	1,060	610
Corporate and unallocated	(220)	190
	7,690	5,620
Segment operating profit margin		
Organics	22.4%	18.6%
Electronics	28.1%	17.9%
Monomers	6.7%	3.8%
Average number of employees		
Organics	718	650
Electronics	98	105
Monomers	313	310
Corporate and central functions	10	11
	1,139	1,076
Revenue per employee (£'000)		
Organics	33	32
Electronics	56	48
Monomers	51	52
Segment return on capital employed		
Organics	22.2%	22.3%
Electronics	34.3%	21.1%
Monomers	9.0%	4.7%
Segment capital expenditure (£'000)		
Organics	4,100	2,610
Electronics	2,630	1,920
Monomers	400	370
Corporate	180	100
	7,310	5,000

Extract from accounting policies note

Segment reporting

Lydford plc presents segment information for its business segments, which is consistent with the internal management and financial reporting systems and reflects the risks and earnings structure of the group. Each segment provides different products and serves different sectors. They include all revenues and expenses which are directly attributable to a segment plus central overheads which are capable of allocation by management on a reasonable basis. Management determines transfer prices for sales between segments in a market-orientated manner.

Segment assets and liabilities include all items that are directly attributable to a segment plus central assets that are allocated on a reasonable basis by management where possible.

Requirements

(a) Analyse the judgements and ethical issues associated with the preparation of segment information.

(3 marks)

(b) Assess and comment on the apparent performance of the directors of Lydford plc, calculating a maximum of five additional relevant ratios to assist in your analysis. Your answer should identify and justify matters that you consider require further investigation. **(18 marks)**

6 Initial review

Section overview

You should start by analysing the requirements and developing a plan.

The mark allocation allows you approximately 30 minutes to formulate your answer to the question. The examiners recommend that you should spend 5 minutes reading the question thoroughly, 5 minutes thinking and planning your answer and 20 minutes in writing your answer.

It is essential that before you begin to answer the question you take this time to understand the requirements and to develop a plan.

Here are a number of questions relevant to any scenario you may encounter. They will provide you with a good basis to answer the question.

- **Context**

    - Who am I?
    - With respect to the context, what is my focus?
    - To whom am I communicating and what are their key information needs?

- **Requirement**

    - What is it?
    - If there is more than one part to the requirement, does the first part lead in to the second? Does that give me some clues to what may be important?

- **Additional information**

    - What am I given?
    - Is there some other information that is obviously omitted?
    - How does the information relate to the requirement?
    - Can the additional information help focus my answer?

- **Economic and business issues**

    - What are the key issues identified in the information?
    - How is this reflected in the financial information?

- **Disclosure notes and accounting policies**

  - Which are reproduced?
  - How can I use this information?
  - What queries does it raise in my mind?

- **Ethical issues and judgements**

  - Are there any that need considering?
  - Does anything look unusual?
  - Are there any areas where significant judgement has been applied?

- **Financial headlines**

  - Growing?
  - Profitable?
  - Cash generative?
  - Solvent or highly geared?

- **Other matters**

  Have I noticed or thought of anything else?

- **Additional ratios**

  Which additional ratios can I calculate that would address the requirement?

Interactive question 2: Lydford: key points [Difficulty level: Exam standard]

Re-read the question Lydford plc and write down the key points you have identified under each of the headings suggested.

- **Context**

- **Requirement**

- **Additional information**

- **Economic and business issues**

- **Disclosure notes and accounting policies**

- **Ethical issues and judgements**

- **Financial headlines**

- **Other matters**

- **Additional ratios**

See **Answer** at the end of this chapter.

7 Structuring the answer

Section overview
- Use your plan to write your answer.
- Answer the question in the order that the requirements are set.
- Use the 'because' rule to turn 'whats' into 'whys'.

You are now in a position to start writing your answer. The examiner has structured the requirements in a particular order for a reason. In most cases it will be a good idea to follow the same order in your answer.

7.1 Judgements and ethics in segment information

In the Lydford plc question, part (a) requires an analysis of the judgements and ethical issues that should be considered in preparing segment information. You should have identified some ideas for these issues from your review of the financial information provided for Lydford plc. You should remember that the mark allocation for this part of the question is only three marks and this should be reflected in the depth of your answer.

Interactive question 3: Completing part (a)   [Difficulty level: Exam standard]

Now re-read the requirement for part (a) and prepare your answer.

See **Answer** at the end of this chapter.

7.2 The ratio calculations

Part (b) requires you to assess the apparent performance of management with a view to advising the investor about her proposal to try to remove the management. Before you can write a meaningful answer you should calculate the maximum of five additional ratios that you identified in your initial review.

Interactive question 4: Calculating the ratios   [Difficulty level: Exam standard]

Calculate the five additional ratios that you identified from your initial review. In the examination the identification and correct calculation of each ratio earns half a mark, with another half mark for its comparative.

See **Answer** at the end of this chapter.

7.3 Part (b) – structuring your answer

You should structure your answer to help demonstrate how you have addressed the question requirement. You will need a short introduction and conclusion. The other sections in your answer should address the requirements of the question.

 Interactive question 5: Headings [Difficulty level: Exam standard]

Write down six headings under which you are going to structure your answer.

-

-

-

-

-

-

See **Answer** at the end of this chapter.

7.4 Writing your answer

Before you make an attempt at writing an answer, it is important that you understand how the points you make will be assessed. It is important that you understand why one script would obtain a better mark on the points made than another. The guidance given below is only guidance; it cannot be exact because the overall mark will be based on the answer coverage as a whole and not just the specific point.

For each of the examples given, there are three versions of comment given. They show a progression from a 'poor' to an 'average' through to a 'good' comment.

- 'Poor' points typically state (or restate) facts from the question without any direct reference to the context of the question.

- 'Average' points generally relate a ratio or fact to the context given.

- 'Good' points build on average points by providing rationale, judgement or a link to further investigation.

As a broad rule of thumb, the 'poor' comment would achieve no mark, the 'average' comment ½ mark and the 'good' comment 1 mark.

Candidates' answers should demonstrate how relevant information can be obtained from the financial reporting data and how it is of benefit to the financial statement analysis. Hence, good answers will show not only that candidates have understood the purposes of the analysis by computing ratios appropriate to the context of the question but also that candidates are able to interpret the resulting information to produce sensible recommendations.

In most cases, good points pass the **'because' test**. When answering an analysis question you should be able to include the word 'because' in your answer. For example, 'EPS has reduced because ….', 'the share price has reduced because…' **The word 'because' changes a 'what' into a 'why'**. In other words, you can demonstrate why something has changed as well as what that change is. You should try to **relate the 'why' to the specific company**, industry or environmental issues given in the question. The reader (in your case examiner) will then appreciate that you understand the relationships between the financial statement information and the business issues.

Finally, within the constraints of these short examples, there are some important features to note, particularly of the good points.

- They are concise – they demonstrate the benefit of careful thought, planning and a logical approach.

- They include succinct financial information.

- They receive credit for reaching conclusions drawn from the information given and the analysis. Such conclusions are not included in poor answers.

Here are some examples of poor, average and good points on the same area.

Area	'Poor' point	'Average' point	'Good' point
Profitability	The return on capital employed (ROCE) has increased from 17.6% to 21.1%. *(Examiner's comment – This is a simple restatement of information given in the question. Nothing has been added from the scenario itself, consequently no marks are awarded.)*	The return on capital employed (ROCE) has increased from 17.6% to 21.1% demonstrating that the overall efficiency of the group in employing the resources available has increased. *(Examiner's comment – This is a generic comment in relation to ROCE that could apply to any company. It provides marginally more information than the 'poor' point. It does not earn a whole mark as it adds little value to the analysis exercise. In practice as a Chartered Accountant clients are only willing to pay for advice if it is focused on their company and the specific circumstances it faces.)*	The return on capital employed (ROCE) has increased from 17.6% to 21.1% demonstrating that the overall efficiency of the group in employing the resources available has increased. The ROCE is still below that of the chemical sector but the sector ROCE has remained almost stagnant and Lydford plc's has grown. *(Examiner's comment – This answer looks at the specific circumstances of Lydford itself, in terms of its own trading position and that of its competitors and the industry it operates in. It passes the 'because' test.)*
Profitability	The revenue of the group has increased by over 4%.	The revenue of the group has increased by over 4%. In contrast to the other segments, the Monomer segment has shown a decline in revenue by 1.7%.	The revenue of the group has increased by over 4%. In contrast to the other segments, the Monomer segment has shown a decline in revenue by 1.7%. In addition, the Monomer division has increased its sales to the other segments (given all inter-segment sales are thought to originate from this segment). Therefore, turnover to third parties has reduced significantly.

Area	'Poor' point	'Average' point	'Good' point
Efficiency	The group has been spending significant amounts of capital expenditure.	The group has been spending significant amounts of capital expenditure. It may be that this capacity has yet to generate operating performance improvements.	The group has been spending significant amounts of capital expenditure. It may be that this capacity has yet to generate operating performance improvements. This would contribute to the reduction in net asset turnover. This idea is supported by the reduction in non-current asset turnover from 1.81 times to 1.57 times.
Investor ratios	The price earnings ratio has fallen from 20.9 times to 15.4 times.	The price earnings ratio has fallen from 20.9 times to 15.4 times. The EPS growth has not been reflected in the share price movement.	The price earnings ratio has fallen from 20.9 times to 15.4 times. The EPS growth has not been reflected in the share price movement. The shares may be less attractive to investors seeking growth.
Further information	A statement of cash flows for Lydford plc. A review of cash flows from operations and those from other activities would be useful.	A statement of cash flows for Lydford plc. A review of cash flows from operations and those from other activities would be useful. In particular an analysis of the quality of the profits by comparing the operating cash flows and operating profits would be useful.	A statement of cash flows for Lydford plc. A review of cash flows from operations and those from other activities would be useful. In particular an analysis of the quality of the profits by comparing the operating cash flows and operating profits would be useful. In addition details of the cash flows of each division.
Profitability	Profitability in the Monomer division has increased.	The improvement in profitability for the Monomer division seems to be inconsistent with its revenue decrease.	The improvement in profitability for the Monomer division seems to be inconsistent with its revenue decrease. The increase in the proportion of inter-segment sales initiated by the division may indicate favourable transfer pricing arrangements on these transactions.

Area	'Poor' point	'Average' point	'Good' point
Profitability		The significant year on year movement in the operating profit allocated to the 'corporate and unallocated' segment raises questions about allocation issues.	The significant year on year movement in the operating profit allocated to the 'corporate and unallocated' segment raises questions about allocation issues. The allocation of expenses, assets and liabilities to the segment may have been made with a view to improving the segment performance before its impending disposal in order to maximise sales proceeds and expedite the process.

Interactive question 6: Attempting part (b)   [Difficulty level: Exam standard]

You can now attempt part (b) of the question. Try to write down 15 'good' points under the six headings that you identified in interactive question 5 and using the ratios you have calculated and the ratios given in the question. You can mark your answer by applying the general principles in the commentary and table above.

1

2

3

4

5

6

7

8

9

10

11

12

13

14

15

See **Answer** at the end of this chapter.

8 Mark plans and model answers

The answer to Interactive question 6 is a mark plan. It covers an analysis of all of the nine additional suggested ratios (calculated in Interactive question 4) and is longer than a candidate would be expected to prepare, as the candidate's discussion will only cover a maximum of five additional relevant ratios.

In the examination a clear pass would include six good points and six average points plus four correct ratios. A model answer of a clear pass is included below which has been constructed on this basis.

Lydford plc

	20X6	20X5
Gross profit %	42.6%	37.7%
Dividend cover	2.2 times	1.4 times
Dividend yield	2.9%	3.4%
Price earnings ratio	15.4 times	20.9 times

Introduction

To assess the directors' performance a detailed analysis of the information provided is required. The initial interpretation of the operating performance suggests that Lydford plc has performed well during the year. However, the reduction in the dividend from 20p to 18p is inconsistent with this interpretation. (Average point) $\frac{1}{2}$

Profitability

The return on capital employed (ROCE) has increased from 17.6% to 21.1% demonstrating that the overall efficiency of the group in employing the resources available has increased. (Average point) $\frac{1}{2}$

The Monomer and Electronics business segments show impressive growth in ROCE. However, the Monomer segment ROCE is significantly below the market ROCE and that of the other segments and this may be a contributing factor to the decision to sell that business. (Average point) $\frac{1}{2}$

The cash return on capital employed has increased to 28.7%. As expected it is higher than traditional ROCE as that ratio takes into account depreciation. (Poor point)

The revenue of the group has increased by over 4%. In contrast to the other segments, the Monomer segment has shown a decline in revenue by 1.7%. In addition, the Monomer division has increased its sales to the other segments (given all inter-segment sales are thought to originate from this segment). This would be expected given the growth of these other segments. Therefore, revenue to third parties has reduced significantly. (Good point)   1

The improvement in profitability is largely attributable to the improvement in gross margin by almost five percentage points to 42.6%. No analysis of gross margins by division is provided and so it is difficult to ascertain whether this is due to improvements by gross margin in each division or due to the mix of revenue from each division changing. (Average point – look at the length of the sentence, could you break it down into shorter points?) $\frac{1}{2}$

Operating expenses have increased by over £500,000. There could be issues with cost control. (Poor point – how could you improve on this?)

The significant year on year movement in the operating profit allocated to the 'corporate and unallocated' segment raises questions about allocation issues. The allocation of expenses, assets and liabilities to the Monomer segment may have been made with a view to improving the segment performance before its impending disposal in order to maximise sales proceeds and expedite the process. (Good point)   1

The effective tax rate has fallen. (Poor point – it adds nothing to the figures calculated)

Efficiency

Net asset turnover has reduced markedly from 1.23 times to 1.12 times. ROCE has increased and this suggests that the increase in operating margin has masked a reduction in the efficiency of sales generation from the overall resources of Lydford plc. (Good point)

The group has been spending significant amounts of capital expenditure. The capital expenditure has been concentrated on the Organics and Electronics divisions. (Poor point – how could it be improved?)

Investor ratios

The EPS has shown strong growth to 40.2p per share. However, investors will be cautious given the reduction in the level of dividend and the dividend yield. The yield has reduced to 2.9% from 3.4% and the shares will be less attractive to investors seeking income. (Good point)

The price earnings ratio has fallen from 20.9 times to 15.4 times. (Poor point – once again this adds no value)

The dividend has probably been cut to restore dividend cover. In 20X5 it was only 1.4 times and even though it has increased to 2.2 times investors may be cautious about the sustainability of future distributions. (Good point)

The capital expenditure requirements of the business also seem to be increasing. The future capital expenditure requirements will have a major influence on the capacity to pay dividends. (Good point – it demonstrates an ability to link historic trends to future capital requirements and the implications)

Further matters for investigation

A copy of the financial statements or press releases issued with the annual results to identify any reasons given for the dividend reduction. (Average point)

Details of arrangements to secure Monomer product for use by the two remaining divisions when the Monomer division is sold. Are there any cost implications? (Good point)

A statement of financial position and statement of cash flows. (Poor point)

Conclusion

The directors have delivered operational performance but shareholder value is less apparent. (Weak point – not focused on requirement. It is 'business speak' and does not help the reader)

9 Examiners' suggestions to improve your answer

Section overview

- The examining team have identified seven ways in which candidates can improve their answers by addressing the common weaknesses listed in section 4 above.

Set out below are the attributes that the examining team looks for when marking answers.

Specific not generic

Comments need to relate to the company's specific circumstances. Too many answers are 'generic', that is the observations made (such as 'receivables days have increased, this could be due to poor credit control') could apply to any company, not only the one that you are reporting about.

Create don't repeat

Use new ratios and new relationships between financial statement data contained in the stem of the question, rather than repeating existing information. Unless accompanied by added value, repetition of figures and comments from the question itself will not earn you any marks.

Use the 'because' rule to add value. This rule was discussed in the earlier study text material and suggests that you explain 'why' things happen as well as 'what' has happened.

Reader not writer

The report contents should focus on the information needs of the supposed readers of the report. Put yourself in their shoes, think about what they want from the report and then give it to them. For example, if a client is considering a takeover of a rival company and has asked you to report back, ask yourself: what does the client want to know? For example:

- Is the target company growing more slowly or quickly than the would-be acquirer?
- How big is the target company compared to the would-be acquirer?
- How much additional debt would be taken on by the combined entity?
- Is there scope for cost savings/economies of scale and so on?

Integration not isolation

Don't just use one ratio or number when making a point or conclusion in a report – try to link some together. For example, if a company's revenues and receivable days have increased significantly, it could be a strategic management decision to expand operations by providing more generous credit terms to customers, OR it could be due to the company expanding and not investing in its credit collection department at the same time. You need to therefore......

Use the clues, don't ignore the news

The examiner will nearly always provide additional information in the question and not just the financial statements. This information normally gives a significant twist to the data contained in the income statement/statement of financial position/statement of cash flows. Ensure you link this information to the financial statements as it will help you formulate explanations for changes in the figures. When reading the additional information try to highlight the three or four important points that are discussed as this will help you plan your answer and ensure that you don't overlook these points once you start writing your answer.

Big picture not trivial pursuits

You have a limited amount of time to write your report, so concentrate on the big issues and not insignificant numbers. For example, if a company has operating profits of £500 million for two years, and finance costs increase from £4 million to £6 million, don't waste time calculating interest cover, and then commenting why it has decreased by 33%, as it is not important in the wider scheme of things.

Three course meal

A good answer should be like a good meal; it should have a short starter (one or two sentences that contextualises the answer), a memorable main course (consisting of separate elements such as commentary on performance, position and solvency and so on) and a dessert (in the form of a conclusion or recommendation) that finishes the meal (one or two sentences).

Using these seven as guidance, critically review your own answers to the interactive questions and see if you could improve your answers.

Summary

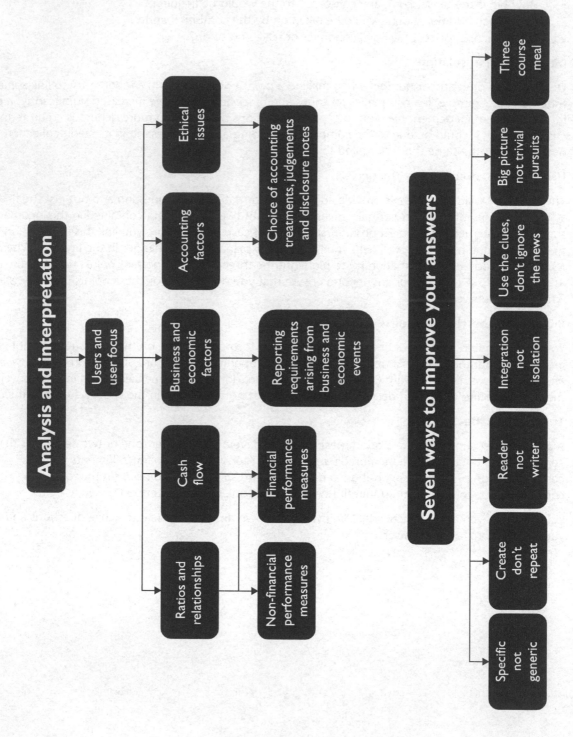

Self-test

Answer the following questions.

1 Ironville plc

Ironville plc is the listed parent company of a group of companies which operate in the oil engineering industry. The group prepares consolidated financial statements in accordance with IFRS.

You have been asked by the finance director of Ironville plc to investigate the financial performance, financial position and liquidity of the group's principal manufacturing subsidiary, Radbourne Ltd. Market conditions in the sector have been poor with raw material prices increasing.

Radbourne Ltd's management have been highly incentivised by targets for profits growth. The draft financial statements show that these targets have been met; this will generate significant cash bonuses for management. The following information has been provided:

Income statements

	Year ended 31 October 20X5 £'000	Year ended 31 October 20X4 £'000
Revenue	16,440	16,510
Cost of sales	(12,600)	(12,200)
Gross profit	3,840	4,310
Operating expenses	(1,710)	(2,530)
Profit from operations	2,130	1,780
Finance costs	(470)	(380)
Profit before tax	1,660	1,400
Income tax expense	(500)	(490)
Profit for the period	1,160	910

Extract from statement of changes in equity for the year ended 31 October 20X5

	Retained earnings £'000
Balance at 1 November 20X4	2,110
Profit for the period	1,160
Final 20X4 dividend on ordinary shares (5p per ordinary share)	(500)
Balance at 31 October 20X5	2,770

No dividends have been declared in respect of the year ended 31 October 20X5.

Statements of financial position

	31 October 20X5		31 October 20X4	
	£'000	£'000	£'000	£'000
ASSETS				
Non-current assets				
Property, plant and equipment		16,200		16,130
Intangibles		500		–
		16,700		16,130
Current assets				
Inventories	3,150		2,760	
Trade and other receivables	5,070		4,200	
Cash and cash equivalents	50		120	
		8,270		7,080
Total assets		24,970		23,210
EQUITY AND LIABILITIES				
Equity				
Issued capital – £1 ordinary shares		10,000		10,000
Share premium		1,000		1,000
Retained earnings		2,770		2,110
		13,770		13,110
Non-current liabilities				
Borrowings – due to Ironville plc	8,500		6,600	
Provisions (see note below)	–		880	
		8,500		7,480
Current liabilities				
Trade payables and other liabilities	2,230		2,040	
Taxation	470		580	
		2,700		2,620
Total equity and liabilities		24,970		23,210

Extract from notes to the financial statements

Restructuring provision

Radbourne Ltd commenced a restructuring and rationalisation of its engineering activities in 20X3. At that time a restructuring provision was created to cover the expected full costs of the programme. The restructuring was completed in June 20X5 and the unused amount was reversed to operating expenses. The movement on the restructuring provision during the year was as follows.

	£'000
Restructuring provision at 1 November 20X4	880
Amounts used during the period	(260)
Unused amounts reversed during period	(620)
Restructuring provision at 31 October 20X5	–

Additional information

	20X5	20X4
Gearing (net debt/equity)	61.4%	49.4%
Operating profit margin	13.0%	10.8%
Inventory turnover	4.0 times	4.4 times
Current ratio	3.1	2.7
Acid test ratio	1.9	1.7
Return on capital employed (ROCE)	9.6%	9.1%
Average number of employees	105	97
Engineering sector operating profit margins	10.5%	11.2%
Research and development expense	£260,000	£640,000

Requirements

(a) Comment on the usefulness to financial statement users of the disclosure information in respect of provisions required by IAS 37 *Provisions, Contingent Liabilities and Contingent Assets*. **(4 marks)**

(b) Comment on the performance, financial position and liquidity of Radbourne Ltd, calculating a maximum of five additional relevant ratios to assist in your analysis. Your answer should identify and justify matters that you consider require further investigation. **(20 marks)**

2 **Tirril plc**

Tirril plc is a listed company that operates in the electronics industry. It prepares financial statements in accordance with IFRS.

You are a manager of an investment fund which has held an investment of 5% of the ordinary share capital of Tirril plc for a number of years. Tirril plc launched 'Millom', a computer design package, some years ago. It has been an industry leader ever since with a 70% current market share in Europe. Tirril plc has tried to develop other complementary products over the past five years but these failed to generate any significant revenue. Tirril plc is widely rumoured to be investigating merger and acquisition opportunities.

The following is an extract from a recent article in a leading international business newspaper:

'Whigham Inc. in Technology Breakthrough

'Reports from the USA have indicated that Whigham Inc. is due to launch a new computer design package in 20X7. Whigham's current computer design package is the industry standard in North America and is now being aggressively marketed in Europe where it is a direct competitor for Tirril plc's Millom package. Whigham's new package is expected to increase operating speeds and reduce operating costs. Tirril plc has yet to comment on the developments.'

The following information has been provided for Tirril plc:

Income statement

	Year ended 31 March 20X6 £'000	Year ended 31 March 20X5 £'000
Revenue	28,300	32,450
Cost of sales	(13,660)	(12,770)
Gross profit	14,640	19,680
Operating expenses	(5,890)	(6,780)
Profit from operations	8,750	12,900
Finance costs	(340)	(600)
Profit before tax	8,410	12,300
Income tax expense	(3,170)	(4,190)
Profit for the period	5,240	8,110

Extract from statement of changes in equity for the year ended 31 March 20X6

	Retained earnings £'000
Balance at 1 April 20X5	9,810
Profit for the period	5,240
Final 20X5 dividend on ordinary shares (30p per ordinary share)	(4,500)
Balance at 31 March 20X6	10,550

A final dividend in respect of the year ended 31 March 20X6 of £4.8 million (32p per share) was declared in May 20X6.

Statement of cash flows

	Year ended 31 March 20X6		Year ended 31 March 20X5	
	£'000	£'000	£'000	£'000
Cash flows from operating activities				
Cash generated from operations (note)		12,970		16,450
Interest paid		(360)		(640)
Tax paid		(4,510)		(4,710)
Net cash from operating activities		8,100		11,100
Cash flows from investing activities				
Purchase of property, plant and equipment	(60)		(960)	
Proceeds on sale of property, plant and equipment	810		340	
Net cash from investing activities		750		(620)
Cash flows from financing activities				
Repurchase of own shares	–		(3,500)	
Dividends paid	(4,500)		(4,125)	
Borrowings	(1,000)		(2,455)	
Net cash used in financing activities		(5,500)		(10,080)
Change in cash and cash equivalents		3,350		400
Cash and cash equivalents brought forward		2,300		1,900
Cash and cash equivalents carried forward		5,650		2,300

Reconciliation of profit before tax to cash generated from operations

	£'000	£'000
Profit before tax	8,410	12,300
Finance cost	340	600
Amortisation	560	600
Depreciation	2,640	2,750
Loss on disposal of property, plant and equipment	160	10
Decrease / (Increase) in inventories	570	(70)
Decrease in receivables	340	210
(Decrease) / Increase in trade payables	(50)	50
Cash generated from operations	12,970	16,450

Extract from notes to financial statements

Development costs

	£'000
Cost	
At 1 April 20X5 and 31 March 20X6	3,550
Amortisation and impairment	
At 1 April 20X5	2,800
Charge for year	560
At 31 March 20X6	3,360
Carrying amounts	
At 1 April 20X5	750
At 31 March 20X6	190

Additional information

	20X6	20X5
Gearing (net debt/equity)	28.2%	49.1%
Number of computer packages sold	26,400	29,100
Operating profit margin	30.9%	39.8%
Inventory turnover	7.0 times	5.1 times
Trade receivables collection period	54 days	51 days
Research expenditure (included in operating expenses)	£125,000	£450,000
Return on capital employed (ROCE)	30.3%	39.7%
Cash return on capital employed	44.9%	50.6%
Cash flow per share	54p	74p
Market share price (at 31 March)	240p	450p
Earnings per share	35p	54p

Requirement

Comment on the performance, cash flow and investor ratios of Tirril plc, calculating a maximum of five additional relevant ratios to assist in your analysis. Your answer should identify and justify matters that you consider require further investigation. **(20 marks)**

Now, go back to the Learning Objectives in the Introduction. If you are satisfied you have achieved these objectives, please tick them off.

Answer to Interactive question 1

The acquisition of a business will require consideration of:

- IFRS 3 *Business Combinations'* requirements as to the separate disclosure of the revenue and profit from operations of the acquired business together with the key terms of the acquisition

- IAS 7 *Statement of Cash Flows'* requirements as to disclosure within investing activities of the cash flows resulting from the acquisition

- IAS 10 *Events After the Reporting Period's* requirements as to events occurring after the end of the reporting period, whether they are adjusting events (for example confirmation of deferred or contingent consideration) or non-adjusting events (for example the disclosure of an agreement to acquire a business)

- IFRS 8 *Operating Segments'* requirements as to segment reporting – an acquisition could give rise to a new reportable segment

- IAS 36 *Impairment of Assets'* requirements as to impairment of goodwill arising from the initial impairment calculation

- IAS 37 *Provisions, Contingent Liabilities and Contingent Assets'* requirements as to provisions, for example, where acquired and existing operations have been merged and a rationalisation programme has begun.

Answer to Interactive question 2

Here are a number of points that you could have identified. You must remember that you may have raised some additional valid points. Examiners will award credit for any valid points that you raise, even if they are not included in the marking guide provided.

- **Context**

  - Adviser to a fund manager

  - Focus is on management's performance – need to consider investor ratios and financial performance – and whether to force a replacement

- **Requirement**

  - Two parts
  - First part would indicate that segmental analysis is important
  - Second part looks at management performance
  - Does the word 'apparent' suggest anything?
  - Need to identify matters for investigation

- **Additional information**

  - Given income statement and segmental information plus some other data

  - Other data includes investor ratios

  - What about statement of financial position and cash flow to assess the management of these aspects (although ratios are given relating to these)?

- **Economic and business issues**

  Extract from *Industrial Chemistry* suggests that:

  - The Monomer division is to be sold
  - A substantial amount of its output is to other divisions (will this continue?)
  - Transfer prices are vague

- **Disclosure notes and accounting policies**

    - Segmental information and policies are given
    - Accounting policy note – 'allocation on a reasonable basis'
    - Vagueness of transfer pricing and allocation information

- **Ethical issues and judgements**

    - Transfer prices and allocations could have been manipulated to affect profitability of Monomer division

    - Profitability of Monomer division has increased substantially whereas revenue has fallen. ROCE still low

    - Sector capex for monomers is minimal

- **Financial headlines**

    - Marginal growth overall – divisions growing at different rates
    - Profitability increasing – variable by division
    - Highly geared and increasing
    - Dividend reduced

- **Other matters**

    - What will disposal proceeds be used for?
    - Which divisions are cash generative?
    - Large capital spend in divisions to be retained

- **Additional ratios**

    - Investor ratios – dividend cover, dividend yield, P/E
    - Interest cover (as gearing is climbing)
    - Gross profit margin

Answer to Interactive question 3

The following is the published answer to part (a) of the question. Remember that the mark allocation is three marks for this part.

There is a great deal of management judgement involved in the presentation of segment information. The exercise of this judgement can have a significant influence on the information provided and its interpretation. Examples of those judgements include:

- Management allocating expenses, assets and liabilities between segments on a reasonable basis. This may allow the profitability of one segment to be dressed up to avoid competitors gaining beneficial information on margins.

- Transfer pricing has a direct effect on segment profitability. It may be driven by taxation motives to minimise liabilities in any given jurisdiction.

The exercise of this judgement has a direct effect on key performance indicators. Management may use the opportunity to present biased information that meets their motives and objectives. It may obscure the true picture of an entity's performance and position.

Chartered Accountants should resist these temptations and the influence of non-financial management in preparing financial statements. They should be objective and ensure the spirit of the reporting requirements is met.

(Remember, this is a mark plan and is more detailed than would be required to obtain three marks in the examination. The key is to remember the requirement of the question. The key term was 'analyse'.)

The answer contains four key issues. The discussion of each, comprising a couple of sentences for each issue, would have gained one mark. The four key issues are:

- Allocation judgements
- Transfer pricing
- Management's motivations
- Chartered Accountants' responsibilities

Answer to Interactive question 4

	20X6	20X5
Gross profit % ((17,420/40,910) × 100%) and ((14,820/39,260) × 100%)	42.6%	37.7%
Operating cost % ((9,730/40,910) × 100%) and ((9,200/39,260) × 100%)	23.8%	23.4%
Operating profit margin ((7,690/40,910) × 100%) and ((5,620/39,260) × 100%)	18.8%	14.3%
Net asset turnover = ROCE/operating profit margin (21.1%/18.8%) and (17.6%/14.3%)	1.12 times	1.23 times
Interest cover (7,690/1,660) and (5,620/1,070)	4.6 times	5.3 times
Dividend cover (40.2/18) and (27.8/20)	2.2 times	1.4 times
Dividend yield ((18/620) × 100%) and ((20/580) × 100%)	2.9%	3.4%
Price earnings ratio (620/40.2) and (580/27.8)	15.4 times	20.9 times
Revenue per employee (40,910/1,139) and (39,260/1,076)	£35,920	£36,490

(Credit would be given for other relevant ratios; the basis of the calculation should be given.)

Answer to Interactive question 5

- Introduction
- Profitability
- Efficiency
- Investor ratios
- Further matters
- Conclusion

You may have considered some other headings.

Answer to Interactive question 6

The following is the examiner's answer to this question. Remember that the maximum mark for part (b) is 18. Five of these marks relate to the calculation of ratios and therefore you need to make 13 'good' points to obtain full marks. The examiner's answer is a mark plan. It is necessarily comprehensive to accommodate a wide range of possible answers. However, markers will award credit for other valid points not included in the mark plan.

As a rule of thumb, each paragraph in the examiner's answer represents a 'good' point for which credit of one mark would be awarded.

Introduction

To assess the directors' performance a detailed analysis of the information provided is required. The initial interpretation of the operating performance suggests that Lydford plc has performed well during the year. Revenue has increased by 4.2% ((40,910/39,260) – 1) and operating profits by almost 37% ((7,690/5,620) – 1). In addition, interest cover, whilst down on last year, remains healthy at 4.6 times. Moreover, EPS has grown by 44.6% ((40.2/27.8) – 1) year on year.

However, the reduction in the dividend from 20p to 18p is inconsistent with this interpretation. The increase in gearing and reduction in the price earnings ratio confirm these causes for concern.

Profitability

The return on capital employed (ROCE) has increased from 17.6% to 21.1% demonstrating that the overall efficiency of the group in employing the resources available has increased. The ROCE is still below that of the chemical sector but the sector ROCE has remained almost stagnant and Lydford plc's has grown. This may be due to the mix of Lydford plc's business segments against that of the sector.

The Monomer and Electronics business segments show impressive growth in ROCE. However, the Monomer segment ROCE is significantly below the market ROCE and that of the other segments and this may be a contributing factor to the decision to sell that business.

The Organics segment ROCE has decreased. The decrease is only marginal and may reflect the significant investment in new capital expenditure which may not yet be generating its expected return.

The cash return on capital employed has increased to 28.7%. As expected it is higher than traditional ROCE as that ratio takes into account depreciation. The cash return on capital employed suggests that whilst operating profits have increased, the effect on operating cash flows has been less marked. This may be due to additional investments in working capital.

The operating profit margin has increased by 4.5 percentage points to 18.8%. All three business segments have shown growth in operating margins. The Organics and Electronics segments are above the group average. The Monomers division shows growth in operating margins but it is significantly below the other business segments. This may be another factor in the decision to dispose of this business segment.

The revenue of the group has increased by over 4%. In contrast to the other segments, the Monomer segment has shown a decline in revenue of 1.7% ((15,810/16,080) – 1). In addition, the Monomer division has increased its sales to the other segments (given all inter-segment sales are thought to originate from this segment). This would be expected given the growth of these other segments. Therefore, sales to third parties has reduced significantly.

The operating cost percentage is almost unchanged at 23.8%. However, the information provided does not indicate how this is allocated by division in accordance with the accounting policy extract. The operating cost control in each segment cannot be commented upon.

The improvement in profitability is largely attributable to the improvement in gross margin by almost five percentage points to 42.6%. No analysis of gross margins by division is provided and so it is difficult to ascertain whether this is due to improvements by gross margin in each division or due to the mix of revenue from each division changing.

The improvement in profitability for the Monomer division seems to be inconsistent with its revenue decrease. The increase in the proportion of inter-segment sales initiated by the division may indicate favourable transfer pricing arrangements on these transactions.

The significant year on year movement in the operating profit allocated to the 'corporate and unallocated' segment raises questions about allocation issues. The allocation of expenses, assets and liabilities to the segment may have been made with a view to improving the segment performance before its impending disposal in order to maximise sales proceeds and expedite the process.

Efficiency

Net asset turnover has reduced markedly from 1.23 times to 1.12 times. ROCE has increased and this suggests that the increase in operating margin has masked a reduction in the efficiency of sales generation from the overall resources of Lydford plc.

The group has been spending significant amounts of capital expenditure. It may be that this capacity has yet to generate operating performance improvements. This would contribute to the reduction in net asset turnover. This idea is supported by the reduction in non-current asset turnover from 1.81 times to 1.57 times.

The capital expenditure has been concentrated on the Organics and Electronics divisions. Additional facilities in these areas appear to be being built. The capital expenditure in the Monomer division is much lower. This may reflect the higher margins available in the other divisions and the disposal decision.

Revenue per employee has remained broadly static. The number of employees in the Electronics division has reduced. The capital expenditure in that division may have generated operating efficiencies. The number of employees in the Organics division has increased significantly. The capital expenditure in that division may have generated additional capacity and a need for more employees.

Investor ratios

The EPS has shown strong growth to 40.2p per share. However, investors will be cautious given:

- The reduction in the level of dividend and the dividend yield. The yield has reduced to 2.9% from 3.4% and the shares will be less attractive to investors seeking income.

- The price earnings ratio has fallen from 20.9 times to 15.4 times. The EPS growth has not been reflected in the share price movement. The shares will be less attractive to investors seeking growth.

The dividend has probably been cut to restore dividend cover. In 20X5 it was only 1.4 times and even though it has increased to 2.2 times investors may be cautious about the sustainability of future distributions.

The capital expenditure requirements of the business also seem to be increasing. Cash dividend cover seems healthy at 3.4 times, but this excludes the capital expenditure requirements of the business. The future capital expenditure requirements will have a major influence on the capacity to pay dividends. This issue is brought into focus by the increase in the gearing to 63%. The ability to borrow further may be restricted and investment may have to be financed largely from operating cash flows.

Cash flow per share has grown to 68.1p from 56.2p. Again, this excludes capital expenditure as this is largely at the discretion of management. It is significantly higher than EPS as the latter includes depreciation.

The key to the future cash flows is also dependent on the future cash resources from the potential disposal. However, it may be imprudent to consider these as no agreements have been made and any transaction is uncertain. Any reinvestment by way of capital expenditure or business acquisition needs also to be considered.

Further matters for investigation

- A statement of cash flows for Lydford plc. A review of cash flows from operations and those from other activities would be useful. In particular an analysis of the quality of the profits by comparing the operating cash flows and operating profits would be useful. In addition details of the cash flows of each division.

- A statement of financial position to determine working capital efficiency.

- A copy of the financial statements or press releases issued with the annual results to identify any reasons given for the dividend reduction.

- Further details of the proposed disposal of the Monomer division including any indicative proceeds, timing of the disposal and post year end performance.

- Details of the basis of any inter-company pricing as this has a direct effect on profitability. Details of any changes in transfer pricing arrangements between 20X5 and 20X6.

- Details of arrangements to secure Monomer product for use by the two remaining divisions when the Monomer division is sold. Are there any cost implications?

- Analysis of the allocation of central costs and assets between divisions. In particular, any costs or assets allocated to the Monomer division but which will continue to be borne by the continuing operations after the disposal.

- Details of any future capital expenditure plans and available financial resources.

- Details of any plans for the utilisation of the disposal proceeds of the Monomer division.

Conclusion

The directors have a major strategic decision to make. If the press reports are correct, they are in the process of disposing of a key business segment. This raises questions about the performance and cash flows of the continuing operations together with the future operational and dividend policies. Whilst EPS has grown investors will be wary about the dividend cuts and the fall in the P/E ratio. The directors have delivered operational performance but shareholder value is less apparent.

Point to note:

When you review these answers, remember that they are mark plans and are more detailed than a candidate would be expected to prepare. They include a discussion of a large number of additional ratios which could have been calculated. For example, question 1 requires candidates to calculate a maximum of five. Remember, that as a rule of thumb, each paragraph in the sample answer represents a 'good' point and would be awarded one mark.

1   **Ironville plc**

(a) The disclosure of information on provisions allows a user of financial information to evaluate their nature, timing and financial effect on the financial statements.

Provisions can be significant liabilities in the statement of financial position. They often involve significant estimates and judgements made by management which can have a material effect on the financial performance and financial position of an entity. Users need to understand the significant estimates and uncertainties involved. The disclosure of a range of outcomes as part of estimation techniques assists in this.

Previous accounting scandals have involved the inappropriate use of provisions either to smooth profits between periods or to use them for a purpose for which they were not created. By requiring the disclosure of the movements on provisions users can assess the appropriateness of their use and their effect on the quality of profits.

Providing details of the provisions' movements during the year helps users to confirm past estimates. The nature and timing of future outflows gives users predictive information with which to assess future cash flows.

Examiner's comment – Poor answers to this question would simply involve listing the IAS 37 disclosure requirements. This does not answer the requirement. Good answers would discuss the usefulness of the information and in particular its predictive and confirmatory value.

(b) Relevant additional ratios (up to a maximum of five) will gain half a mark each, with another half for its comparative. Their calculation could be included in an appendix.

Further ratios could be calculated. For example

	20X5	20X4
Gross profit %		
((3,840/16,440) × 100%) and ((4,310/16,510) × 100%)	23.4%	26.1%
Operating cost %		
((1,710/16,440) × 100%) and ((2,530/16,510) × 100%)	10.4%	15.3%
Trade receivables collection period		
((5,070/16,440) × 365) and ((4,200/16,510) × 365)	113 days	93 days
Trade payables payment period		
((2,230/12,600) × 365) and ((2,040/12,200) × 365)	65 days	61 days
Non-current asset turnover		
(16,440/16,200) and (16,510/16,130)	1.01 times	1.02 times
Net asset turnover (16,440/(13,770 + 8,500 – 50)) and		
(16,510/(13,110 + 6,600 – 120))	0.74 times	0.84 times
Interest cover (2,130/470) and (1,780/380)	4.5 times	4.7 times
Interest cover (exc. provision reversal)		
20X5 = ((2,130 – 620)/470)	3.2 times	4.7 times
Operating cost % (exc. provision reversal)		
20X5 = ((1,710 + 620)/16,440)	14.2%	15.3%
Operating margin (exc. provision reversal)		
20X5 = ((2,130 – 620)/16,440)	9.2%	10.8%
Revenue per employee (16,440/105) and (16,510/97)	£157,000	£170,000
Operating profit per employee (2,130/105) and		
(1,780/97)	£20,286	£18,350

(Credit will be given for other relevant ratios; the basis of the calculation should be given.)

Introduction

The financial statements and ratios provided by the directors show a 27.5% ((1,160/910) – 1) increase in net profit year on year. Initially this performance looks creditable in the light of stagnant revenues, poor market conditions and increases in raw material prices.

Profitability

The ROCE has increased by one half of a percentage point to 9.6%. This has principally arisen from a 19.7% ((2,130/1,780) – 1) increase in profit from operations. Capital employed has risen due to a £1.97 million ((8,500 – 50) – (6,600 – 120)) increase in net borrowings and a £660,000 (13,770 – 13,110) increase in equity.

Revenue has fallen by 0.4% ((16,440/16,510) – 1) year on year. Given the raw material price increases it would be interesting to understand whether these have been passed onto customers. If this is the case, sales volumes may have decreased.

Revenue per employee has decreased markedly by 7.6% ((157/170) – 1). Average employee numbers have increased by eight people (8%) from 97. Given that the restructuring was completed during the year, it is surprising to see employee numbers increase so markedly. The restructuring may have been over aggressive and additional staff may have subsequently been hired to replace those who have left.

The gross profit margin has decreased by 2.7 percentage points (23.4% – 26.1%). This is consistent with the increase in raw material input prices. This would confirm that price increases have not been passed onto customers. Alternatively, the restructuring may have created inefficient manufacturing practices which have eroded margins.

Operating expenses have reduced by 32.4% ((1,710/2,530) – 1) and now represent 10.4% of revenue (20X4 – 15.3%). At first sight this looks a creditable achievement. However, £620,000 of the restructuring provision has been reversed against operating expenses. If this is adjusted for, the operating expenses become 14.2% of revenue which still represents a reduction of 1.1 percentage points (14.2% – 15.3%). This may represent the benefits of the restructuring.

However, research and development expenditure has fallen by £380,000 (260 – 640) and this could explain the improved cost efficiency. Research and development is a discretionary expense and whilst a reduction may boost performance in the short term, it may have adverse long-term consequences on business development. The development expenditure may have been capitalised; an intangible asset has been recognised during the year.

Operating profits have increased by 19.7% ((2,130/1,780) – 1) and the operating profit margins have increased by over two percentage points (13.0% – 10.8%). Whilst gross margins have eroded, this has been more than compensated for by the reduction in operating expenses.

Operating profit margins of 13.0% are significantly above the sector average of 10.5%, having been slightly below in 20X4 (10.8% v 11.2%). The sector operating margin reduction is probably due to raw material price increases.

However, if the provision is adjusted for, the operating margin is only 9.2%. This is significantly below the sector average. Year on year the operating margins have fallen further behind competitors.

Interest cover has remained healthy at about 4.5 times. Again, this is before adjusting for the provision release. When adjusted for, it falls to 3.2 times. Whilst the fall is of concern, this level of cover is still reasonable. However, the increased borrowings and falling interest cover may give lenders cause for concern.

The effective rate of tax has fallen from 35% ((490/1,400) × 100%) to 30% ((500/1,660) × 100%). This has contributed to the increase in net profits. This may be due to the tax treatment of the restructuring costs.

No dividend has been declared in respect of 20X5. Within groups this is not unusual, as tax and treasury are often decided at a group level. However, sustainable profits have fallen and debt (see below) has increased, which raises concerns about the ability to maintain high dividend payouts.

Operating profit per employee has increased from £18,350 to £20,286. However, this is distorted by the provision release and should not be seen as an indicator of increased efficiency.

Financial position

Gearing has increased significantly to 61.4%. Borrowings have increased from £6.6 million to £8.5 million. Significant operating cash flows do not appear to be being generated. This funding has been provided by the parent company.

The carrying amounts of property, plant and equipment are comparable year on year which, in the absence of disposals, would indicate that capital expenditure is at the level of the depreciation expense. This indicates that expansion of facilities is unlikely to be occurring.

The non-current asset turnover (1.01 compared to 1.02) has not changed significantly. Net asset turnover (0.84 to 0.74 in 20X5) figures show a year on year decline. Revenue has reduced slightly whilst operating assets have increased. It appears that efficiency has fallen.

The statement of financial position includes an intangible asset of £500,000. No further details are given. This is in a year when the research and development expense has reduced by £380,000 which may indicate that the IAS 38 criteria for recognition as an asset have been met. The future benefits of this asset need reviewing carefully.

Liquidity

The current ratio (3.1 v 2.7) and acid test ratio (1.9 v 1.7) both show improvements year on year. It appears that a key factor is increased inventory levels which have changed significantly. However, receivables have increased by £0.87 million (5,070 – 4,200) whilst revenue is virtually unchanged.

Inventory turnover has reduced to 4.0 times (20X4 4.4 times). This is low but may reflect a long production cycle in the sector. In addition raw material prices have increased and inventory holding volumes may not have increased significantly.

The trade receivables collection period has increased from 93 days to 113 days. This period was already significant and now it is of concern. It may result from the seasonality of sales. It will raise concern over recoverability. In the poor market conditions extended credit periods may have been offered. Credit control procedures should be reviewed.

Trade payables payment period has increased marginally from 61 days to 65 days. This has not been sufficient to compensate for changes in inventory turnover and the trade receivables collection period.

The increase in inter-company borrowings together with the lack of a dividend in the current year may indicate that liquidity is of concern.

Conclusion

The reversal of the restructuring provision of £620,000 is a significant contributor to the year on year performance. It is a one-off, non-cash profit and analysts would regard it as a low quality profit. High quality profits arise from increased revenues or reduced costs. This does not appear to be the case here.

Further matters for investigation

- An analysis of the sales revenue by segment, including an analysis of price and volume changes within revenue, to understand better the components of the revenue change.

- A statement of cash flows for Radbourne Ltd, to be able to analyse the quality of the profits by comparing the operating cash flows and operating profits.

- Details of the movements in other judgemental items in the financial statements such as allowances against inventory and trade receivables. This will help determine the quality of the profits and whether management have used judgements to improve profits.

- Details of the intangible asset capitalised during the year. Was it separately acquired or internally generated? Does it really meet the recognition criteria if it was internally generated? Does it explain the reduction in the R&D expense?

- Details of the restructuring undertaken. This should assist an understanding of any future costs and the benefits of the restructuring, including an analysis of what they are expected to be and when they will be realised.

- Details of the increase in the number of employees. This should include an analysis of the reasons for the increase. This appears to be contrary to normal restructurings where headcount reduces.

- Details of the basis of any inter-company pricing because this has a direct effect on profitability.

- An analysis of the terms and conditions of the inter-company finance because this has a direct effect on profitability.

- Analysis of the year on year movement in the effective tax rate which has fallen by 5%.

2 Tirril plc

Relevant additional ratios (up to a maximum of five) will gain half a mark each, with another half for its comparative. Their calculation could be included in an appendix.

Further ratios could be calculated. For example:

	20X6	20X5
Gross margin %		
((14,640/28,300) × 100%) and ((19,680/32,450) × 100%)	51.7%	60.6%
Operating expenses %		
((5,890/28,300) × 100%) and ((6,780/32,450) × 100%)	20.8%	20.9%
Operating expenses exc. research costs %		
(((5,890 – 125)/28,300) × 100%) and (((6,780 – 450)/32,450) × 100%)	20.4%	19.5%
Interest cover (8,750/340) and (12,900/600)	25.7 times	21.5 times
Dividend cover (5,240/4,800) and (8,110/4,500)	1.1 times	1.8 times
Dividend yield ((32/240) × 100%) and ((30/450) × 100%)	13.3%	6.7%
Price earnings ratio (240/35) and (450/54)	6.9	8.3
Cash from operations to profit from operations		
((12,970/8,750) × 100%) and ((16,450/12,900) × 100%)	148%	128%
Cash interest cover (12,970/360) and (16,450/640)	36.0 times	25.7 times
Cash dividend cover (8,100/4,500) and (11,100/4,125)	1.8 times	2.7 times
Capital expenditure to depreciation expense		
(60/2,640) and (960/2,750)	0.02 times	0.35 times
Revenue per computer package sold		
(28,300/26,400) and (32,450/29,100)	£1,072	£1,115
Operating profit per computer package sold		
(8,750/26,400) and (12,900/29,100)	£331	£443

(Credit will be given for other relevant ratios; the basis of the calculation should be given.)

Introduction

The financial statements and ratios provided show a 12.8% ((28,300/32,450) – 1) decrease and a 35.4% ((5,240/8,110) – 1) decrease in revenue and net profit year on year respectively. However, the cash flows remain strong with significant increases in cash and repayments of borrowings. The operating environment remains very competitive.

Profitability

ROCE has fallen significantly, by over nine percentage points to 30.3%. This shows that the overall efficiency of the group in employing available resources has decreased.

Revenue has fallen by 12.8% year on year. This probably reflects the increasingly competitive operating environment and the aggressive marketing strategy by Whigham Inc. The revenue per computer package sold has fallen by 4% to £1,072 from £1,115. Hence, the primary factor in the revenue decrease is the fall in the number of units sold. Tirril plc may need to consider reducing price levels to remain competitive against Whigham Inc.

The gross profit margin has decreased by 8.9 percentage points (51.7% – 60.6%). If costs of sales are variable, this would appear to indicate that cost increases might be a significant factor.

However, if some production overheads are fixed, a fall in gross margin might have been expected with lower production levels. The operating gearing levels may be high. Cost of sales has increased in absolute terms, suggesting cost increases per unit. This requires further investigation.

Operating expenses have reduced by 13.1% ((5,890/6,780) – 1) and now represent 20.8% of revenue (20X5 – 20.9%). This would appear to be quite an achievement. The expenses have been reduced in direct proportion to the reduction in revenue.

However, research expenditure has fallen by £325,000 (125 – 450). Excluding this, operating expenditure has increased to 20.4% of revenues (20X5 – 19.5%). R & D is discretionary expenditure and this may have been reduced due to the falling revenue levels.

However, given the technological advances suggested for Whigham Inc, it is of concern that no significant research expenditure has been undertaken and no development expenditure has been capitalised. Tirril plc may not be in a position to respond to product advances made by its competitors.

The capitalised development expenditure is almost fully written-off. This may indicate that the technology developed by Tirril plc is nearing the end of its useful life. It may be obsolete compared to the competitors.

Operating profits have decreased by 32.2% ((8,750/12,900) – 1) and the operating profit margins have decreased by 8.9 percentage points (30.9% – 39.8%). Whilst gross margins have eroded, this has been compensated for by the reduction in operating expenses.

Interest cover has remained healthy and increased to 25 times operating profit. The rising interest cover, falling debt levels and falling gearing will provide comfort for debt providers given the competitive and uncertain operational environment. The fall in interest costs is consistent with other information and the strong cash flows.

The profit per package sold has fallen by 25% ((331/443) – 1). With only a slight reduction in selling price per unit, the costs per unit must have increased. This has arisen from either an increase in variable costs per unit or the spreading of fixed costs over fewer units manufactured.

Statement of cash flows

Tirril plc's cash flow in both years is very strong. There has been a net increase in cash in both years, despite significant cash outflows from financing activities.

Gearing has decreased significantly (by over 20 percentage points) to 28.2%. This is a result of the strong operating cash flows and despite the reductions in equity that would arise from share repurchases and increasing dividend payments.

The cash return on capital employed has fallen from 50.6% to 44.9%. This ratio is usually higher than ROCE as it excludes cash payments for capital expenditure (even though these are small) and ROCE is calculated after deducting depreciation. It does show that cash returns are falling in line with reductions in profitability and cash from operations.

The quality of profits is good. The cash flow from operations to profit from operations has increased from an already healthy 128% to 148%. A key factor in this is the reduction in working capital in both years. In 20X6 the reduction in working capital is £860,000 (570 + 340 – 50).

- This is reflected in the inventory turnover increasing to 7 times (20X5 – 5.1 times).

- Trade receivables have fallen but not as quickly as revenue has fallen. Trade receivable days have increased by three days to 54 days. This is not significant but Tirril plc should be wary of increasing credit periods as a competitive response to the operating environment.

Capital expenditure has reduced significantly in 20X6 to only £60,000. This represents only 2.2% of the annual depreciation expense and this may result in future reductions of operating capacity. At this level it is questionable whether any replacement of worn out plant is occurring.

Significant disposals of property, plant and equipment have occurred in both years. This may reflect the reductions in operating levels and the sale of surplus assets.

Cash interest cover is healthy at over 36 times (20X5 – 25.7 times). It is normally higher than interest cover calculated from the income statement as it excludes capital expenditure whereas the income statement measure is after deducting depreciation.

Debt providers may be concerned about the long-term prospects for the business but the current measures for interest cover and gearing will be reassuring. Those measures may also suggest that raising debt finance is a possibility for potential investment in acquisitions.

Significant cash outflows from financing activities have occurred. During 20X5 almost £8 million (3,500 + 4,125) was returned to investors through share buybacks and dividend payments. Debt repayments have also been made. The cash balances have increased in 20X6. This may suggest that cash resources are being accumulated for the suggested acquisitions.

Investor ratios

EPS has fallen by over a third ((35/54) – 1) to 35p. This reflects the fall in profitability. The PE ratio has also fallen from 8.3 times to 6.9 times. This probably reflects investors' caution over the prospects for the company, the competitive operating environment and the new products developed by Whigham Inc.

Dividends have grown by 6.7% (32/30) – 1) year on year. However, even this increase has failed to underpin the share price. Dividend yield is now 13.3% (20X5 – 6.7%). This high yield probably reflects the risks associated with the business.

The cash flow per share has fallen from 74p to 54p. This ratio is calculated by excluding capital expenditure. However, this remains relatively small. The ratio is declining as profitability declines.

Cash dividend cover at 1.8 times has reduced from 2.7 times in the prior year. Traditional profits-based dividend cover has also fallen to 1.1 times from 1.8 times. The current dividend levels will be unsustainable if profits fall further. Even if profits remain stable, it will be questionable whether this level of payout can continue. Any investment in capital or acquisitions will further reduce the possibility of future high dividend payments, unless borrowings are increased.

Further matters for investigation

- An analysis of the current research expenditure activities undertaken by Tirril plc, to see whether it is working to improve the technological attractiveness of its products.

- Comments from Tirril plc on the suggested technological improvements by Whigham Inc. and the potential impact on the business including details of Tirril plc's strategic response.

- Details of Tirril plc's future acquisition targets and the strategic objectives of the acquisitions, to understand the direction the company is trying to take.

- Details of the changes in the number of employees. This should include details of changes in key personnel such as software designers, because any decrease would restrict product development and therefore future revenue.

- Details of the share buybacks and any future plan to repurchase equity, to understand the likely effect on future cash flows.

- Other comments in trade and local press about technological changes in the market place including timescales and actions of other competitors. This will provide an understanding of the threats faced by Tirril plc.

- Price lists for Whigham Inc. within Europe, to understand the extent of its price competition.

- The financial statements of Whigham Inc. An analysis of its financial performance and position can be undertaken to determine its strategic and financial competitiveness.

- A statement of financial position to show the principal assets (including non-current) to determine the equity invested in the business and any recoverability risks associated with the assets.

Conclusion

The market position of Tirril plc's products is under significant pressure from competitors. The volume of products sold has reduced significantly with consequential adverse effects on profitability. Cash flows have remained strong with share buybacks, increased dividend payments and debt repayments occurring. However, investment in R&D and capital has dried up and the long-term strategy of management must be questioned.

CHAPTER 14

Scenario-based, open-ended questions

Introduction

Examination context

Topic List

1   Scenario questions

2   Approach to examination questions

3   Examination question – Windgather plc

4   Deconstruction

5   Reconstruction

Summary and Self-test

Answers to Interactive questions

Answers to Self-test

Introduction

The ability of Chartered Accountants to identify and resolve financial reporting issues is essential to meeting the needs of their employers, firms and clients. These issues are often not apparent at first sight. Whilst some financial reporting problems relate to one area, it is more common for issues to be more complex. Financial reporting issues are most often driven by both planned and unplanned business events. These business scenarios create interesting reporting challenges for Chartered Accountants.

Learning objectives

Tick off

- Prepare and present extracts from the financial statements of a single entity undertaking a wide range of transactions according to its accounting policies, subject to the international financial reporting framework

- Identify from financial and other data any subsidiary, associate or joint venture of a single entity according to the international financial reporting framework

- Calculate, from financial and other data, the amounts to be included in an entity's consolidated financial statements in respect of its new, continuing and discontinued interests in subsidiaries, associates and joint ventures, according to the international financial reporting framework

- Prepare and present extracts from the consolidated financial statements of an entity undertaking a wide range of transactions in accordance with its accounting policies and the international financial reporting framework

- Define and calculate from information provided the distributable profits of an entity and allocations of distributable profit

- Identify financial and operational information in documents containing audited financial statements (for example, reports on operations by management or those responsible for governance, financial summaries and highlights) that could be relevant to the legal entity or consolidated financial statements, and assess whether those financial statements adequately reflect that information

- Formulate accounting and reporting policies in accordance with laws, regulations, accounting standards and other requirements for use in the single entity and consolidated financial statements

Due to the integrated nature of the syllabus, other learning objectives could be combined with any or all of those above in any one question. For example, learning objectives from syllabus section 1, Current Issues in the Reporting Framework, such as those related to the FRSSE, UK GAAP and ethics could be incorporated into questions.

Syllabus links

In the Financial Accounting syllabus you developed the basic knowledge and application skills for a number of financial reporting standards. You have extended these knowledge and application skills for those and other financial reporting standards during your studies of Chapters 1 to 10 of this Study Manual. This chapter will help you develop your ability for questions that require 'integrated' answers covering several financial reporting standards in depth.

In the technical integration papers at Advanced Stage you will be faced with further scenario questions where you will be required to identify and resolve more complex financial reporting issues. In some questions you will also be required to resolve taxation, assurance and business analysis issues relating to the same scenario.

Examination context

In an examination you will be faced with questions based upon 'real life' scenarios. The questions will be 'open-ended'. You will be required to deconstruct the scenario given and then reconstruct the facts, issues and judgements as part of your answer. Ethical issues and professional judgement are regular features in these types of questions. Open-ended questions are a common feature of the Financial Reporting examination.

The questions involve a significant proportion of higher-level skills as they involve analysing events and formulating the most appropriate reporting treatments.

Chapter 15 will review a different question type, the 'closed-ended' or 'consequential' question type. A number of the skills discussed in this chapter will be relevant to that chapter also.

The requirements of the questions dealt with in this chapter are open-ended. In the assessment, candidates may be required to:

- Discuss the financial reporting treatment for the issues arising from a business event or series of events

- Quantify the effects of the financial reporting issues on the financial statements

- Identify the choice of accounting treatments adopted in financial statements and other financial information and assess how they affect the view presented

- Recognise the ethical and professional issues for a professional accountant undertaking work in and giving advice on accounting and financial reporting

- Prepare and present financial statement extracts from structured and unstructured data

- Explain in non-technical language the application of accounting and disclosure requirements to information provided

- Develop and advise upon accounting policies for an organisation

1 Scenario questions

In the examination you will meet questions that are based closely upon 'real life' scenarios. The scenarios, like other questions in the Financial Reporting paper, are based upon the financial reporting requirements for common business events.

Common business events that may occur in scenario questions **could** include:

- Business start up
- Business transformation
- Mergers and acquisitions
- Demergers and disposals
- Refinancing and financial strategy changes
- Outsourcing
- Strategy changes
- Competitors entering and leaving markets
- Regulatory changes
- Contractual terms re-negotiated

These questions will test the technical knowledge that you have developed through the Accounting, Financial Accounting and Financial Reporting modules. However, clients and employers expect Chartered Accountants to provide advice, solutions to complex issues and options about strategy, in addition to technical excellence. These scenario questions test your ability to identify issues and apply technical knowledge when providing solutions.

Strong answers to scenario style questions require methodology and planning. This mirrors the way that you should approach challenges in the workplace.

The examiners are looking for the following characteristics in **strong** answers:

- Evidence of **planning** which demonstrates that thought has been applied before the answer is written out.

- Well structured answers addressing the **key issues** in a logical format.

- **Technical excellence** through identifying the relevant business issues and the related financial reporting issues.

- Focused **discussion** of the issues arising with arguments applied to the specific circumstances of the scenario in the question.

- **Quantification** of the issues and where necessary preparation of financial statement extracts and ratios.

- Advice where a **range of solutions** is available by discussing a range of factors rather than simply one solution.

- Answers that demonstrate **higher skills** by synthesising, integrating, analysing and evaluating the material in the question.

Weaker answers would fail to display many or all of the above characteristics. **Weaker** answers may have the additional features:

- Points made are merely **repetition** from the question, without any 'added value' in the form of analysis or drawing of inferences.

- Points are made **randomly** without any focus or argument.

- The **requirements are not addressed** directly or fully.

- **Failure** to provide a clear explanation of the point or **to communicate** a clear understanding.

- **Lack of any consideration** of the broader aspects of an issue and its wider implications.

- Technically incorrect solutions or answers that include **content copied** from the set text without a focus on the scenario.

- Too much **emphasis on demonstrating knowledge** as opposed to problem solving.

- Lack of prioritisation of the key, as opposed to **peripheral**, parts of the question.

2 Approach to examination questions

In helping you to develop an approach to open-ended questions, we will base our discussions around the question Windgather plc. Windgather plc is a sample question that was produced by the examination team when the syllabus was first introduced to demonstrate the style of a common open-ended, scenario-based examination question. This chapter will lead you through the Windgather plc question. You will be able to develop a range of skills that should help you in the real examination.

You need to focus particularly on the requirements of the question and those attributes of an answer that demonstrate your ability to identify financial reporting issues and then resolve them.

When working through this chapter you should bear in mind the attributes of strong and weak answers discussed above.

3 Examination question – Windgather plc

Read the following examination question.

Worked example: Windgather plc

Windgather plc acquired, from the licensing authority, a ten-year licence to operate a unique, ten channel satellite television network at a cost of £3.7 million on 1 January 20X5. The licence commenced on that date.

The licence purchase was funded by the issue of five million £1 ordinary shares at a premium of 20p. Professional fees of £500,000 were incurred of which £300,000 related to the issue of the ordinary shares. The remainder related to legal negotiations for the network operating licence. All of the professional fees are deductible for tax. The current tax rate is 30%. Sateast plc subscribed for 10% of the shares issued. It also paid £500,000 for five million warrants. Each warrant entitles Sateast plc to subscribe for one new ordinary share in Windgather plc from 1 April 20X7 for £2 per share. The market value of one Windgather plc warrant at 31 December 20X5 has been estimated at 11p.

Windgather plc has signed a four-year agreement with Stars plc to utilise its satellite network for the delivery of its television channels. That agreement commenced on 1 April 20X5. Windgather plc paid Stars plc £1 million on 1 April 20X5. Three further annual payments of £600,000 are payable commencing on 1 April 20X6. Windgather plc utilises approximately 10% of the operating capacity of Stars plc's network, which has an estimated useful life of eight years. Stars plc has agreed a minimum level of service that will be provided.

Windgather plc operates a simple business model involving only one customer package. Each customer pays Windgather plc £45 per month for television services and commits to an initial 12 month contract. After that initial period the customer may cancel the contract. Once the initial contract is signed each customer receives free receiver equipment (needed to receive the programmes) and free equipment installation. These have a retail value of £90 and £30 if purchased without the contract. Stars plc offers customers a similar television package without receiver equipment and installation for £40 per month. Windgather plc signed up 20,000 customers during 20X5. The average unexpired term of a customer contract is eight months.

Windgather plc's business plan includes ambitious growth targets. The customer take up has been disappointing. The business plan target number of customers who were needed to have subscribed to the service by 31 December 20X5 in order to achieve eventual break even has been calculated at 75,000. Sateast plc, who wishes to break into this market, has made an indicative offer of £3.2 million for Windgather plc's operating licence. The net selling price of the other intangible and tangible assets is believed to approximate to their carrying amount.

Requirements

Discuss the financial reporting treatment in the 31 December 20X5 financial statements of Windgather plc for the issues arising from the establishment of the satellite television network business. Your answer should quantify the effects on the 31 December 20X5 financial statements.

Point to note:

The preparation of financial statement extracts or disclosure notes is not required. **(20 marks)**

On first reading, you should notice some common key attributes of these questions:

- They are based upon business events, in this case the establishment of the satellite television network.

- There are no references to any financial reporting standards either in the body of the text or the requirement.

- The requirement is unstructured. It is open-ended. There are no parts (a), (b) and so on to lead you through the issues.

- It requires you to discuss the issues. This may involve the consideration of different perspectives. In other words, there may be more than one single answer to the issues and a range of answers may be possible.

The examiners described this question as follows.

'This is a scenario question surrounding a key business event – the formation of a new business and the formulation of the required accounting practice. The requirements of the question are largely un-structured so that the candidate has to identify the reporting issues and consider information from throughout the question in formulating the answer. The higher-level skills involve analysing the events and formulating the most appropriate reporting treatments. Credit would be given to candidates who raised valid, alternative issues or suggested other issues that needed investigation'.

These comments confirm that these questions are open-ended and a range of valid, alternative solutions is possible. You should bear this in mind as we walk through a process to answer this question.

4 Deconstruction

4.1 Focus on the requirement

It is essential that before you begin to answer the question you take a few minutes to understand the requirements and develop a plan.

Firstly you should read and consider the requirement. Ask yourself the following.

- What am I being asked to do?
- Am I required to give advice in a particular context (for example reporting to a third party)?
- Is there a particular format such as a report or memorandum?
- Is there anything I need to be aware of in formulating my answer?

Interactive question 1: Windgather plc – requirement

[Difficulty level: Exam standard]

Identify the salient features of the Windgather plc question requirement.

-
-
-
-

See **Answer** at the end of this chapter.

4.2 Read the question thoroughly

Next, you should read the question thoroughly. As you read, it may be advisable to annotate the question or highlight anything that appears unusual to you. This should give you a basis on which to plan your answer.

4.3 Planning your answer

The next challenge is to identify the key aspects of your answer by identifying the key business and financial reporting issues. The following questions will assist you in developing a plan of your answer and the key points that the examiners are seeking.

- **Business issues**

    - What is the business issue(s) in the question?

    - How is this reflected in the scenario?

    - Am I aware of any industry issues surrounding this industry that may help my consideration of the financial reporting issues?

- **Financial reporting issues**

    - What are the financial reporting issues?
    - Are any of the issues linked or are they independent of one another?

- **Ethical issues and judgements**

    - Are there any that need considering?
    - Are there any areas where significant judgement has been or needs to be applied?
    - What are the consequences of such judgement on the key issues of profit, cash and debt?

- **Additional information**

    Is there any additional information that may be required to complete my analysis of the issues identified?

It is important that you don't forget that the examiners have structured the question in the order the information is given for a reason. The basic issues are kept together to help you formulate your answer. For example, the second paragraph relates to raising finance. In general, the issues are confined to the paragraphs in which the information is given and the facts required to discuss most financial reporting issues are located together.

Interactive question 2: Windgather plc – planning your answer
[Difficulty level: Exam standard]

Identify the key issues in the Windgather plc question.

- **Business issues**

- **Financial reporting issues**

    - Paragraph 1
    - Paragraph 2
    - Paragraph 3
    - Paragraph 4
    - Paragraph 5

- **Ethical issues and judgements**

- **Additional information**

See **Answer** at the end of this chapter.

4.4 Financial reporting standards

On your plan, you can now annotate the financial reporting standards that you need to consider in answering the question.

Interactive question 3: Windgather plc – financial reporting standards
[Difficulty level: Exam standard]

Identify the financial reporting standards that you need to consider in completing your answer for each of the issues identified in the paragraphs.

*   Paragraph 1 – operating licence

*   Paragraph 2 – fund raising

*   Paragraph 3 – outsourcing agreement

*   Paragraph 4 – revenue recognition

*   Paragraph 5 – impairment of licence

*   Paragraph 5 – going concern

See **Answer** at the end of this chapter.

You could complete Interactive questions 2 and 3 by preparing a mind map to help plan your answer.

5 Reconstruction

5.1 Writing your answer

You are now in a position to start writing your answer. Because the examiner will have ordered the issues in the given order for a reason, it will in most cases be a good idea to answer them in that order. This is consistent with how you have planned the question. Lay your answer out using headings that relate to the six issues you have identified so far.

Before you make an attempt at writing an answer, it is important that you think through how the points you make will be assessed. It is important that you understand why one script would obtain a better mark on the points made than another. This suggested evaluation is given for guidance only and cannot be exact, since the overall mark will be based on the answer coverage as a whole and not just the specific point.

Strong answers will address the requirements of the question. They will identify the issues. For each issue candidates should ensure that their answers:

- **Identify the issue** and **discuss the financial reporting treatment**. The analysis should be appropriate to the context of the question. It should refer to the facts given in the question and relate these to the financial reporting treatment. Alternative treatments should be discussed and where possible a conclusion drawn as to the most appropriate.

- **Quantify the effects**. In quantifying the effects you should consider both the initial measurement and subsequent remeasurement of an item where appropriate. The effect on the statement of financial position, the income statement (including earnings) and the statement of cash flows should be considered. Where appropriate, your answers could mention the impact of the conclusions you draw. For example, the classification of an instrument as debt or equity will have an effect on gearing.

You might like to use the following model in formulating answers. However, remember that your answer should address the question requirement. In the Windgather plc question, disclosure notes are not required and therefore that area of the analysis is not needed.

Recognition	Measurement
How should the item be recognised?	How should the item be measured both on initial recognition and then subsequently?
For example	For example
• Asset or expense	• Historical cost or fair value

Presentation	Disclosure
How should the item be presented in financial statements?	What disclosures should be made either in the key statements or in the notes?
For example	For example
• Debt or equity	• Key judgements

In most cases, **good points pass the 'because' test**. When suggesting a solution to the financial reporting issue you should explain 'why', ie your reason for suggesting it. For example, the financial instrument should be classified as debt because …., the amortisation period should be ten years because… The word **'because' changes a 'what' into a 'why'**. In other words you can demonstrate what approach is most appropriate and why. You should try to relate the 'why' to the specific business issues given in the question. The reader (in your case, the examiner) will then appreciate that you understand the **relationships between** the **financial reporting** treatment and the **business issues**.

5.2 Overall issues – focus

It is important when writing your answer to consider the depth that you will need to go into. This is where you can demonstrate your understanding and added value. As a general rule, you will be able to demonstrate more 'added value' where the issues are of significant magnitude (materiality) and where judgement is required in discussing the issue and developing solutions.

In this question, the revenue recognition policy is the most sensitive issue. In most cases, revenue is the most significant number in the financial statements and IAS 18 often only provides limited guidance. In this case the formulation of a revenue policy will have significant bearing on the view developed by users and any financial statement analysis.

Interactive question 4: Attempting the question [Difficulty level: Exam standard]

You can now attempt the question. Try to write down the solutions to the issues with explanation and quantification where possible. You can mark your answer by applying the general principles in the commentary and table above.

See **Answer** at the end of this chapter.

Summary and Self-test

Summary

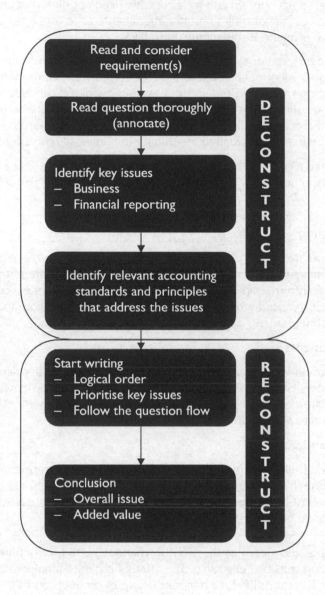

Self-test

Answer the two following questions.

1 **Bluejohn plc**

You are a Chartered Accountant and have recently been appointed as an independent, non-executive director of Bluejohn plc, a multi-national enterprise that operates in the pharmaceuticals sector and prepares financial statements using IFRS.

Various governments, national and international regulators monitor Bluejohn plc. The company is aware of this high level of political risk and public scrutiny and of the sensitivity of reporting high gross and operating margins in certain business and geographical sectors due to the industry that it operates in. Bluejohn plc has a reputation for non-transparent financial reporting. You have been concerned about this and as Bluejohn plc's shares have recently started trading on the London Stock Exchange, you have decided to investigate the financial reporting practices.

You have obtained a copy of the draft financial statements for the year ended 31 March 20X7 from the chief financial officer (CFO). You have identified the following extracts from the accounting policies note.

Segment reporting

The company operates in the pharmaceutical market. The directors are of the opinion that the market for pharmaceuticals is single and global. No analysis by different product or service is provided because information is not reported regularly to the chief executive on this basis. Information is not reported internally on a regional basis, so no geographical analysis is presented in the financial statements.

Treasury investments

The company has an active treasury department which manages the risks associated with the company's business. Short-term cash surpluses are invested in long-dated government securities. These securities are classified as available-for-sale financial instruments. They are subsequently sold when cash resources are required.

Freehold land and buildings

Freehold land and buildings are carried at revalued amount less subsequent depreciation and impairment losses. The revaluation surplus included in equity in respect of an item of property, plant and equipment is transferred directly to retained earnings when the asset is derecognised either upon disposal or through depreciation.

You have also obtained a copy of the monthly management information pack provided to the directors, including the chief executive. The internal organisational structure is reported through five divisions, each responsible for a different group of products and services. It also includes revenue details by country. The CFO has said 'We're in the pharmaceutical industry. It's one big sector. We don't need to provide segment information. It would be detrimental for us to do so as it would increase the scrutiny of our businesses'.

The divisions have no trading with each other, and the external revenue can be analysed as follows.

	£m
Oils products	45
Established products	28
Contract products	15
Emerging solutions	9
Licensing division	3
	100

On 1 June 20X5 the company acquired a government bond at a cost of £4 million. The fair value of the government bond at 31 March 20X6 was £4.4 million and a gain of £0.4 million was recognised in other comprehensive income and held in equity. In accordance with the company's treasury policy the bond was sold on 28 February 20X7 for £4.3 million. A loss of £0.1 million has been recognised in operating expenses.

On 31 March 20X7 Bluejohn plc sold an unoccupied freehold land and building site for £4 million, being the fair value of £4.2 million less disposal costs of £0.2 million. The net proceeds of £4 million were credited to revenue. The carrying amount of the freehold land and buildings was £2 million. This amount was debited to operating expenses on that date and the revaluation surplus relating to the asset of £0.6 million was transferred directly to retained earnings. The held for sale classification criteria of IFRS 5 *Non-current Assets Held for Sale and Discontinued Operations* were met on 31 March 20X7.

A junior employee approached you in the company car park. She said 'I've heard that you've been asking questions. I hope that you sort out the sale of that old building. The purchaser was the pension fund of the executive directors. It was sold before the company's shares were listed on the stock exchange so they could hide it'.

Requirements

(a) Discuss the financial reporting treatment in the 31 March 20X7 financial statements of Bluejohn plc arising from this situation. Your answer should quantify the effects on the 31 March 20X7 financial statements. **(16 marks)**

(b) Comment on the ethical issues arising from the scenario and the actions that you should consider. **(6 marks)**

(22 marks)

Note:

The preparation of financial statement extracts or disclosure notes is not required.

2 **Frodsham plc**

Frodsham plc is a listed food products manufacturer. It operates from three factory locations. Each factory operates as a separate operating division of Frodsham plc under a different brand name. The three divisions are called Tarlton, Catworth and Euxton.

Certain technical functions are provided on a company wide basis by the central technical team which serves all three divisions. The following is an extract from the Operating and Financial Review included in the 20X5 financial statements:

Food safety and quality: the technical assurance team assesses and approves raw material suppliers, audits the quality control systems across all divisions, provides guidance on compliance with relevant legislation, sets technical standards and offers expertise on a wide range of food science and technology matters. The systems continually meet the highest standards.

Finance: Each division prepares detailed annual budgets and strategic plans, which are reviewed and updated on a regular basis. Weekly and monthly financial reports are prepared for each operating division and performance is monitored against the original budget and updated forecasts. The group's management board meets on a monthly basis to review divisional performance. Each division is reported as a separate operating segment in the annual financial statements because the results for each are regularly reported to the chief executive.

The Tarlton division produces 'premium' poultry products for Buyit, a national supermarket, in addition to selling own brand products through independent outlets.

On 1 December 20X6 a salmonella health scare at the Tarlton division was reported in national newspapers and on national television. The Government Health Department (GHD) immediately closed the production facility. Production recommenced on 1 March 20X7. At that time GHD initiated legal proceedings under food hygiene law against Frodsham plc for failing to maintain adequate food safety systems. The maximum fine payable is £1 million and Frodsham plc's lawyers have indicated that the case will be heard in January 20X8 and their advice is that Frodsham plc should not contest the case.

Buyit returned its entire inventory of poultry products on hand at 1 December 20X6. These products had been purchased by Buyit at a cost of £400,000. The contaminated products were disposed of by Tarlton by 31 December 20X6. A number of production assets were deemed to be contaminated and their carrying amounts were reduced to zero. £50,000 was incurred in January 20X7 to ensure that these production assets were safely disposed of. Under the terms of the contract between Frodsham plc and Buyit, Buyit is entitled to £250,000 compensation for each month that Frodsham plc is unable to supply products to it.

The adverse publicity has had a negative effect on all of Frodsham plc's three divisions. Buyit, who is a major customer of all three divisions, has reduced its level of business and overall sales volumes of products have reduced significantly. On 27 December 20X6 Frodsham plc announced a relaunch of all three divisions. This includes revising all product offerings and incurring additional promotional expenditure of £2 million.

At the end of 20X6 the following information is available for each division:

	Tarlton £'000	Catworth £'000	Euxton £'000
Carrying amount of assets	3,000	2,500	3,500
Remaining useful life	5	10	10
Recoverable amount	1,000	3,200	3,800

Corporate assets comprise the central functions including food safety and hygiene and finance functions. The carrying amount of corporate assets at the end of 20X6 is £900,000. Frodsham plc allocates corporate assets to divisions on a weighted basis on the basis of the estimated remaining useful lives of each division's assets.

The pre-tax discount rate that represents risks specific to Tarlton's production of food products is 10%.

Requirement

Discuss the financial reporting treatment in the 31 December 20X6 financial statements of Frodsham plc arising from the food hygiene incident. Your answer should quantify the effects on the 31 December 20X6 financial statements. **(20 marks)**

Note:

The preparation of financial statement extracts or disclosure notes is not required.

Now, go back to the Learning Objectives in the Introduction. If you are satisfied you have achieved these objectives, please tick them off.

Answers to Interactive questions

Answer to Interactive question 1

The salient features of the Windgather plc question requirement are

- There is no particular context given. No report is required and the issues are not being viewed from any particular perspective

- A discussion is required of the financial reporting issues – this is a wide ranging requirement

- The requirement specifically requires the issues to be quantified

- The preparation of disclosure notes and extracts is not required

- The mark allocation is 20 marks. As a rule of thumb this will be 30 minutes

Answer to Interactive question 2

Here are a number of suggested points that you could have identified. It may be the case that you have raised some additional valid points. Examiners will award credit for any valid points that you raise even if they are not included in the marking guide provided.

- **Business issues**

  - Business set-up
  - Poor performance to date – going concern?
  - Technology business – cash flow sufficient?
  - Television services – subscriber revenue and 'churn'

- **Financial reporting issues**

  - Paragraph 1 – operating licence
  - Paragraph 2 – fund raising
  - Paragraph 3 – outsourcing agreement
  - Paragraph 4 – revenue recognition
  - Paragraph 5 – impairment of licence; going concern

- **Ethical issues and judgements**

  None noted

- **Additional information**

  Information regarding events after the reporting period to assess going concern

Answer to Interactive question 3

The following is a suggested answer. You may have identified additional financial reporting standards to consider.

- Paragraph 1 – operating licence

  IAS 38 – measurement on initial recognition of the licence and its subsequent amortisation.

- Paragraph 2 – fund raising

  IAS 32 – presentation of warrants and issue expenses

- Paragraph 3 – outsourcing agreement

  IAS 17 – finance or operating lease?

- Paragraph 4 – revenue recognition

  IAS 18 – unbundling of revenue between equipment and service fees

- Paragraph 5 – impairment of licence

    IAS 36 – CGU impairment test

- Paragraph 5 – going concern

    - IAS 1 – going concern issues
    - IAS 10 – events after the reporting period

A mind map could be used to plan your answer. Here's a suggestion.

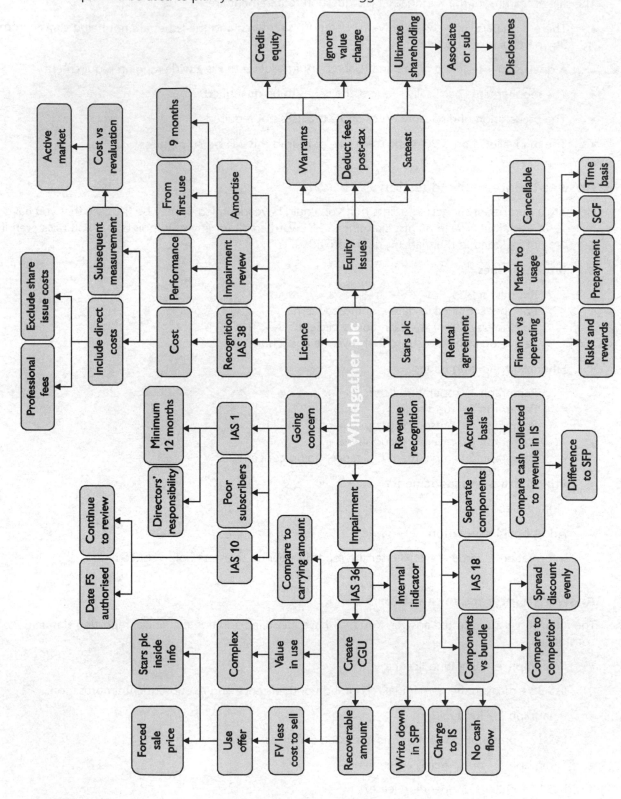

Answer to Interactive question 4

The following is the published answer to the question.

Operating licence

Intangible assets should be measured on initial recognition at cost. The cost of a separately acquired intangible asset, such as the licence, should include any direct costs incurred in preparing the asset for its intended use. These direct costs include professional fees. The asset should be measured at initial recognition at £3.9 million (£3.7m plus (£500,000 - £300,000)).

IAS 38, *Intangible Assets*, allows subsequent measurement using either the cost or revaluation model. However, the latter can only be used when an active market in the intangible asset exists. This is unlikely to be the case here and IAS 38 recognises that the revaluation model will not be used frequently.

The licence has a finite ten-year period and the initial cost should be fully amortised by the end of the licence period, as no residual value exists. Amortisation should commence when the asset is available for use. Whilst the licence period commences on 1 January 20X5, no infrastructure is available until 1 April 20X5 when the agreement with Stars plc commences. It would be reasonable to use the latter date, as this is when the licence can be put to use.

The amortisation for the nine months that the infrastructure is available in 20X5 should be £300,000 ((3.9m/9.75) × 9/12) and the carrying amount at year end should be £3.6 million (£3.9m less £0.3m).

Equity issue

The professional fees relating to the issue of new ordinary shares, net of any tax benefit, should be deducted from equity.

The total amount recognised in equity should be £5.79 million (5m × £1.2 less (100 - 30)% × £300,000)).

The £500,000 proceeds from the issue of the warrants should be credited directly to equity. Any subsequent movement in the fair value of the warrant should not be recognised in the financial statements of Windgather plc as it is only of concern to the warrant holder.

Agreement with Stars plc

The substance of the agreement with Stars plc needs to be considered. As Windgather plc is using less than 10% of the operating capacity, it appears that Stars plc is providing a service. The substance of the transaction does not appear to be a finance lease because Windgather is not taking on the risks of ownership of the equipment.

The fees paid should be recognised in profit or loss on a straight-line basis over the four-year term. An amount of £525,000 (9/12 × (1m + 3 × 0.6m)/4) should be recognised as an expense. The difference between this and the cash flow is £475,000, which should be recognised as a pre-payment.

Revenue recognition

Whilst Windgather plc may believe it has a simple business model, it provides challenges as each transaction contains several components. IAS 18 *Revenue* provides limited guidance in this area, other than stating that the recognition criteria may need to be applied to the separate components of a transaction to reflect substance. However, it provides no detailed guidance on how this is achieved. The application of the general principles would mean that each component should be considered against the recognition criteria in IAS 18.

The fair value of the consideration over the 12 month contract is £540 (12 × £45) and the fair value of the individual components is £600 (£90 + £30 + (12 × £40)). The discount of £60 (10%) should be allocated to each component on a reasonable basis, such as pro rata.

	Individual fair value £	Discount £	Bundled fair value £
Receiver equipment	90	9	81
Installation	30	3	27
Monthly subscription	480	48	432
Total	600	60	540

On installation revenue of £108 (£81 + £27) should be recognised. The average elapsed time of a contract is four months, so the total revenue recognised to date should be £252 (£108 + 4/12 × £432). For 20,000 contracts the total revenue should be £5.04 million.

The total cash collected will be £3.6 million (20,000 × £45 × 4). The difference between this and the revenue recognised of £1.44 million should be recognised as a receivable.

Impairment

The subscriber numbers to date are significantly below target. This is an indicator of impairment per IAS 36, *Impairment of Assets*. An impairment review should be undertaken.

The licence does not generate cash flows independently of the other assets and so the impairment test should be undertaken on a cash generating unit (CGU) basis. The recoverable amount of the CGU containing the licence should be determined. Given the nature of the business, Windgather plc itself would be the CGU.

A value in use exercise should be undertaken for the CGU. However, given the poor subscriber numbers and the operating performance being below break even, it is unlikely that the value in use will support the asset carrying amounts.

The offer from Stars plc of £3.2 million is a reasonable approximation for the fair value less costs to sell of the licence. The fair value less costs to sell of the other assets approximates to their carrying amount and so no impairment will arise on them.

Therefore it is likely that the carrying amount of the licence should be adjusted to £3.2 million and an impairment loss of £400,000 recognised in profit or loss.

Going concern

The business issues regarding poor subscriber numbers and below target performance raise questions about the going concern assumption and whether Windgather plc can continue to operate.

IAS 1 *Presentation of Financial Statements* requires Windgather plc's management to assess whether the going concern assumption is appropriate for a period of not less than 12 months from the end of the reporting period. They may have to consider the availability of additional sources of finance, and disclosure of the significant uncertainties should be made in the financial statements.

IAS 10 *Events after the Reporting Period* requires management to consider events occurring in 20X6 in determining the appropriateness of the going concern assumption. Further detail of subscriber numbers in 20X6 would assist in drawing a conclusion.

Point to note:

Credit would be given to candidates who raised valid, alternative issues or suggested other issues that needed investigation. The examiner's answer is a mark plan. It is necessarily comprehensive to accommodate a wide range of possible answers. This answer is comprehensive and to obtain a clear pass, candidates would not have to identify all of the areas. However, to obtain a pass, the examiners would expect candidates to discuss five of the six areas in detail. The maximum marks available for each area are:

• Operating licence	**(4 marks)**
• Equity issue	**(4 marks)**
• Agreement with Stars plc	**(3 marks)**
• Revenue recognition	**(6 marks)**
• Impairment	**(4 marks)**
• Going concern	**(3 marks)**

1 Bluejohn plc

Examiner's comments – this is a scenario based question. You have been put in the role of an independent director. This independence is important as there are several ethical issues in the question and the question (part (b)) requires a careful consideration of these issues. Part (a) is open-ended. There is no guidance and candidates who develop the necessary skills to identify and present solutions to the issues could score high marks.

(a) Financial reporting issues

Segmental reporting

IFRS 8 *Operating Segments* requires entities to provide disaggregated financial information about their different operating segments, together with some information about products and services and about geographical areas.

The standard applies to an entity whose equity is publicly traded. The recent listing of Bluejohn plc's shares requires the presentation and disclosure of segment information.

Bluejohn plc needs to look at its internal organisation and reporting systems to identify its operating segments, because IFRS 8 requires segments to be identified by reference to how the organisation reports internally. Bluejohn plc is organised along business divisions and the internal reporting as five divisions is persuasive evidence to contradict the CFO's argument that Bluejohn plc operates in a single industry.

These operating segments should each be reported separately if one of the following reaches a 10% threshold:

- Segment total revenue as a percentage of the total revenue of all operating segments.

- Segment profit or loss as a percentage of the greater of the total profit of all operating segments reporting a profit and the total loss of those reporting a loss.

- Segment assets as a percentage of the total assets of all operating segments.

The external revenue of the reportable segments must be at least 75% of total revenue.

For Bluejohn plc the oil products, established products and contract products divisions all meet the test of generating 10% or more of revenue and account for 88% of external revenue. The three are the separately reportable segments. The other divisions can be reported together.

The minimum information to be reported for each operating segment is a measure of segment profit or loss.

Bluejohn plc is under an obligation to report information, measured in accordance with IFRS, about geographical areas unless the information is not available and the cost to develop it would be excessive. The reporting of a geographical revenue analysis in the management information is evidence that the information is available. Bluejohn plc should report external revenues attributable to its country of domicile and to all foreign countries, with a similar analysis of non-current assets by their location. In each case, the amounts for individual foreign countries should be disclosed if they are material. The draft accounting policy should be changed.

Available-for-sale investments

The government securities are appropriately classified as available-for-sale financial instruments. They are not held for trading and so do not meet the criteria to be classified as at fair value through profit or loss. Similarly, they were not acquired with the positive intention of holding to maturity, so the held-to-maturity categorisation is not appropriate.

The £0.1 million loss on disposal has been calculated by comparing the disposal proceeds of £4.3 million with the carrying amount of £4.4 million at that date. However, at disposal the

£0.4 million cumulative gain previously recognised in other comprehensive income and held in equity should also be reclassified to profit or loss. Therefore the loss on disposal of £0.1 million should be corrected to a gain of £0.3 million.

The net effect is to eliminate the previous reserve in equity and to increase draft operating profit by £0.4 million. There will be no impact on the overall equity total of Bluejohn.

Held for sale asset

When an entity becomes demonstrably committed to sell an asset, IFRS 5 *Non-current Assets Held for Sale and Discontinued Operations* requires the asset to be classified as held for sale and it is no longer depreciated. In this case the asset is being measured using the revaluation model and so:

- It should be revalued to fair value immediately prior to being classified as held for sale and any gain or loss accounted for in accordance with IAS 16 (usually through the revaluation surplus); and

- It should then be adjusted to fair value less costs to sell. The costs to sell should be recognised as an impairment loss in profit or loss.

On 31 March 20X7 the asset should be classified as held for sale. Immediately before this it should be revalued to fair value of £4.2 million and the revaluation surplus should become £2.8 million (0.6m + (4.2m – 2.0m)).

The asset should then be reclassified as held for sale and the £0.2 million of disposal costs recognised as an impairment loss in profit or loss.

On the same day the asset was disposed of it should be derecognised and the revaluation surplus of £2.8 million transferred directly to retained earnings in the statement of changes in equity.

No further gain or loss should be recognised in profit or loss. The proceeds from the sale and the impairment loss should not be included in revenue. The adjustments required are:

- Revenue should be reduced by £4 million

- Operating expenses should be reduced by £1.8 million (£2 million less £0.2 million impairment loss).

These changes have a direct effect on gross profit percentage.

The identity of the purchaser of the property needs to be confirmed with the executive directors. If the purchaser is the executive directors' pension fund, then the requirements of IAS 24 *Related Party Disclosures* need to be investigated. IAS 24 specifically states that a post-employment plan for the benefit of a reporting entity's employees is a related party of that entity. In addition, an entity controlled by the reporting entity's management is also a related party of the reporting entity.

Details of the transaction, including a description of the related party relationship, should be disclosed. It may be useful for the executive directors to provide evidence that the transaction was on terms equivalent to those on an arm's length basis so that a statement disclosing this fact can be made.

(b) **Ethical issues and actions**

The range of errors within the application of financial reporting standards raises questions about the ethical behaviour and professional standards of management. For example, the segmental reporting issue is relatively straightforward for a qualified accountant to deal with. It is a concern that statements in the draft financial statements about the internal reporting of management information appear to contradict the facts of the matter. Is this a mistake or an intention to mislead?

Many observers have commented that the application of recent financial reporting standards has become a complex area. For example, the held for sale criteria and the related accounting is relatively complicated and a significant change from past practice. However, qualified accounting staff have responsibilities for continuing professional development and they should ensure that their technical knowledge and professional skills are kept up to date.

It is unlikely that these issues are oversights. It appears that the issues have the effect of reducing financial transparency and managing the profit margins that are scrutinised by public and regulatory authorities. I should discuss them with my fellow non-executive directors and executive management to obtain an explanation of the treatments. In any event, I should request amendments to be made to the draft financial statements.

Bluejohn plc has a poor reputation for financial reporting. This is an area I should encourage my fellow directors to seek to address. In addition, I should consider the professional values of management and their ethical behaviour in other business areas. There appears to have been an attempt to cover up the sale of the freehold property to the executive directors' pension fund. It may be appropriate to obtain evidence that the fair value of the property was realised for the benefit of Bluejohn plc.

I should advise those other non-executive directors who are members of professional bodies that they should be conscious of the guidance issued by those bodies. It may be appropriate to obtain guidance from any professional ethics mentors or ethics departments of our professional bodies. In any event, it may be appropriate for me to consider my long-term position at Bluejohn plc.

2   Frodsham plc

Examiner's comments – this is an open question with unstructured requirements based on the scenario of an unfortunate business event. Candidates who followed the approach suggested in the Study Manual would be able to analyse the issues in a logical manner. Candidates should consider the scenario carefully. The business issue could give rise to additional liabilities and bring into question the recoverability of business assets. This should be the focus of a candidate's answer. Whilst the following answer is designed to be comprehensive, credit would be given to candidates who raised valid alternative issues or suggested other issues that needed investigation.

Government Health Department (GHD) Legal Case

IAS 37 *Provisions, Contingent Liabilities and Contingent Assets* requires that a provision should be made for the potential fine for the failure to maintain adequate food systems. The three criteria in IAS 37 are met

- A legal obligation exists as a result of a past event. The obligating event was the salmonella outbreak which occurred during the year.

- The transfer of economic benefits is probable. Frodsham plc's legal advisors have advised that a defence of the case should not be contested.

- The provision can be measured reliably since a maximum liability is known.

The advice of the legal advisor is so strong that it would be appropriate to provide for the maximum amount of the fine (£1 million). The amount is likely to be payable in 12 months' time. The provision should be discounted where the effect of discounting is material. A pre-tax discount rate should be used reflecting the time value of money and the risks specific to the liability.

The provision should be for £909,000 (£1m/1.1). In 20X7 the discount should be unwound as a finance cost. Disclosures surrounding the uncertainties involved and judgements made are required.

The statements in the 20X5 corporate responsibility statement appear to be inconsistent with the financial statements. The corporate responsibility statement will need to be updated to ensure that it is consistent with the financial statement issues.

Buyit contract

The inventory returned by Buyit has no resale value. Trade receivables from Buyit should be reduced by £400,000 with an equivalent reduction in revenue. The costs of disposing of the contaminated production assets should be provided for at the year end, so a provision of £50,000 should be recognised in the statement of financial position at 31 December 20X6.

IFRS 5 *Non-current Assets Held for Disposal and Discontinued Operations* does not apply to these contaminated production assets; they are being abandoned, not sold, so their carrying amount is not being recovered principally through a sale transaction.

Frodsham plc will have to pay £750,000 of compensation to Buyit. This is £250,000 per month for each of the three months that no production is undertaken. Two of these months fall after the financial year end. However, the obligating event occurred before the year end and a provision for the full amount of what is in effect an onerous contract should be recognised.

Products relaunch

The announcement of the relaunch of the products does not create an obligation that is independent of the entity's actions. No provision for the relaunch costs should be recognised. The promotional expenditure should be included in the financial statements as it is incurred.

Impairment test

The salmonella scare and the significant reduction in sales volumes is an indicator of impairment. An impairment test is required in accordance with IAS 36, *Impairment of Assets*.

As the three divisions both operate and report their financial results separately, they should be classified as three separate cash-generating units (CGUs). The corporate assets are not revenue generating but contribute to the cash-generating activities of the overall business. The corporate assets should be allocated on a reasonable and consistent basis to the CGUs under review. The recoverable amounts for the units should then be compared to the carrying amounts of the CGUs including the allocated corporate assets.

The carrying amount of the corporate assets (£900,000) is allocated to CGUs on a weighted average basis as the remaining life of the Tarlton division assets is shorter than the other divisions. The revised carrying amounts should then be compared to the recoverable amount to quantify any impairment loss.

End of 20X6	Tarlton	Catworth	Euxton	Total
	£'000	£'000	£'000	£'000
Carrying amount of assets (A)	3,000	2,500	3,500	9,000
Useful life	5 years	10 years	10 years	
Weighting based on useful life	1	2	2	
Carrying amount after weighting	3,000	5,000	7,000	15,000
Pro rata allocation of corporate assets	3/15	5/15	7/15	100%
Allocation of corporate assets based on pro rata weightings (B)	180	300	420	900
Carrying amount including building (C = A + B)	**3,180**	**2,800**	**3,920**	**9,900**
Recoverable amount (D)	1,000	3,200	3,800	8,000
Impairment losses (C-D)	2,180	Nil*	120	2,300

* No impairment loss as recoverable amount exceeds CGU carrying amount.

The impairment losses should be allocated between the assets of the CGUs and the corporate assets.

	Tarlton		Euxton	
	£'000		£'000	
Corporate assets	123	(2,180 × 180/3,180)	13	(120 × 420/3,920)
Cash generating unit assets	2,057	(2,180 × 3,000/3,180)	107	(120 × 3,500/3,920)
	2,180		120	

The impairment losses in the cash generating units should be apportioned to the assets within each CGU. The impairment should be apportioned to any goodwill first and then pro rata to other assets. A similar pro rata approach should be undertaken for the corporate assets.

Disclosure

The costs related to the health and safety incident are significant. The presentation of the non-recurring expenses as a separate line item in the income statement and an explanation of the liabilities recognised would provide relevant information. In accordance with IFRS 8 any 'exceptional' expenses should be analysed by operating segment if they are separately reported to the chief operating decision maker. The disclosure of performance measurement analysis figures such as 'adjusted' EPS excluding the effects of the incident should be considered.

CHAPTER 15

Scenario-based, consequential questions

Introduction

Examination context

Topic List

1 Scenario questions

2 Approach to examination questions

3 Examination question – Stragglethorpe Ltd

4 Deconstruction

5 Reconstruction

Summary and Self-test

Answers to Interactive questions

Answers to Self-test

Introduction

Chartered Accountants are regularly required to resolve technical financial reporting issues. This is achieved by considering the facts relating to the reporting issues, researching the technical consequences and presenting solutions. In many cases, more than one solution may be feasible, for example when financial reporting standards allow alternative treatments or where judgement or estimation is required.

It is essential that Chartered Accountants can resolve technical issues and provide a definitive solution or range of possible solutions to clients or their managers. When providing solutions, the consequences of the proposals nearly always require explanation at the same time. For example, what is the effect of the proposed treatment on ROCE (return on capital employed), gearing or EPS, as these metrics have a significant impact upon the perception of companies by many user groups. It is this 'added value' analysis that Chartered Accountants regularly demonstrate.

Learning objective

Tick off

- In the assessment, candidates may be required to demonstrate any of the learning outcomes detailed in the Professional stage financial reporting syllabus. The objective of this chapter is to provide a framework to assist candidates in addressing the requirements of this question type.

Syllabus links

In the Financial Accounting syllabus you developed the basic knowledge and application skills for many financial reporting standards. You have extended these knowledge and application skills for those and other financial reporting standards during your studies of Chapters 1 to 10 of this Study Manual. In this chapter you will learn how to use quantitative and qualitative analysis skills to consider the consequential effects of resolving financial reporting issues.

In the technical integration papers at Advanced Stage you will be faced with further scenario questions where you will be required to identify and resolve more complex financial reporting issues and consider the ethical and consequential issues that arise.

Examination context

In an examination you will be faced with questions based upon 'real life' scenarios. The questions will be 'closed-ended', in that the requirements will be very specific. You will be required to resolve financial reporting issues and then consider the consequences of the solutions that you have derived. Question types include the following:

- You may be asked to resolve a number of financial reporting issues where the financial statements are in draft form. You may be required to process any adjustments to the financial statements and then to recompute financial performance indicators and consider the impact on users.

- You may be asked to formulate accounting policies or prepare financial statement extracts. The question requirements may focus upon a single accounting issue, or upon two or more accounting issues. You may also be required to consider the financial and non-financial consequences of an accounting policy formulation or presentation of financial statements.

Such questions involve a high proportion of higher level skills as they require the analysis of the consequences of financial reporting solutions. A common theme of these questions will be ethics and the related judgement required in formulating solutions.

Commonly, the questions will be structured with a number of requirements. Each requirement leads from the one that precedes it ('consequential requirements'). In the examination, candidates may be required to:

- Discuss the financial reporting treatment for the issues arising from a business event or series of events

- Quantify the effects of the financial reporting issues on the financial statements

- Identify the choice of accounting treatments adopted in financial statements and other financial information and assess how they affect the view presented

- Recognise the ethical and professional issues for a professional accountant undertaking work in and giving advice on accounting and financial reporting

- Prepare and present financial statement extracts from structured and unstructured data

- Explain in non-technical language the application of accounting and disclosure requirements to information provided

- Develop and advise upon accounting policies for an organisation

1 Scenario questions

Section overview

An introduction to scenario questions and how they reflect work-based practice.

Examination questions mirror the way Chartered Accountants work in practice. Chartered Accountants demonstrate technical excellence, analyse situations carefully and reflect on possible different solutions before presenting the optimal approach and alternatives to interested parties.

Examination questions will follow the work-based process. Your work-based experiences will benefit your examination performance and vice versa. In these situations Chartered Accountants demonstrate their skills and add value through working through the process in a conscientious and thorough manner. It is essential that the ethical and judgemental issues associated with different potential solutions are considered as part of providing advice.

These 'closed-ended' questions have structured requirements. Each requirement follows on from the previous part and they are focussed on the specific facts of the given scenario. They are often referred to as 'consequential' questions, because the answer to an earlier part of the question is the basis for the next requirement.

The examiners are looking for the following characteristics in **strong** answers:

- **Planning** which demonstrates that thought has been applied before the answer is written out.

- **Technical excellence** through addressing the relevant financial reporting issues and providing alternative solutions where required.

- **Focussed discussion** of the issues arising with arguments applied to the specific circumstances of the question scenario.

- **Quantification** of the issues and where necessary preparation of financial statement extracts.

- Well presented answers appropriately **cross-referenced** to workings.

- Demonstration of **higher skills** by analysing and evaluating the revised financial information.

Weaker answers would fail to display many or all of the above characteristics. **Weaker** answers may have the additional features:

- **Repetition** of points from the question, without any 'added value' in the form of analysis or drawing of inferences.

- Points made randomly **without any focus** or argument.

- **Requirements are not addressed** directly or fully.

- **Failure** to provide a **clear explanation** of the point or to communicate a clear understanding.

- **Lack** of any **consideration** of the broader aspects of an issue and its wider implications.

- **Failure to consider ethical issues** and judgements.

- **Technically incorrect** solutions or answers that include paragraphs copied from the set text without a focus on the scenario.

2 Approach to examination questions

Section overview

This section will help you develop an approach to tackling examination questions through a sample question.

In helping you to develop an approach to consequential questions, we will base our discussions around the question Stragglethorpe Ltd. Stragglethorpe Ltd is a sample question that was produced by the examination team when the syllabus was first introduced. This chapter will lead you through the Stragglethorpe Ltd question. You will be able to develop a range of skills that should help you in the real examination.

Focus particularly on the consequential requirements of the question and those attributes of an answer that demonstrate your ability to resolve financial reporting issues and consider the matters that arise from their resolution.

When working through this chapter you should bear in mind the attributes of strong and weak answers discussed above.

3 Examination question – Stragglethorpe Ltd

Read the following examination question.

Worked example: Stragglethorpe Ltd

You are an accountant at Stragglethorpe Ltd, a small UK company with ambitious plans in the retail and property sectors. It prepares financial statements in accordance with IFRS because it is considering a listing on the London Stock Exchange. Stragglethorpe Ltd has grown rapidly and is highly geared. The financial statements for the year ended 31 March 20X5 included the following accounting policies extract:

'Non-current assets

Non-current assets are stated at cost less accumulated depreciation and impairment charges. Depreciation is computed using the straight-line method using estimates of average useful lives.

Grants and subsidies receivable to assist the promotion of investment are carried in the statement of financial position as deferred income. The amounts are reversed to income during the useful life of the respective assets.'

At 31 March 20X6, Stragglethorpe Ltd has two freehold properties as follows:

(1)   A retail outlet acquired on 1 April 20X2 for £10 million, of which £1 million relates to land. The useful life of the building was assessed at 30 years.

On 31 March 20X6 the fair value of the property was assessed at £12 million, of which land amounted to £2 million. The useful life was reassessed as 25 years from that date.

(2)   An office building was acquired on 1 October 20X5 for a cost of £4 million of which £0.5 million related to land. Its useful life was estimated at 35 years at that date. It is rented to local businesses under short-term agreements with a view to generating returns from rental income. Stragglethorpe Ltd has not previously owned any investment property. On 31 March 20X6 the fair value was assessed at £4.2 million of which land amounted to £0.6 million. The useful life remained unchanged.

The building is located in an area of high unemployment. The Government contributed £0.3 million to the cost of the office building to support the creation of new employment opportunities. As a condition of the grant, Stragglethorpe Ltd has agreed to reduce rents payable by local businesses by £0.1 million per annum for the three years ended 30 September 20X8.

The managing director of Stragglethorpe Ltd has called you. He would like to meet you in two weeks' time. He said:

'I think we should consider very carefully how we account for non-current assets. We should change from using cost to current value. I did this at the last company I worked for, even though they used UK GAAP. That'll reduce our gearing and enable us to borrow further without compromising the gearing covenant in our banking agreements'.

Requirements

Prepare notes for the meeting with the managing director which should:

(a) Explain, using extracts from financial statements, the possible financial reporting treatments for the non-current assets issues identified above for the year ended 31 March 20X6 under the cost and fair value models. **(11 marks)**

Note:

The preparation of disclosure notes is not required.

(b) Assess the potential impact on the financial statements and key financial ratios in future years if fair value accounting policies are adopted. **(4 marks)**

(c) Discuss the financial reporting, ethical and other matters that you need to consider in formulating the accounting policies for non-current assets. **(5 marks)**

(d) Explain the differences between IFRS and UK GAAP in respect of the required accounting treatment for these matters. **(5 marks)**

(25 marks)

On first reading, you should notice some **common** key attributes within this question.

- It is based within a scenario and a context. You are an accountant.

- There are no references to any financial reporting standards either in the text or the requirements.

- The requirements are structured. They are closed-ended. There are parts (a), (b) and so on and they are linked.

- It requires you to explain alternatives in part (a) and prepare extracts.

- Part (b) is a consequence of matters discussed in part (a) and part (c) relates to the scenario.

- Part (d) relating to UK and IFRS differences is a common aspect of this examination.

The examiners described this question as follows.

'This question examines the choices surrounding accounting policies for non-current assets. The question develops the ethical and other considerations that management must consider in developing accounting policies and it requires candidates to consider the future as well as current financial reporting effects'.

These comments confirm that these questions often surround choices and the consequential effects of different approaches by considering current and future issues.

4 Deconstruction

Section overview

Before answering the question you need to plan the answer by deconstructing the question.

4.1 Focus on the requirement

Whilst this question has a structured set of requirements from (a) to (d), it is important that you analyse them carefully. Your answers to latter parts will be influenced by answers to earlier parts.

Firstly you should read and consider the requirements. Ask yourself the following

- What are they?

- Am I required to give advice in a particular context (for example meeting with a client?)

- What level of information/knowledge does the deemed recipient (if any) of the answer possess?

- Is there a particular format such as notes, a report or a memorandum?

- Is there anything I need to be aware of in formulating my answer or particular things I need to prepare?

- What is the weighting of each part of the requirements? Where does my emphasis need to go?

Interactive question 1: Stragglethorpe Ltd – requirement   [Difficulty level: Exam standard]

Identify the salient features of the Stragglethorpe Ltd question requirement.

-
-
-
-
-
-

See **Answer** at the end of this chapter.

4.2 Read the question thoroughly

Next, you should read the question thoroughly. As you read, it may be advisable to annotate the question or highlight anything that appears unusual to you. This should give you a basis on which to plan your answer.

4.3 Planning your answers

The key to these consequential questions is part (a). The remainder of the question follows from it.

These questions focus on technical issues but you can quickly write down the key points for each part of the question.

- **Part (a)**

    - What financial reporting treatments require resolution?
    - What are the relevant financial reporting standards?
    - What are the alternative treatments (if any)?
    - What extracts do I need to prepare?

- **Part (b)**

    - What are the key financial statements effects (statement of comprehensive income, statement of financial position, statement of changes in equity and statement of cash flows)?

    - What key financial ratios are affected?

- **Part (c)**

    - What are the financial reporting issues?
    - What are the ethical and judgemental issues?
    - What other things need considering?

- **Part (d)**

    What are the differences under UK GAAP from those treatments identified in part (a)?

Interactive question 2: Stragglethorpe Ltd – planning your answer

[Difficulty level: Exam standard]

Identify the key issues in the Stragglethorpe Ltd question using the questions above. You could do this as a mind map.

- **Part (a)**

- **Part (b)**

- **Part (c)**

- **Part (d)**

See **Answer** at the end of this chapter.

5 Reconstruction

Section overview

You can now consider how you put your answer together.

5.1 Writing your answer

The examiner has ordered the requirements in the given order for a reason. You should answer them in that order. This is consistent with how you have planned the question.

It is worth reiterating the marking approach used in your examination. It was introduced in Chapter 14 and it is repeated here. Before you make an attempt at writing an answer it is important that you understand how the points you make will be assessed. It is important that you understand why one script would obtain a better mark on the points made than another. This suggested evaluation is given for guidance only and cannot be exact, since the overall mark will be based on the answer coverage as a whole and not just the specific point.

Strong answers will address each of the question requirements. For each part candidates should ensure that their answers:

- **Focus and discuss** in a way that is appropriate to the context of the question. It should refer to question facts and relate these to the answer. Alternative treatments should be discussed and where possible a conclusion drawn as to the most appropriate.

- **Quantify the effects**, such as in your extracts. The effect on the statement of financial position, the statement of comprehensive income (including earnings) and the statement of cash flows should be considered. Your supporting calculations should be clearly referenced to your answer.

In 'consequential' questions where later parts rely on your answers to previous parts of the question, a **'single jeopardy'** or 'follow through' approach is used by the examining team. If your answer to part (a) is incorrect, the examiners will take account of this by looking to see whether you have used your own information correctly in part (b). In other words, you could obtain maximum marks in part (b) even if part (a) was only partially correct. To facilitate this you should clearly set your work out to allow the marker to assess the method and principles you have employed.

Consider the following model in formulating answers.

Recognition	**Measurement**
How should the item be recognised?	How should the item be measured both on initial recognition and then subsequently?
For example	For example
• Asset or expense	• Cost or fair value

Presentation	**Disclosure**
How should the item be presented in financial statements?	What disclosures should be made either in the key statements or in the notes?
For example	For example
• Debt or equity	• Key judgements

However, remember that your answer should address the question requirement. In the Stragglethorpe Ltd question, disclosure notes are not required and therefore that area of the analysis is not needed. The question focuses on measurement and presentation. This may be different in other questions.

Remember the '**because**' test. In most cases, good points pass the 'because' test. When suggesting a solution to the financial reporting issue you should explain why. For example, gearing will be higher because …., the fair values are most appropriate because… The word '**because**' changes a '**what**' into a '**why**'. You can demonstrate what approach is most appropriate and why. You should try to relate the 'why' to the specific scenario given in the question. The reader (in your case the examiner) will then appreciate that you understand the relationships between the financial reporting treatment and the scenario or context.

5.2 Overall issues – focus

Consider depth when writing your answer. This is where you can demonstrate your understanding and added value. As a general rule, you need more focus in the earlier parts of the question where the technical issues are explored.

In this question your focus needs to be on the measurement alternatives for PPE and investment property and how this affects the user's perception of financial performance and financial position.

Interactive question 3: Attempting the question [Difficulty level: Exam standard]

You can now attempt the question. Use your plan or mind map to structure your work. Mark your answer by applying the general principles in the commentary and table above.

See **Answer** at the end of this chapter.

Summary

The approach to closed-ended questions requires similar planning techniques to those used for open-ended questions.

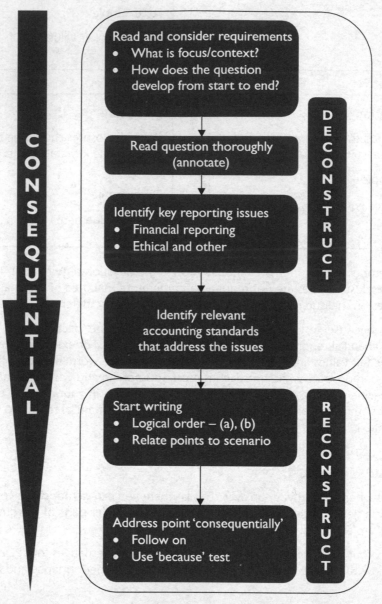

Self-test

Answer the following questions.

1   **Calne plc**

Calne plc is the holding company for a group of manufacturing companies. Its ordinary shares have recently been listed on a public market. You have just been appointed as the finance director. The previous finance director resigned suddenly following adverse market reaction to recently published earnings updates.

The Board of Directors has asked you to finalise the financial statements for the year ended 31 March 20X6. They are particularly concerned about the reported earnings per share (EPS) figures. They have asked you to document your findings in a memorandum addressed to them. They have provided you with the following draft consolidated income statement and consolidated statement of financial position:

	Year to 31 March 20X6 £'000
Revenue	20,440
Cost of sales	(12,600)
Gross profit	7,840
Operating expenses	(2,710)
Profit from operations	5,130
Finance costs	(270)
Profit before tax	4,860
Income tax	(300)
Profit for the period	4,560
Attributable to:	
Owners of parent	4,200
Non-controlling interest	360
	4,560

	As at 31 March 20X6 £'000
Non-current assets	
Property, plant and equipment	19,200
Goodwill – acquisition of Shotton Ltd	1,500
	20,700
Current assets	8,270
Total assets	28,970
Equity attributable to owners of Calne plc	
Issued capital	4,800
Retained earnings	8,400
Non-controlling interests	4,570
Equity	17,770
Non-current liabilities	8,500
Current liabilities	2,700
Total equity and liabilities	28,970

The following information about three issues has been provided:

(1)   Calne plc acquired 75% of the issued ordinary share capital of Shotton Ltd on 1 October 20X5 for £4.2 million in cash. The carrying amount of the identifiable net assets at that date was £3.2 million and there was no material difference from their fair values except for land, where the fair value was £400,000 greater than the carrying amount at acquisition. Shotton Ltd had no contingent liabilities at the date of acquisition. Professional fees of £200,000 were incurred on the acquisition and the costs of the management time involved have been estimated at £100,000. These amounts have been included in operating expenses. Calne plc chose to measure any non-controlling interest in Shotton Ltd at its proportionate share of net assets at the acquisition date.

The carrying amount of Shotton Ltd's identifiable assets and liabilities in its separate financial statements at 31 March 20X6 can be summarised as follows:

	£'000
Land (excludes fair value adjustment)	1,000
Other identifiable assets	1,800
Liabilities	(500)
	2,300

The assets of Shotton Ltd are the smallest group of assets that generate cash inflows that are largely independent of other assets. The recoverable amount of Shotton Ltd's assets has been assessed at 31 March 20X6 as £3.6 million. This was determined without considering the liabilities.

(2) Calne plc has one other subsidiary, Kilton Ltd, in which it acquired a 60% equity holding when the subsidiary was formed. On 1 April 20X5 Kilton Ltd sold its freehold interest in an office building, with a carrying amount of £1.4 million, to a bank for its fair value of £2 million and leased it back over a period of 20 years at a rental of £175,000 per annum payable annually in arrears commencing on 31 March 20X6. The useful life of the building has been assessed at 20 years, the rate of interest implicit in the lease is 6% and the present value of the minimum lease payments is £2 million.

Kilton Ltd has derecognised the property and recognised a gain of £600,000 in revenue. The first rental payment has been included in operating expenses.

(3) An issue of 500,000 7% £10 convertible bonds was completed by Calne plc on 1 April 20X5. The bonds were issued at a discount of 5% to their par amount and on 31 March 20X8 can either be redeemed for cash at their par value or converted into ordinary shares. Each £10 bond is convertible to two new ordinary shares. The proceeds of the convertible bond issue have been credited to non-current liabilities. The interest paid, which is payable annually in arrears commencing on 31 March 20X6, has been debited to finance costs. Calne plc's advisors have calculated that the effective rate of interest on the convertible bond is 9% per annum and that the effective rate of interest on an equivalent bond without the convertibility option is 11% per annum.

The issued share capital on 1 April 20X5 was 3,600,000 ordinary shares. A 1 for 4 bonus issue was made on 1 July 20X5. 300,000 shares were issued on 1 October 20X5 at market value. These share transactions have been correctly reflected in the draft financial statements.

The financial statements for the year ended 31 March 20X5 disclosed an EPS of 75p. No diluted EPS was disclosed.

Requirements

Draft a memorandum to the Board of Directors of Calne plc that includes:

(a) An explanation of the required IFRS accounting treatment of these issues, preparing relevant calculations where appropriate. **(20 marks)**

(b) A revised draft of the consolidated income statement for the year ended 31 March 20X6 and the consolidated statement of financial position at that date. **(8 marks)**

(c) A calculation of the basic and diluted EPS figures, including comparative figures. **(6 marks)**

(34 marks)

Note:

The preparation of disclosure notes is not required. Your answers should be to the nearest £'000. Ignore taxation.

2 Hart plc

You have recently been appointed as an interim financial manager at Hart plc, a company whose previous finance director, Dave Belotty, left the company part way through the year. The company has produced draft financial statements based on the notes prepared by Dave Belotty before he left.

Hart plc has decided always to measure any non-controlling interest in an acquiree at its proportionate share of net assets at the acquisition date.

The main transaction in the year was the acquisition of 49% of the ordinary share capital of Sheepcote Ltd on 1 June 20X6. This has been accounted for using the equity method in accordance with IAS 28 *Investments in Associates*.

Upon further investigation, you discover that on the same date, Hart plc's professional advisers acquired 2% of Sheepcote Ltd, and signed a 'memorandum of understanding' in which the advisers agreed always to vote as instructed by Hart plc.

You have been provided with the draft consolidated financial statements of the Hart plc Group, along with the separate financial statements of Sheepcote Ltd.

Income statement for year ended 31 May 20X7

	Hart plc Group £'000	Sheepcote Ltd £'000
Revenues	34,520	17,640
Expenses	(21,940)	(13,880)
Operating profit	12,580	3,760
Share of profit of associate	490	–
Finance costs	(1,460)	(1,720)
Profit before tax	11,610	2,040
Income tax	(3,270)	(1,040)
Profit for the year	8,340	1,000

Statement of financial position at 31 May 20X7

	Hart plc Group £'000	Sheepcote Ltd £'000
ASSETS		
Property, plant and equipment	34,880	20,000
Goodwill	9,540	–
Investment in associate	10,090	–
	54,510	20,000
Current assets (nil cash)	6,300	4,500
Total assets	60,810	24,500
EQUITY AND LIABILITIES		
Equity		
Issued ordinary shares of £1	1,500	1,000
Share premium account	23,060	–
Retained earnings	9,230	4,400
	33,790	5,400
Non-current liabilities		
Debt	17,310	16,300
Current liabilities	9,710	2,800
Total equity and liabilities	60,810	24,500

You are provided with the following information:

1 The consideration for the investment in Sheepcote Ltd was satisfied by a cash payment of £9.6 million on 1 June 20X6. The share purchase agreement stated that if the profit after tax of Sheepcote Ltd, excluding intra group transactions, exceeded £1.2 million in the year ended 31 May 20X7 then Hart plc would make a cash payment of £2 million as further consideration in October 20X7. Hart plc's advisers estimated that the probability of Sheepcote Ltd achieving this earnings target was such that the fair value at the acquisition date of this possible cash payment was £500,000. Despite this estimate Hart plc has, on Dave Belotty's advice, not accounted for this additional consideration, because the draft profit after tax is only £1 million.

2   The carrying amounts of Sheepcote Ltd's net assets at the acquisition date were the same as their fair values.

3   Hart plc's bankers have a clause in their loan agreement that states that should the total debt in the consolidated financial statements of Hart plc exceed £30 million, then a penalty charge of £1 million arises. This penalty is allowable for tax purposes and Hart plc pays tax at the rate of 30%.

4   During the year ended 31 May 20X7, Sheepcote Ltd sold goods to Hart plc for £500,000, at a mark up of 25% on cost. One quarter of these goods were held as inventories by Hart plc at 31 May 20X7. Hart plc owes Sheepcote Ltd £140,000 in respect of these transactions at 31 May 20X7. Hart plc has not made any adjustments for these inventories in the equity accounting calculations for Sheepcote Ltd.

5   Hart plc charged Sheepcote Ltd £250,000 as a management fee in November 20X6, in accordance with an instruction from Dave Belotty. Hart plc has included the full £250,000 in revenue. Sheepcote Ltd paid the amount on 12 December 20X6 and presented it in expenses.

6   Sheepcote Ltd has not paid any dividends in the year ended 31 May 20X7.

Requirements

Draft a memo to the Hart plc board that includes:

(a)   Advice to them about the treatment of the acquisition of Sheepcote Ltd and the other transactions listed above.   **(9 marks)**

(b)   A revised consolidated statement of financial position at 31 May 20X7 and income statement for year then ended, taking into account the advice you gave in part (a).   **(12 marks)**

(c)   Calculations of earnings per share, gearing and interest cover from both the draft financial statements and those you have prepared in part (b). Explain why there are differences (if any) between the two sets of figures.   **(6 marks)**

      (27 marks)

Note:

The preparation of disclosure notes is not required. Your answers should be to the nearest £'000.

Now, go back to the Learning Objective in the Introduction. If you are satisfied you have achieved this objective, please tick it off.

Answers to Interactive questions

Answer to Interactive question 1

The salient features of the Stragglethorpe Ltd question requirements are:

- Acting as an accountant – need to prepare notes for managing director

- Key to question is part (a) – requires **explanation** of possible financial reporting treatments plus preparation of extracts

- Part (a) states 'cost and fair value models' – answer must meet this expectation

- Part (b) is a follow on but **only** refers to fair value accounting policies

- Part (c) is wide ranging. It is not limited to ethical matters. However, it is directly related to the context

- The mark allocation is 25 marks. As a rule of thumb this will be 37 minutes of time allocation.

Answer to Interactive question 2

Here are a number of suggested points that you could have identified. You must remember that you may have raised some additional valid points. Examiners will award credit for any valid points that you raise even if they are not included in the marking guide provided.

- **Part (a)**

  - What financial reporting treatments require resolution?

    - Non-current asset – measurement
    - Investment property – measurement
    - Government grants – recognition

  - What are the relevant accounting standards?

    - IAS 16
    - IAS 40
    - IAS 20

  - What are the alternative treatments?

    - Both IAS 16 and IAS 40 allow the use of cost and fair value models
    - IAS 20 – recognition of grant income

  - What extracts do I need to prepare?

    - Statement of financial position and income statement
    - No impact on presentation in statement of cash flows

- **Part (b)**

  - What are the key financial statements effects in future years (income statement, statement of financial position and statement of cash flows)?

    - Retail outlet – increased depreciation, increased asset carrying amounts (and capital employed)
    - Office building – volatility, difficult to predict, increases and decreases taken to income

  - What are the key financial ratios and how are they affected?

    - Retail outlet – lower EPS, gearing and ROCE
    - Office building – uncertain effect due to year on year movements

- **Part (c)**

  - What are the financial reporting issues?

    - Retail outlet – voluntary change of accounting policy if move to fair value
    - Office building – subsequent changes to policy difficult

  - What are the ethical issues?

    Influence and dominance by managing director?

  - What other things need considering?

    - Costs of revaluing assets and keeping asset carrying amounts up to date
    - Qualified valuers
    - Lender's view

- **Part (d)**

  What are the differences under UK GAAP from those treatments identified in part (a)?

  - Market value or EUV (lower)
  - Frequency of valuation
  - Non-availability of cost model
  - Treatment of investment property gains/losses

You might find it useful to plan using a mind mapping technique.

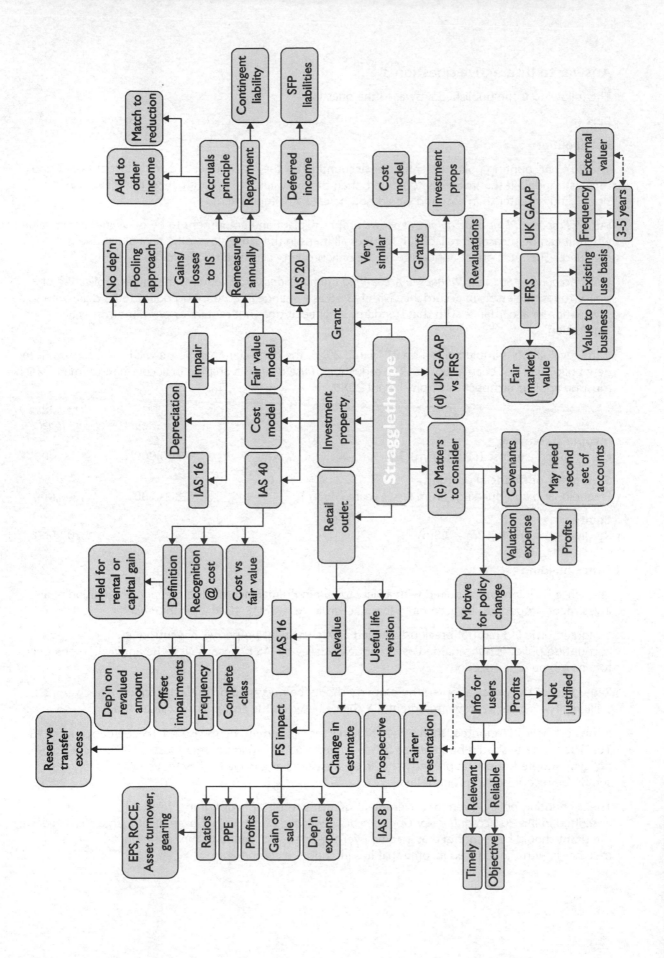

Answer to Interactive question 3

The following is the published answer to the question.

Part (a)

Retail outlet

The 20X5 accounting policy describes the accounting for the retail outlet as a non-current asset using the cost model. If that model is continued, then the fair value at 31 March 20X6 is irrelevant as it is significantly greater than cost and would not indicate any impairment.

IAS 16 *Property, Plant and Equipment* allows property, plant and equipment to be measured at fair value where it can be measured reliably. It requires all items in the same class to be revalued if one is revalued. The retail outlet appears to be the only property classified under IAS 16.

IAS 8 *Accounting Policies, Changes in Accounting Estimates and Errors* requires the initial application of a policy to revalue assets in accordance with IAS 16 as a change in accounting policy to be dealt with as a revaluation in accordance with that standard. In effect it does not require or permit retrospective application.

If the revaluation is implemented on 31 March 20X6, the depreciation expense will be the same as if the new policy had not been adopted. The reduction in useful life is a change in accounting estimate which must be applied prospectively from 1 April 20X6.

	Cost Model £	Revaluation Model £
Income statement		
Depreciation expense ((10m – 1m)/30)	300,000	300,000
Statement of financial position		
Freehold land and buildings (10m less 4 years × 0.3m)	8,800,000	12,000,000
Equity		
Revaluation surplus (12m – 8.8m)	–	3,200,000

Office building

The office building was acquired with a view to earning rental income and meets the definition of an investment property to be accounted for in accordance with IAS 40 *Investment Property*.

Stragglethorpe Ltd has not previously owned any investment property. The introduction of a new accounting policy is not regarded as a change of policy by IAS 8, because it is the application of a policy to a new type of transaction.

Regardless of the policy adopted the property should be measured on initial recognition at cost of £4 million. The subsequent measurement is a choice between the cost and fair value model.

If the cost policy is adopted, then IAS 40 requires the property to be measured in accordance with IAS 16. The property should be stated at cost less depreciation and impairment losses. If the fair value policy is adopted, then the property should be measured at fair value. Any movement in fair value should be recognised in profit or loss.

The accounting policy given for government grants is consistent with grants related to assets as described in IAS 20 *Accounting For Government Grants and Disclosure of Government Assistance*. However, the grant should be recognised as income over the three-year period of the rent reduction. This matches it with the reduced income that it is intended to compensate.

	Cost Model £	Fair Value Model £
Income statement		
Depreciation expense ((4m – 0.5m)/35 × 6/12)	(50,000)	–
Increase in fair value of investment property	–	200,000
Other income (0.3m/3 × 6/12)	50,000	50,000
Statement of financial position		
Investment property (cost model 4m less 50,000)	3,950,000	4,200,000
Current liabilities: Government grants	(100,000)	(100,000)
Non-current liabilities: Government grants	(150,000)	(150,000)

Part (b)

Retail outlet

The depreciation expense will increase under the revaluation model because of the increase to fair value and the reduction in useful life. The annual depreciation charge should be £400,000 ((12m – 2m)/25) rather than £312,000 ((8.8 – 1)/25).

Profits and hence EPS and performance measures such as operating margin will be lower.

The revaluation surplus should be transferred to retained earnings in the statement of changes in equity as the asset is depreciated, ie at the rate of £88,000 (400 – 312) per annum. Retained earnings will be the same regardless of which accounting policy is adopted.

The capital employed will be higher and as a result gearing will be lower. However, other key ratios such as return on capital employed and net asset turnover will be lower than under the cost model.

The fair values must be kept up to date. Therefore any increases or decreases should be recognised in other comprehensive income and held in equity. However, a reduction below depreciated historical cost should be recognised in profit or loss.

Office building

Fair values should be updated annually and any change recognised in profit or loss. These changes may be hard to predict and will potentially create volatility, short-term market changes being recognised in profit or loss.

If prices rise, then profits will be higher than under the cost model. If prices fall, the reverse will probably be true. The effect on financial ratios is difficult to predict. Gearing is likely to be lower but the effect on ROCE will depend upon the magnitude of the changes in fair value.

Part (c)

In general, management are restricted in the accounting policies that they may adopt. They must comply with IFRS and can only exercise judgement where IFRS provide a choice between alternatives.

The adoption of the revaluation model for PPE is a voluntary change in accounting policy and should only be made if it results in reliable and more relevant information for users. The key considerations are whether reliable fair values are available and the information is more relevant to users. The latter may be true if other entities in the industry use the revaluation model or if stakeholders are making representations about the policy.

Such considerations are not required for the investment property, as no previous accounting policy had applied. However, it would be appropriate to consider users and their information needs. IAS 40 does not prefer either model explicitly. However, if the fair value model is chosen it is highly unlikely that a subsequent voluntary change to the cost model would provide more relevant information to users.

Management will wish to place the financial position and results in the best possible light. A change in accounting policy could possibly help this if it enhances profitability, reduces gearing and so on. Non-financially qualified managers may consider that such policies may be more relevant.

Financially qualified managers should ensure that policies are only changed where the qualitative criteria in IAS 8 are met. They may have to argue that a policy change is not appropriate and stand by their professional judgement.

Other matters management should consider are:

- The need to update the fair values of PPE on a regular basis. This may prove costly. The cost and benefit of adopting the policy should be considered.

- The fair value must be determined regardless of the investment property accounting policy adopted. Valuations of investment properties will always be required, because even if the cost model is adopted, fair value should be disclosed by way of note.

- The use of a qualified, independent valuer is not required but is encouraged. This will provide reliable valuations that may be perceived as being more objective.

- The fact that the policies adopted will need to be applied to any further freehold properties acquired for own use or investment purposes in the future.

- Lenders' covenants may stipulate that ratios such as gearing are based on historical cost amounts, so a switch to current values may not have the desired effect of facilitating further borrowing.

Part (d)

Both IAS 16 and UK GAAP require that where a policy of revaluation is adopted, the revalued amounts should be carried at current values. IAS 16 requires such PPE to be measured at fair value, which is usually market value and considers the alternative uses for the asset. Where market value is not available, IAS 16 requires the use of depreciated replacement cost. UK GAAP is based on a value to the business model and requires non-specialised properties to be measured by reference to their existing use value, with the addition of notional directly attributable acquisition costs, if material, to reflect replacement cost (EUV).

EUV is usually lower than market value used in IAS 16 and as a result the depreciation expense is likely to be lower also. Hence earnings and ROCE will be more favourable.

IAS 16 requires subsequent revaluations of assets where the fair value is materially different from carrying amount. UK GAAP has a similar requirement but provides more detailed requirements about the procedures to be adopted in satisfying this requirement. This involves the use of a full valuation every five years, interim valuations in Year 3 and updates where necessary in the other years.

UK GAAP requires each full and interim valuation to be undertaken by a qualified valuer. Each full valuation should be undertaken by an external valuer or reviewed by one. IAS 16 states that qualified valuers normally undertake valuations. The independence or otherwise has to be disclosed but is not mandated.

The UK accounting standard on investment property uses a fair or open market value model. The cost model option is not available.

As under IAS 40, investment properties should not be depreciated, but under UK GAAP movements in open market value are recognised in an investment revaluation reserve in equity, rather than in profit or loss. Where a deficit (or its reversal) on an individual investment property is expected to be permanent. it should be recognised in the profit and loss account of the period. If it is not permanent, then a temporary deficit on the investment revaluation reserve may occur.

Point to note:

Credit would be given to candidates who raised valid, alternative issues or suggested other issues that needed investigation. The examiner's answer is a mark plan. It is necessarily comprehensive to accommodate for a wide range of possible answers. This answer is comprehensive and to obtain a clear pass, candidates would not have to identify all of the areas. However, to obtain a pass, the examiners would expect candidates to discuss each part of the requirement. The maximum marks available for each area can be analysed as follows.

Part (a)

- Retail outlet   **(7 marks)**
- Office building   **(7 marks)**

Part (b)

- Retail outlet   **(3 marks)**
- Office building   **(2 marks)**

Part (c)

- Available marks   **(7 marks)**

Part (d)

- Available marks   **(5 marks)**

1   You should have planned your answer. The following mind map would be useful in preparing your answer.

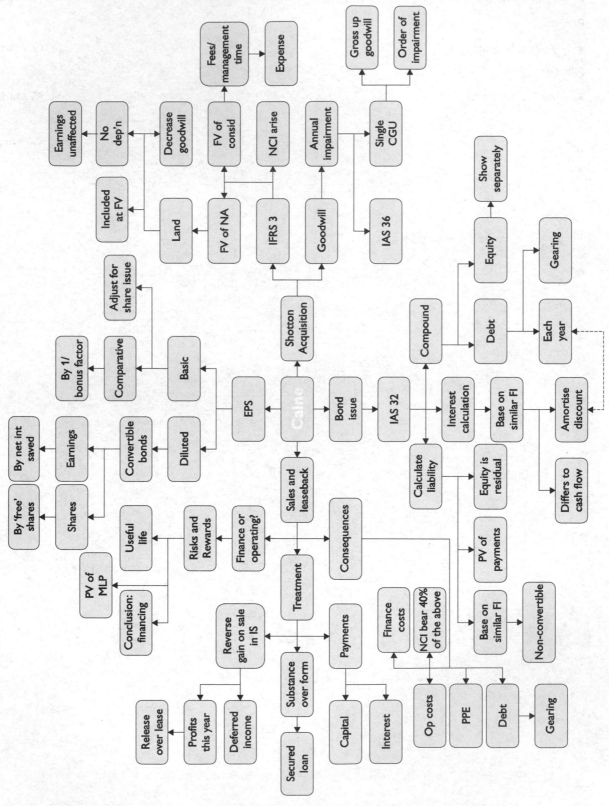

(Note: up to two marks will be awarded for the professional style and layout of the answer)

1 Calne plc

MEMORANDUM

To   Board of Directors
From   Finance Director
Date   1 June 20X6

Subject: Financial Reporting Issues for the Year Ended 31 March 20X6

In accordance with our discussions, I have reviewed the draft financial statements and the financial reporting issues identified in the preparation of the 31 March 20X6 financial statements. My analysis, explanations, calculations, revised income statement, revised statement of financial position and EPS calculations are set out below.

(a) Financial reporting issues

CGU impairment

The consideration transferred in the business combination with Shotton Ltd is correctly measured at £4.2m. IFRS 3 *Business Combinations* states that both the directly attributable professional costs (£0.2m) and the cost of the management time involved (£0.1m) should be recognised as expenses in profit or loss.

In determining the goodwill acquired, the £3.2 million carrying amount of the identifiable net assets should be increased by the £400,000 excess of the fair value of land over its carrying amount.

The goodwill acquired in the business combination should be measured as:

	£'000
Consideration transferred	4,200
Non-controlling interest at the acquisition date (25% × £3.6m)	900
	5,100
Less: fair value of identifiable net assets acquired	3,600
	1,500

The goodwill is subject to an annual impairment test. This test can be performed at any time during the year provided it is at the same time every year. In the year of acquisition the test should be performed before year end. Data is readily available and so the impairment test can be undertaken at that date.

Shotton Ltd is a cash generating unit since it is the smallest group of assets that generate independent cash flows that can be measured. The carrying amount of the CGU should exclude the liabilities, as this is how the recoverable amount has been assessed.

A portion of the recoverable amount of the CGU is attributable to the unrecognised non-controlling interest in goodwill. The carrying amount of the CGU must be notionally adjusted to include the unrecognised goodwill relating to the non-controlling interest before comparing it to the £3.6 million recoverable amount.

The carrying amount of the CGU and comparison to recoverable amount are (in £'000):

	Carrying amount	Impairment	Revised amount
Goodwill – including NCI element (1,500/75%)	2,000	(1,600)	400
Land (1m plus 0.4m fair value adjustment)	1,400	–	1,400
Other identifiable assets	1,800	–	1,800
	5,200	(1,600)	3,600

In accordance with IAS 36 *Impairment of Assets* the impairment loss should be allocated to goodwill first. However, because the goodwill is only recognised to the extent of Calne plc's 75% interest, Calne plc should only recognise 75% of the impairment loss. An impairment loss of £1.2 million should be recognised and the carrying amount of goodwill should be £300,000 (75% × 400).

Point to note:

The journal (provided for tutorial purposes and not required to obtain full marks) is

DR	Operating expenses	£1,200,000	
CR	Non-current assets – goodwill		£1,200,000

To recognise the goodwill impairment loss

Sale and finance lease transaction

The sale and leaseback is essentially a financing transaction. The risks and rewards of ownership of the building have not been disposed of. The leaseback should be classified as a finance lease because:

- The lease term is the same as the remaining useful life of the building
- The present value of the minimum lease payments is the same as the asset fair value

As such the operating expense of £175,000 should be reversed, as the treatment as an operating lease is inappropriate.

The profit on disposal of £600,000 should be deferred and amortised over the lease term. The effect is to adjust the depreciation of the property to the amount consistent with its carrying amount before the transaction. The net effect on profit or loss is to reduce profit by £570,000 (19/20 × 600,000) and it would be more appropriate to show the amount in net operating expenses rather than revenue.

The asset and the related debt (proceeds received) should be recognised on 1 April 20X5 at £2 million. The property should be depreciated over 20 years (being the lease term and useful life). Depreciation of £100,000 (2m/20) should be recognised in profit or loss and the property carrying amount should be £1.9 million.

The movement in the lease liability can be analysed as follows (in £'000):

	B'fwd	Interest at 6%	Repayment	C'fwd
20X6	2,000	120	(175)	1,945
20X7	1,945	117	(175)	1,887

The lease liability (£1.945m) should be split between current liabilities of £58,000 (£1,945,000 less £1,887,000) and long-term liabilities of £1,887,000.

As Kilton Ltd is a 60% subsidiary, the net reduction in the profits attributable to the owners of Calne plc is £369,000 (60% × (£600,000 – £175,000 – £30,000 + £100,000 + £120,000)) and in those attributable to the non-controlling interest effect is £246,000.

Point to note:

The journals (for tutorial purposes) are

DR	Non-current liability	£175,000	
CR	Operating expenses		£175,000

To reverse the payment charged to operating expenses

DR	Revenue	£600,000	
CR	Deferred income		£570,000
CR	Operating expenses		£30,000

To reverse the profit recognised as revenue, set up deferred income and release an amount to income for the year

DR	Leased property – carrying amount	£2,000,000	
CR	Non-current liability		£2,000,000

To recognise the leased property

DR	Finance expense	£120,000	
CR	Non-current liability		£120,000

To recognise finance charge during year

| DR | Operating expenses | £100,000 | |
| CR | Leased property – carrying amount | | £100,000 |

To depreciate the leased property

| DR | Non-current liability | £58,000 | |
| CR | Current liability | | £58,000 |

To recognise short-term liability

Issue of convertible bonds

A convertible bond is a compound financial instrument per IAS 32 *Financial Instruments: Presentation*, in that it has both equity and liability components. It should be accounted for using 'split accounting'. The components should be measured and presented separately at the time of issue.

The liability component should be measured first at the present value of the capital and interest payments. The discount rate should be that for an instrument with the same terms and conditions except for the convertibility (being 11%).

	Cash flow £'000	Discounted at 11%	Present value £'000
31 March 20X6	350	1/1.11	315
31 March 20X7	350	1/1.11²	284
31 March 20X8	5,350	1/1.11³	3,912
			4,511

The bonds should be recognised at £4,511,000. The equity component should be calculated as the residual amount and should be recognised at £239,000 (5m × 0.95 less 4.511m).

The interest expense should be calculated at 11% of the liability's carrying amount. It includes the amortisation of the discount. Therefore the interest expense should be £496,000 (£4.511m × 11%) even though the interest paid is only £350,000. This increases the debt to £4,657,000 (4,511+(496-350)) at 31 March 20X6 and the finance costs by the same amount of £146,000.

Point to note:

The journal (provided for tutorial purposes and not required to obtain full marks) is

| DR | Non-current liabilities | £239,000 | |
| CR | Equity | | £239,000 |

To recognise the equity component within the convertible bonds

| DR | Finance costs | £146,000 | |
| CR | Non-current liabilities | | £146,000 |

To increase finance costs in line with the effective rate of interest on the convertible bonds

(b) **Consolidated income statement for the year ended 31 March 20X6**

	Draft	(1)	(2)	(3)	Revised
			Issues		
	£'000	£'000	£'000	£'000	£'000
Revenue	20,440		(600)		19,840
Cost of sales	(12,600)				(12,600)
Gross profit	7,840				7,240
Operating expenses	(2,710)	(1,200)	175 + 30 + (100)		(3,805)
Profit from operations	5,130				3,435
Finance costs	(270)		(120)	(146)	(536)
Profit before tax	4,860				2,899
Income tax	(300)				(300)
Profit for the period.	4,560				2,599
Attributable to:					
Owners of parent	4,200	(1,200)	(369)	(146)	2,485
Non-controlling interest	360		(246)		114
	4,560				2,599

Consolidated statement of financial position at 31 March 20X6

	Draft	(1)	(2)	(3)	Revised
			Issues		
	£'000	£'000	£'000	£'000	£'000
Non-current assets					
Property, plant and equipment	19,200		2,000 + (100)		21,100
Goodwill	1,500	(1,200)			300
	20,700				21,400
Current assets	8,270				8,270
Total assets	28,970				29,670
Equity attributable to owners of Calne plc					
Issued capital	4,800				4,800
Equity component of convertible	0			239	239
Retained earnings	8,400	(1,200)	(369)	(146)	6,685
Non-controlling interest	4,570		(246)		4,324
Equity	17,770				16,048
Non-current liabilities	8,500		(175) + 2,000 + 120 + (58)	(239) + 146	10,294
Current liabilities	2,700		570 + 58		3,328
Total equity and liabilities	28,970				29,670

(c) **Basic EPS**

The earnings attributable to the equity owners of Calne plc are £2.485 million (see part (b)).

The weighted average number ('000) of shares should be calculated as

Date	Number ('000)	Fraction	Bonus	Weighted average ('000)
1 Apr X5	3,600	3/12	5/4	1,125
1 Jul X5	4,500	3/12		1,125
1 Oct X5	4,800	6/12		2,400
				4,650

Earnings per share is 53.4p (2,485/4,650). The prior year earnings should be adjusted for the effect of the bonus to 60p (75p x 4/5).

Diluted EPS

The diluted earnings per share should be calculated as:

	£'000
Basic earnings	2,485
Add: convertible bond interest saved	496
Diluted earnings	2,981

	Number '000
Basic number of shares	4,650
Add: number of shares on conversion (500,000 × 2)	1,000
	5,650

Diluted EPS (2,981 ÷ 5,650)	52.8p

Conclusion

A number of material adjustments to the financial statements are required. The adjustments significantly change earnings and the profile of our financial statements. Please contact me if you require any further information.

2 Hart plc

Memorandum

To	Board of Directors, Hart plc
From	A. Accountant
Date	13 July 20X7

Subject Treatment of acquisition of Sheepcote Ltd and impact on financial statements

(a) Explanation of financial reporting issues

Introduction

In accordance with your instructions I have prepared revised drafts of the financial statements for the year ended 31 May 20X7 together with an explanation of the changes and a quantification of the effects on key metrics.

Treatment of acquisition

The current treatment of Sheepcote Ltd is inappropriate. Although Hart plc has legal ownership of 49% of the voting shares, it controls 51% of the voting rights, through the memorandum of understanding with the professional advisers.

IAS 27 *Consolidated and Separate Financial Statements* explicitly states that control of an entity is obtained where the parent owns less than half of the voting power of an entity but has power over more than half of the voting rights through an agreement with other shareholders.

Consequently Sheepcote Ltd should be treated as a subsidiary per IAS 27 and consolidated in the financial statements as a business combination using the acquisition method. The income, expenses, assets and liabilities of Sheepcote Ltd should be fully incorporated into the group financial statements on a line by line basis, instead of the 'one line' approach undertaken when using equity accounting.

A 51% non-controlling interest now arises in both the profit of the subsidiary for the year and its consolidated net assets at 31 May 20X7.

Contingent consideration

The £500,000 fair value of the additional consideration potentially payable in October 20X7 should be recognised at the acquisition date as part of the consideration transferred, with a liability being recognised for the same amount.

Although the draft profit after tax for the relevant period is below the £1.2 million target figure, this is partially due to the £250,000 management fee that is included in the expenses of Sheepcote Ltd. As this is an intra-group item, it should be adjusted for, as should the intra-group trading transactions. The adjusted profit after tax of Sheepcote Ltd rises above the £1.2 million threshold (Appendix 1) and the full £2 million becomes payable.

Under IFRS 3 the £1.5 million additional amount payable arises as a result of events after the acquisition date, rather than from further information becoming available about conditions existing at that date. Therefore it should be recognised as expense in profit or loss, rather than being added to the consideration for the acquisition.

Banking covenant fee

When Sheepcote was accounted for using the equity method, its debt and finance costs were not presented in the consolidated statement of financial position and consolidated income statement. Under the acquisition method of accounting, these debts and finance costs should be aggregated with those of Hart plc.

The revised debt total of £33.61 million (17,310 + 16,300) exceeds the £30 million total included in the loan covenant. Hart plc should provide for the penalty charge of £1 million, although this is diminished to a degree by the tax deduction arising on the penalty of £300,000. The penalty should be treated as a finance cost or presented elsewhere in the income statement.

Intra-group trading and unrealised profits

When using equity accounting, only the group share of the intra-group profit is eliminated upon consolidation. No adjustment is made to group revenues, because sales made by the associate company are not group revenues.

If the acquisition method of accounting is used, then both revenues and operating costs are reduced by the level of intra-group sales. A further adjustment should be made for the remainder of the unrealised profit. The risks and rewards of ownership of these goods have not been transferred to parties outside of the group, so it would be inappropriate to include the profits.

The amount of unrealised profit is £25,000 (W7). The inventory was sold by Sheepcote Ltd and the non-controlling interest will be affected as a result.

Management fee

The management fee appears to have been charged to Sheepcote Ltd with the objective of reducing profits below the threshold for the contingent consideration. No adjustment is required when using equity accounting as far as revenues are concerned, because an associate company is not deemed to be part of the group.

When using the acquisition method, both revenues and expenses are reduced by the full amount of the management fee. This is because Sheepcote Ltd is now deemed to be a subsidiary company and all transactions between parent and subsidiary companies should be eliminated on consolidation.

(b) **Revised drafts of the consolidated income statement and statement of financial position**

Consolidated income statement for year ended 31 May 20X7

	£'000
Revenues (W1)	51,410
Expenses (W1)	(37,595)
Operating profit	13,815
Finance costs (W1)	(3,180)
Profit before tax	10,635
Income tax (W1)	(4,010)
Profit for the year	6,625
Attributable to:	
Owners of Hart plc (bal)	6,128
Non-controlling Interest (W2)	497
	6,625

Consolidated statement of financial position at 31 May 20X7

	£'000
Non-current assets	
Property, plant and equipment (34,880 + 20,000)	54,880
Goodwill (9,540 + 7,944 (W4))	17,484
	72,364
Current assets (6,300 + 4,500 – 25 (W7) – 140 intra-group)	10,635
Total assets	82,999
EQUITY AND LIABILITIES	
Equity attributable to the owners of Hart plc	
Issued ordinary shares	1,500
Share premium account	23,060
Retained earnings (W6)	7,018
	31,578
Non-controlling interest (W5)	2,741
Equity	34,319
Debt (17,310 + 16,300)	33,610
Current liabilities	
(9,710 + 2,800 + 500 + 1,500 + 1,000 – 300 – 140 intra-group)	15,070
Total equity and liabilities	82,999

(c) **Impact on financial ratios**

Ratios	Original	Revised
Interest cover (((12,580 + 490)/1,460) and (13,815/3,180))	8.95	4.34
Interest cover (treating interest penalty as a finance cost) (14,815/4,180)	–	3.54
Gearing ((17,310/33,790) and (33,610/34,319))	51%	98%
Earnings per share (W8)	£5.56	£4.09

When Sheepcote Ltd is consolidated using the acquisition method, its debts are added to those of the parent company and have a disproportionate impact on debt compared to equity. Interest cover has fallen and gearing has risen because Sheepcote Ltd is significantly funded by debt.

Earnings per share has fallen because of the reduction in profits caused by the need to provide for the interest penalty and the smaller adjustment for unrealised profits.

Summary

The amendments to the financial statements show significant changes from the original drafts. They result in the need to pay additional substantial amounts of consideration to the vendors of Sheepcote Ltd. In addition, a penalty is due to our bankers and I suggest we discuss how the financial presentation of the subsidiary affects this with a view to negotiating revised terms or a lower penalty.

Appendix 1: Revised profit figure for Sheepcote Ltd

	£'000
Draft profit after tax per income statement	1,000
Add: management fee	250
Less: profit on intra-group sales (49% of 500 x 25/125)	(49)
Revised draft profit after tax	1,201

WORKINGS (All in £'000)

(1) Consolidated income statement

	Hart	Sheepcote	Adjust	Total
Revenues	34,520	17,640	(500)	
			(250)	51,410
Expenses	(21,940)	(13,880)	500	
	(1,500)		(1,000)	
			250	(37,595)
PURP (W7)		(25)		
Finance costs	(1,460)	(1,720)		(3,180)
Tax (30% × 1,000)	(3,270)	(1,040)	300	(4,010)
Profit for the period		975		

(2) Non-controlling interest – income statement

51% × 975 = 497

(3) Net assets

	At period end	At acquisition	Post-acquisition
Shares	1,000	1,000	–
Retained earnings (at acq = 4,400 - 1,000 for year)	4,400	3,400	1,000
PURP adjustment (W7)	(25)		(25)
	5,375	4,400	975

(4) Goodwill

Consideration transferred	
Cash paid on 1 June 20X6	9,600
Fair value of contingent consideration at acquisition date	500
Non-controlling interest at the acquisition date (51% × 4,400 (W3))	2,244
	12,344
Less: net assets at acquisition (W3)	(4,400)
Goodwill	7,944

(5) Non-controlling interest – statement of financial position

At acquisition ((51% × 4,400 (W3))	2,244
For year (W2)	497
	2,741

(6) Retained earnings

Draft total	9,230
PURP adjustment (49% × 25)	(12)
Less: Finance penalty accrued	(1,000)
Tax adjustment (30% × 1,000)	300
Revision to liability for contingent consideration	(1,500)
	7,018

(7) Unrealised profit

	%	£'000
Cost	100	100
Profit	25	25
Sales price (1/4 × 500)	125	125

49% (Hart's share) of this PURP will have been adjusted for in the share of profit of associate recognised in profit or loss under the equity accounting for Sheepcote, but this share has been excluded from (W1). So the full PURP needs to be adjusted for.

(8) EPS

	Draft	Revised
Earnings	8,340	6,128
Shares	1,500	1,500
EPS (8,340/1,500) and (6,128/1,500)	£5.56	£4.09

Index

A

Accounting policy choices, 499
Accounting Standards Board, 15, 16
Acquistion method, 313
Adjusting events, 428
Approach to examination questions, 535, 569, 592
ASB *Statement*, 6

B

Basic EPS, 390
Borrowing costs, 180
Business, 326
Business combination, 313
Business issues, 496

C

Cash, 422
Cash dividend cover, 477
Cash equivalents, 422
Cash flow headings, 475
Cash flow per share, 477
Cash flow ratios, 476
Cash from operations/profit from operations, 476
Cash interest cover, 476
Cash return on capital employed, 476
Cash-generating unit, 118
Classification of financial instruments, 277
Close members of the family of a person, 66
Compound financial instruments, 273
Conceptual Framework, 3, 13
Consolidated income statement, 314
Consolidated statement of changes in equity, 318
Consolidated statement of financial position, 314
Construction contract, 246
Constructive obligation, 430
Contingent asset, 433
Contingent consideration, 337
Contingent liability, 431
Control, 66, 326
Control achieved in stages, 328
Convergence process, 10
Convergence progress, 13
Convergence projects, 14
Cost model, 97
Cost plus contract, 247
Credit crisis, 14
Credit risk, 292
Current ratio, 463

D

Dealer lessors, 212, 214
Deferred consideration, 243, 336
Deferred income method, 175
Derecognition, 285
Derivative, 270
Diluted earnings per share, 396
Diluted EPS – convertible debt, 397
Directors' report, 72
Discontinued operations, 51
Disposal group, 126
Disposal of associate, 345
Disposal of subsidiary, 323
Distributable profits, 399
Dividend cover, 470
Dividend yield, 470

E

EBIT, 506
EBITDA, 506
EBITDAR, 506
Economic factors, 496
Effective interest rate, 281
Efficiency ratios, 466
Elements of financial statements, 5
EPS - bonus issue, 393
EPS - rights issue, 394
Equity instrument, 269
Equity method of accounting, 320
Ethical issues, 502
Ethics, 21, 293, 539, 555, 571, 584, 604
European Union, 11
Events after the reporting period, 428

F

Fair presentation, 20
Fair value, 169, 284
Fair value less costs to sell, 113, 114
Fair value model, 168
Faithful representation, 4, 244
FIFO, 420
Finance lease: manufacturer and dealer lessors, 212
Financial analysis, 532
Financial asset, 268
Financial instrument, 267
Financial liability, 268
Financial Reporting Standard for Smaller Entities (FRSSE), 18
Fixed price contract, 246
FRS 1 *Cash Flow Statements*, 435
FRS 2 *Accounting for Subsidiary Undertakings*, 357
FRS 3 *Reporting Financial Performance*, 75

FRS 5 *Reporting the Substance of Transactions*, 252

FRS 6 *Acquisitions and Mergers*, 357

FRS 7 *Fair Values in Acquisition Accounting*, 357

FRS 8 *Related Party Disclosures*, 78

FRS 9 *Associates and Joint Ventures*, 357

FRS 10 *Goodwill and Intangible Assets*, 357

FRS 11 *Impairment of Fixed Assets and Goodwill*, 132, 134

FRS 15 *Tangible Fixed Assets*, 132, 184

FRS 18 *Accounting Policies*, 75

FRS 22 *Earnings per share*, 403

FRS 28 *Corresponding Amounts*, 75

Gearing ratio, 464

Goodwill and non-controlling interests, 333

Government, 70

Government assistance, 173

Government grants, 174

Government-related entity, 70

Gross investment in the lease, 210

Gross profit percentage, 461

IAS 1 *Presentation of Financial Statements*, 45

IAS 2 *Inventories*, 419

IAS 10 *Events After the Reporting Period*, 428

IAS 11 *Construction Contracts*, 246

IAS 12 *Income Taxes*, 54

IAS 16 *Property, Plant and Equipment*, 97

IAS 17 *Leases*, 207

IAS 18 *Revenue*, 241

IAS 20 *Accounting for Government Grants and Disclosure of Government Assistance*, 173

IAS 23 *Borrowing Costs*, 178

IAS 24 *Related Party Disclosures*, 64

IAS 27 *Consolidated and Separate Financial Statements*, 313

IAS 28 *Investments in Associates*, 320

IAS 31 *Investments in Joint Ventures*, 346

IAS 32 *Financial Instruments: Presentation*, 272

IAS 33 *Earnings per Share*, 389

IAS 36 *Impairment of Assets*, 111

IAS 37 *Provisions, Contingent Liabilities and Contingent Assets*, 429

IAS 38 *Intangible Assets*, 103

IAS 39 *Financial Instruments: Recognition and Measurement*, 277

IAS 40 *Investment Property*, 165

IAS 7 *Statement of Cash Flows*, 422, 474

IAS 8 *Accounting Policies, Changes in Accounting Estimates and Errors*, 49

ICAEW Code of Ethics, 22

ICAEW/ICAS Technical Release 01/08, 402

IFRS 3 *Business Combinations*, 313

IFRS 5 *Non-current Assets Held for Sale and Discontinued Operations*, 51, 124, 125

IFRS 7 *Financial Instruments: Disclosures*, 290

IFRS 8 *Operating Segments*, 57

IFRS for SMEs, 19

IFRS Foundation structure, 8

Indications of impairment, 112

Industry analysis, 504

Interest cover, 465

Interest rate implicit in the lease, 210

International Federation of Accountants, 9

Inventory turnover, 466

Investment property, 165

Investor, 347

Investors' ratios, 470

Joint control, 66, 347

Joint venture, 346

Jointly controlled assets, 349

Jointly controlled entities, 350

Jointly controlled operations, 348

Judgements and estimates, 501

Judgements required, 63, 71, 101, 123, 131, 172, 178, 182, 218, 245, 251, 293, 356, 399, 421, 427, 435

Key management personnel, 66

Legal obligation, 430

Lessor accounting: finance lease, 210

Lessor accounting: operating lease, 213

Liquidity risk, 292

Long-term solvency ratios, 464

Major needs of users, 6

Market risk, 292

Measurement in financial statements, 5

Measurement of financial instruments, 279, 280

Measurement of non-controlling interest, 330

Measurement period, 341

Minimum lease payments, 210

Net asset turnover, 466

Net asset value, 471

Net investment in the lease, 210

Net realisable value, 420

Netting-off method, 175
Non-adjusting events, 428
Non-current asset analysis, 468
Non-financial performance measures, 505
Non-mandatory government grants, 177
Norwalk Agreement, 12
Not-for-profit entities, 19, 52, 478

O

Offsetting, 276
Onerous contracts, 430
Operating and financial review, 72
Operating cost percentage, 461
Operating lease incentives, 218
Operating margin, 461
Operating segment, 58
Owner-occupied property, 166

P

Performance ratios, 459
Potential voting rights, 327
Price/earnings (P/E) ratio, 470
Private companies, 17, 400
Profit in financial statements, 52
Proportionate consolidation, 351
Provision, 430
Public companies, 400

Q

Qualifying asset, 179
Qualitative characteristics of useful financial
    information, 4
Quick ratio, 463

R

Reclassification adjustments, 53
Reclassification of financial assets, 288
Recognising an impairment loss, 117, 120
Recognition of elements in financial statements,
    5
Recoverable amount, 113
Regulatory framework, 8
Related party, 65
Related party transaction, 68
Relevance, 4
Relevance of information, 101, 109, 123, 131,
    172, 178, 182, 219, 245, 251, 356, 399,
    421, 427, 429, 435
Reportable segments, 59
Reporting requirements for UK companies, 16

Return on capital employed (ROCE), 459
Return on shareholders' funds (ROSF), 460
Revaluation model, 97
Reversal of impairment losses, 122

S

Sale and leaseback transactions, 215
Scenario questions, 568, 592
Short-term liquidity ratios, 463
Significant influence, 66
Special Purpose Entity (SPE), 327
SSAP 4 *Accounting for Government Grants*, 184
SSAP 9 *Stocks and Long-term Contracts*, 252
SSAP 13 *Accounting for Research and
    Development*, 132
SSAP 19 *Accounting for Investment Properties*,
    184
SSAP 21 *Accounting for Leases and Hire Purchase
    Contracts*, 220
SSAP 25 *Segmental Reporting*, 78
Standard setting process, 9
Statement of changes in equity, 49, 54
Statement of comprehensive income, 47
Statement of financial position, 46
Statements of cash flows interpretation, 474
Substance over form, 244

T

Terminology, 74
Theoretical Ex rights Price (TERP), 395
Trade payables payment period, 467
Trade receivables collection period, 467
Treasury shares, 277
'True and Fair Override', 21
True and fair view, 20

U

UK regulatory framework, 10
Underlying assumption, 4
Unguaranteed residual value, 210
User information needs, 457

V

Valuation of inventories, 419
Value in use, 113, 115
Venturer, 347

W

Weighted average cost, 420
Working capital cycle, 468

Notes

Notes

Notes

Notes

REVIEW FORM – FINANCIAL REPORTING STUDY MANUAL

Your ratings, comments and suggestions would be appreciated on the following areas of this Study Manual.

	Very useful	Useful	Not useful
Chapter Introductions	☐	☐	☐
Examination context	☐	☐	☐
Worked examples	☐	☐	☐
Interactive questions	☐	☐	☐
Quality of explanations	☐	☐	☐
Technical references (where relevant)	☐	☐	☐
Self-test questions	☐	☐	☐
Self-test answers	☐	☐	☐
Index	☐	☐	☐

	Excellent	Good	Adequate	Poor
Overall opinion of this Study Manual	☐	☐	☐	☐

Please add further comments below:

Please return to:

The Learning Team
Learning and Professional Department
ICAEW
Metropolitan House
321 Avebury Boulevard
Milton Keynes
MK9 2FZ
ACAFeedback@icaew.com
www.icaew.com